BIOLOGICAL ANTHROPOLOGY

BIOLOGICAL ANTHROPOLOGY
The Natural History of Humankind

Craig Stanford
University of Southern California

John S. Allen
University of Iowa

Susan C. Antón
New York University

PEARSON

Prentice
Hall

Upper Saddle River, New Jersey 07458

Library of Congress Cataloging-in-Publication Data

Stanford, Craig B.
  Biological anthropology : the natural history of humankind / Craig Stanford, John S. Allen, Susan
  C. Antón.
    p. cm.
  Includes bibliographical references and index.
  ISBN 0-13-182892-4 (alk. paper)
  1. Physical anthropology—Textbooks. I. Allen, John S. (John Scott) II. Antón, Susan C. III. Title.

GN25.S73 2006
599.9—dc22

2004060138

Editorial Director: Leah Jewell
AVP, Publisher: Nancy Roberts
VP, Director of Production and Manufacturing: Barbara Kittle
Director of Marketing: Brandy Dawson
AVP, Editor-in-chief of Development: Rochelle Diogenes
Manufacturing Manager: Nick Sklitsis
Prepress and Manufacturing Buyer: Ben Smith
Senior Marketing Manager: Marissa Feliberty
Development Editors: Carolyn Viola-John and Elisa Adams
Production Editor: Cheryl Keenan
Copyeditor: Carol Anne Peschke
Proofreader: Susan Plog
Editorial Assistant: Lee Peterson
Marketing Assistant: Jennifer Lang
Creative Design Director: Leslie Osher
Senior Art Director: Anne Bonanno Nieglos
Interior and Cover Design: Jill Lehan

Illustrator (Interior): Maria Piper
Scientific Illustration (Interior):
    Precision Graphics
Digital Design Assistance: Bruce Killmer
Director, Image Resource Center: Melinda Reo
Manager, Rights and Permissions: Zina Arabia
Manager, Visual Research: Beth Brenzel
Image Permission Coordinator: Debbie Latronica
Photo Researcher: Teri Stratford
Cover Image Specialist: Karen Sanatar
Cover Art: Martin Harvey/Peter Arnold Inc.; Demitri
    Vervits/Image State International Stock Photography Ltd.;
    Kenneth Garrett Photography
Cover Illustrator: Bruce Killmer
Supplements Editor: Erin Katchmar
Media Editor: Kate Ramunda
Media Production Manager: Lynn Pearlman

This book was set in 10.5/12 Sabon by Seven Worldwide and was printed
and bound by Courier Kendallville. The cover was printed by Phoenix Color Corp.

For permission to use copyrighted material, grateful acknowledgment is made to the copyright
holders listed on page 583, which is considered an extension of this copyright page.

Pearson Education LTD.
Pearson Education Singapore, Pte. Ltd
Pearson Education, Canada, Ltd
Pearson Education—Japan
Pearson Education Australia PTY, Limited

Pearson Education North Asia Ltd
Pearson Educación de Mexico, S.A. de C.V
Pearson Education Malaysia, Pte. Ltd
Pearson Education, Upper Saddle River, New Jersey

10 9 8 7 6 5 4

ISBN 0-13-182892-4

CBS: For Erin, Gaelen, Marika, and Adam

*JSA: For my wife, Stephanie Sheffield,
and our sons, Reid and Perry*

*SCA: For Mr. Carl, My Folks, and
the wet noses of Four Dog Farm*

BRIEF CONTENTS

Contents

Chapter 5
THE FORCES OF EVOLUTION
AND THE FORMATION OF SPECIES   99

Chapter 6
HUMAN VARIATION: Evolution, Adaptation,
and Adaptability   126

PART III
Primates

Chapter 7
THE PRIMATES   163

PREFACE

A new biological anthropology textbook? After teaching biological anthropology for 15 years we feel there is a great need for a new textbook. Biological anthropology was once commonly called physical anthropology. This is because decades ago the field was mainly about human anatomy, human fossils, and the study of racial variation. Over the past 20 years, the field has evolved into biological anthropology, the evolutionary biology of humankind based on information from the fossil record and the human skeleton, the genetics of both individuals and populations, our primate relatives, human adaptation, and human behavior, among other topics. Our book combines up-to-date, comprehensive coverage of the material that any good physical anthropology text explains, with a modern biological approach that includes fields that have become major areas of research by biological anthropologists over the past decade. Though comprehensive, the book is written as accessibly as possible to be useful from community college to research-oriented university levels. We three coauthors conduct our research in three of the main areas of biological anthropology: the human fossil record (Susan Antón), primate behavior and ecology (Craig Stanford), and human biology and the brain (John Allen). This has allowed us to provide a specialist approach to each of the broad divisions of the field covered by the text.

Undergraduate enrollment in introductory biological anthropology courses has increased sharply as biological anthropology has become one way to fulfill the basic natural science requirement at many colleges and universities. We believe the changing field and the new audience have created a need for a text such as this one, integrating traditional physical anthropology with a modern Darwinian framework.

The authors are anthropologists with extensive backgrounds in both biological and social sciences and are both teachers and researchers. In a field changing as rapidly as human evolutionary science is today, we feel it is critical for active researchers to produce textbooks that serve the needs of students. In addition to the strong biological orientation of the book, we try to frame questions about humankind in light of our understanding of culture and the ways in which culture interacts with biology to create the template for human nature.

We have made an effort in *Biological Anthropology* to add topics not covered in many of the existing texts while preserving a comprehensive coverage of traditional topics.

For instance, we have included an appendix in the book on forensic anthropology, a topic not traditionally covered in introductory biological anthropology texts. We have also featured biomedical anthropology, including a large feature (much of Chapter 17) on the behavior and biology of modern people, from the study of foragers (hunter-gatherers) to that of the human psyche (evolutionary psychology), and a more extensive discussion of the geological background necessary for human paleontology (Chapter 9).

We have also tried to keep polemic out of the book; in a field famous for intellectual disagreements over the meaning of fossils or interpretations of Darwinian theory, we feel it is essential to provide students with well-rounded views of the evidence. There are places where, because of the introductory nature of the text, we have not delved deeply into the details of some debates, but we have nevertheless tried to balance multiple views of ongoing unresolved questions.

FORMAT OF THE BOOK

The book is organized in much the same way that we three authors have taught introductory courses in biological anthropology. We have different backgrounds within biological anthropology but a common intellectual thread, which is the heart and soul of any book on biological anthropology: the theory of evolution by natural selection. This is the unifying aspect of each chapter, and indeed for the entire discipline. Part I, Foundations (Chapters 1 and 2) reflects this. The text begins with an overview of the field of biological anthropology in the larger context of the social and life sciences, including a brief history of the field. Chapter 2 reviews the roots of evolutionary thinking and how it became central to biological anthropology. Part II, Mechanisms of Evolution (Chapters 3 through 6) reviews at length the mechanisms of evolution and describes the applications of modern genetic research techniques in unraveling some of the mysteries of human evolution. Chapters 3 and 4 review cellular, molecular, and population genetics. Chapter 5 takes the discussion of genetics into modern evolutionary theory: the formation of species and the central topics of natural selection and adaptation. Chapter 6 surveys the field of human adaptation and the ways in which evolutionary forces mold human populations.

Part III, Primates (Chapters 7 and 8) is about the living nonhuman primates. We review their classification, their anatomical and behavioral adaptations, and their social life. We cautiously use the behavior of living monkeys and apes to understand what their ancestors, and therefore ours, may have been like.

Part IV, The Fossil Record (Chapters 9 through 15), describes the fossil record for humanity. We begin with the environmental context in which fossils are found and describe the periods of Earth's history during which primates arose (Chapter 9). After a review of primate evolution (Chapter 10), we discuss the anatomical transition from an ape to human ancestor (Chapter 11), a change that set off a cascade of effects that we feel to the present day. Chapter 12 describes the most up-to-date information on the earliest known hominids in Africa. Chapter 13 introduces the genus *Homo* and the causes and consequences of dispersal from Africa. Chapters 14 and 15 cover the more recent hominid fossils, including Neandertals, and the origins of our own species. We have tried to provide up-to-the-minute information on the discovery of new human fossils. As this book went to press, an important new hominid fossil was announced (Flores Women), which you will read about in Chapter 15.

Part V, Biology and Behavior of Modern Humans (Chapters 16 through 18) is about the biology of modern people. We include coverage of the human brain and its evolutionary aspects (Chapter 16), biocultural issues of biomedical anthropology (Chapter 17), and the biocultural aspects of the lives of traditional foraging people (Chapter 18).

The appendices offer a section on forensic anthropology (Appendix A), and additional reference material on the primate skeleton (Appendix B), the Hardy–Weinberg equilibrium (Appendix C), and metric to imperial conversion factors (Appendix D).

SPECIAL FEATURES

As you read the book, you will notice a few special features in addition to the main body of text. We begin each chapter with a short **vignette** depicting the main topic of the chapter. Some of these are quotes taken from famous works by biological anthropologists, such as Dian Fossey describing a day with mountain gorillas at the beginning of Chapter 8. For other chapters, one of the authors has written a short description of how someone studying human fossils, for example, might experience a day in the field. In a few chapters, we depict the lives of early humans drawn from our imagination, fleshed out with details as accurate as our science currently possesses. You should use the vignettes as a way to get a feel for the chapter topics and as an enjoyable and informative reflection on the text material.

We have also presented some text material in **boxes** inset into each chapter. The purpose of the boxes is to expand on text material or call your attention to current events connected to our field, to emerging debates, or sometimes just to fascinating side stories. The material in the boxes is generally distinct from that in the text.

Other special features of the text are a margin **glossary** to define new terms as students encounter them and a complete glossary at the back of the book. Each chapter is summarized by a list of questions and answers and each chapter also ends with several **critical thinking questions** intended to provoke as well as summarize. We have listed a few **suggested readings** with each chapter, with an emphasis on books that are highly readable, nontechnical accounts that an introductory student may want to pursue. And the book contains a **bibliography** of all the references used and cited in the text.

ILLUSTRATIONS

Illustrations play a major role in any textbook, and they are crucial learning tools in introductory science texts. The publisher and authors have worked together to try to provide you with the best possible photos and drawings of every topic covered in the book. Many of the photographs of living primates, and some of fossils and fossil sites, were taken by one of the authors, and others were contributed by other biological anthropologists. Prentice Hall has worked hard to produce some of the finest images of everything from molecular genetics to stone tools that have ever been published in a biological anthropology textbook. The maps have been specifically created for this book by Dorling Kindersley, a leading publisher of atlases for both the educational and consumer markets. These maps describe the geography of everything from the distribution of living primates in the world today to the locations of the continents in the distant past. We authors worked with Prentice Hall to be sure everything in this first edition is depicted accurately and clearly, and we hope you will gain a better understanding of the text by studying the visual material as well.

Special two-page feature illustrations appear in a number of chapters, especially in Part IV, and provide a snapshot of evolutionary development through time. These special feature illustrations provide a concise way for the reader to easily grasp the evolutionary changes through a vast sweep of time that are presented in greater detail in the text.

A Note about Language Authors must make decisions about language and terminology, and textbook authors make those choices with the knowledge that they may be influencing the mindset of a generation of young scholars. Some of these choices are modest. For instance, we use the modern American spelling *Neandertal* instead of the more traditional European spelling *Neanderthal*. Other language choices are more central to the subject matter. Perhaps the most significant choice we have made is with regard to primate classification. Although the primate order historically has been subdivided into anthropoids (the apes and monkeys, including us) and prosimians (the "lower" primates, including lemurs, galagos, lorises, and tarsiers), the majority of scholars today think this dichotomy does not reflect evolutionary reality as well as a subdivision into haplorhines and strepsirhines. Haplorhines include all anthropoids and tarsiers, and strepsirhines include all prosimians except tarsiers. We discuss this distinction in some depth in Chapter 7 and use the terms *strepsirhine* and *haplorhine* rather than *prosimian* and *anthropoid*. In another case, we have opted to use the more traditional family-level designation *hominid* to refer to humans and our ancestors rather than the alternative tribal-level *hominin*, which is less broadly used in the literature. We discuss this classification in Chapter 11.

Regarding Abbreviations and Time Because of the plethora of sometimes conflicting abbreviations used to refer to time throughout the text, we have attempted to spell out time ranges (e.g., "millions of years ago" or "thousands of years ago"). Where this is not feasible, such as in tables, we use the abbreviations most common to anthropology textbooks (*mya* for "millions of years ago" and *kya* for "thousands of years ago"). However, students should note that the standard usage in geology and paleontology is *Ma* (mega-annum) and *ka* (kilo-annum).

SUPPLEMENTAL RESOURCES

The ancillary materials that accompany *Biological Anthropology* are part of a complete teaching and learning package and have been carefully created to enhance the topics discussed in the text.

PRINT SUPPLEMENTS

Instructor's Resource Manual with Tests For each chapter in the text, this valuable resource provides a detailed outline, list of objectives, discussion questions, and classroom activities. In addition, test questions in multiple-choice and short answer formats are available for each chapter; the answers to all questions are page referenced to the text.

TestGEN-EQ This software allows instructors to create their own personalized exams, to edit the existing test questions, and to add new questions. Other special features of this program include random generation of test questions, creation of alternative versions of the same test, question sequence scrambling, and test preview before printing.

MEDIA SUPPLEMENTS

A one-stop shop for both professors and students, this innovative, premium Website will help professors more effectively prepare lectures and help students more efficiently review the course material. For professors, it includes PowerPoint presentations, instructor supplements, and testing software. For students, it includes flashcards, quizzes, and concept tips. Professors can gain access to OneKey by contacting their Prentice Hall representative or by visiting http://www.prenhall.com/onekey for registration. Students can access OneKey when professors order a special package of *Biological Anthropology* with a free OneKey access code wrapped with the text. OneKey can be used with WebCT™, BlackBoard™, or Course Compass.

Instructor Resource CD-ROM This interactive CD pulls together all the print and media assets available to instructors. In addition, instructors can insert media—PowerPoint slides, graphs, charts, and maps—into their interactive classroom presentations.

Companion Website™ This online study guide provides unique support to help students with their studies in biological anthropology. Featuring a variety of interactive learning tools, including online quizzes with immediate feedback, this site is a comprehensive resource organized according to the chapters in *Biological Anthropology*. It can be found at http://www.prenhall.com/stanford.

The New York Times/Prentice Hall Themes of the Times The New York Times and Prentice Hall are sponsoring *Themes of the Times*, a program designed to enhance student access to current information relevant to the classroom. Through this program, the core subject matter provided in the text is supplemented by a collection of timely articles downloaded from one of the world's most distinguished newspapers, *The New York Times*. These articles demonstrate the vital, ongoing connection between what is learned in the classroom and what is happening in the world around us. Access to *The New York Times*/Prentice Hall *Themes of the Times* is available on the *Biological Anthropology* Companion Website™.

ACKNOWLEDGMENTS

Textbooks require the collaboration of many people with many areas of expertise, and this book made good use of all of those involved. The process begins with each author compiling his or her notes from years of teaching biological anthropology and thinking about how the course could be more effectively taught. Over the years the students in our courses have helped us to assess what did and did not work in conveying the information and excitement of biological anthropology, and for this we are extremely grateful. For her vision and steady guidance over the past two and a half years we are most grateful to Nancy Roberts, publisher of anthropology at Prentice Hall. We also thank Nancy's assistant, Lee Peterson, for keeping the chapters flowing, and media editor Kate Ramunda for the media that accompanies this text. We owe a debt of gratitude to our project manager and development editor, Carolyn Viola-John, and to development editor Elisa Adams for their tireless and careful editing and for their patience and diplomacy in dealing with the logistics of working with three different authors. The outstanding efforts of Anne Bonanno Nieglos and Jill Lehan in coordinating and creating all design elements resulted in this beautiful text. Cheryl Keenan, production editor at Prentice Hall, did a remarkable job of coordinating the entire production process. Maria Piper was tireless in coordinating the extensive art program that accompanies this book. We appreciate the diligence of copyeditor Carol Anne Peschke and the creativity of photo researcher Teri Stratford. Thanks also to senior marketing manager Marissa Feliberty for directing the marketing campaign.

For discussions on the book outline and organization and insights about introductory texts and primate evolution we thank Monte McCrossin.

For contributing photos and published or unpublished material to help in writing the text, we thank Brad Adams, Christopher Boehm, David Brill, Peter Brown, Joel Bruss, Hanna Damasio, Eric Delson, Todd Disotell, Craig Feibel, Ken Garrett, John Krigbaum, The National Museum of Kenya, Lisa Matisoo-Smith, William McComas, Monte McCrossin, Amy Parish, Briana Pobiner, Paul Sledzik, Josh Snodgrass, Fred Spoor, Carl Swisher, Ian Tattersall, Brent Turrin, Alan Walker, Randy White, Tatiana White, Andrea Wiley, and Milford Wolpoff.

All three of us cut our teeth teaching introductory biological anthropology as graduate students apprenticing as teaching assistants at the University of California. Our fellow TAs shared their ideas and our tasks, for which we are thankful. We are most grateful to the triumvirate of faculty with whom we apprenticed and from whom we learned much about the subject matter, how to teach it, and how an introductory course can be made a rewarding, enriching experience for undergraduates. Our heartfelt thanks go to Katharine Milton, Vincent Sarich, and Tim White.

Graduate teaching assistants in our own courses at the University of Southern California, the University of Auckland, the University of Florida, Rutgers University, and New York University brought new enthusiasm and ideas, and we are grateful to them all.

For their constructive reviewing of the manuscript, we thank

Robert L. Anemone, Western Michigan University
John R. Baker, Moorpark College
Art Barbeau, West Liberty State College
Anna Bellisari, Wright State University
David W. Frayer, University of Kansas
Sarah A. C. Keller, Eastern Washington University
Andrew Kramer, University of Tennessee
John R. Lukacs, University of Oregon
Peer H. Moore-Jansen, Wichita State University
Leanne T. Nash, Arizona State University
Robert R. Paine, Texas Tech University
Jill D. Pruetz, Iowa State University
J. Richard Shenkel, University of New Orleans
Lynnette Leidy Sievert, University of Massachusetts-Amherst
Larissa Swedell, Queens College – CUNY
Trudy R. Turner, University of Wisconsin-Milwaukee
Daniel J. Wescott, University of Missouri-Columbia
Bruce P. Wheatley, University of Alabama-Birmingham
Linda D. Wolfe, East Carolina University

We've made a great effort to produce a comprehensive and fully accurate text, but as in any book's first edition, errors may remain. We would be grateful for comments or corrections from students and instructors using *Biological Anthropology.* And we hope you find this account of human evolution as fascinating and compelling as we do.

Craig Stanford
John S. Allen
Susan C. Antón

Craig Stanford is a professor of anthropology and biological sciences at the University of Southern California, where he also directs the Jane Goodall Research Center and chairs the Department of Anthropology. He has conducted field research on primate behavior in south Asia, Latin America, and East Africa. He is well known for his long-term studies of meat-eating among wild chimpanzees in Gombe, Tanzania, and of the relationship between mountain gorillas and chimpanzees in the Impenetrable Forest of Uganda. He has authored or coauthored more than 100 scientific publications. Craig has received USC's highest teaching awards for his introductory *Biological Anthropology* course. In addition, he has published seven books on primate behavior and human origins, including *Significant Others* (2001) and *Upright* (2003). He and his wife, Erin Moore, a cultural anthropologist at USC, live in South Pasadena, California, and have three children.

John Allen is a research scientist and adjunct associate professor in the Department of Neurology at the University of Iowa College of Medicine. Previously, he was a faculty member in the Department of Anthropology at the University of Auckland, New Zealand, for several years. His primary research interests are the evolution of the human brain and behavior, and behavioral disease. He also has research experience in molecular genetics, nutritional anthropology, and the history of anthropology. He has conducted fieldwork in Japan, New Zealand, Papua New Guinea, and Palau. He has received university awards for teaching introductory courses in biological anthropology both as a graduate student instructor at the University of California and as a faculty member at the University of Auckland. John and his wife, Stephanie Sheffield, have two sons, Reid and Perry (the Berry).

Susan Antón is an associate professor in the Center for the Study of Human Origins, Department of Anthropology at New York University, where she also directs the M.A. program in Human Skeletal Biology. Her field research concerns the evolution of genus *Homo* in Indonesia and human impact on island ecosystems in the South Pacific. She is best known for her work on *H. erectus* and dispersal. She is joint editor of the *Journal of Human Evolution*. She received awards for teaching as a graduate student instructor at the University of California and was Teacher of the Year at the University of Florida. She has been twice elected to *Who's Who Among America's Teachers*. Susan and her husband, Carl Swisher, a geochronologist, raise Anatolian shepherd dogs.

PART I

FOUNDATIONS

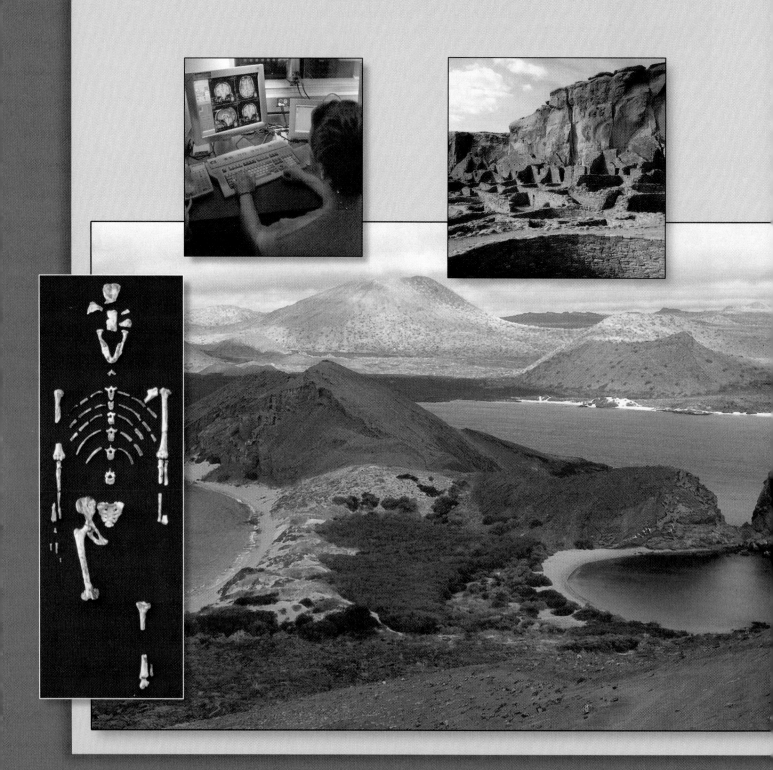

Chapter 1

INTRODUCTION: What Is Biological Anthropology?

O N A SUNNY MORNING IN EAST AFRICA, with the temperature already climbing past 90 degrees, a scientist stands in a shallow pit, carefully examining the dusty ground. All around her are the tools of her trade: shovels, dental picks, whisk brooms, surveying equipment. Something glinting in the morning light catches her eye. She bends over to examine a tiny fragment of whitish bone, then another and another. Realizing that her week of hard, sweaty work has just paid off, she beckons her assistants to see the prize, then carefully begins to map the spot for the work that now begins: unearthing the fossilized skeleton of an ancient primate, perhaps the forerunner of all modern apes. Weeks later, returning to the capital city and its museum, the scientist compares the new fossils with previously collected specimens. She finds that a few of the pieces her team has excavated fit together with the long-neglected bones of a fossil ape discovered at the site in the 1930s. The scientist devotes long hours to studying every detail of the skeleton. A new picture emerges: This ancient ape may have been the first to come down from the trees and venture forth on the ground below.

A FEW HUNDRED MILES AWAY, ANOTHER SCIENTIST sits in the tall grass of a high mountain meadow. All around him are massive, shaggy-haired mountain gorillas, happily munching on wild celery. A bright-eyed baby gorilla ambles up to the scientist and toys with the laces of his boot, then runs quickly back to its mother. Two silverbacks, majestic 400-pound males wearing saddles of gray hair across their backs, sit like enormous statues a few yards away. The scientist uses the tools of his trade: a notebook and checklist to record behavior, plus a handheld global positioning system unit to map the animals' travels. As the gorilla group finishes its lunch, the silverbacks get up and head off into the forest, bulldozing a trail that the females, babies, and scientist obediently follow.

AT THE SAME TIME, HALF A WORLD AWAY, a third scientist is sitting in a laboratory intently studying a computer monitor. He looks at a three-dimensional, high-resolution image of a human brain. Millimeter by millimeter, he examines the frontal lobe, a region of the brain thought to be of key importance in the evolution of modern people. By moving the screen cursor slightly, he can study the brain's surface from every possible angle, making virtual slices through it to study its internal organization. Unlike skulls, brains do not become preserved as fossils, so the scientist uses images of the brains of living humans and other primates to reconstruct the way in which the brains of long-dead ancestors may have been organized.

What do these three scientists—one studying ancient fossils, another observing primate behavior, and the third studying the evolution of the human brain—all have in common? They are biological anthropologists, engaged in the scientific study of humankind (from *anthropos*, meaning human, and *-ology*, the study of). Despite our exalted intellect, our mind-boggling technology, and our intricately complex social behavior, we are nonetheless biological creatures. Humans are **primates** and share a recent ancestry with the living great apes. Like the apes, we are the products of millions of years of **evolution** by natural selection.

The famed geneticist Theodosius Dobzhansky once said, "Nothing in biology makes sense except in the light of evolution." Biological anthropologists spend their careers trying to understand the details of the evolutionary process and the ways in which it has shaped who we are today. They use a central, unifying set of biological principles in their work, first set down by Charles Darwin nearly 150 years ago. The frequency of a particular trait and the genes that control it can change from one generation to the next; this is evolution. This elegantly simple idea forms the heart and soul of **biological anthropology.**

The evolutionary process usually is slow and inefficient, but over many generations it can mold animals and plants into a bewildering variety of forms. Our ancestry includes many animals that little resemble us today. Biological anthropology is particularly concerned with the evolutionary transformations that occurred over the past 6 million years, as an apelike primate began to walk on two legs and became something different: a **hominid.** From the perspective of evolutionary theory, humans are like all other biological species, the product of the same long process of **adaptation.**

THE SCOPE OF BIOLOGICAL ANTHROPOLOGY

The scope of biological anthropology is vastly wider than the study of primates, fossils, and brain evolution. Any scientist studying evolution as it relates to the human species, directly or indirectly, could be called a biological anthropologist. This includes a number of related disciplines (see Figure 1.1).

PALEOANTHROPOLOGY

When an exciting new fossil of an extinct form of human is found, paleoanthropologists usually are responsible (Figure 1.2 on page 4). **Paleoanthropology** is the study of the fossil record for humankind, and fossilized remains are the most direct physical evidence of human ancestry that we have to understand where we came from. The discovery of skeletal evidence of new ancestral species, or additional specimens of existing species, revises our view of the human family tree. Discoveries of hominid fossils—some as famous as Peking Man or Lucy (Figure 1.3 on page 4) but many less known—have profoundly changed the way we view our place in nature. Paleoanthropology also includes the study of the fossil record of the other primates—apes, monkeys, and prosimians—dating back at least 65 million years. These early fossils give us key clues about how, where, and why hominids evolved millions of years later. There are fossil sites producing important fossils all over the world, and with more and more students and researchers searching, our fossil history grows richer every year. In fact, although the first half of the twentieth century witnessed discoveries of new human fossils every decade or so, the pace of discovery of new species of fossil humans has accelerated rapidly in recent years. This is because more students and researchers are searching for fossils and because global and regional political changes have allowed researchers into areas that were long off limits because of civil war or political unrest.

Paleoanthropological research begins in the field, where researchers search the landscape for new discoveries. Much of the scholarly work then takes place in museums and university laboratories around the world, where the specimens are archived and preserved for detailed study. Because we can safely assume that the evolutionary process taking place in the present also took place in the past, the study of the meaning of human and nonhuman primate fossils proceeds from comparisons between extinct and living forms. For example, the presence of large canine teeth in the male specimens of a fossil monkey species implies that in life, the species lived in multiple male groups in which males competed for mates, because

primate Member of the mammalian order Primates, including prosimians, monkeys, apes, and humans, defined by a suite of anatomical and behavioral traits.

evolution A change in the frequency of a gene or a trait in a population over multiple generations.

biological anthropology The study of humans as biological organisms, considered in an evolutionary framework; sometimes called physical anthropology.

hominid A member of the primate family Hominidae, distinguished by bipedal posture and, in more recently evolved species, large brain.

adaptation A trait that increases the reproductive success of an organism, produced by natural selection in the context of a particular environment.

paleoanthropology The study of the fossil record of ancestral humans and their primate kin.

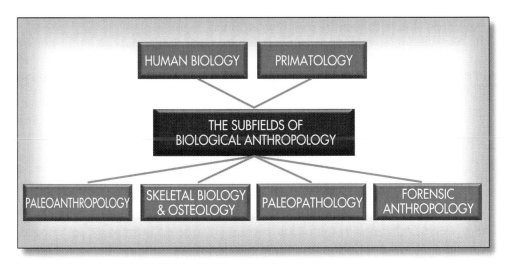

FIGURE 1.1 Subfields of Biological Anthropology.

FIGURE 1.2
Paleoanthropologist Jane
Moore maps sites at Kanapoi,
Kenya.

major differences in canine tooth size between males and females indicates mate competition in living monkeys.

As the fossil record has grown, we have begun to see that the evolutionary history of our species is extremely complicated; most lineages are now extinct, but many thrived for millions of years. The ladder of progress notion—an older, more linear view of our ancestry in which each species evolved into more complex forms—has been replaced by a family tree with many branches.

SKELETAL BIOLOGY AND HUMAN OSTEOLOGY

osteology   The study of the skeleton.

paleopathology   The study of diseases in ancestral human populations.

Osteology is the study of the skeleton. The first order of business when a fossil is discovered is to figure out what sort of animal the fossil—often a tiny fragment—may have been in life, so osteologists must possess extraordinary skills of identification and a keen spatial sense of how a jigsaw puzzle–like array of bone chips fits together when they are trying to understand the meaning of fossils they have found.

Among the first generation of biological anthropologists (Figure 1.4) were the *anthropometrists,* who made detailed measurements of the human body in all its forms, and their work is still important today. Understanding the relationship between genetics, human growth and stature, and geographic variation in human anatomy is vital to identifying the origins and patterns of human migration across the globe during prehistory, for example. When a 9,000-year-old skeleton was discovered some years ago on the banks of the Columbia River in the Pacific Northwest, osteologists with expertise in human variation in body form were among those who sought to identify its ethnic affinities.

Skeletal biology, like osteology, is the study of the human skeleton, but because the bones of the body develop in concert with other tissues, such as muscles and tendons, a skeletal biologist must know the patterns and processes of human growth, physiology, and development, not just anatomy.

PALEOPATHOLOGY

Hand in hand with skeletal biology is **paleopathology**: the study of disease in ancient human populations, as evidenced by telltale signs on the skeleton. When the Neandertal fossils first appeared in the mid-nineteenth century, there was much scientific debate about whether they represented a true species or "race," or whether they were simply modern individuals who had suffered from some pathological condition. It took nearly 30 years and the discovery of several additional specimens to resolve the issue. Today, paleopathologists would help resolve such a debate much more quickly.

FIGURE 1.3   Lucy, a partial hominid skeleton.

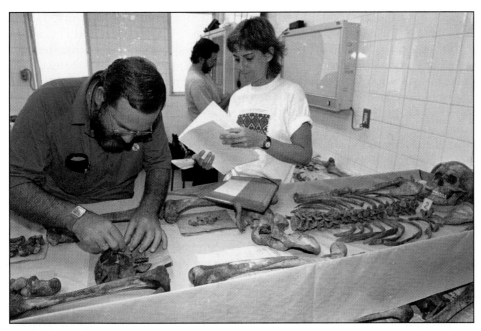

FIGURE 1.4 An osteologist at work.

Paleopathologists also work with archaeologists excavating ancient humans to study the effects of trauma, epidemics, nutritional deficiencies, and infectious diseases. If archaeologists find evidence that an ancient civilization crashed precipitously, a paleopathologist will study the remains of the bodies for signs of anything from outbreaks of sexually transmitted disease to poor nutrition.

FORENSIC ANTHROPOLOGY

Although biological anthropology is concerned primarily with basic research into human origins, biological anthropologists also play roles in our daily lives. **Forensic anthropology,** the study of the identification of skeletal remains and of the means by which the individual died, is a contemporary application of biological anthropology. Forensic anthropologists take their knowledge of osteology and paleopathology and apply it to both historical and criminal investigations (Figure 1.5). During the war crime investigations into mass graves in Bosnia,

forensic anthropology
The study of human remains applied to a legal context.

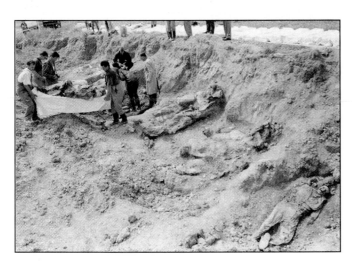

FIGURE 1.5 Forensic anthropologists use skeletal remains to identify victims of war in Bosnia.

FIGURE 1.6 Recovery team at work at the World Trade Center Ground Zero following the September 11, 2001 attack.

forensic anthropologists were called in to attempt to identify victims, as they also were after the terrorists attacks in New York, Washington, and Pennsylvania on September 11, 2001 (Figure 1.6). When police were investigating the murder of the wife of football star O. J. Simpson, forensic scientists used the footprints in blood left at the murder scene to try to reconstruct the height and weight of the murderer. This is not so different from what paleoanthropologists did when they discovered a set of tiny human-like footprints imbedded in fossilized ash at Laetoli in northern Tanzania. They used forensic skills to try to reconstruct the likely height and weight of the creatures that had left those prints nearly 4 million years ago.

PRIMATOLOGY

Primatology is the branch of biological anthropology that is best known to the public through the highly publicized work of renowned primatologists Jane Goodall and Dian Fossey. Primatologists study the anatomy, physiology, behavior, and genetics of both living and extinct monkeys, apes, and prosimians. Behavioral studies of nonhuman primates in their natural environments gained prominence in the 1960s and 1970s, when the pioneering work of Jane Goodall was publicized widely in the United States and elsewhere. In the early days of primate behavior study, the researchers were mainly psychologists. By the late 1960s, however, biological anthropology had become the domain of primate behavior study, especially in North America.

Primatologists study nonhuman primates for a variety of reasons, including the desire to learn more about their intrinsically fascinating patterns of behavior (Figure 1.7). Within an anthropological framework, primatologists study the nonhuman primates for the lessons they can provide on how evolution has molded the human species. For example, male baboons fight among themselves for the chance to mate with females. They are also much larger and more aggressive than females. Do larger, more macho males father more offspring than their smaller and gentler brothers? If so, these traits appear to have appeared slowly through generations of evolutionary change, and the size difference between males and females is the result of selection for large body size. Then, what about the body size difference between men and women of our own species? Is it the result of competi-

primatology The study of the nonhuman primates and their anatomy, genetics, behavior, and ecology.

FIGURE 1.7 Jane Goodall is a pioneering primatologist whose studies of wild chimpanzees changed our view of human nature.

tion between men in prehistory, or perhaps a preference by women in prehistory for tall men? The clues that we derive about human nature from the behavior and anatomy of living primates must be interpreted cautiously but can be vitally important in our understanding of who we are and where we came from.

Biological anthropologists trained as primatologists find careers not only in universities but also in museums, zoos, and conservation agencies. Many important wildlife conservation projects seeking to protect endangered primate species are being carried out around the world by biological anthropologists.

HUMAN BIOLOGY

In addition to paleoanthropology and primatology, biological anthropologists span a wide range of interests that are often labeled **human biology**. Some work in the area of *human adaptation,* learning how people adjust physiologically to the extremes of Earth's physical environments. For instance, how are children affected by growing up high in the Andes mountain range of South America at elevations over 14,000 feet (4,270 m)? Other human biologists work as *nutritional anthropologists,* studying the interrelationship of diet, culture, and evolution. Biological anthropologists interested in demography examine the biological and cultural forces that shape the composition of human populations. Other biological anthropologists are particularly interested in how various hormones in the human body influence human behavior and how, in turn, the environment affects the expression of these hormones. The study of *human variation* deals with the many ways in which people differ in their anatomy throughout the world.

At an earlier time in history, the scholarly study of physical traits such as height, skull shape, and especially skin color was tainted with the possibility that the researcher had some racially biased preconceptions. Today, biological anthropologists are interested in human variation, both anatomical and genetic, simply because it offers clues about the peopling of the world by the migrations of early people. Understanding when, where, and how people left Africa and colonized Europe, Asia, and eventually the New World can tell us a great deal about the roots of modern languages, diseases, population genetics, and other topics of great relevance in the world today.

Many contemporary biological anthropologists are interested in research problems that require an understanding of both biological and cultural factors. Biological anthropologists with these interests sometimes are called *biocultural anthropologists.* One area in which a biocultural perspective is vitally important is *biomedical anthropology* (Figure 1.8). Biomedical anthropologists might study how human cultural practices influence the spread of infectious disease and how the effects of pollution or toxins in the environment affect human growth. Biomedical anthropologists are particularly interested in looking at the effects that adopting an urbanized (and Western) lifestyle has on people who have lived until recently under more traditional, non-Western conditions. The expression of many human diseases is influenced by genetic factors, and biomedical anthropologists often look at the long-term evolutionary consequences of disease on human populations.

Finally, an increasing number of biological anthropologists work in the field of genetics (Figure 1.9 on page 8). *Molecular anthropology* is a genetic approach to human evolutionary science that seeks to understand the differences in the genome between humans and their closest relatives, the nonhuman primates. Because genetic inheritance is the basis for evolutionary change, a geneticist is in a perfect position to be able to address some of the fundamental questions about human nature and human evolution. We know that the human DNA sequence is extremely similar to that of an ape, but what exactly does this mean? At which points do the differences result in some key shift, such as language? These are some of the questions that may be answerable in the very near future with the help of anthropological geneticists.

human biology Subfield of biological anthropology dealing with human growth and development, adaptation to environmental extremes, and human genetics.

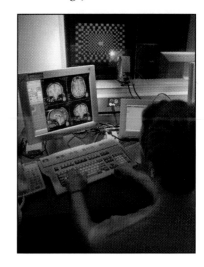

FIGURE 1.8 Biomedical anthropologists study, among other things, the human brain.

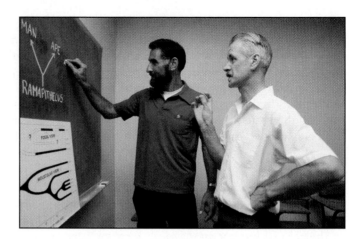

FIGURE 1.9 Vincent Sarich and Allan Wilson helped pioneer the molecular anthropological approach to studying primate and human evolution.

THE ROOTS OF MODERN BIOLOGICAL ANTHROPOLOGY

In 1856, the fossil of an ancient human ("Neandertal Man") was discovered in Germany (Schaaffhausen, 1858). In England in 1859, Charles Darwin published *On the Origin of Species*. Darwin's work had a greater immediate impact than the Neandertal's appearance because it was some time before scientists agreed that the Neandertal was an ancient human rather than just an odd-looking modern one. Darwin's introduction of an evolutionary perspective made many of the old debates about human origins irrelevant. After Darwin, scientists no longer needed to debate whether humans originated via a single creation or the different races were created separately (*monogenism* versus *polygenism*); the study of the natural history of humans became centered on the evolutionary history of our species. Human variation was the product of the interaction between the biological organism and the environment. Apes and monkeys—the nonhuman primates—became our "cousins" almost overnight.

The field known in North America as **physical anthropology** was established as an academic discipline in the second half of the nineteenth century (Spencer, 1997). In France, Germany, and England, it was called simply *anthropology*. Most early physical anthropologists were physicians who taught anatomy in medical schools and had an interest in human variation or evolution. In the first half of the twentieth century, much of physical anthropology was devoted to measuring bodies and skulls (*anthropometry* and *craniometry*), with particular attention paid to the biological definition of human races. Physical anthropologists also studied the comparative anatomy of nonhuman primates and the limited fossil record of humans and other primates.

By the mid-twentieth century, a new physical anthropology emerged, led by a generation of scholars who were trained as anthropologists first and foremost and who in turn trained hundreds of graduate students who benefited from the expansion of higher education fueled by the Baby Boom generation. The new physical anthropology, whose main architect was Sherwood Washburn of the University of Chicago and later of the University of California, Berkeley, embraced the dynamic view of evolution promoted by the adherents of the neo-Darwinian synthesis. This synthesis of genetics, anatomy, ecology, and behavior with evolutionary theory emerged in the biological sciences in the 1930s and 1940s. In the new physical anthropology, primates were not simply shot and dissected; their behavior and ecology were studied in the natural environment as well as in the laboratory (Goodall, 1963). The study of human races as pigeonholed categories gave way to the study of evolving populations, with a particular emphasis on how human populations adapt to environmental conditions. The field of paleoanthropology was revolu-

physical anthropology
The study of humans as biological organisms, considered in an evolutionary framework.

tionized by the introduction of new dating techniques and the adoption of a multidisciplinary approach to understanding ancient environments. Molecular genetics research in anthropology gave us a whole new way to reconstruct the biological histories of human populations and of primate species as a whole (Goodman, 1962; Sarich and Wilson, 1967).

Today, biological anthropology embraces a wide variety of approaches with the goal of answering a few basic questions: What does it mean to be human? How did we become who we are today? How does our biological past influence our lives in the environments of the present? What is the place of human beings in nature?

ANTHROPOLOGY AND ITS OTHER SUBFIELDS

Anthropology is the study of humankind in all its forms. But of course this would not distinguish it from other disciplines that study the human condition, such as psychology, history, and sociology. The critical aspect of anthropology that sets it apart is its cross-cultural, holistic nature. That is, we try to understand the inner workings of a group of people who hold different worldviews, values, and traditions than we do. The unusual thing about the human animal is that we have **culture**. Although it often seems that anthropologists spend their careers arguing about how to define culture, we can say simply that culture is the sum total of learned traditions of a group of people. Language is culture (although the ability to use language is biological), as is religion, as are the way people dress and the foods they eat. These human behaviors vary greatly from one culture to the next. But what about the universal taboo on incestuous relations with one's siblings? Or the observation that across many human societies, women tend to marry older men? Are these common threads of human cultures the result of learned traditions, passed down across the generations, or is there a biological influence at work? As we will see, the interplay between biology and culture provides many of the most intriguing and perplexing clues about the roots of our humanity. It also creates many of the most intense debates; for decades scholars have debated whether genes or the environment have played the more important role in molding intelligence and other human qualities.

The dichotomy between biological and cultural influences on humankind is a false one, as we examine in detail later in the book. In earliest humans, biological evolution produced the capacity for culture: Intelligence had to evolve before learned traditions such as tool using could flourish, as we see in wild apes today. Our biology produced culture, but culture can also influence biology. We study these patterns under the rubric of **biocultural anthropology**.

Anthropology is divided into four subfields: biological anthropology, cultural anthropology, linguistic anthropology, and archaeology (Figure 1.10 on page 10). Some anthropologists consider linguistics and archaeology as subfields within cultural anthropology. In addition, applied anthropology—a method more than a discipline—is sometimes considered a fifth subfield. The majority of practicing anthropologists in the United States are cultural anthropologists, who typically make up more than half of the faculty of anthropology departments in universities and who also are employed in a variety of nonacademic settings, as you will see in this section.

Cultural Anthropology

Cultural anthropology is the study of human societies in a cross-cultural perspective. The amazing variety of ways in which people lead their daily lives is at the heart of the field. Although biological anthropology straddles the life sciences and social sciences and is often treated as a life science in undergraduate education, cultural

anthropology The study of humankind in a cross-cultural context. Anthropology includes the subfields cultural anthropology, linguistic anthropology, archaeology, and biological anthropology.

culture The sum total of learned traditions, values, and beliefs that groups of people, and a few species of highly intelligent animals, possess.

biocultural anthropology The study of the interaction between biology and culture, which plays a role in most human traits.

cultural anthropology The study of human societies, especially in a cross-cultural context; the subdivision of anthropology that includes ethnology, archaeology, and linguistics.

FIGURE 1.10 The Subfields of Anthropology.

ethnology The study of human societies, their traditions, rituals, beliefs, and the differences between societies in these traits.

ethnography The practice of cultural anthropology. Ethnographers study the minute-to-minute workings of human societies, especially non-Western societies.

anthropology is squarely in the social sciences. In fact, recent trends in cultural anthropology that have tended to deemphasize quantitative data about other cultures in favor of interpretive, subjective accounts have moved some anthropologists further away from science and toward the humanities. This trend has stretched the spectrum of anthropology even further, as faculty members in the same academic department may run the gamut from molecular biochemists to political philosophers. (Box 1.1)

Ethnology, one of the subfields of cultural anthropology, is the study of human societies and of the behavior of people within those societies. It might include everything from the way marriages and funerals are arranged, to the economic system, to the kinship system. The practice of ethnology is called **ethnography** (literally, the describing of culture). The study of the way in which foraging people track down their prey is ethnography. So is a written account of the initiation rituals of street gangs in Los Angeles. And so is the study of how parents in Boston care for their children relative to parenting among the Sherpas of highland Nepal. The common thread that runs through all these studies is that they seek to understand the workings of another culture by comparing it with the culture of the investigator (Figure 1.11). Although sociologists could also say they study culture, ethnologists immerse themselves in the hour-to-hour process of human lives in a way that is different from other academic fields, both in the degree of immersion and the emphasis on cross-cultural differences.

Traditionally, ethnologists aligned themselves with the geographic area in which they worked. A cultural anthropologist studying the practice of witchcraft in Africa would also be an Africanist, an authority on all aspects of African culture. These

FIGURE 1.11 Cultural anthropologist Erin Moore interviews a family in a village in Rajasthan, India. Ethnographers immerse themselves in local cultures in order to understand them.

Box 1.1   A Paradigm Split in Anthropology?

A *paradigm* is a conceptual framework that allows scholars to make sense of existing information. It is the rules and methods by which a scientist works. Newtonian physics is a paradigm; so is Freudian psychology. Darwin's theory of evolution is the paradigm anthropologists have used for a century and a half to make sense of the natural world. But in the first decade of the twenty-first century, the field of anthropology is experiencing sharp growing pains. Many cultural anthropologists have come to reject biological influences on human behavior, and a debate over paradigms has ensued. During most of the twentieth century, all anthropologists shared a common mindset: that we can study human societies scientifically by gathering information about them and testing ideas in much the same way that scientists in other fields work. In the 1960s, a cultural anthropologist might have gone off to rural Africa to spend a year studying the religious practices and beliefs of a tribal culture there; she made an educated guess about the reasons that a given religious ritual was performed and then collected data to test her hypothesis or idea. She would then come home and write a book that would become the authoritative work on the subject, partly because the culture she studied would not have had literate scholars of its own.

In the past decade, there has been a movement to reconsider the role that the anthropologist plays in describing a culture. A white male anthropologist from an urban background will have a very different perspective on the culture under study than a black female anthropologist from a rural background. If these two anthropologists, both highly trained in the practice of ethnography, see the same culture differently, what does this say about the notion of objective science? The view that scholarly study is subject to the biases inherent in the background and philosophy of the researcher is part of a worldview called *postmodernism,* in which a new age of scholars seek to "deconstruct" the conclusions of an earlier generation of anthropologists. The benefit of this approach is the open acknowledgement that an observer brings his or her own background into a scientific question. We are never fully objective observers of events around us: Postmodernists reflect on their own role in these events and in how they tend to interpret them. This movement has swept the humanities and social sciences in recent years and is having a profound impact on how cultural anthropology and the other subfields of anthropology are prac-

ticed today in America and abroad. It has meant that some of the new generation's cultural scholars regard the time-honored ethnographies of the past with skepticism. One healthy result has been an increase in importance of ethnographies written by scholars of color, especially those who are from the culture they study.

The result of this paradigm shift is that many anthropology departments in American universities are split between cultural and biological approaches to their research. Biological anthropologists are universally empirical, testing hypotheses within an objective scientific framework. Many cultural anthropologists now reject this framework, preferring to interpret what they see in other cultures in light of issues of power, gender, and ethnicity. Many biological anthropologists consider the interpretive approach to be so subjective that little of long-term merit can come from it.

Although some see this split as a natural outgrowth of the fields, most anthropologists savor the cross-fertilization of ideas that occurs when cultural and biological perspectives are present in the same academic program. Whether this trend toward separation of the disciplines will continue and result in a breakup of the field or is only a temporary fissure, only time will tell.

regional studies have become somewhat less important for a combination of reasons. First, many anthropologists now work in subcultures of their own society, such as corporate America or Latino gangs in New York City. Second, the world is a much smaller place than it was 50 years ago, with increasingly fewer groups of little-known people in the world and greater migration of people from far-flung regions to where anthropologists live. Anthropologists have broadened their perspective from regional to global and from the strictly exotic to the more common and local. Many universities now have ethnic studies programs, in which the Asian American or African American cultural experience is studied by scholars in a variety of fields.

One subfield of cultural anthropology that is growing rapidly is *medical anthropology.* Medical anthropologists used to study mainly traditional healing practices and the ways in which health and illness are conceptualized in other cultures. More recently, they have been interested in looking at how Western medicine embodies cultural biases and power asymmetries pervasive in Western culture as whole. For example, the medicalization of pregnancy (and a person's reaction to it) over the course of the twentieth century can be understood not only as an example of medical progress but as a cultural phenomenon, the result of the interaction of a variety of economic, political, and social forces.

In contrast, biological anthropologists working as biomedical anthropologists study human disease using an approach that integrates research on organic diseases with an appreciation for how the local culture may influence the way the disease is prevented, understood, and treated. Biomedical anthropologists attempt to understand disease in an evolutionary context, whereby some diseases may actually be viewed as the results of adaptive processes. They in turn study how human bodies adapt to the diseases to which they are exposed. Today, biomedical anthropologists work in collaboration with cultural medical anthropologists, clinicians, and others who take a comprehensive view of human health and illness.

Other prominent subfields of cultural anthropology include *folklore*, the collection and analysis of folktales from around the world, which often follow universal themes. *Kinship* is the study of how people define themselves in relation to their descent groups: the lineage of descent, of either genetic or fictional ancestry, that the community one lives in recognizes. Kinship patterns vary widely but follow certain universal patterns in human societies, following either maternal or paternal lines of inheritance, residence, and affiliation. Kinship patterns are of great interest to many biological anthropologists because of the biocultural nature of human behavior. Are human marital and kinship patterns derived from our primate past, or are they subject to the whims of cultural variation? This is a longstanding unanswered question in the field.

Economic anthropology, another subfield of cultural anthropology, is the study of how other cultures arrange the use of their resources. Because not all societies accumulate wealth in the way that Western cultures do, this is often the study of labor in all its forms. Hunter-gatherers engage in subsistence labor but do not accumulate material wealth. They display a sex division in labor that anthropologists feel may reveal something of the human past. Nomadic pastoralist societies accrue wealth in the form of livestock. Other, more settled agricultural and industrialized societies create economic orders, which in turn strongly influence social status of individuals.

Another subfield of cultural anthropology, *ecological anthropology* (or cultural ecology), is the study of how cultures and their physical environments interact. Adaptation is a biological concept, but people and cultures adapt themselves to local environmental circumstances in myriad nonbiological ways, too. People living in the highlands of New Guinea must cope with an entirely different set of ecological pressures than Native Americans living on the Great Plains of the United States. The ways in which these differences in environmental context have molded the tools, rituals, marital and kinship patterns, and other cultural practices are at the heart of ecological anthropology.

The work of all subfields of cultural anthropology is reflected in the field of *applied anthropology*. Anthropologists no longer do just the theory making and field research they have long been known for. Increasingly, they work to solve social problems using the cross-cultural information and perspective they bring to a cultural problem. Many of these anthropologists—biological anthropologists and archaeologists in addition to cultural anthropologists—work outside the university, in international development organizations, the health professions, and various government agencies.

archaeology The study of the material culture of past peoples.

artifacts The objects, from tools to art, left by earlier generations of people.

material culture The objects or artifacts of past human societies.

ARCHAEOLOGY

Archaeology is the study of how people used to live, based on the materials, or **artifacts**, they left behind. These artifacts, art, implements, and other objects of **material culture**, form the basis for the analysis and interpretation of everything from what an ancient culture ate to how they imagined the afterlife. Archaeologists come in many different stripes (Figure 1.12).

Prehistoric archaeologists study cultures that did not leave any recorded written history, from the early hominids to the preliterate antecedents of modern cultures from Hawaii to Africa. When a biological anthropologist excavates a 2-million-year-old fossil site in East Africa, a prehistoric archaeologist often works with the team to document the discovery, map the site, and analyze the primitive stone tools that may be found alongside the fossilized bones. The bones are the direct physical evidence of humanity, and the stone tools are the material cultural evidence. From the study of such stone tools, a prehistoric archaeologist may be able to reconstruct whether the maker of the tool was a hunter or a scavenger, and left- or right-handed.

Archaeologists work at sites all over world, studying time periods from the advent of stone tools 2.5 million years ago until the much more recent past. There are Iron and Bronze Age archaeologists working at sites across Europe and New World archaeologists studying pre-Columbian civilization in Latin America. The history and pattern of settlement of the New World and subsequent migrations of early native Americans are also studied by archaeologists. *Historical archaeologists* study past civilizations that left a written record of their existence, whether in the hieroglyphics of Egyptian tombs, the Viking runes scratched onto rock across northern Europe, or the diaries kept by the colonial settlers of New England. Other archaeologists study Revolutionary War battlefields, or sites of former slave plantations, or the land beneath New York City in an effort to understand how people lived and how their societies were structured.

In addition, an entire industry exists, *cultural resource preservation* (often called *salvage archaeology*), because construction or road-building projects that threaten to destroy burial sites or artifacts of early Americans are required to hire archaeologists to examine and evaluate artifacts found in the path of construction. Many such archaeologists work for state and local governments. Some archaeologists even work in the present, rather than the past; they study how household waste in American communities, for example, informs us about social and economic trends in society.

What kinds of insight can we gain from the things left behind? Archaeologists in the American Southwest have been embroiled in a fierce debate in recent years about whether the Native Americans we call Anasazis were peaceful farmers or violent warriors. The rapid abandonment of their elaborate stone dwellings in the Southwest by Anasazi people about 800 years ago traditionally was linked to

FIGURE 1.12 Archaeologists doing fieldwork.

drought and food shortages (Figure 1.13). The Anasazi then scattered across the Southwest, where their descendents live today. But studies of that drought by archaeologists (who studied tree rings to understand how severe the drought may have been, as recorded in patterns of tree growth) led some archaeologists to argue that drought was not enough to move the Anasazi (LeBlanc and Register, 2003). This new view holds that social factors, specifically intertribal and even internal warfare, were the driving causes that sent the Anasazi from their traditional home.

Unfortunately, some aspects of culture do not preserve as well over time as artifacts. One of these is language, because we have only the written record of humankind, plus the body's soft tissues that produce sound but do not fossilize, to guide us. Therefore, some anthropologists study the structure and context of language use to gain a deeper understanding of human behavior.

LINGUISTIC ANTHROPOLOGY

Language is perhaps the only uniquely human social behavior. Whereas other animals have communication systems based on a variety of sounds and calls that you might consider a language—chimpanzees use pant-hoots, pant-grunts, and several dozen other sounds to communicate, for example—only humans have a richly *symbolic* language. Linguists often study language structure: the grammar and sentence structure that are the mechanisms of speaking and writing. They also study the function and development of human speech and language.

Linguistic anthropology is the study of the form, function, and social context of language. Linguistic anthropologists usually are more interested in language use and the role that language plays in shaping culture than they are in the technical aspects of language structure. For instance, an anthropological linguist might study the aspects of Black English that set it apart from mainstream English—its word choice and usage—and be interested in the roots of Black English on slave plantations and in west Africa. People tend to use language to conform with their cultural, environmental, and social needs. In India, for instance, Hindi and Bengali speakers have specific labels for a far wider variety of kinship categories (such as a wife's older brother) than English speakers use.

Another research area for anthropological linguists is the roots of human language. In the same way that we can use detailed comparisons of bones to gener-

linguistic anthropology
The study of language, its origins, and use; also called anthropological linguistics.

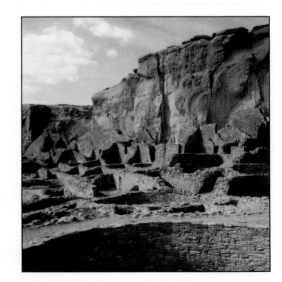

FIGURE 1.13 Archaeologists were able to understand why the Anasazi disappeared by studying their material culture.

ate a family tree of the human family, linguists construct family trees and paths of migration for human languages. Studying languages in use today, combined with archaeological records of written languages from the past, linguists attempt to understand which languages, and therefore which human cultures, are descended from which others. Such language trees can then be compared with other trees constructed using skeletal or genetic data to try to obtain a cross-referenced, comprehensive picture of humanity's past.

BIOLOGICAL ANTHROPOLOGY TODAY

Anthropologists no longer limit themselves to academic studies of people in remote corners of the world, and biological anthropologists are no exception. Biological anthropologists who undertake field studies of African hunter-gatherers with purely academic scholarly research questions in mind often become advocates for indigenous people. Because local people who cannot read or write usually lack the ability to speak out effectively against their government, biological anthropologists often end up on the front line of efforts to protect the culture, language, and way of life of such groups, whether they are hunter-gatherers in the Amazon basin or war refugees in central Africa.

Likewise, some of the most important primate conservation projects, such as the protection of mountain gorillas in Rwanda or of chimpanzees across Africa, began as the result of long-term field studies by anthropologists, who later became environmental activists. Today, as tropical forests are felled at an increasing rate and primates everywhere are threatened with imminent extinction, primatologists often form the backbone of tropical forest conservation efforts, working with conservation groups and local governments to set aside protected land for the long-term preservation of primate biodiversity. For example, primatologist Karen Strier began a study of one of the most endangered primates in the world, the muriqui of the Atlantic coastal forests of Brazil, as a graduate student at Harvard University. Some 20 years later, she continues to conduct research at the same site but has also helped to persuade the local landowners, as well as the Brazilian government, to actively help ensure the continued survival of the species.

Paleoanthropologists often are as active in preservation movements to protect the natural fossil heritage of the countries in which they work as they are in the research itself. And geneticists, while probing the mysteries of the DNA molecule, contribute to important advances in biomedical research. Applied biological anthropologists with training in forensic techniques were deeply involved in the recovery efforts at ground zero of the World Trade Center after the terrorist attacks of September 11, 2001. These efforts, and many others like them, are an essential part of what biological anthropologists do in the modern world.

SUMMARY

1. **How is anthropology different from other disciplines that involve the study of humankind?**

   Anthropology is the study of humankind in a cross-cultural perspective. Anthropologists study cultures in far-flung places, and they also study subcultures in our own society, typically immersing themselves in other cultures in ways scholars in other disciplines do not.

2. **What exactly is culture, and why do anthropologists care so much about it?**

   Culture is a set of learned behavior traditions. Every human group has its own distinctive culture, which includes its collective values and beliefs. Our capacity for culture itself is biological, and the evolution of intelligence in humans that allowed us to learn much of our behavior is a defining feature of our humanity.

3. **How does biological anthropology differ from the other subfields of anthropology?**

   Biological anthropology is the study of humans as biological creatures. It is the study of where we came from, our evolution, and how our biology interacts with our culture today. Biological anthropology is one of anthropology's four subfields, along with archaeology, cultural anthropology, and linguistic anthropology.

4. **What is the central unifying theory of biological anthropology?**

   Evolution by natural selection is the principle by which biological anthropologists understand the place of humans in the natural world.

CRITICAL THINKING QUESTIONS

1. For centuries, people have argued about whether biology or culture is the more important influence on human behavior, intelligence, and a wide range of other human qualities. This has sometimes been called the genes-environment debate or the nature-nurture debate. Why is the dichotomy between biology and culture a false one? Considering any human trait, from aggression to intelligence to courtship, how might human biology and culture interact with one another?

2. How might a forensic anthropologist be useful to a paleoanthropologist? Can you think of other special training, apart from that described in this chapter, that someone studying the human fossil record might want to have to more fully understand what he or she is studying?

KEY TERMS

primate
evolution
biological anthropology
hominid
adaptation
paleoanthropology
osteology
paleopathology

forensic anthropology
primatology
human biology
physical anthropology
anthropology
culture
biocultural
  anthropology

cultural anthropology
ethnology
ethography
archaeology
artifacts
material culture
linguistic anthropology

SUGGESTED READING

Darwin, Charles. (1859). *On the Origin of Species by Means of Natural Selection; or, The Preservation of Favoured Races in the Struggle for Life.* Murray, London.

Mead, Margaret. (1972). *Blackberry Winter: My Earlier Years.* William Morrow & Company, New York.
Spencer, Frank. (1997). *A History of Physical Anthropology.* Academic Press, New York. Garland.

Chapter 2
Origins of Evolutionary Thought

I N A MIDDLE-CLASS SUBURBAN TOWN in southern California, a heated debate about the nature of public education, science, and politics erupted in 1993. The town of Vista, a community of 76,000 near San Diego, became a battleground in the war that *creationists* (people who prefer religious explanations for the origins of humankind) have waged against the teaching of evolution in public schools. School board elections in Vista in 1993 brought a three-person majority of creationism advocates to power. The United States Supreme Court had repeatedly ruled that the teaching of theological beliefs in public school science classrooms was unconstitutional because it violated the principle of separation of church and state. Despite these rulings, the newly elected board passed a policy allowing it. The school board declared that "weaknesses that seriously challenge theories of evolution" warranted religious alternatives to be taught alongside scientific theories.

In 1993 and 1994, school gymnasiums were filled with shouting parents and educators, both for and against the new Vista policy. Many parents, even those who were conservative Christians, were firmly against allowing politics and religion to bend a science curriculum away from science. In the end, science won: In the next round of school board elections, the creationist board members were voted off and replaced by those who favored teaching science in science classrooms.

The Vista case was only one of the most recent highly publicized battles between evolution and creationism that occurred in the United States in the twentieth century. The best-known case was the "Scopes Monkey Trial," which pitted two famous lawyers against each other and focused national attention on the issue in 1925 (Figure 2.1). The 1920s was a decade of rapid social change, and conservative Christians, in an effort to preserve traditional values, wanted to ban the teaching of evolution in public schools. The state of Tennessee passed an antievolution statute in 1925. In the summer of that year, in the small town of Dayton, famed trial attorney Clarence Darrow defended John Scopes, a young schoolteacher charged with illegally teaching evolution. The legendary William Jennings Bryan, a former U.S. secretary of state, represented the state of Tennessee and argued that Scopes should be fired for espousing views that ran counter to literal acceptance of the age of the earth and of humankind as described in the Old Testament. On the witness stand, Darrow forced Bryan to acknowledge that the 6-day creation of the Book of Genesis, along with the idea that the earth was very young, were powerful myths not meant to be taken literally. In the end, Scopes was found guilty, was fined $100, and lost his job. It took decades and numerous court battles before all the states dropped antievolution laws from their books. In each case contested before a federal court, the court has ruled in favor of the separation of church and state, meaning that religious views should not be taught in a public school classroom. The courts have also stated that evolution is the unifying principle of the life sciences, without valid competition in a science curriculum from theological explanations.

For centuries, people considered the earth to be young and life on it to be unchanging. Perhaps this is because the reality of evolutionary change is inconceivable to some people. You can't see it, touch it, or sense

FIGURE 2.1 The Scopes Trial: William Jennings Bryan (right) represented the state of Tennessee, and Clarence Darrow (left) represented John Scopes.

it happening in any way, unlike more easily perceived physical laws such as gravity. The 80-year human life span is far too short to watch evolution, a process that typically happens on a scale of thousands of years. The enormous time scale of evolution is one reason that religious fundamentalists in the United States can continue to argue that "evolution is only a theory" and therefore campaign for equal time in public schools for biblical explanations for the origins of life and of humankind. As we shall see in this chapter, evolution is a theoretical framework that is the only way to make sense of a tremendous amount of evidence in support of the theory that is all around us. Fossilized dinosaur bones and ancient hominid skulls are evidence of evolution. But so are disease resistance to antibiotics and the need to develop new pesticides in order to cope with the evolution of resistance in insect pests.

In this chapter we will examine the history of ideas about how life came to be and the proponents and opponents of evolutionary theory and fact. We will also consider the issue of creationist opposition to evolutionary science. Biological anthropologists, as human evolutionary scientists, often find themselves on the front line of the debate over science and creation. First, we need to consider what science is and how it works.

WHAT IS SCIENCE?

Science is a process, not a result. The process involves **deduction** and **observation**, formulating a **hypothesis** or preliminary explanation, testing, and **experimentation**, or the collection of evidence (data) that either supports or refutes the hypothesis. This is the **scientific method** (Figure 2.2 on page 20). It is the way scientists proceed when they have a question that needs answering, or a possible explanation for a natural phenomenon that needs testing. Suppose a scientist proposes that the reason that humans walk upright and apes do not is that walking upright uses less energy (in the form of calories burned) per mile of walking, thereby giving early humans who stood up to walk an advantage over their ape ancestors (Rodman and McHenry, 1980). This is the hypothesis. The scientist would then gather quantitative evidence—the data—to test this hypothesis. He might compare the caloric output of two-legged and four-legged walking by having a human and a chimpanzee walk on a treadmill while measuring the oxygen consumption of each. If chimpanzees were discovered to be less efficient walkers than humans, then the hypothesis would be supported. Of course, there are always alternative hypotheses; perhaps another researcher would argue that chimpanzees are *more* efficient walkers than other four-legged animals, in which case a whole new study that measures walking efficiency of many other animals will be needed before the first researcher can truly stake his claim.

deduction A conclusion that follows logically from a set of observations.

observation The gathering of scientific information by watching a phenomenon.

hypothesis A preliminary explanation of a phenomenon. Hypothesis formation is the first step of the scientific method.

experimentation The testing of a hypothesis.

scientific method Standard scientific research procedure in which a hypothesis is stated, data are collected to test it, and the hypothesis is either supported or refuted.

FIGURE 2.2   The Scientific Method.

data   The scientific evidence produced by an experiment or by observation, from which scientific conclusions are made.

falsifiable   Able to be shown to be false.

paradigm   A conceptual framework useful for understanding a body of evidence.

immutability (or fixity)   Stasis, lack of change.

Science is an *empirical* process that relies on evidence and experiment. Science is not a perfect process, because **data** can be subject to differences in interpretation. But science has the essential property of being *self-correcting*. If one scientist claims to have found evidence that the Earth is flat but others claim it is round, this question can be resolved by examining all the data, which can be published for the scientific world to scrutinize. If the data supporting the flat-Earth hypothesis are weak, and the weight of scientific evidence indicates that Earth is round, the flat-Earth research will be ignored or overturned. In other words, the hypothesis that the Earth is flat is **falsifiable**. Such falsifiability is a defining trait of science. It means that rarely does a scientist claim to have "proven" anything. Instead, results are presented, and a hypothesis is either supported or rejected. Falsifiability is also a primary reason why science is such a powerful way to understand the world around us: The opportunity always exists for others to come along and correct earlier mistakes. This can be a long, slow process. Once a **paradigm**—an intellectual framework for understanding a given set of information—is in place, it may take a great deal of conflicting evidence and debate between scientists before that paradigm is overturned and replaced by a new one. In the next section we examine the great intellects whose ideas changed the paradigm of how we see the natural world.

THE EARLY THINKERS

Although Darwin is the central intellectual figure in biology and in biological anthropology, his ideas did not reach the public until the publication of his first great work, *On the Origin of Species,* in 1859. For hundreds of years before this event scholars had been thinking about the nature of life and of humanity. The ancient Greeks often are credited with the first written efforts to understand the natural world and our place in it. In the fourth century B.C., Aristotle (Figure 2.3) described the animal and plant life of the Mediterranean region; he believed that each living form possessed an absolutely fixed essence that could not be altered (**immutability** of species) and that all life was arranged in an orderly, hierarchical ladder, with humans at the very top. Ironically, both Aristotle and Plato considered experimental science to be a crude endeavor compared with the innate beauty and elegance of mathematical theory (White, 2001). Although we often think of these natural philosophers as the first real scientists, they did not see themselves this way.

THE ROOTS OF MODERN SCIENCE

The idea of the fixity of species was simply part of the static worldview during the Middle Ages. Theology was a pervasive force during this period, not only spiritually but also legally and politically. The church set doctrine that could be op-

FIGURE 2.3   Aristotle

posed only under penalty of imprisonment, or worse. Part of this doctrine was that the natural world had always existed in the same form as it exists today. Aristotle's Great Chain of Being, the idea that all organisms existed in a hierarchical ladder of sorts, with people at the top rung, was very much in place as both a natural philosophy and a legal code. Under this mindset, it is easy to see why science barely progressed.

During the Renaissance (fourteenth through sixteenth centuries), three critical developments laid the foundation for the establishment of an academic discipline devoted to a scientific understanding of the human condition (Hodgen, 1964; Rowe, 1965). First, Renaissance scholars saw themselves as "rediscovering" the knowledge of the ancient Greeks and Romans. From our perspective, what they discovered was not so important as their approach to science, which was "modern." Renaissance scholars developed a strong sense of time, their own past, and the process whereby that past is reconstructed. They also developed a sense of cultural variation as they came to realize that the people of antiquity were not like them. Indeed, science became modern when it overturned the old notions of fixity and hierarchy that held sway in the Middle Ages and were reinforced by powerful religious doctrine.

Second, great artists of the Renaissance, such as the Italian Leonardo da Vinci (1452–1519) and the Belgian Andreas Vesalius (1514–1564), raised the scientific study of human anatomy to new heights. Leonardo was perhaps the first true scientist in the modern sense. Representations of the human body in medical texts of the Middle Ages were simplistic and inaccurate, and the anatomical works of the classical physician Galen were still taken to be definitive into the Renaissance period. However, by combining scientific curiosity—culminating in the systematic dissection of the human body—and consummate artistic skill, Renaissance artist-scientists literally changed the way scholars looked at the human body. Vesalius's *De Humani Corporis Fabrica* (*On the Structure of the Human Body,* 1543) became a standard medical text replacing Galen's works (Figure 2.4). Vesalius even demonstrated that Galen's descriptions of human anatomy had been based on the dissection of animals.

Finally, the Renaissance coincided with the first circumnavigation of the globe and the European discovery and exploration of the New World. European naturalists got their first look at thousands of exotic plant and animal species at about the same time that they were trying to be more systematic and accurate in describing the natural world around them. Europeans were exposed to a greater range of human variation, both biological and cultural, than they ever knew existed. Although it was clear that the peoples of the New World were not the monsters of Medieval travelers' tales, questions were raised as to their basic humanity. Were they fully human? Did they possess souls? Could their origins be traced to Adam and Eve and the Garden of Eden? Could they be converted to Christianity? The church was definitive on this issue: By proclamation of Pope Paul III in 1537, the Indians of the New World were declared to be, in the eyes of the church, "truly men," sharing a common creation with all other men. This was used as the rationale for converting them to Christianity. This edict was strongly enforced. Sixteenth- and seventeenth-century scholars who argued for multiple origins of humanity—**polygenism**—as opposed to a single, divine origin—**monogenism**—were imprisoned or even burned at the stake. Unfortunately, the declaration that the people of the New World were indeed people did not prevent their enslavement or exploitation by Christian colonizers.

As classification, including the classification and naming of different types of people, took precedence in the seventeenth and eighteenth centuries, the issue of the ultimate biological origins of humans was pushed aside. Monogenism, the Biblical orthodoxy that all humans were derived from a single creation, held sway in

polygenism Ancient belief that people are derived from multiple creations.

monogenism Ancient belief that all people are derived from a single creation.

FIGURE 2.4 Vesalius' *De Humani Corporis Fabrica* was an important early work on the human species.

both Protestant and Catholic countries. At the turn of the nineteenth century, natural historians who wrote about people, such as the American Samuel Stanhope Smith (1750–1819) and the German Johann Friedrich Blumenbach (1752–1840), indicated their strong support for the basic unity of humankind via monogenesis. However, in the first half of the nineteenth century, an increasing number of scholars supported polygenism or multiple orgins (see Chapter 6).

If most natural historians and philosophers before the nineteenth century believed that there was a single creation event, when did they think this happened? Anglican archbishop James Ussher (1581–1656) calculated the date of the creation of Earth using the only evidence of the age of Earth available to him: the Old Testament of the Bible. By counting backward using the ages of the main characters as given in the books of the Old Testament, Ussher arrived at 4004 B.C. as the year of the creation. Although it sounds a bit silly today, Ussher had no other chronological evidence available to him. He knew that Adam had lived to a ripe old age and begat Cain and Abel; the cumulative ages of these founders and all their descendants added up to about a 5,500-year history of the world. Ussher's date provided the timeframe for understanding the natural history of Earth for more than two centuries and to this day is accepted by fundamentalist Christian creationists as a reasonably accurate estimate for the age of Earth.

During this period of European history, the church exerted enormous influence over scientific thinking. Speaking out against church doctrine was a crime punishable by death. When Italian mathematician Galileo Galilei (1564–1642) turned his homemade telescope to the night sky in 1609 and saw that the giant planet Jupiter had four large moons orbiting it, he immediately realized that he had proof of Copernicus's sun-centered theory of a century earlier. The universe was not, as church doctrine held, Earth-centered and stationary; the planets of the solar system obviously were in orbit around our sun. But this was heresy, and Galileo spent years under house arrest by order of the pope for publishing his findings in a famous little book called *The Starry Messenger,* published in 1610. The law of the church was simple and steadfast: God created Earth and everything on it, and life as we know it today was unchanged since the moment of the creation.

Over time, with the advent of more powerful telescopes and with the work on motion and gravity by German mathematician and astronomer Johnannes Kepler (1571–1630) and English physicist Isaac Newton (1642–1727), it became impossible for the church to argue against the burgeoning evidence of a sun-centered solar system constantly in orbital motion. But the official doctrine that humans were the center of the creation and that all forms of life existed today in the form they always had remained firmly entrenched.

LINNAEUS AND THE NATURAL SCHEME OF LIFE

In the seventeenth and eighteenth centuries, naturalists became more concerned with developing classification schemes for naming and organizing plants and animals. Nevertheless, they did not part company with the theological view of a static, unchanging world. The classification scheme we use in the biological sciences today (now called the *Linnaean system*) dates from this period.

Anglican minister John Ray (1627–1705) was the first naturalist to use the terms *genus* and *species* to designate types of animals and plants. Later, Carolus Linnaeus (1707–1778), an eminent Swedish botanist and the author of the *Systema Naturae,* built on Ray's writings to create the most comprehensive classification of the plant world compiled at the time (Figure 2.5). In addition to his work on plants, Linnaeus studied the diversity of animal life, often based on specimens shipped to his laboratory from far-flung corners of the world. He used the physical characteristics of plants

FIGURE 2.5   Carolus Linnaeus

and animals to assign them to a scheme of classification. The science of classifying and naming living things that Linnaeus invented is called **taxonomy**. Sorting organisms into categories was a vital way to make sense of their patterns of relationship, so he applied a hierarchy of names to the categories of similarity, which today we call the Linnaean hierarchy. The two-level genus-species labels, or **binomial nomenclature**, were at the heart of taxonomy; a **taxon** is any unit of this formal hierarchy. Linnaeus followed the naming pattern of the ancient Greeks by using Greek and Latin languages for his scheme. But Linnaeus was intellectually hidebound by his theology. He believed firmly in the immutability of species—that each species existed as a completely separate entity from every other species and that these separations were fixed by God. Influenced further by his belief that apes and humans could not be closely related by common descent, Linnaeus assigned people to the family Hominidae and great apes to the family Pongidae. This separation stands to this day although, as we shall see, it may not be justifiable on biological grounds.

An obvious example of how Linnean categorizing could have helped to make sense of human nature is the taxonomic comparison of apes and humans. One of the earliest anatomical descriptions of an ape—a young, female chimpanzee—was published in 1699 by Edward Tyson. In his description, the chimpanzee is referred to variously as a "pygmie" and an "orang-outang." Tyson wrote,

> Now notwithstanding our *Pygmie* does so much resemble a *Man* in many of its parts, more than any of the *Ape-kind,* or any other *Animal* in the World I know of: Yet by no means do I look upon it as a product of mixt Generation; 'tis a *Brute-Animal sui generis,* and a particular *Species of Ape.* For when I was dissecting it, some Sea-Captains and Merchants who came to my House to see it, assured me, that they had seen a great many of them in *Borneo, Sumatra,* and other Parts, tho' this was brought from *Angola* in *Africa.* (McCown and Kennedy, 1972, p. 43)

Tyson considered this African ape to be very similar to humans and to the Asian ape (the orangutan). He saw it as different from both humans and monkeys but sharing many features with each. Nonetheless, Tyson was certain that the ape was a species of animal and not a mixture of species. Not until Linnaeus, however, did anyone undertake a truly systematic study of anatomical comparisons among the primates.

THE ROAD TO THE DARWINIAN REVOLUTION

In the eighteenth and early nineteenth century, a number of European natural historians made their mark in explaining the nature of the diversity of flora and fauna on Earth. Some of these directly influenced Darwin's thinking decades later; most were also following in Linnaeus' taxonomic footsteps. Prominent among these were three eminent French natural historians.

Comte de Buffon Georges-Louis Leclerc, Comte de Buffon (1707–1788), accepted the notion of biological change in general. Buffon (Figure 2.6) observed that animals that migrate to new climates often change in response to new environments, although like others of his day he had no idea about the mechanism of change. He famously claimed that the animals of the New World were weaker and smaller than their counterparts in the Old World, a result of a generally less healthy and productive environment. This claim was vigorously refuted by Thomas Jefferson in his *Notes on the State of Virginia* (1787).

Georges Cuvier By the turn of the nineteenth century, discoveries of dinosaur bones across western Europe had made it difficult for biblically driven scholars to

FIGURE 2.6 Comte de Buffon

taxonomy The science of biological classification.

binomial nomenclature Linnaean naming system for all organisms, consisting of a genus and species label.

taxon A group of organisms assigned to a particular category.

FIGURE 2.7 Georges Cuvier

catastrophism Theory that there have been multiple creations interspersed by great natural disasters such as Noah's flood.

theory of inheritance of acquired characteristics Discredited theory of evolutionary change proposing that changes that occur during the lifetime of an individual, through use or disuse, can be passed on to the next generation.

Lysenkoism Soviet-era research program that tried to apply Lamarckian thinking to agricultural production.

FIGURE 2.8
Jean-Baptiste Lamarck

continue to deny the importance of change to the history of Earth. Georges Cuvier (born Jean-Léopold Cuvier; 1769–1832) rose rapidly in the ranks of the world's foremost natural scientists at the Natural History Museum of Paris, where he spent his entire career. Cuvier (Figure 2.7) was a steadfast opponent of the modern concept of evolutionary change. The existence of extinct creatures such as dinosaurs was a large problem for Cuvier and other creationist scientists of the day because they presented compelling evidence of a past world very different from that of the present day. Cuvier and his supporters sought to explain away these fossils by embracing the concept of extinction and change, but with a biblical twist. They advocated a theory now known as **catastrophism**, in which cataclysmic disasters were believed to have wiped out earlier forms of life on Earth. One such natural disaster that Cuvier had in mind was Noah's flood. After such an event, Cuvier argued, more advanced animals from other regions of world moved in to repopulate the flooded area. These replacement populations were thought to be more advanced than the originals.

Geoffroy Saint-Hilaire Cuvier's contemporary Geoffroy Saint-Hilaire (1772–1844) was an anatomist and a strong advocate of evolutionary change. He engaged in acrimonious public debate with Cuvier on the subject after he corrected Cuvier on identification of a crocodile skeleton, which Cuvier had called an unknown modern species but Saint-Hilaire correctly identified as a fossil. Saint-Hilaire's work led him to support his senior colleague Jean-Baptiste Lamarck, who had proposed a system to explain the process of evolution.

Jean-Baptiste Lamarck In 1809, Lamarck (1744–1829) proposed his **theory of inheritance of acquired characteristics**, which is today often called simply *Lamarckianism*. Lamarck (Figure 2.8) argued that all organisms make adjustments to their environment during their lifetime that could be passed on to their offspring, making those offspring better adapted to their environment. It relied on the concept of *need and use*. For example, if an animal that lived by the seashore spent much of its time swimming in the ocean, its offspring, according to Lamarck, would be better swimmers than its parents had been. In postulating this sort of evolutionary process, Lamarck made one laudable breakthrough and one major error. The breakthrough was seeing the crucial relationship between the organism and its environment. But the fundamental error was thinking that evolutionary change could occur during the lifetime of an individual. This error is easily seen by taking Lamarck's theory to its logical extension: If a mouse loses its tail to a cat, does the mouse later give birth to babies lacking tails? Likewise, no amount of body-building will enable you to give birth to muscular children.

Larmarck's idea is often ridiculed today, but it was a brilliant notion in light of the evidence of evolutionary change available in the eighteenth century. Lamarck knew nothing about the mode of inheritance—genes—and his theory of the inheritance of acquired characteristics served as a natural antecedent to Darwin's theories (Figure 2.9).

The so-called **Lysenkoism** incident in the twentieth century illustrated the failure of Lamarck's theory in a dramatic way. Trofim Lysenko, although never formally educated in biology, was one of the top-ranking botanists in the Soviet Union from the 1930s to 1960s. He argued that Darwinian thinking was inherently capitalist in its focus on the individual struggle for existence. He also rejected the "capitalist" model of population growth and ensuing fierce competition for scarce resources described by British social theorist Thomas Malthus (1766–1834). Malthus had observed that if left unchecked, human populations would grow rapidly, outstripping their resources and ultimately crashing because of famine.

Lysenko campaigned successfully for a Lamarckian (he called it Stalinist-Marxist) model of evolution to be applied to Soviet agricultural production. He took the environmental focus of Larmarck's work to an illogical extreme. For years Soviet scientists stored winter wheat grain at low temperatures, on the theory that such exposure during the seeds' lifetime would create a new generation of wheat

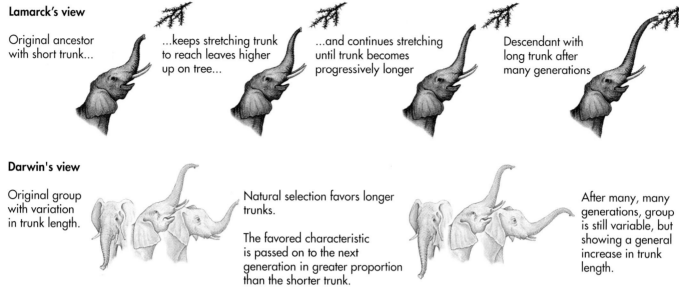

Lamarck's view

Original ancestor with short trunk...

...keeps stretching trunk to reach leaves higher up on tree...

...and continues stretching until trunk becomes progressively longer

Descendant with long trunk after many generations

Darwin's view

Original group with variation in trunk length.

Natural selection favors longer trunks.

The favored characteristic is passed on to the next generation in greater proportion than the shorter trunk.

After many, many generations, group is still variable, but showing a general increase in trunk length.

FIGURE 2.9 Lamarckian and Darwinian views of evolution.

that was cold tolerant, thereby turning the colder parts of the Soviet Union into a new breadbasket. Of course, the experiment was an embarrassing and tragic failure. Soviet biology was set back decades (many of their best genetic scientists were exiled to concentration camps, never to be seen again), and Lysenkoism is a good example of why political ideology should never drive scientific practice.

THE UNIFORMITARIANS: HUTTON AND LYELL

At about the same time that Lamarck's ideas were being debated, a key piece of the evolution puzzle fell into place. Along the rocky Scottish seacoast, James Hutton (1726–1797) spent his career studying, among other things, layering of rock formations. One of the fathers of modern geology, Hutton saw clear evidence of past worlds in the upthrusting of the earth. A devout Christian, Hutton attempted to shoehorn his observations into a biblical framework. However, he did assert a central principle that stands to this day: **uniformitarianism**. Hutton asserted that the geological processes that drive the natural world today are the same as those that prevailed in the past. Hutton was not prepared to extend this theory to the living world; that was left for Charles Darwin many years later. But his views of the changing Earth strongly influenced a generation of geologists.

Charles Lyell (1797–1875), another British geologist, was a strong proponent of uniformitarianism, arguing that slow, gradual change was the way of the physical world and that if one looked in older and older rock sediments, one would find increasingly primitive forms of life. Although an ardent creationist, Lyell (Figure 2.10) became the leading geologist of his day; through his research and his prominence in the social hierarchy of nineteenth-century London, Lyell exerted an enormous influence over his academic peers. His acquaintance with Darwin certainly was a strong influence on the latter's evolutionary ideas. His book *Principles of Geology,* published in three volumes beginning in 1830, was a work that Darwin carried and read time and again during his voyage of discovery on the sailing ship H.M.S. *Beagle.* Lyell played a key role in convincing both the scientific world and the public that the earth's history could be understood only in the context of deep, ancient changes in geology, which necessarily cast creationist explanations for life in a different, more dubious light.

uniformitarianism   Theory that the same gradual geological process we observe today was operating in the past.

FIGURE 2.10   Charles Lyell

THE DARWINIAN REVOLUTION

Charles Darwin (1809–1882) was one of six children born into a life of affluence. His father, Robert Darwin, was a physician, his maternal grandfather was famed potterymaker Josiah Wedgwood, and his paternal grandfather was Erasmus Darwin (1731–1802), an eminent naturalist and philosopher. His mother, Susanna Darwin, died when Darwin was 8 years old. An ardent naturalist from an early age, Darwin wandered the English countryside in search of animals and plants to study. However, he was a lackluster student. When Darwin was 16, his father sent him to study medicine at the University of Edinburgh. Uninterested in his studies and appalled at the sight of surgery, young Darwin did not fare well academically. He did, however, make his initial contacts with evolutionary theory, in the form of Lamarck's ideas about evolutionary change.

FIGURE 2.11   Charles Darwin

Darwin subsequently left Edinburgh and headed to Cambridge University, where he planned to study for the ministry in the Church of England (Figure 2.11). He received a degree in 1831, but more importantly continued his studies in the natural sciences and left Cambridge more eager for adventure and natural history study than for the ministry. Two key events in Darwin's career took place there. One of his professors at Cambridge was John Henslow, a botanist and eminent naturalist who deeply influenced Darwin's scientific thinking. Second, Darwin read the travel and natural history accounts of the renowned German explorer and scientist Baron Friedrich Heinrich Alexander von Humboldt and was greatly inspired by them.

FIGURE 2.12   Map of Darwin's voyage on the HMS *Beagle*.

FIGURE 2.13 Darwin was deeply influenced by his stop in the Galápagos Islands, isolated volcanic rocks off the coast of Ecuador.

In the summer of 1831, while Darwin was on a natural history field trip in Wales, Henslow was meeting with Captain Robert Fitzroy (1805–1865). Fitzroy, an officer in the Royal Navy and himself a keen amateur naturalist, was planning a voyage to map the coastlines of the continents, particularly South America, on the sailing ship H.M.S. *Beagle.* He had invited Henslow to accompany him, but Henslow turned down the offer, as did Henslow's first choice of alternates, his brother-in-law. Henslow then put Darwin's name forward, and Fitzroy accepted. Charles Darwin thus departed in December 1831 as the "gentleman" amateur naturalist aboard the *Beagle,* a trip that changed not only Darwin but also modern science. It also changed Captain Fitzroy, whose deep Christian beliefs eventually led him to regret his decision to take Darwin along on the voyage.

THE GALÁPAGOS

It's hard for us to fully appreciate today what a rare gift a trip around the world was for a naturalist in the early nineteenth century. The 22-year-old Darwin, who had left the Britain Isles only once before his voyage on the *Beagle,* spent 5 years of his life exploring the seacoasts of South America, Australia, and Africa, with many stops along the way (Figure 2.12). From 1831–1836, unburdened by other distractions, he was able to devote most of his waking hours to observing myriad plants and animals in their natural environment.

Contrary to the popular image of Darwin spending 5 years at sea, most of his time was spent on land expeditions or in seaside ports in South America. He rode horses in Patagonia, trekked in the Andes, and explored oceanic islands in the Atlantic and Pacific Oceans. Of these oceanic island stops, one had a profound influence on Darwin: the Galápagos Islands.

The *Beagle* dropped anchor amid a cluster of rocky islands 600 miles off the coast of Ecuador on September 15, 1835. The two dozen Galápagos Islands, most of them tiny lumps of rock, are of recent volcanic origin (Figure 2.13). Most of the islands are rather barren, possessing only a few species of large animals, most notably reptiles and birds. Darwin was amazed by the bizarre and oddly approachable animal life of the islands, including iguana-like lizards that dived into the sea to forage for seaweeds and enormous tortoises that weighed more than 400 pounds (Darwin, 1839) (Figures 2.14 and 2.15).

Each of the Galápagos Islands had its own varieties of animals. There was a distinctive variety of giant tortoise on each, many of which still survive today. It was the birds, however, that provided Darwin with the key piece of evidence for his eventual theory of evolution. Each of the islands has its own species of finch. Some live on the arid rocky islets, and others on lusher parts of the island group. There are finches with rather generic-looking beaks, finches with long slender beaks, and finches with remarkably large, strong beaks. Altogether, Darwin collected at least thirteen different varieties of small, brownish or black finches in the islands, skinning them and packing them into crates to carry back to the British Museum in London.

There are many myths about the influence the Galápagos had on Darwin. He certainly did not immediately formulate the theory of natural selection upon spending a month there. In fact, Darwin left the Galápagos an uneasy creationist, his heretical ideas taking shape only months and years later (Larson, 2001). And although history often records Darwin immediately recognizing something of evolutionary importance when he began to see the variations among finch species, this was not the case. Darwin collected hundreds of the little birds but never saw the importance of their small differences in appearance. In fact, he never even labeled the specimens as to the specific island on which he collected them. It was ornithologist John Gould in London who studied the expedition's collection of finches, now stuffed, and realized that they could be sorted into an array of different species according to island. In his published journal of voyage of the *Beagle*, written the year after he returned home, Darwin said,

> Seeing this gradation and diversity of structure in one small, intimately related group of birds, one might really fancy that from an original paucity of birds in this archipelago, one species had been taken and modified for different ends. (Darwin, 1839)

FIGURE 2.14 Darwin observed that tortoises on islands with trees tend to have shells that allow them to reach up to browse.

FIGURE 2.15 But tortoises living on islands where the main foods are grasses lack such saddle-shaped shells.

In light of Gould's discovery of bill differences, Darwin realized the importance of the finches for his budding theory. He surmised that the various animal varieties of the Galápagos, from giant tortoises to mockingbirds, probably were descended from a very small number of creatures that had reached the islands (presumably from the South American mainland) long ago and had then diversified in response to the different island habitats they found there (Figure 2.16). Darwin referred to this process of many species emerging from one or few ancient ones, like the spokes of wheel emerging from the hub, as **adaptive radiation**. The process of biological change in a species by which such a radiation occurs, Darwin referred to as **natural selection**. In fact, the Galápagos were the perfect setting for Darwin to see evolution in action. Because they are islands, isolated from the mainland, and because they are relatively young, they are biologically simple. Only a few species had managed to reach the islands. Perhaps the ancestors of the finches had been blown off course while flying in a storm and ended up there; ocean currents probably had carried the tortoises and iguanas there as they floated or clung to pieces of driftwood. Finding rocky islets that had food and shelter but few competitors, the species flourished, and eventually their descendants had radiated into the available space in the archipelago.

In setting out his theory of evolution, Darwin used what he had learned from the Galápagos in three ways. First, he observed that isolated oceanic islands seem to hold many species found nowhere else, many of them closely related. Second, isolated islands often lack whole groups of animals found on the mainland; for example, the Galápagos Islands lack any large mammals. Darwin therefore suggested that because only a few tenacious species reach such islands, others fill the place of missing species. In the Galápagos, the place of land mammals may be taken by gigantic tortoises and oversized iguanas. Third, the distinctive animals and plants of isolated islands tend to resemble close relatives on the mainland, even when the environment of the island differs greatly from that of the mainland.

REFINING THE THEORY OF EVOLUTION BY NATURAL SELECTION

Home in England, Darwin took up a life of nature study, contemplation, and writing. He married his cousin Emma Wedgwood and purchased a manor house in the village of Downe, some 15 miles south of London (Figure 2.17 on page 30).

adaptive radiation   The diversification of one founding species into multiple species and niches.

natural selection   Differential reproductive success over multiple generations.

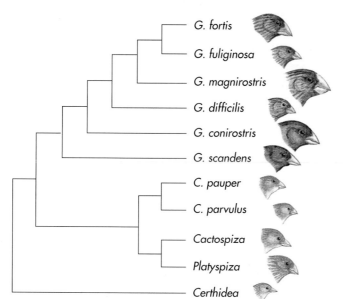

FIGURE 2.16   Darwin's finches: Adaptive radiation of bill types.

FIGURE 2.17 Darwin spent most of his life after the voyage of the *Beagle* at Down House in the village of Downe, south of London.

Beset by a variety of health problems, foremost among them a likely case of Chagas's disease contracted in South America, he rarely left Downe and was bedridden for long periods. But he spent years developing his theory of natural selection, drawing extensively on the parallel process of artificial selection. When animal breeders try to develop new strains of livestock, they select the traits they want to enhance and allow only those individuals to breed. For example, a farmer who tries to boost milk production in Guernsey cows must allow only the best milk producers to breed, and over many generations milk production will indeed increase. Darwin developed friendships with some of the local breeders of fancy pigeons and drew on their work to elaborate on his theory of natural selection. Pigeons, horses, cows, dogs: All are fine examples of what selective breeding can achieve in a few generations. What artificial breeders do in captivity natural selection does in the wild, with one key exception. The animal breeder chooses certain traits, such as floppy ears or a long tail, and pushes the evolution of the breed in that direction generation after generation (Figure 2.18). He or she has a goal in mind with respect to animal form or function. Natural selection has no such foresight. Instead, it molds each generation in response to current environmental conditions.

As Darwin worked his theories into publishable form, he had frequent discussions with his two closest colleagues. One of these was Joseph Hooker, Henslow's brother-in-law and a well-known botanist. The other was T. H. Huxley (Figure 2.19), an ally whose support Darwin relied on time and again during his life after the publication of *On the Origin of Species* and who remained a loyal advocate of Darwinian theory long after the author's death. Darwin was content to ruminate on his ideas, reworking them over and over and publishing only short sketches of the theory in the 1840s, even as his friends pushed him to go public. For years Darwin demurred, fearing the public reaction to his controversial, potentially heretical idea.

Alfred Russel Wallace   In 1858 an event occurred that galvanized Darwin into action. He received a letter and manuscript from Alfred Russel Wallace (1823–1913),

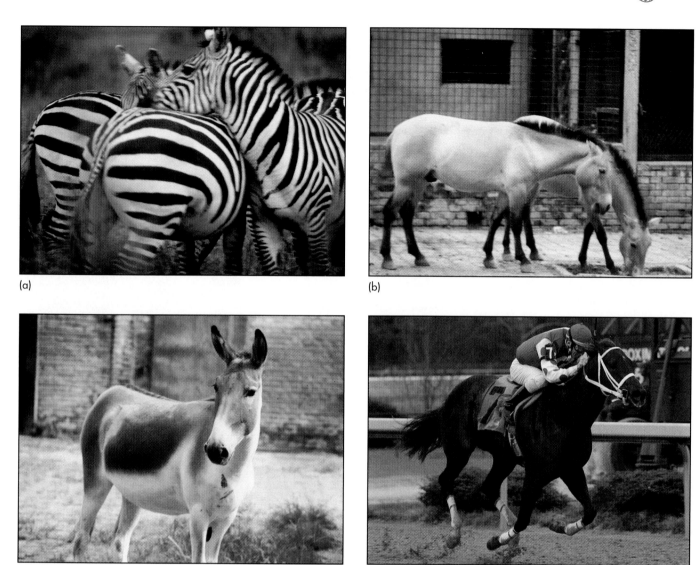

FIGURE 2.18 Species of horses: (a) zebra, (b) Przewalski's horse, (c) Mongolian ass, and (d) thoroughbred race horse.

another field biologist then collecting plant and animal specimens in Indonesia (Figure A in Box 2.1). Wallace's life paralleled Darwin's only in his citizenship and lifelong fascination with nature. Otherwise, in the class-conscious society of nineteenth-century England, the two men were from different worlds. Whereas Darwin was from wealthy landed gentry, Wallace grew up in a working-class family, leaving school at an early age. His employment as a specimen collector for wealthy patrons took him on far-flung adventures and set the stage for him to gain many of the same insights that Darwin had gained on the *Beagle*. Wallace had come up with his own version of the theory of evolution by natural selection and was writing to Darwin for advice as to whether the idea was sound and worthy of publication (Box 2.1 on page 32). With prodding from Hooker and Huxley, Darwin wrote up his own theory and readied it for presentation before the Royal Linnaean Society and for publication.

Twelve hundred copies of *On the Origin of Species* were published on November 24, 1859, and quickly sold out of every bookshop in London. Alongside the expected best-sellers that autumn—Charles Dickens's *Tale of Two Cities* and Alfred Lord Tennyson's *Idylls of the King*—it was a surprise hit. Darwin wrote, as did many scientific authors of his day, with both a scientific audience and the

FIGURE 2.19
Thomas H. Huxley

BOX 2.1   Darwin versus Wallace?

Imagine you are a prominent scientist who has been working day and night for 20 years on a groundbreaking theory that you are certain will revolutionize the life sciences. Then one day you receive a thin parcel in the mail, sent by a colleague who has innocently enclosed a manuscript detailing exactly the same theory. Furthermore, the letter asks your help in improving the theory and your advice on how best to publicize it to the world.

This is the situation in which Charles Darwin found himself one day in June 1858. The mail delivery to his home in England included a package sent by steamship from the remote reaches of the Indonesian islands. The parcel from Alfred Russel Wallace had been 2 months in transit. Darwin and Wallace had corresponded for several years since the publication of a short paper Wallace had written on his early ideas about evolutionary change in animal populations.

Wallace's cover letter described a handwritten manuscript he had enclosed that detailed a theory he had been working on for many years. Wallace titled the manuscript "On the Tendency of Varieties to Depart Indefinitely from the Original Type." We can picture the mailing envelope opening and that cover page sliding before Darwin's eyes. As he no doubt immediately saw, it was a slight variant of the theory of evolution by natural selection. Beginning with a rejection of Lamarckian notions of change, Wallace outlined the way in which some variations in nature are favorable and others unfavorable and the tendency for such variation to produce new forms better suited to their environments. He even paralleled Darwinian thinking in his use of Thomas Malthus's work on populations. Wallace's idea differed in two important ways from Darwin's. Wallace rejected artificial selection—selective breeding—as analogous to natural selection, while Darwin felt animal breeders were essentially mimicking the lengthy process of natural selection. Wallace also placed more emphasis on the replacement of groups and species by other groups and species than did Darwin, who

focused on individuals (in this Wallace was certainly wrong).

Although the exact date that Darwin replied to Wallace's letter and manuscript is not known, journals and letters written by the two men suggest that Darwin waited for several weeks, during which he chronicled his worries about receiving proper credit for the theory in his journal. He characterized the similarities between Wallace's theory and his own:

> I never saw a more striking coincidence, if Wallace had my m.s. [manuscript] sketch written out in 1842 he could not have made a better abstract.

Darwin finally wrote back to Wallace, responding politely but with a note of territoriality. He reminded Wallace that "this summer marks the twentieth year since I opened my first notebook on the question how and in what way do species and varieties differ from each other." He apparently spent weeks fretting that his own work has been rendered unoriginal by Wallace. But Darwin's allies Lyell and Hooker would have none of this. They insisted that Darwin had priority of place and that he should assert his primacy in responding to Wallace and presenting their ideas before the British scientific community.

Darwin and his ally Hooker proposed in separate letters to Wallace that Darwin be allowed to present a jointly authored paper with an introduction by Lyell and Hooker at a meeting of the Linnean Society of London, announcing both theories simultaneously. Wallace was delighted that his work would receive such prominent attention in the scientific world and that his ideas would be linked to those of such eminent thinkers. Several months later, Wallace received another letter from Hooker, informing him that the joint Darwin-Wallace presentation had taken place and that the two papers had been read: first Darwin's, then Wallace's. The paper was then published as one paper in the proceedings of the event, with Darwin as first author and Wallace listed second. The title of Wallace's original manuscript had been altered, however: The

FIGURE A   Alfred Russel Wallace

term *natural selection,* which Darwin had coined, had been inserted into it.

Although Wallace's theory described how natural selection could produce new species, Darwin modified his paper somewhat to explain how species gave rise to endless variations of form by natural selection, a shift in focus that did not really correspond to Wallace's writing. Furthermore, in Hooker and Lyell's introduction to the paper, Wallace read "neither of them [Darwin or Wallace] having *his* published views." Wallace, sitting half a world away from London and having published an essay four years earlier that Darwin had read, would have known this not to be the case.

Three factors may have guaranteed Darwin's fame as the founder of the theory of natural selection. First, Wallace recognized that Darwin had been thinking and writing about his ideas for 20 years and had published a sketch of his theory as early as 1845 (in a revised version of his journal of the voyage of the *Beagle*). Second, Wallace granted enormous respect to Darwin, who was a member of the upper class and had powerful scientific allies. Third, Wallace was living in the jungles of Malaysia and so was unable to argue his own case or present his own paper to the Linnean Society. Had Wallace been in London at the time, and had he been a bit less respectful of his senior colleague, the theory of the origin of species might have emerged quite differently.

reading public in mind. He was immediately besieged by letters and requests for personal appearances. He turned down most of the opportunities to speak publicly but received and wrote hundreds of letters in the next few months. Darwin was suddenly one of the most famous men in the world.

In presenting his theory of evolution by natural selection as laid out in *On the Origin of Species,* Darwin explained his three observations and two deductions:

Observation 1. All organisms have the potential for explosive population growth that would outstrip their food supply. Darwin took this idea directly from Malthus, who had been concerned with human population growth. A female bullfrog may lay 100,000 eggs every spring, but we don't see bullfrogs hopping everywhere. Even humans, with their very low reproductive potential compared with most animals, can undergo exponential population growth, as evidenced by the global population explosion.

Observation 2. But when we look at nature, we see populations that are roughly stable.

Deduction 1. Therefore, there must be a struggle for existence. That is, the bullfrog's 100,000 eggs may yield no more than a handful, or even just one, adult frog. This, Darwin labeled *natural selection* to parallel the term *artificial selection* in use by animal breeders of the period.

Observation 3. Nature is full of variation. Even in one animal group, every individual is slightly different from every other individual. If you look closely enough, even a basketful of uniform-looking bullfrogs will resolve into myriad small differences in size, shape, color, and other features.

Deduction 3. Therefore, some of these variations must be favored, and other must be disfavored, in a process we can call natural selection.

This elegantly simple set of ideas is the heart of evolutionary theory. Famed biologist Julian Huxley, the grandson of Darwin's ally T. H. Huxley, referred to the idea as bringing about "the greatest of all revolutions in human thought, greater than Einstein's or Freud's or even Newton's." Far from the eternally static cubbyholes that most earlier thinkers had conceived, species were dynamic units, constantly in flux in response to changing environments and the unceasing pressure of competitors (Figure 2.20). Natural selection was a filtering process

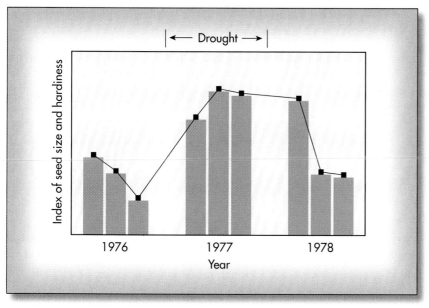

FIGURE 2.20 Index of seed size and hardiness prior to, during and after drought.

fitness Reproductive success.

population An interbreeding group of organisms.

mutation An alteration in the DNA, which may or may not alter the function of a cell. If it occurs in a gamete, it may be passed from one generation to the next.

in which unfavorable traits lost the race with more favorable traits. As Darwin saw it, natural selection is all about reproductive success. Therefore, the time-honored definition of natural selection as "'survival of the fittest'" is misleading. That phrase was coined by social theorist Herbert Spencer and does not really apply well to natural selection. It is much more about the number of offspring an organism leaves in the next generation who themselves survive to reproductive age, a measure we call **fitness,** a biological measure of reproductive success (not a reference to physical fitness). This can be measured, and the qualities that contribute to reproductive success can often be determined. Natural selection can therefore be succinctly defined as differential reproductive success across multiple generations and among the individuals of a given population of animals or plants.

For natural selection to work, three preconditions must be met (Figure 2.21). First, *the trait in question must be inherited.* For example, if you incubate the eggs of some animals, such as reptiles, at temperatures that are too high or too low, the resulting baby will have odd color patterns. These are not genetic and so are not under the control of natural selection. Second, *the trait in question must show variation between individuals.* Natural selection cannot distinguish good from bad traits if all individuals are genetically identical clones. This is rarely the case in nature, where variants abound, and is the key difference between organisms that reproduce by asexual splitting, such as amoebas, and higher animals that reproduce sexually. Higher animals are all genetically unique, so their traits can be selected or not selected. Third, *the filter between the organism and its genetic makeup is the environment, which must exert some pressure in order for natural selection to act.* Many scholars believe that humans evolved rapidly in part because the environment in which our ancestors lived underwent many dramatic fluctuations caused by world climate swings.

Evolution is about change. Although in common English usage *evolution* sometimes is used to describe the changes an individual goes through in the course of a lifetime ("in my evolution as an artist . . ."), in biology this is never the case. It is a change in a **population** (a breeding group of organisms of the same kind) in the frequency of a trait or a gene from one generation to the next. The currency of change is the genetic material, in which alterations in the DNA sequence provide the raw source of variation—**mutation**—on which natural selection can act. Whereas evolution happens at the level of the population, natural selection occurs at the level of the individual organism. As we will see, this has important implications for understanding how the evolutionary process produces the myriad forms we see in nature.

THE RESPONSE TO DARWIN

Although many people think that Darwin's (and Wallace's) theory of evolution by natural selection was a dramatically new view that replaced the old view of immutability, this is only partly true. Scholars had held evolutionary views for gen-

(a) Mode of inheritance

(b) Variation among individuals

(c) Environmental pressure

FIGURE 2.21 The prerequisites needed for natural selection to occur.

erations; recall Lamarck and his many advocates right up to the time of Darwin. Darwin simply offered a mechanism, one so elegantly simple and effective that many scholars were surprised that they had not themselves seen it.

But the response to Darwin by some scholars was not immediate acceptance. The church and many religious people were offended and outraged by the implication that there was no meaning to existence other than the random sorting of traits by natural processes. Even in the scientific community, there were many holdouts who continued to argue for other forms of evolutionary change into the mid-twentieth century. For instance, Louis Agassiz of Harvard University was one of America's most prominent naturalists around the time of the publication of *On the Origin of Species*. Darwin's book rendered Agassiz's work on animal classification instantly obsolete. Agassiz not only repudiated natural selection but also set out to refute it (Larson, 2001). He offered his own view, based on Cuvier's theory of catastrophism and multiple new creations, to explain the appearance of fossil animals that no longer existed. Agassiz fought Darwin tooth and nail, motivated by both professional jealousy and a deeply held belief that natural selection's failure to invoke the power of a divine creator made it fatally flawed. He mounted expeditions to the Galápagos and elsewhere to seek evidence that natural selection was wrong. He seized on Darwin's prediction that the creatures of the Galápagos, ridiculously tame and approachable in the 1830s, would evolve a fear of humans once they had been hunted for generations. Agassiz tried to demonstrate that the creatures' continued tameness in the 1860s showed that Darwinian theory must be flawed. Most other naturalists chastised Agassiz for this futile attempt to refute natural selection since intense hunting of the Galápagos animals had begun only a century earlier. Agassiz's death after his return from the 1873 expedition silenced his voice of opposition.

Failure to accept natural selection came from other scientific quarters as well. Neo-Lamarckian views surfaced in the decades after the publication of the *Origin* and persisted well into the twentieth century. Darwin himself, challenged repeatedly by critics and hampered by the general lack of understanding of genetic transmission, acknowledged that Lamarckian mechanisms might have some role in evolutionary change. Not until the so-called neo-Darwinian modern synthesis of the 1940s and 1950s, when Ernst Mayr and other biologists integrated ecology with Darwinian theory, genetics, anatomy, and other fields, did the full weight and influence of Darwin pervade the biological sciences and, by extension, the field of biological anthropology.

THE SCIENCE AND CREATIONISM QUESTION

Ever since the publication of *On the Origin of Species,* a small but vocal minority in the United States (and other countries) have argued against the teaching of the principles of evolution. They argue instead for a biblical, creationist view of the origin of species and of humanity. But what exactly is a *creationist?* A scientist who studies the origins of the known universe but who believes that the universe may have been created 14 billion years ago by a single supernatural force is a creationist. So is a fundamentalist who believes the earth and every living thing on it were created in 6 days, that dinosaurs and other extinct animals never existed, and that we are all descendants of Adam and Eve. Creationism is simply a belief in a single creative force in the universe.

The ongoing conflict between evolution and creationism lies in the claim by some fundamentalist religious groups that the creation story in the Book of Genesis is a viable alternative to science as the explanation for how humans came to be. These groups argue that evolution is a theory that has no

creation science A creationist attempt to refute the evidence of evolution.

more scientific validity than biblical explanations for the origins of life and of people. The intellectual centerpiece of their thinking is that the Earth is very young (i.e., it is approximately the age calculated by Ussher) and that the sedimentary layers of the earth that provide scientists with evidence of antiquity, and also yield most of our fossils, were really the product of Noah's flood and are of very recent origin. They consider the species found alive today and in the most recent fossil beds to be the species that could swim well enough to escape the rising flood waters. Not surprisingly, this belief can be easily overturned by quick examination of the fossil record and by the study of radiometric dating of the age of the earth's layers.

A religious belief in a divine creation relies entirely on faith. The sole evidence of this faith is the Book of Genesis in the Old Testament of the Bible. Although the Bible is a profoundly important book, its contents are not testable evidence. Nowhere in the evaluation of the truth of the Old Testament does the scientific method come into play; either you accept the reality of the Old Testament or you don't. A literal interpretation of Genesis would mean accepting a 6-day creation. However, many Christians accept the Old Testament as a powerful and important work that is not intended to be taken literally. The problem that most scientists have with teaching religion in public schools therefore is not due to lack of respect for religion—some are quite religious themselves—but rather that science classes are intended to teach children how to think like scientists.

The political agenda of some American antievolution fundamentalist groups belies their stated belief in offering diverse approaches to human origins. Religious fundamentalists often support the teaching of the Judeo-Christian creation story as fact but do not want to allow other creation stories to be taught alongside them in classrooms. Christianity, Judaism, and Islam are creationist faiths: They identify a single creator. Other major religions of the world, such as Hinduism, do not accept a single creator. Fundamentalists fight politically for the right to teach the Judeo-Christian belief system in public schools but generally do not support and sometimes even oppose teaching other religious points of view.

Repeated state court and Supreme Court decisions have ruled that creationism should not be taught alongside science in public schools. For example, the U.S. Supreme Court ruled that a Lousiana law requiring public school teachers to read a disclaimer about evolution (saying it did not address the validity of biblical accounts of the creation) to their students was unconstitutional. Nevertheless, creationists continue to fight. Many teachers themselves support offering religious views of life in science classes. A local public school board in the suburbs of Atlanta recently approved the teaching of "alternatives to evolution" in science classes only to back down after national and regional condemnation from many quarters (Figure 2.22).

All the pieces of evidence for evolution, from fossils to DNA, are facts that add up to a body of evidence for a scientific theory without viable competitors. In recent years, however, challenges have come to evolution in the form of new incarnations of creationism. **"Creation science"** is one recent approach taken by fundamentalists. Recognizing that the Old Testament is not scientific evidence for life's origins, many creationists have argued in the negative, trying to refute the voluminous evidence for evolution. They ask why there are gaps in the fossil record; where, they ask, are the intermediate forms that ought to exist between *Homo erectus* and modern humans? Don't these gaps support the notion of a divine power molding our species? The fossil record is fragmentary, and always will be because of the low odds of fossils being formed, preserved, and then found millions of years later. Creationists seize on this fragmentariness, attempting to portray early humans as apes and later humans as aberrant forms

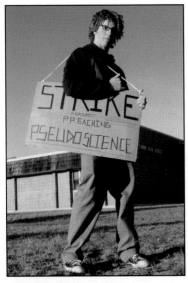

FIGURE 2.22 A student protesting the teaching of creationism.

Box 2.2 What Is Intelligent Design?

Intelligent design is a recent attempt to repackage creationist ideas in a way that might be more palatable for society and the scientific community. Instead of arguing outright for a biblical or divine basis for life, intelligent design advocates claim they have evidence that evolution by natural selection cannot fully explain the diversity of form and function that exists in nature. This school of thought is fond of using the argument of "irreducible complexity": There are aspects of the design of some organisms that are so complex that gradual, successive small modifications of earlier forms could not have produced them. If removal of one part of an organism's adaptive complex of traits causes the entire complex to cease functioning, advocates of intelligent design say, then a supernatural force must have been the actual creator. The example of a mousetrap is often cited. Without each essential feature of a mousetrap—the wooden platform, the spring mechanism, and the latch holding it—the device fails to function at all. Intelligent design advocates say that unless the trap were assembled all at once, it would be useless and therefore could not be created by natural selection. Michael Behe, a biologist and an influential advocate of intelligent design who seeks to reconcile evolution

with religious faith, has claimed that there are examples of irreducible complexity in biology that make natural selection an inadequate mechanism for all change. For instance, Behe claims that the working of cells at the biochemical level, in which cellular function can occur only after numerous working integrated parts are in place, might be an example of irreducible complexity (Behe, 1996).

Unfortunately for adherents of intelligent design, their few examples of irreducible complexity have been met with refutations in the scientific literature. Behe himself acknowledges that whereas gradual, Darwinian change by natural selection can be studied and tested using the scientific method, intelligent design cannot. By definition, if the original design is supernatural, understanding this design must be beyond the reach of science or rational explanation. In other words, the intelligent design movement asks us to accept on blind faith that supernatural forces are at work in designing life. Rather than offering rational explanations for features that might challenge Darwinian theory, advocates of intelligent design offer criticisms that cannot be addressed by further research. The whole belief system of intelligent design therefore stands well outside of

FIGURE A

science in the realm of faith rather than offering a scientific alternative to evolution by natural selection.

As the latest addition to the beliefs of the creationist movement, intelligent design is unlikely to go away any time soon. Indeed, because it is an intellectual, if not scientific, approach to evolutionary change, it is held by some academics, including university-level science instructors. Because instructors in universities can cite the legal right of academic freedom, the teaching of intelligent design belief, even though it lies outside the sciences, is hard to prevent.

of modern people. In the resulting gap they argue that God must have played his hand. As we shall see in later chapters, the fossil record for human ancestry is rich, with a progression of brain size and anatomical changes bridging the apes, early hominids, and modern humans. Creation science is a denial of science rather than science itself and has not been any more successful in the U.S. court system than were earlier approaches by creationists. In recent years other attempts have been made to resurrect creationism in American education. "Intelligent Design" is one such school of thought (Box 2.2).

The relationship between the church and the teaching of evolution remains an uneasy one even in the twenty-first century. Pope John Paul II has stated publicly that the Roman Catholic Church accepts the reality of evolution, even though the essence of humanity is still maintained to be a divine product.

Most biological scientists have deep respect for all religious beliefs. Scientists want only that creationist thinking be excluded from science curriculum in government-supported schools because that is the place where children are being

intelligent design A creationist school of thought that proposes that natural selection cannot account for the diversity and complexity of form and function seen in nature.

trained to think like scientists. In addition, the U.S. Constitution mandates a separation of the influence of church and state in our society, so that the rights of those of other religious faiths, or those without religious faith, can be fully respected. If public schools offered courses in comparative world religion, it would be entirely appropriate to consider Judeo-Christian creation beliefs about the creation alongside those of other cultures, from Native Americans to Buddhists.

SUMMARY

1. **What are the key features that distinguish the scientific from the religious view of the origins of life?**

   Science is a form of inquiry based on hypothesis testing via evidence collection. It is falsifiable and self-correcting. Religious ideology is based on faith and on the Bible; it cannot be tested in an empirical way.

2. **Before Darwin, why was the notion of evolutionary change forbidden?**

   The church had decreed that the world was created by God and had existed in its original form until the present; to contradict that was heresy punishable by imprisonment or worse.

3. **What is catastrophism, and can you think of a modern idea that is similar to it?**

   Catastrophism is the eighteenth-century theory that natural disasters had wiped out life on parts of the earth multiple times, and each time new forms of life moved in from other regions. This would account for the existence of past life forms that no longer existed without invoking evolutionary change.

4. **How did the false view of evolution expressed in Lamarckian theory differ from Darwinian theory?**

   Lamarck proposed that the use of a trait could influence an offspring's phenotype in the next generation; Darwin showed that change could occur across gener-

ations based only on the selective retention of some traits and the filtering out of others.

5. **Why does Alfred Russel Wallace deserve a great deal of credit for formulating the theory of evolution by natural selection?**

   Wallace independently developed the theory of natural selection at the same time as Darwin did. He corresponded with Darwin, who agreed to a joint presentation of their ideas to the scientific world.

6. **How was Darwin's *On the Origin of Species* influenced by his association with geologist Charles Lyell?**

   In addition to being the most influential geologist of his time, Lyell was Darwin's close friend and trusted advisor. When Darwin learned of Wallace's manuscript on evolution, it was Lyell, along with botanist Joseph Hooker, who persuaded their friend to write up his theory of evolution by natural selection. Darwin's paper eventually was read jointly with Wallace's to the scientific community.

7. **What are the three conditions necessary for natural selection to work?**

   Natural selection can occur only if a trait can be inherited, there is variation within a population, and there is pressure from the environment.

CRITICAL THINKING QUESTIONS

1. Was it really so absurd for Bishop James Ussher to come up with a date of 4004 B.C. as the moment of creation ? If you had only your own intuition and observation to guide you, how could you prove to others that the world is round or that the earth is ancient? This leads to the question, What exactly is a fact?

2. How would you handle the science versus creationism issue?

3. Despite Linnaeus's contribution to the study of animal and plant life through the invention of the classification scheme we call taxonomy, his approach hampers us today in understanding what a species is. Why do you think this is true?

KEY TERMS

deduction
observation
hypothesis
experimentation
scientific method
data
falsifiable
paradigm
immutability

polygenism
monogenism
taxonomy
binomial nomenclature
taxon
catastrophism
theory of the inheritance
   of acquired
   characteristics

Lysenkoism
uniformitarianism
adaptive radiation
natural selection
fitness
population
mutation
creation science
intelligent design

SUGGESTED READING

Brooks, J. L. (1984). *Just before the Origin*. ToExcel Publishing, New York.

Browne, Janet. (1995). *Charles Darwin: Voyaging*. Alfred A. Knopf, New York.

Browne, Janet. (2002). *Charles Darwin: The Power of Place*. Alfred A. Knopf, New York.

Dennett, Daniel C. (1995). *Darwin's Dangerous Idea*. Simon and Schuster, New York.

Weiner, J. (1994). *The Beak of the Finch*. Vintage Books, New York.

PART II

MECHANISMS OF EVOLUTION

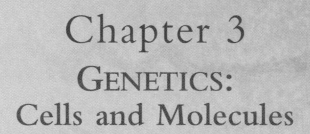

Chapter 3
GENETICS:
Cells and Molecules

THE PACKAGE THE MOLECULAR ANTHROPOLOGIST HAD BEEN WAITING FOR finally arrived. After taking it to an isolated part of her laboratory, she opened it carefully. Wrapped inside were ten small vials, each containing a very small piece of bone. She knew that two of the vials held bone fragments from humans who had recently died, and two contained human bone recovered from an archaeological site several thousand years old. There were also single bone samples from a chimpanzee and a baboon. But most exciting of all, the remaining four vials held bone fragments from an extinct kind of person: a Neandertal. Her job was to extract the genetic material of life—DNA—from each of these samples. If the DNA remained in good condition, the information it contained could provide vital clues about the course of human evolution over the past several hundred thousand years.

The vials were labeled only with the letters A–J. The molecular anthropologist's colleagues were well aware of some of the pitfalls in analyzing ancient DNA, and they wanted the experiment to be done blind to see whether her methods and techniques were good enough to deliver reliable results without knowledge of the source of the samples. This was fine with her. She was thrilled with the opportunity to recover genetic material from people who had lived so long ago. As she gazed at the vials, she reflected on the DNA contained in the bones: The information (or at least some of it) that provided the recipe for these long-dead beings was still there. This was a great responsibility, she told herself, especially given that fossils were so rare and she would have to destroy the samples to get the DNA out of them.

As she stared at the vials, lost in deep thought, her technician walked up behind her. "Are those the bones?" he asked.

"Yes," she said, "they finally arrived."

"When you consider how old those Neandertal samples are," he said, "how they reach back to the dawn of humanity, to the time when people were just beginning to become people, all I can say is, we'd better not screw it up."

One of the most striking examples of the power of modern genetic science is the extraction of DNA from the fossilized remains of long-dead organisms. Although the complete resurrection of extinct animals (as in the movie *Jurassic Park*) remains in the realm of science fiction, we should nonetheless be impressed—even in the case of Neandertal DNA, where recovery is limited to small portions of the total DNA present in life—that such an essential aspect of the living organism can be recovered after tens of thousands of years.

Some argue that our current age is almost too focused on genetics and on what genetic science might someday do for us, but a concern with genetics and its applications is nothing new. Ideas about heredity can be found in all human cultures. There is no more basic observation of nature than "like begets like"; it applies to plants, animals, and people. Without some understanding of heredity, the domestication of plants and animals, which began at least 10,000 years ago, would not have been possible. Another example of the importance of heredity across cultures is the universal existence of kin naming systems. Although these systems vary from culture to culture, their very existence in all cultures indicates the importance of identifying and labeling groups of people who are linked to one another via heredity (kin naming systems can also incorporate nonrelated people, of course).

From the perspective of contemporary science, we can say that many older ideas about the nature of heredity were incomplete, irrelevant, or simply wrong. For example, although it is true that "like begets like" in the sense that dogs beget dogs and horses beget horses, it is strictly true only for clones and only if there are no differences that arise in the course of reproduction and development. Over the past hundred years, the modern science of *genetics* has developed to give us a much better understanding of the biological processes underlying heredity. We need to understand genetics if we are to understand how evolution happens because genetic variation provides the raw material for evolutionary change.

In this chapter, we will begin our exploration of genetics—which will continue in Chapter 4—with an overview of genetic science today. We will then look at the fundamental building block of life, the cell, and consider its structure and function. Then we will discuss DNA, the genetic material itself, and how it carries out the important functions of replication and protein synthesis. We will also look at how DNA is packaged into structures called chromosomes, which become visible during the two kinds of cell division, meiosis and mitosis, and conclude the chapter with a discussion of the molecular methods biological anthropologists use to study human and primate evolution.

GENETICS

The term *gene* was coined in the early 1900s by a Danish botanist named Wilhelm Johannsen (1857–1927). Neither Johannsen nor any of his colleagues at that time knew exactly what a gene was in a biochemical sense, but Johannsen thought it was a good little word to describe the "something"—the particulate unit of inheritance—that was being passed on from generation to generation. The early 1900s were an exciting time in the history of genetics, with researchers inspired by the rediscovery in 1900 of the groundbreaking research and theories (published in 1866) of Austrian monk Gregor Mendel (see Chapter 4). Ironically for Johannsen, although the word *gene* continues to be used, his own theories about the relationship between genes and evolution have largely been forgotten. The twentieth century saw a steady increase in our understanding of the biological mechanisms underlying heredity, with the gene evolving from a theoretical construct to a well-described biochemical entity.

THE STUDY OF GENETICS

If a scientist says that he or she works on the genetics of an organism, that can mean several different things. Biological organisms differ greatly from one another, ranging from the very simple (such as a bacterium) to the very complex (such as a mammal), and the role genetics plays in influencing what an animal is and does varies correspondingly. In complex animals, genetics can be approached from several different levels, depending on what aspect of the organism is of interest. These include the following:

- *Cellular and molecular genetics.* Cellular and molecular genetics involves the study of genetics at the level of the basic building blocks of bodies (cells) and at the most fundamental level of genetic transmission (the DNA molecule). We often hear about exciting advances in molecular genetics in the news as scientists attempt to devise genetic therapies for disease or determine the precise makeup of our DNA and that of other animals.

- *Classical or Mendelian genetics.* Classical genetics, such as that done by Mendel or Johannsen, involves looking at *pedigrees* of related individuals (plant or animal) and tracking how various traits are passed from one generation to the next. Although pedigree studies go back to the beginning of genetic science, they are still essential in the age of molecular genetics. After all, we are usually not interested in the variation of the molecules per se but in the observable traits they influence. These traits must first be identified as genetic features using pedigree analysis or a related technique.

- *Population genetics.* Biological species usually are divided into populations composed of groups of individuals who associate more with one another than with members of another population. Different populations within species almost always vary at the genetic level. By examining the genetic variation within and between populations (at both the molecular level and at the level of observable traits), we can gain insights into the evolutionary history of those populations and of the species as a whole.

- *Phylogenetics.* This field is concerned with determining evolutionary relationships between species, usually by constructing treelike diagrams that visually indicate how closely or distantly species are related to one another. Although traditionally it has been done by comparing observable traits, over the last 30 years the methods of molecular genetics have come to the forefront of phylogenetic analysis.

- *Behavioral genetics.* When one honeybee transmits information to another honeybee about the location of a flower, the behavior of both honeybees is under strong genetic control. When we look at other animals, especially animals who engage in more complex forms of behavior that may involve learning, the role of genetics is more difficult to ascertain. Behavioral genetics involves trying to understand how the behavior of animals, including humans, is influenced by genetics. It is a controversial field, especially in regard to human behavior, because human behavior is especially complex and the product of multiple, interacting influences.

Biological anthropology is concerned with the evolution of the human species in all its aspects. Because genetic variation underlies all evolutionary processes, each of the different approaches to the study of genetics listed here is relevant to understanding human evolution. The field of biological anthropology is also fundamentally concerned with understanding human biological variability, which arises from both genetic and environmental influences. Biological anthropologists often work at the intersection of biological (genetic) and environmental (cultural) sciences in their attempt to develop a comprehensive understanding of human variation and its evolution.

GENETIC METAPHORS: BLUEPRINTS, RECIPES, OR WHAT?

Even the most hardened scientists resort to the use of metaphor to explain the "big picture" of how genes somehow become bodies. So before getting to the actual biological mechanisms of heredity, let us consider how we might characterize the role of genetics in producing an individual organism. Do genes provide the "blueprint" for an individual, as is sometimes claimed? Not really. The idea of a blueprint is reminiscent of Medieval notions that a tiny version of a fully formed individual, a *homunculus*, is what is passed between generations (Figure 3.1). The blueprint metaphor also implies construction—a builder—and the potential for deconstruction. You cannot "unbuild" a body by breaking it down into its original component parts. Throughout the course of biological development, a body maintains a unity that is quite different from the process of constructing a building by starting with the foundations, and then the walls, and so on.

Some scientists have suggested that our genes, in their totality, are much more akin to a recipe than a blueprint. A recipe includes two things: a list of ingredients and the instructions for what to do with those ingredients. To some extent, the genetic material is a recipe for converting energy and a host of essential components into a body, an organism that cannot in any sense be "unmade." However, the main difference between our genes and a recipe is that in cooking, the environment specified by the recipe can be controlled and modified as needed to produce a final product. In contrast, the environments in which genes exist cannot be controlled, although humans have a biologically unprecedented ability to modify their environments, thus making them more hospitable for the genes they carry.

FIGURE 3.1 An old concept of genetic transmission—a homunculus in a sperm cell. The drawing was done by Nicolas Harsoeker, in his *Essai de dioptrique*, 1694.

More recently, as befits the Information Age, there has been a tendency to consider genetic material to be a form of information storage. There can be no doubt that our genes carry information about the bodies they make and that they contain information for the growth and development of those bodies. The problem with seeing genetic material principally as an information storage device is that it is so much more than that. As you read this, genes in your body are doing at least a thousand tasks. Some are being turned on while others are being turned off. Genes are not just information but are part of the essential machinery of the living body. In the fossil remains of an extinct species, of course, genetic material is more like pure information, to be used by molecular anthropologists to reconstruct evolutionary relationships between species, including humans.

The genetic system underlying the development of life on Earth is a unique and truly extraordinary thing. No simple metaphor can encompass all of its properties and functions. Although our discussion will now turn to the somewhat unromantic realm of cell structure and function, we should not cease to wonder at the exquisite machinery of heredity, which has been shaped by nearly 4 billion years of evolution.

THE CELL

The basic building block of life is the cell. A cell is a microscopic organic entity in which genetic material and other structures are separated from the surrounding environment by a semipermeable membrane. Some organisms, such as bacteria or protozoans, are made up of only a single cell. Others, including humans and every other form of life that can be seen with the naked eye, are *multicellular* organisms. Complex multicellular life forms are made up of hundreds of billions of cells. The attraction of studying simpler creatures to understand basic cellular mechanisms is easy to understand when one considers that each cell in the body works in concert with numerous other cells in an ever-increasing web of complexity. The marine sea slug (*Aplysia californica*) has long been the object of scientific study in part because its central nervous system consists of a manageable 20,000 cells (Kandel et al., 2000). In contrast, the human brain, which has approximately 10 billion nerve cells, is complicated.

Based on cellular structure, the basic division of life on Earth is not between single-celled and multicellular creatures but between **prokaryotes** and **eukaryotes**. The prokaryotes, which include bacteria and blue-green algae, are all single-celled organisms with no major compartments within the cell to separate the genetic material from all other components of the cell. The eukaryotes, which include all other forms of life, are characterized by a cellular anatomy that separates the genetic material from the rest of the cell in a structure known as the **nucleus**. The outer boundary of the cell is defined by a *plasma membrane*, which regulates the transport of material into and out of the cell and governs communication and coordinated activity between cells. The fluid-filled space within the cell and surrounding the nucleus is known as the **cytoplasm**. The cytoplasm contains a number of structures, known collectively as *organelles*, that are essential in maintaining the cell and carrying out its functions. Fossil prokaryotes appear in the fossil record about 3.4 billion years ago, whereas eukaryotes do not appear until about 1.5 billion years ago. Eukaryotes that more closely resemble those found today evolved around 850 million years ago, and multicellular organisms (such as plants and animals) made their first appearance only 600 million years ago (Kostianovsky, 2000). Thus single-celled creatures have dominated most of the history of life on Earth.

Complex organisms have a variety of different somatic cell types. **Somatic cells** are simply the cells of the body that are not **gametes**, or sex cells; gametes are the germ cells that are directly involved in propagation or reproduction. Humans have around 200 different types of tissues, each of which is composed of a characteristic

prokaryotes Single-celled organisms, such as bacteria, in which the genetic material is not separated from the rest of the cell by a nucleus.

eukaryotes A cell that posesses a well-orgainzed nucleus.

nucleus In eukaryotic cells, the part of the cell in which the genetic material is separated from the rest of the cell (cytoplasm) by a plasma membrane.

cytoplasm In a eukaryotic cell, the region within the cell membrane that surrounds the nucleus; it contains organelles, which carry out the essential functions of the cell, such as energy production, metabolism, and protein synthesis.

somatic cells The cells of the body that are not sex cells.

gametes The sex cells: sperm in males and eggs (or ova) in females.

somatic cell type (Klug and Cummings, 2003). We have nerve cells (neurons), muscle cells, skin cells, bone cells, cells that secrete hormones, and so on. At the earliest stages of its development, the human embryo contains a population of cells known as **stem cells**. These cells are *totipotent*, which means they can differentiate into any of the somatic cell types found in the fetus or adult. Stem cells are also found in adults, but adult stem cells can differentiate into a more limited variety of cell types (Stewart and Pryzborski, 2002).

Stem cell research has become an important and controversial topic in recent years. Given their totipotent capacity, embryonic stem cells may be useful for treating diseases that are characterized by the loss of specific types of cells. An example of this is *Parkinson disease,* a nervous system disorder characterized by movement problems, which is caused by the loss of a certain population of cells in the brain. It is hoped that embryonic stem cells may be able to replace (i.e., take on their form and function) the specific cells lost in Parkinson disease. The controversy surrounding embryonic stem cell research lies in the fact that human embryos (produced in the laboratory through in vitro fertilization) are our only source of totipotent stem cells; after the stem cells are removed, the embryos are no longer viable (Box 3.1). Research is also being done on adult stem cells to see whether they can be coaxed into forming a greater variety of cell types than they would under more natural conditions.

CELL ANATOMY

It should come as no surprise that different types of cells have different anatomies, which serve the functional or structural needs of a particular tissue. Nonetheless, almost all somatic cells share a host of characteristics that can be represented in the figure of a generic cell. Although gametes share some of the characteristics of somatic cells, there are also some fundamental differences, which we'll discuss separately.

In most eukaryotic cells (Figure 3.2), the most prominent structure in the cytoplasm is the nucleus. The nucleus is bounded by its own membrane or envelope, which separates its contents from the rest of the cytoplasm. Within the nucleus, the

stem cells   Undifferentiated cells found in the developing embryo that can be induced to differentiate into a wide variety of cell types or tissues. Also found in adults, although adult stem cells are not as totipotent as embryonic stem cells.

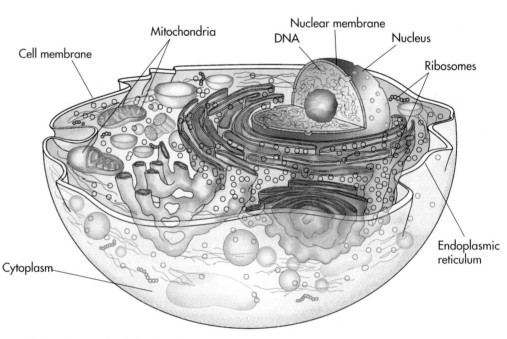

FIGURE 3.2   A typical eukaryotic cell.

Box 3.1 Cloning Controversies

On July 5, 1996, a sheep was born at the Roslin Institute in Edinburgh, Scotland. This sheep, named Dolly, was as unremarkable as any other sheep with the exception of one fact: She was a clone, an exact genetic copy of another sheep (Figure A). Dolly was the first mammal ever cloned, and her birth raised many questions about the nature and even the moral status of cloning. If a sheep could be cloned, why not a human?

The process of cloning is straightforward, which is not to say that it is easy (Solter, 2000). First, the nucleus of a somatic cell (which contains a copy of all of the genetic material of an individual) is carefully removed. The cell often comes not directly from the body but from a cell line that has been established in the laboratory. At the same time, the nucleus of an egg (or *oocyte*) is carefully removed, preserving the cell membrane and the cytoplasm as much as possible. The nucleus from the somatic cell is then transferred to the oocyte either mechanically via microinjection or by using an inactivated virus as a vector. Once the new nucleus is introduced to the egg, the egg is *activated,* which initiates the development of the embryo. In normal fertilization, the introduction of the sperm to the egg causes activation. In cloning, an electrical current applied to the egg (with the new nucleus) activates the egg. It is possible to use a fertilized egg that has already been activated (after removal of both the egg and sperm nuclei), but they are harder to come by than unfertilized eggs. Activation is essential to reprogram the donor nucleus away from whatever its original function was and toward the development of a new individual. Once the embryo begins to develop, the egg can be implanted into a surrogate mother, and the pregnancy proceeds in the usual way.

Sheep, cows, mice, and pigs have all been cloned. For each group, the success rate of growing a clone (egg with a new nucleus) to adulthood is about 1%. The live birth rate is perhaps twice as high as this, but a number of cloned newborns have problems and die before adulthood. It is likely that one barrier to successful cloning arises in the reprogramming stage after activation (Fairburn et al., 2002).

Another problem that arises with cloned individuals is that even if they survive to adulthood, they do not live as long. In a study of cloned mice, it was found that only two of twelve cloned mice lived as long as 800 days, compared with ten of thirteen control mice (Ogonuki et al., 2002). The famous sheep Dolly lived less than 7 years, whereas sheep usually live to be 11–12 years (Coghlan, 2003). One possible cause of the short life span of cloned individuals involves structures called *telomeres.* Telomeres are pieces of DNA that cap the ends of chromosomes. As an individual ages and cells divide, the telomeres shorten. Shortening telomere lengths are a sign of aging in cells. If cloning is done with the genome of an adult, then the short telomeres may be passed on directly to the cloned individual, resulting in accelerated aging or the development of diseases early in life that are associated with aging.

Why do we need cloning? Agricultural scientists are working on cloning in order to develop methods for efficiently propagating animals who have desired characteristics. After all, sexual reproduction leads to an inefficient genetic mixing (recombination or crossing over) every generation. Other scientists see cloning as a potential tool to save endangered or even extinct species, such as the giant panda or the extinct Tasmanian wolf (Mazurek, 1999). The largest wild populations of our closest relatives, the chimpanzee and gorilla, declined by one-half between 1983 and 2000 (Walsh et al., 2003), and the development of efficient cloning techniques may someday help save these very threatened species.

Arguments in favor of human reproductive cloning are harder to come by. The poor survival rate of cloned individuals from other mammal species is reason enough to consider human reproductive cloning to be an unethical undertaking. On the other hand, many consider therapeutic cloning to be a different matter. Imagine a patient who has a disease that may be curable by the introduction of a working cell type to replace cells that are nonfunctional or have been destroyed. Somatic cells from that patient could be used to make cloned embryos. At a very early stage of development (the blastocyst stage), embryonic stem cells could be recovered and then coerced in the lab into growing into the cell type the patient needs. Once a population of these cells has grown, they are transferred to the patient. Because the patient is the original source for the cells, there would be no worry about immunological rejection. It is clear that even if some countries ban therapeutic cloning, other countries will work hard to develop this technique.

FIGURE A Dolly, the cloned sheep.

hereditary material, **deoxyribonucleic acid (DNA)**—the stuff that genes are made of—is found. DNA is a double-stranded complex molecule, and the elucidation of its structure by James Watson and Francis Crick in 1953 launched the modern era in molecular genetics. Two of the primary functions of DNA are making **proteins** for the body, or **protein synthesis**, and cellular replication. Another complex molecule, **ribonucleic acid (RNA)**, which is similar structurally to DNA but is single stranded, is also found in large quantities in the nucleus and in the cytoplasm, as well. RNA is essential for carrying out the protein synthesis function of DNA.

Floating in the cytoplasm of the cell are several other important structures or organelles (Figure 3.2). These structures are analogous to the organs of the body, and they are responsible for functions such as metabolizing nutrients and eliminating waste, energy synthesis, and protein synthesis. The **mitochondria** (sing., *mitochondrion*) are capsule-shaped organelles that number in the hundreds or thousands in each cell. Mitochondria are the site where a series of metabolic reactions take place, resulting in the production of an energy-rich molecule, *adenosine triphosphate (ATP)*, which fuels the activities of the cell. Mitochondria are known as the "powerhouse" of the cell. Another important feature of mitochondria is that they have their own DNA, which is not contained in a nucleus and is different from the DNA found in the nucleus of the cell. It is likely that the mitochondria (and their plant analogs, chloroplasts) had their origins as a prokaryotic cell that evolved in symbiosis with a nucleated cell to produce the eukaryotic cell. As we will see later in the chapter, *mitochondrial DNA* (mtDNA) has proved to be an important tool in evolutionary and anthropological research.

The **endoplasmic reticulum (ER)** is another organelle found in the cytoplasm. The ER is a complex structure, with a folded-sheet appearance. It provides increased surface area within the cell for metabolic reactions to take place. Some of the endoplasmic reticulum has a knobby appearance; this is known as *rough endoplasmic reticulum*. The knobs are **ribosomes**, the site in the cell where proteins are synthesized. Molecules of ribosomal RNA (rRNA) form a large component of ribosomes. The synthesis of ribosomes begins in the nucleus but can be completed only in the cytoplasm. Because completed ribosomes cannot pass through the nuclear membrane, protein synthesis always occurs in the cytoplasm.

DNA STRUCTURE AND FUNCTION

Hereditary material—DNA—has to be able to do three things. First, it must be able to make copies of itself, or *replicate*, so that it can be passed from generation to generation. Second, it has to be able to make proteins, which are the most important components of cells. Third, it must coordinate the activity of proteins to produce bodies, or at least have some way to translate the information it carries about making bodies into growing actual bodies (i.e., development). As it turns out, the chemical structure of DNA lends itself to self-replication and to carrying the information necessary for making proteins; we will discuss these two DNA functions in detail. However, the third function—directing development—is much more complex and is beyond the scope of this text.

DNA STRUCTURE I: THE MOLECULAR LEVEL

The structure of the DNA molecule is a double helix, resembling a ladder twisted around its central axis. The basic unit of DNA (and RNA) is a molecule called a **nucleotide** (Figure 3.3). A nucleotide consists of three parts: a sugar (deoxyribose in DNA and ribose in RNA), a phosphate group, and a nitrogenous **base**, a mol-

---

deoxyribonucleic acid (DNA)
A double-stranded molecule that is the carrier of genetic information. Each strand is composed of a linear sequence of nucleotides; the two strands are held together by hydrogen bonds that form between complementary bases.

proteins   Complex molecules formed from chains of amino acids (polypeptide) or from a complex of polypeptides. They function as structural molecules, transport molecules, antibodies, enzymes, and hormones.

protein synthesis   The assembly of proteins from amino acids, which occurs at ribosomes in the cytoplasm and is based on information carried by mRNA.

ribonucleic acid (RNA)   Single-stranded nucleic acid that performs critical functions during protein synthesis and comes in three forms: messenger RNA, transfer RNA, and ribosomal RNA.

mitochondria   Organelles in the cytoplasm of the cell where energy production for the cell takes place. Contains its own DNA.

endoplasmic reticulum (ER) An organelle in the cytoplasm consisting of a folded membrane.

ribosomes   Structures composed primarily of RNA, which are found on the endoplasmic reticulum. They are the site of protein synthesis.

nucleotide   Molecular building block of nucleic acids DNA and RNA; consists of a phosphate, sugar, and base.

base   Variable component of the nucleotides that form the nucleic acids DNA and RNA. In DNA, the bases are adenine, guanine, thymine, and cytosine. In RNA, uracil replaces thymine.

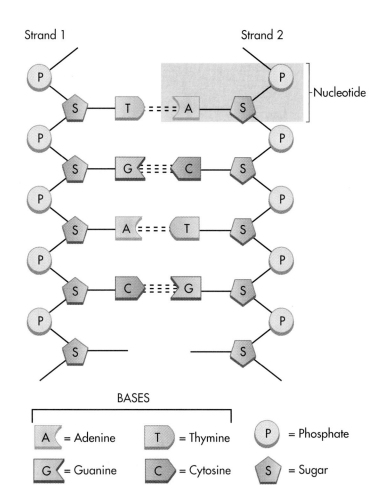

Strand 1   Strand 2

Nucleotide

BASES

A = Adenine   T = Thymine   P = Phosphate

G = Guanine   C = Cytosine   S = Sugar

FIGURE 3.3 The nucleotide structure of DNA. The dashed lines between the A-T and C-G pairings indicate hydrogen bonds.

ecule that includes one or two rings composed of carbon and nitrogen atoms. The DNA molecule is assembled from four different nucleotide units, which vary according to the base they carry. There are two classes of bases: the *purines* and the *pyrimidines*. The purines are *adenine* (A) and *guanine* (G); the pyrimidines are *cytosine* (C) and *thymine* (T). DNA consists of two separate strands, corresponding to the two sides of the ladder, each of which is made up of a chain of nucleotides (Figure 3.4 on page 50). The sugar of one nucleotide bonds to the phosphate group of the next one; thus, each side of the DNA ladder is composed of alternating sugar and phosphate molecules. The bases point toward the center of the ladder and form its rungs. The rungs are formed by two bases, one projecting from each side of the ladder.

In the late 1940s and early 1950s, biochemist Erwin Chargaff and his colleagues found a curious pattern in the distribution of nucleotides in DNA: The amount of A present in the sample was always about the same as the amount of T, and the amount of C equaled the amount of G. This information, along with an X-ray crystallograph of the DNA molecule provided by physical chemists Rosalind Franklin and Maurice Wilkins, helped Watson and Crick formulate their model of DNA structure (Figure 3.5 on page 51). As they surmised, the rungs of the DNA ladder are composed of two bases, and the base combinations are always A-T or C-G. For example, if there is a sequence of nucleotides on one side of the DNA that goes ATCGATCG, then on the other side of the ladder, the sequence will be TAGCTAGC. The two sides of the DNA double helix complement each other (sometimes the two strands are nicknamed "Watson" and "Crick"). A purine (A or G) is always opposite a pyrimidine (C or T)

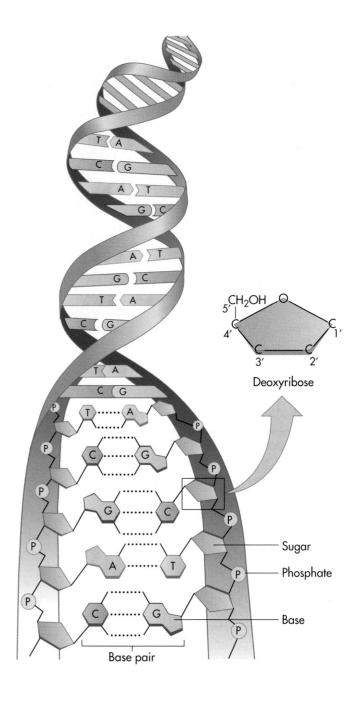

FIGURE 3.4 The double-helix structure of DNA.

because purines are larger molecules than pyrimidines, and the purine-pyrimidine combination is necessary for the two sides of the ladder to maintain a constant distance from each other. The more specific A-T and C-G pairings occur because these combinations form hydrogen bonds (three for G-C and two for A-T), which hold the two sides of the ladder together. Such hydrogen bonding cannot occur between A and C or G and T. Hydrogen bonds are quite weak (compared with the chemical bonds that form between the sugars and phosphates, for example), but in a DNA molecule, thousands of nucleotides line up against thousands of other nucleotides, thus giving strength to the entire molecule.

RNA is very similar to DNA except that it is a single-stranded molecule, and ribose replaces deoxyribose as the sugar in the nucleotide. In addition, thymine is not found in RNA but is replaced by another pyrimidine base, *uracil* (U), which also bonds to adenine.

(a)   (b)

FIGURE 3.5   (a) The 1962 Nobel Prize winners. Francis Crick is at far left, Maurice Wilkins is next to Crick, and James Watson is third from the right. At his right is John Steinbeck. (b) Rosalind Franklin made an essential contribution to the discovery of DNA structure, but died four years before these Nobel Prizes were awarded.

DNA FUNCTION I: REPLICATION

A complete copy of the DNA is found in the nucleus of almost every cell of the body. When a mother cell divides into two daughter cells, other cell components can be split between the cells, but a faithful copy of the genetic material must be deposited in each daughter cell. After all, once the two cells have split from each other, they no longer have access to the genetic material of the other cell.

The very structure of the DNA molecule suggests a mechanism for its replication (Figure 3.6 on page 52). Watson and Crick immediately recognized this after they determined the structure of the molecule. In simple terms, DNA replication occurs in the following manner. The DNA molecule, or a portion of it, divides into two separate strands. The two strands can be separated when the weak hydrogen bonds between the base pairs are broken. After separation, each of the strands serves as a template for the assembly, nucleotide by nucleotide, of a new complementary strand of DNA. When the process is completed, there are two copies of the mother DNA molecule, each of which is made up of one original side and one newly synthesized side.

Each step of DNA replication, from the uncoiling of the DNA double helix to "proofreading" and correcting the occasional errors that occur in the process, is mediated by a particular **enzyme**. An enzyme is a complex protein molecule in the body that mediates a chemical or biochemical reaction. One of the first enzymes associated with DNA replication to be discovered is called *DNA polymerase I* (Kornberg, 1960). If you place a single-stranded template strand of DNA in a test tube with all four nucleotide bases (A,T, C, and G) and add DNA polymerase I, you will get synthesis of double-stranded DNA. The observation of its action in the test tube led to the discovery of other DNA polymerases more critical to DNA replication (as it turned out, DNA polymerase I was more critical for proofreading DNA in prokaryotes than for DNA replication).

We will see in this chapter that the proofreading and repair of DNA are critically important because errors in DNA replication can have important consequences for the survival of an organism. If these errors in DNA replication are not corrected, they can lead to permanent changes in the DNA of cell. These changes

enzyme   A complex protein that is a catalyst for chemical processes in the body.

= Adenine   = Thymine

= Guanine   = Cytosine

FIGURE 3.6
DNA replication.

are known as mutations. Mutations can alter cell function in many different ways. For example, a mutation can transform a cell, causing it to replicate at an accelerated rate; such uncontrolled cell growth is the basis of cancer. Mutations that occur in gametes can be passed from one generation to the next and may have profound effects on the biology of offspring.

DNA FUNCTION II: PROTEIN SYNTHESIS

Proteins are the workhorse molecules of biological organisms and the most common large molecules found in cells. Structural tissues, such as bone and muscle, are composed primarily of protein. Proteins such as **hemoglobin**, a protein molecule in red blood cells, bind to oxygen and transport it throughout the body, and other transport proteins facilitate the movement of molecules across cell membranes. Some proteins function as **hormones** and hormone receptors and regulate many bodily functions. Antibodies or immunoglobulins are proteins of the immune system, which our bodies use to fight disease or any biochemical invader. The largest class of proteins in the body are the enzymes, such as DNA polymerase I. These proteins lower the activation energy of (*catalyze*) countless biochemical reactions in cells. Many biochemical reactions happen at physiological temperatures (body temperature) only if catalyzed by enzymes. So enzymes are essential for life.

Proteins are complex molecules made up of smaller molecules known as **amino acids** (Figure 3.7). Amino acids share a common chemical structure that allows them to bond to one another in long chains. There are twenty different amino acids that function as building blocks for proteins (Table 3.1). Of these

TABLE 3.1		
AMINO ACID	DNA TRIPLET	mRNA CODON
Alanine	CGA, CGG, CGT, CGC	GCU, GCC, GCA, GCG
Arginine	GCA, GCG, GCT, GCC, TCT, TCC	CGU, CGC, CGA, CGG, AGA, AGG
Asparagine	TTA, TTG	AAU, AAC
Aspartic acid	CTA, CTG	GAU, GA
Cysteine	ACA, ACG	UGU, UGC
Glutamine	GTT, GTC	CAA, CAG
Glutamic acid	CTT, CTC	GAA, GAG
Glycine	CCA, CCG, CCT, CCC	GGU, GGC, GGA, GGG
Histidine[*]	GTA, GTG	CAU, CAC
Isoleucine[*]	TAA, TAG, TAT	AUU, AUC, AUA
Leucine[*]	AAT, AAC, GAA, GAG, GAT, GAC	UUA, UUG, CUU, CUC, CUA, CUG
Lysine[*]	TTT, TTC	AAA, AAG
Methionine[*] (initiation codon)	TAC	AUG
Phenylalanine[*]	AAA, AAG	UUU, UUC
Proline	GGA, GGG, GGT, GGC	CCU, CCC, CCA, CCG
Serine	AGA, AGG, AGT, AGC, TCA, TCG	UCU, UCC, UCA, UCG, AGU, AGC
Threonine[*]	TGA, TGG, TGT, TGC	ACU, ACC, ACA, ACG
Tryptophan[*]	ACC	UGG
Tyrosine	ATA, ATG	UAU, UAC
Valine[*]	CAA, CAG, CAT, CAC	GUU, GUC, GUA, GUG
Termination codons	ATT, ATC, ACT	UAA, UAG, UGA

[*] Essential amino acids.
Source: Laidlaw and Kopple (1987).

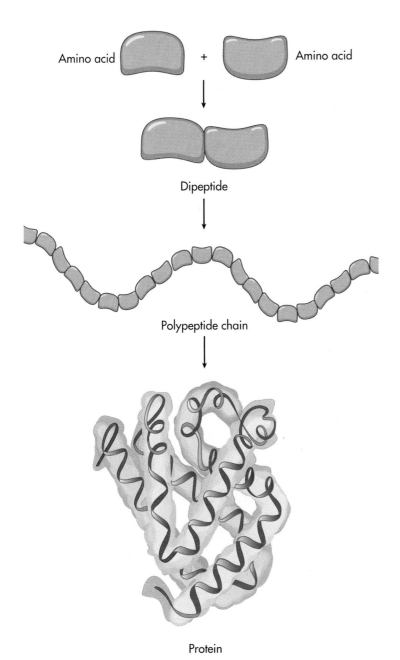

Amino acid + Amino acid

Dipeptide

Polypeptide chain

Protein

FIGURE 3.7 Schematic representation of protein structure.

twenty, nine are essential amino acids (Laidlaw and Kopple, 1987). This means they cannot be synthesized by the body and must be obtained from protein in the diet. The nonessential amino acids can be synthesized from the essential amino acids.

A typical protein may be made up of a chain of 200 amino acids; such a chain can also be called a **polypeptide**. Any combination of the twenty different amino acids may go into this chain. Thus the number of possible 200–amino acid proteins that may be generated from the twenty kinds of amino acids is immense (20^{200}). At a primary level, proteins differ from each other by length and by the sequence of amino acids in the polypeptide chain. Protein structures generally are much more complex than a simple linear chain, however. The sequence

hemoglobin   Protein found in red blood cells that transports oxygen.

hormone   A natural substance (often a protein) produced by specialized cells in one location of the body that influences the activity or physiology of cells in a different location.

amino acids   Molecules that form the basic building blocks of protein.

polypeptide   A molecule made up of a chain of amino acids.

of amino acids in a polypeptide governs how the chain may be folded in space or how it may associate with other polypeptide chains to form a larger, complex protein. For example, the protein hemoglobin is composed of four separate polypeptide chains, which in conjunction assume a complex three-dimensional form. The three-dimensional conformation a protein takes is integral to its function (Figure 3.8).

As we saw earlier, proteins are made of chains of amino acids. The structure and therefore the function of proteins are determined by the sequence of amino acids in their polypeptide chains. The structure of DNA, in which different bases are lined up in sequence, is ideal for carrying other kinds of sequential information, such as the sequence of amino acids in a protein. The system that has evolved to represent protein amino acid sequences in the base pair sequence of DNA is known as the **genetic code**.

There are twenty different amino acids in proteins, but there are only four different bases in DNA. Obviously, there are not enough types of bases to represent each amino acid. If two bases in sequence were used to represent an amino acid, there would still be only sixteen possible combinations (4^2), which is not enough to represent the twenty amino acids. However, three bases in sequence produce sixty-four (4^3) unique triplet combinations—more than enough to have a unique triplet sequence of bases represent each of the twenty amino acids. The genetic code therefore consists of three-base sequences, called **codons**, each of which represents a single amino acid. There is *redundancy* in the code: Given that there are sixty-four possible codons and only twenty amino acids, most of the amino acids are represented by more than one codon. Three of the codons (termination codons) do not code for any amino acid but instead signal that the protein chain has come to an end. Another codon (TAC) represents the amino acid methionine and also typically serves as an initiation codon, signaling the beginning of a polypeptide chain.

The information to make proteins is represented, via the genetic code, in the sequence of bases in a portion of a DNA molecule. The part of a DNA molecule that contains the information for one protein (or for one polypeptide chain that makes up part of a protein) is called a **gene**. One DNA molecule can have many genes arrayed along its length. Given the triplet codons of the genetic code, a protein with 300 amino acids would need 900 bases to represent it (not including initiation or termination signals) in a gene. If the first twelve bases of that gene were TGA CCA CTA CGA, the first four amino acids of the protein would be threonine, glycine, aspartic acid, and alanine. A single gene can consist of hundreds of thousands of bases, and current estimates are that human beings have between 30,000 and 40,000 genes in total.

genetic code The system whereby the nucleotide triplets in DNA and RNA contain the information for synthesizing proteins from the 20 amino acids.

codon A triplet of nucleotide bases in mRNA that specifies an amino acid or the initiation or termination of a polypeptide sequence.

gene The fundamental unit of heredity. Consists of a sequence of DNA bases that carries the information for synthesizing a protein (or polypeptide), and occupies a specific chromosomal locus.

FIGURE 3.8 The complex structure of the hemoglobin protein, which comprises four polypeptide chains in association with iron-based heme groups that are essential for oxygen binding and transport.

So how does the information to make a protein, encoded in the DNA, actually become a protein? It involves two steps, *transcription* and *translation,* along with the participation of RNA molecules with specialized functions. Transcription occurs in the nucleus of the cell, while translation (protein synthesis) occurs in the cytoplasm. Each step is mediated by specialized enzymes (Figure 3.9).

Transcription begins when the two DNA strands split apart in a region where a gene is represented on one of the strands. The whole molecule does not split apart because only the region where the gene is located must be read. When the DNA molecule separates, the strand corresponding to the gene can serve as a template for the synthesis of a single-stranded RNA molecule. As mentioned previously,

TRANSCRIPTION
The two DNA strands separate at the site of a gene—the sequence of bases on one of the strands that carries the information to make a protein. The gene serves as a template to form a complementary mRNA molecule that will carry the information to assemble a protein from the gene (DNA) in the nucleus to a ribosome in the cytoplasm.

TRANSLATION (1)
When the mRNA binds to the ribosome, protein synthesis is initiated. As each codon in the mRNA sequence is "read," a tRNA brings the corresponding amino acid to the ribosome.

TRANSLATION (2)
The mRNA is read by the ribosome codon by codon. A second amino acid is brought to the ribosome by a tRNA, and it is linked to the first amino acid to start forming the protein amino acid chain.

TRANSLATION (3)
As each codon is read, tRNA transports the appropriate amino acid to the ribosome where it can be added to the growing protein chain. The ribosome moves down the mRNA, codon by codon, until the end of the molecule is reached. At this point, the synthesis of one protein molecule is complete.

FIGURE 3.9 Protein synthesis. Transcription occurs within the nucleus, while translation takes place in the cytoplasm.

RNA is a nucleic acid, like DNA, composed of nucleotide bases (C, G, A, and U, instead of T). At the site of the gene, a complementary RNA molecule is synthesized: In effect, the information of the gene is transcribed from the language of DNA to the related language of RNA. When an RNA molecule has been synthesized that corresponds to the entire gene, it separates from the DNA and exists as a free-floating, single-stranded molecule. The two strands of the DNA reattach to each other, returning the DNA to its intact double helix structure. The free RNA molecule is called **messenger RNA (mRNA)**. This is an appropriate name because the mRNA carries the information of the gene from the nucleus of the cell to the cytoplasm, which is where protein synthesis or translation takes place.

Protein synthesis occurs at ribosomes, thousands of which are found in the cytoplasm of every cell. At the ribosome, the information the mRNA carries is translated into a protein molecule. The mRNA is read at the ribosome, from beginning to end, two codons at a time. At this point in the process, another critical molecule enters the picture: **transfer RNA (tRNA)**. The job of tRNA is to transport a single, specific amino acid to the ribosome, so that it can be attached to the growing protein chain. The tRNA has a three-base region called the *anticodon* that is complementary to the codon on the mRNA. When an mRNA codon (ACU, for example, which corresponds to the DNA triplet TGA) is read at the ribosome, a tRNA with the anticodon UGA temporarily aligns to the mRNA and brings the amino acid threonine into position. Then the next codon on the mRNA is read, and a second tRNA brings the appropriate amino acid into position next to the first amino acid. Once the two amino acids are next to each other, a chemical reaction requiring energy occurs, and a bond is formed between the two amino acids. The ribosome then moves down one codon, while the growing peptide chain moves in the opposite direction.

This process continues until the entire mRNA has been read and the complete protein (or polypeptide chain) has been assembled. A single mRNA molecule can be read by several ribosomes at the same time, and thus one mRNA molecule can lead to the synthesis of several copies of the same protein molecule (Figure 3.10).

Of course in the real world of cells, protein synthesis is a bit more complicated than outlined here. Two of these complicating factors deserve mention. First, in most cases, after an mRNA is formed but before it reaches the ribosome, it undergoes posttranscriptional processing whereby intervening sequences in the mRNA are spliced out, and the mRNA molecule is reassembled. The parts of the gene that correspond to the intervening sequences of the mRNA are called *introns,* and the parts of the gene that are actually translated into a protein (that is, they are expressed) are called *exons.* In some cases, posttranscriptional processing means that a single gene can produce different (but related) protein products depending on which intervening sequences are processed out (Figure 3.11).

messenger RNA (mRNA)
Strand of RNA synthesized in the nucleus as a complement to a specific gene (transcription). It carries the information for the sequence of amino acids to make a specific protein into the cytoplasm, where at a ribosome it is read and a protein molecule is synthesized (translation).

transfer RNA (tRNA)   RNA molecules that bind to specific amino acids and transport them to ribosomes to be used during protein synthesis.

FIGURE 3.10 Electron microscope photo of an mRNA molecule being read by ribosomes, (the dark round structures) with growing polypeptide (protein) chains forming at the ribosomes as the mRNA is read.

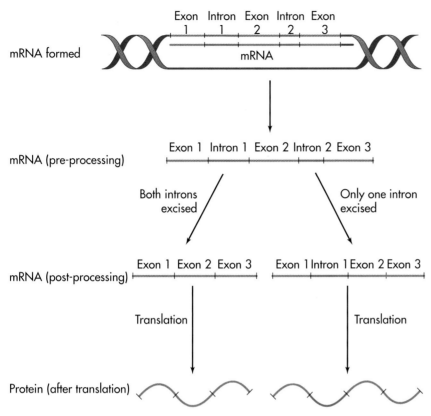

Post-Transcriptional Processing

FIGURE 3.11   Processing of an mRNA molecule after transcription.

The second complicating factor to keep in mind is that most of our DNA does not code for anything; in other words, it is not made up of exons. According to recent results from the attempts to elucidate the complete human DNA structure, only about 1.1% of the bases are expressed (Venter et al., 2001). Another 24% are introns; they are transcribed into mRNA but are not translated into protein. From the organism's perspective, the rest of the DNA does not do anything but replicate. As we will see later, this noncoding DNA has important ramifications for a variety of genetic processes.

DNA STRUCTURE II: CHROMOSOMES AND CELL DIVISION

We have 2–3 meters (6–9 feet) of DNA in the nucleus of each somatic cell. Most of the time, the DNA in these cells exists in dispersed, uncoiled strands, supported by proteins. DNA in this state is called **chromatin**. However, during **mitosis** and **meiosis**, the two processes of cell division or replication, the chromatin condenses and coils into larger, tightly wound, discrete structures called **chromosomes** (which, like chromatin, are composed of DNA and supporting proteins) (Figure 3.12 on page 58). Because chromosomes are visible under the light microscope, scientists were able to study them and learn something about genetic mechanisms before the age of molecular biology. Each chromosome has a distinctive size and shape. The shape is determined in part by the position of the **centromere**, a condensed and constricted region of chromosomes that is of critical importance during cell replication. The size is determined by the size (in numbers of base pairs) of the DNA molecule that makes up the chromosome.

Except for the gametes or sex cells, each somatic cell in an individual's body has the same number of chromosomes. In fact, chromosome number is a constant

chromatin   The diffuse form of DNA as it exists during the interphase of the cell cycle.

mitosis   Somatic cell division in which a single cell divides to produce two identical daughter cells.

meiosis   Cell division that occurs in the testes and ovaries that leads to the formation of sperm and ova (gametes).

chromosome   Discrete structures composed of condensed DNA and supporting proteins.

centromere   Condensed and constricted region of a chromosome. During mitosis and meiosis, location where sister chromatids attach to one another.

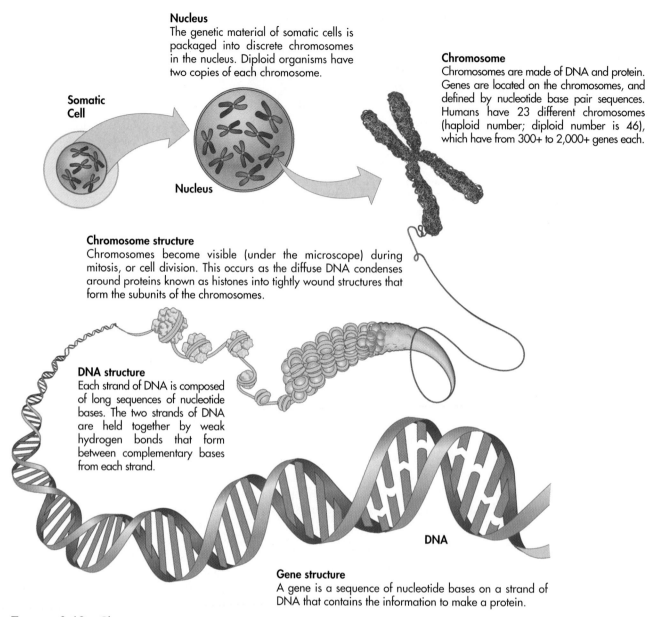

Nucleus
The genetic material of somatic cells is packaged into discrete chromosomes in the nucleus. Diploid organisms have two copies of each chromosome.

Somatic Cell

Nucleus

Chromosome
Chromosomes are made of DNA and protein. Genes are located on the chromosomes, and defined by nucleotide base pair sequences. Humans have 23 different chromosomes (haploid number; diploid number is 46), which have from 300+ to 2,000+ genes each.

Chromosome structure
Chromosomes become visible (under the microscope) during mitosis, or cell division. This occurs as the diffuse DNA condenses around proteins known as histones into tightly wound structures that form the subunits of the chromosomes.

DNA structure
Each strand of DNA is composed of long sequences of nucleotide bases. The two strands of DNA are held together by weak hydrogen bonds that form between complementary bases from each strand.

DNA

Gene structure
A gene is a sequence of nucleotide bases on a strand of DNA that contains the information to make a protein.

FIGURE 3.12   Chromosome structure.

diploid number   Full complement of paired chromosomes in a somatic cell. In humans, the diploid number is 46 (23 pairs of different chromosomes).

haploid number   The number of chromosomes found in a gamete, representing one from each pair found in a diploid somatic cell. In humans, the haploid number is 23.

across entire species. Most organisms have two copies of each chromosome in each cell; in each of these pairs of chromosomes, one is maternally derived and the other is paternally derived. The total number of chromosomes in each somatic cell is called the **diploid number**. Sex cells have only half as many chromosomes as somatic cells (one copy of each chromosome), so the total number of chromosomes in a sex cell is known as the **haploid number**. In a diploid cell, the members of each pair of chromosomes are known as **homologous chromosomes**.

The genes are distributed across the chromosomes, and the locations of specific genes can be mapped to specific chromosomes (Figure 3.13). Sometimes the term **locus** (pl. *loci*) is used interchangeably with the term *gene*. More specifically, we can think of the locus as the location of a gene on a chromosome. Because somatic cells have two copies of each chromosome, they also have two copies of each gene, one at each locus. Genes come in different versions, called **alleles**. For example, there might be a gene for eye color, but it could have two alleles, one for brown and one for blue; the locus of this gene could be mapped to a specific chromosome. A real example

FIGURE 3.13 Homozygosity and heterozygosity.

involves the ABO blood type system (which is discussed in more detail in Chapter 6). At that locus (which is on chromosome 9), there are three possible alleles, called A, B, and O, which determine blood type. When an individual has the same allele for a gene at each locus on each chromosome, this individual is called **homozygous** for that gene. If the individual has different alleles of the gene at each locus, then he or she is **heterozygous** for that gene. When we consider that each individual has thousands of genes, each of which may be represented by several alleles, it is easy to see that the number of possible different combinations of alleles is enormous (Box 3.2 on page 60).

Mitosis   As stated previously, Mitosis is the process whereby a somatic cell replicates, leading to the formation of two identical daughter cells. Mitosis is the basis of all cell proliferation, which can occur in the context of the growth of an organism, during healing, or during any physiological process in which new cells are needed to replace the loss of cells (Figure 3.14 on page 61).

The ongoing process of cell division and nondivision sometimes is known as the *cell cycle.* The cell cycle can be divided into several stages. The *interphase* is the stage of a cell's life when it is not involved in mitosis; instead, most of its energies are devoted to metabolism and growth. Although the interphase is not part of mitosis, an important premitotic activity occurs toward the end of interphase: The DNA is replicated in preparation for mitosis. During interphase, DNA is packaged into chromatin, and discrete chromosomes are not visible.

The first stage of mitosis is the *prophase.* Three important things happen during the prophase:

1. The nuclear envelope breaks down and disappears.

2. The diffuse chromatin fibers condense and begin to form dense chromosomes. The individual chromosomes actually are doubled chromosomes, composed of two identical sister *chromatids.*

3. The polar orientation of the cell for the division into two daughter cells is established. The prophase often takes up at least half of the process of mitosis.

After prophase, the chromosomes migrate to the equatorial center of the cell, where they line up in an orderly fashion. When they have reached this position, the cell is in the *metaphase.* The *anaphase* follows the metaphase as the sister chromatids split apart and migrate to opposite ends of the cell. This is usually the shortest part of mitosis. Once the anaphase is completed, there will be a complete diploid complement of *daughter chromosomes* at each end of the cell.

homologous chromosomes Members of the same pair of chromosomes (or autosomes). Homologous chromosomes undergo crossing over during meiosis.

locus The location of a gene on a chromosome. The locus for a gene is identified by the number of the chromosome on which it is found and its position on the chromosome.

alleles Alternative versions of a gene. Different alleles are distinguished from one another by their different effects on the phenotypic expression of the same gene.

homozygous Having the same allele at the loci for a gene on both members of a pair of homologous chromosomes (or autosomes).

heterozygous Having two different alleles at the loci for a gene on a pair of homologous chromosomes (or autosomes).

Box 3.2　Biochemical Individuality

Individual human beings differ from one another in physical appearance. Even identical twins have subtle physical differences that allow others to tell them apart. But individuality extends to the biochemical and genetic levels as well. We are as much unique individuals at the biochemical level as at the anatomical level.

In the 1950s, biochemist Roger Williams wrote a monograph called *Biochemical Individuality* in which he argued, based on innumerable biochemical measures, that everyone deviated from the norm in some way. In other words, at the biochemical level, everyone was an individual. For example, Williams measured amino acid secretion in saliva. He found that every individual secreted a different combination of amino acids and in different amounts. There were amino acids that were secreted by a small percentage of the people, and others that were more commonly secreted. Williams pointed out that people varied from each other in levels of enzymatic activity, nutritional metabolism, and many other phenotypic expressions of biochemical processes.

Williams's work anticipated later developments in genetics that made it possible to develop unique biochemical profiles for every individual. These methods have come to be used in a variety of forensic settings, especially in the analysis of blood (*forensic serology*). The ability of investigators to identify different alleles of proteins provides a valuable tool for individual identification. Blood types, such as the ABO system, represent one such allelic system, but several other proteins that can be isolated from blood samples also show allelic variation. These proteins allow individual identification because it is very unlikely that two individuals will share exactly the same combination of alleles from a number of variable proteins. For example, if we examine ten blood proteins, each with two alleles that are represented in the population at a frequency of 0.5, the chance that any two individuals from that population will have the same combination of ten alleles is 0.5^{10}, or about 0.00098. If you add some more proteins or if the individual has some alleles that are very rare in the population, you can develop an allelic profile that is unique among the entire human population. It is important to keep in mind that the allele frequencies used to make these calculations must be derived from the individual's own biological population because allele frequencies vary from population to population.

Over the last 15 years, a technique known as *DNA fingerprinting* has been developed to further refine the ability of investigators to make individual genetic identifications (Jeffreys et al., 1985). DNA fingerprinting is based on the fact that there are segments of DNA (called *minisatellites*) dispersed throughout the genome at different loci, which are composed of different numbers of repeated base pair sequences. These sequences do not code for anything and are highly variable. When the DNA from an individual is digested using an enzyme called a *restriction endonuclease,* a unique pattern of DNA fragments derived from these minisatellites will emerge for each individual (Figure A). They are truly as unique as fingerprints.

FIGURE A　DNA fingerprint

The final stage of mitosis is the *telophase*. During this period, the cytoplasm is split into two, resulting in the complete separation of the two daughter cells, each with its daughter chromosomes. Once the separation is complete, the chromosomes uncoil into chromatin, and the nucleus of the cell forms around the genetic material. The new cell then enters interphase, restarting the cell cycle.

Meiosis　The process of meiosis (Figure 3.14) leads to the formation of the gametes (sperm in males and eggs in females), which are cells that have the haploid number of chromosomes (that is, one copy of each chromosome as opposed to the two copies of each found in diploid somatic cells). Meiosis occurs only in the testes of males and the ovaries of females. Like mitosis, meiosis begins with diploid cells, but through an additional cell division, haploid gametes eventually result. The sex cells must be haploid because when the sperm and egg unite to form the **zygote** (fertilized egg), the resulting zygote should reestablish the diploid number of chromosomes.

The first meiotic prophase is similar in some ways to prophase in mitosis but with some critical differences. It is similar in that the replicated DNA condenses

zygote　A fertilized egg.

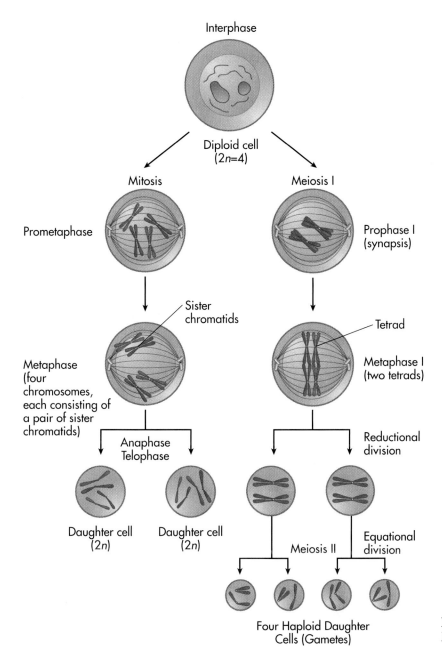

Interphase

Diploid cell
(2*n*=4)

Mitosis

Meiosis I

Prometaphase

Prophase I
(synapsis)

Sister
chromatids

Tetrad

Metaphase
(four
chromosomes,
each consisting of
a pair of sister
chromatids)

Metaphase I
(two tetrads)

Anaphase
Telophase

Reductional
division

Daughter cell
(2*n*)

Daughter cell
(2*n*)

Meiosis II

Equational
division

Four Haploid Daughter
Cells (Gametes)

FIGURE 3.14
Mitosis and meiosis.

into chromosomes, and sister chromatids form. However, unlike in mitosis, in meiosis the double-stranded homologous chromosomes pair up, forming units that are in effect made up of four chromatids (that is, two pairs of sister chromatids); this unit is known as a *tetrad*. At this stage, an important process called **crossing over** occurs. Crossing over is the process whereby genetic material is exchanged between pairs of homologous chromosomes. This process results in a **recombination** of alleles on the chromosomes.

Crossing over is extremely important because it enables new genetic combinations (although not new genes) to be assembled along each chromosome. Crossing over increases the available genetic variability in a population, thereby increasing the amount of variability available for natural selection to act on. The rate of evolution in sexually reproducing species therefore is much faster than in asexually reproducing species. Without sexual reproduction, it is likely that the complexity of plant and animal life on Earth could never have been achieved. Only mutation can

crossing over Exchange of genetic material between homologous chromosomes during the first prophase of meiosis; mechanism for genetic recombination.

recombination The rearrangement of genes on homologous chromosomes that occurs during crossing over in meiosis. Source of variation arising out of sexual reproduction; important for increasing rates of natural selection.

provide wholly novel new variants in a population, but the new combinations of genes that arise from sexual reproduction are of critical importance in evolution by natural selection. One advantage of nonsexual reproduction is that it is possible to make sure that an exact copy of a parent is created. Although this would not be an advantageous long-term evolutionary strategy, some people today think that there may be commercial and other reasons to develop artificial cloning techniques.

After crossing over occurs in the first meiotic prophase, a metaphase follows and tetrads align along the equator of the cell. During the *first meiotic division* (also known as the *reduction division*), the chromatid tetrads split, and a double-stranded chromosome is sorted into each daughter cell. This is very different from what happens in mitosis. In mitosis, the doubled-chromosomes separate so that each daughter cell winds up with one paternally derived chromosome and one maternally derived chromosome, just as the mother cell had. In the first meiotic division, one daughter cell has two copies of the maternal chromosome and the other has two copies of the paternal chromosome (although after crossing over, of course, they are no longer identical to the parental chromosomes).

Once the first cell division is complete and after another round of prophase and metaphase, the *second meiotic cell division* occurs. During this division, the paired chromatids split—as they do in mitosis—resulting in a total of four haploid gametes (two from each of the two daughter cells of the first meiotic division) with only one copy of each chromosome.

Different Kinds and Numbers of Chromosomes   As mentioned previously, chromosomes come in different sizes and shapes, and different species have different numbers of chromosomes. During mitosis, when the chromosomes become visible, it is possible to study the chromosomes by taking a photograph of them through a microscope. From such a photograph, a **karyotype** of an individual can be made (Figure 3.15). A karyotype shows all the chromosomes in a single somatic cell. Humans have twenty-three different chromosomes (haploid number) and a diploid number of forty-six. Of the forty-six chromosomes in humans, forty-four can be distributed into twenty-two homologous pairs. These are called **autosomes**. The twenty-third pair are the **sex chromosomes**. In mammals, the sex chromosomes

karyotype   The complete chromosomal complement of an individual; usually based on a photograph of the chromosomes visualized under the microscope.

autosomes   Any of the chromosomes other than the sex chromosomes.

sex chromosomes   In mammals, chromosomes X and Y, with XX producing females and XY producing males.

FIGURE 3.15   A human karyotype.

are labeled X and Y, and the autosomes are numbered (in humans, from 1 to 22). Mammalian males have one X chromosome and one Y chromosome, whereas females have two X chromosomes. Because females have only X chromosomes, it is the sex cells of the male, who can produce gametes with one X and one Y chromosome, that determine the sex of the offspring.

Even closely related species can have different numbers of chromosomes. In chimpanzees, our closest living biological relatives, the haploid number is twenty-four chromosomes, and the diploid number is forty-eight. At some point since humans and chimpanzees last shared a common ancestor, the packaging of DNA into chromosomes changed. As it turns out, the other great apes, the gorilla and orangutan, to whom we are also closely related, have the same number of chromosomes as a chimpanzee. Thus, along our unique evolutionary lineage, humans had a fusion of two chromosomes, resulting in the loss of one chromosome. Note that this does not mean a loss of DNA because chromosomes are indicative only of the packaging, but not the amount, of DNA. We do not know whether the fusion of these two chromosomes was a critical event in human evolutionary history. Among the gibbons—small-bodied Asian apes—there are several species whose diploid chromosome numbers vary from thirty-eight to fifty-two, and yet in physical appearance and behavior the species are not all that different from one another (Marks, 1992). Certainly they are nowhere near as different from each other as humans are from any of the great apes.

Chromosomal Abnormalities   In humans, individuals with abnormalities in chromosome number usually suffer from a range of medical and developmental problems; chromosomal abnormalities probably are also a common cause of miscarriages. **Nondisjunction errors** that occur during meiosis result in the misdistribution of chromosomes to the sex cells (that is, one receives both copies of the chromosomes and the sister cell receives none). If fertilization occurs with either of these sex cells, this leads to an inappropriate number of chromosomes in the fertilized egg, or zygote. Two common kinds of nondisjunction errors are *monosomy,* which occurs when one chromosome in a pair is absent, or *trisomy,* which occurs when there is an extra chromosome, resulting in three copies of the chromosomes rather than a pair. An example of monosomy is *Turner syndrome.* Females with Turner syndrome have only a single X sex chromosome (represented as XO) rather than XX or XY. The absence of the second X chromosome leads to a delay or absence of sexual maturation, small physical stature, delayed mental maturation, and other physical abnormalities.

An example of trisomy, *Down syndrome,* or *trisomy 21,* occurs when an individual has three rather than two copies of chromosome 21. Individuals with Down syndrome share a constellation of features, including a common facial anatomy and head shape, short stature, a furrowed tongue, and short, broad hands with characteristic palm and fingerprint patterns. People with Down syndrome also show retarded physical and mental development, and they are also prone to heart disease and leukemia. Another striking feature of Down syndrome is that as they age, people with the condition almost always develop *Alzheimer disease,* the most common form of age-related dementia. Alzheimer disease is characterized by the development of microscopic plaques in the brain (which cause the death of neurons); a primary component of these plaques is a protein called *beta-amyloid.* As it turns out, the gene for beta-amyloid is on chromosome 21. The susceptibility of people with Down syndrome to Alzheimer disease probably is a result of the overexpression of this gene caused by the fact that three copies are present rather than two.

It is important to keep in mind that for most chromosomes, monosomy or trisomy is incompatible with life. Down syndrome and Turner syndrome are the exceptions rather than the rule. The rate for Down syndrome is only 0.05% in pregnancies in 20-year-old women but rises to 3% in women over 45. When

nondisjunction error
The failure of homologous chromosomes (chromatids) to separate properly during cell division. When it occurs during meiosis, it may lead to the formation of gametes that are missing a chromosome or have an extra copy of a chromosome.

you consider that all of the chromosomes are vulnerable to trisomy, it is easy to see why it is so difficult for older women to produce a viable zygote (Figure 3.16). Studies show that about 2% of all recognized pregnancies (including those that result in miscarriage) in women 25 years or younger are trisomic for some chromosome; this compares with 35% in pregnancies in women over 40 years (Hassold and Hunt, 2001). Nondisjunction errors obviously are more common with increasing maternal age; evidence of an effect of increasing paternal age is not strong.

MOLECULAR TOOLS FOR BIOANTHROPOLOGICAL RESEARCH

Understanding genetics is critical to understanding evolutionary phenomena such as adaptation and the biological histories of populations and species. Over the years biological anthropologists have used a variety of molecular genetics techniques to study the natural history of people and other primate species. The application of these techniques to anthropological problems and issues will be considered in later chapters.

INDIRECT METHODS

The ultimate indirect method to study genetics is to look at the visible *phenotype:* the anatomy and physiology of an organism. But as we will discuss in more detail in Chapter 4, individual organisms are a result of complex interactions between genes and the environment. Molecular structures provide a more straightforward way to compare populations or species because they are not strongly influenced by environmental variables.

The problem with molecules is that they are very small and difficult to see. Clever techniques have been developed to visualize molecular structures. The visual representation did not have to be an exact replication of the molecule, but it had to provide enough information so that inferences about structure could be made. In anthropology, the concern was to find techniques that would provide

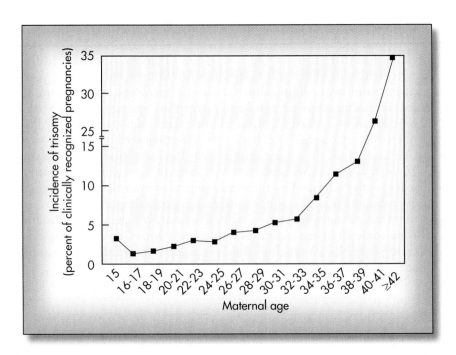

FIGURE 3.16 Increased risk of trisomy with maternal age.

information about *variation* in molecular structures without necessarily worrying about the exact structure of the molecules.

In the 1960s and 1970s, biological anthropologists made extensive use of three indirect molecular techniques to study evolutionary relationships between and within primate species, including humans. The *immunological method* was used to compare protein structure between species (Goodman, 1963; Sarich and Wilson, 1967). This method takes advantage of the great sensitivity of the immune system and its ability to make antibodies that are very specific for *antigens* or foreign invaders (such as viruses or bacteria). For example, the same protein found in the blood of a chimpanzee and a human probably will be very similar and will differ by only a few amino acids; it is reasonable to expect that the same protein from a monkey species will be more different because monkeys clearly are more distantly related to us and the great apes. The antibody made against the human protein will then show a higher cross-reactivity to the chimp protein than to the monkey protein (Figure 3.17). It is possible to do numerous cross-reactions of this kind and determine evolutionary relationships between a large number of species, based on the similarity or dissimilarity of a single protein.

An indirect method used to compare DNA sequences between species involves making hybrid DNA molecules composed of one strand from one species and another strand from a different species. This *DNA hybridization method* compares the total genomic DNA of two species to give an overall measure of DNA sequence difference (Sibley and Ahlquist, 1984; Marks et al., 1988). Again, it is assumed that the more similar the DNA sequences of two species are, the more closely they are related. If DNA is heated to about 95 degrees Celsius, the weak hydrogen bonds between the base pair rungs of the DNA ladder break down, and the two strands

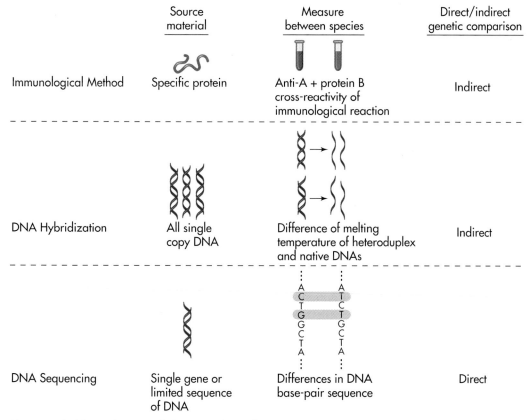

FIGURE 3.17 Indirect and direct methods for molecular genetic analysis.

separate from each other ("melt"), leaving single-stranded DNA. Hybrid DNAs made from two different species have many base pair mismatches, which means that there are fewer hydrogen bonds (compared with nonhybrid, native DNA) holding the two DNA strands together. It therefore takes less energy to separate the two hybrid DNA strands, and the melting temperature of the hybrid DNA is lower than the melting temperature of the native DNA (Figure 3.17). The more closely related two species are—the more similar their DNA is—the higher the melting point of their hybrid DNA.

The immunological method and DNA hybridization are useful only for looking at molecular differences between species. Within a species, the differences are too subtle for these methods to detect. But within-species variation can be very important. We know that allele frequencies vary between human populations, as in the case of the ABO blood type system (see Chapters 4 and 6). The most commonly used method for uncovering protein variation (that is, allelic variation) is *protein electrophoresis*. Proteins vary not only by size but by electrical charge, which is determined by the amino acid composition of the protein. If you place small amounts of a protein in a thin sheet of agarose gel and run an electric current through it, the proteins will migrate across the gel, driven by the current. The protein can be visualized on the gel by using a variety of dyes. This technique is useful for detecting protein and allelic variation because different versions of a protein migrate at different speeds across the gel, depending on their amino acid composition. For example, an individual who is heterozygous at some locus may produce two different bands on a gel, reflecting the two slightly different versions of the same protein his body produces. Electrophoresis techniques are also widely used in experiments involving DNA and RNA.

DIRECT SEQUENCING METHODS

In recent years, advances in molecular genetics techniques have allowed the direct sequencing of molecules such as DNA. However, the direct study of genetic structures extends back almost a century. *Cytogenetics,* the study of chromosome structure, has long been available as a way of comparing different species. Besides chromosome number, species vary in the size and shape of their chromosomes. In addition, when stains are used, banding patterns on chromosomes emerge under the microscope that can also be used to provide insights into the relationships between species and to track evolutionary events.

Although *protein sequencing* is another direct method that has been used for evolutionary research, *DNA sequencing*—determining the actual base sequence of a gene or stretch of DNA—is by far the most widely used tool in molecular anthropology today (Figure 3.17). DNA sequencing provides the most direct kind of evidence about the genetic makeup of individuals and species, and it can yield insights about both coding and noncoding regions of the genome. The automated methods currently used to directly sequence DNA are beyond the scope of this text, but it is important to know that the development of these methods in the 1970s and 1980s made possible much of the "molecular revolution" of the end of the twentieth century. Without automated DNA sequencing, for example, it would have been impossible for molecular biologists to sequence the entire genomes of humans, rats, and other species.

PCR, MITOCHONDRIAL DNA, AND ANCIENT DNA

In addition to automated DNA sequencing, the other essential tool of the molecular revolution is a technique known as the **polymerase chain reaction (PCR)**

polymerase chain reaction (PCR) Method for amplifying DNA sequences using the Taq polymerase enzyme. Can potentially produce millions or billions of copies of a DNA segment starting from a very small number of target DNA.

(Mullis, 1990). The key feature of PCR is that an extraordinarily small amount of DNA can be used to make millions or even billions of copies of a specific DNA segment. The technique depends on a specialized enzyme, called *Taq polymerase,* which causes the extension of a single strand of DNA (if free nucleotide base pairs are available). Once the *target sequence,* the specific region of DNA that is to be amplified, has been identified, two *primers* must be designed, one for each end of the sequence. These primers are short segments of DNA (about fifteen to twenty base pairs long), which are necessary for the Taq polymerase to begin extension of the two DNA strands. They attach to the DNA at each end of the target sequence because they are designed to complement the DNA sequence in that region.

Here's how the process works (Figure 3.18). DNA containing the target sequence, base pair nucleotides (A,T,C, and G), the two primers, and Taq polymerase are placed in a test tube that is then heated to the point where the DNA strands

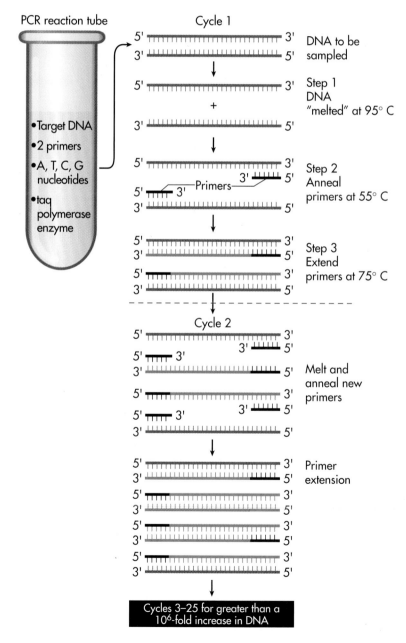

FIGURE 3.18 The polymerase chain reaction (PCR).

Human Mitochondrial Genome
16,569 base pairs in total

D-Loop

Complex I genes (NADH dehydrogenase)

Complex III genes (ubiquinol: cytochrome c oxidoreductase)

Transfer RNA genes

Complex IV genes (cytochrome c oxidase)

Complex V genes (ATP synthase)

Ribosomal RNA genes

FIGURE 3.19 Schematic map of the human mitochondrial genome.

separate—about 95 degrees Celsius. After this, the solution is cooled to about 55 degrees Celsius. This allows the primers to attach to the single DNA strands at the positions flanking the DNA segment of interest. Then, the temperature is then raised to somewhere around 75 degrees Celsius. At this temperature, the Taq polymerase works to extend the target segment's DNA strands starting at each of the primer positions. Copies of the target DNA are being made during this step in the process. This heating-cooling-heating cycle is then repeated twenty-five or thirty times. Every newly synthesized strand of DNA becomes a target for copying in each new cycle, which results in an exponential increase in the number of target DNA sequences in the reaction tube.

PCR allows the recovery of DNA sequences from miniscule samples, such as a single hair or dried saliva on an envelope obtained at a crime scene. In biological anthropology, PCR often is used to study evolutionary patterns in mitochondrial DNA and nuclear DNA recovered from bone, or *ancient DNA*.

mitochondrial DNA (mtDNA)
Small loop of DNA found in the mitochondria. It is clonally and maternally inherited.

Mitochondrial DNA As you recall, the mitochondria are the organelles found in cells in which energy metabolism occurs. **Mitochondrial DNA (mtDNA)** is a circular structure of about 16,600 base pairs (Figure 3.19). Each mitochon-

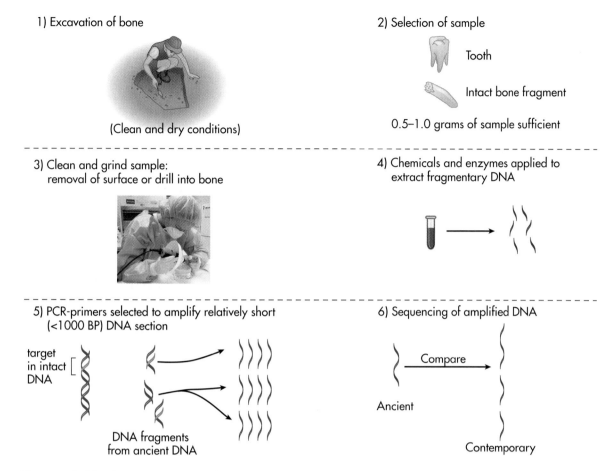

1) Excavation of bone

(Clean and dry conditions)

2) Selection of sample

Tooth

Intact bone fragment

0.5–1.0 grams of sample sufficient

3) Clean and grind sample:
   removal of surface or drill into bone

4) Chemicals and enzymes applied to
   extract fragmentary DNA

5) PCR-primers selected to amplify relatively short
   (<1000 BP) DNA section

target
in intact
DNA

DNA fragments
from ancient DNA

6) Sequencing of amplified DNA

Compare

Ancient

Contemporary

FIGURE 3.20   Recovery process of ancient DNA.

drion may have several copies of its DNA, and because each cell can have hundreds or thousands of mitochondria, each cell also has hundreds or thousands of mtDNA copies. Although there are several genes in the mtDNA genome, there are also regions that do not code for anything. These regions (such as one called the D-loop) are highly variable, so they tend to evolve quickly. They are very useful for looking at evolutionary patterns between closely related species, or even between populations within a single species (as we will see in Chapter 15). These regions are so variable that families may have mutations or sequences specific to them. Sequences of these highly variable mtDNA regions therefore are very important in forensic investigation because they allow otherwise unidentifiable pieces of tissue or bodily fluids to be linked to a known individual (provided an appropriate DNA sample from the individual or a relative is available for comparison).

There are two important things to keep in mind about mtDNA. First, unlike nuclear DNA, mtDNA has no exchange (crossing over) between maternal and paternal DNA as it is passed down through the generations. Instead, mtDNA is passed on clonally from generation to generation. Second, mtDNA is passed on only through the mother because an offspring's mtDNA comes from the mitochondria floating in the cytoplasm of the egg. The mitochondria of the sperm are concentrated in the tail region of the cell and are not injected into the egg with the nuclear DNA at fertilization. All of your mtDNA came from your mother, and if you are a male, you are an mtDNA evolutionary dead-end. The

Y chromosome acts as the male version of the mtDNA: It undergoes minimal recombination and is passed on only through males. It is also being used in evolutionary studies of populations.

Ancient DNA Bones up to 100,000 years old can yield DNA. Because the DNA in bone often is fragmentary or degraded, PCR is essential for recovering ancient DNA sequences. In most cases, the DNA amplified from bone is mtDNA. Because there are thousands of copies of mtDNA per cell, there are potentially many more individual copies of mtDNA than nuclear DNA in bony remains, which may be used as a target for amplification (Figure 3.20 on page 69).

Because the recovery of DNA in bone often involves pushing the PCR technique to its limits, contamination is a major worry. If the PCR primers find complementary DNA sequences to attach to, amplification of DNA will occur, even if it is not the target sequence. This is especially a concern if one is looking at human bones because the experimenters themselves become the source of contamination: The primers designed to work on the ancient sample might also work on the researcher's DNA. Given the sensitivity of PCR, even a single molecule of contamination can distort the results of an experiment. Some molecular archaeologists specialize in looking at the ancient DNA from domestic animals, such as cows, and commensal animals, such as rats, which inevitably share living spaces with humans in many parts of the world (Matisoo-Smith et al., 1998). This tends to limit the possibility of contamination, at least from the excavators or the laboratory workers. As we will discuss in Chapter 15, recovery of DNA from one extinct hominid species, the Neandertals, has shed new light on our evolutionary relationship with this close cousin of modern humans.

In this chapter, we have reviewed some of the most fundamental aspects of life on earth: DNA, cells, proteins, and the basics cell growth and organismal reproduction. Although humans may in some ways be unique among our planet's life forms, molecular genetics reaffirms the evolutionary continuity between us and other organisms, ranging from bacteria to plants to all other animals.

SUMMARY

1. **What are the different levels at which scientists study genetic phenomena?**

   Genetics can be studied at the cellular and molecular, individual, population, and species levels. The genetic bases of physical and behavioral traits of an organism can also be studied. The ultimate goal of genetic science is to understand how genes interact with each other and the environment to produce complex organisms. This requires understanding genetic expression at each level.

2. **Why is the cell called the fundamental building block of life?**

   All of the different tissues and structures of the body are composed of cells. Although the cells from different tissues become specialized and differ substantially in appearance, all cells have a similar basic design. Even single-cell organisms have the same basic structure as cells from more complex, multicellular life forms.

3. **What is the difference between prokaryotes and eukaryotes?**

   Prokaryotes, such as bacteria, are single-celled life forms in which the genetic material is not contained within a

nucleus in the cytoplasm. In eukaryotes, the genetic material is contained within a structure in the cytoplasm known as the nucleus. Eukaryotes include single-celled and multicelled life forms, including all complex plants and animals.

4. **What are DNA and RNA? What functions do they serve in the cell?**

   In both prokaryotes and eukaryotes, the genetic material is composed of DNA. DNA is a double-stranded nucleic acid made up of a sequences of bases. The sequence of bases is used to carry the information (in genes) to synthesize proteins and direct growth and development via cellular replication. RNA is a single-stranded nucleic acid. Different kinds of RNA (e.g., messenger RNA, transfer RNA, and ribosomal RNA) have specific roles in protein synthesis.

5. **What are proteins, and what functions do they serve in living organisms? How are proteins synthesized?**

   Proteins are large molecules composed of amino acids. An amino acid chain is also known as a polypeptide; a protein may be formed from several polypetide chains.

Protein synthesis occurs via a two-step process occurring in the nucleus and cytoplasm. Transcription occurs in the nucleus and involves the synthesis of an mRNA molecule that is complementary to the base sequence of a gene. The mRNA molecule carries the genetic information to make a protein from the nucleus to the cytoplasm. At ribosomes located in the cytoplasm, translation occurs, a process in which the information carried by the mRNA is read and a polypeptide or protein is assembled. The language of protein synthesis that allows the conversion of DNA base pair sequences into protein amino acid sequences is known as the genetic code.

6. **How are mitosis and meiosis different from one another? How does crossing over during meiosis increase genetic variability?**

   Mitosis is the process of somatic cell replication in which the diploid chromosome number is maintained in each of the daughter cells after a cell divides. Meiosis is the process of cellular replication that results in the production of sex cells, or gametes. Meiosis has one more step of cell division than mitosis, which results in four daughter cells with the haploid number of chromosomes. Crossing over during meiosis leads to new combinations of genes on chromosomes, which in turn provides new variants on which natural selection can work.

7. **Why is mitochondrial DNA important in the recovery of ancient DNA?**

   DNA in bony remains degrades over time and becomes fragmented. In order for DNA to be recovered from bone, the PCR method is used to amplify target sequences. Because there are thousands of copies of mtDNA per somatic cell, target sequences from mtDNA are more likely to be present intact than target sequences from nuclear DNA (for which only one or two copies would be present per cell).

CRITICAL THINKING QUESTIONS

1. What is a gene? Compare physical and theoretical definitions. How do you think laypeople conceive the gene and how it works?

2. What do you think about the ethics of cloning and stem cell research? Should they be allowed to continue, or be restricted by society and the government?

KEY TERMS

prokaryotes
eukaryotes
nucleus
cytoplasm
somatic cells
gametes
stem cells
deoxyribonucleic acid
   (DNA)
proteins
protein synthesis
ribonucleic acid (RNA)
mitochondria
endoplasmic reticulum
   (ER)
ribosomes
nucleotide
base

enzyme
mutation
hemoglobin
hormone
amino acids
polypeptide
genetic code
codon
gene
messenger RNA
   (mRNA)
transfer RNA (tRNA)
chromatin
mitosis
meiosis
chromosome
centromere
diploid number

haploid number
homologous
   chromosomes
locus
alleles
homozygous
heterozygous
zygote
crossing over
recombination
karyotype
autosomes
sex chromosomes
nondisjunction error
polymerase chain
   reaction (PCR)
mitochondrial DNA
   (mtDNA)

SUGGESTED READING

Maddox, Brenda. (2003). *Rosalind Franklin: The Dark Lady of DNA*. Perennial, New York.
Ridley, Matt. (2000). *Genome*. HarperCollins, New York.

Watson, James D. (2001). *The Double Helix: A Personal Account of the Discovery of the Structure of DNA*. Touchstone Books, New York.

Chapter 4

GENETICS:
From Genotype to Phenotype

Pisum sativum L.

ON A SPRING DAY IN 1900, A SCIENTIST FROM CAMBRIDGE named William Bateson was riding on a train to London. Although relatively young, Bateson was widely recognized among scientists interested in heredity and evolution. He had conducted field and experimental research on both plants and animals and had been involved in theoretical debates about the nature of evolutionary change. Bateson was heading to London to give a talk to the Royal Horticultural Society. In his talk to the society in the previous year, Bateson had forthrightly argued that if the mechanisms of heredity were ever to be worked out, it would only be through the careful breeding of plants or animals, with precise recording of the expression of characters in parent and offspring generations. The expression of these characters would have to be statistically analyzed to make sense of the patterns of hereditary transmission.

As he rode on the train, Bateson read a scientific paper that he had recently seen mentioned in a new publication by a Dutch botanist named Hugo de Vries. The paper, in an obscure Austrian journal, was not hot off the presses; in fact, it had been published 35 years before. Bateson was not familiar with the author, Gregor Mendel, whom he realized had probably been dead for some time.

As he read, one word came to Bateson: remarkable. Mendel had conducted a long series of painstaking hybridization experiments using the common garden pea. Bateson was impressed by the scale of the experiments, his description of them, and, most particularly, the analysis of the results Mendel provided. Bateson immediately recognized that the research program he had so boldly advocated the year before had already been implemented more than four decades earlier by Mendel.

Bateson had prepared his talk to the Royal Horticultural Society before leaving Cambridge, but after arriving in London he hurriedly added a long section to the end discussing and lauding Mendel's work. During his presentation, he admitted some puzzlement as to how research as significant as Mendel's could be all but forgotten or unnoticed for so many years. He proclaimed that Mendel's ideas would "play a conspicuous part in all future discussions of evolutionary problems." Bateson was confident that the "laws of heredity" were finally within reach.

Bateson returned to Cambridge a self-avowed "Mendelian" and, within two years, published a book-length defense of "Mendelism." He devoted the rest of his career to the promotion of Mendel's ideas and to explaining what Mendelism meant to understanding evolutionary change (taking time out to father a son, Gregory, born in 1904, who grew up to be one of the most famous cultural anthropologists of the twentieth century). Strictly speaking, Bateson did not rediscover Mendel. Rather, he did something that was even more important: He recognized the significance of the rediscovery of Mendel and that a whole new science—genetics (a term Bateson coined in (1908)—was at hand.

In Chapter 3, we discussed the cellular and molecular bases of heredity. As the story about William Bateson (1861–1926) indicates, geneticists had a concept of the gene long before anyone knew what DNA was or how it played its role in heredity. In this chapter, we explore in greater detail the observable effects of genes on the structures of plants and on the bodies and behavior of animals, including humans. As we will see, the relationship between gene and structure sometimes is very simple and straightforward and at other times is much more complex.

Human genetics encompasses a wide range of phenomena, which are of evolutionary, cultural, and medical significance. As we cover these diverse topics in this chapter, it is useful to keep in mind the universality of the system of inheritance shared by all forms of life. After all, modern human genetics has its beginnings in research conducted on the common garden pea, a species with whom humans last shared a common ancestor hundreds of millions of years ago.

FROM GENOTYPE TO PHENOTYPE

Little-known Austrian scientist Gregor Mendel (1822–1884), who was "rediscovered" by Bateson and his contemporaries, had a sense of how genes worked almost 90 years before Watson and Crick figured out the structure and function of DNA. This was a striking achievement when you consider that Mendel and his followers could not explore the laws of heredity by looking at the genes themselves. Instead, they had to make inferences about how genes worked based on observations of how specific traits of plants and animals were passed from generation to generation. Such research was painstaking and took years to complete.

How do we make the connection between genes and the physical traits we can observe? As we learned in Chapter 3, DNA functions include replication and protein synthesis. But DNA must do more than this: The genetic information of the DNA must somehow be translated into the physical reality of working bodies. Even today, as some investigators deduce the base composition of the entire human genome, we are far from understanding the exact molecular mechanisms linking genes to bodies.

The local control of gene expression is reasonably well understood. Genes that contain information to make proteins are called **structural genes**. Structural genes are surrounded by *regulatory regions,* sequences of bases that are important in initiating, promoting, or terminating transcription. If these regulatory regions are altered or missing, the expression of the gene can be affected. Beyond these regulatory regions, however, there must also be **regulatory genes** that further guide the expression of structural genes.

Structural genes may be quite similar across divergent (but related) species, so regulatory genes probably are critical in determining the form an organism, or species, takes. For example, two species may have several differences in the structural gene for some protein. Given the redundancy of the genetic code and the fact that the function of a protein may not change even with one or more amino acid substitutions, the structural protein may function in the same way in both species despite the changes at the structural gene level. However, a single change in a regulatory gene could result in the synthesis of the protein being shut down in one species while it is maintained in the other. This could lead to major differences between the two species in anatomy, physiology, or behavior. Recent estimates indicate that DNA base sequences in humans and chimpanzees are 95% identical (including coding and noncoding regions) (Britten, 2002). The small number of differences between human and chimpanzee DNA indicates that the physical and behavioral differences between the species result primarily from regulatory rather than structural genes (Figure 4.1).

When Wilhelm Johannsen introduced the term *gene* in the early twentieth century (see Chapter 3), he introduced two other terms that remain in use today: **genotype** and **phenotype**. The genotype is the set of specific genes (or alleles) an organism carries; it is the genetic constitution of that organism. The phenotype is the observable physical feature of an organism that is under some form of genetic control or influence. In some cases, the relationship between genotype and phe-

structural genes Genes that contain the information to make a protein.

regulatory genes Guide the expression of structural genes, without coding for a protein themselves.

genotype The genetic makeup of an individual. *Genotype* can refer to the entire genetic complement or more narrowly to the alleles present at a specific locus on two homologous chromosomes.

phenotype An observable or measurable feature of an organism. Phenotypes can be anatomical, biochemical, or behavioral.

FIGURE 4.1 Genetically closely related species can have profound anatomical differences, as this movie still from the 1938 film *Her Jungle Love*, featuring Dorothy Lamour and one of her chimpanzee co-stars, indicates.

notype is direct: The observed phenotype is a direct product of the underlying alleles. In other situations, the genotype interacts with factors in the environment to produce a phenotype. In phenotypes that are the result of complex gene–environment interactions, it can be difficult to ascertain the contributions each makes to the variation we observe. Two divergent examples of the relationship between genotype and phenotype in humans are the ABO blood type system and obesity.

THE ABO BLOOD TYPE SYSTEM

The **ABO blood type system** illustrates a straightforward relationship between genotype and phenotype. The ABO system which is important in typing for blood transfusions, refers to a protein found on the surface of red blood cells, which is coded for by a gene located on chromosome 9. This gene has three alleles: A, B, and O. A and B stand for two different versions of the protein, and O stands for the absence of the protein (more precisely, A and B represent versions of the protein modified by enzymes from a common precursor, whereas O has only the precursor version of the protein). Because we are diploid organisms, we have two copies of each gene, one on each chromosome. As we discussed in Chapter 3, if an individual has the same allele of the gene on each chromosome, he or she is said to be homozygous for that gene; if the alleles are different, then the individual is heterozygous. In many cases, the phenotypic expression of the alleles for a gene depends on whether the genotype is heterozygous or homozygous.

An allele that must be present on both chromsomes to be expressed (that is, homozygous) is called a **recessive** allele (or gene). In the ABO system, O is a recessive allele: In order for it to be expressed, you must be homozygous for O (that is, have two copies of it). An allele that must be present at only one chromosomal locus to be expressed is called a **dominant** allele (or gene). Both A and B are dominant to O and **co-dominant** with each other: Only one copy is needed. See Table 4.1 on page 76. As you can see, there are six possible genotypes and four possible phenotypes. Even though this example illustrates a direct relationship between genotype and phenotype, knowing an ABO blood type does not necessarily tell you what the underlying genotype is if you are type A or B. But no amount of environmental intervention will change your blood type. The phenotype is a direct product of the genotype.

ABO blood type system   Refers to the genetic system for one of the proteins found on the surface of red blood cells. Consists of one gene with three alleles: A, B, and O.

recessive   In a diploid organism refers to an allele that must be present in two copies (homozygous) in order to be expressed.

dominant   In a diploid organism, an allele that is expressed when present on only one of a pair of homologous chromosomes.

co-dominant   In a diploid organism, two different alleles of a gene that are both expressed in a heterozygous individual.

TABLE 4.1 ABO Blood Type System Genotypes and Phenotypes		
	GENOTYPE	PHENOTYPE
Homozygous	AA	Type A
	BB	Type B
	OO	Type O
Heterozygous	AO	Type A
	BO	Type B
	AB	Type AB

OBESITY: A COMPLEX INTERACTION

Obesity provides a more complex example of the interaction between genes, environments, and phenotypes (Shell, 2002). Studies have shown that some people with an obese phenotype, defined as some percentage of body weight greater than population norms or ideals, are in some way genetically predisposed to such a condition. Recent research in both lab animals and humans indicates that there are specific genes that are critical to regulating appetite, which would be an important factor in overall body development. Some individuals have alleles for these genes that make it difficult for them to regulate their appetites (Figure 4.2). Genes that regulate fat storage, metabolism, and so on, would also be critical in the development of an obese phenotype. If we could look at all the genes underlying the development of body size and shape, we might be able to come up with combinations of alleles that might indicate that an individual is prone to developing obesity.

Of course, the development of obesity depends on the availability of food in the environment (Figure 4.3). No one becomes obese, even those in possession of alleles predisposing them to obesity, if there is not enough food to maintain an adequate body weight. On the other hand, the obese phenotype in some modern populations—characterized by abundant food and sedentary lifestyles—is becoming so common that the environment is unleashing the potential for obesity in the majority of people rather than a small number who may be exceptionally prone to developing the condition. This "epidemic of obesity"—which is associated with increased rates of heart disease and diabetes, among other medical conditions—probably is a clear example of the mismatch between the environment in which humans evolved and the environment in which people in developed countries now live. People in general are genetically adapted for an environment where food is not so plentiful and where simply accomplishing everyday tasks uses a substantial amount of energy. The obesity phenotype is the product of genes and the environment even in people who do not have an "obesity genotype."

FIGURE 4.2 Laboratory mice demonstrate that genetic differences can have profound effects on the propensity to gain weight.

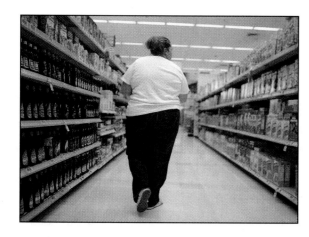

FIGURE 4.3 Obesity is becoming an epidemic in the United States and other developed countries due in part to a mismatch between genes and the environment.

Despite the very different biological levels at which they are expressed, both ABO blood types and obesity are phenotypes. They are both measurable traits that are under a greater or lesser degree of genotypic control. However, in neither case does the observation of the phenotype necessarily provide an unequivocal understanding of the underlying genotype.

MENDELIAN GENETICS

Many of the basic mechanisms of heredity seem obvious once you know something about DNA structure, chromosomes, meiosis, and mitosis. But what is now obvious was once quite mysterious. In the nineteenth and early twentieth century, scientists embraced ideas about heredity that were ill-conceived or later proved to be simply wrong.

One such nineteenth-century notion (supported by Charles Darwin, among others) was **blending inheritance**. Blending inheritance was based on two assumptions: Each parent contributes equally to the offspring, and these contributions are halved at each successive generation. The first assumption is valid. The second assumption only *appears* to be valid, based on selected observations. Blending inheritance was commonly used in the late nineteenth century as an argument against evolution by natural selection because it was thought that it would be virtually impossible to select for any trait if it was being "blended out" with each passing generation (Figure 4.4 on page 78). The logic for this argument went as follows: Suppose a trait appeared in a population that greatly enhanced the fitness of the individual who possessed it. With blending inheritance, it would be expected that if this individual mated with an individual who did not possess that advantageous trait, their offspring would represent some intermediate form between the phenotypes of the parent. As such, the offspring would not have the fitness advantage possessed by the parent with the new trait. With each passing generation, the advantageous trait would be diminished, blended out of existence. It was very difficult to see how natural selection could work under such circumstances, although convoluted and wholly speculative theories of genetic inheritance (such as Darwin's pangenesis theory) were offered to try to counter this argument.

Gregor Mendel's careful experimental work demonstrated the nonblending, particulate (that is, genetic) nature of heredity, or **particulate inheritance**. Unfortunately for Mendel, his research was so far ahead of its time—a time when ideas about blending inheritance held sway—that his work was not discovered until 16 years after his death and 35 years after he published it.

Mendel was an Austrian monk who, between about 1856 and 1868, conducted plant breeding experiments in the garden of the abbey in which he lived and taught

blending inheritance
Discredited nineteenth-century idea that genetic factors from the parents averaged-out or blended together when they were passed on to offspring.

particulate inheritance The concept of heredity based on the transmission of genes (alleles) according to Mendelian principles.

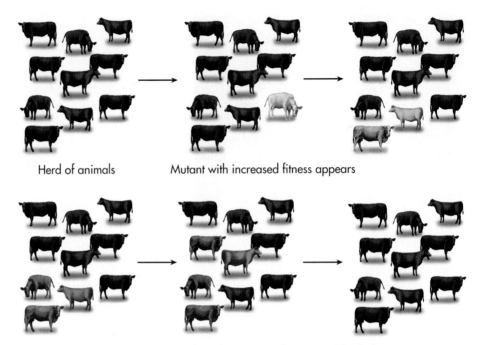

Herd of animals   Mutant with increased fitness appears

With each passing generation, the advantageous feature is "blended out"

FIGURE 4.4 Blending inheritance formed the basis of nineteenth-century critiques of evolution by natural selection.

FIGURE 4.5 Gregor Mendel

(Figure 4.5). These experiments were conducted on different varieties of the common garden pea (genus *Pisum*) and involved a series of hybridizations or crosses in which Mendel carefully recorded the transmission of several characters across generations. As it turned out, the garden pea was an ideal organism for elucidating the particulate nature of genetic transmission. Its best feature is that it displays two alternative phenotypes, or *dichotomous variation*, for several different and independent traits: They appear in one distinct form or the other with no apparent blending.

In his breeding experiments, Mendel focused on the following seven features of the pea: seed coat (round or wrinkled), seed color (green or yellow), pod shape (full or constricted), pod color (green or yellow), flower color (violet or white), stem form (axial or terminal), and stem size (tall or dwarf) (Figure 4.6). In his simplest experiments, Mendel looked at the expression of just one trait at a time in the first generation (the F_1 generation) when he crossed two lines that were true-breeding (e.g., wrinkled seeds $\times$ smooth seeds, green seeds $\times$ yellow seeds, and so on); a true-breeding line is one that reliably produced the same phenotype generation after generation. In the next stage of the experiment, he bred the F_1 generation plants with themselves ($F_1 \times F_1$), and looked at the distribution of characters in the second generation (F_2). He obtained similar results for each feature he examined:

1. Although the F_1 generation plants were the result of crosses between different true-breeding lines, only one of the parental generation traits was expressed. For example, when he crossed full pea pod plants with constricted pea pod plants, the F_1 generation consisted entirely of full pea pod plants. For none of the 7 traits he examined did Mendel find evidence of blending inheritance.

2. In the F_2 generation, the version of the trait that had disappeared in the F_1 generation returned, but was found in only one quarter of the offspring plants. The other three quarters of the plants were the same as those in the F_1 gen-

eration. In other words, there was a 3:1 ratio in the expression of the original parental lines. For example, in the cross involving seed color, in which yellow is dominant to green, Mendel counted 6022 plants with yellow seeds and 2001 with green, for a ratio of 3.01:1. Similar results were obtained for other 6 traits. Mendel called the version of the trait that appeared in the F_1 generation dominant, while the trait that reappeared (as one quarter of the total) in the F_2 generation was called recessive.

From these basic observations, Mendel developed a series of postulates (or laws or principles) that anticipated the work of later generations of geneticists.

Mendel's Postulates

In the postulates listed (Klug and Cummings 2003), the Mendelian insight is in italics while the modern interpretation of his insight is discussed below it.

CHARACTER	CONTRASTING TRAITS		F₁ RESULTS	F₂ RATIO
SEEDS	round/wrinkled		all round	3 round:1 wrinkled
	yellow/green		all yellow	3 yellow:1 green
PODS	full/constricted		all full	3 full:1 constricted
	green/yellow		all green	3 green:1 yellow
FLOWERS	violet/white		all violet	3 violet:1 white
STEM	axial/terminal		all axial	3 axial:1 terminal
	tall/dwarf		all tall	3 tall:1 dwarf

FIGURE 4.6 The traits Mendel used in his experiments, and the results of the F_1 and F_2 generation crosses.

F₁ cross

Gamete formation by F₁ parents

Setting up Punnett square

Filling out squares representing fertilization

F₂ results

Genotype	Phenotype	
1 GG		
2 Gg	3/4	
1 gg	1/4	
1 : 2 : 1	3 : 1	

FIGURE 4.7
The Punnett square demonstrates how the F₂ ratio arises from an F₁ X F₁ cross.

1. Hereditary characteristics are controlled by particulate unit factors that exist in pairs in individual organisms.
The unit factors are genes, and they exist in pairs because in diploid organisms, chromosomes come in pairs. Each individual receives one copy of each chromosome from each parent, thus he or she receives one of his or her pair of unit factors from each parent. Different versions of the unit factors (alleles) may exist. An individual may have two that are the same (homozygous) or two that are different (heterozygous).

2. When an individual has two different unit factors responsible for a characteristic, only one is expressed and is said to be dominant to the other, which is said to be recessive.
In heterozygous individuals, those who have different versions of a gene on each chromosome, the allele that is expressed is dominant to the allele that is not expressed. Thus in Mendel's experiments, round seed form was dominant to wrinkled seed form, yellow seed color was dominant to green, and so on. Mendel did not examine a co-dominant character, such as AB in the ABO blood type system.

3. During the formation of gametes, the paired unit factors separate, or segregate, randomly so that each sex cell receives one or the other with equal likelihood.
This is known as **Mendel's law of segregation**, and it reflects the fact that in diploid organisms, the chromosomes in a pair segregate randomly into sex cells during meiosis. Mendel formulated this law based on his interpretation of the phenotypes expressed in the F₁ (100% of which had the dominant phenotype) and F₂ generations (dominant:recessive phenotype ratio of 3:1). It is easy to understand Mendel's insight if we use a kind of illustration known as a *Punnett square,* named after British geneticist R. C. Punnett (1875–1967).

The Punnett square allows us to illustrate parental genetic contributions to offspring and the possible genotypes of the offspring (Figure 4.7). For example, in the cross between green peas and yellow peas, yellow is dominant to green. Let us call the alleles G and g, for the dominant yellow seed and recessive green seed, respectively. The yellow seed parent can contribute only the G allele and the green seed parent can contribute only the g allele to the offspring. In the Punnett square, you can see that all of the offspring will be heterozygous Gg. Because G is dominant to g, all of the offspring have yellow seeds. Now, if we cross the heterozygous offspring (Gg) of the F₁ generation with each other, we get three possible genotypes: GG (25%), gg (25%), and Gg (50%). As we can see from the Punnett square, 75% of the offspring will produce yellow seeds and 25% of them will have green seeds. Thus the 3:1 phenotypic ratio of Mendel's F₂ generation is obtained. Punnett squares are quite handy and can be used to illustrate the parental contributions to offspring for any gene.

4. During gamete formation, segregating pairs of unit factors assort independently of each other.
This is known as **Mendel's law of independent assortment** (Figure 4.8). Mendel did a series of more complex pea breeding experiments known as *dihybrid crosses* that looked at the simultaneous transmission of two of the seven genetic characters of peas. For example, Mendel looked at how both seed color and seed shape might be transmitted across generations. What he found was that the unit factors (alleles) for different characters were transmitted independently of each other. In other words, the segregation of one pair of chromosomes into two sex cells does not influence the segregation of another pair of chromosomes into the same sex cells. Mendel explored the transmission of seed color (yellow dominant to green) and seed shape (round dominant to wrinkled) in a dihybrid cross experiment (Figure 4.9 on page 82). He started by crossing yellow–round with green–wrinkled and yellow–wrinkled with green–round. In both crosses, he obtained peas that expressed the dominant characters of both traits (yellow and round) but were heterozygous for

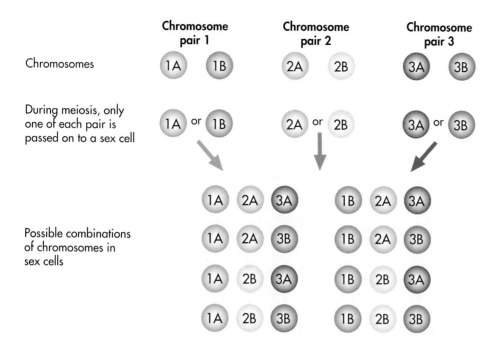

FIGURE 4.8 Mendel's law of independent assortment. Each sex cell receives one chromosome (either A or B) from each of the three paired chromosomes. The assortment of one pair of chromosomes is not influenced by either of the other chromosome pairs, hence "independent assortment." There are 8 possible combinations of chromosomes in the resulting sex cells.

both as well. So the genotype of these plants (the F1 generation) was GgWw. He then crossed the F_1 generation (GgWw x GgWw) with itself. There are sixteen possible genotypes resulting from this cross, with four possible phenotypes (yellow–round, yellow–wrinkled, green–round, green–wrinkled). Mendel found that approximately 9/16 were yellow–round, 3/16 were yellow–wrinkled, 3/16 were green–round, and 1/16 were green–wrinkled. This 9:3:3:1 ratio is what would be expected if the two characters are transmitted independently of each other. Hence, we can say that they are independently (and randomly) assorted during meiosis.

LINKAGE AND CROSSING OVER

The law of independent assortment applies only to genes that are on different chromosomes. Because the chromosome is the unit of transmission in meiosis, genes that are on the same chromosome should segregate together and find themselves in the same sex cells. This is known as **linkage**. A chromosome may have thousands of genes, and these genes are linked together during meiosis by virtue of being on the same chromosome.

However, decades of genetic research on fruit flies and other organisms have shown that independent assortment of genes on the same chromosome is not only possible but relatively common. How does this happen? It occurs through the process of crossing over, or recombination, which we discussed in Chapter 3. As you recall, during meiosis there is a physical exchange of genetic material between nonsister chromosomes (that is, the chromosomes that originally came from different parents), so that a portion of one chromosome is replaced by the corresponding segment of the other homologous chromosome. Through this process of

Mendel's law of segregation
The two alleles of a gene found on each of a pair of chromosomes segregate independently of one another into sex cells.

Mendel's law of independent assortment Genes found on different chromosomes are sorted into sex cells independently of one another.

linkage Genes that are found on the same chromosome are said to be linked. The closer together two genes are on a chromosome, the greater the linkage and the less likely they are to be separated during crossing over.

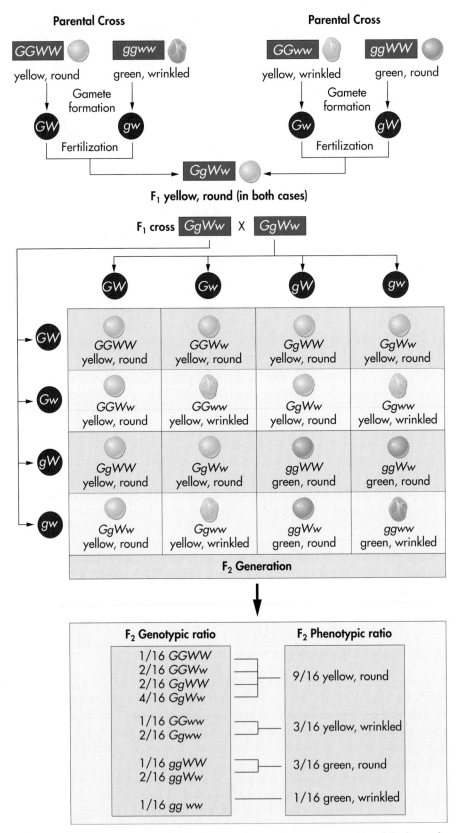

FIGURE 4.9 The Punnett square of a dihybrid cross demonstrates Mendel's law of independent assortment. The F₁ heterozygous plants are self-fertilized to produce an F₂ generation. Mendel was able to infer the genotypic ratios from observing the phenotypic ratios.

crossing over, new allele combinations are assembled on the recombinant chromosomes (Figure 4.10). The likelihood of any two genes on a chromosome being redistributed through crossing over is a function of distance, or how far apart they are physically along the length of the chromosome. Genes that are located near one another on a chromosome are more strongly linked than genes that are far apart and thus are less likely to be separated or "independently assorted" during meiosis through crossing over.

Given the obvious complexities that linkage and crossing over introduce to the genetic process, it may occur to you that Mendel was not only extraordinarily insightful but also a bit lucky. How did he get such consistent results for seven different genes without being distracted or derailed by linkage or crossing over? As it happens, the garden pea has seven chromosomes, and Mendel looked at seven genes; it is easy to assume that this is the reason why Mendel had no problems with linkage. Two of the genes Mendel looked at were on chromosome 1 of the pea, and three others were on chromosome 4; the other two were alone on chromosomes 5 and 7, respectively (Blixt, 1975). The two genes on chromosome 1 are so far apart that very little linkage is detected between them (due to crossing over), and the same is true for some of the gene combinations on chromosome 4. In addition, one of the characters on chromosome 4 (pod shape) is also controlled by a gene on chromosome 6, and we do not know which gene Mendel was using. Some have accused Mendel of detecting linkage but ignoring it in his published work, but a recent reanalysis of these claims supports the view that Mendel did not have to deal with linkage because he never observed it (Fairbanks and Rytting, 2001).

MUTATION

A mutation is essentially an error that occurs in the replication of DNA (see Chapter 3). Given that Mendel did not know about the biochemical mechanisms of heredity, he was not too concerned with mutations as we know them. However, Mendel and his contemporaries were acutely aware that the spontaneous appearance of new variants in a species, or "sports" as Darwin called them, could have important consequences for an individual, a population, or even an entire species.

Getting back to the DNA level, a mutation is any change in a DNA sequence that becomes established in a daughter cell. Any time somatic cells divide, a mutation may occur and be passed to the daughter cells. However, mutations that occur in sex cells are especially important because they can be passed to subsequent generations and will be present in all cells of the bodies of offspring. Mutations can occur in any part of the DNA, but obviously those that occur in structural or regulatory genes are much more critical than those that occur in noncoding regions or introns (see Chapter 3).

POINT MUTATION AND SICKLE CELL DISEASE

There are several different kinds of mutations. A **point mutation** occurs when a single base in a gene is changed. A number of diseases can be attributed to specific point mutations in the gene for a protein. One of the most well-known and anthropologically important is the mutation that results in **sickle cell disease**. Sickle cell disease is caused by an abnormal form of the protein hemoglobin, which is the protein that transports oxygen throughout the body in red blood cells (it makes up 95% of the protein found in a red blood cell). Hemoglobin molecules normally exist separately in the red blood cell, each binding to a molecule of oxygen. In sickle cell disease, the hemoglobin molecules are separate from each other when they bind oxygen, but upon the release of oxygen, the abnormal hemoglobin molecules stick together, forming a complex structure with a helical shape. These long helical fiber

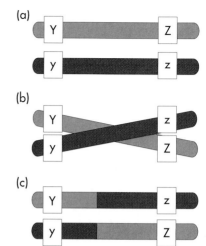

FIGURE 4.10 Crossing over during meiosis leads to allele combinations in sex cells that are not present in the parent chromosomes. (a) A pair of homologous chromosomes is represented, carrying alleles YZ and yz respectively. (b) Crossing over occurs during meiosis. The more distant from each other two genes are on a chromosome, they more likely they are to be separated during meiosis. (c) Two recombinant chromosomes, with allele combinations of Yz and yZ, may now be passed into sex cells.

point mutation   A change in the base sequence of a gene that results from the change of a single base to a different base.

sickle cell disease   An autosomal recessive disease caused by a point mutation in an allele that codes for one of the polypeptide chains of the hemoglobin protein.

bundles deform the red blood cells from their normal, platelike shape to something resembling a sickle, hence the name of the disease (Figure 4.11).

Red blood cells, which lose their nucleus not long after they are formed, are remarkably flexible and malleable in order to squeeze through tiny blood vessels. In contrast, sickled red blood cells lose this flexibility. They clump together in small blood vessels and impair circulation in capillaries; they also collect in the spleen, causing damage to that organ. The sickling also damages the red blood cells themselves. If a sickled red blood cell can make it back to the lungs and become reoxygenated, then the cell returns to its normal shape and can be used to transport oxygen. But repeated sickling shortens the life span of the red blood cells, contributing to the development of anemia. In addition, abnormal complexes of hemoglobin cause the body's immune system to make antibodies against these cells, further exacerbating the anemia. During periods of oxygen stress, such as during exercise, oxygen uptake and release increases, which leads to an increase in the formation of sickle cells. Sickle cell disease is characterized by chronic anemia, but the secondary effects of the circulation of sickled cells can also be deadly during a crisis.

Hemoglobin (Hb) is a protein that consists of four polypeptide chains (two *alpha* chains and two *beta* chains) (Chapter 3). The *beta* chains consist of 146 amino acids. The normal, adult hemoglobin is called HbA. In the *beta* chain, the sickle cell hemoglobin, or HbS, is one amino acid different from HbA: The sixth amino acid in HbA is glutamic acid, whereas in HbS it is valine (Figure 4.12). This amino acid substitution is caused by a mutation in the codon from CTC to CAC. Out of 438 bases, this is the only change. A striking feature of the mutation in sickle cell is that it does not directly affect the ability of the hemoglobin to carry oxygen but rather causes the hemoglobin molecules to stick together, leading to the deformed cell shape. Of course, a mutation that rendered a red blood cell totally incapable of carrying oxygen probably would be directly fatal.

Sickle cell disease appears in people who are homozygous (have two copies) for the HbS allele. A disease of this kind that is caused by being homozygous for a recessive, disease-causing allele is known as an **autosomal recessive disease**. People who are heterozygous HbA HbS produce enough normal hemoglobin to avoid the complications of sickle cell disease under most circumstances, but they are *carriers* of the disease: They do not suffer from the disease but can pass on the allele that causes the disease. If a carrier mates with another individual who is a heterozygous carrier, then following Mendelian laws, there is a 25% chance that the offspring will be a homozygous sufferer of the disease. We will discuss the biological anthropology of sickle cell disease in greater detail in Chapter 6.

autosomal recessive disease A disease caused by a recessive allele; one copy of the allele must be inherited from each parent for the disease to develop.

FIGURE 4.11 Comparison of normal and sickle cell red blood cells.

Normal Hemoglobin Beta Chain		Sickling Hemoglobin Beta Chain	
DNA sequence	Amino acid	DNA sequence	Amino acid
•	#1	•	#1
•		•	
•		•	
•		•	
•		•	
T G A	#4 threonine	T G A	#4 threonine
G G A	#5 proline	G G A	#5 proline
C T C	#6 glutamic acid	C A C	#6 valine
C T C	#7 glutamic acid	C T C	#7 glutamic acid
T T T	#8 lysine	T T T	#8 lysine
• • • • •	• • • • •	• • • • •	• • • • •
#1652 (including intron sequences)	#146	#1652	#146

β chain — β chain
— α chain
α chain   heme group

FIGURE 4.12 A single base substitution leading to a single amino acid substitution in the hemoglobin beta chain is the cause of sickle cell disease.

TRINUCLEOTIDE REPEAT DISEASES

In addition to point mutations, another common kind of mutation involves the **insertion mutation** or **deletion mutation** of several bases in sequence. In the last decade, at least sixteen genetic diseases have been found to be caused by a specific kind of insertion mutation, which involves the multiple, repeated insertion of trinucleotide (three-base) repeat sequences (Fischbeck, 2001). The best-known of **trinucleotide repeat diseases** may be *Huntington disease* (which claimed the life of folksinger Woody Guthrie), a degenerative neurological disorder that is caused by a dominant allele: It is an **autosomal dominant disease.**

The gene that causes Huntington disease (which produces a protein called *huntingtin*) is located on chromosome 4. In normal individuals, a trinucleotide sequence, CAG, which codes for the amino acid glutamine, usually is repeated 10–35 times. In contrast, people who have Huntington disease have 40–120 CAG repeats. Huntington disease usually is thought of as a disease that strikes people in middle age, with a gradual onset of symptoms, including loss of motor control

insertion mutation A change in the base sequence of a gene that results from the addition of one or more base pairs in the DNA.

deletion mutation A change in the base sequence of a gene that results from the loss of one or more base pairs in the DNA.

trinucleotide repeat diseases A family of autosomal dominant diseases that is caused by the insertion of multiple copies of a three-base pair sequence (CAG) that codes for the amino acid glutamine. Typically, the more copies inserted into the gene, the more serious the disease.

autosomal dominant disease A disease that is caused by a dominant allele: Only one copy needs to be inherited from either parent for the disease to develop.

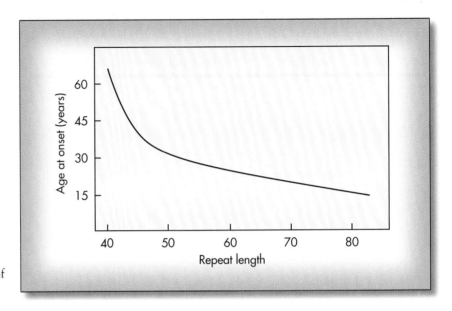

FIGURE 4.13 Relationship between the number of CAG repeats in a gene and the age of onset of Huntington disease.

and ultimately dementia. However, there is variability in the age of onset, and it is directly related to the number of CAG repeats a person is carrying. If someone has more than 80 repeats, the age of onset could be in the teenage years, whereas someone with 40 repeats may not show signs of illness until he or she reaches 60 years of age (Figure 4.13). In addition, the more repeats, the more severe the disease. About half of the known trinucleotide repeat diseases are characterized by CAG repeats; they are also known as *polyglutamine expansion* diseases.

MUTATIONS: BAD, NEUTRAL, AND GOOD

The idea that mutations are bad pervades our popular culture. After all, you would probably not consider it a compliment if someone called you a mutant. However, although several diseases arise as a result of mutations in normal genes, it is important to keep in mind that the vast majority of mutations probably are neutral.

Mutations that occur in noncoding regions are by definition neutral because they make no contribution to the phenotype. Mutations that occur in a gene but do not alter the amino acid in a protein also have no phenotypic effect. These kinds of mutations are common because of the redundancy in the genetic code. For example, if a codon changes from CGA to CGG, alanine is still placed in the corresponding position in the polypeptide chain. On top of that, proteins can endure amino acids substitutions without changes in function. There are usually some parts of a protein that are more critical to function than other parts. Amino acid substitutions in noncritical parts of a protein may not affect the function of the protein at all. In fact, protein variation in nature is extensive, and in many cases it does not appear to have any functional consequence. If protein function is not affected, then there is likely to be no change to the physiology or anatomy of the organism.

Finally, a mutation may affect the anatomy or physiology of an organism and still have no direct affect on the fitness of an individual. A famous example of such a trait is the *Habsburg face,* which is composed of a characteristic combination of facial features, including a prominent lower lip (hence the name *Habsburg jaw,* by which it is also known). This trait is found in many European noble families, and its transmission has been traced over twenty-three generations (Wolff et al., 1993). Because these European nobles were painted and sculpted with some regularity, there are many accurate historical representations of people with this condition (Figure 4.14). It is caused by an autosomal dominant allele.

FIGURE 4.14 King Charles V, Holy Roman Emperor and ruler of Spain from 1516–1556, possessed the distinctive Habsburg jaw.

Can mutations be good? Absolutely. Mutations are the ultimate source of variation, and variation is the raw material on which evolution acts. Without mutation, there could be no natural selection. Although chromosomal processes such as crossing over create new allele combinations and thereby increase phenotypic variability, mutation is the only source for new alleles that can be combined in novel ways. "Good" mutations—those that increase an organism's chance of surviving and reproducing—do not have to be common. The process of natural selection makes their spread throughout a population possible. Once this happens, they are no longer considered to be mutations but are the normal or wild type (Figure 4.15).

If we focus on any given gene, we will find that mutations are not very common. However, if we consider the genome as a whole, then mutations are not so hard to find. The calculation of mutation rate is very complicated. It is made even more complicated by the fact that the mutation rate varies between species, and within species, different genes appear to undergo spontaneous mutation at different rates (Eyre-Walker and Keightley, 1999).

Many autosomal dominant disorders (such as *achondroplasia,* a disorder characterized by dwarfism caused by impaired long bone growth) occur at rates on the order of 1 in 10,000 births, and they result almost entirely from new mutations. Let us suppose that the mutation rate in humans for any given gene averages about 1 in 10,000 per generation (a very rough estimate). That might not seem very high, but when we consider that humans have two copies each of 30,000–40,000 genes, then it is likely that every individual carries a mutation in some gene. And if we search in a population of individuals, the chance of finding mutations in more than one gene is very high indeed.

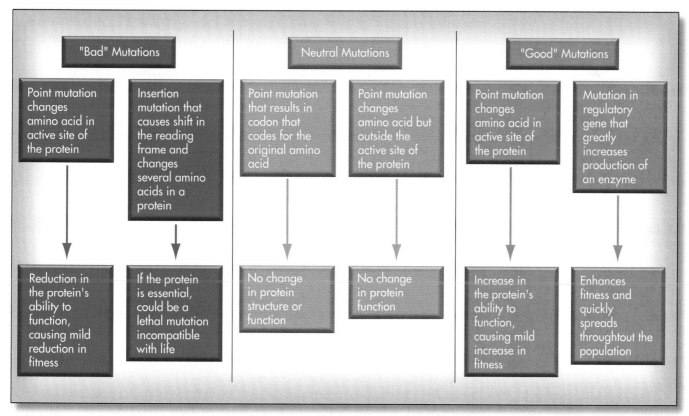

FIGURE 4.15 "Bad," neutral, and "good" mutations.

X-LINKED DISORDERS

We discussed chromosomal mutations or abnormalities in an earlier section. However, there is one class of gene mutations that is directly related to chromosome structure. These are the **X-linked disorders**. As discussed in Chapter 3, the sex chromosomes in human males are XY, and in human females they are XX (technically speaking, males are the *heterogametic* sex and females are the *homogametic* sex). The Y chromosome is very small compared with other chromosomes and contains a small number of genes. In contrast, the X chromosome contains a large number of genes.

Because human males have only one copy of the X chromosome, they are susceptible to a host of diseases that are caused by mutations in X chromosome genes. These diseases are much less common in females because they are essentially autosomal recessive disorders and will appear in a female only when they are present in two copies. Female children of affected males are all carriers of the condition because one of their X chromosomes is a copy of their father's (only) X chromosome. **Pedigrees** of families affected by X-linked disorders show a typical pattern whereby the disorders appear to skip a generation. If a male has an X-linked disorder, he cannot pass it on to his sons because he does not pass an X chromosome to them. His daughters will not have the disease but will be carriers. Their sons then have a 50% chance of getting the disorder because they have a 50% chance of receiving the affected X chromosome.

X-linked disorders that cause death before reproductive age, such as *Lesch–Nyhan syndrome*, which is characterized by mental and motor retardation, self-mutilation, and early death, and some severe forms of muscular dystrophy, are never seen in females because they are on X chromosomes that are never transmitted to the next generation. A female can develop an X-linked disorder if her father has one of the disorders and her mother is a carrier (or via an extremely unlikely combination of family genetics and a new mutation).

Hemophilia, a disease characterized by the absence of one of the clotting factor proteins in blood, is perhaps the most well-known X-linked disorder. Boys and men with this condition are very vulnerable to hemorrhage and severe joint damage. With advances in the treatment of hemophilia, males with the condition are able to live long and productive lives. Several of the male descendants of Queen Victoria suffered from this condition (Figure 4.16). *Red color blindness* and *green color blindness* are both also X-linked disorders and therefore are much more common in men than women. In European-derived populations, the frequency in men is about 7% and in women about 0.4%. The genes affecting red and green color vision are located next to each other at one end of the X chromosome (Vollrath et al., 1988). The high frequency of color blindness may reflect the absence of selective pressure against the condition. In addition, studies of the alleles of color-blind individuals indicate that those alleles have all arisen via recombination events. Recombination rates often are higher at the end of a chromosome, which is where the genes for red and green color vision are located.

MENDELIAN GENETICS IN HUMANS

Over the past century, hundreds of conditions and diseases have been cataloged in humans that can be explained in terms of Mendelian genetic transmission (Table 4.2 on page 90). Besides those discussed previously, there are traits such as ear lobe form (free hanging is dominant to the recessive attached form) or the ability to taste the chemical phenylthiocarbamide (PTC; tasting is dominant to nontasting) that appear to conform to simple Mendelian rules of transmission. The Online Mendelian Inheritance in Man (OMIM) Web site (http://www3.ncbi.nlm.nih.gov/Omim/) provides an extraordinary database on genetic conditions in humans, from the most innocuous to the most lethal. An examination of this

X-linked disorders Genetic conditions that result from mutations to genes on the X chromosome. They are almost always expressed in males, who have only one copy of the X chromosome; in females, the second X chromosome containing the normally functioning allele protects them from developing X-linked disorders.

pedigree A diagram used in the study of human genetics that shows the transmission of a genetic trait over several generations of a family.

FIGURE 4.16 Queen Victoria and her family and a pedigree showing the transmission of hemophilia in the British royal family.

database conveys a sense of the complexity inherent in studying even the simplest genetic conditions. Even such classic examples as ear lobe form and the ability to taste PTC are not necessarily as clear-cut as they have appeared to be (although the dominant–recessive model works well enough for them).

GENETICS BEYOND MENDEL

Mendelian genetics provided a beginning for our understanding of the biological mechanisms of heredity and evolution. By studying the genetics of phenotypes that are determined by a single gene, which have a small number of alleles, scientists have gained a significant understanding of many other more complex biological phenomena. However, it is important to keep in mind that a single-gene, dominant–recessive model of heredity cannot explain much of the biological world we see around us. As Kenneth Weiss (2002, p. 44) has pointed out, although Mendelian genetics provides a foundation for understanding heredity, "a misleading, over-simplified, and overdeterministic view of life is one of the possible consequences." Not long after the rediscovery of Mendel, the overly enthusiastic application of Mendelian principles to human affairs, in combination with certain political and nationalistic movements, had a number of important consequences (Box 4.1 on page 91).

Mendelian genetics is most useful in examining characters for which there are different and nonoverlapping phenotypic variants. This is called **qualitative variation**. Seed color in peas (green or yellow) or the different phenotypes in the ABO

qualitative variation
Phenotypic variation that can be characterized as belonging to discrete, observable categories.

TABLE 4.2　Mendelian Inheritance in Humans

DISORDERS	DESCRIPTIONS
AUTOSOMAL RECESSIVE DISORDERS	
Cystic fibrosis	Causes abnormal mucous secretions, which affect several organs, especially in the respiratory system. In European and European-derived populations has a frequency of about 50/100,000 births.
Sickle cell disease	Abnormal hemoglobin molecule causes sickling of red blood cells, impairing oxygen transport in the body. Particularly common in some African and African-derived populations.
Tay–Sachs disease	Most common in Ashkenazi (European) Jews, caused by an abnormal form of an enzyme that breaks down a fatty substance known as ganglioside GM2. When this substance builds up, it is toxic to nerve cells, and death usually occurs before 5 years of age.
Phenylketonuria (PKU)	Defects in the enzyme phenylalanine hydroxylase cause a buildup of the amino acid phenylalanine, which results in mental retardation and physical abnormalities if phenylalanine is not removed from the diet.
AUTOSOMAL DOMINANT DISORDERS	
Huntington disease	Polyglutamine expansion disease that causes uncontrolled movements, mental and emotional problems, and progressive loss of thinking ability (cognition).
Neurofibromatosis type I	Causes the growth of noncancerous tumors along nerves called neurofibromas, usually in the skin but also in the brain and other parts of the body. Causes mental retardation in about 10% of cases, and about half of afflicted individuals have learning disabilities.
Myotonic dystrophy	Most common form of muscular dystrophy in adults. Causes a progressive wasting of the muscles, particularly in the lower legs, hands, neck, and face.
Achondroplasia	Form of dwarfism caused by a failure to convert cartilage to bone, especially in long bones. Individuals have a slightly enlarged head, with prominent forehead, and other physical anomalies in addition to short stature.
X-LINKED DISORDERS	
Fragile X syndrome	Causes mild to severe mental retardation. Result of the insertion of hundreds of copies of the triplet CGG into a gene on the X chromosome (normal is about 40 repeats).
Hemophilia	Absence of one of the clotting factors in the blood leads to uncontrolled bleeding upon even mild injury. In severe cases, spontaneous bleeding can occur in joints and muscles.
Lesch–Nyhan syndrome	Caused by the overproduction of uric acid, leading to the development of goutlike joint problems, kidney and bladder stones, and involuntary flexing and jerking movements. Self-injury through biting and head banging is common.

quantitative variation
Phenotypic variation that is characterized by the distribution of continuous variation (expressed using a numerical measure) within a population (for example, in a bell curve).

polygenic traits　Phenotypic traits that result from the combined action of more than one gene; most complex traits are polygenic.

blood system are examples of qualitative variation. In contrast, **quantitative variation** refers to continuous variation for some trait, which emerges after we measure a character in a population of individuals. It is not possible to divide the population into discrete groups reflecting one variant or another because the variation is overlapping. For many characters, if we measure enough individuals, we find that there is a normal (or bell-shaped) distribution in the individual expression of the character. Individuals who have extremely high or low measurements are most rare, and individuals who have measurements near the population mean, or average, are most common. Stature in humans is a classic example (Figure 4.17 on page 92). Very short and very tall people are much less common than people of average height. Stature is influenced by genes, but except for rare kinds of dwarfism, the phenotypic distribution of stature in humans does not lend itself to a simple Mendelian explanation.

Stature and other complex phenotypes, such as the timing of puberty, skin color, and eye color, are **polygenic traits**. Their expression depends on the action of multiple genes, each of which may have more than one allele. The more genes and alleles that contribute to a polygenic trait, the more possible genotypes—and phenotypes—are possible. Thus when continuous variation for a trait is observed

BOX 4.1 State Fair Mendelism and the Eugenics Movement

In the 1920s, if one attended a state fair or similar public gathering, it would not have been unusual to see a display explaining the finer points of Mendelian inheritance. These displays were not simply meant to be educational; rather, they served as a warning to the dangers and costs of "bad heredity." One might learn that the cross between a "pure" and "abnormal" parent would result in the production of "normal but tainted" children and some "abnormal" grandchildren. A cross between a "tainted" individual and another "tainted" individual would produce the Mendelian F2 ratio of one "abnormal," one "pure normal," and two "tainted" offspring (Kevles, 1985). Such a display would certainly make a person think twice about the genetic quality of a prospective mate, which was exactly the point of the display.

The popular enthusiasm for Mendelism was directly linked to a broader social and intellectual movement known as *eugenics*. The term was coined in 1883 by Francis Galton (1822–1911), cousin of Charles Darwin and a pioneer in the application of statistical methods to biological phenomena. *Eugenics* was derived from a Greek root meaning "good in birth" or "noble in heredity." In the view of Galton and his followers, eugenics was fundamentally about "the future betterment of the human race." Of course, not everyone can agree on what direction the human race should take.

Eugenics had a remarkably widespread appeal (Figure A). In the first decades of the twentieth century, eugenics societies were founded in countries throughout the world, and the ideals of eugenics could be shaped to serve any number of causes. Women often were active in eugenics societies, and the increasing control of women over their reproductive lives may be one of the ultimate outcomes of the eugenics movement. In Western countries, eugenics tended to be more enthusiastically embraced by middle- and upper-class people, many of whom worried about the decline in the quality of their compatriots caused by the unchecked population growth of lower-class people and other "undesirables."

The eugenics movement called for deliberate intervention in the "natural" evolutionary processes that were ongoing in human populations. This intervention could take either positive or negative forms. In many countries, many upper-class people believed that there was a disturbing trend for the better-educated, more intelligent, and sensitive young people to marry later and to have fewer children than the less-educated, coarser, and less intelligent lower classes. Positive eugenics was devoted to reaching out to the "right kind" of people and encouraging them, for the sake of the "race," to have more babies.

Negative eugenics was far less benign and had more serious and longstanding consequences. It focused on removing the "wrong kind" of people from the population by preventing them from having children, banning their entry into a country, expelling them from a country, or killing them. In the United States, legislation in the 1920s allowed the involuntary sterilization of "mental defectives" and the exclusion of immigrants from certain (that is, non–northern European) countries; both actions were strongly influenced by an ideology of negative eugenics. In Nazi Germany, the implementation of the "final solution"—the genocidal killings of Jews, Gypsies, and others whom the Nazis considered undesirable—was the most horrifying form of negative eugenics. Although these killings may represent the culmination of various historical trends, historian Robert Jay Lifton argues that the bureaucratic and practical origins of mass killings in Nazi Germany began with programs to "euthanize" all chronic mental patients and other medical undesirables. It is estimated that 80,000–100,000 chronic mental patients were killed by Nazi doctors as a grisly prelude to the millions killed during the Holocaust.

The popularity of the eugenics movement waned in the United States even before the start of World War II, but the term *eugenics* often arises, usually from critics, any time when human genetics intersects with broader social issues. One can only hope that critics who use *eugenics* as a contemporary pejorative do not have as simplistic and deterministic a view of history as the eugenicists did of human biology, genetics, and behavior.

FIGURE A Eugenics display at the Kansas Free Fair in the 1920s.

in a population (whether or not it is normally distributed), it is much more likely to be caused by polygenic inheritance rather than a single gene effect.

Single genes that produce qualitative variants often are referred to as though they produced the whole trait, when in fact the trait in question results from the concerted efforts of several genes. For example, Mendel focused on a specific gene and two alleles that influenced the height of pea plants, such that he was able to

FIGURE 4.17 The normal distribution of height in a sample of 3,808 adult men and women. Mean is 165.2 cm (standard deviation 11.3).
NOTE: Data taken from the National Health and Nutrition Survey 2001-2002, National Center for Health Statistics.

pleiotropy The phenomenon of a single gene having multiple phenotypic effects.

dichotomize the phenotypes as short and tall. However, stem height in peas is really under the control of several genes, some of which have several alleles (Weiss, 2002). Similarly, we often hear that the gene for some disease in humans has been discovered, but that does not mean that the single gene is responsible for the organ system in question. For example, the most common form of short-limbed dwarfism in humans, achondroplasia, is caused by a single dominant gene (Figure 4.18). Although this gene certainly influences stature in a fundamental way, the development of stature in humans is nonetheless a polygenic trait.

Just as one trait can be the result of the interaction of more than one gene, one gene can have multiple phenotypic effects (Figure 4.19). This is called **pleiotropy**. For example, the gene that causes achondroplasia—the fibroblast growth factor receptor–3 gene—has the paradoxical effect of shortening limb length while leading to larger than average head size (megalencephaly). Artificial breeding for docility in foxes leads to the development of coat colors not found in wild foxes; this is undoubtedly a pleiotropic effect of whatever genes underlie that behavioral pattern. As we will discuss in Chapter 17, aging patterns in human may best be explained as resulting from the pleiotropic effects of genes selected for their effectiveness during the reproductive phase of life.

POLYGENIC TRAITS, THE PHENOTYPE, AND THE ENVIRONMENT

FIGURE 4.18 Achondroplastic dwarf represented in a carved pipe made by Adena Indians who inhabited the central and southern regions of Ohio in the first millennium BC.

Bell curve distributions for the expression of a trait may result from polygenic inheritance. However, phenotypes, especially complex phenotypes, tend to be the result of an interaction between the genotype and the environment. The variation we observe in the expression a complex trait may result from genetic factors or environmental factors that may influence phenotypic expression.

When scientists investigate the relative contributions of genes and environment to the production of the phenotype, they often use a statistical concept called **heritability**. If we look at variation for some trait in a population, we can be certain that the total variation we observe is caused by some combination of environmental and genetic factors. Heritability is a measure of the proportion of the total variation observed in a population that can be attributed to genetics rather than to the environment:

$$\frac{\text{Variability caused by genetics}}{\text{Variability caused by genetics} + \text{Variability caused by the environment}}$$

Heritability can range from 0 to 1. It is easy to measure heritability if you can control all the critical factors in the environment, as a scientist working on a short-lived experimental animal might be able to do. In humans, heritability is more difficult to measure because we obviously cannot use humans in breeding experiments.

There are several methods for using pedigree and adoption data to estimate heritability in human populations. The most commonly used is the **twin method** (Figure 4.20). As is well known, there are two kinds of twins: *identical* or *monozygotic (MZ) twins* and *fraternal* or *dizygotic (DZ) twins*. Monozygotic twins are genetically identical to each other, and they are the result of the fertilization of a single egg that splits into two embryos very early in development. Dizygotic twins result from the separate fertilization of two eggs during the same ovulatory cycle. They are no more alike than any other full siblings, and they share, on average, half of their genes.

If two twins share a common phenotype or if both get a certain disease, we say that they are *concordant* for that trait; if the twins are dissimilar, then they are *discordant*. Twins raised together typically share a very similar environment. If we compare the MZ and DZ concordance for a trait, a significantly higher concordance rate in the MZ twins indicates that genetic factors may be important in the expression of that trait. Both MZ and DZ twins share a common environment (some critics have argued that MZ twins may share a more similar environment than DZ twins, which may be true, but how much this may contribute to similarities or differences must be assessed for each condition examined), but MZ twins share a

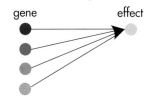

(a) Polygenic trait: many genes contribute to a single effect.

gene   effect

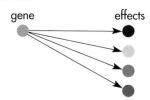

(b) Pleiotropy: one gene has multiple effects.

gene   effects

FIGURE 4.19 Contrasting (a) polygenic and (b) pleiotropic effects.

heritability   The proportion of total phenotypic variability observed for a given trait that can be ascribed to genetic factors.

twin method   A method for estimating the heritability of a phenotypic trait by comparing the concordance rates of identical and fraternal twins.

FIGURE 4.20 The twin method can be used to investigate genetic and environmental influences on the development of phenotypes.

much stronger genetic link than DZ twins. For example, concordance for ABO blood type is 100% in MZ twins and 66% in DZ twins. This indicates that blood type is totally under genetic control. Allergy patterns have a concordance rate of 59% in MZ twins and 18% in DZ twins. This indicates that genetics plays an important role in developing allergies. However, the fact that the concordance rate is not 100% in MZ twins indicates that the environment plays a substantial role as well. Many complex diseases such as schizophrenia and heart disease have MZ and DZ concordance rates that indicate that both genetic and environmental factors play a role in their expression.

Although concordance rates cannot be used directly to compute heritability values, they can be incorporated into mathematical models for estimating heritability. In addition, they indicate the possible roles of genetic and environmental factors in the expression of a trait or disease, providing useful directions for future research or intervention.

Heritability is an extremely important tool in trying to understand genetic influences on complex phenotypes. However, the discovery of significant heritability for a trait does not provide information about which or even how many genes are responsible for a phenotype. Heritability is a population statistic and provides no direct insight into individual genetic mechanisms. Also, heritability does not provide an absolute measure of the genetic contribution to the development of a phenotype. It is a relative statistic that measures the influence of genetics in a specific environment. If that environment is highly variable and most of the variation results from environmental factors, then the heritability will be low. On the other hand, if the environment is uniform and all members of the population are affected equally by environmental factors, then heritability will be high. As variation caused by environmental factors decreases, any remaining variation we observe can result only from genetic factors. Thus heritability changes with changing environments, even as the genetics remains the same.

HERITABILITY AND IQ TEST SCORE PERFORMANCE

Perhaps the most well known and controversial use of heritability statistics has been in the study of variation in IQ test score performance (Mackintosh, 1998). Let us consider them as a measurement that exhibits continuous variation in human populations, with a normal distribution. Innumerable studies of the heritability of IQ test score in industrial societies have been conducted over the years, and they almost all agree that genetics is an important factor in producing the variation observed within populations (heritability ranges from 0.3 to 0.75). Most scientists, although not all, interested in IQ test score would agree that in a population with an absolutely uniform environment, you would still observe variation for IQ test score performance, which would result from genetic factors.

Most people would not argue with the idea that genetics and environment both play some role in IQ test score performance. But what does heritability tell us about an issue of anthropological importance: ethnic differences in IQ test score performance? There is much empirical evidence to demonstrate that American whites score on average about 100 (the designed mean for the test) on IQ tests, with American blacks scoring substantially lower (7–12 points less), and Asian Americans somewhat higher (about 5 points higher, with most of the difference on the nonverbal portions of the test). Do the heritability studies of IQ test score performance indicate that the ethnic differences we observe result from genetic differences? No. Heritability scores apply only *within* a population or environment, not *between* populations. Heritability may give us some insight into the production of variation within each ethnic group, but it cannot be used to address issues of population variation between groups. The variation between groups could result from genetics, the environment, or both, but heritability scores, whether high or low, have no bearing on between-group differences.

In fact, it is theoretically possible that you could observe within-group heritabilities of 0 for some trait, whereas the between-group differences could result entirely from genetic factors. For example, imagine that we have two distinct populations, one with a substantially greater mean stature than the other one. Let's say that this difference in stature reflects the presence of "tall" alleles in one population that are absent in the other. If in both populations access to food while growing up is highly variable, then within each population the distribution of stature would result primarily from environmental factors (that is, food availability). There would still be a difference in mean stature between the populations, caused entirely by genetics. However, if we measured heritability within each population separately, we would find that little of the observed variation could be ascribed to genetics (that is, heritability would be low). Thus low within-group heritability does not mean that between-group differences cannot be caused by genetic differences, and vice versa.

PHENYLKETONURIA: ILLUSTRATING MENDELIAN AND POST-MENDELIAN CONCEPTS

Before the advent of universal neonatal screening for the condition (Lindee, 2000), **phenylketonuria (PKU)** was one of the most common causes of mental retardation. Pedigree studies have shown that the transmission of PKU appears to follow classic Mendelian rules. It is caused by a recessive allele and therefore is seen only in people who are homozygous for this allele. People who have just one copy of the allele are heterozygous carriers of the condition.

Individuals with PKU accumulate large quantities of the amino acid phenylalanine in the blood (up to forty times the normal amount) (Scriver et al., 1985). In newborns and infants, a high level of phenylalanine is toxic to the developing nervous system. The most prominent feature of the PKU phenotype is mental retardation, which is a direct result of the neurotoxic effects of high levels of phenylalanine. However, people with PKU also tend to have light skin and hair and abnormal gait, stance, and sitting posture, among other characteristic features. It is quite clear that the allele for PKU has multiple pleiotropic effects.

At a biochemical level, PKU is the result of a deficiency of an enzyme, *phenylalanine hydroxylase,* which converts phenylalanine to another amino acid, tyrosine. Phenylalanine builds up in the bloodstream because the PKU phenylalanine hydroxylase either is inactive or has much lower than normal activity. Because the phenylalanine is not converted to tyrosine, people with PKU also tend to have less tyrosine available for metabolic reactions. Tyrosine is the starting point for the body's synthesis of melanin, which is one of the most important components of skin pigment. This explains one of the pleiotropic effects of the PKU allele: Light skin and hair is a result of low tyrosine levels and low production of melanin.

Over the past 20 years, there have been many advances in our understanding of the molecular genetics of PKU. The gene for phenylalanine hydroxylase has been localized to chromosome 12, and hundreds of different point mutations in the gene have been identified. The effects of these mutations on phenylalanine hydroxylase activity vary tremendously, with some of them rendering the enzyme inactive, whereas others show no effect or only a mild depression in activity (Benit et al., 1999). The variability in the alleles of the phenylalanine hydroxylase gene explains why PKU exhibits a good deal of phenotypic variability. Remember that PKU is an autosomal recessive disorder: Individuals who have one normal phenylalanine hydroxylase allele are phenotypically normal.

Screening for PKU in newborns is done by assessing phenylalanine levels in the blood not long after birth. Profoundly elevated levels of phenylalanine indicate the presence of PKU and the need for dietary intervention. This intervention takes the form of drastically reducing the amount of phenylalanine in the diet. This is easier said than done because phenylalanine is an important component of proteins

phenylketonuria (PKU)
Autosomal recessive condition that leads to the accumulation of large quantities of the amino acid phenylalanine, which causes mental retardation and other phenotypic abnormalities.

FIGURE 4.21 Two sisters with PKU. The younger sister (left) was diagnosed at birth and followed a strict phenylalanine-limited diet. The older sister (right) was not diagnosed until she was one year of age. She is symptomatic of PKU.

found in meat, fish, eggs, cheese and other milk products, legumes, and some cereals. Babies with PKU must take special formula that provides calories and essential nutrients, and children with the condition must adhere to a very limited diet. They must also learn to be wary of dietary additives such as the artificial sweetener aspartame, which is a dipeptide composed of phenylalanine and aspartic acid. The good news is that when they become adults, most PKU sufferers can adopt a normal diet because their nervous system is no longer developing. However, if a woman with PKU wants to become pregnant, she must resume the restricted diet, or the elevated levels of phenylalanine in her blood will damage the developing nervous system of her developing child.

PKU provides a striking example of the relationships between genotype, phenotype, and the environment. People with PKU are different from other people because they have two copies of an abnormal allele for a single enzyme. If they grow up in a typical dietary environment—which is basically the dietary environment you have if you live on the planet Earth—their nervous systems will not develop normally and they will have a seriously dysfunctional phenotype. On the other hand, if we place children with PKU in a different, highly artificial nutritional environment, they will develop normally. Figure 4.21 depicts two sisters with PKU. The older sister was born before there was routine screening of newborns and intervention for PKU, and she suffers from the disease. The younger sister was identified as having PKU immediately after birth, avoided phenylalanine while growing up, developed normally, and later had a healthy child. The sisters have the same PKU genotype, but their divergent phenotypes were shaped by different nutritional environments.

GENES AND ENVIRONMENTS

When we hear the word *environment* we usually think about the world around us—things such as the air and water, trees and other plants, and all the other critters with whom we share the world. But from a gene's perspective, the environment is made up mainly of other genes. Concepts such as pleiotropy and polygenic inheritance emphasize that the genetic environment is just as critical to the production of phenotypes as any other kind of environment.

Mendelian concepts such as independent assortment and segregation were useful in establishing the activities of genes in isolation from one another. This was essential for doing away with concepts such as blending inheritance. But it is clear that the challenge of genetics in the twenty-first century will be to determine how genes work together, not separately, to produce complex phenotypes in the context of complex environments.

SUMMARY

1. **What is the difference between structural genes and regulatory genes?**

   Structural genes carry the information to make proteins. Regulatory genes guide the expression of structural genes. Given that the DNA of humans and chimpanzees is so similar—their DNAs are about 95% identical—many scientists believe that changes in regulatory genes have been critical in producing the profound physical and behavioral differences between the species.

2. **What are genotypes and phenotypes?**

   The genotype consists of the specific genes (or alleles) an organism carries; it is the genetic constitution of an individual. The phenotype is an observable or measurable feature of an organism. Phenotypes can be anatomical, biochemical, or behavioral. If we look at the expression of a phenotype among a group of organisms in a population, we will probably see some variation. This variation could be caused by genetic factors; individuals may have different genotypes that influence the expression of the phenotype differently. It could also be caused by environmental factors if the expression of the phenotype changes with changes in the environment. In many cases, the observed phenotypic variation is caused by a combination of genetic and environmental factors.

3. **What is heritability?**

   Heritability is a measure of the proportion of the total phenotypic variation that is caused by genetics. It can range from 0 to 1. For example, in a population where all organisms have exactly the same environment, all observed variability would have to be caused by genetic factors, and the heritability would be 1.

4. **What did Mendel's experiments on the garden pea show us about the nature of genetic transmission?**

   Mendel's work demonstrated first and foremost the particulate nature of genetic inheritance: There was no "blending" of the basic genetic factors (that is, genes) during sexual reproduction. Mendel showed that genes for a single phenotypic trait come in pairs and that these are passed to the next generation independently of each other (law of segregation). He also showed that the pairs of genes for one trait are passed on independently of the pairs of genes for other traits (law of independent assortment).

5. **What are X-linked disorders?**

   X-linked disorders are diseases or conditions that are almost always seen in males and appear in pedigrees to skip a generation after their appearance in a male sufferer. An X-linked disorder is caused by a mutation in a gene on the X chromosome. If a woman carries this mutated allele on one of her X chromosomes, she does not develop the disease because she also has a normal allele on the other X chromosome. However, if her son receives a copy of the mutant allele from his mother, he will develop the disease because he has only the single copy of the X chromosome (along with the Y chromosome). Because he can pass on an X chromosome only to his daughters, they will be carriers of the condition but not suffer from it, and they can later pass it on to their sons. Therefore, it appears to skip a generation. Hemophilia is the best-known X-linked condition.

6. **Compare and contrast polygenic traits and pleiotropy.**

   Polygenic traits are those that are the product of the action of more than one gene, each of which may have more than one allele. Observed quantitative variation in a polygenic trait often follows a bell curve distribution because of the many possible genotypes that may underlie the expression of single phenotype. Pleiotropy is the converse: A single gene can influence more than one phenotypic trait. This is seen in the condition known as achondroplasia, in which several changes in the phenotype result from a change in a single allele.

CRITICAL THINKING QUESTIONS

1. What is the role of genetic knowledge in our day-to-day lives? Should information about the alleles we carry be available to employers or health insurance providers? Would you want to know if you are carrying an allele that might cause you to have a fatal illness 20 years from now?

2. Mendel often is said to have been "ahead of his time." Why? Do you think such a delay between the discovery and the recognition of the discovery could happen today?

KEY TERMS

structural genes
regulatory genes
genotype
phenotype
ABO blood type system
recessive
dominant
co-dominant
blending inheritance
particulate inheritance
Mendel's law of
  segregation

Mendel's law of
  independent
  assortment
linkage
point mutation
sickle cell disease
autosomal recessive
  disease
insertion mutation
deletion mutation
trinucleotide repeat
  diseases

autosomal dominant
  disease
X-linked disorders
pedigree
qualitative variation
quantitative variation
polygenic traits
pleiotropy
heritability
twin method
phenylketonuria (PKU)

SUGGESTED READING

Dawkins, R. (1989). *The Selfish Gene* (new edition). Oxford University Press, Oxford.

Mackintosh, N. J. (1998). *IQ and Human Intelligence.* Oxford University Press, Oxford.

Mendel, G. (1866). Versuche über Plflanzenhybriden (Experiments in plant hybridization). *Verhandlugen des natur-forschenden Vereines in Brünn, Bd. IV für das Jahr 1865,* 3–47. (English translation available at www.esp.org/foundations/genetics/classical/gm-65.pdf.)

Provine, W. B. (1971). *The Origins of Theoretical Population Genetics.* University of Chicago Press, Chicago.

Chapter 5

THE FORCES OF EVOLUTION AND THE FORMATION OF SPECIES

THE LITTLE BOAT SLOSHES DANGEROUSLY CLOSE to the cliffs of a tiny islet, little more than a rock among the Galápagos Islands. The passengers—biologists and their students—carefully climb the rocky shoreline. For the next 6 months they live like monks, watching the tiny finches that are the major inhabitants of the island of Daphne Major. They catch the birds in mist nets, measuring their beaks, feet, and wings, and also measure everything in the finches' island habitat.

The scientists come and go for 30 years, spanning about thirty generations of finches and a large portion of their own life spans. The island is subjected to a terrible drought. The drought is followed by several years of plentiful rainfall, turning the island green and lush. Throughout these periods of plenty and famine, the scientists dutifully collect their birds and record their measurements.

Then one day they notice that something astounding is happening. The dimensions of the beaks of the finches have changed in direct relationship to the periods of drought and plenty. When food is scarce, the major available seeds are thick-shelled and very tough to crack. The birds that were born with minutely larger, stronger beaks survive better and leave more baby finches than their smaller-beaked neighbors. When the rains come again and food is plentiful, the trend reverses. The evidence is indisputable: The species is evolving. In the span of just a few years, climate and food conditions have changed the appearance of the tiny finches because finches with stronger beaks are better able to crack open hard-shelled seeds and therefore produce more offspring than their smaller-beaked neighbors.

Demonstrating natural selection in the wild is not easy. It takes many generations and a great deal of tedious field research. However, the results show the truth of Darwin's ideas. The now-famous field study just described, conducted by biologists Peter and Rosemary Grant, is one of the best demonstrations of evolution by natural selection under natural conditions. In this chapter we will examine the principles of the evolutionary process. These include but are not limited to Darwinian natural selection. We will consider where variation in nature comes from and how the forces of evolution act on this variation to mold the form and function of animals and plants. We also examine another important question: what is a species?

HOW EVOLUTION WORKS

We speak of the forces of evolution as those factors occurring in natural populations that cause changes in gene frequencies over multiple generations. These include both adaptive and nonadaptive causes. Natural selection is the most cited cause of evolution, and much evidence suggests that it is the most important force. But, as we will see, several other causes of evolutionary change exist as well. Moreover, evolution can only occur in the presence of a source of variation, which is mutation.

WHERE DOES VARIATION COME FROM?

In Chapter 3, we saw that alterations occur in the DNA sequence during the course of replication, changing the allelic expression at a given locus. A change in a base on the DNA molecule is a *point mutation.* Larger-scale errors during replication can result in *chromosomal mutations,* when entire chunks of chromosomes are transposed with one another. Such changes in the genetic material, whether large or small, are the stuff from which new variation springs. Mutations of great significance occur very rarely. Many mutations are neutral and have no effect on the offspring's viability, survival, and reproduction. Only through the accumulation of mutations do new traits enter a population, allowing natural selection and other evolutionary forces to filter out undesirable traits and perpetuate favorable ones.

HOW NATURAL SELECTION WORKS

Natural selection takes the package of traits each animal or plant inherits from the previous generation and then tweaks it in response to the current environment. Natural selection is not simply about genes and traits. The environment is the filter through which traits—and the genes that control their expression—are selected for or against. As we saw in Chapter 4, each organism's genetic makeup, or genotype, is fixed from conception. Natural selection acts on the organism's phenotype, the actual expression of the alleles present in the genotype. The environment can play a critical role in how the genotype is expressed, even when basic Mendelian principles are operating at single gene loci. Such environmental effects include sunlight, nutrition, and exposure to toxins, all of which can have profound biological effect on one's phenotype without affecting the genotype. If you spend years sunbathing to acquire a deep tan, your phenotype—skin color in this case—has changed while your genotype stayed the same. However, skin cancer from ultraviolet rays in sunlight is a biological effect on which natural selection can forcefully act by removing afflicted individuals from the breeding population. *Natural selection operates on the phenotype of an individual organism.* As individuals with the greatest genetic susceptibility to skin cancer—perhaps those with the palest skin—are removed from the breeding population, the frequency of genes influencing skin color will change too. This is evolution, so cultural practices such as sunbathing, can potentially have evolutionary effects.

Populations evolve as the frequency of certain genes changes; individual organisms don't evolve. The result is that the frequency at which a gene or a trait governed by genes occurs in a population changes over time. This change generally happens very slowly, although it can be seen easily when researchers study animals with very short generation lengths, such as fruit flies or mice, or when animal breeders take selection into their own hands and choose which animals will breed and which will not. In this latter case, selection is not necessarily based on survival and reproductive value of traits. For instance, cattle breeders may select cows for milk production, or they may select them for purely aesthetic reasons such as body size, temperament, or color. The process is analogous to natural selection, as Darwin himself understood.

The case of natural selection pushing the size of finch beaks larger and stronger when food is scarce and pushing it back the other way when food is plentiful is an example of **directional selection** (Figure 5.1 on page 102). Of course, it could also be the case that selection is intense for certain beak dimensions when times are lean, and this pressure is diminished when the rains come again. A relaxation of selection pressure in a population might be difficult to distinguish in nature from selection in the opposite direction from earlier generations.

If natural selection can drive gene frequencies in a certain direction by elaborating or eliminating a certain trait, can it also be responsible for keeping

directional selection Natural selection that drives evolutionary change by selecting for greater or lesser frequency of a given trait in a population.

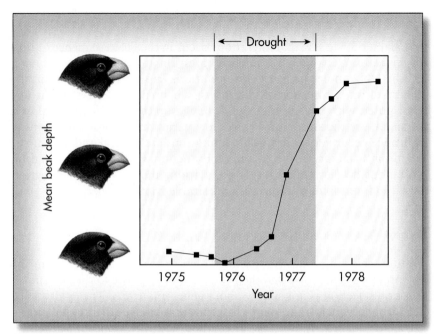

FIGURE 5.1 Directional selection pushes a phenotype one way or another.

populations uniform? It can, by a process known as **stabilizing selection**. The first demonstration of stabilizing selection was an early study of natural selection in the wild. In the winter of 1898, 136 house sparrows were found lying on the icy ground the morning after a severe snowstorm in Providence, Rhode Island. They were taken to biologist Herman Bumpus at nearby Brown University. Seventy-two of the birds recovered; the other 64 died of exposure to the frigid conditions. Bumpus (1899) then measured nine traits of the birds to see whether there were anatomical differences between the sparrows that survived the storm and those that died. He found that there were anatomical differences between survivors and nonsurvivors. Surviving birds were smaller-bodied and had shorter wings than those that died, and they were more similar to the average size of birds in the local population. In other words, natural selection favored certain *phenotypes* in an environmental crunch. We don't know the exact mechanism—why smaller-bodied birds survived the storm better—but we can say that birds that deviated greatly from certain sizes and shapes were not favored by natural selection.

There are many such examples of natural selection in populations of wild animals. Showing natural selection at work in a human population is far more difficult: People reproduce slowly, and the genetic code for specific human traits is rarely known. One well-documented case of natural selection in human populations is birth weight. Producing a healthy baby is a critical precondition for reproductive success (Figure 5.2). Studies have shown conclusively that birth weight of newborns is a key factor influencing the probability of their survival. In one study of nearly 6,000 births in a New York City hospital, researchers analyzed mortality rates in relation to a number of anatomical measures of newborns and found that male and female babies had optimal birth weights of 7.96 pounds (3.62 kilograms) and 8.5 pounds (3.84 kilograms), respectively (Van Valen and Mellin, 1967). Other studies have produced similar results (Karn and Penrose, 1951) (Figure 5.3). The likelihood of mortality caused by congenital abnormalities was directly related to the deviation from the optimal birth weight. Factors that influence birth weight, such as length of the pregnancy and ethnic background, were controlled for. In

stabilizing selection Selection that maintains a certain phenotype by selecting against deviations from it.

FIGURE 5.2 Human infants are like all other placental mammals, except they are born at a less developed state.

other words, natural selection played a role at the time of birth, favoring survival of infants who were healthy, as indicated by lack of congenital abnormalities and within a certain optimal range of birth weights. Over human history, natural selection operated on birth weights and perhaps on other factors related to birth weight. Birth weights that deviated far from the mean were selected against, producing a normal distribution of birth weights with a well-defined optimum.

OTHER WAYS IN WHICH EVOLUTION HAPPENS

The power of natural selection remains a topic of debate. Some scholars argue that natural selection alone cannot account for the rapid evolution of wholesale changes in anatomy that we sometimes observe. These critics are not creationists; they simply question whether natural selection can or should be expected to have produced all the myriad traits we see in nature. There are at least two other important natural processes that produce evolutionary change in populations that are unrelated to natural selection: gene flow and genetic drift.

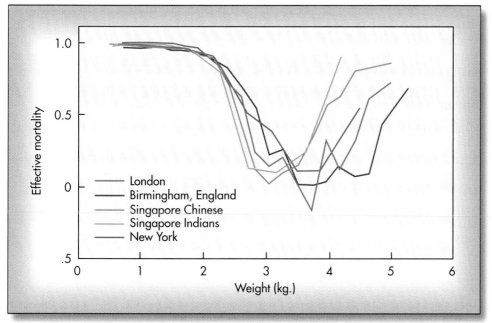

FIGURE 5.3 The birth weight of human infants is tightly constrained by natural selection. Note the high mortality of newborns of very high or low body weight based on hospital records.

Gene Flow   When humans or other animals migrate from one place to another, or when wind carries airborne seeds hundreds of miles from where the parent tree stands, **gene flow** has occurred. *Migration* refers to whole animals on the move; *gene flow* refers to the genetic material they carry with them in their genotypes. The exchange of genes between populations in different geographic locations can produce evolutionary change, as can stopping the exchange of genes between two areas. Movements, both permanent and temporary, of people to new locales have characterized human history. These migrations have become widespread and rapid as regional and global transportation has improved in recent centuries. When migrants produce offspring in new populations, whether they remain in the population long term or not, their genes enter the new gene pool and provide biological diversity and new traits that may eventually change the evolutionary character of the population. An excellent example of how gene flow can change a population occurred in 1789, when the crew of the British sailing ship H.M.S. *Bounty* mutinied against Captain William Bligh. Surviving crew members ended up on Pitcairn Island in the South Pacific, and after much battling among the crew (primarily over Tahitian women they brought to the island), one sailor named Adams ended up as a permanent resident. Over the ensuing years, Adams fathered many children, and his genes, including those for his blue eyes, became widespread in the population of Pitcairn.

The cessation of gene flow can be just as important an evolutionary force as gene flow itself. If a population receives genetic contributions (*admixture*) from other nearby populations for a long period of time, it may create one large gene pool spread across two areas through extensive interbreeding. Suppose that interbreeding stops because of changes in social behavior (two neighboring tribes go to war, and all exchange between them is halted for centuries) or changes in geography (a flood creates a wide river barrier between the two populations). In either case the lack of gene flow means that random mutations that were formerly passed back and forth are now confined to only one population. As they accumulate, the two populations will diverge genetically and perhaps anatomically as well.

Studies of the genetics of human and other populations have generally concluded that despite our long-standing belief that **inbreeding**, or reproduction between close kin, is always bad for the health of a population, very limited amounts of gene flow can eliminate the harmful effects of inbreeding. A study of rhesus macaque monkeys conducted in the mountains of Pakistan showed only limited migration between breeding groups. Nonetheless, very limited gene flow from males who immigrated to the valley where the study was conducted were enough to maintain high levels of genetic diversity (Melnick and Hoelzer, 1996). Studies such as this do not imply that inbreeding is normal and healthy, only that a low level of immigration apparently can offset its harmful effects in a population.

Genetic Drift   Despite the importance of selection pressure on animal phenotypes, evolution can also result from nothing more than chance. **Genetic drift** is a change in the frequency of a gene in a population over time caused entirely by random factors. The odds that genetic drift will have great importance in changing the frequency of a trait are greatest in very small populations. Consider this analogy: Someone wagers you that if you flip a coin ten times, it will land heads-up nine times. You take the bet, knowing that the odds of a heads-up coin flip are 50% on each flip, and ten flips should produce about five heads-ups. But in fact the coin lands heads-up nine times in ten flips. Do you accuse the person making the wager with you of cheating? You do not, because we all know that although each flip has a random chance of landing either heads or tails, ten coin flips sometimes produce very skewed results. But suppose the person now wagers that if you flip the same coin a million times, it will land heads-up 900,000 times. This is extremely unlikely to happen, simply because of the very low statistical probability of having the coin lands heads-up so many consecutive times.

gene flow   Movement of genes between populations.

inbreeding   Mating between close relatives.

genetic drift   Random changes in gene frequency in a population.

The comparison between small and large samples of coin flips and small and large populations is apt in the case of genetic drift. Each flip of the coin is analogous to the likelihood that a given allele for a gene is passed to the next generation during reproduction. Although on average, each cross of two people who are heterozygous for a trait should produce half heterozygous children, one-quarter homozygous dominant, and one-quarter homozygous recessive (recall Mendelian crosses from Chapter 4), this does not always occur. At a population level, genetic drift brings about evolutionary change through the same principle of alleles appearing or disappearing by random chance. This is important mainly in small populations, where an allele can easily disappear entirely or become prevalent in all individuals (going to *fixation*, in genetic terms). The smaller the population, the larger the potential effect of genetic drift on gene frequencies. Distinguishing drift from the effects of natural selection is not always easily done because selection in a small population would have similar visible results to the gene pool.

There are many examples of genetic drift in human and other mammalian populations, most often caused by another aspect of genetic drift, called **founder effect**. When a small subset of a much larger population becomes isolated or cut off from genetic contact with its parent gene pool, its gene pool consists only of the genotypes of the individuals in the new, small subpopulation. Only through a long and slow accumulation of mutations can the genetic diversity of the subset increase. If you and a boatload of fellow travelers were stranded permanently on a desert island, the genetic makeup of the new human population of that island would consist only of the combined genotypes of all the passengers. Founder effect and gene flow often are linked, as in the case of the Pitcairn Islanders receiving new residents in the form of the *Bounty* mutineers. The combination of immigration and very small population size of the island enabled the genes of one British mutineer to become widespread in a short period of time.

Some immigrant groups to the United States who have chosen to live in closed societies experience the effects of genetic drift. The Amish, a well-known religious sect, immigrated to the United States from Germany and the Netherlands in the 1800s (Figure 5.4). They practice farming with nineteenth-century technology, avoiding contact with the larger American culture around them; until recently very few Amish married outside the Amish community. As a consequence, some genetic

founder effect A component of genetic drift theory, stating that new populations that become isolated from the parent population carry only the genetic variation of the founders.

FIGURE 5.4 A child with Ellis-van Creveld (EVC) syndrome.

genetic bottleneck Temporary dramatic reduction in size of a population or species.

diseases that were rare in the parent population in western Europe are common among the Amish in America. *Ellis–van Creveld (EVC) syndrome,* a genetic disease common among the Amish, is a form of dwarfism, and its victims always possess an extra finger on each hand and sometimes extra toes on the feet, a condition known as *polydactyly.* Not only is the EVC gene more common among the Amish than in the larger American gene pool, but it is restricted mainly to the Amish settlements in Lancaster County, Pennsylvania, and is extremely rare elsewhere. It appears that one or a few Amish individuals carried the gene with them from Europe to Lancaster County and, by virtue of their high reproductive rate (the Amish often have ten or more children), spread the gene rapidly through the very small founding population of other Amish (McKusick et al., 1964).

A phenomenon associated with the founder effect that can bring about evolutionary change is a **genetic bottleneck.** A bottleneck occurs when a large, genetically diverse population undergoes a rapid reduction in size and then increases again (Figure 5.5). When the population size declines, a large percentage of the alleles present may be lost, and after the bottleneck, only the accumulation of mutations will rebuild genetic diversity. For example, Native Americans, Russians, and then Americans hunted the southern elephant seal, a minivan-sized marine mammal, nearly to extinction from the eighteenth to twentieth centuries. By the time complete protection was enacted, there were only a few dozen southern elephant seals left in the wild. But elephant seals breed rapidly, and over the past several decades their numbers have grown exponentially. They are returning to former breeding beaches up and down the California coast (including a few bathing beaches, to the shock of human sunbathers). However, the new elephant seal population has a potential problem. It possesses only the genetic diversity present in the new postbottleneck population. Should a disease strike the seals, it could well be that a gene for disease resistance that existed in the population before the bottleneck is gone, and the disease could devastate the remaining seals. Hundreds of generations will have to pass before mutations can begin to restore this diversity.

Natural selection is not the only mechanism by which evolution can occur, although it is considered by most researchers to be the predominant way the variation present in nature is molded into new forms.

Sexual Selection: Darwin's Other Great Idea Although Darwin's *Origin of Species* in 1859 laid the groundwork for all research on evolution by natural selection that followed, he made another contribution in a later book, the importance of which is less appreciated. In his 1871 book *The Descent of Man,* Darwin extended his evolutionary principles directly to humankind. In it, he explained an-

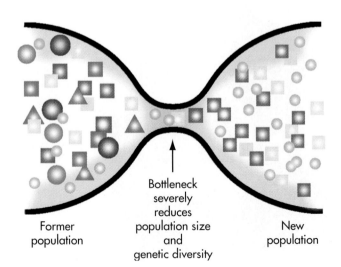

FIGURE 5.5 A genetic bottleneck reduces a population temporarily to very low levels, removing much of its genetic diversity.

Former population

Bottleneck severely reduces population size and genetic diversity

New population

other major evolutionary force: nonrandom mating brought about by **sexual selection**. Social animals don't mate and bear offspring simply because they bump into each other like balls on a pool table. Females choose particular males as their mates, and they make their choices based on natural variations in male traits (Figure 5.6).

Just as the struggle for existence defined natural selection, Darwin identified two components to sexual selection: the struggle between males to gain access to mates and the struggle by a female to choose the right mate. Sexual selection can be defined as differential reproductive success among the members of the same sex within a given species. Female choice of particular genetically based male traits, such as antlers or large muscles or bright colors, leads to the evolution of males that exhibit those traits because these males enjoy greater reproductive success. Many animal traits that we once believed had evolved to allow males to defend themselves and their group against predators, such as horns and antlers, are now believed to be the products of sexual selection.

Although Darwin considered sexual selection to be an aspect of natural selection, the two forces can operate independently and even in opposition. Although early research on the topic tended to focus on competition between males for mates and assumed that male competition was the driving force behind sexual selection, scientists today recognize that the opposite is more likely. Females of many animal species drive evolutionary change through their selection of certain male phenotypes. For example, female choice has been shown to drive the appearance of long tail feathers in male birds (Andersson, 1992), bright colors in male guppies (Endler, 1983, 1986), and male mating calls in frogs (Ryan, 1990). Increased male body size is a common outcome of sexual selection; in a few primate species, males are nearly twice as large as females. This results from female choice for larger body sizes, and implies competition between males for access to females. **Sexual dimorphism**, a difference in size, shape, or color between the sexes, usually is brought about by evolutionary changes in male appearance caused by female mate preferences.

But why should females prefer males with large antlers, outlandish tail feathers, or brilliant colors? Females are thought to be under selection pressure to choose a male that offers her a direct benefit, such as help in offspring rearing or protection against predators. She may use physical features of the male to judge his quality in these areas (Kirkpatrick, 1982). If the capacity for judging males on this basis evolves in females, then males are expected to evolve more and more elaborate features to impress females. Or females may choose males by selecting for indirect benefits. In species where males offer nothing to a female except their genes at conception, we expect a female to choose a mate based on his genetic quality. To judge a potential mate's genetic quality, a female may use a male's ornamental features as clues (Figure 5.7 on page 108). Brightly colored feathers may indicate a male's underlying genetic health. Elaborate male ornaments, such as a peacock's

sexual selection Differential reproductive success within one sex of any species.

sexual dimorphism Difference in size, shape or color, between the sexes.

FIGURE 5.6 A male peacock displays his genetic worth for a female.

reproductive potential The possible offspring output by one sex.

reproductive variance A measure of variation from the mean of a population in the reproductive potential of one sex compared with the other.

enormous tail feathers, may be the result of what famous geneticist R. A. Fisher (1958) called *runaway sexual selection*. In this process, female preference for a trait and male evolution of that trait to compete for females reinforce each other endlessly. A more recent theory to account for elaborate male traits is *costly signaling*, which derived from the *handicap principle* posed by Israeli biologist Amo Zahavi. Males may display outlandish ornaments in order to state to a female just how vigorous they must be to survive the appendage or brilliant color they bear. Peacocks must escape from tigers and leopards despite their heavy tails; a male who has a large tail may be signaling his genetic quality to females (Zahavi, 1975).

Why is it that males compete for females, and females choose male traits, rather than the other way around? The theory of sexual selection, as developed by more recent generations of evolutionary biologists, proposes that the sex with the more limited **reproductive potential** should be competed over by the sex with the greater reproductive potential. For nearly all higher animals, this means that females are competed over by males because females are the limited commodity that males need to achieve reproductive success. Whereas a male mammal's fitness often is limited only by access to females, a female must bear most of the costs of reproduction: gestation, lactating, and nurturing. Her level of *parental investment* is far greater than that of males.

The difference in reproductive potential in males and females can be as dramatic in a slow-reproducing animal such as humans as in any other organism. Consider the maximum number of children you've ever heard of a woman giving birth to. The *Guinness Book of World Records* cites a woman in Taiwan with twenty-four children born in 33 years as the largest number of offspring of any woman alive (an eighteenth-century Russian woman is alleged to have had sixty-nine children). By contrast, the same source confirms the maximum recorded children for a man to be 888, by the Moroccan ruler Ismail the Bloodthirsty. In addition to the disparity in reproductive potential, males and females often differ greatly in their **reproductive variance**, the degree of variation from the mean of a population in the reproductive potential of one sex compared with the other. One consequence of a female's lower reproductive potential—she can be fertilized only once in each breeding season—is that whereas nearly all the females find mates, many males fail to find females. This reproductive asymmetry between males and females holds major consequences for how males and females behave toward one another during courtship, as we will see in Chapter 8.

We can test whether certain male ornaments evolved to display quality to females as a mating strategy by considering animal species with sex role reversal. In a few bird species, such as the small sandpiper-like phalaropes, males rather than females invest the most time and energy in offspring care. In those species, females

FIGURE 5.7   *"What's the matter? Not puffy enough for you?"*

compete over males, females are larger than males, and females are more brightly colored than males. Phalaropes and a few other sex role–reversed species appear to be the exceptions that prove the sexual selection rule. Sexual selection is currently a hot research area for evolutionary biologists, and new discoveries are being made all the time. For example, only recently have evolutionary biologists begun to appreciate that the loss of male ornaments, caused by loss of female preference for them, may be as common in the animal kingdom as the evolution of those traits in the first place (Wiens, 2001).

CLASSIFICATION AND EVOLUTION

In order to understand the natural world, we categorize plants and animals according to the similarities of their features. The science of taxonomy that Linnaeus devised forms the basis for the study of biological classification today. But as we saw in Chapter 2, Linnaeus' scheme did not incorporate modern notions of evolutionary change. Instead of considering species as dynamic entities that are formed from combination and recombination of gene pools, he saw them as immutable cases of God's handiwork.

TAXONOMY AND SPECIATION

Linneaus classified species in much the same way that we all classify things in our everyday lives, lumping types together based on physical characteristics that were readily apparent to the eye. Presented with an assortment of glasses of wine at a wine tasting, you could quickly sort them into two general "taxa": reds and whites. You could then sort the reds into a wide variety of lower-level categories: merlot, cabernet sauvignon, pinot noir, and so on. Each of these could in turn be subdivided based on other descriptive features such as taste (dry or fruity), geographic origin (France or California), vintage (2002 or 1902), and other qualities.

Unfortunately, sorting species is not exactly like sorting wines. Wines are made to human-desired specifications, and so a finite number of varieties exist. Animal or plant species are dynamic units, always changing in ways that may be too small or slow for us to see in comparing any two or three generations. Furthermore, species themselves don't care whether we can identify them; animals themselves determine the boundaries of species units by their willingness to mate or not with animals from other similar species. Our natural tendency to treat species as distinct, separate categories even when this does not reflect biological reality has contributed to great confusion about species and their formation.

Linnaeus established a hierarchy of categories to classify all living things (Table 5.1). Each of these levels of the hierarchy is like a set of nested Russian dolls. As one descends the categories, the distinctions between related forms become increasingly small. The only "natural" category is the species. All others are a taxonomist's way of making sense of the evolutionary past of clusters of related species. Notice that humans and chimpanzees are classified in the same taxonomic categories

TABLE 5.1	The Linnaean Hierarchy		
LINNAEAN CATEGORY	HUMAN	CHIMPANZEE	TORTOISE
Kingdom	Animalia	Animalia	Animalia
Phylum	Chordata	Chordata	Chordata
Class	Mammalia	Mammalia	Reptilia
Order	Primates	Primates	Testudines
Family	Hominidae	Pongidae	Testudinidae
Genus	Homo	Pan	Manouria
Species	Homo sapiens	Pan troglodytes	Manouria emys

until the level of the family, and if Linnaeus had not been so driven by theology he would have placed us in the same family. Tortoises, on the other hand, are separated from humans and chimpanzees at the level of the class. To Linnaeus, this indicated that tortoises had been created in a different image than primates in God's plan. Today, we recognize that the class-level distinction indicates distant evolutionary relatedness.

Evolutionary biologists use a variety of methods to determine relationships between related evolutionary groups. Today the study of taxonomy usually is called **systematics**. Systematists rely on the principle of **homology**, the notion that similar features in two related organisms look alike because of a shared evolutionary history. The bones of your arm have homologous counterparts in the flukes of a whale; despite the whale's aquatic lifestyle, its evolution as a land animal is revealed in the bones it shares with all other land animals. On the other hand, some features are similar because of similar patterns of use rather than shared ancestry. The wings of a bird and the wings of a bat are both used for powered flight, but they evolved independently (Figure 5.8). Although both are warm-blooded vertebrates, bats and

systematics   Branch of biology that describes patterns of organismal variation.

homology   Similarity of traits resulting from shared ancestry.

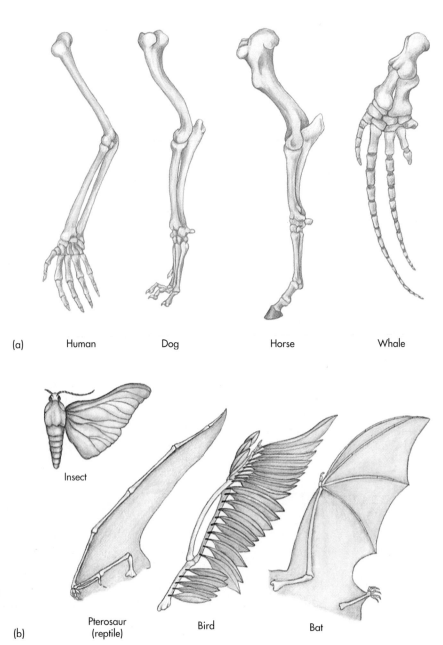

(a)   Human   Dog   Horse   Whale

Insect

FIGURE 5.8   (a) Homologous traits are similar due to shared ancestry. (b)Analogous traits (bat, bird and fly wings) evolved independently but serve a similar purpose.   (b)

Pterosaur (reptile)   Bird   Bat

birds have not had a common ancestor for tens of millions of years. Bird and bat wings are **analogous** and have evolved through **convergent** (or parallel) **evolution**. The problem of convergence has vexed systematists because natural selection can produce stunningly similar adaptations in distantly related creatures that happen to live in similar environments. Animals with placentas and marsupials that reproduce without a placenta are two distantly related groups of mammals that nevertheless have members that bear striking resemblances to one another. There are marsupial mice in Australia that look so much like placental mice in North America that a biologist would have to dissect them to tell the difference.

We use anatomical *characters,* meaning physical features, to categorize organisms. Two principles are commonly used. First, all organisms are composed of many *ancestral* characters, inherited from ancestors they share with living relatives. Second, organisms also possess *derived* characters: features they alone possess that distinguish them from all related species. By identifying the derived characters, systematists can begin to establish a family tree, or *phylogeny,* of the degree of evolutionary relatedness of one form to another. Phylogenies are the evolutionary histories of groups of related organisms, illustrated in a way that the relationship and the time scale of splitting between ancestors and descendants is shown.

Another brand of evolutionary classification has emerged more recently. This new school of thought is called **cladistics** (from the Greek word *clados,* meaning "branch"), a science of classification in which certain traits are considered more evolutionarily important and informative than others. After establishing which traits are ancestral and which are derived, cladists then analyze the uniquely derived characters. If a cladist is trying to build a taxonomy of all monkeys, he will study the anatomies of enough known species to identify which traits are shared by all and which are possessed by only a few species. If a cluster of species displays a trait that no other group displays, then this *clade,* or cluster of species linked by a set of unique traits, can be studied further to distinguish which traits of the cluster are ancestral and which are derived. The cladist might identify monkeys that possess a grasping tail as a clade and then try to determine the evolutionary path by which grasping tails evolved, studying the presence or absence of other traits in the same clade in which the grasping tail appears. The result of this analysis is a **cladogram**, or branching order of the origins of the lineage of monkeys (Figure 5.9 on page 112). A cladogram does not depict the distance in time between the clades, only the relative degree of anatomical and evolutionary difference.

You may see that there is at least one potential problem with this approach. What about the possibility that the trait in question, a monkey's prehensile tail, evolved twice? The separate, convergent evolution of very similar traits is a confounding factor in cladistic analyses. One way around this problem is to make a very reasonable assumption: A given feature is unlikely to have evolved twice independently in the same lineage or to have disappeared and then re-evolved later in the same lineage. This is called the *law of parsimony,* nicknamed *Occam's razor* after medieval English philosopher William of Ockham (1285–1349). Ockham often used his "principle of unnecessary plurality" in his writings, arguing that one should always seek the simplest explanation for a natural phenomenon.

A second approach to systematics, one less used in anthropology than cladistics, is called *phenetics,* or numerical taxonomy. Pheneticists use all traits that link two organisms, not worrying whether they are similar because of homology or analogy. Phenetics relies solely on numerically describing degrees of similarity and difference between organisms, without biases created by knowing some groups are more closely related than others. Unrelated animals sometimes are lumped in the evolutionary group under this scheme. Taxonomies created by phenetics often differ in important ways from those assembled by cladists or other systematists. Phenetics is now out of fashion, and most scholars studying nonhuman primate and human evolution use the principles and language of cladistics in their work.

analogous Having similar traits due to similar use, not due to shared ancestry.

convergent evolution Similar form or function brought about by natural selection under similar environments rather than shared ancestry.

cladistics Method of classification using ancestral and derived traits to distinguish patterns of evolution within lineages.

cladogram Branching diagram showing evolved relationships among members of a lineage.

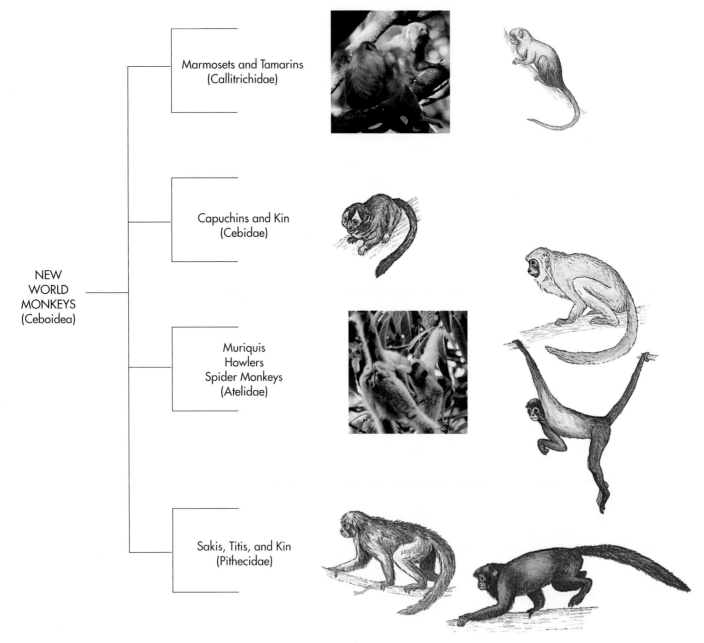

FIGURE 5.9 Example of a cladogram, or branching order, of the New World monkey Superfamily Ceboidea. A cladogram is a family tree but does not show evolutionary time scales.

WHAT IS A SPECIES?

There is no issue more confusing to both students and scientists of evolution than the question "What is a **species**?" It is really two questions. First, what does the word *species* mean? Second, how should we identify species in nature? You might think these are easy questions because we all believe we can distinguish a lion from a tiger or a horse from a donkey. In Linnaeus's time the answer was easy: Species were fixed pigeonholes without evolutionary pasts or connections to other species in the present. But ever since Darwin, we recognize that species are dynamic, ever-changing entities, and finding a consensus on concepts of species has proved vexing. The formation of new species, or **speciation**, is a fundamental evolutionary process.

Species are difficult to define because of the amount of variation found in nature. What we call species tend to be overlapping categories, rather than completely distinct units. So taxonomists who apply names to species are superimposing their labeling scheme onto natural variation, and the result can be contrived and subjective. And as a result of the artificial nature of labeling species, there are many concepts and definitions of how species are formed. Whereas earlier generations of scientists had only outward appearance to go by to identify species, modern evolutionary biologists can use DNA analysis and studies of physiology, ecology and behavior. Yet the problem of unambiguously answering the question "What is a species?" remains.

A GUIDE TO SPECIES CONCEPTS

Evolutionary biologists have a wide variety of species concepts from which to choose. The most widely used definition of species is the **biological species concept**, first proposed by biologist Ernst Mayr (1942, 1963). Scientists who argue for their own new concept of species must first show why the biological species concept is inadequate. Mayr defined species as "groups of actually or potentially interbreeding natural populations which are reproductively isolated from other such groups." This definition has two key phrases. *Reproductive isolation* is at the heart of this concept. If two types of related animal can be distinguished absolutely, then they must have been reproductively isolated for some period of time. But the phrase *actually or potentially* indicates that populations of animals that could cross-breed to create hybrid offspring in nature but don't should be considered separate species. Therefore, Mayr's definition referred to *natural populations* only.

Consider lions and tigers. They seem to be two obviously distinct species, the lion with its mane and tawny body, the tiger with its bold black stripes and orange fur. But these differences are only skin deep. The two species are closely related, and if housed together in the same zoo exhibit, a male lion and female tiger will produce a hybrid cub (often called a liger), as will a male tiger that mates with a lioness (yielding a tiglon). These hybrid cubs are fully fertile and can be bred to one another or to a lion or tiger to produce another generation of tiger–lion hybrids. In the one natural habitat the two species share (the Gir Forest in western India), lions and tigers have never been seen mating. So are lions and tigers considered separate species according to the biological species concept? The answer is yes, because in nature the species are reproductively isolated: There is no overlap between the two species' phenotypes and no evidence of them interbreeding naturally. They also differ ecologically, the lion preferring more open country and the tiger preferring dense thickets. There are many such examples of animals that do not ever meet in nature, because they live thousands of miles apart or occupy different niches in the same habitat, but hybridize readily if placed in the same cage or pond. Nevertheless, these have been traditionally considered separate species.

species An interbreeding group of animals or plants that are reproductively isolated through anatomy, ecology, behavior, or geographic distribution from all other such groups.

speciation Formation of one or more new species via reproductive isolation.

biological species concept Defines species as interbreeding populations reproductively isolated from other such populations.

evolutionary species concept
Defines species as evolutionary lineages with their own unique identity.

ecological species concept
Defines species based on the uniqueness of their ecological niche.

recognition species concept
Defines species based on unique traits or behaviors that allow members of one species to identify each other for mating.

There are many alternatives to the biological species concept; no fewer than twenty-five definitions of *species* have been proposed in the scientific literature. The **evolutionary species concept** is used by many scientists who study the fossil record and therefore cannot directly observe the reproductive isolating mechanisms on which the biological species concept relies. Proponents of the evolutionary species concept consider the enormous geologic time needed to establish the evolutionary history of a species to be an important criterion of a species. Its proponents say that a species not only should be phenotypically distinct from all other species but also should have its own evolutionary identity. As paleontologist George Gaylord Simpson (1961) put it, a species should be a lineage evolving separately from other lineages, having its own evolutionary tendencies. The **ecological species concept**, proposed by Leigh Van Valen (1976), says that a species should occupy its own unique ecological niche, or role, that distinguishes it clearly from all other species. This concept has never been widely applied, although it may be useful in distinguishing species that are very similar genetically and anatomically but differ in how they divide up the resources in their habitat.

The most influential current alternative to the biological species concept is the **recognition species concept** (Paterson, 1986). It argues that the emphasis on reproductive isolation found in the biological species concept is flawed in that such isolation may be only a side effect of the splitting of two populations into separate species for other reasons. The recognition species concept states that species have their own unique systems for recognizing mates. For example, galagoes (bush babies) are small nocturnal primates that use calls to recognize one another in dark tropical forests. Each species has a unique set of calls that apparently prevents accidental matings between members of different galago species. Studying these calls with an emphasis on how galagoes of one species find each other for mating uses the principle of the recognition species concept.

TABLE 5.2 Reproductive Isolating Mechanisms (RIMs)	
PREMATING ISOLATING MECHANISMS	
1. Habitat isolation	Species A and B occupy different habitats, such as tree limbs versus the ground beneath the tree.
2. Temporal isolation	Species A and B breed in different seasons or in different months, or are active in day versus at night.
3. Behavioral isolation	Courtship or other behavior or calls by male of Species A do not elicit mating response by female of Species B.
4. Mechanical incompatibility	Species A and B cannot mate successfully because of anatomical difference, especially in the reproductive organs.
POSTMATING ISOLATING MECHANISMS	
1. Sperm–egg incompatibility	Mating occurs, but sperm of Species A is unable to penetrate or fertilize egg of Species B because of biochemical incompatibility.
2. Zygote inviability	Species A and B produce fertilized egg, but it dies at early stage of embryonic development.
3. Embryonic or fetal inviability	Offspring of hybrid mating dies before birth.
4. Offspring inviability	Hybrid offspring is carried to term but dies after birth.
5. Offspring sterility	Hybrid offspring is healthy but reproductively sterile, as in mules born from horse–donkey matings.

The difficulties raised by applying multiple species concepts create problems for anthropologists trying to understand the human fossil record. Just as species in the present day are best seen as dynamic entities that overlap genetically in many cases, drawing the line in history where one species has evolved into another species often is problematic. We will see in Chapters 11 through 14 that some early human species can be considered one species or four depending on which taxonomist one listens to and which species concept that taxonomist uses.

In addition to confusion over species concepts, interpreting fossils is complicated by individual variation. If we identify a species in the fossil record, some individuals will look more alike than others because of random variation of the kind that makes one person taller or thinner than another today. Moreover, individuals can harbor diseases or other physical conditions that make them look somewhat different from other members of their species. And often whole populations, the breeding subunits of each species, look a bit different from other populations of the same species (Box 5.1 on page 116). Such subunits often—but not always—are the embryonic stages of formation of new species.

REPRODUCTIVE ISOLATING MECHANISMS

If species are reproductively isolated from other species, then what factors keep species apart? Such mechanisms can be sorted into two categories: premating isolating mechanisms and postmating isolating mechanisms (Table 5.2). Such **reproductive isolating mechanisms (RIMs)** have been built into the phenotypes of animals to prevent them from accidentally mating with members of another, similar species. Such a mistaken hybrid mating in most cases would be a wasted reproductive effort, and natural selection promotes mechanisms to prevent such matings. Although premating and postmating barriers to accidental cross-species breeding have evolved, premating barriers are prevalent because they prevent lost mating efforts and prevent wasting of sperm and eggs.

THE ORIGIN OF SPECIES: HOW SPECIES ARE FORMED

The process of speciation can occur in a variety of ways. One species can evolve into another over time, a process known as **anagenesis**. In this mode of change, Species 1 would slowly become Species 2, and Species 1 would no longer exist or be identifiable in the fossil record (Figure 5.10). The question then becomes when taxonomists should stop referring to the species as 1 and begin calling it 2. Species 1 might also branch into two or more new species, a process called **cladogenesis**. In cladogenesis, Species 1 might or might not still exist as one of the new array of species.

reproductive isolating mechanisms (RIMS) Any factor—behavioral, ecological, or anatomical—that prevents a male and female of two different species from hybridizing.

anagenesis Evolution of a trait or a species into another over a period of time.

cladogenesis Evolution through the branching of a species or a lineage.

FIGURE 5.10 Two modes of evolutionary change. (a) In cladogenesis, one species branches into multiple new species. (b) In anagenesis one species evolves into another new species over time.

Box 5.1 What's in a Name? Species Concepts, Genetics, and Conservation

With many of the world's primate species in danger of extinction, scientists are trying to determine the population size of each remaining species. One factor complicating this effort is confusion about species concepts. Whether one species of primate with a population of 3,000 remaining individuals should be split taxonomically into three with only 1,000 each has critical consequences for conservation efforts. Scientists studying these issues have a new arsenal of genetic research tools at their disposal. But these new tools of an evolutionary biologist's trade have not necessarily resolved species identity problems.

Recent fieldwork has identified numerous populations of great apes across Africa that had not previously been described. With the advances in DNA technologies, it is now possible to collect fecal material from these little-known populations and conduct genetic analysis to tell us how closely related new populations are to other, known ape populations. In some cases the combination of new genetic data and traditional studies of the skeletal anatomy of apes and other primates has led researchers to claim that multiple species exist in places where we previously believed there was one.

Recent genetic studies of gorillas (*Gorilla gorilla*) have revealed an amazing amount of genetic diversity (Gagneux et al., 1996; Jensen-Seaman and Kidd, 2001) and demonstrate how misleading the outward appearance of the animals can be for understanding evolutionary relationships. In eastern Africa, mountain gorillas occur in two populations—the Virungas Volcanoes and in the nearby Bwindi Impenetrable National Park (Figure A). Separated by only 25 miles (40 kilometers), these two populations are genetically indistinguishable. They are similar in appearance but can be distinguished by subtle differences in hair color and length (Virungas gorillas are jet black, with longer, shaggier coats). Their behavior differs, too: The Bwindi gorillas climb trees routinely, whereas their Virungas counterparts rarely climb. But despite their geographic separation and differences in appearance and behavior, no one would advocate considering the two variants of mountain gorillas to be separate species.

Meanwhile, lowland gorillas in western Africa also exist in multiple separate populations (Figure B). Unlike their mountain cousins, lowland gorilla populations show a startling degree of genetic divergence. In fact, some western lowland gorilla populations are as different from one another genetically as gorillas are from chimpanzees. Their genetic diversity has prompted some scientists to propose splitting lowland gorillas into at least two species, although this remains controversial. This implies a very long history of separation among the populations. However, despite this genetic divergence, western lowland gorillas all look very much alike; in other words, their phenotypes have remained the same.

The lesson vividly illustrated by lowland gorillas is that the genetic distance between two species does not necessarily correspond to the formation of new species. So learning that two species have been on separate phylogenetic paths for a million years does not necessarily mean that they will look less similar than two other species that have been on separate paths for 100,000 years. This complicates an already thorny conservation question. If gorillas, long considered to be one species across Africa, are really three or more species, how should this change the way we try to protect their future? Splitting one species into three means we would have two additional, even more critically endangered populations. It might also discourage future generations of conservationists from introducing animals to new populations as a means of increasing genetic diversity. On the other hand, creating new gorilla species may help focus world attention on the plight of endangered populations. So when it comes to gorillas, the question "What is a species?" is far from academic.

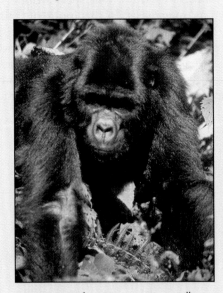

FIGURE A Only 650 mountain gorillas remain in two tiny forests in East Africa.

FIGURE B Most of the world's remaining gorillas are western lowland gorillas.

Beyond these two general modes of evolutionary change, there are specific processes by which new species are formed. One of these is **allopatric speciation** (Mayr, 1942). In allopatric speciation, the trigger to the emergence of new species is geographic separation between two populations of the same species (Figure 5.11). For example, a river that cuts into its banks grows wider and wider over eons. Eventually the river's course becomes a canyon that separates the populations of animals that live on one side from those on the other side. If the animals are small and unable to cross the chasm, gene flow is interrupted. Over thousands of generations, random mutations accumulate in each population until each is different enough that they can be considered separate species. Such circumstances of isolation and divergence happen frequently in nature; islands and river course changes both create fragmented animal habitats that lead to allopatric speciation all the time. In fact, one squirrel species is believed to have speciated into two because of the formation of the Grand Canyon in Arizona; as the chasm grew deeper and wider, what had been one species was fragmented into two. Today, the north and south rims of the canyon support separate, closely related squirrel species.

Darwin's finches, speciating in isolation on the many islands of the Galápagos, are another good example of allopatric speciation. Scientists studying the great apes believe the closely related chimpanzee and bonobo may have been formed when the great Congo River split and isolated two populations of an ape species that was their common ancestor (Figure 5.12 on page 118). Apes do not swim, and with a lack of gene flow over thousands of generations, two apes with differing anatomies and behavior emerged where there had been one.

But what happens if the individuals from the two now-separated species contact each other again? Do the species merge again, or are they forever split? If ocean levels drop and islands become reconnected to the mainland, many species that had been isolated for thousands of generations may be exposed to potential mates from what are now distinct but closely related species. The differences between the two new species can be reinforced through secondary contact. In a

allopatric speciation Speciation occurring via geographic isolation.

FIGURE 5.11 How allopatric speciation works.

(a)

(b)

FIGURE 5.12 Chimpanzees (a) and bonobos (b) likely diverged from a common ancestor due to allopatric speciation in central Africa.

process called *reinforcement*, random mating between the two species is discouraged by natural selection because the hybrid would be less genetically fit than the offspring of two mates of the same species. Because natural selection favors premating reproductive isolating mechanisms, new points of difference between the two species often evolve (perhaps courtship behavior or structure of the reproductive anatomy) that make hybrid mating unlikely.

A second process of species formation is **parapatric speciation**, which appears to be a much less important force than allopatric speciation. When two populations occur adjacent to one another, with continuous gene flow back and forth between them, speciation of one from the other is nevertheless possible, especially if one or both species occur over a very large geographic area. This can make one part of a population remote enough from another that new traits can appear, and over time parts of the original populations diverge more than others. Often, a zone of overlap remains where the new populations, now two species, continue to interbreed. Such hybrid zones are confusing to evolutionary biologists because they can remain stable, without disappearing or growing, over many years. In northeastern Africa, a hybrid zone exists between savanna and hamadryas baboons. In the strip of arid land that is the hybrid zone, but nowhere outside of it, baboons exist that share a mosaic of traits between the two species. These traits are not only morphological ones such as hair color or body size; they include aspects of mating behaviors in hybrids that resemble a mixture of the behavior of both species. Such hybrids therefore allow primatologists to better understand the degree of genetic influence over particular traits.

Another mode of speciation, more controversial than allopatric speciation, is **sympatric speciation**. In theory, sympatric speciation occurs when multiple phenotypes exist in a single species, some of which have greater reproductive success than others. No spatial separation of the parent species is needed. However, there have been very few widely accepted demonstrations of sympatric speciation, and it is probably occurs rarely in nature, although it can be induced in laboratory studies of fruit flies and other simple animals. The most common cases of sympatric speciation in nature are found in plants, in which a single mistake made during reproduction produces large-scale chromosomal mutation. The mutation isolates a whole new form of plant reproductively from its neighbors, thereby creating a new species, which can lead to very rapid speciation because of its dramatic genetic effects.

parapatric speciation
Speciation occurring when two populations have continuous distributions and some phenotypes in that distribution are more favorable than others.

sympatric speciation
Speciation occurring in the same geographic location.

THE TEMPO OF SPECIATION

When Darwin considered evolution by natural selection, he considered mainly one kind of change. Lineages of animal and plant species evolve slowly, gradually evolving into new species over vast periods of Earth's history. This is known as **gradualism** and is widely accepted as the most important and prevalent type of biological evolution. Although Darwin knew about the occurrence of "sports," as he called mutations that differed radically in color or shape from their parents, he considered these extremely rare aberrations. Darwin and most biologists since have accepted gradualism based on the occurrence of so many intermediate forms in the fossil record and the intricate relationships between an organism's adaptations, which imply small incremental evolutionary changes because rapid major changes would disrupt the way an organism functions.

Given this evidence of gradual evolution, how do we explain the presence of gaps in the fossil record? Creationists point to these gaps as evidence that a divine power has created at least some species, and therefore they lack an evolutionary history. Scientists point out that the fossil record is fragmentary, and if complete it would reveal all the gradual changes that evolution has produced.

An alternative explanation for gaps in the fossil record is **macroevolution,** meaning rapid, large-scale evolutionary changes. The most commonly cited mode of macroevolution is **punctuated equilibrium** (Eldredge and Gould, 1972). The theory of punctuated equilibrium holds that most species' phenotypes remain static, changing very little over long periods of time. These long periods of stasis are punctuated by bursts of evolutionary change that happen rapidly (Figure 5.13). Such a process would produce gaps in the fossil record because intermediate forms would occur only in brief windows in time. The theory's advocates claim that this may explain large gaps in the fossil record for the most ancient invertebrates, in which wholesale changes in the phenotypes of lineages appear suddenly and without evidence of immediate ancestors.

Punctuated equilibrium is a radical variation on the traditional Darwinian theory of gradual evolutionary change. Most scientists studying the fossil record of more recent animal life are skeptical of punctuated evolution, for at least two reasons. First, the fossil record is extremely fragmentary, and in cases where abundant fossils are discovered for a lineage of animals, evidence of gradual change exists. Second, there is much evidence that species change slightly over time without evolving into new species, as opposed to the claim of punctuated equilibrium theorists that species remain static for long periods.

gradualism Darwinian view of slow, incremental evolutionary change.

macroevolution Evolution of major phenotypic changes over relatively short time periods.

punctuated equilibrium Model of evolution characterized by rapid bursts of change, followed by long periods of stasis.

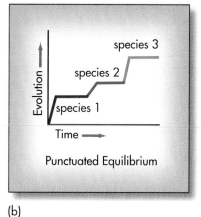

(a)   (b)

FIGURE 5.13 The tempo of evolution. (a) Gradual evolution involves small, steady changes over a long period. (b) Punctuated equilibrium involves long periods of stasis punctuated by bursts of change.

However, scientists who study the deep history of life on Earth have a very different view of punctuated equilibrium. The fossil record of very primitive life forms living hundreds of millions of years ago provides strong evidence that punctuated equilibrium might have been an important mode of speciation. Most evidence of punctuation events comes from patterns of wholesale changes in communities of ancient marine animals, in which large-scale change can been seen in short periods of time. Punctuated equilibrium is a good example of how scientists' views differ widely depending on their perspective of nature. Those looking at only recent evolution on Earth see little evidence of punctuation events, whereas those studying enormously long time scales and more complete fossil records see ample evidence.

An even more extreme version of punctuation theory, called *saltation* (literally, evolution by leaps), argues that macroevolutionary changes were so sudden and so large in effect that intermediate forms did not exist at all. Unlike punctuated equilibrium, which is a Darwinian theory working on large time scales, saltation is departure from Darwinian explanations for the evolution of life.

As we saw in Chapter 1 and will examine in detail in the next section, adaptation is a fundamental aspect of evolution by natural selection. Many scientists question whether punctuated equilibrium can account for the ever-present force of adaptation in nature.

ADAPTATION

Adaptations are evolved phenotypic traits that increase an organism's reproductive success. The eye is an obvious adaptation, and the ways in which eyes differ (nocturnal animals possess very different eye adaptations from other animals) are further examples of adaptations. The concept of adaptation is central to modern biology, but it is also much debated. Some evolutionary biologists consider any well-designed trait an organism possesses to be an adaptation. Others use a stricter definition; they consider an adaptation to be a trait that evolved for a purpose and is still serving that purpose. A trait that evolved for a purpose other than what it does today would not be considered an adaptation.

For instance, we can be sure that the wings of birds did not evolve for powered flight. We know this because natural selection sorts among the available adaptive advantages an organism possesses *in each generation*. There would have been no selective advantage to an ancient bird in having wings that were just slightly adapted for flight. Instead, wings must have evolved for another function entirely and then were co-opted for flight. Some evolutionary theorists think that feathered wings were initially adaptive as organs that absorbed solar radiation, allowing a proto-bird to bask in the sun and warm up more effectively (as some birds use them today). As feathered wings evolved, they became useful for gliding and then eventually were modified for powered flight (Figure 5.14). As in other cases of explaining retrospectively the origin of an adaptation, finding intermediate stages of its evolution during which it would have been adaptive is the key.

IS EVERYTHING ADAPTIVE?

If you were asked to develop a hypothesis in the next 5 minutes to describe the evolutionary origin of the human chin, you probably could think of something plausible. The chin, you might argue, evolved to aid our ancestors in the days when they ran across the savanna, protecting their eyes by jutting out from the face to absorb the first shock if they tripped and fell. Or perhaps the chin evolved to provide a place to catch soup as it dribbled out of the mouth. Such scenarios, though silly, are hard to disprove. As we saw in Chapter 2, evolutionary science works by posing a reasonable hypothesis to explain a feature or behavior and then figuring out

FIGURE 5.14 A feathered dinosaur.

the sort of data one needs to collect to test that hypothesis. In practice, this means that assuming that a trait may be adaptive at the outset of a study is the way to proceed. The premise of your hypothesis would be that the human chin is an adaptation, evolved for a purpose related to reproduction and survival.

It would be naive to think that all evolution is adaptive; we saw that genetic drift and its components are notable exceptions. Some scientists tend toward **adaptationism**, accepting that every aspect of an organism is the product of natural selection or sexual selection. Others, including members of one school we can call *holism*, are skeptical that natural selection is all-powerful and consider many apparent adaptations to be merely the byproduct of other evolutionary changes. Holists would point out that the chin is only the meeting point of the two halves of the lower jaw, which do not fuse until infancy in human development. The chin exists because of the position of the teeth, not because the chin has any adaptive role of its own.

These two schools of thought represent very different ways of understanding how evolution works. Adaptationists tend toward **reductionism**, trying to understand the function of each component of an organism in order to understand the organism as a whole. They make the working assumption that each part of the organism is adaptive. Holists claim that reductionists oversimplify the nature of adaptation and see natural selection in places where it had not occurred. In a well-known 1979 article, biologists Steven Jay Gould and Richard Lewontin argued that adaptationists overlook or ignore many nonadaptive means by which evolution may occur. They analogized evolution to the arches of a cathedral. As a graceful architectural feature, the spaces between the archways (spandrels) appear to have been created for aesthetic reasons. In fact, spandrels are merely the byproduct of building an arch (Mayr, 1983; Gould and Lewontin, 1979).

Adaptationists respond that assuming that traits are adaptive is the only rational starting point for using the scientific method to test their hypotheses. Just as there are both evolved and immediate causes in biology, there are both adaptive and nonadaptive explanations for what an organism looks like. Using an adaptive, reductionist framework as the way to begin investigating those traits is the best, and perhaps the only, way to conduct scientific research into human evolutionary biology. The holistic approach cautions us against assuming that all features of an organisms are adaptive. But in practice, biological anthropologists tend to begin with adaptive hypotheses and test them until they appear to be poor explanations for a phenomenon, and then turn to other possible explanations.

adaptationism A premise that all aspects of an organism have been molded by natural selection to a form optimal for enhancing reproductive success.

reductionism Paradigm that an organism is the sum of many evolved parts and that organisms can best be understood through an adaptationist approach.

null hypothesis The starting assumption for scientific inquiry, that one's research results occur by random chance. One's hypothesis must challenge this initial assumption.

HARDY–WEINBERG EQUILIBRIUM

What would populations be like if evolutionary change never occurred? Although this is not possible in nature, it can be studied in a mathematician's laboratory, and the experiment is extremely useful for understanding the **null hypothesis**, that natural selection and other evolutionary forces have no effect on a population. In 1908, English mathematician G. H. Hardy (Figure 5.15) published a short article in the journal *Science*, which had a peculiarly apologetic beginning:

> I am reluctant to intrude in a discussion concerning matters of which I have no expert knowledge, and I should have expected the very simple point which I wish to make to have been familiar to biologists. However, some remarks of Mr. Udny Yule, to which Mr. R. C. Punnett has called my attention, suggest that it may still be worth making.

In other words, Hardy was saying that the point he had to make was so mathematically elementary that it was almost embarrassing for him to publish it. But we are fortunate that he did because Hardy's paper played a vital role in

FIGURE 5.15 G. H. Hardy

the reconciliation of Mendelian and Darwinian views of nature. It also laid the foundations for the modern field of population genetics and other mathematical approaches to understanding evolution.

Before 1908, geneticists struggled with concepts of equilibrium in biological populations. At what point would genetic stability be reached in these dynamic populations? Looking at it from the simplest perspective of one gene with two alleles (one dominant and one recessive), Yule (1902) argued that equilibrium would be reached in a population when there was a 3:1 ratio of the dominant to the recessive phenotype. Most geneticists with practical experience, such as R. C. Punnett, knew this was wrong but did not know how to prove it was wrong. This is where Hardy stepped in.

Suppose we have a population of diploid, sexually reproducing organisms. Assume that this population is not subject to any evolutionary forces that might lead to changes in allele frequencies: no mutation, no natural selection, no migration. Assume that it is infinitely large (that is, no genetic drift) and that mating is random (that is, allele frequencies cannot be influenced by assortive or disassortive mating practices). This is obviously an "ideal" population, but that is not a problem, as we will see. Let us take the case of a single gene A with two alleles, A_1 and A_2. The frequencies of these alleles in the population can be represented by p and q, respectively (see also Appendix C). By definition, $p + q = 1$.

Hardy showed that after one generation, the genotype frequencies in the population can be represented by a simple quadratic equation:

$$(p + q)^2 = p^2 + 2pq + q^2 = 1$$

This means that the frequencies of the homozygous genotypes A_1A_1 and A_2A_2 are p^2 and q^2, respectively, and the frequency of the heterozygote A_1A_2 is $2pq$. No matter what values p and q have, if the assumptions of no evolution, infinitely large population, and random mating hold, these allele (and genotype) frequencies will not change over generations of breeding. The population is in equilibrium, at least for this single gene or locus.

Despite the fact that ideal populations rarely exist in nature, Hardy's equation, which later became known as the **Hardy–Weinberg equilibrium**, has proved to be valuable in many ways. It can be mathematically expanded to model the distribution of more complex genetic systems, including polygenic traits and those for which more than two alleles exist. One can also use it to calculate approximate allele frequencies based on knowledge of the phenotypic frequency of a homozygous recessive trait. For example, there is a chemical called phenylthiocarbamide (PTC), which can be tasted by about 75% of the European population but cannot be tasted by the other 25%. It is known that this is controlled by a single gene with two alleles, where "tasting" is dominant to "nontasting." Thus the allele frequency of "nontasting" (homozygous recessive) equals the square root of 0.25, or 0.5.

Finally, although ideal populations rarely exist, the allele distributions of many genes often are found to be in equilibrium. Of course, when we find an allele distribution that is not in equilibrium, that can be the most exciting finding of all: It may mean that an evolutionary force is at work in the population, waiting to be uncovered by a curious investigator.

Hardy's article put to rest any ideas of "blending" inheritance. He demonstrated not only that in the absence of evolution allele frequencies are in equilibrium but also that phenotype frequencies are in equilibrium. There would be no averaging out of beneficial traits, which for many years was the standard argument against Darwinian evolution by natural selection.

And who is Weinberg? Hardy did not know Wilhelm Weinberg, a German physician, who in 1908—and some months before Hardy—presented an equilibrium model of allele frequency stability identical to Hardy's. Wilhelm published several articles on population genetics in 1909, many of which anticipated later developments in the field. They were all ignored and therefore had no influence on

Hardy-Weinberg equilibrium
The theoretical distribution of alleles in a given population in the absence of evolution, expressed as a mathematical equation.

the development of population genetics. It was many years later, after the rediscovery of Weinberg's work, that the Hardy equilibrium became universally known as the *Hardy–Weinberg equilibrium.*

LEVELS OF SELECTION

A final consideration about the nature of selection and evolution is the level at which evolution by natural selection occurs. Darwin considered an individual's lifetime reproductive success as the bottom line for natural selection. Challenges to this idea have consistently been shown to be in error. Biologist V. C. Wynne-Edwards (1962) attempted to show that natural selection could sometimes occur for the good of a whole group animals, which he called **group selection**. He claimed that when animals are overcrowded, they regulate their reproduction rather than overpopulate their range and outstrip their food resources. But biologist George C. Williams (1966) showed clearly that in such a situation, the individual that is concerned only with itself always prospers evolutionarily. Consider a herd of 100 antelope that are beginning to run out of food because of overpopulation. Ninety-nine antelope stop bearing offspring for 1 year because natural selection has a mechanism that is intended to prevent overpopulation, but one antelope continues having babies. That one selfish antelope would eat heartily and pass its genes for selfish behavior to the next generation, whereas its altruistic neighbors did not. In time, *altruism* would be extinguished in favor of selfish behavior. Williams showed succinctly that in the face of selfish behavior, there are few scenarios in which self-sacrifice in the animal kingdom could proliferate.

INCLUSIVE FITNESS

More recent evolutionary thinkers argue that selection may operate at other levels as well. Individual selection leads us to believe that all behavior should be selfish; altruism should be very rare. But social animals such as primates behave in ways that benefit their close relatives, often to the detriment of their nonrelatives. Such behavior, called **kin selection**, first framed by biologist William D. Hamilton (1964), is part of a larger concept known as **inclusive fitness**. Instead of considering only an animal's own reproductive success, evolutionary biologists realized that the reproductive success of one's kin also matters because it can contribute indirectly to the animal's fitness by helping its offspring survive and reproduce. Inclusive fitness predicts that social animals should behave less competitively toward close kin because of their shared genes.

The field of study that incorporates the concepts of inclusive fitness and kin selection is *sociobiology.* The majority of scientists who study animal social behavior in the wild today use an evolutionary framework to understand why animals behave as they do. Because full siblings share more of their genetic material than distant cousins, we can make predictions about how animals will behave in nature. For example, food-sharing between chimpanzees is far more likely to occur between close relatives than between nonrelatives. Ground squirrels sitting near their burrows give piercing alarm calls when hawks or coyotes appear. Isn't this altruistic behavior hard to explain in Darwinian terms because the call attracts attention to the caller, making him more likely to be eaten than his neighbor? Researchers found that alarm calls are given mainly when the nearest neighbor is a close relative; when a squirrel is sitting near nonrelatives, he is the first animal to flee into the burrow when danger approaches (Figure 5.16) (Sherman, 1977).

Kin selection operates based on a *coefficient of relatedness*, expressed as $rb > c$, or Hamilton's rule, where r is the degree of kinship between two animals, b is the benefit of altruism to the recipient, and c is the cost of altruism to the altruist (the alarm caller, for instance). The closer the degree of kinship, the more likely

group selection Notion largely discredited by the rise of Darwinian theory proposing that animals act for the good of their social group or of their species.

kin selection Principle that animals behave preferentially toward their genetic kin; formulated by William Hamilton.

inclusive fitness Reproductive success of an organism plus the fitness of its close kin.

FIGURE 5.16 Ground squirrel predator warnings illustrate how kin selection may work.

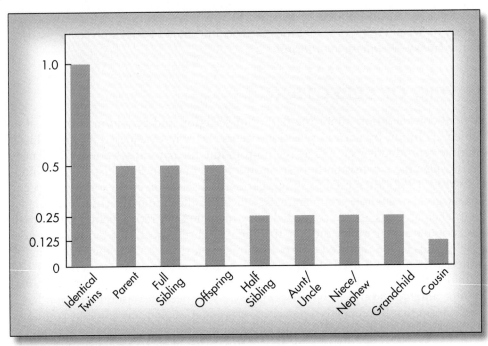

FIGURE 5.17 Coefficients of relatedness: How kin selection works.

altruistic behavior becomes, and the more likely an animal is to engage in dangerous behavior to help its kin (Figure 5.17). This principle guides much of the modern-day research into the social behavior of our closest relatives. We will return to the subject of kin selection when we consider the relevance of sociobiology to primate social behavior in more detail in Chapter 8.

SUMMARY

1. How does natural selection work to mold adaptations?

Natural selection filters genetically inherited traits by favoring some phenotypes in a given environment and disfavoring others. The process perpetuates and enhances mutations that have positive effects on an organism's survival and reproduction. The same process can remove harmful or nonadaptive traits from a population.

2. What is the goal of taxonomic analysis?

Taxonomists attempt to categorize organisms based on their phenotypes. Cladists use ancestral and derived traits to separate lineages and to sort members of a single lineage.

3. What is the difference between Linnaeus's way of classifying species and our modern notion of species?

Linnaeus used a typological pigeonholing scheme for sorting species by similarities to other species. Modern evolutionary biologists recognize that species are dynamic entities that are in flux.

4. Are there nonadaptive modes of evolution?

Genetic drift, including the founder effect, is an example of evolution without adaptation.

5. How does population size affect the impact of random forces such as genetic drift?

Genetic drift and other random factors are much more powerful in very small populations because traits can become fixed (100% occurrence) or lost more easily.

6. Does sexual selection ever work against the effect of natural selection? How?

Sexual selection promotes the elaboration of male traits that enhance reproductive success but not necessarily phenotypic traits that enhance survival. In some cases sexual selection appears to favor traits that adversely affect survival.

7. **What is the reproductive asymmetry between males and females?**

   Males typically have a far greater potential for reproductive success than females and also a far greater variance in mating and reproductive success.

8. **How can we resolve the paradox of animals behaving altruistically toward each other, when Darwin predicted that all behavior should enhance one's own reproductive success?**

   Through kin selection, animals act in ways that enhance their own fitness. When an animal shares genes with another through kinship, altruistic or cooperative behavior helps the giver as well as the recipient of the cooperation.

9. **Is every aspect of an organism adaptive?**

   As an initial working hypothesis, we can presume that a trait evolved to enhance an organism's fitness; this is the reductionist approach. We attempt to understand adaptations by considering each element of an organism's phenotype as the product of natural selection.

CRITICAL THINKING QUESTIONS

1. How can sexual selection sometimes work against natural selection? How can we decide whether sexual selection is a part of or acts in opposition to natural selection?

2. How should we choose which species concept to apply? Is it acceptable to use different species concepts in different circumstances? Shouldn't a species be unambiguously identifiable in all cases?

3. Can behavior be a phenotype? What conditions must be met for natural selection to mold a given behavior?

KEY TERMS

directional selection
stabilizing selection
gene flow
inbreeding
genetic drift
founder effect
genetic bottleneck
sexual selection
sexual dimorphism
reproductive potential
reproductive variance
systematics
homology
analogous
convergent evolution

cladistics
cladogram
species
speciation
biological species
   concept
evolutionary species
   concept
ecological species
   concept
recognition species
   concept
reproductive isolating
   mechanisms (RIMs)
anagenesis

cladogenesis
allopatric speciation
parapatric speciation
sympatric speciation
gradualism
macroevolution
punctuated equilibrium
adaptationism
reductionism
null hypothesis
Hardy–Weinberg
   equilibrium
group selection
kin selection
inclusive fitness

SUGGESTED READING

Endler, J. (1986). *Natural Selection in the Wild*. Princeton University Press, Princeton, NJ.

Hey, J. (2001). The mind of the species problem. *Trends in Ecology and Evolution* 16: 326–329.

Mayr, Ernst. (2001). *What Evolution Is*. Basic Books, New York.

Weiner, Jonathan. (1994). *The Beak of the Finch*. Vintage Books, New York.

Williams, G. C. (1966). *Adaptation and Natural Selection*. Princeton University Press, Princeton, NJ.

Chapter 6

HUMAN VARIATION:
Evolution, Adaptation, and Adaptability

IN THE FAR NORTH COUNTRY, approaching the Arctic Circle, late September can start to feel like winter. The biological anthropologist would have preferred to collect his samples during the warm summer, but his negotiations with the tribal council had gone a bit more slowly than he had expected. He was relieved that he had finally convinced the councilors and other members of the community that a genetic study of their group would have both scientific and social benefits for them as a people.

At several meetings, the anthropologist had explained why he was interested in their group and what they might gain from his genetic research. He pointed out that their biology, along with their culture, was part of their ethnic identity as a people. Tribal identity had been officially suppressed during much of the twentieth century, and the anthropologist argued that genetic study could help them reclaim some of their heritage, in part by reconstructing their biological history. He said that his work would provide a "biological snapshot" of the tribe today, which future generations could refer to for scientific, cultural, or medical reasons. Although he could not promise immediate health benefits as a result of his work, he pointed out that he was creating a genetic database that could be important in the future and that it would belong to them as a people. After much consultation, the tribe agreed that he could conduct the research as long as members of the tribe were collaborators in the research and not merely subjects.

So on a cold morning in late September, the anthropologist prepared for the big day, when he would collect blood, hair, and saliva samples from 70–80 of the tribe's 600 members. He was nervous: There was so much to keep track of. The room was full of test tubes, ice chests, and plastic bags. One of the anthropologist's graduate students was ready to record everything on a laptop.

The first participant to arrive was a woman in her mid-70s. She took off her coat and walked up to the anthropologist, who was sitting at a small table, a list of community members in front of him. She rolled up one sleeve, thrust her arm out toward him, and said, "OK, now what?" The anthropologist decided that maybe things might not go too badly that day.

The origins of biological anthropology go back to the first half of the nineteenth century, an era when evolution had yet to be accepted by most natural historians and fossils representing human ancestors were all but unknown. At that time, biological anthropology was essentially the study of human variation. Unlike the modern anthropologist described in the vignette, most of the earliest anthropologists did not go into the field to meet their research subjects. Instead, they relied on travelers' accounts of exotic peoples from faraway places and waited in their universities, hospitals, and museums for specimens, such as skeletal remains, to be sent to them.

Today, the study of human variation covers a wide range of topics, encompassing population genetics and the evolutionary history of human populations, how natural selection influences human biology, and how humans biologically and culturally adapt to environmental stress. However, before considering how biological anthropologists now approach the topic of human variation, it is important to examine past approaches, many of which were centered around the concept of race and the goal of racial classification.

HUMAN VARIATION AT THE INDIVIDUAL AND GROUP LEVEL

It is obvious that modern humans show substantial *individual variation*. Except for identical twins, our genetic differences alone make each of us unique. At the anatomical and behavioral levels, even identical twins are not truly identical. Twins reared in different environments develop different phenotypic characteristics despite having the same genotype (although they may still be more similar to each other than two people picked at random). The "twin environment" itself leads to the development of variation: In the uterus, one twin often receives more nutrients than the other, leading to a difference between the two in birth weight. Thus it is clear that human phenotypes are shaped by both genetic and environmental factors.

Human variation can also be measured at the *group level*. In Chapter 5, we discussed sexual dimorphism. Some of the variation we observe in the human species results from the fact that men and women vary in the expression of certain phenotypic features, such as body size. Another profound source of variation at the group level is age. Children differ in many ways from adults, and younger adults differ from older adults. Phenotypic traits that vary according to age are very common. Body size is again an obvious one (children are little and adults are big), but all sorts of anatomical, physiological, and behavioral features change as we age. We will discuss this aspect of variation in Chapter 17.

For as long as the field has existed, variation at the *population level* has been of particular interest to biological anthropologists. Humans have long noticed that people from different populations may look different from one another. They also noticed that they may behave differently. The science of anthropology developed in order to systematically examine biological and cultural differences observed between different human populations. *Homo sapiens* is a **polytypic species**, one that is divided into local populations that differ by one or more phenotypic traits. As anthropology has developed over the years, methods for disentangling genetic, cultural, and environmental factors responsible for producing population variation have become more refined (Figure 6.1).

WHAT IS A POPULATION?

The word *population* often is used to describe groups or communities of animals that are identifiable within a species. As we discussed in Chapter 5, the members of a biological population constitute a potentially interbreeding group of individuals. From the perspective of an individual organism, it will find its reproductive mates from among the other members of its population. As you will see, *population* can be a very flexible term.

Many other terms have also been suggested for groups below the species level. Population geneticists have used several that emphasize that populations are assemblages of genes as well as individuals: *gene pool, local Mendelian population,* and *panmictic unit* (a local population in which mating is completely random) (Mettler et al., 1988). In general, geneticists use the term **deme** to refer to populations that are being defined in terms of their genetic composition (such as allele frequencies). All of these terms are meant to convey the notion that although these groups are in some way stable and identifiable, they are by no means genetically impermeable. After all, we study gene flow *between* populations.

Subspecies is another term some biologists use to describe variation below the species level. A subspecies is defined as a group of local populations that share part of the geographic range of a species and can be differentiated from other subspecies based on one or more phenotypic traits (in rare cases, a subspecies could consist of a single local population). Theoretically, the identification of a

polytypic species Species that consist of a number of separate breeding populations, each varying in some genetic trait.

deme A local, interbreeding population that is defined in terms of its genetic composition (for example, allele frequencies).

subspecies A group of local populations that share part of the geographic range of a species, and can be differentiated from other subspecies based on one or more phenotypic traits.

FIGURE 6.1   Humans vary according to age, sex, and population of origin.

subspecies is done somewhat more formally than the identification of a population. In the biological sciences, the term **race** has been used interchangeably with *subspecies*. As we will see in this chapter, however, the historical use of the race concept in anthropology has not been a simple matter of identifying biological subspecies. In the past, some anthropologists subscribed to the idea that human races, like biological subspecies, correspond to groups of populations that are found in or derived from a particular geographic area (Figure 6.2 on page 130).

All terms used to describe groups of individuals or populations within species share some basic shortcomings. There can be no objective way to decide how much variation (genetic or anatomical) is enough to consider two groups worthy of separate identification, nor is it possible to declare that all individuals in a geographic area are by definition members of a single population. For some scientists, these shortcomings are so problematic that they would never formally identify any group below the species level. On the other hand, most species are made up of distinct local groups of individuals who tend to interbreed within their group and may be genetically or anatomically distinct from other such groups.

The identification of particular populations can depend on the research questions a particular scientist is interested in. For example, if a scientist were interested in studying the effects of geographic isolation on gene flow in urban-dwelling ground squirrels, then his populations might be groups of squirrels living in different city blocks. If another scientist wanted to know about the long-term evolution of North American squirrels, she might identify populations based on samples taken from large geographic areas, and so her populations would be very different from those identified in a small city environment. To some extent, then, the identification of populations is a pragmatic matter depending on what hypothesis is being tested or which genetic phenomenon is being investigated.

Modern bioanthropological, medical, and genetic researchers also seem to apply the term *population* in a pragmatic way. For example, investigations of diseases in the United States often are conducted by measuring the rates in different groups that have biological, historical, and cultural relevance in this setting, such as "American black" and "American white." An anthropologist investigating the evolution of modern humans as a species might not find these categories useful, nor would a geneticist who is looking at gene flow between Africa and different North and South American populations. But, the issues being

race In biological taxonomy, same thing as a subspecies; when applied to humans, sometimes incorporates both cultural and biological factors. The term is not used by biological anthropologists today.

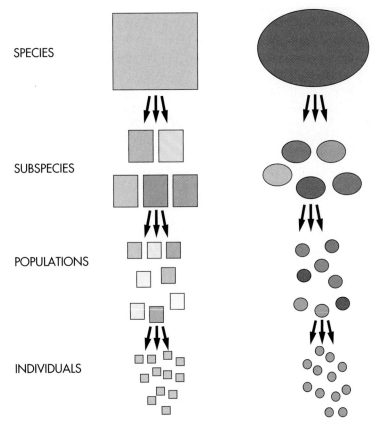

FIGURE 6.2 Species, subspecies, populations, and individuals. Species are reproductively isolated from one another, but all members of a species can interbreed.

examined and the groups accessible for research influence how populations are identified.

One problem that has arisen repeatedly in the investigation of variation within our species is that in the past the pragmatic concerns of some people were centered on identifying inferior and superior races, and using "racial science" to reinforce and justify the prevailing social order. The science of anthropology was born in the nineteenth century, when there were incendiary debates about the moral and scientific correctness of slavery. Was it the natural right of a "superior race" to enslave the members of an "inferior race"? In the twentieth century, Nazi Germany used "racial science" to justify the genocide of Jews and Gypsies.

HISTORICAL PERSPECTIVES ON HUMAN VARIATION

The most basic and universal classification of human variation at the group level is "us" and "them." The field of **ethnobiology** is dedicated to understanding the different systems that cultures have developed to classify the objects and organisms in the world around us (Berlin, 1992; Atran, 1998). One thing that ethnobiology makes clear is that human beings are masters at making up categories and classifications in which to place things. It comes as no surprise that humans have made efforts to classify people as well.

ethnobiology The study of how traditional cultures classify objects and organisms in the natural world.

RECORDING HUMAN VARIATION IN PAST CIVILIZATIONS

In the nineteenth century, archaeologists discovered that the ancient Egyptians depicted human variation in some of the hieroglyphic records they left behind (Stanton, 1960). The Egyptians had extensive contacts with peoples to their north and south and were well aware of the physical differences between them. As the great antiquity of the Egyptian civilization began to be appreciated, Egyptology figured strongly in two major nineteenth-century racial debates. One involved the origins of races themselves. Did evidence of human variation (and races clearly recognizable to nineteenth-century scientists) in ancient Egypt, which existed not long after the biblical creation (4004 B.C.), indicate that races were created by God and were therefore immutable (see Chapter 2)? The other debate focused on the physical constitution of the Egyptians themselves: Were they "African Negroes" or a more typically Middle Eastern people? Because the Egyptian civilization was viewed as one of the first great Western civilizations, this was considered to be an issue of some importance.

The ancient Greeks also knew of dark-skinned Africans, whom they called "Ethiopians," a term meaning "scorched ones" in Greek (Brues, 1977). Homer and Herodotus also make reference to Africans in their work. In his *Histories,* Herodotus also made note of nomads from the north, the "Scythians," who had light skin and red or light hair, in obvious contrast to the darker skin and hair of the Greeks themselves, and he was aware of darker-skinned peoples from India.

The ancient Romans had at least as extensive knowledge as the Greeks of the variety of peoples that could be found in the western part of Eurasia and north Africa; they even had limited contact with Han Chinese traders who had ventured as far west as Turkestan (Brues, 1977). However, in general the Romans made very little of the biological differences between its subject peoples.

After the collapse of the (western) Roman Empire in the fifth century A.D., the peoples of Europe entered the Dark Ages (as the Early Middle Ages were characterized), and their knowledge of the world and peoples beyond their local borders diminished along with many other aspects of learning. It was during this period that tales of monsters and other fantastic beasts took center stage (de Waal Malefijt, 1968). Greek and Roman writers had reported the existence of monstrous sorts of people, with greater and lesser degrees of skepticism. There were tales of cyclops, headless people, and people who hibernated or transformed themselves into wolves during the summer (Figure 6.3 on page 132). The Bible mentions monsters and many missionaries were the sources of tales of monstrous people.

When the European age of discovery began in 1492, Europeans came into contact with many peoples who were new to them, but the basic question was, Were these actually people? Shakespeare's depiction of the strange and brutish Caliban (an anagram of *cannibal*) in *The Tempest* illustrates a common European view of people from the New World. In 1537, when Pope Paul III declared that American Indians were humans, he established a policy that became church orthodoxy for centuries: that all people, of all races, were the product of a single creation. In later scientific debates, this position became known as *monogenism* (see Chapter 2).

THE MONOGENISM–POLYGENISM DEBATE

During the eighteenth century, Linnaeus introduced a biological classification system that formed the basis of the one we use today (see Chapter 2). In the tenth edition of *Systema Naturae* (1758), Linnaeus provided a new name for our species, *Homo sapiens,* and with it he identified five subspecies or races:

Homo sapiens afer (Africans)

Homo sapiens americanus (American Indians)

Homo sapiens asiaticus (Asians)

Homo sapiens europaeus (Europeans)

Homo sapiens ferus (Wild Men)

Linnaeus also identified a second species, *Homo monstrosus*, which included a variety of human- and ape-like forms.

German anatomist Johann Friedrich Blumenbach (1752–1840), in many ways the father of physical anthropology, established one of the first large collections of biological anthropological material, including a large number of skulls, for which

FIGURE 6.3 Monstrous people from distant lands depicted in a fifteenth-century European woodcut.

he carefully noted their place of origin in order to better understand the biological diversity of the human species. Like Linnaeus, Blumenbach was also a monogenist, and he fully recognized the pitfalls of naming races:

> There is but one species of the genus Man; and all people of every time and climate with which are acquainted, may have originated from one common stock. All national differences in the form and colour of the human body are not more remarkable nor more inconceivable than those by which the varieties of so many other organized bodies, and particularly of domestic animals, arise, as it were, under our eyes. All these differences too, run so insensibly, by so many shades and transitions one into the other, that it is impossible to separate them by any but very arbitrary limits (Blumenbach 1779, 1780, in McCown and Kennedy 1972).

Despite the fact that he knew the limits were arbitrary, Blumenbach identified five races for the sake of convenience:

Caucasian

Mongolian

Ethiopian

American

Malayan

Blumenbach was the first to use the term *Caucasian* to describe the people of western and southern Eurasia because he believed that a likely source of these peoples was to be found somewhere in the Caucasus region in present-day Georgia (Keith, 1940).

A basic problem for the monogenists was how to explain where the different races came from if they all had a recent common origin. Many believed in a very strong form of **environmentalism**, which held that the human body was biologically quite plastic and that the environment had great power to shape our anatomy. An example of strong environmentalism is to be found in the writings of the Reverend Samuel Stanhope Smith (1751–1819), a president of Princeton University and one of the first American writers to address the natural history of human beings. As an example of the power of the environment to shape anatomy, Smith (1965[1810]) looked to the "blacks in the southern states." Smith claimed that the field slaves were darker and retained more of their "African" features, both physical and behavioral, than the domestic slaves, who were more "refined" in appearance, with lighter skin and elegant manners. He argued that the effects of civilization on the domestic slaves shaped their anatomy to make them more like their "civilized" masters (of course, Smith did not acknowledge that the domestic slaves might resemble their masters because they were related to them). By the standards of his day, Smith was not a racist; he believed that exposure to European-based civilization would cause people (African or Indians) to take on a European appearance.

In the early nineteenth century, as more information on the diversity of humanity became available, many scientists found it harder to believe that all of the racial diversity they observed could have arisen within the biblical timeframe. Samuel George Morton (1799–1851), a Quaker anatomist and physician from Philadelphia, was one of the most prominent advocates of polygenism, or multiple creations or origins (Stanton, 1960). He argued that given only 6,000 years of Earth history and the fact that different races were represented in ancient Egyptian monuments, there was not enough time for the differentiation to occur. The polygenists rejected the idea that the environment had almost unlimited powers to

environmentalism The view that the environment has great powers to directly shape the anatomy of individual organisms.

reshape the human body. By the mid-nineteenth century, the polygenist position became increasingly accepted by serious scientists.

The issue of slavery often was associated with debates about racial origins, although not in a consistent way (Figure 6.4). In England, early anthropological societies were split on the basis of their adherence to monogenesis or polygenesis, a split that also reflected differing views on the equality of races and the legitimacy of slavery (Stocking, 1987). In the United States, before the Civil War (1861–1865), although the origin of races became an issue in the abolition debates, advocates of polygenism and monogenism did not consistently line up on one side of the debate or the other (Haller, 1970).

After the publication of Darwin's *On the Origin of Species* in 1859, the polygenism–monogenism debate subsided. To some extent, the evolutionary viewpoint could be made to accommodate aspects of both positions. Clearly, all humans were members of one species that shared a common evolutionary history, a viewpoint that was consistent with monogenism. On the other hand, the different races could be viewed in terms of their own evolutionary histories, and it was not difficult to construct hypothetical evolutionary scenarios that underscored racial differences and the "evolution" of racial inequality.

THE RACE CONCEPT IN THE TWENTIETH CENTURY

Throughout the twentieth century, the scientific study of human population variation was shaped by political and cultural forces. Of course, this has always been the case, but an increased recognition of the impact of these factors on "objective" science has developed, especially since the end of World War II (1939–1945). There has also been an increasing awareness of **racism**, scientific and otherwise. At one level, racism is simply prejudice against a person based on his or her racial heritage. The basis of such prejudice is the idea that important qualities of an individual (such as intellect, physical ability, and temperament) are biologically determined by his or her membership in a racial group. *Stereotyping*, in which the qualities of an individual are projected onto a larger group or vice versa, is also an important component of racism, especially of the more "everyday" variety.

racism A prejudicial belief that members of one ethnic group are superior in some way to those of another.

FIGURE 6.4 This watercolor depicts the miserable conditions Africans endured as they made the passage across the Atlantic and into slavery in the New World. In the mid-nineteenth century, debates about the abolition of slavery were often focused on concepts of racial origins.

Racial issues were of critical importance, in different ways, in three of the principal nations involved in World War II: Germany, Japan, and the United States. In Depression-era Germany, the Nazi party rose to power on the basis of an ideology that was centered on a celebration of "Aryanism," a form of racism that was, in effect, a mythical rendering of the racial history of northern Europeans. The Aryan myth celebrated the "true" German as being the member of a "superior race" and was used to justify the subjugation and ultimately the extermination of "inferior races," such as Jews and Gypsies (Roma). Nazi ideology tapped into and amplified racial prejudices that had long existed, and the Nazis themselves acted on these impulses on an unprecedented scale. In prewar Japan, the imperial government and military also fostered an ideology of racial superiority, focused on the godlike status of the emperor (Bix, 2000). Some Japanese leaders were particularly attuned to racial issues in conflicts between Japan and Western powers, arguing that they were fueled in part by Western concepts of Japanese racial inferiority. Japanese imperialists justified their invasions of the Chinese province of Manchuria and other Asian nations as being in part a war of liberation from non-Asian colonizers while asserting their superiority over their subject peoples.

The United States in the first half of the twentieth century was a fundamentally racist country. The conquest of the Native Americans was complete, and their demise was celebrated in the literature and films of the time. Blacks and whites lived separate and unequal lives, the second-class status of African Americans was reinforced legally by Jim Crow laws and extralegally by lynchings and other violent means of coercion. Immigration laws restricted the entry of "undesirables" such as Asians and southern, central, and eastern Europeans. During World War II, Japanese Americans and Japanese nationals living in the continental United States were interned in "relocation" camps for the duration of the war. After the war, advocates of civil rights and racial equality recognized how ironic it was that the United States had helped to defeat two racist regimes while maintaining racist policies and cultural attitudes at home.

CHANGING ATTITUDES TOWARD RACE IN ANTHROPOLOGY

Anthropologist Franz Boas and his followers instigated a reappraisal of the race concept early in the twentieth century. Boas was a true general anthropologist who conducted research in the cultural, biological, and linguistic realms. Although he did not reject the race concept, he took great pains to emphasize that biology, culture, psychology, and language needed to be carefully studied in any group so that they may be understood in local terms. In *The Mind of Primitive Man* (1938[1911]), Boas argued that there was little evidence of a strong relationship between racial biology and cultural achievement. Boas's biological work focused on craniometry and **anthropometry**, the measurement of different aspects of the body, such as stature or skin, and culminated in his large-scale study comparing head and body form in immigrants to the United States and their U.S.-born children (Boas, 1940 [1912]; Allen, 1989). The differences he observed between parents and offspring led Boas to emphasize that there was a good deal of biological plasticity within "racial" types. Boas had a much "softer" view of race than many of his contemporaries. Although the validity of Boas's work on bodily form changes in immigrants continues to be debated (Sparks and Jantz, 2002; Gravlee et al., 2003), and his own particular type of cultural anthropology goes in and out of fashion, there can be no doubt that the critique of race and racism that Boas initiated was one of the greatest scientific achievements of the twentieth century.

A tireless opponent of the use of the term *race* was anthropologist and writer Ashley Montagu (1905–1999). Although he did not invent it, Montagu was a proponent of the term **ethnic group** to describe human populations (Montagu, 1974). Ethnic

anthropometry The measurement of different aspects of the body, such as stature or skin color.

ethnic group A human group defined in terms of sociological, cultural, and linguistic traits.

BOX 6.1   Traits in Folk Racial Taxonomies

A few key traits loom large in the folk racial taxonomies that have been used in Western cultures over the past 200 years. Even if the race concept itself is not considered valid in biological anthropology, what about the features people have been focusing on for so many years? What is their biological relevance or irrelevance?

Skin Color   Skin color is perhaps the most important morphological feature in social racial categories. Variation in human skin color is of no small biological significance. Because humans do not have fur, our skin is more directly exposed to the environment, and skin color probably is influenced by natural selection. Many of the insights we have about the evolution of skin color come from looking at the associations of skin color with various medical conditions (such as severe sunburn, cancer, and vitamin synthesis), so we will discuss it in more detail in Chapter 17.

On a global scale, skin color is not a particularly good indicator of geographic origins. Populations from different parts of the world may have similar skin colors because they share a common environmental feature, namely the intensity of sunlight exposure. Very dark-skinned populations can be found in Africa, India, and Melanesia, but these populations do not share a recent common ancestry compared with other populations. The amount of variation in skin color of people classified as "white Americans" is substantial and reflects the diverse population origins (in terms of sunlight exposure, among other things) of this "race," which ranges from the Middle East and Mediterranean regions to the far north of Europe.

Eye Form   North and east Asians, as well as some of their descendant populations in the New World, have a high frequency of a morphological feature known as an *epicanthic fold*. This is the classic racial marker of "Oriental" or "Mongoloid" populations, although it can appear in individuals from other parts of the world. The epicanthic fold is a small flap of skin extending from the eyelid to the bridge of the nose. It has no known biological function. Alice Brues (1977) suggests that it is a secondary anatomical feature that results from a combination of a fatty eyelid and a low nasal bridge, both of which, she argues, may reflect adaptations to cold. She points out that epicanthic folds are more common in women than men in some Native American populations and in children rather than adults in European populations; both patterns may be a function of the relative development of the nasal bridge.

Hair Color and Form   Human populations vary significantly in the color and form of the hair. There are no generally accepted functional explanations for why hair color, form, or thickness varies. It is clearly a polygenically inherited trait. Hair color is determined in part by the same substance as skin color (melanin), so it is no surprise that the two are correlated. However, some dark-skinned Australian aborigine populations have a large number of individuals with blond hair, especially when they are children. This may indicate that a different set of alleles may be governing hair color in these populations than in others (Molnar, 2002). Hair form varies from straight to tightly spiraled

---

groups are separated from one another primarily by social barriers, which may lead to biological differentiation or be a marker of biological difference. Although the term has come into widespread usage, in many cases as a replacement for *race*, it is far from ideal for use in biologically oriented research because it explicitly incorporates sociocultural factors in group identification.

Today, biological anthropologists do not typically use the term *race*, preferring almost always to use the term *population*. But if biological anthropologists do not use the term race, does that mean that races do not exist? In a formal sense, the answer is "yes," but the word race is commonly used every day, by all sorts of people, in all kinds of contexts. These people are talking about something, and other people understand what they are referring to, so in that sense races must exist. Take "racial profiling" in law enforcement, for example. Say that a police force has a policy of pulling over young African American men when they drive through certain neighborhoods in a community. We can be fairly certain that the police force is not pulling over young men who are predominantly of Scandinavian origin. It *is* possible to sort Scandinavians from Africans or, for that matter, to sort Chinese from Cherokees or Lapplanders from Inuit people (Box 6.1). Population-level biological differences do exist and often are quite significant.

or woolly. Again although there may be differences in the insulation properties of straight and spiraled hair, arguments can be made that this would be an advantage in either warm or cold climates. African and Melanesian populations both have woolly hair, but at a microscopic level their hair forms are quite different, indicating separate genetic origins.

Head Shape In the 1840s, Swedish anatomist Anders Retzius (1796–1860) introduced a statistic, the cranial or cephalic index (CI), to characterize the shape of the human skull. The CI is simply the width of the skull divided by the length multiplied by 100. Skulls that are narrow, or *dolichocephalic,* have CIs in the 70s, whereas those that are rounder, with CIs in the 80s, are called *brachycephalic.* Despite the fact that the CI was used to categorize skulls (and people) as "long-headed" or "rounded-headed," all normal skulls are longer than they are wide. Retzius's work introduced cranial shape as a widely used marker of racial affiliation. Some racist scientists of the late nineteenth and early twentieth centuries seemed to put an inordinate amount of emphasis on the shape of the skull as a key racial feature. One reason for this may have been that the CI was something that was not immediately obvious and required scientific measurement to be obtained, which was important as precise measurements were incorporated into essentially folk racial typologies. Although racial schemes based (in part) on cranial shape are not considered valid today, it remains true that human populations show substantial variation in cranial shape and other cranial measures. In an analysis of a large number of skulls from populations around the world, Kenneth Beals and colleagues (1984) found that there is a relationship between skull shape and climate, with skull breadth increasing in colder climates. From a volume–to–surface ratio perspective, this makes sense in terms of the conservation of heat in a cold climate (see text).

FIGURE A   An 1827 portrait by George Catlin of Eeh-Nis-Kin (Crystal Stone), a Blackfoot woman.

FIGURE B   A nineteenth-century Japanese portrait of Commodore Matthew Perry, who "opened up" Japan in 1854.

POPULATION GENETICS

The field of **population genetics** is concerned with uncovering genetic variation within and between populations of organisms. In Chapter 5 we discussed several evolutionary processes, such as natural selection, gene flow, and genetic drift, which are all studied by population geneticists. Studying the dynamic distribution of alleles across populations can require complex mathematical tools (Cavalli-Sforza et al., 1994), many of which are derived from the Hardy–Weinberg equilibrium (see Chapter 5 and Appendix C). Although discussing these tools in detail is beyond the scope of this text, we will consider some of the results they have produced.

Population genetics is concerned primarily with **microevolution**, or evolutionary processes that occur within a species (in contrast to *macroevolution;* see Chapter 5). With increasingly sophisticated molecular biological techniques now available, the line between microevolutionary and macroevolutionary studies is becoming less clear-cut.

POLYMORPHISMS: ABO AND OTHER BLOOD TYPE SYSTEMS

If we look at a population and find that there are at least two alleles present for a given gene, and the alleles are both present at a frequency greater than 1%, then we can say that the population is **polymorphic** for that gene. The term is also used

population genetics   The study of genetic variation within and between groups of organisms.

microevolution   The study of evolutionary phenomena that occur within a species.

polymorphic   Two or more distinct phenotypes (at the genetic or anatomical levels) that exist within a population.

to describe variation at the more observable phenotypic level (see Chapter 4). For example, in a population where both blue- and brown-eyed people live, we can say that it is polymorphic for eye color, assuming that it is a genetic feature and that both phenotypes are present at a frequency of at least 1%. Many protein polymorphisms have no phenotypic effect other than the fact that they are slightly different versions of the same protein. The 1% figure is used as a cutoff because it is substantially above the level you would expect if a rare allele or phenotype were present simply because of the occurrence of mutations.

Different populations can be polymorphic for the same trait or gene but differ in the frequency of alleles. In Chapter 4 we discussed the ABO blood type system, which is a classic example of a polymorphic genetic system. Although Karl Landsteiner discovered the ABO system in 1901 (for which he received the 1930 Nobel Prize in Medicine), it was not until 1919 that Polish physicians Ludwik and Hanka Hirszfeld published the first report on "racial" variation in the ABO system. They did this study at the end of World War I, on the Macedonian battlefront, where soldiers from Europe, the Middle East, Africa, and Southern Asia could be tested. It is interesting to note that ABO distribution initially was of little interest to many anthropologists because they did not correlate particularly well with traditional notions of racial classification (Boyd, 1950), a fact pointed out by the Hirszfelds themselves. In Figure 6.5 *clinal* maps of the distribution of the ABO alleles throughout the world's populations are presented. A **cline** represents the distribution of a genotype or phenotype across geographical space.

The clinal maps in Figure 6.5 clearly illustrate that the ABO system is highly polymorphic across the species but that some populations are essentially monomorphic for type O, including several South American Indian groups. The allele frequencies for A and B never exceed 50% and typically are much lower than this. High A frequencies are found in some European populations, in some North American Indian groups, in Inuit living in arctic North America and Greenland, and in some Australian aborigine tribes. High B frequencies are found in central Asia, especially in the Himalayan region, declining gradually as one moves away from this high-frequency zone. There are also pockets of high B frequency in sub-Saharan Africa. The B allele is almost entirely absent from the Americas or Australia. One worldwide estimate for the frequencies of the three alleles is 62.5% O, 21.5% A, and 16.0% B (MacArthur and Penrose in Harrison et al., 1988).

The distribution of ABO alleles in populations raises some interesting evolutionary issues. Why are the polymorphisms maintained in different populations? Why do we not see more alleles at fixation in different populations because of the effects of genetic drift or bottlenecks? Why are the A and B allele frequencies always less than 50%? Recent research on A and B antigens strongly suggests that natural selection has influenced their population distribution in some way (Koda et al., 2001). Over the years, several investigators have suggested that infectious disease plays a key role in the distribution of ABO alleles in different populations. Robert Seymour and his colleagues (2004) recently suggested that a balance between A and B alleles is maintained in populations with a heavy load of bacterial disease, whereas O would be expected to predominate in populations that are more vulnerable to viral disease. Their mathematical genetic models suggest that the relative frequencies of A, B, and O alleles are maintained by the relative impact of bacterial and viral diseases in a population.

Maternal–Fetal Incompatibility   Another factor that influences the distribution of ABO alleles in a population arises out of the immune response of a pregnant woman and how it influences the health of her fetus. **Maternal–fetal incompatibility** occurs when a mother has type O blood and her infant has type A, B, or AB or when a woman has type A and the infant has type B and vice versa. In the case of a type O mother and a type B infant (the father must carry an B allele), because the mother does not possess the B antigen on her red blood cells, she will make

cline   The distribution of a trait or allele across geographical space.

maternal-fetal incompatibility   Occurs when the mother produces antibodies against an antigen (for example, a red blood cell surface protein) expressed in the fetus that she does not possess.

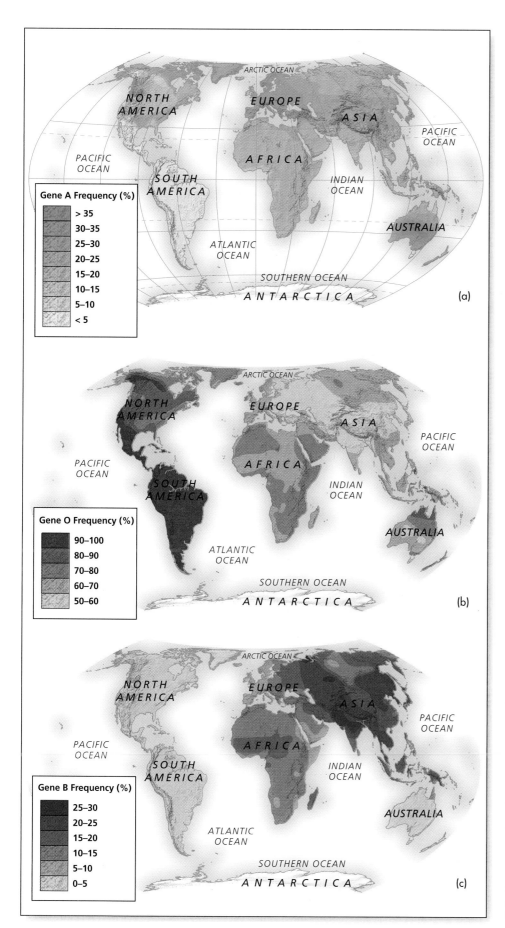

FIGURE 6.5 Clinal maps of ABO allele distributions in the indigenous populations of the world. (a) Frequency distribution of the *A* allele. (b) Frequency distribution of the *O* allele. (c) Frequency distribution of the *B* allele. *Source:* Adapted from Mourant et al, 1976.

rhesus (Rh) system Blood type system that can cause hemolytic anemia of the newborn through maternal-fetal incompatability if the mother is Rh-negative and the child is Rh-positive.

anti-B antibodies upon exposure to the fetus's blood. For much of the pregnancy, the maternal and fetal blood do not mix; however, at birth the mother is almost always exposed to fetal blood through ruptures in tissues caused by the delivery or separation of the placenta from the uterine wall. Upon exposure to the B antigen, the mother's immune system is primed to produce anti-B antibodies. In subsequent pregnancies, the red blood cells of fetuses that carry the B allele are subject to attack by the maternal anti-B antibodies, which can cross the placental barrier. When the infant is born, he or she can be anemic because of the reduction in the number of oxygen-carrying red blood cells. This is known as *hemolytic anemia.*

Hemolytic anemia caused by ABO maternal–fetal incompatibility is rare, and when it occurs it is usually mild. However, it is important to keep in mind that a mild illness in a traditional culture could have far more serious consequences than it would in a contemporary medical facility. There is some evidence that ABO incompatibilies can have a damaging affect early in pregnancy, resulting in a higher rate of spontaneous abortion (Bottini et al., 2001).

The **rhesus (RH) system,** another blood group, was originally identified by using antibodies made against rhesus macaque red blood cells. It is of particular clinical importance because maternal–fetal incompatibility in this system leads to the development of a much more severe form of anemia in the newborn, resulting in a disease called *erythroblastosis fetalis,* than does ABO incompatibility (one reason for this is that unlike the Rh factor, the A and B antigens are expressed in tissues other than the red blood cells, so there are fewer maternal antibodies available to attack the fetal red blood cells). The genetics of the Rh system are complex and involves three major genes with at least two alleles apiece (Cavalli-Sforza et al., 1994). For our purposes we can concentrate on one of these loci, which has two alleles, D and d. Individuals who are homozygous DD or heterozygous Dd are called *Rh-positive,* and those who are homozygous dd are *Rh-negative* (Figure 6.6). Similar to cases in which the

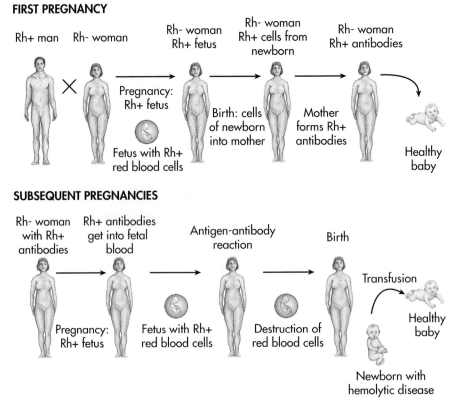

FIGURE 6.6 Maternal-fetal incompatibility in the Rh system.

mother is type O and the infant is type A, B, or AB, maternal–fetal incompatibility arises when the mother is Rh-negative and the infant is Rh-positive. The first pregnancy usually is fine, but subsequent incompatible pregnancies can lead to the development of severe hemolytic anemia in the newborn, which may necessitate blood transfusions. It has been found that giving the mother anti-D antibodies early in pregnancy can suppress her immunological response: The anti-D antibodies "intercept" the fetal red blood cells before the mother's immune system is exposed to them. This prevents development of anemia in the at-risk newborn.

Maternal–fetal incompatibility in both the ABO and Rh systems influences the distribution of their alleles in populations. For example, in the Rh system, only heterozygous offspring of an Rh-negative mother and an Rh-positive father are at risk of developing anemia. In a traditional culture, these infants would be at great risk of dying without reproducing. Simple genetic models indicate that in a population that has a D allele frequency of 50% or more, the d allele eventually will be lost. The opposite case is also true if the d allele frequency reaches 50% (assuming that no selection or other evolutionary factors are at play) (Cavalli-Sforza and Bodmer, 1999[1971]). Because of factors such as genetic drift, founder effect, and genetic bottlenecks, high rates of Rh-negative or Rh-positive individuals could evolve. However, only one population has a majority of Rh-negative individuals: the Basques of southern France and northern Spain. The Basque population was historically isolated and is well known for having a language unrelated to any other in Europe. Although one might predict that Rh-negative alleles should go to fixation, there is enough admixture with the predominantly Rh-positive surrounding populations that this may be unlikely.

The Human Leukocyte Antigen (HLA) System   Besides the ABO and Rh systems, several other blood systems are used in population genetic studies. These include the Diego, Duffy, Kell, Kidd, Lewis, Lutheran, and MNS systems. A different class of blood group markers is formed by the **human leukocyte antigen (HLA) system**. These antigens are proteins found on the surface of white rather than red blood cells. There are many classes of white blood cells, all of which are critical in the immune response (an elevated white blood cell count indicates that the body is fighting an infection). As most people know, the ABO antigens are critical for determining who can donate blood to whom. The HLA system is critical in matching donors and hosts for organ and skin transplants.

The HLA system is organized into two classes, more than a dozen loci, and hundreds of alleles (Meyer and Thomson, 2001). These genes are all located on the short arm of chromosome 6. Besides their critical importance in tissue typing for transplantation, HLA-A and HLA-B have also been used extensively in population genetics studies. Different HLA alleles are also associated with increased susceptibility to different diseases. Many of these are **autoimmune diseases**, those in which the pathological process involves the body's immune system attacking its own tissues. Allele HLA-B27 is associated with the development of *ankylosing spondylitis,* a form of arthritis that affects the pelvis and lower back. Rates of this disease (and of rheumatoid arthritis) are particularly high in some native North American groups and correspond to high frequencies of the HLA-B27 allele (Peschken and Esdaile, 1999). Another disease associated with a particular HLA genotype is *celiac disease,* an autoimmune disorder characterized by a digestive intolerance to gluten, a protein found in wheat, rye, and barley. Celiac disease causes damage to the small intestine, preventing the absorption of nutrients through its walls. The highest rates of celiac disease are found in Europe, where screening of newborns for the disease is routine in some countries (Volta et al., 2001).

Negative selection operates on the HLA alleles that are associated with the development of serious genetic diseases. However, some HLA alleles are associated with protection from a variety of infectious diseases, including malaria, HIV, hepatitis B, and bacterial diseases (Cooke and Hill, 2001). The high degree of variability

human leukocyte antigen (HLA) system Class of blood group markers formed by proteins expressed on the surface of white blood cells (leukocytes).

autoimmune diseases Occur when a body's immune system attacks its own tissues.

within the HLA system is evidence in itself that natural selection and other non-random evolutionary forces have been critical in shaping the distribution of its alleles (Meyer and Thomson, 2001).

GENE FLOW AND PROTEIN POLYMORPHISMS

Because allele frequencies for countless proteins vary from population to population, genetic polymorphisms can be used to look at patterns of gene flow and migration from one population to another. For example, because the A and B alleles are so rare in indigenous South American populations, the ABO system can be used to measure gene flow or admixture with European or African populations that have migrated to the region since 1500 A.D. This is despite the fact that on a worldwide basis, there is much overlap in the distribution of ABO alleles in different populations.

The history of the human species has been characterized by events involving migration and gene flow. Even when there are cultural prohibitions against mating with others outside the group, there is ample evidence that such matings occur. Official written records do not always indicate the scope of admixture between distinct cultural groups living in the same area.

Gene Flow in Contemporary Populations　Countless gene flow studies have been done on populations throughout the world. For example, the complex origins of the Hungarian people, who live in central Europe at the crossroads between Asia and Europe, have recently been examined using a variety of classic (protein) markers (Guglielmino et al., 2000). One Hungarian ethnic group, the Örség, were found to be particularly closely related to populations from the Ural Mountains in Central Asia. Hungarian is a non–Indo-European language of Uralic orgin, and these results confirmed oral histories and traditions that linked the Örség to populations that had migrated from the Ural region in the ninth century.

Numerous studies have also been done to trace the complex genetic history of Jewish populations in western Eurasia and Africa. The migrational history of Jews is complex, dating back to the *diaspora* or dispersal of the Jews from ancient Palestine to Babylonian exile in 586 B.C. The diaspora became a permanent feature of Jewish life and included events such as the expulsion of Jews from Spain in 1492. Gene flow studies have produced conflicting results, some indicating substantial admixture between Jewish and other populations located in an area and others indicating much less gene flow. More recently, Y-chromosome markers have provided new insights into the histories of some Jewish populations. The Lemba, or "Black Jews," of southern Africa have a long oral tradition of Jewish ancestry (a claim that has been regarded with more than a little skepticism). Consistent with this tradition, genetic studies indicate that about half of the Y-chromosomes in the Lemba population are of Semitic origin (Figure 6.7) (Spurdle and Jenkins, 1996). Michael Hammer and colleagues (2000) looked at Y-chromosome **haplotypes** in Jewish and non-Jewish men from populations throughout Europe, Africa (including a Lemba sample), and the Middle East. Haplotypes are combinations of alleles (or, at the sequence level, of mutations) that are found together in an individual. In many cases, combinations of alleles or mutations are more informative than alleles or mutations considered singly. Hammer and colleagues found that the Jewish populations closely resembled non-Jewish Middle Eastern populations, with whom they are presumed to share a common ancestry, in the distribution of Y-chromosome haplotypes, more so than non-Jewish populations near which they may currently be living. Thus Jewish populations, despite numerous migrations across a broad geographic area, appear to be more similar to one another and to non-Jewish Middle Eastern populations than to other populations, at least in terms of the Y-chromosome.

Several gene flow studies have been done in African American populations to assess the contribution of European alleles in the composition of their genet-

haplotypes　Combinations of alleles (or at the sequence level, mutations) that are found together in an individual.

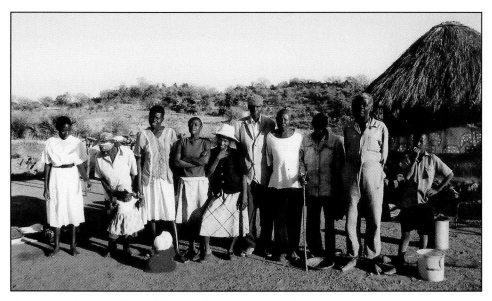

FIGURE 6.7   Members of the Lemba ethnic group from southern Africa.

ic structures. Although for much of U.S. history admixture between African and European Americans has been strongly proscribed, gene flow studies indicate that it was not an unusual occurrence. A classic genetic study using a **Duffy blood group** allele that is largely absent in Africa but common in European populations showed that European admixture in five African American populations ranged from 4% in Charleston, South Carolina, to 26% in Detroit (Reed, 1969). In a more recent study using autosomal DNA markers, mtDNA haplotypes, and Y-chromosome polymorphisms, Esteban Parra and colleagues (1998) confirmed these high rates of admixture. Looking at nine communities, they found admixture rates ranging from 11.6% in Charleston to 22.5% in New Orleans (Table 6.1). A sample from a Jamaican population showed a European proportion of only 6.8%, indicating a substantial difference between Afro-Caribbean and African American communities. The mtDNA (maternally inherited) and the Y-chromosome (paternally inherited) data indicated that gene flow from European to African American populations was strongly sex-biased, with men making a substantially greater contribution than women. This comes as no surprise, given that sexual contacts between male slave owners and female slaves were not uncommon.

Duffy blood group   Red blood cell system useful for studying admixture between African- and European-derived populations.

TABLE 6.1 European Genetic Contribution to African American and Jamaican Populations	
LOCATION	PERCENTAGE
Detroit	16.3
Maywood, Illinois	18.8
New York	19.8
Philadelphia	13.0
Pittsburgh	20.2
Baltimore	15.5
Charleston, South Carolina	11.6
New Orleans	22.5
Houston	16.9
Jamaica	6.8

Source: Parra et al. (1998).

Morphological Features and Gene Flow   Morphological features (such as eye or hair color) are rarely used today to study gene flow between populations. There are several reasons for this: Many morphological features have complex genetics, thus making patterns of inheritance difficult to discern; their expression in an individual may be highly subject to environmental factors during development; and more so than genetic markers, morphological markers may be subject to the forces of natural selection, leading, for example, to convergent evolution. Of course, even with our ability to recover ancient DNA, morphological features may be all we have to study gene flow in past populations.

One set of morphological features, dental traits, has been extensively used to study gene flow in skeletal populations. Some discrete dental traits appear to be transmitted in a simple genetic fashion, are resistant to environmental factors (except wear), and can be easily examined in large numbers of skeletal specimens. Christy Turner (1989, 1990) has argued that a constellation of dental features, known collectively as *sinodonty*, links northern Asian populations with the populations of the New World. Not all North American populations have high frequencies of sinodonty, but because it is absent elsewhere, it provides evidence of a migrational link or gene flow between the northern Asian and Native American populations. East Asian, Australian aborigine, and Ainu (aboriginal Japanese) populations exhibit a different dental pattern, which Turner calls *sundadonty*. Turner used eight dental features to distinguish sinodonts from sundadonts. For example, shovel-shaped incisors are more common among sinodonts than sundadonts, and four-cusped lower molars (cusps are the bumps on the chewing surfaces of molars; five is the typical number) are significantly more common in sundadonts than sinodonts (Figure 6.8). Turner places the origins of sinodonty at 18,000 years ago or earlier in northern China.

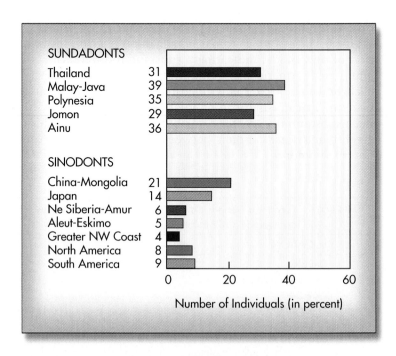

FIGURE 6.8   Number of lower molar cusps is one of the features used to distinguish sundadonts from sinodonts. Graph shows that 4-cusped molars are more common in sundadont populations rather than sinodont populations.

POLYMORPHISMS AND PHYLOGENETIC STUDIES

Allele frequencies, haplotype frequencies, and DNA and protein sequence information can all be used to construct an evolutionary tree, or **phylogeny**, relating populations (if frequency data are used) or individuals from different populations (if sequence data are used). The statistical mathematics underlying the construction of these trees is beyond the scope of this text, but the basic principles are not.

Constructing a Phylogenetic Tree   Any phylogenetic tree aims to cluster closely related populations together (Figure 6.9). Closely related populations share a *branch:* a lineage or a clade (see Chapter 5). Branching points, or *nodes,* in the tree should be placed with as high degree of statistical certainty as possible. These nodes represent evolutionary events leading to the separation of any pair (or groups) of populations. Longer branches and deeper nodes indicate that more evolution has occurred and thus that more time has elapsed since the separation of the two populations (assuming that evolutionary change is occurring at similar rates in different populations—not always the case when a nonneutral trait is being used). Whatever the source of data, the overriding concern in constructing an evolutionary tree is that it should be parsimonious. In other words, the phylogenetic tree produced from a dataset should be the one that incorporates the fewest number of evolutionary steps or events.

Phylogenetic trees are not precise reconstructions of evolutionary events. They are hypotheses about the way evolution happened, inferred from genetic or other kinds of data collected from extant or extinct populations. Even a tree that is statistically rigorous may be subject to different kinds of interpretation.

phylogeny   An evolutionary tree indicating relatedness and divergence of taxonomic groups.

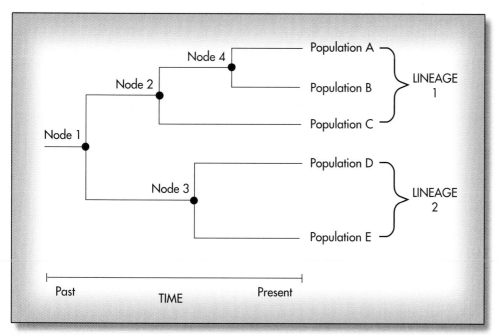

FIGURE 6.9   A generic phylogenetic tree. Populations A, B, and C share a lineage (or clade) and are more closely related to each other than populations D and E of lineage 2. Populations A and B share a more common ancestor (at node 4) with each other than they do with population C. The last time all five populations shared a common ancestor was at node 1.

A Genetic Tree of the World's Populations   Geneticist Luigi Luca Cavalli-Sforza and colleagues (1994) provided an extensive analysis of the distribution of 120 alleles (29 of which come from the HLA system) in forty-two populations throughout the world. The selection of these forty-two populations was based on several criteria, not least important of which was the availability of genetic data for inclusion in the analysis. They provide a good sample of the world's populations as they were distributed at the arbitrary cutoff date of 1492 A.D. The phylogenetic tree of these forty-two populations divides into nine major clusters: Africans (sub-Saharan), Caucasoids (Europeans), Caucasoids (non-Europeans), northern Mongoloids (excluding arctic populations), northeast Asian arctic populations, southern Mongoloids (mainland and island Southeast Asia) (Figure 6.10), New Guineans and Australians, inhabitants of the minor Pacific islands, and Americans.

Although slightly different trees result depending on the method used and how the populations are constructed, some basic conclusions are possible. First, the deep separation of the African populations from others is an indication that this reflects the earliest genetic event in human history. This event could have happened outside Africa, although palaeontological evidence indicates that modern humans evolved first in Africa, followed by migration to other parts of the world (see Chapters 14 and 15). A northern Eurasian cluster clearly includes both Caucasoid and northeast Asian (including arctic and American) populations. The relationships between Australians, New Guineans, and Southeast Asians are less clear-cut. One tree groups the Southeast Asians with the Australians and New Guineans, and another places them as an early split from the northern Eurasian cluster. Given the complex patterns of population movements throughout Southeast Asia and Melanesia into Polynesia and Micronesia, it is not surprising that unambiguous clusters are not always possible.

POLYMORPHISMS AND NATURAL SELECTION IN HUMAN POPULATIONS

We have already discussed several examples of the effects of natural selection on polymorphisms in human populations. For example negative selection probably is also working to reduce the frequencies of any number of HLA alleles associated

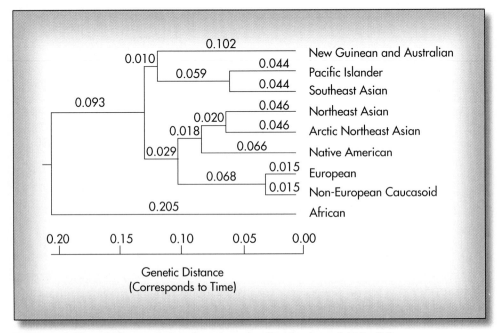

FIGURE 6.10   Phylogenetic tree based on the distribution of 120 alleles in 42 populations from around the world, clustered into 9 major groups. *Source:* Cavalli-Sforza et al. 1994.

with the development of autoimmune diseases, which may have initially reached high frequencies because of genetic drift or founder effects. On the other hand, it is clear that some HLA variants confer resistance to various infectious diseases. Why don't these variants go to fixation? If they confer resistance to a serious disease, then why do they remain polymorphisms rather than becoming a monomorphism? We will address this issue, but first let us look at a straightforward example of natural selection that has led to the evolution of a polymorphism at the species level.

lactose intolerant The inability to digest lactose, the sugar found in milk; most adult mammals (including humans) are lactose intolerant as adults.

THE EVOLUTION OF LACTOSE TOLERANCE

One of the main characteristics of mammals is that newborns and young animals suckle milk from their mothers. After weaning, young mammals are no longer directly dependent on their mothers for food, and they never drink milk again. The main carbohydrate in mammal milk is a sugar called *lactose*. Lactose is actually a *disaccharide*—or a sugar made up of two smaller sugars—composed of the monosaccharides glucose and galactose. In order for lactose to be metabolized, it must first be split into glucose and galactose; this is done by an enzyme called *lactase*, which is present in the small intestine of most young mammals. As mammals get older, their bodies shut down production of lactase, so older mammals cannot digest lactose. As adults, they are *lactose malabsorbers*. Indeed, many older mammals suffer gastric distress if they consume milk, with symptoms such as abdominal distention, flatulence, cramps, acidic stools, and diarrhea. These digestive problems are caused by the accumulation of lactose in the small intestine, which changes the osmotic activity in that part of the gut, leading to an influx of fluid (that is, diarrhea), and excess lactose in the large intestine, which is fermented by bacteria in the colon (that is, gas production). An individual who has these symptoms after consuming milk products is **lactose intolerant** (Figure 6.11).

It was once thought that humans were unique among mammals in the continued production of lactase through adulthood, which allows humans to digest lactose (milk products) as adults. However, research in the 1960s on European and African Americans demonstrated that only *some* humans were lactose tolerant as adults

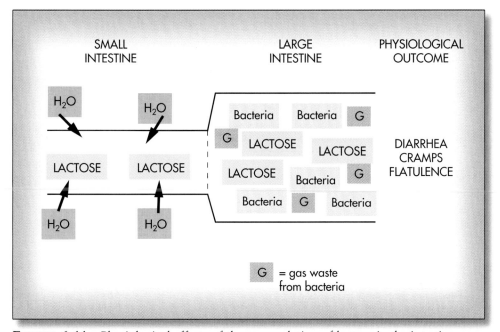

FIGURE 6.11 Physiological effects of the accumulation of lactose in the intestines of a lactose intolerant individual.

(Cuatrecasas et al., 1965). Indeed, as more research was done, it was discovered that most people in the world are lactose intolerant as adults and that lactase production is a highly polymorphic trait across the human species (Allen and Cheer, 1996). Table 6.2 presents lactose absorption rates for populations throughout the world. High-absorber populations are concentrated in Europe or in populations with a high degree of European admixture (such as Polynesian populations in New Zealand). In addition, some African ethnic groups, such as the Tussi, Fulani, and Hima, also have high rates of lactose tolerance (the African figures in the table are for countries, not ethnic groups). Other populations, such as many in Asia, some African, and many Native American groups, have very low frequencies of lactose absorbers.

The Genetics of Lactase Production   The genetics of lactase production is reasonably well understood. The lactase gene is located on chromosome 2. Continued lactase production in adulthood is caused by a dominant allele (called the *lactase persistence allele,* or *LCT*P*), so heterozygous and homozygous individuals with this allele can produce lactase. The lactase enzymes produced by lactose tolerant and lactose intolerant adults are identical in structure and function, although there are many "silent mutations" in the base pair sequence that can be used for phylogenetic studies of this locus (Hollox et al., 2001). Variants found in regions several thousand base pairs from the lactase gene differentiate lactase persistent from lactase nonpersistent individuals (Enattah et al., 2002). These regions clearly have a regulatory function (as yet undetermined) in the timing of lactase synthesis.

TABLE 6.2 Lactose Absorption Rates in Different Populations	
POPULATION	PERCENTAGE LACTOSE ABSORBERS
AFRICA	
Bantu (West Africa)	4
Watutsi (East Africa)	83
Nilotic (Sudan)	39
South Africa	17
ASIA	
South India	33
Japan	0
Thailand	2
Taiwan Chinese	0
EUROPE	
Britain	94
Germany	85
Sweden	100
Italy	25–50
NORTH AMERICA	
European American	80–94
African American	25–30
Apache	0
Chippewa	30
PACIFIC	
Fiji	0
New Zealand Maori	36
Australian Aborigines	16
Papua New Guinea	11
Sources: Allen and Cheer (1996), Molnar (2002).	

Explanations for the Lactase Polymorphism   Lactose tolerant individuals are found at high frequency in populations with a long history of dairying and using milk products (Simoons, 1970; McKracken, 1971; Durham, 1991). There has been strong selection for LCT*P in these populations. In nondairying populations, the distribution of haplotypes associated with lactase nonpersistence are consistent with evolution primarily by genetic drift (Hollox et al., 2001). The *cultural historical hypothesis,* suggested by Simoons and McKracken independently, proposes that in populations where animals were domesticated and milk products used (dating back to about 9,000 B.C. in the Middle East), there has been strong selection for lactase tolerant individuals. Milk is a valuable food providing both carbohydrates and proteins, and in an environment where other nutritional resources might be scarce, individuals who could digest milk as adults would have a substantial survival advantage. Modest selective advantages (relative increases in fitness) of 5–10% could account for the high frequencies of lactose tolerance found in northern European populations over a period of about 6,000 years (Aoki, 1986; Feldman and Cavalli-Sforza, 1989).

There are populations in which dairying is present but lactose tolerance frequencies are low, such as those in central and southern Asia. In many of these populations, milk is not drunk raw but is processed into yogurt or cheese. In the making of yogurt and cheese, bacteria are used to convert lactose to lactic acid. Thus the ability to digest lactose is not critical in obtaining the nutrients from these products, and lactose tolerant individuals historically have had no selection advantage in these populations.

The evolution of lactose tolerance is a clear-cut example of the interaction of biological and cultural factors in shaping microevolutionary processes within our species.

BALANCED POLYMORPHISMS: SICKLE CELL AND OTHER CONDITIONS

In any population, the polymorphism for lactose digestion ability in adulthood can be explained in terms of cultural practices, natural selection, gene flow, and genetic drift. There are no particular reasons for a population to be polymorphic for this feature: Some populations approach 100% lactose tolerant, and others approach 100% lactose intolerant. However, when we look at other genetic systems and populations, it appears that there are polymorphisms that are quite stable and are not the result of obvious historical factors. Something is preventing alleles from going to fixation or being lost. This is called a **balanced polymorphism**. A fascinating aspect of microevolution is the attempt to explain mechanisms underlying balanced polymorphisms.

The large number of variants present in the HLA system may be evidence of a balanced polymorphism in this genetic system. If HLA variants are useful for conferring resistance to infectious diseases, then some HLA polymorphisms may be maintained as a **frequency-dependent balanced polymorphism** (Cooke and Hill, 2001). In this situation, an allele (or trait) has an advantage in a population relative to other alleles until it reaches a certain frequency in the population. If it becomes more common than this frequency, it loses its advantage, and the balanced polymorphism is maintained. In the HLA system, an HLA variant may confer resistance to a specific infectious disease. While it is rare in the population, it will have an advantage because the infectious agent itself has not evolved to overcome whatever defense it confers. However, as the resistant variant becomes more common in the population, there will be selection on the infectious agent to adjust to it. Eventually, a frequency will be reached at which the disease-resistant variant loses its advantage. A high degree of polymorphism in a population may result as this process is repeated for multiple alleles, and the resulting polymorphism is stable or balanced.

Heterozygous Advantage   It has been noted that genetic diversity in breeding plants and animals often results in improved yields; this is called hybrid vigor or *heterosis.* It is assumed that this may result from a high frequency of heterozygosity at many

balanced polymorphism
A stable polymorphism in a population in which natural selection prevents any of the alternative phenotypes (or underlying alleles) from becoming fixed or being lost.

frequency-dependent balanced polymorphism   Balanced polymorphism that is maintained because one (or more) of the alternative phenotypes has a selective advantage over the other phenotypes only when it is present in the population below a certain frequency.

heterozygous advantage With reference to a particular genetic system, the situation in which heterozygotes have a selective advantage over homozygotes (for example, sickle cell disease); a mechanism for maintaining a balanced polymorphism.

loci underlying a complex genetic trait. However, **heterozygous advantage** has been observed in much simpler genetic contexts. In a one-gene, two-allele situation, a balanced polymorphism will be maintained if the heterozygotes have a selective advantage over both of the homozygotes. This is just the opposite of what happens in cases of maternal–fetal incompatibility, which actually works against the maintenance of a polymorphism.

The classic example of a balanced polymorphism maintained by heterozygous advantage is the high frequency of the *sickle cell trait* in some populations with endemic *malaria*. In Chapter 4, we discussed the molecular and cellular genetics of sickle cell disease, which is caused by an abnormal hemoglobin protein, HbS (as opposed to the normal HbA), that impairs the ability of red blood cells to deliver oxygen to the tissues of the body. It is an autosomal recessive disease, and people who are heterozygotes are carriers of the condition. In a nonmalarial environment, the carriers show few signs of illness, although they may be slightly at risk in low-oxygen environments.

Malaria may have killed more people—especially children—than any other infectious disease. According to the World Health Organization, more than 40% of the world's population lives in malarial regions, it affects 300–500 million people per year, and it kills a million children per year under the age of 6 in Africa alone. In addition, chronic malaria has incalculable negative economic, social, and political effects. There is no doubt that malaria has exerted a strong selection pressure on human populations for many thousands of years.

Malaria is caused by protozoa from the genus *Plasmodium*. Of the 120 species in this genus, 4 cause malaria: *P. malariae*, *P. vivax*, *P. falciparum*, and *P. ovale*. The symptoms of malaria include fever, anemia, inflammation of the spleen, and headache. Cerebral malaria is especially serious and may lead to insanity, unconsciousness, and death.

Humans are infected with the *Plasmodium* parasite via the bite of a female *Anopheles* mosquito, which is an essential carrier or *vector* of the disease. The *Plasmodium* life cycle requires both human and mosquito hosts. Because malaria depends on the mosquito for its spread from human host to host, the ability of the mosquito to survive and breed is a critical factor in local patterns of malarial expression. For example, in regions that have a pronounced dry season, mosquito breeding is highly seasonal, and malaria does not become a stable and constant aspect of life. In contrast, malaria is endemic in wet, equatorial climates in Africa and southeast Asia, where mosquito breeding continues year-round.

Although human intervention has worked to limit the range of malaria, human cultural practices have also helped to increase its impact on human populations. The development of slash-and-burn agriculture in Africa led to clearing of tropical forests, an increase in the amount of standing, stagnant water, and higher human population densities (Figure 6.12) (Livingstone, 1958). All of these worked to increase the disease's spread. In addition, the disrupted tropical forest conditions fa-

FIGURE 6.12 Slash and burn agriculture in Africa.

vored breeding of a particular species of mosquito, *A. gambiae,* which is the vector for *P. falciparum,* which in turn causes the most lethal form of malaria. This was the context for the evolution of high frequencies of the HbS allele (Allison, 1954).

In malarial environments, individuals who are heterozygous HbS HbA have higher reproductive fitness than either HbA HbA or HbS HbS homozygotes (Figure 6.13). Individuals who are homozygous HbS HbS have sickle cell anemia, a disease that, in traditional settings, drastically shortens the life span, precluding reproduction. However, heterozygous individuals with sickle cell trait are more resistant to developing malaria than homozygous HbA HbA individuals because the presence of abnormal hemoglobin in the red blood cells of heterozygous individuals, though not enough to affect human physiology in any meaningful way, seriously affects the life cycle of the *P. falciparum* parasite. In these malarial regions, heterozygote individuals are overrepresented in populations over age 45, indicating their enhanced survival. The HbS allele cannot go to fixation because the homozygotes are seriously impaired. Thus the HbA–HbS polymorphism is maintained by heterozygous advantage.

Sickle cell carrier frequencies are almost 40% in some African populations. High HbS frequencies are also found in Mediterranean, Middle Eastern, and Indian populations, reflecting former and present malarial loads in these regions. African Americans also have a high frequency of HbS, which reflects their ancestral populations. However, without malaria in the environment, heterozygotes are no longer at an advantage, and the frequency of HbS is declining because of the reduced fitness of HbS homozygotes.

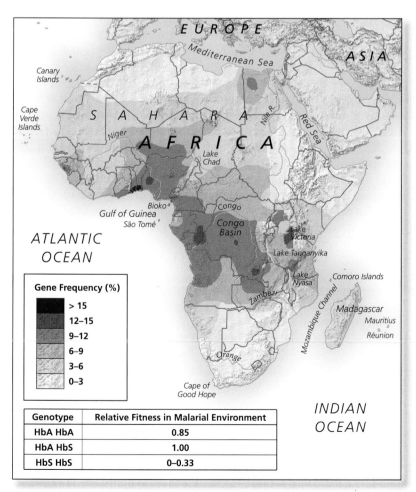

Gene Frequency (%)
> 15
12–15
9–12
6–9
3–6
0–3

Genotype	Relative Fitness in Malarial Environment
HbA HbA	0.85
HbA HbS	1.00
HbS HbS	0–0.33

FIGURE 6.13 Clinal map of the distribution of HbS in Africa.

Several other alleles that directly or indirectly affect red blood cell physiology (such as the thalassemias, which directly affect the structure of hemoglobin, and G6PD polymorphisms, which affect key metabolic pathways) are also found in high frequency in malarial areas. These conditions, along with sickle cell trait, are compelling evidence of the importance of malaria as a selective force in human evolution.

Other Possible Disease-Associated Balanced Polymorphisms   The sickle cell polymorphism is the best example we have of a balanced polymorphism maintained by heterozygous advantage. It is often said that it is the only example we have. However, the high frequencies in some populations of alleles responsible for two other autosomal recessive diseases—*Tay–Sachs disease* and *cystic fibrosis*—have led some to suggest that a similar mechanism may be underlying their polymorphisms (Smith, 1998). For both of these genetic diseases, the hypothesized selective agent in the environment was *tuberculosis,* a bacterial disease that was once one of the main causes of death in urban populations in Europe and the United States.

Tay–Sachs disease (TS) causes the accumulation of a fatty substance in the nerve cells of the brain. There is no treatment for the disease. Although a child with TS is normal for the first few months of life, as the disease takes hold there is a progressive loss of mental and physical function, resulting in death within a few years. Tay–Sachs is found at high frequency in Ashkenazi (European) Jewish populations and occurs at a rate of about 0.2–0.4 in 1,000, which makes it about 100 times more common in these populations than others. A rate of 0.4 in 1,000 would indicate a TS allele frequency of 2% and a heterozygote carrier frequency of 3.9% (0.98 * 0.02 * 2) in Ashkenazi populations. Several geneticists have argued that given the ancient origins of the TS allele in Palestine, some selection advantage—specifically resistance of the heterozygotes to tuberculosis or typhoid (Myrianthopolous and Aronson, 1966; Chakravarti and Chakraborty, 1978)—must be working to maintain its presence in the historically isolated and diverse Ashkenazi populations.

Cystic fibrosis (CF) is the most common autosomal genetic disorder in northern European–derived populations (Ratjen and Döring, 2003). Although it is found in other populations, the rates are much higher in populations with European ancestry. CF is a disease of the mucus- and sweat-producing glands, characterized by symptoms such as excessive sweating (leading to mineral imbalances in the blood, which can in turn lead to heart problems) and the accumulation of thick mucus in the lungs and intestine. Lung disease is the most common cause of death in CF; today, with medical treatment, the average life span of a CF sufferer is about 30 years. In European populations, the rate of cystic fibrosis is about 0.5 in 1,000 births. As with Tay–Sachs, given the obvious reduction in fertility of the homozygous sufferers, several investigators have suggested that the heterozygote CF carriers may be more resistant than normal homozygotes to developing disease. Meindl (1987) argued specifically that CF carriers have a greater ability to resist damage caused by pulmonary (lung) tuberculosis and that there has been selection for the CF allele in European populations since tuberculosis first became a public health problem in the sixteenth century. Other investigators have suggested that the CF allele may confer a resistance to intestinal bacteria that are known to induce diarrhea, which can pose a serious health risk, especially to children (Hansson, 1988).

Although intriguing and plausible cases can be made for heterozygous advantage in CF and TS, it is important to keep things in perspective: HbS carrier frequencies approach 40% in some malarial populations, compared with 3–5% for CF and TS carriers in their high-frequency populations. The HbS heterozygous advantage may simply be that much greater, or its allele frequencies may have had more time to evolve. It seems likely that heterozygous advantage is an important factor in determining CF and TS allele frequencies, but we do not know whether sickle cell disease is a particularly accurate model for the maintenance of these other polymorphisms.

ADAPTATION AND ADAPTABILITY

A variant that can be demonstrated to increase fitness in a specific environment (such as the ability to digest lactose as an adult) is an adaptation in the classic evolutionary sense. However, adaptation is a more general phenomenon. All organisms exhibit some degree of *biological plasticity:* an ability on the part of individuals to physiologically respond to changes in the environment. This is obvious in poor environments; for example, if there is not enough food, an animal will become thinner. When the phenotype of an organism reflects *positive* changes that arise in the context of short- or long-term exposure to a set of environmental conditions, this is called **adaptability**. Differences in environments can thus lead to population- level differences, as individuals within the populations biologically adapt to local conditions. Because of biological plasticity and adaptability, populations may phenotypcially differentiate from one another without any underlying changes to the genotypes.

Adaptation and adaptability are not always separate and distinct issues. The ability of a phenotype to respond differently to different environments an organism may encounter in a lifetime may in itself be an adaptation. When we look at different populations adapting to similar environmental conditions, one population may have adapted to the environment in a more genetic sense, whereas the other may be adapting in the context of biological plasticity. Or populations may vary in their adaptability to specific environmental conditions depending on the biological variation present in those populations.

LEVELS OF ADAPTABILITY

The process of very short-term changes in physiology that occur in response to changes in environmental conditions is called **acclimatization**. We are all familiar with acclimatization. When people from sea level move to high altitude, they have to cope with a reduction in the amount of oxygen available in the atmosphere. Initially, the body physiologically adapts by breathing more quickly and increasing heart rate. Over time, more profound changes in the body occur, such as an increase in red blood cell production, which allows the individual to cope with a lower-oxygen environment. Tanning is another example of acclimatization. The transient darkening of the skin in lighter-skinned individuals is an acclimatization response to increased ultraviolet radiation in the atmosphere (see Chapter 17).

In contrast to acclimatization, adaptability refers to the physiological changes that arise in individuals who have lived their entire lives under a certain set of environmental conditions (Figure 6.14 on page 154). Thus their bodies reflect the influence of the environment on development as they were growing up and the long-term effects of continued exposure to such an environment.

Again, acclimatization, adaptability, and genetic adaptation are all interacting forces in the production of individual phenotypes. They reflect different mechanisms that organisms possess to adapt to the environments in which they live. Humans also use cultural adaptations to cope with the environment (Box 6.2 on page 155). These cultural adaptations can interact with biological adaptations to shape patterns of human variation.

HEAT AND COLD

From the arctic to the desert, humans live in a vast array of thermal environments, some of them with marked seasonality. One way we cope with changes in ambient temperature is through the cultural adaptation of wearing more or less clothing. But in addition to clothing, humans display a variety of physiological adaptations to heat and cold, some of which reflect adaptations of a genetic kind, whereas others are better described in terms of acclimatization and adaptability (Moran, 2000; Beall and Steegman, 2000).

adaptability The ability of an individual organism to make positive anatomical or physiological changes after short- or long-term exposure to stressful environmental conditions.

acclimatization Short-term changes in physiology that occur in an organism in response to changes in environmental conditions.

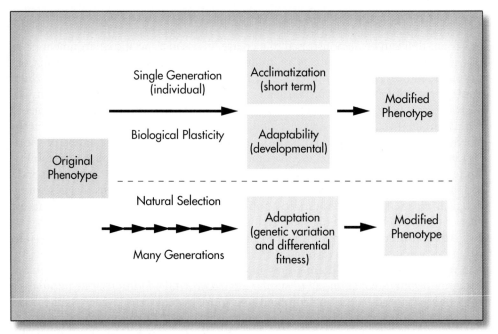

FIGURE 6.14   Adaptability and adaptation.

When people get too hot, the body responds through a process of *vasodilation* and sweat. Vasodilation (which appears as flushing in lighter-skinned people) increases blood flow to the surface of the body, which allows heat from the core of the body to be dissipated into the environment. The primary mechanism for dissipating heat at the surface of the body is sweating. The human body is unusual (although not unique) among mammals in having more than a million specialized sweat glands distributed over the skin. Despite the great range of thermal environments in which people live, there is almost no population variation in the number of sweat glands per person. This may reflect the fact that we are ultimately of tropical origin and that our bodies are well adapted to this kind of environment.

The evaporation of 1 liter of sweat removes 560 kcal of heat from the body, and people can sweat up to 4 liters/hour (Beall and Steegman, 2000). Heat stroke—when the core temperature of the body reaches 41°C (105.8°F)—is a serious condition, with the depletion of fluid from the body unleashing a cascade of events that ultimately leads to the coagulation of blood and the death of brain tissue. Even today, heat waves in urban environments kill hundreds or even thousands of people. Heat is a strong selective force.

Cold is also a strong selective force in environments where temperatures go significantly below freezing. Death from hypothermia is likely to result if the body's core temperature falls to 31–32°C (88–90°F). Because the body's reaction to cold is to decrease blood flow to the periphery—*vasoconstriction*—in order to maintain core temperature, frostbite, resulting in serious damage to the appendages and face, is another serious consequence of prolonged exposure to cold. Another basic acclimatization mechanism to cold is shivering. A decline of the body's core temperature by 2–3°C brings on the shivering response, which generates heat.

Human populations show significant variation in response to cold. In the Korean War, U.S. soldiers of African ancestry suffered higher rates of frostbite than those of European ancestry (Schuman, 1953). However, there is no particular evidence that European-derived populations are particularly cold-adapted; the difference between European American and African American soldiers in frostbite susceptibility may have resulted from the fact that African Americans in general show a more acute sympathetic nervous response to stress, which may lead to a more pronounced vasoconstriction response to cold (Beall and Steegman, 2000).

Box 6.2 Technology and Extreme Environments

Human beings have had thousands of years to adapt to certain kinds of natural environments. However, our technological prowess allows us both to exploit and to create new environments. These new environments require a physiological response from our bodies if we are to survive within them.

A *zero-gravity* or *microgravity* environment is one of the most exotic to which any human being would have to adapt (Williams, 2003) (Figure A). Since the advent of extended (weeks and months) stays in space, with the Skylab and Mir programs and the development of the International Space Station, dozens of people have had to deal with how their bodies react to an environment essentially free of the effects of gravity. Over time, people in a microgravity environment have muscle atrophy and loss of muscle strength. There are also cardiovascular changes, which can affect the ability to maintain blood pressure after one returns to Earth. The most critical change may be the loss of calcium in bone. In certain bones, prolonged microgravity exposure causes calcium levels to drop two standard deviations below normal levels. Although this loss is mostly reversible when one returns to gravity, it is not known what the effects would be after a very long-range flight, such as would be needed for a manned mission to Mars. Another medical issue that arises with pro-

longed microgravity exposure involves how the symptoms of various diseases might be influenced by bodily changes. For example, physicians recognize appendicitis by the presence of pain in a certain part of a patient's abdomen (although it varies widely). In space, the effects of microgravity on both the structure and function of the gastrointestinal tract could totally change how appendicitis presents to physician (Williams, 2003).

In contrast to the small numbers of people affected by the space environment, billions of people around the world are subject to the effects of industrial pollution in the environment. Lawrence Schell and Elaine Hills (2002) argue that polluted environments, as much as high-altitude or hot or cold climates, should be considered extreme environments to which humans must adapt. Industrial pollution has been a problem for some human populations for more than 150 years, and even as some parts of the developed world clean up their air and water, people living in developing countries are increasingly being exposed to toxic substances in their environments. Air pollutants, such as carbon monoxide, sulfur dioxide, and ozone, contribute to increased mortality rates and may also affect prenatal and postnatal growth. Exposure to lead, mercury, and other substances may also affect growth and have cognitive effects. Schell and Hills point out that

people with the highest exposure to one pollutant are also likely to have high exposure to others. These people also tend to be the poorest in a society, thus the human biology of pollution exposure interacts with social issues such as access to food, health care, and adequate housing.

Human technological achievements can be characterized as triumphant, as in the "conquest of space," or tragic, as in the "poisoning of the environment" by pollution. In either case, technology places individual human bodies into new environments to which they are not well adapted. It will be interesting to see what the long-term effects of exposure to these environments will be.

FIGURE A A human in a microgravity environment.

Humans can cope with temperatures in the freezing range via a combination of shivering and vasoconstriction. Subcutaneous fat also helps insulate the core of the body from the external cold. Populations vary in how these mechanisms are used to deal with cold. Arctic Inuit populations, who must deal with extreme cold, use cultural adaptations such as clothing, combined with biological adaptations, such as subcutaneous fat storage and vasoconstriction, to cope with cold on an ongoing basis. In addition, research involving hand immersion in a cold water bath indicates that Inuit maintain higher hand temperatures than European or African Americans after prolonged exposure to cold (Meehan, 1955). At the other extreme, desert-dwelling Australian aborigines must cope with a great range of temperatures on a daily and seasonal basis. In winter, they sleep in near-freezing temperatures uncovered and without shelter. They cope with the cold by using an extreme vasoconstriction response, which causes the skin surface temperature to fall 2.5°C. Given that the temperatures they must cope with are not severely cold, frostbite does not

Bergmann's rule   Stipulates that body size is larger in colder climates to conserve body temperature.

Allen's rule   Stipulates that in warmer climates, the limbs of the body are longer relative to body size to dissipate body heat.

occur, and they conserve energy while maintaining adequate core body temperatures. It is assumed that the adaptive responses seen in these populations are a result of both genetic adaptation and the process of developmental adaptability.

BODY SIZE AND SHAPE

In the nineteenth century, two biologists, Carl Bergmann (1814–1865) and Joel Asaph Allen (1838–1921), looked at the relationship between body size and climate in a wide range of mammals. They found that within polytypic species, there were predictable relationships between body form and proportions and temperature. **Bergmann's rule** (1847) focuses on body size. He found that the colder the climate, the larger the body. This makes geometric sense in that as volume increases, surface area decreases as a proportion of the volume. This would decrease the rate of heat dissipation through the surface, which helps to maintain a higher core temperature. **Allen's rule** (1877) focuses on the appendages of the body. For example, limbs should be longer relative to body size in warmer climates because that would help to dissipate heat, whereas shorter limbs in colder climates would conserve body heat. An example of Bergman's and Allen's rules can be found in comparing artic and desert hares (Figure 6.15). The ears of the desert hare are much longer than those of the arctic hare and the body much leaner and rangier; both are features that dissipate heat.

Do Allen's and Bergmann's rule hold for human populations? In general, yes. If we look at humans adapted to extreme environments, such as Inuit in the Arctic and Nilotic peoples from East Africa, we see that the Inuit body seems to be structured to conserve heat, whereas the African body is designed to dissipate heat (Figure 6.16). Looking at a broad range of populations, there is a general trend among humans for larger body size and greater sitting height (that is, body length) to be associated with colder climates, whereas relative span (fingertip to fingertip length divided by height) tends to be greater in warmer temperatures (that is, longer appendages relative to body size) (Roberts, 1978).

Because it seems unlikely that an Inuit person raised in East Africa would grow up with drastically modified limb and body proportions, should we assume that the associations between body form and climate in humans always result from genetic differences? The evidence that body size proportions reflect developmental adaptability is not particularly strong. The results of a classic study conducted in

(a)   (b)

FIGURE 6.15   Bergmann's and Allen's rules expressed in two rabbit species.   (a) A snowshoe hare.   (b) A desert-living black-tailed jack rabbit.

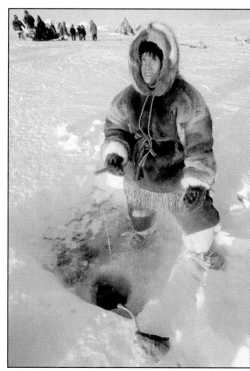

(a)

(b)

FIGURE 6.16 Bergmann's and Allen's rule expressed in two human populations. (a) Sudanese tribesman have body types adapted to warm climates. (b) Inuit people have body types adapted to cold climates.

the 1950s on U.S. soldiers showed a relationship between state of origin (that is, warmer or colder) and body proportions (Newman and Munroe, 1955) and was interpreted to represent an example of adaptability or acclimatization rather than adaptation. However, a recent analysis of updated Army data shows that if one takes into account whether the soldiers are of African or European ancestry, the climate association disappears (Steegman, 2003). Whites have shorter legs and longer trunks than blacks, and warmer (that is, southern) states may have a greater representation of blacks than colder states.

One study shows that climate change may affect primate phenotypes in accordance with Allen's and Bergmann's rules (Paterson, 1996). In the 1960s, two troops of Japanese macaques (*Macaca fuscata*) were transferred from one location in Japan to an Oregon primate center. Subsequently, one of the troops was moved to a facility in Texas. Analysis of long-term records (more than 20 years) on body size and proportions in the troops showed that by the 1990s, the Oregon monkeys were significantly larger than their Texas cousins, whereas the Texas monkeys had significantly longer limbs. The Oregon monkeys lived at a latitude of 45° N, whereas the Texas troop was at 28° N; the Texas site was substantially warmer. Thus the results were in accordance with predictions based on Allen's and Bergmann's rules. Although natural selection could have been responsible for the body changes, it would be surprising to see such effects after only two generations and in the absence of any obvious differences in fertility.

LIVING AT HIGH ALTITUDE

Humans originally evolved in a warm, humid climate, which was at low altitude. But millions of people today live at very high altitudes of 3,500–4,000 m

(11,600–13,200 ft), in environments that are typically dry and cold (Figure 6.17). Another major difference between high- and low-altitude environments is that atmospheric pressure is much less at high altitude. Although oxygen makes up the same proportion of the air at high and low altitude (21%), the lower pressure means that hemoglobin molecules in red blood cells take in fewer oxygen molecules with each breath—about one-third less at 4,000 m than at sea level (Harrison et al., 1988; Beall, 2001). The effects of altitude on oxygen availability start to become an issue at around 2,500 m.

Any person accustomed to breathing at sea level who goes to one of these high-altitude locations is at risk of *hypoxia,* or "oxygen starvation." Immediate acclimatization to hypoxia involves increasing heart and breathing rates in order to increase circulation of oxygen. This is only a temporary solution, and the long-term effects of increased lung ventilation include headaches, tunnel vision, and fainting. Hemoglobin concentrations are increased by initially reducing the volume of blood plasma, followed by an increase in the production of red blood cells. Over time, the maximal oxygen consumption capacity reduces, which is an adaptation to the reduction in oxygen available. There are few indications that high altitude alone poses any particular long-term health problems. Growth is slower in children, but the total growth period is prolonged, so overall size is not decreased (Frisancho and Baker, 1970). High altitude has been no barrier to the development of large-scale, well-populated civilizations.

The inhabitants of three high-altitude populations have been extensively studied to determine the mechanisms underlying adaptation to hypoxia. These include Andean populations in South America, Tibetans in south Asia, and Ethiopians in Africa (Beall, 2001; Beall et al., 2002). A striking result of these studies is that there does not appear to be a single way in which humans adapt to high altitude: A variety of mechanisms or combinations of mechanisms are observed. For example, the increase in ventilation induced by hypoxia, the *hypoxic ventilatory response* (HVR), is initially very high in lowland people who go to high altitude, although it reduces significantly over time as they acclimatize. Andean and Tibetan populations show significant differences in HVR. The Andean populations show a marked blunting in HVR, resembling the acclimatization response of lowlanders at high altitude. In contrast, Tibetan populations maintain a higher ventilation response, which is close to those observed in sea level populations and twice that of Andean populations.

We mentioned that hemoglobin concentrations increase in low-altitude individuals going to high altitude. Another difference between Andean and Tibetan

FIGURE 6.17 Anthropologist Andrea Wiley (left) investigates the effects of high altitude living on reproductive health in Ladakh, India.

populations is that whereas increased hemoglobin concentration is seen in Andean individuals, it is not seen in Tibetans. Cynthia Beall's (2001) analysis of several studies shows that at a mean elevation of 3,859 m, the hemoglobin concentration for acclimatized lowlanders was 18.2 g/dL, for Andean men it was 18.1 g/dL, and for Tibetan men it was only 16.9 g/dL. Ethiopian males have a concentration of 15.9 g/dL, which is within 2% of the U.S. male sea level value of 15.3 g/dL (Beall et al., 2002). Ethiopians living at only 2,400 m have similar hemoglobin concentrations to those living at about 3,500 m, indicating that there is no increase of hemoglobin with altitude in this population. Although Ethiopian and Tibetan populations have similarly low (for high altitude) levels of hemoglobin, they differ in the extent of oxygen saturation in arterial blood. Tibetans have low oxygen saturation compared with sea level populations, which is not surprising because they do not produce more hemoglobin to deal with the reduced atmospheric pressure. However, the Ethiopians have oxygen saturation percentages similar to those seen in sea level populations. Basically, the Ethiopian population at high altitude has a blood oxygen profile that resembles most other populations at sea level.

ADAPTIBILITY TO WATER

There are no human populations that live under water. However, there are populations whose inhabitants traditionally have made a living on what they can harvest from the sea. Tribal groups in Southeast Asia known as "sea gypsies" have long been known for their diving and swimming ability, which they use to collect shells, clams, and sea cucumbers (Gislén et al., 2003). The Moken are one such group living in coastal areas of Burma and Thailand. Moken children are expert divers and are noted for their ability to locate objects under water without the benefit of diving goggles or masks (Figure 6.18).

Being terrestrial animals, humans are not well adapted to seeing under water. We lose about two-thirds of our focusing power under water, which explains why everything appears blurry to us and it is almost impossible to pick out small objects. Given this limitation, the ability of Moken children to pick out small objects under water is remarkable. In a study comparing a group of Moken children with a group of European children, Anna Gislén and her colleagues (2003) found that both groups of children had equivalent vision out of the water. The underwater visual acuity of the Moken children, however, was twice as good as that of the European children.

How do they see under water? The eye focuses through a process known as accommodation, which involves, among other things, constricting the pupil.

FIGURE 6.18   Moken children can see small objects under water.

Gislén and colleagues found that unlike European children, Moken children accommodate under water by constricting their pupils. Underwater environments typically are darker than open-air environments, so the natural response of the pupil is to expand under water, not constrict. Somehow, accommodation in Moken children takes precedence over pupil expansion to compensate for the reduction in light. Furthermore, underwater pupil constriction and accommodation in the Moken children are at the known limits of human performance for children their age.

As in other examples of coping with extreme environments, it is not clear whether the Moken ability to see under water results from a genetic adaptation or is an example of human adaptability or acclimatization. People can be taught to voluntarily accommodate to some extent, so this may simply represent an extreme version of that kind of learning. However, there is no evidence that Moken children trained to accommodate except by diving under water. On the other hand, given their traditional lifestyle, the ability to accommodate under water may have been strongly selected for.

Human variation is a truly multifaceted topic. It goes right to the heart of what it is to be a human being. Although in the past some scientists looked at human variation as a means of dividing our species into competing groups, contemporary views emphasize differences without resorting to division. Human diversity is a beautiful thing, and that diversity reflects our extraordinary ability to adapt to different environments and our penchant for migrating across great swaths of the planet. Our individual biologies reflect where we came from, in both a genetic and environmental sense. We are all products of a dual heritage.

SUMMARY

1. Why do we say that *Homo sapiens* is a polytypic species?

A polytypic species is one that can be divided into local populations that differ from each other by more than one phenotypic trait. Human populations exhibit substantial population-level diversity, which can be observed both genetically and anatomically.

2. How do the biological and genetic definitions of *population* differ?

The classic biological definition of *population* focuses on the organism: A population is a potentially interbreeding group of individuals. A genetic population—sometimes called a deme—is defined in terms of that genetic composition of a group of animals, expressed, for example, in terms of allele frequencies. Both viewpoints agree that populations defined within a species are fluid and that gene flow or migration can occur between populations.

3. Compare and contrast the terms *race* and *subspecies*.

A subspecies is defined as a group of local populations within a species that share a geographic range and can be distinguished from other subspecies based on one or more phenotypic traits. In biology, a subspecies is the same thing as race. Historically, however, many classifications of human races, both formal and informal, have incorporated behavioral, cultural, and sociological factors that have extended the definition of human race beyond that of a biological subspecies.

4. What is maternal–fetal incompatibility, and how does it influence allele frequencies in a population?

Maternal–fetal incompatibility arises in the context of the ABO blood type system and, more critically (from a medical point of view), in the Rh system. It occurs when the mother does not possess a red blood cell surface protein, while the fetus does (inherited from the father). In the case of an Rh-negative mother, the Rh-positive fetus causes her to create antibodies against the Rh-positive blood cells. Although the first incompatible pregnancy usually is normal, in subsequent incompatible pregnancies, her immune system will produce antibodies that attack the red blood cells of the infant, resulting in severe anemia of the newborn.

5. Why did lactose tolerance evolve in some human populations?

Mammals typically lose the ability to digest lactose, the sugar found in milk, after weaning. Most humans share this mammalian characteristic. However, in human populations that have a long history of dairying, a high frequency of individuals continue to produce the enzyme lactase through adulthood, and they can therefore digest lactose as adults. In these populations it is likely that lactose tolerance is an adaptation that has been selected for in an environment where raw milk products are available and consumed.

6. **What do sickle cell anemia, Tay–Sachs disease, and cystic fibrosis have in common?**

All three are autosomal recessive diseases whose disease-causing alleles are found in higher than expected frequency (given the low fitness of homozygous individuals who have the diseases) in certain populations. It has been suggested that the alleles underlying these diseases are maintained in these populations as balanced polymorphisms by heterozygous advantage. Sickle cell carriers are more resistant to developing malaria than unaffected homozygotes. Similarly, it has been suggested that Tay–Sachs and cystic fibrosis carriers may have increased resistance to tuberculosis.

7. **What role does temperature play in influencing the distribution of body size and shape in the human species?**

In cold climates, body heat must be conserved, whereas in hot climates, it is necessary to dissipate heat.

Bergmann's rule states that animals in colder climates should have larger bodies because the greater the volume, the smaller the relative surface area and the less loss of heat through the body's surface. Allen's rule states that in hotter climates, appendages should be longer compared with the size of the body because that will increase surface area and promote heat dissipation. These rules are expressed in human populations adapted to extreme temperatures, such as in the arctic Inuit and Nilotic tribes of Africa.

8. **Why are high-altitude environments considered to be stressful?**

Humans originally evolved in warm and humid environments at low altitude. High-altitude environments tend to be dry and cold. In addition, the decrease in atmospheric pressure at higher altitudes reduces the ability of hemoglobin molecules to carry oxygen. This becomes an issue at altitudes greater than 2,500 m. Individuals from different high-altitude populations (Andes, Tibet, Ethiopia) have different physiological adaptations to high-altitude conditions.

CRITICAL THINKING QUESTIONS

1. How is the concept of race currently being used in your community? Are you comfortable with its usage? Is it consistent with what we know about human biological variation?

2. In what ways is natural selection acting on human populations today? Is it possible to identify these selective forces now, or can it be done only retrospectively after their effects are more apparent?

KEY TERMS

polytypic species
deme
subspecies
race
ethnobiology
environmentalism
racism
anthropometry
ethnic group
population genetics
microevolution

polymorphism
cline
maternal–fetal
   incompatibility
rhesus (Rh) system
human leukocyte
   antigen (HLA) system
autoimmune disease
haplotypes
Duffy blood group
phylogeny

lactose intolerant
balanced polymorphism
frequency-dependent
   balanced
   polymorphism
heterozygous advantage
adaptability
acclimatization
Bergmann's rule
Allen's rule

SUGGESTED READING

Cavalli-Sforza, L. L. and Cavalli-Sforza, F. (1996). *The Great Human Diasporas: The History of Diversity and Evolution.* Perseus, Reading, MA.

Molnar, S. (2002). *Human Variation: Races, Types, and Ethnic Groups* (5th edition). Prentice Hall, Upper Saddle River, NJ.
Montagu, A. (1974). *Man's Most Dangerous Myth: The Fallacy of Race* (5th edition). Oxford University Press, London.

PART III

PRIMATES

Chapter 7
THE PRIMATES

Ranomafana National Park in Madagascar is a range of rugged, rain-soaked hills and rushing streams, and is home to some of the world's most unusual, beautiful, and endangered primates. We've come here to spend a few days looking for them.

Unlike monkeys and apes, which are active in the daytime and sleep all night, many of the most interesting primates in Madagascar are nocturnal. Finding them means hiring a guide who can lead us with his headlamp along muddy trails in the rainy dark. We have high hopes of seeing some of the forest's more exotic residents, such as aye-ayes, dwarf lemurs, and avahis. For several hours we follow in our guide's footsteps as the beam of his light falls across prehistoric-looking chameleons clinging to tree limbs along our path.

Around midnight we cross our umpteenth muddy ravine, and I am cold and tired and beginning to privately curse my guide for leading me on this wild primate chase. Just then he stops and points at the tree branches overhead. Looking up, I see movement in the foliage and spot several small rat-sized creatures bounding about. We stare at them, and one stares back. It's a mouse lemur, one of the world's smallest primates, weighing in at only a few ounces.

If I were not in Madagascar, I would assume it was a rodent. But due to Madagascar's isolation, natural selection took the primate path in an idiosyncratic direction, and primates evolved along some bizarre lines. I reflect on the difference between a mountain gorilla, with a close genetic kinship to me, and this little creature that seems more rat than primate. But the mouse lemur is just as much a primate as the gorilla is; the two species share an ancestor that lived over 60 million years ago before they and the monkeys and apes went separate evolutionary ways. If we look back far enough into Earth's past, this tiny mammal's ancestor and my ancestor are the same.

The mouse lemur takes a last look at us, its eyes glowing in the beam of our headlamps, then turns and bounces off into the rainy night.

—Craig Stanford, Madagascar, August 1998

Biological anthropologists are interested in nonhuman primates for three reasons. First, as our closest living kin, nonhuman primates share with us a recent ancestry. By carefully testing hypotheses about their diet, social behavior, and anatomy, we can reconstruct aspects of how extinct primates, including hominids, probably behaved. In other words, studying nonhuman primates offers us a window onto our own evolutionary past.

Anthropologists also want to know how the forces of natural selection and sexual selection molded our ancestors after the human lineage split from the rest of the primate order. Therefore, when we study nonhuman primates we are studying not just the animals but also the evolutionary process itself.

Finally, biological anthropologists study nonhuman primates simply because they are intrinsically fascinating animals. Most living nonhuman primate species are under threat of extinction because human activities are destroying their habitat and the animals themselves. To develop strategies for primate conservation, we must first have detailed information about their habitat needs and behavioral biology. Only with this knowledge can we hope to ensure their survival.

This chapter introduces the nonhuman primates, their habitat, and their anatomical and ecological adaptations. After considering the place of the order Primates among the mammalian orders, we examine the suite of traits that characterizes the order. We then survey primate taxonomy and general traits of the major primate groups. In the latter part of the chapter, we turn to the topic of primate ecology—the role of nonhuman primates in tropical ecosystems—and look at the ecological factors that have molded primate behavior.

THE PRIMATE RADIATION

About 5–10 million species of animals and plants inhabit Earth today. Only a tiny fraction of these, about 4,000 species, are mammals. Taxonomists divide the mammals into three groups:

1. The **metatheria,** or marsupials, reproduce without use of a placenta. Instead, their offspring are born in an almost embryonic state. They leave the mother's reproductive tract and crawl into her pouch, where they attach themselves to a nipple. After a further period of development, the offspring leave the pouch at a well-developed stage. Metatheria include the kangaroos (Figure 7.1), koalas, opossums, and a wide variety of other mammals, most of which are confined to Australia and nearby islands. Recent evidence suggests that marsupials and placental mammals have occurred together in Australia for long periods. This may mean that a long-held notion that marsupials diversified

FIGURE 7.1 Kangaroos and other marsupials lack a placenta; they give birth to poorly developed offspring that grow and develop in a pouch.

FIGURE 7.2 Most modern mammals are placentals.

only because they did not face competition from placentals in Australia is not accurate. You should not consider marsupials "primitive" and other mammals "advanced"; marsupials possess a number of adaptations to their habitat that other mammals lack. For instance, many marsupials can undergo diapause, in which females are able to stop the development of an embryo when food is scarce and continue the embryo's development months later when environmental conditions improve.

2. The **prototheria** are the monotremes, a small and unusual taxonomic group that includes only the Australian platypus and echidna. These species reproduce by egg-laying, but they nurse their young with milk in the manner of other mammals. Paleontologists believe that monotremes were more diverse and numerous in the past than they are today.

3. The **eutheria**, or placental mammals, include some two dozen orders, one of which is the order Primates. Primates and other placental mammals reproduce by means of internal fertilization, followed by implantation of the fertilized zygote on the wall of the uterus. The developing embryo is nourished via thickened tissue that connects the circulatory system of the mother with that of her offspring. The pattern of reproduction, length of gestation, and degree of development of the newborn offspring vary widely among placental forms (Figure 7.2).

THE EXTRAORDINARY DIVERSITY OF NONHUMAN PRIMATES

Some 250 species of nonhuman primates are currently recognized (Table 7.1 on page 166), but including all the minor taxonomic variations of these species, there are more than 350 varieties, or *taxa* (Groves, 2001). This is a small percentage of overall mammalian diversity, but nonhuman primates nonetheless exhibit an amazing variety of size and form. Adult body weights range from less than 2 ounces (40 g) in mouse lemurs to more than 450 pounds (200 kg) in gorillas. Body shapes range from the graceful arm-swinging gibbon to the bizarre aye-aye.

metatheria Mammals that reproduce without a placenta, including the marsupials.

prototheria Mammals that reproduce by egg-laying, then nurse young from nipples. The Australian platypus and echidna are the only living monotremes.

eutheria Mammals that reproduce with a placenta and uterus.

TABLE 7.1 Some Mammalian Orders and the Number of Species in Each	
ORDER	NUMBER OF SPECIES
Chiroptera (bats)	>1,000
Rodentia (rodents)	1,700
Insectivora (hedgehogs, tree shrews, and kin)	380
Carnivora (dogs, cats, weasels, raccoons, and kin)	240
Marsupials	270
Nonhuman primates (strepsirhines, monkeys, and apes)	250

Source: Adapted from Nowak and Paradiso (1983).

WHAT EXACTLY IS A PRIMATE?

Primates are mammals with grasping hands, large brains, a high degree of learned rather than innate behavior, and a suite of other traits. However, the primates are a diverse group, and not all species share the same suite of traits. The order Primates is divided into two suborders: the **Strepsirhini**, or **strepsirhine** primates (lemurs, lorises, and galagos), and the **Haplorhini**, or **haplorhine** primates (tarsiers, monkeys, apes, and humans) (Figure 7.3 and Figure 7.4). We should not consider strepsirhines more primitive than haplorhines; both groups have been evolving on their own paths for more than 60 million years. But many of their adaptations are clear holdovers from the early days of the Primate order (Figure 7.6 on pages 168–169). The strepsirhine– haplorhine classification system reflects genetic relationships and was developed by St. Hilaire in the late eighteenth century, long after Linnnaeus's earlier primate taxonomy. Many taxonomists use another traditional naming system, which is based on aspects of anatomy, for the major primate groups: the **prosimian** and **anthropoid** suborders. We'll see how the strepsirhine–haplorhine classification differs from the prosimian–anthropoid classification later in the chapter.

ANATOMICAL TRAITS

We distinguish primates from other mammals by a set of traits that all primates share.

Grasping Hands with Opposable Thumbs or Big Toes   The grasping hand with opposable thumb is believed to be the fundamental primate adaptation, although some prosimians don't fully exhibit this trait. Like most other mammals, primates typically have five digits per hand or foot. Having a thumb and big toe that are anatomically opposed to the other four digits allows primates to grasp objects with greater precision than other mammals. In some primates, such as colobine monkeys, gibbons, and spider monkeys, the four fingers are so elongated or the thumb is so reduced that

strepsirhine (Strepsirhini) Infraorder of the order Primates that includes the prosimians, excluding the tarsier.

haplorhine (Haplorhini) Infraorder of the order Primates that includes the anthropoids and the tarsier.

prosimian   Member of the primate suborder Prosimii that includes the lemurs, lorises, galagos, and tarsiers.

anthropoid   Members of the primate suborder Anthropoidea that includes the monkeys, apes, and hominids.

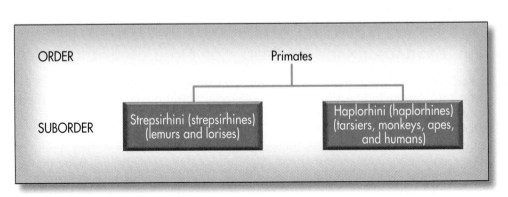

FIGURE 7.3   The major groupings of living primates.

FIGURE 7.4 Primate body size and shape vary widely from the 440 lb (200 kg) gorilla to the 2 oz. (40 g) mouse lemur.

the digits do not meet, rendering them less useful for gripping. Nonhuman primates also have an opposable hallux (the big toe).

For example, an ape uses its feet in much the same way that we use our hands. Humans have instead evolved a foot in which all the toes line up in the same plane, at the cost of a loss of dexterity of the foot.

Flattened Nails The primate grasping hand has flattened nails at the ends of the digits instead of claws. This is the case for all primates except one group, the marmosets and tamarins. In addition, many strepsirhines have a combination of nails and a single clawed digit on their hands and feet.

Forward-Facing Eyes with Stereoscopic Vision Consider the way you see the world and compare it with the view of most other mammals (Figure 7.5).

FIGURE 7.5 The primate skull is generalized compared to many other mammals.

(a) Skeleton of a terrestrial quadruped

Baboon

(b) Skeleton of an arboreal quadruped

Uakari

FIGURE 7.6   The Primate order displays a diversity of ways of moving around.

For example, a horse has eye sockets mounted on either side of its head. It has a field of vision that extends nearly 360 degrees, except for a blind spot directly behind. However, the horse's forward vision is not very good because the fields of vision of its two eyes don't fully overlap in front. Now consider your own vision. Like those of nonhuman primates, your eyes are mounted flush on the front of your head; your peripheral vision to the sides and behind you is severely constrained by this anatomy. But your forward field of vision is covered by both eyes. This stereoscopic view enables you to have excellent *depth per-*

Indri

(c) Skeleton of a vertical clinger and leaper

Gibbon

(d) Skeleton of a brachiator

FIGURE 7.6 *(continued)*

ception because the overlapping fields of vision provide a three-dimensional view of the world.

   Why are horses and primates built so differently? Horses are built for running on flat ground and for detecting predators, against which their ancestors had to be vigilant. Being able to perceive depth is less important to them, in large part because they don't have hands to use for grasping.

   Stereoscopic vision, grasping hands, opposable thumbs, and nails rather than claws seem like an obvious suite of adaptations to life in the trees. This was the thinking of Frederic Wood-Jones and George Elliot-Smith, two British anatomists who proposed the idea in the 1920s. Their **arboreal hypothesis** was widely accepted and stood unchallenged for a half-century. But in the 1970s Matthew Cartmill, a young primate anatomy student, pointed out some key flaws in that model. Squirrels, he noted, lack the primate stereoscopic vision and grasping hand with nails, yet they scamper up and down trees with great agility. To understand primate origins, Cartmill argued, we should consider how the very earliest primates and their close kin lived. The fossil record shows that early on, primates were anatomically very much like modern insectivores. Today, such small creatures live in the tangled thickets that grow around the base of tropical forest trees, where they live by stalking and capturing insects and other fast-moving prey. Cartmill hypothesized that these creatures are a useful analog for early primates; his **visual predation hypothesis** proposed that forward-facing eyes, depth perceptive vision, and grasping hands for catching their prey, not for climbing in trees, were the key adaptations of ancient primates (Cartmill, 1974). Many predators have forward-facing eyes—eagles, owls, and cats, for instance—and this is thought to aid them in precisely homing in on their prey.

The arboreal hypothesis and the visual predation hypothesis are not mutually exclusive; at some point ancient nonhuman primates did indeed live in the trees. Variants of these two theories have been put forward by scholars such as Robert Sussman (1991), who proposed that excellent stereoscopic vision and grasping hands were essential for foraging for flowering plants, which arose during the same geologic period in which early primates emerged.

Generalized Body Plan   The primate body plan is generalized, not specialized. Many mammals have extremely specialized body designs; consider a giraffe's neck, a seal's flippers or an elephant's trunk. Primates typically lack such specializations. Their generalized body plan gives them versatility; most primate species engage in a wide variety of modes of travel, for instance, from arm-swinging (in apes) to running, leaping, and walking.

Because primates evolved from ancient mammalian stock, they have inherited the many traits of that lineage (Figure 7.6 on pages 168–169). All nonhuman primates are quadrupeds, designed for moving about using all four limbs, but there is great variation in the way they use their limbs. Many strepsirhines move by *vertical clinging and leaping* (VCL). Their hind limbs are longer than their front legs. This allows them to sit upright against a tree trunk or bamboo stalk, then launch themselves from a vertical posture through the air, turning as they leap and landing upright against a nearby upright support. For instance, sifakas bound from tree trunk to tree trunk at high speed using this locomotor technique.

Contrary to the commonly depicted image of them swinging through treetops, monkeys actually walk and run (on the ground and in trees) in much the same way that dogs, cats, and other four-legged mammals do. Rather than arm-swing, monkeys run and leap along branches, their arms and legs moving in a limited plane of motion. The palms of the hands and feet make contact with the surface they are walking on. The skeleton of a monkey such as a baboon, which lives both on the ground and in trees, shows this clearly (Figure 7.6). The running motion of any four-legged animal, whether a dog or a monkey, features a limited range of motion of the limbs, which are adapted for fast forward running, not three-dimensional climbing. The shoulder blade, or scapula, is oriented vertically across the upper arm and shoulder, allowing the arms to swing back and forth in a rapid pendulum motion but not rotate. Although a few monkey species use their arms in what appears to a semi–arm-swinging motion, this is by no means a widespread or well-developed adaptation in monkeys.

By contrast, an ape's arm has a full range of motion (Figure 7.6). As we shall see, this is an adaptation to arm-hanging for feeding. Arm-hangers need a scapula that is oriented across the back rather than on the sides of the upper arms to allow

arboreal hypothesis   Hypothesis for the origin of primate adaptation that focuses on the value of grasping hands and stereoscopic vision for life in the trees.

visual predation hypothesis   Hypothesis for the origin of primate adaptation that focuses on the value of grasping hands and stereoscopic vision for catching small prey.

this freedom of motion. Apes also possess a cone-shaped rib cage and torso, long, curved digit bones, small thumbs, and long arms to aid in arm-swinging.

Generalized Teeth Teeth are an extraordinarily important part of a nonhuman primate from an anthropologist's perspective. Their shape tells us a great deal about everything from a species' diet to its mating system (Figure 7.7). Fossilized teeth also allow us to cautiously infer patterns of behavior and diet in extinct primates we study. Most nonhuman primates eat a diet that is some combination of leaves, fruit, and other plant products, with occasional animal protein in the form of insects, small mammals, or other animals. Only one, the tarsier, eats mainly animal protein.

Nonhuman primates do not possess enormous canine teeth for tearing food, as carnivores do, nor do they have the heavy grinding molars that grazing animals have. Scientists believe that nonhuman primates have undergone an evolutionary reduction in the degree of specialization of the teeth, evident in the small canines and incisors and the rounded molars of most of them. If we consider the **dental arcade**, the arc of teeth along either the bottom or top of the mouth, beginning at the midline of the mouth there are four types of teeth arranged in the following dental formula: two incisors, one canine, two premolars (what your dentist calls bicuspids), and three molars. The exceptions to this pattern are most of the New World monkeys, which have a third premolar, and the strepsirhines, which have varying dental formulas.

Activity Patterns Most primate species are active during daylight hours, possess color vision, and have limited olfactory senses. Many mammal species are nocturnal and rely on their sense of smell to negotiate their physical and social environment. Consider a cat, rat, or wolf, all of which are primarily nocturnal and have a sense of smell thousands of times more powerful than that of any haplorhine primate. Many strepsirhines are **nocturnal** (active at night), but all haplorhines except one, the night monkey *Aotus,* are **diurnal** (active during the daylight hours). Primates made a fundamental shift from an olfactory-based lifestyle to a visually based one. This entailed shifting from being primarily nocturnal to being diurnal. Diurnal animals have a greater need for color vision, and haplorhine primates in particular use their eyes to find plant foods, including brightly colored fruits, in a complex forest environment. At the same time, diurnal primates evolved complex patterns of visual communication, such as bright colors and communicative behaviors, in place of the scent-marking communication that nocturnal primates use. In addition, some nonhuman primate species are active mainly at dusk and dawn, and others are active irregularly throughout the day and night.

dental arcade The parabolic arc that forms the upper or lower row of teeth.

nocturnal Active at night.

diurnal Active during daylight hours.

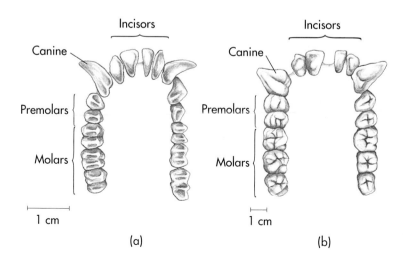

FIGURE 7.7 The primate dental formula illustrated for (a) the lower dentition of an Old World monkey and (b) the upper dentition of a gorilla.

Petrosal Bulla   The petrosal bulla is the tiny bit of the skeleton that covers and protects parts of the inner ear. Its importance to primate taxonomists is that this is the single bony trait that is shared by all primates, living or extinct, which occurs in no other mammalian group. When a fossil of questionable status is uncovered, researchers examine the ear portion carefully in search of the petrosal bulla.

Enclosed Bony Eye Orbits in the Skull   Primates also have an apparent anatomical adaptation to the importance of vision: enclosed (or partially enclosed) bony eye orbits in the skull, which may protect the eye more effectively than the open orbit of lower mammals (Figure 7.5). This orbital closure is more complete in haplorhines than it is in strepsirhines.

LIFE HISTORY TRAITS

The life history of mammals—their trajectory from conception to death—varies widely. In general, mammals that reproduce slowly, live long lives, and acquire information about their world through learning and not their genes, have delayed maturation and drawn-out life histories. Primates take this trend to an extreme.

Single Offspring   Nearly all primates give birth to single offspring. Many mammals, especially smaller species, give birth to litters or twins. The only exception among nonhuman primates is the marmosets and tamarins, which give birth to twins. Single births, combined with the long maturation period and the amount of time and energy mothers invest in their offspring, represent a strategy in which investment of time and energy in a few babies has replaced the more primitive mammalian pattern of litters of offspring that receive less intensive care.

Large Brains   Primates have large brains. They possess a high degree of *encephalization*, or evolved increase in the volume of the **neocortex** of the brain, which is involved in higher cognitive processes. This is more obvious in the brains of haplorhine primates than in strepsirhines, and we see it in the greater number of convolutions that compose the ridges and fissures (sulci and gyri) of the brain's surface. These convolutions increase the effective surface area of the brain and are believed to contribute to higher cognitive function.

There is much debate among scientists about the reasons for the evolutionary expansion of brain volume in primates and for the survival value of a big brain itself. The primate brain is such a large, metabolically expensive organ to grow and maintain that it must have important survival and reproductive benefits. We will consider these in Chapter 8.

Extended Ontogeny   Primates live by learned behaviors as much as they do on hard-wired instinct. For example, many primates live in social groups, so a baby monkey or ape must learn how to be a member of a social group if it intends to successfully court a mate and rear offspring itself; these are largely learned behaviors. Thus it is important for primates to be socialized within their communities, a process that can take up a large proportion of their infancy and maturation.

Many animals live much longer life spans than primates. Giant tortoises may live 150 years, and even among mammals some whale species may live more than 100 years. But primates are notable for the extended length of each stage, from infancy to adulthood, of their life cycle. The life cycle is also called **ontogeny** (Figure 7.8). The gorilla life span is about 20 times longer than that of a mouse, but the time it takes from gestation to sexual maturity is almost 80 times longer (about 15 years, compared with 10 weeks). Why?

neocortex   The part of the brain that controls higher cognitive function; part of the cerebrum.

ontogeny   The life cycle of an organism from conception to death.

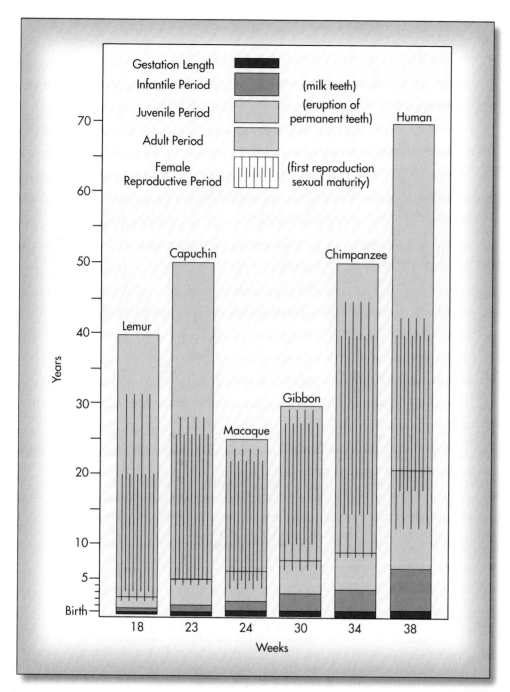

FIGURE 7.8 Primates exhibit prolonged life histories, spending more time in each stage of life than most other mammals do.

Consider the sort of information a growing primate must learn in order to survive in the world. In addition to learning how to find food and water, the primate must learn how to live in a social group. The process of learning to live in a group is a long one, and the behaviors involved tend not to be purely instinctual. An infant monkey or ape reared in isolation will end up severely deficient in the social skills it needs to be part of a social group. Parental investment in the infant is dramatically greater in primates than it is in rodents or most other mammals because social skills require years of maturation and practice.

BEHAVIORAL TRAITS

Sociality, or the characteristic of living in groups, is perhaps the most fundamental social adaptation that characterizes most primates. It is the adaptation by which a primate survives and reproduces because it provides the animal with ready access to mates and may help it find food and avoid predators.

Of the haplorhine primates, only one—the orangutan—is not normally found in a social group of some sort. There are many variations in sociality among the nonhuman primates, and we will examine the diversity of social grouping patterns in detail in Chapter 8.

All the characteristics in the previous descriptions do not apply to every primate species. Many strepsirhines are nocturnal and solitary, navigating by olfaction, whereas others are highly social, diurnal, and visually oriented. Strepsirhines often possess a mixture of primate traits, such as a combination of claws and nails on the hands. Don't make the mistake of thinking that lemurs and their kin are necessarily "less evolved" or more primitive than monkeys. The simple fact is that, as we will examine in detail in Chapter 11, monkeys and strepsirhines share a common ancestor, and after the split between the two lineages, each group evolved in separate lines. Natural selection favored diurnality and sociality more in monkeys than it did in strepsirhines.

A GUIDE TO THE NONHUMAN PRIMATES

As we discussed on page 166, we consider the nonhuman primates as two major groups within the order Primates: the suborders Strepsirhini and Haplorhini (Figure 7.9). Alternately the primates can be subdivided into suborders Prosimii and Anthropoidea. Recall that the Linnaean system for naming includes not only order, family, genus, and species but also higher and lesser categories (see Chapter 5). So primate families that are anatomically similar are lumped in the same superfamily, and subgroups of families are called subfamilies. Not all taxonomists agree on how to classify the primates, and one nonhuman primate, the tarsier, straddles the two suborders. The geographic distribution of nonhuman primates is presented in Figure 7.10 on pages 176–77.

THE STREPSIRHINES

The primates of the suborder Strepsirhini include the lemurs of Madagascar and the lorises and galagos of mainland Africa and tropical Asia. Linnaeus originally subdivided the primates into two major groups—the prosimians (sometimes called the lower primates) and the anthropoids (higher primates)—based on a number of anatomical features. *Strepsirhine* and *prosimian* are not completely synonymous; one prosimian primate, the tarsier, is a haplorhine, not a strepsirhine. But all strepsirhines and prosimians share some common anatomical features: a reliance on olfaction, nocturnality, and a lack of complex social behavior patterns. Their incisor teeth protrude from the front of the mouth to form a comblike surface, known as the *tooth comb*, used for grooming. Many also have specialized clawed toes that serve as grooming tools. Some lemurs violate these general traits, however, as we shall see next.

The Lemurs The superfamily Lemuroidea is found only on Madagascar and consists of the families Lemuridae (true lemurs), Cheirogalidae (dwarf lemurs), Indriidae (the sifakas and indri), and Daubentoniidae (the aye-aye). The fourth largest island on Earth, Madagascar is home to perhaps the best example of an adaptive

sociality Group living, a fundamental trait of haplorhine primates.

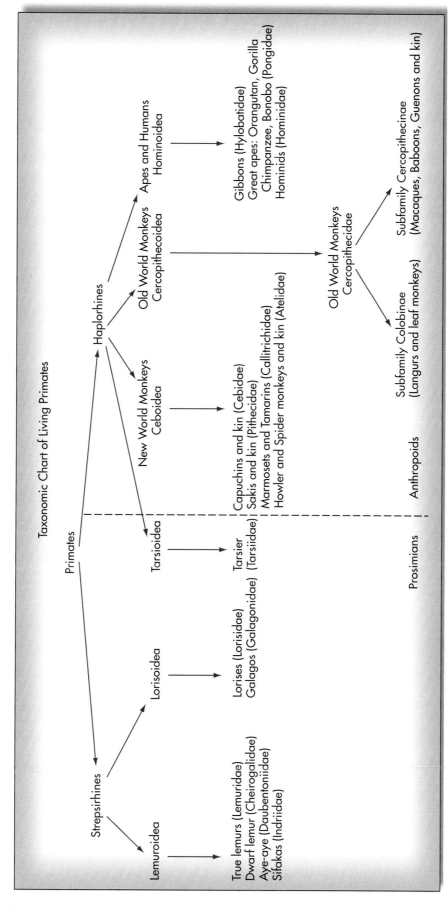

Figure 7.9 A taxonomic chart of the living primates.

Figure 7.10 A WORLD MAP OF LIVING NONHUMAN PRIMATES

NORTH AND SOUTH AMERICA

Primates in the New World tend to be small-bodied compared to those elsewhere. All species are primarily arboreal, and some have grasping tails to aid in tree-top feeding. New World primates are found from central Mexico to Argentina, and in some equatorial forests numerous species can be found sharing the same habitat.

UAKARI Native to seasonally flooded rain forests

MURIQUI Highly endangered, the largest new world monkey

GOLDEN LION TAMARIN One of Brazil's endangered primates

EUROPE AND ASIA

Nonhuman primates are found across tropical Asia, occurring as far north as central Japan (the Japanese macaque). They occur in only the tiniest bit of Europe, on the island of Gibraltar (where they may have been introduced by people). Asia is the home of gibbons and orangutans, many species of Old World Monkeys (the langurs, leaf monkeys and macaques) plus numerous strepsirhines.

DeBrazza's Guenon
A diverse group found in African forests

Galago Live in many African forests; Also called Bushbabies

Golden Snub-Nosed Monkey One of China's beautiful and endangered primates

Savanna Baboon
Baboons are found across subsaharan Africa

Chimpanzee
Found in suitable habitat across equatorial Africa

Hanuman Langurs
Found all across the Indian Subcontinent

Lar Gibbon Found in forests from India through South East Asia

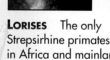

Lorises The only Strepsirhine primates in Africa and mainland Asia

Gorillas Live in both lowland and mountain forests

Tarsier The only entirely carnivorous primate, found in Southeast Asia rain forests

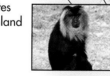

Red-Bellied Lemur
Found only on Madagascar

Lion-Tailed Macaque One of the world's most threatened primates, found in hilly forests of Southern India

Orangutan Live only on the Islands of Sumatra and Borneo in Indonesia

AFRICA

Primates are found across subSaharan Africa and also in small areas of northwestern Africa and in the Arabian peninsula. Primate biodiversity peaks in the central African Congo Basin, where more than fifteen species can be found in the same tropical rain forest habitat. Africa provides primate habitat ranging from rain forest to savanna to high mountain meadows, across a vast area. Moreover, since humans evolved in Africa, we can study African primates with a eye toward learning something about the environment of the human past.

FIGURE 7.11 Lemurs are found only in Madagascar.

FIGURE 7.12 A sifaka, a member of the lemur family.

radiation we know of among living nonhuman primates (Figure 7.11). Madagascar broke away from the eastern coast of the continental mainland of Africa, through the process of continental drift, beginning some 100 million years ago. By the time the separation was complete, the earliest members of the primate order had evolved in Africa. As Madagascar drifted slowly out of contact with the rest of Africa, the primitive primates stranded on its land mass began to evolve without gene flow from other primates.

Over time, these animals developed a wide range of adaptations to exploit the many available habitats and niches on Madagascar (Figure 7.12). In the absence of large predators (there are no big carnivores or large eagles on the entire island), a diverse array of forms radiated from the ancestral colonizing forms. Sadly, many of those species are now extinct, presumably because of hunting by people, who arrived on the island beginning 1,500–2,000 years ago. We know about the extinct forms through the skeletal remains we have found; we call these remains *subfossils* because they are found as bones, rather than fossils, due to the recent date of the animals' disappearance (in about the past 1,000 years).

There was once an adaptive radiation on Madagascar of large-bodied, slow-moving lemurs, both arboreal and terrestrial. Many of the extinct species were quite large; *Archaeoindris* and *Megaladapis* ambled along the ground like large bears (Figure 7.13). One entire subfamily, the Paleopropithecines, were sloth lemurs; some of these species apparently hung upside down from tree limbs, as New World sloths do. Lacking natural predators, they would have been plentiful prey for the human colonizers. The species still alive today may be those that were simply too small or too elusive for human colonizers to bother hunting (Box 7.1 on page 182 and Box 10.1 on page 275).

FIGURE 7.13 A subfossil lemur, *Megaladapis*.

The four families of lemurs alive today range in size from the 2-ounce (40-g) mouse lemur to the 20-pound (8-kg) indri. The families are quite distinct from one another. The dwarf lemurs are small, dull-colored insect- and fruit-eaters and tend to be nocturnal and solitary. True lemurs tend to be diurnal and social, living in social groups like those of many haplorhine primates. The well-studied ring-tailed lemur (Figure 7.14) lives in groups of up to 25 in which, as among many true lemurs (Figures 7.15 and 7.16), females are dominant to males (Ganzhorn and Kappeler, 1993). The indri and several sifaka species are the largest living prosimians. The indri is noted for its monogamous social system, its loud, haunting call, and its diet of leaves. The aye-aye is nocturnal and largely solitary. It feeds on bird eggs, fruit, and insect larvae that it locates by tapping fallen tree trunks with its long middle finger. Grubs respond to the tapping by wriggling, and the aye-aye then digs under the bark to find its meal.

The Lorises   The lorises are a diverse group of strepsirhines in tropical Africa and Asia (Figure 7.17 on page 180). They include the various species of galago, or bushbaby, which occur only on Africa and are now considered to be in their own family, the Galagonidae. Recent behavioral and genetic studies have warranted the splitting of many new species from this group (Bearder et al., 1995; Groves, 2001).

FIGURE 7.14 The ring-tailed lemur is the best-known of the Madagascar primates.

FIGURE 7.15 This red-bellied lemur shows clearly the traits that characterize strepsirhine primates.

FIGURE 7.16 The endangered ruffed lemur.

FIGURE 7.17 The distribution of lorises and galagos.

Lorises (Figure 7.18) and galagos (Figure 7.19) probably resemble the primitive ancestors of modern haplorhines. They communicate both vocally and olfactorily, by scent-marking objects in their environment. They are nocturnal and largely solitary and spend their nights feeding on fruits and hunting for insects and other small animals. In a classic study, Pierre Charles-Dominique (1977) found that in West African forests, multiple species of lorises and galagos shared their habitat by dividing up the available food items and by foraging at different heights within the forest canopy and understory. During the daylight hours, many lorises and galago species stay curled up in a nest in a tree cavity, and some species also park their offspring in such nests when they are out searching for food.

Lorises include the slender and slow loris of Asia and the potto and angwantibo of tropical Africa. All are slow-moving, deliberate stalkers, capturing small prey. Galagos are active, leaping animals (using VCL) that range in size from a housecat to a rat and generally are more insectivorous than lorises.

FIGURE 7.18 A loris.

FIGURE 7.19 A galago, or bushbaby.

THE HAPLORHINES

The nonhuman primates of the suborder Haplorhini include the tarsier, New World monkeys, Old World monkeys, apes, and hominids. The tarsier is a haplorhine but also a prosimian. It is closely related to the anthropoids but occupies an evolutionary status intermediate between the lower and higher primates. All the other haplorhines can also be called anthropoid primates. Haplorhines possess the full suite of adaptations that characterize the living primates. Without exception haplorhines are guided more by vision than by olfaction. This emphasis on vision is reflected in the full closure of the back of their eye orbits, providing bony protection for the eye that strepsirhines and most other mammals lack. Living haplorhines also possess a lower jaw that is fused at the midline in adulthood; in prosimians and most other mammals the jaw is two pieces joined in the middle with cartilage.

With few exceptions (the owl monkey and tarsier), haplorhines are diurnal. And with one exception (the orangutan), they live in social groups. The ratio of brain to body size in haplorhines is higher than in strepsirhines; cognition is part of the haplorhine suite of adaptations. Cognition also is related to the degree of social complexity we observe among haplorhines, greater than what we usually see among the strepsirhines. The haplorhines include all extinct forms of hominids, as well as humans.

The Tarsiers   Tarsiers are haplorhine primates that occupy an evolutionary position between the lower and higher primates. The tarsier represents either an evolutionary enigma or modern-day evidence of an evolutionary bridge. Tarsiers possess a mixture of traits of anthropoid and prosimian primates, but they are generally considered to be closer to anthropoids (Figure 7.20). Frederick Szalay and Eric Delson (1979) tried to resolve the status of tarsiers by classifying them as both Prosimians and haplorhines to indicate their mixed evolutionary bridge. That is, they are haplorhines but have anatomical links to the strepsirhines.

The several species of tarsier recognized today live in Indonesia and nearby island groups (Figure 7.21). They occupy an owl-like ecological role as

FIGURE 7.21   The tarsier is a haplorhine, and may represent an evolutionary bridge between lower and higher primates.

FIGURE 7.20   The distribution of the tarsier.

BOX 7.1   The Rarest of the Rare

Although extinction has always been a natural event in the history of life on Earth, humans have dramatically increased the odds of extinction for many species. Of the 250 living nonhuman primate species, the majority are threatened with extinction. For perhaps half of these, the new century may bring an end to their existence on Earth.

At least 50 species are critically endangered. Many of these endangered species live in one of several hotspots of biodiversity, geographic regions known for a unique assortment of highly diverse animals and plants (Mittermeier et al., 2002). Not surprisingly, these areas are centered in equatorial regions, where large tracts of forests in the Amazon Basin of South America and the Congo Basin of central Africa remain. In these strongholds it is still possible to find 15 or more nonhuman primate species in a single tract of forest. Other areas, such as Madagascar, harbor whole ecosystems full of primates that exist nowhere else on Earth.

These vanishing treasures include the following:

- *Golden bamboo lemur* Discovered only in the late 1980s, this beautiful 5-pound (2-kg) prosimian (*Hapalemur aureus*) lives in Ranomafana National Park, a densely forested preserve of lemur biodiversity in eastern Madagascar (Figure A). It feeds on bamboo, which it shares with two other species of bamboo lemur in the same forest. The golden bamboo lemur eats the inside of the stem of the bamboo, whereas the other two species eat the leaves. The pith contains high levels of cyanide; every day the lemur consumes enough cyanide to kill a horse (Meier et al., 1987; Glander et al., 1989). An estimated 300–400 of the animals exist in

FIGURE A   The golden bamboo lemur.

the only remaining forest habitat left to this species.

- *Zanzibar red colobus* Zanzibar, a palm-covered tropical island just off the coast of the East African nation of Tanzania, is home to a small and dwindling population of red colobus monkeys (*Procolobus badius kirkii*) (Figure B). They are gorgeous animals, with a crimson back and black face fringed with white tufts of hair. A remnant population lives in tiny patches of forest amid villages and palm groves on both Zanzibar and neighboring islands. Their long-term prospects are bleak in the face of land development and human population increase.

- *Golden snub-nosed monkey* Snub-nosed monkeys are still little known to Western science because their several species live in China and Vietnam, which until recently were closed to foreign scientists. The golden snub-nosed monkey (*Rhinopithecus roxellanae*) has the largest population, about 20,000, centered in the high mountain ranges of Sichuan and Hubei provinces in cen-

tral China (Figure C). Males weigh nearly 50 pounds (22 kg) and possess a thick mane of golden-orange hair that drapes across its back. This, combined with a pale blue face, gives the species a dramatic appearance. In Shennongjia Nature Reserve, it lives in pine and fir forest not unlike the Rocky Mountains of the United States, and it survives the snowy winters eating pine needles and lichens. Two close relatives, *Rhinopithecus bieti* and *R. brelichi*, are more critically endangered, with populations of only a few hundred each.

- *Lion-tailed macaque* The western Ghat mountains of southern India are home to a number of rare primates. Among these is the lion-tailed macaque (*Macaca silenus*), so named for its long

FIGURE B   The beautiful Zanzibar red colobus.

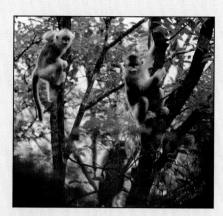

FIGURE C   The golden snub-nosed monkey.

FIGURE E   The muriqui.

tail ending in a tuft and its mane of white hair (Figure D). The species has never been common, and its limited habitat of lush mountain valleys is threatened by construction of a controversial hydroelectric project by the Indian government, which will flood part of the macaque's range.

• *Muriqui*   The largest nonhuman primate in the Western Hemisphere is also one of the rarest (Figure E). The muriqui, or woolly spider monkey, lives in forest fragments in the Atlantic coastal forest of Brazil, where ranching has eaten up almost all its remain-

ing habitat. Conservation efforts have focused on preserving existing habitat on private lands; fewer than 1,000 animals may remain.

• *Golden lion tamarin*   This flame-colored, 1-pound (0.4-kg) monkey lives in the same region as the muriqui and is also critically endangered because of habitat loss (Figure F). A novel project has reestablished golden lion tamarins in forests in which they had gone extinct by releasing monkeys that have been reared in zoos and then "rehabilitated" to survive in the wild. After years of shaky progress, this project has restored healthy populations of golden lion tamarins to some former habitats and shows how sound knowledge of a species' needs in nature can be essential for its long-term conservation.

The current approach to nonhuman primate conservation is to try to protect hotspots of nonhuman primate diversity that are home to species such as these and to prevent people from exploiting the forest resources at unsustainable levels. The threat is clear: If we do not act now, a large proportion of the diversity of nonhuman primates will be gone within a generation.

Nearly all threatened nonhuman primate species live in developing countries. The challenge is to help these countries develop without casting aside regard for the health of the environment.

In the whole of the twentieth century, not one primate taxon went extinct. It seems very unlikely we will be able to make the same statement about the twenty-first century. Indeed, in the few years since the new century opened, one species, Miss Waldron's red colobus, has already been reported to be on the brink of extinction in West Africa.

FIGURE D   The lion-tailed macaque.

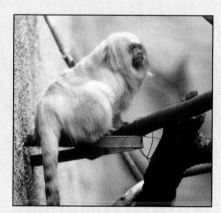

FIGURE F   The golden lion tamarin.

nocturnal predators on small vertebrates and are the most highly carnivorous of all nonhuman primates, eating small prey such as lizards, frogs, and insects. They live in monogamous pairs, are exclusively nocturnal, and park their young in tree nests while out foraging (Gursky, 1994, 1995).

THE NEW WORLD MONKEYS

The New World monkeys are classified in the infraorder **Platyrrhini** (referring to the flat shape of the nose) and are all in the superfamily Ceboidea. They live in the tropical and subtropical forests of the Western Hemisphere, from Argentina northward to within a few hundred miles of the U.S. border in the state of Veracruz, Mexico (Figure 7.22). All the New World monkeys share three features:

- *Small body size.* The largest New World monkey, the muriqui (Figure 7.23), weighs only about 25 pounds (12 kg). The smallest, the marmosets and tamarins, range from 1.5 pounds (0.6 kg) down to just a few ounces.

Platyrrhini Infraorder of the order Primates that is synonymous with the New World monkeys, or ceboids.

- *Three premolar teeth.* Whereas all other haplorhine primates have two premolars (bicuspids) and three molars in each quadrant of the mouth, New World monkeys have three. (The ceboid monkeys possess three molars and the Callitrichidae only two).

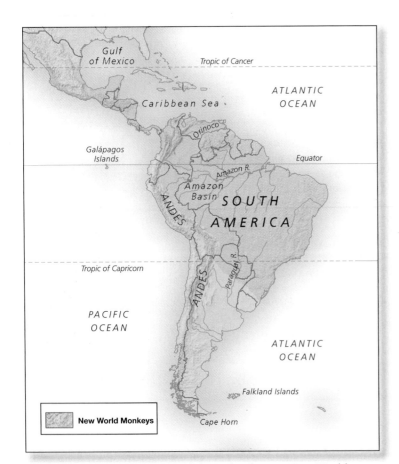

FIGURE 7.22 Distribution of the Ceboidea, or New World monkeys.

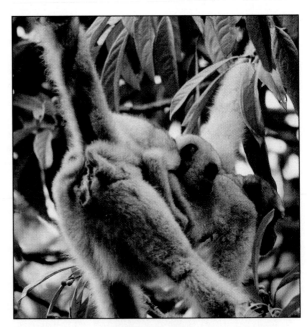

FIGURE 7.23 The muriqui of Brazil, the largest New World monkey.

FIGURE 7.24 A prehensile tail is an adaptation to grasping branches for support while feeding.

FIGURE 7.25 The red-faced uakari, a bizarre-looking New World monkey.

• *Arboreality.* There are no primarily terrestrial New World nonhuman primates, even though there are large stretches of grassland in parts of South America (as opposed to Africa, where baboons and other nonhuman primates make use of open country). In addition, some New World monkeys have grasping **prehensile tails**; this trait occurs in some members of the families Cebidae and Atelidae (Figure 7.24). The prehensile tail is an adaptation to feeding, allowing a monkey to hang beneath slender branches to reach food.

The Ceboidea are currently classified as four families: Cebidae (capuchins), Pithecidae (sakis and related species; Figure 7.25), Atelidae (howlers, spider monkeys, and muriquis), and Callitrichidae (marmosets and tamarins; Figure 7.26). A few taxonomists (Fleagle, 1999; Groves, 2001) consider the Callitrichidae to be so closely allied with the Cebidae that it should be a subfamily within it. The callitrichids are unique among primates for their suite of traits that resemble those of lower mammals: small body size, claws instead of nails, and the routine birthing of twins rather than a single offspring. In some species a **polyandry** mating system, in which one female has more than one male mate, is characteristic.

prehensile tail Grasping tail possessed by some species of the primate families Cebidae and Atelidae.

polyandry Mating system in which one female mates with multiple males.

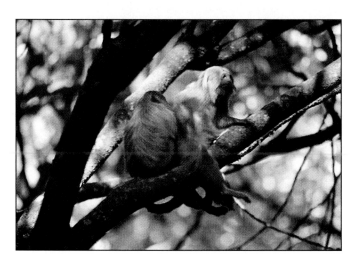

FIGURE 7.26 The rare golden lion tamarin is the largest callitrichid monkey.

The evolutionary reasons behind these traits are complex; we will discuss them further when we consider the diversity of nonhuman primate mating systems.

THE OLD WORLD MONKEYS

The Old World monkeys, along with the apes and humans, are in the infraorder **Catarrhini** (or primates with downward-facing nostrils). Old World monkeys occur in many parts of Africa and Asia and also in small areas of the Middle East (Figure 7.27). They are in the superfamily Cercopithecoidea, which contains the single family Cercopithecidae. Old World monkeys have exploited a wider variety of habitats than their New World counterparts, occupying every ecological setting from tropical rain forest to savanna to desert.

As a family, the Old World monkeys share *ischial callosities:* thickened calluses on the rump that presumably make sitting on rough surfaces more comfortable. They also possess double-ridged molar teeth. These *bilophodont molars* are believed to be an evolutionary advance for biting through fibrous plant material. Old World monkeys display a greater size range than New World monkeys, from 2-pound (0.8-kg) talapoins (*Miopithecus talapoin*) to 70-pound (32-kg) baboons (*Papio* ssp.). Some groups also display a greater degree of sexual dimorphism than we see in any New World monkey species.

Two subfamilies within the Cercopithecidae merit special attention. Colobines are the so-called leaf-monkeys, langurs, and odd-nosed monkeys of Asia (Figure 7.28) and the colobus of Africa (Figure 7.29). They have evolved a semichambered stomach that resembles that of a cow and can digest tough, cellulose-laden foods in an organ called a foregut, using a community of microbes that break down the cellulose compounds in their food for them. This adaptation enables colobines to live at high population densities in forests where they would otherwise be hardpressed to find edible foods. The gruesome but intriguing behavior of infanticide also occurs more widely among colobines than any other monkey taxonomic group (Box 8.2 on page 222).

Catarrhini Infraorder of the order Primates that includes the Old World monkeys, apes, and hominids.

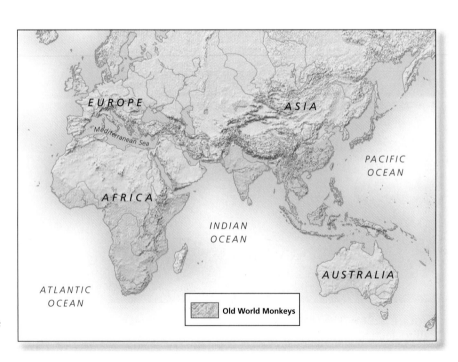

FIGURE 7.27 Distribution of the Old World monkeys.

FIGURE 7.28 The Hanuman langur, a widely distributed Asian colobine.

FIGURE 7.29 The black-and-white colobus is an African colobine.

FIGURE 7.30 Baboons are African cercopithecines.

FIGURE 7.31 De Brazza's monkey and its fellow guenons are in the subfamily Cercopithecinae.

The cercopithecines include the macaques of Asia and the baboons, guenons, drills, mangabeys, and patas monkeys of Africa (Figures 7.30 and 7.31). They share the presence of cheek pouches for food storage. Females of some Old World monkey species undergo a regular period of sexual receptivity, or **estrus**, during which skin around the genital area inflates with fluid and serves as a billboard of her fertility. Sexual dimorphism is generally more pronounced in cercopithecines than in colobines. Some of the cercopithecines—the baboons of Africa and the rhesus macaque in Asia—are among the most studied species of all primates.

THE HOMINOIDS

The apes and humans, past and present, are classified in the superfamily Hominoidea. This includes the ape families **hylobatid (Hylobatidae)** and **pongid (Pongidae)** and the human family **hominid (Hominidae)**. As we saw earlier, had Linnaeus not been so bound by his theology, humans and apes probably would have been placed in the same family, based on their many shared anatomical traits (Box 12.1 on page 322).

The hominoids extend many haplorhine traits: increased brain volume and intelligence, extended ontogeny, increased complexity of social interactions, and

estrus Hormonally influenced period of sexual receptivity in some female mammals, which corresponds to the timing of ovulation.

hylobatid (Hylobatidae) Member of the gibbon, or lesser ape, family.

pongid (Pongidae) One of the four great apes species: gorilla, chimpanzee, bonobo, or orangutan.

hominid (Hominidae) Member of our own human family, past or present.

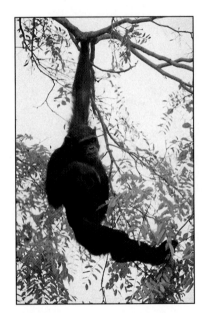

FIGURE 7.32 All living apes possess rotating, suspensory shoulders, as do humans.

large body size. The hylobatids, or gibbons, often are called the lesser apes, based on minor anatomical differences from the four pongids, or great apes: the chimpanzee, bonobo, gorilla, and orangutan.

Apes and humans share several key postcranial anatomical traits. Foremost among these is the suspensory, rotating shoulder apparatus that allows for arm-hanging and arm-swinging, or **brachiation**. The anatomy that allows a quarterback to throw a football or a gymnast to perform on the high bar is the same as that which allowed fossil apes to hang from branches in the canopy of ancient forests (Figure 7.32), although it probably did not evolve for the purpose. Instead, researchers believe that arm-hanging initially was adaptive for suspending a large-bodied ape underneath a tree limb from which ripe fruit was growing. A branch that could not support the weight of an ape walking on top of it could support the same weight hung beneath it. In this way, the rotating shoulder of the ape may have an evolved function similar to that of the prehensile tail of many New World monkeys.

The four great apes move about by a modified form of quadrupedalism called knucklewalking (Figure 7.33) or, in the case of the orangutan, fist-walking. Apes also lack tails.

The social complexity of the hominoids does not apply to all taxa. We see it to its greatest extent in chimpanzees, bonobos, and human societies. Anthropologists study ape behavior because, in addition to being intrinsically fascinating, apes are among the most intelligent animals with which we share the planet. Only in great apes do we see tool technologies that resemble simple versions of human tool industries, lethal aggression between communities that resembles human warfare, and cognitive development, including language acquisition, that parallels that of children.

Gibbons   Gibbons are 14 species of closely related apes, all currently classified in the genus *Hylobates* (although some taxonomists divide the genus into three or four genera). Gibbons live in Asian tropical and subtropical forests from easternmost India and Bangladesh through mainland southeast Asia and the Indonesian archipelago (Figure 7.34). They range in size from the 10-pound (4-kg) Kloss's gibbon of the Mentawai Islands to the 25-pound (12-kg) siamang of peninsular Malaysia.

Gibbons are rain forest canopy inhabitants, their bodies well adapted for a highly arboreal existence of brachiating among and hanging beneath tree limbs (Figure 7.35). They possess long arms, extremely elongated fingers, shortened thumbs, and a suspensory shoulder designed for treetop life. Most gibbon species are highly **frugivorous** or fruit-eating, using their high-energy diet to engage in a high-energy lifestyle of brachiating and singing. They are among the most vocal of all non-human primates; their whooping songs are given from morning until night and serve as declarations of territorial boundaries for other members of their species. Mated pairs also sing duets that reinforce the bond between male and female.

brachiation   Mode of arm-hanging and arm-swinging that uses a rotating shoulder to suspend the body of an ape or hominid beneath a branch or to travel between branches.

frugivorous   An animal that eats a diet composed mainly of fruit.

FIGURE 7.33 Great apes knucklewalk when traveling on the ground.

FIGURE 7.34 Distribution of the gibbons.

FIGURE 7.35 Gibbons are lesser apes, and live in the forests of south and southeast Asia

Gibbons have long been considered the most monogamous of the higher primates, living in pair bonds that last many years (Brockelman et al., 1998). However, recent field studies have shown that secretive matings outside the pair bond are not uncommon (Palombit, 1994). Gibbons are best considered to be socially monogamous but not necessarily reproductively monogamous. Whereas early gibbon researchers believed that monogamy among gibbons benefited the females, with the male providing protection against predators and other gibbons, modern researchers believe much the opposite. A female tolerates a male because he provides an essential service, helping to defend the patch of forest on which she must find food to nourish herself and her offspring (Sommer and Reichard, 2000).

Orangutans   Orangutans (*Pongo pygmaeus*) are the most enigmatic of all the hominoid primates. These red apes are among our closest living kin and among the largest-brained animals on Earth. But compared with other apes, they are largely solitary. Found in the rapidly disappearing rain forests of the Indonesian islands of Sumatra and Borneo (Figure 7.36 on page 190), orangutans are large-bodied and extremely sexually dimorphic. Males may weigh 200 pounds (78 kg), more than twice the size and weight of adult females (36 kg) (Figure 7.37 on page 190).

Orangutans are highly arboreal, traveling slowly through the forest canopy in search of fruit. Adult females and their dependent offspring occupy territories that they defend from other adult females. Adult males attempt to maintain control over a number of female territories, moving over a much larger area to attempt to monopolize them for mating purposes. Surplus males that cannot obtain access to their own females live as transients, attempting to approach females without being detected by the resident adult male. Resident adult males use resonating, loud calls to warn transients away. Birute Galdikas (1985), who did pioneering field research on Bornean orangutans in the 1960s, first observed transient males trying to forcibly mate with females, sometimes successfully. It became clear only recently that these transient males, long assumed to be adolescents because of their small size and lack of adult male physical features, often are adult males that have retained adolescent features. In fact, these "pseudo-adolescents" possess the physical features of immature males but produce male sex hormones and sperm (Maggioncalda et

FIGURE 7.36 Orangutans are limited to the islands of Sumatra and Borneo, where their numbers are rapidly declining.

al., 1999). This appears to be a case of sexual selection for *bimaturism,* in which adults can take two different forms, allowing males to approach females by "posing" as adolescents without arousing the ire of resident adult males.

Orangutan reproduction is strongly influenced by the food supply. Cheryl Knott (1998) has documented that *mast-fruiting,* the unpredictable ripening of many fruit trees at the same time in Indonesian rain forests, triggers ovulation among female orangutans. At times of fruit abundance, orangutans form temporary associations of several individuals, presumably for mating purposes.

When times are lean, orangutans cope with the lack of fruit by feeding on whatever foods are available, including tree bark. They possess thickened molar enamel, unlike that of the African apes, which may be an adaptation to eating seeds and unripe fruits (Leighton, 1993).

Orangutans share the extended ontogeny of the other great apes; females reach sexual maturity at age 11–15 and males not until 15. The interval between successive births is longer in orangutans than in any other primate, nearly 8 years (Galdikas and Wood, 1990). When females mature, they disperse from their mother's territory to a nearby area to establish themselves as breeding adults. Males disperse more widely and often are alone for long periods (Delgado and van Schaik, 2000).

Sumatran and Bornean orangutans are quite different morphologically, and many researchers advocate considering them separate species (Delgado and van Schaik, 2000). Bornean males have enormous flanges of flesh around the face and long, pendulous throat sacs (probably used to produce their resonating long calls).

Gorillas   The largest primates, weighing more than 400 pounds (200 kg) in the wild, gorillas today have a severely fragmented geographic distribution (Figures 7.38, 7.39). Most of the estimated 80,000 gorillas in equatorial Africa are lowland gorillas and live in forests across central and western Africa. Lowland gorillas are extraordinarily diverse genetically, and some isolated populations are being elevated to full species status on the basis of the degree of their divergence from other gorillas (Gagneux et al., 1996). In eastern Africa, mountain gorillas also live in a highly fragmented distribution, but their overall numbers are far lower. Only 600 remain in the wild in two mountain ranges, the Virunga Volcanoes and the Bwindi Impenetrable Forest, along the border of Uganda, Rwanda, and the Democratic Republic of the Congo (Box 7.2 on pge 192). The two populations are nearly identical genetically and were separated by forest clearing only in the last several hundred years (Garner and Ryder, 1996; Stanford, 2001). Between the ranges of

FIGURE 7.37 Orangutan males are twice the size and weight of females.

FIGURE 7.38 Distribution of the African great apes.

western lowland and mountain gorillas live eastern lowland gorillas, which occur across a wide elevational range in eastern Congo. Only a few thousand eastern lowland gorillas are believed to remain in the wild.

Gorillas are extremely sexually dimorphic, with males outweighing females by more than 50%. In their mid-teen years, males reach sexual maturity and acquire a gray saddle of hair on their backs, hence the label *silverback* for an adult male gorilla and *blackback* for an adolescent male. Females give birth about every 4 years. At or after sexual maturity, females tend to migrate to other groups, often in the company of sisters or close female kin (Figure 7.40). Life can be difficult for a female if she migrates with offspring; infanticide by silverbacks is a leading cause of mortality among mountain gorillas (Watts, 1989).

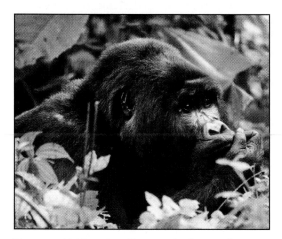

FIGURE 7.39 Gorillas are the largest living primates.

FIGURE 7.40 Gorillas live in one or multi-male groups, from which females emigrate at sexual maturity.

BOX 7.2 The Impending Extinction of the Great Apes?

For more than 20 million years, apes have flourished in the tropical forests of the Old World. But today, throughout their geographic distribution in equatorial Africa and southeast Asia, the great apes are in grave peril of extinction. For the most critically endangered, the orangutan and bonobo, this could mean extinction in the wild within your lifetime. Can this be prevented? Conservation efforts must begin with an understanding of the threats to the endangered species. These threats exist in several key areas:

- *Habitat destruction* The loss of tropical forest habitat is the single greatest factor causing the decline in nonhuman primate populations worldwide (Figure A). From Congo to Indonesia, forest clearing is accelerating, and with it comes the loss of thousands of animal and plant species. Forests are cut by local farmers so they can plant crops, but forests are also cut by government-sanctioned logging companies in many regions.

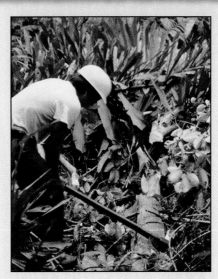

FIGURE A The destruction of tropical forests, the habitat of living great apes, continues at an alarming rate.

Recent estimates on the Indonesian island of Sumatra place the loss of orangutan habitat at 80% in the past two decades, and the population de-

clined 45% just from 1993 to 1999 (van Schaik et al., 2001). At current rates of habitat loss, the 20,000 orangutans remaining in the wild face extinction within 15 years.

- *Bushmeat* A major cause of population decline among apes in central and western Africa is the bushmeat trade. Bushmeat is simply the meat of any wild animal that is eaten by people.

  In Africa, the smoked flesh of gorillas, chimpanzees, and bonobos is highly valued. People have been hunting and eating apes for thousands of years, but recently the pattern has changed. No longer is ape hunting practiced only by local villagers trying to put some protein in their children's stomachs. As international logging companies from Europe cut logging roads deep into pristine rain forests, they create a pipeline by which ape carcasses can be easily transported from remote areas. Businessmen in towns and cities pay hunters to send them as many apes

Gorillas live in highly cohesive groups, ranging in size from several animals to several dozen. Males have two reproductive options. They can remain in their birth group, waiting to join the ranking silverback as a breeding adult male someday (or wait for him to die or be driven out). Alternatively, they can emigrate and attempt to find mates elsewhere. Young silverbacks often spend months or years on their own or live in bachelor groups of other silverbacks. Such bachelors wait for opportunities either to take over a male–female group by driving out the resident silverback or to steal a female or two away from an established group. Female gorillas are prone to emigrate just after encounters between groups occur; they may be sizing up the males in the new group to assess whether the time is right to leave with them (Harcourt, 1978). Contrary to the image of a "harem" of females led by a single silverback male, many gorilla groups have two or more silverbacks.

Our view of gorillas as slow-moving, terrestrial leaf-eaters living in one-male harems was shaped by the pioneering study of mountain gorillas begun by Dian Fossey in the Virunga Volcanoes. Following early work by George Schaller, Dian Fossey gave up her training as an occupational therapist to begin the first long-term study of wild gorillas. She established a research camp in the mountains of Rwanda and began to document the daily lives of her study subjects. Fossey's mountain gorillas ate a diet that was nearly 100% high-fiber, poor-quality plants, for which they foraged slowly, almost exclusively on the ground (Fossey, 1983).

as they can kill, the meat of which is sold on the black market, and sometimes in the open market, for several times the price of beef. In Africa, government officials and wealthy people exhibit their affluence by serving ape meat to visitors, occasionally including stunned foreigners.

Apes have withstood low levels of hunting for millennia, but the recent intense pressure, combined with the very slow reproductive rate of the great apes (perhaps one baby every 4 years), has resulted in dramatic population decline even in forests that have seen little human use. Stopping the bushmeat trade entails not only law enforcement but also a change in cultural values so that Africans do not consider the eating of apes to be a status symbol.

- *International zoo, laboratory, and pet trade* Despite increased public awareness of the evils of taking apes from the wild, poaching for the live animal trade still occurs. Hundreds of baby orangutans are caught every year to be sold illegally as pets in Southeast Asia.

Some years ago, conservationists estimated that there were more baby orangutans being kept as household pets on the island of Taiwan than were being born in all of Borneo each year. For every baby entering the pet trade alive, many others die before reaching the market.

Poaching has been outlawed, but the practice continues. Although most labs in Europe and the United States now use captive-bred apes, gorillas and chimpanzees sometimes are poached for their value as laboratory animals in other countries and for sale to unscrupulous zoos.

- *Disease* Emerging viruses, including ebola and anthrax, have recently been discovered in wild ape populations and pose a great threat.

What can we do? The first step is habitat protection. Many conservation organizations work in Africa to preserve ape populations. This goal can be achieved only by providing local people with an economic incentive to protect the animals and other forest resources. Because apes are valued as tourist attractions, ecotourism sometimes provides that incentive.

In Bwindi Impenetrable National Park in southwestern Uganda, tourists pay up to $350 per hour to view wild mountain gorillas. A percentage of this fee goes to local villages, for building and staffing clinics and funding other entrepreneurial endeavors. Ecotourism does not work everywhere, however, and is highly vulnerable to the political instability that plagues much of Africa. In addition, close contact between tourists and apes increases the risk of disease transmission from us to them. Most wild ape populations have no immunity to flus, colds, and other human diseases that, because of their genetic kinship with us, they easily catch.

Conservationists must provide a simple economic rationale for local people and governments: How will protecting the forest and its inhabitants, rather than destroying them, help people living near great apes? The answer to nonhuman primate protection lies in improving the living conditions of people. Scientists from wealthier countries help to train students in countries where apes live to become conservation leaders themselves. In this way, we hope to help people in Asia and Africa preserve their natural heritage for future generations.

As more recent studies of gorillas elsewhere in Africa have been carried out, it has become clear that most wild gorillas do not behave much like those in the Virungas. At Bai Hokou in the Central African Republic, Melissa Remis found that lowland gorillas ate a highly varied diet containing many fruit species. At the same site, Michele Goldsmith found that gorillas walked nearly 2 miles (3 km) per day in search of food (Remis, 1997b; Goldsmith, 1999). It appears that gorillas all over Africa prefer to eat fruit but can fall back on fibrous leaves as a staple when fruit is not widely available. Contrary to their terrestrial image in the Virungas, gorillas in other forests, including mountain gorillas in the Bwindi Impenetrable Forest (Uganda), climb trees readily and often are seen feeding on fruits more than 100 feet (30 m) from the ground. Socially, lowland gorillas appear to forage in a more dispersed way than mountain gorillas and may live in less cohesive groups (Remis, 1997a). In some sites in central Africa, lowland gorilla groups use open swampy clearings to gather and feed, even wading into water in search of aquatic plants to eat.

Chimpanzees Along with bonobos, chimpanzees (*Pan troglodytes*) are our closest living relatives (Figure 7.41 on page 194). The genetic similarity between a chimpanzee and us is greater than the chimpanzee's evolutionary affinity to a gorilla. The most abundant of the three living African apes, with a total wild population estimated at 150,000–200,000, chimpanzees are extraordinarily adaptable animals, found across equatorial Africa from lowland rain forest to nearly open grasslands. Males may weigh up to 150 pounds (68 kg) and are 10–15% larger and heavier than females.

Unlike most nonhuman primates, chimpanzees do not live in cohesive, stable social groups but rather in a multimale, multifemale community called a **fission–fusion** mating system. A community may number 20–120 individuals, in which the only stable unit is a mother–offspring pair. Its members come together in unpredictable social groupings to form foraging subgroups, the size and composition of which seem to be determined by a combination of fruit distribution and the presence of fertile females (Figure 7.42). The community occupies a territory, which is defended by its males with great ferocity. Males band together to patrol the territorial boundaries on a regular basis and may attack and attempt to kill any chimpanzee, male or female, that is found encroaching on their land. The only exception occurs when male patrols encounter sexually receptive females from other communities, in which case the female may be coercively brought back to the home community (Goodall, 1986).

Within the community, males and females have very different social behavior patterns. Males tend to be highly social with one another, forming strong, long-lasting coalitions that they use to try to control females, patrol, and hunt. These alliances are not necessarily based on genetic relatedness among the males (Goldberg and Wrangham, 1997). Females travel more independently, apparently in order to avoid feeding competition from other adults. After an 8-month pregnancy, a 4-year infancy, and a prolonged juvenile period, a female chimpanzee reaches sexual maturity at about age 12. After this time, most females begin to visit neighboring communities, eventually settling there as breeding adults. The result is that adult females tend to be unrelated immigrants with few bonds in the new community (Goodall, 1986). Males remain in their birth community their entire lives, reaching maturity at 15 years of age. In the wild, chimpanzees live to a maximum age of 45; in captivity some have been known to reach 60 years of age.

Chimpanzees eat a highly diverse diet that is composed mainly of ripe fruit. In addition, they eat leaves and other plant products, plus insects such as termites and ants, which they extract from termite mounds using hand-fashioned tools

fission-fusion   Form of mating system seen in chimpanzees, bonobos, and a few other primates in which there are temporary subgroups but no stable, cohesive groups.

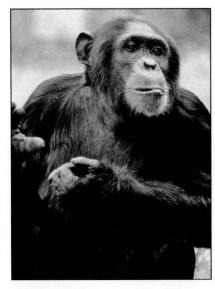

FIGURE 7.41   Chimpanzees and humans share a very close genetic and evolutionary kinship.

FIGURE 7.42   Chimpanzees live in complex kin groups in which life-long bonds and individual personalities play key roles, as in human societies.

FIGURE 7.43 Wild chimpanzees make and use simple tools to obtain food, learning tool-making from one another.

(Figure 7.43) Some West African chimpanzee populations use stones and clubs collected from the forest floor to crack open hard-shelled nuts. The pattern of tool use varies across Africa and is a prime example of another aspect of chimpanzee sophistication: culture (Whiten et al., 1999). More than any animal other than humans, chimpanzees live by learned traditions and pass these traditions on to their offspring. Tool use is not genetic, although the intellectual capacity to understand how a tool is used certainly is.

Chimpanzees also relish meat, in the form of monkeys, wild pigs, young antelope, and other small animals. In some forests, chimpanzees kill and eat hundreds of animals every year (Stanford, 1998a). Meat-eating patterns vary from site to site and seem to be subject to the same learned traditions that characterize tool use and other behaviors. Anthropologists find chimpanzee hunting behavior intriguing as a model for how early hominids may have behaved. Jane Goodall's pioneering research on chimpanzees, followed by research by Toshisada Nishida (1990), set the stage for much modern primate research.

Bonobos   Bonobos (*Pan paniscus*), sometimes called pygmy chimpanzees because of their slightly more slender build, are close relatives of chimpanzees and are classified in the same genus (Figure 7.44 on page 196). They exhibit more modest sexual dimorphism than the other great apes. Males and females have similar body sizes but males have larger skulls and canine teeth. They occur only in a limited region south of the Congo River in the Democratic Republic of the Congo (formerly Zaire), mainly in lowland rain forest habitat. Their total population is estimated at only about 25,000 (Box 7.2). Far less is known about bonobos than about chimpanzees; the first detailed field studies were conducted only in the 1980s, and political turmoil in Congo has repeatedly disrupted long-term research (Susman, 1984).

Bonobos eat a largely fruit diet but rely more on leafy plant material from the forest floor than chimpanzees do. Their more consistently available food supply may allow bonobos to live in larger parties than do chimpanzees (Malenky et al., 1994). Although they hunt and kill other mammals, bonobos do not necessarily eat them. At Lilungu, bonobos have been observed to capture young monkeys and use them as playthings, releasing them unharmed after they became bored with their prey (Sabater-Pi et al., 1993). At other sites, however, bonobos catch and eat small antelopes (Hohmann and Fruth, 1993).

Like chimpanzees, bonobos live in large, fluid social groupings we call communities. Males remain in the community of their birth, whereas females migrate between communities after sexual maturity. Males engage in border clashes with

FIGURE 7.44   Bonobos are close relatives of chimpanzees, and of humans.

males from neighboring communities (Kano, 1992). But there are some striking differences between bonobo and chimpanzee societies. Unlike female chimpanzees, female bonobos forge strong bonds and use female coalitions to prevent males from dominating them. Females engage in *genital-genital (or GG) rubbing,* a sociosexual behavior that reduces tensions between individuals. Immigrant females ally themselves with individual resident females and slowly extend their social network (Furuichi, 1987). Females achieve dominance status in bonobo communities far beyond that of female chimpanzees (Parish, 1996).

Bonobos have become well known to the public because of reports of their hypersexuality. The contrast between their behavior and that of chimpanzees has led to a debate over which species is the better model for how early humans may have behaved. Bonobos are said to be closer in sexual behavior and biology to humans than any other animal. Whether this is fully accurate has been questioned by a number of researchers (Box 8.1 on page 218).

In addition to their interesting behavior patterns in the wild, bonobos have been the subjects of exciting research on the origins of human language. Kanzi, a male bonobo at Georgia State University, understands several hundred words in spoken English and communicates using a symbol board (Savage-Rumbaugh and Lewin, 1994).

PRIMATE ECOLOGY

It's important to remember that despite their interesting social behavior, primates are first and foremost parts of ecosystems. A revolution has taken place in the way we see primates and other animals in their natural habitat, as a result of advances in the field of ecology. **Ecology** is the study of the interrelationships of animals, plants, and their physical environment. The environment provides the template on which natural selection molds behavior. At the same time, primates influence the ecology of many tropical forests, as dispersers of seeds and even as pollinators of flowering plants. Primate behavior evolved in direct response to environmental pressures, and we can understand most aspects of primate behavior only in the context of the natural environment in which the primate evolved.

Several key ecological factors have shaped the evolution of nonhuman primates and continue to shape them today. Finding and eating food is a constant, chronic concern that occupies much of the day for nonhuman primates. They are bound by the same equation that faces all other wild animals: The energy that is expended to find food (calories burned) must be balanced by the quantity (calo-

ecology   The study of the interrelationships of plants, animals, and the physical environment in which they live.

ries consumed) and quality (nutrients such as fats, proteins, and carbohydrates) of the food eaten. This need is even greater for females because of the physical cost of reproduction. To understand how nonhuman primates live, we must therefore understand something about the nature and distribution of their favorite foods and how that affects aspects of their behavior. In this section we consider primate ecology, which will allow us, in Chapter 8, to understand how primate social systems may be adapted to the environment.

Diet

Most primates are *herbivores*, living largely on a plant food diet (Figure 7.45). Exceptions to this pattern are many of the lower primates, which eat insects as a substantial portion of the diet, and a few higher primates (including humans) that also eat meat. Only one primate group is entirely carnivorous: The tarsier of southeast Asia, which subsists on insects, lizards, frogs, and other small animals. For the rest, much of the diet is composed of two items: fruits and leaves.

We tend to think of the natural world in a very human-centric way. But for a moment, consider a tropical forest from the point of view of a tree. As a tree, you produce several products that are highly valued by the animals you share the forest with: fruit, leaves, flowers, seeds, and so forth. All around you there are birds, monkeys, and small mammals that hunger after the fruit you produce. There are also millions of leaf-eating insects, monkeys, and other animals that eat your leafy foliage. But fruit and leaves have very different values to the potential herbivore. Leaves are the factories of a tropical tree; they take in sunlight and synthesize energy for the tree by the process of photosynthesis. For this reason, if a horde of insects or leaf-eating monkeys comes along and eats all its leaves, the tree will be unable to produce energy or obtain the nutrients it needs. At best it will have to endure a difficult period until new leaves can be grown, and at worst it could die. So ecologists predict that natural selection should endow trees with the means to protect their leaves.

Fruits have a very different value. They are the vessels that hold the seeds, which are the reproductive opportunities for the tree—its embryos for the next generation. Therefore, a tree "wants" its fruit to be eaten by animals, carried away somewhere, and then excreted out so that its seeds can germinate on the forest floor some distance away from their parents. Whereas trees and leaf-eaters, or **folivores**, are in a constant evolutionary battle, trees and fruit-eaters, called *frugivores*, are in a long-running symbiosis. So ecologists predict that natural selection should build traits into fruit that encourage frugivores to seek out the fruit crop and eat it.

There is abundant evidence that this is exactly what has happened. Consider how you choose a peach in the market that is ripe and ready to eat. First you look at it; is it orange and red, or still green? Then you touch it; is it soft, or still rock hard? Finally, you may smell it; does it have a pleasant, sweet smell? Wild primates use exactly the same criteria for choosing their fruits in tropical forests. And all these qualities—bright color, soft texture, and a good smell—were built into fruits by natural selection to convince frugivorous animals that they are delicious, nutritious, and ready to be eaten. These signals show a foraging primate that the fruit contains high levels of carbohydrate in the form of sugars, providing a caloric boost for an active day of foraging. Certainly brightly colored fruit did not evolve solely in response to primates; many birds eat fruit too, and their ancestors predate those of modern primates. But like birds, many primates are color-visioned fruit foragers.

Fruit-eating primates reap the benefit of a carbohydrate-rich diet, but at a cost. Fruits are temporary tree products that ripen and rot quickly, so fruit availability is far less predictable than leaf availability. And fruit is sought after by a wide range of animals because of its high caloric content (fruits tend to be high in carbohydrates and low in proteins). A primate must be able to efficiently locate fruits and then compete successfully for access to them. Fruits also tend to be patchily distributed on the tree.

Figure 7.45 Like all animals, primates must balance their calories expended searching for food with calories, protein, fat, and other nutrients obtained.

folivores Animals who eat a diet composed mainly of leaves, or foliage.

Leaves are an entirely different story when it comes to foraging. Leaves are found everywhere in a tropical forest, so you might think all a monkey has to do is reach out and pluck its breakfast. But a tropical forest is not the cornucopia of food that it might appear. Leaves tend to be poor sources of nutrients and calories compared with fruits, but they can contain large amounts of protein. Because leaves are such a valuable and dependable resource, trees protect them against folivores in a variety ways. First, many leaves are coated with bristles, spines, or hairs that make it difficult or painful to ingest them. A primate must also have a digestive system designed to cope with *fiber*. Fiber is a barrier to digestion, as anyone who eats raw corn or other high-fiber vegetables knows. Young tender leaves contain minimal fiber because the cell walls in each leaf have not yet built up layers of cellulose and hemicellulose that later become the structural support of the plant (Figure 7.46). Mature leaves are tougher and highly fibrous.

In addition to physical barriers, folivorous primates must cope with chemical defenses that plants put into their leaves. Leaves often contain an array of chemicals, called **secondary compounds** (because they are the byproducts of plant metabolism), which are toxic or at least indigestible to a primate. We're all familiar with secondary compounds; the reason tea becomes bitter when brewed too long is the presence of *tannins* in the tea leaves. Alkaloids and phenols are other secondary compounds commonly found in tropical forest foliage. The presence of secondary compounds is greatest in mature trees growing in poor soil, apparently because the tree needs to protect its leaves most in circumstances where nutrients for new growth are most limited.

THE CYCLES OF A TROPICAL FOREST

Tropical trees do not influence primate behavior only by the nutritional content of their food products. The distribution of foods is also profoundly important. In a temperate forest in the northern United States, an acre of forest might contain 500 trees of several species: oaks, maples, pines, and so forth. In an acre of tropical rain forest the diversity of species would be dramatically higher; 400 different species might be represented among the 500 trees. The cycle of a forest's trees producing new leaves, fruit, and flowers is its **phenology**. However, many tropical forest trees have *asynchronous cycles,* meaning that while one individual tree is laden with ripe fruit, the other trees of the same species standing nearby have no fruit at all. This is apparently an evolved strategy to protect trees by preventing predators ranging from insects to monkeys from homing in on a whole stand of trees and devouring all of their leaves in one swoop.

The staggering level of species diversity and the existence of asynchronous cycles in the tropics mean that wild primates must know their habitat intimately in order to find food. In Bwindi Impenetrable National Park, Uganda, chimpanzees travel from ripe fig tree to ripe fig tree. But even researchers cannot predict when a given tree will next produce ripe fruit (fruiting may happen once a year or every third year) or whether any of the fig trees will have fruit at a particular time.

secondary compounds Toxic chemical compounds found in the leaves of many plants which the plants use as a defense against leaf-eating animals.

phenology The leafing and fruiting cycles of a forest.

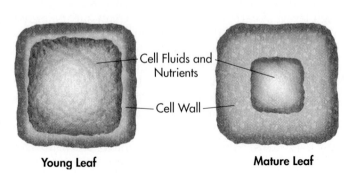

FIGURE 7.46 Comparison of a tender and mature leaf. As leaves mature, they become fiber-filled and harder to digest.

Young Leaf　　**Mature Leaf**

Cell Fluids and Nutrients

Cell Wall

Climate seasonality is another very important dietary factor to primates because they must locate tender new leaves and ripening fruit before other animals in the forest find it. In a northern climate, seasons are obvious: Autumn arrives and all the leaves fall. In the tropics, seasons exist, contrary to widespread belief, but they are staggered and asynchronous. While one species is dropping its leaves, another species standing nearby may be growing new ones.

In addition to leaves and fruit, most primates eat at least small quantities of other foods. Many species eat insects and other small invertebrates such as spiders, grubs, scorpions, and (for those leaving near water) crayfish and crabs. Many strepsirhine species rely heavily on small, living prey. And a few species, primarily the marmosets and tamarins, rely on another source: the resin that flows from tree trunks. These monkeys use well-shaped front teeth to scrape away the uppermost layer of bark from trees in their home range, causing sap to flow. They then return to the spot over and over to eat the gummy resin. Like people tapping maple trees to obtain syrup, marmosets reap a bounty of carbohydrates from such behavior.

A final source of nutrition for wild primates is the meat of other mammals. Chimpanzees are the most avid hunters of mammalian prey, but many other species hunt as well. In some Brazilian forests, capuchin monkeys hunt the endangered golden lion tamarin. The highest daily meat consumption ever recorded among nonhuman primates was by savanna baboons at Gilgil, Kenya, in a field study by Shirley Strum. Strum's baboon group ate nearly one mammal, usually a rabbit or baby antelope, per day (Strum, 1981).

YOU ARE WHAT YOU EAT: DIETARY AND DIGESTIVE STRATEGIES

For most primates, finding a suitable diet means foraging in the right place at the right time and then selecting the most edible and nutritious plant foods available. But as we saw earlier, the best foods often are fiercely competed for. So many primates have evolved dietary or digestive specializations that allow them to coexist with other species by carving out their own ecological niche. For example, colobine monkeys of Africa and Asia possess a specialized digestive tract that allows them to consume large amounts of high-fiber, low-quality leaves and derive maximum nutrients from them. They can do this because all colobines possess a digestive system somewhat similar to that of a cow, with a semichambered stomach and the clear division of a *foregut* from the main gut. In the foregut, symbiotic bacteria break down dietary cellulose fiber in much the same way that microbes in a termite's gut break down wood. There is also evidence that this specialized gut can partially detoxify leaves that are high in some secondary compounds. This adaptation has allowed colobines to invade habitats in which other monkeys do not thrive and to live at higher densities than other monkeys where several species are sympatric.

In general, the largest-bodied primates rely the least on insect prey, although a few primates, such as chimpanzees and capuchin monkeys, forage for insects very intensively and at times consume large numbers of them. Gorillas don't eat many insects, and very small-bodied primates rarely eat large quantities of leafy matter. This is because of the time and energy needed to make a living on these diets in relation to the time and energy needed to properly digest leaves, fruits, and live prey. The very largest primates tend to be folivorous, although there are exceptions. So gorillas are able to subsist on a diet of high-fiber plants, which they slowly pass through a very long digestive tract that provides the space for maximal breakdown of food before excretion. The smallest primate that is highly folivorous is a species of dwarf lemur (*Lepilemur mustelinus*).

DIET AND ACTIVITY BUDGETS

In nature, there are only so many hours of daylight during which a diurnal primate can make its living. A primate's **activity budget** allows it to compensate for calories expended with calories consumed. Diurnal primates forage during the day, nocturnal primates come out of hiding at night, and *crepuscular* primates forage at dawn and dusk. *Cathemeral* primates have irregular active periods during both the day and night. Each activity period has its share of foods available and predators lurking to catch unwary prey.

Activity budgets are tightly linked to dietary quality. Primates that live on high-fiber, low-calorie diets also tend to be more sedentary than those living on a high-fruit diet; compare the fission–fusion social system of the chimpanzee or spider monkey with the slowly moving cohesive groups in which howlers or mountain gorillas live. Gibbons brachiate acrobatically through Asian forests, eating fruit as their dietary staple. Muriquis of the Atlantic coastal forest of Brazil wake up late, go to sleep early, and in between forage slowly through their treetop habitat for a diet that consists largely of leaves. Mountain gorillas in Rwanda move at a glacial pace, walking as little as a few hundred yards in a day. Their high-mountain habitat contains practically no fruit trees, so their diet is mainly wild celery and other highly fibrous plants. But lowland gorillas a few hundred miles to the west live in tropical forests with a high diversity of fruiting trees, and they eat a great deal of fruit. Lowland gorillas travel up to 2 miles (3 km) per day. They travel such great distances to find widely scattered fruit trees, and the energy they burn in their travels is replaced by the high carbohydrate value of their fruity diet.

Katharine Milton (1980) conducted a field study of howler and spider monkeys that illustrates the contrasts between frugivore and folivore activity patterns and what they may mean for primate evolution. On Barro Colorado Island in Panama, Milton observed howlers eating a diet high in leaves. The howlers carefully selected the most tender, young growing parts, but their diet contained little other than fiber. They were also very sedentary, moving very slowly through the forest canopy in a cohesive group. Meanwhile, spider monkeys ate a diet high in ripe fruit and traveled many times further per day than howlers. Milton (1981) further considered the relative brain sizes of the two species; spider monkeys have larger brain–body size ratio than do howlers. She hypothesized that the evolutionary pressure of finding and remembering the changing locations of ripe fruit trees had placed a premium on cognition in spider monkeys, leading to brain size increase in this primate but not in the related howlers.

FEEDING COMPETITION

Primates live in communities with a host of other animals, both primates and nonprimates. In many tropical forests, when a large tree bears ripe fruit it becomes an arboreal banquet table for a wide variety of animals, both mammals and birds, day and night. The problem for the primate is that it competes for the bounty of energy-rich food with numerous other species. Primatologists have debated for years over which is the more important influence on the evolution of primate social systems: competition between the members of a group, called *intragroup feeding competition*, or competition between two groups, or *intergroup feeding competition*.

When animals feed together in social groups, feeding competition is likely to occur. Such competition is more intense when the quality of the food is high, and especially when the food is distributed in small, scattered parcels that concentrate feeding at a few spots. When a group of monkeys enters a fruit tree, they all want to eat the ripest fruit. But inevitably, higher-ranking animals, older animals, and

activity budget　The pattern of waking, eating, moving, socializing, and sleeping that all nonhuman primates engage in each day.

males tend to control and monopolize the food at the expense of smaller, weaker, lower-ranking animals and females. This direct squabbling over food is called *contest feeding competition* and is very common among frugivorous group-living primates. Although contest competition usually is considered an aspect of intragroup competition, it can also occur between groups.

When feeding competition occurs but enough food exists so that every animal nevertheless gets some food, *scramble feeding competition* has occurred. Folivorous primates often are scramble competitors: Leaves are everywhere, and everybody will find some, even if some animals find more than others. Primate species that practice scramble competition often lack rigid dominance hierarchies, perhaps because there is less pressure to compete intensely when food is evenly distributed. Scramble competition often characterizes intragroup competition in folivorous primate groups.

The effects of feeding competition are cumulative: Over time, if you can't get quite enough good food to eat, you will be stressed, and such stress may lead to poor health, lower dominance rank, and lowered fertility. There is ample evidence of the negative effects of feeding competition in nature. For example, Charles Janson showed that for a population of cebus monkeys in Manu National Park, Peru, the amount of food eaten by each monkey was limited by aggressive competition with other monkeys in the same group (Janson, 1985). In some primates, competition is lessened when males and females have slightly different diets, as Natalie Vasey demonstrated for two lemur species on the Masoala Peninsula of Madagascar. Vasey (1996) found that among red ruffed lemurs, females ate a lower-fiber, higher-protein diet than males, and this difference was even more pronounced during the breeding season.

Sue Boinski studied two squirrel monkey species in forests in Central and South America and found that despite similar feeding patterns and similar levels of predation, the two species differed in the degree of intragroup feeding competition. Females of the Costa Rican species, in which feeding competition was intense, formed rigid dominance hierarchies, whereas the Peruvian species in which feeding competition was lower did not exhibit such rigid hierarchies (Boinski, 1994).

Natural food shortages have a severe effect on wild primate populations. A long-term study of ring-tailed lemurs in Beza-Mahafaly Reserve, Madagascar, by Michelle Sauther and colleagues (1999) showed that nearly one-third of all adult females died during a particularly harsh drought in the 1990s, during which infant mortality reached 80%. Some primate ecologists believe that feeding competition matters mainly when the environment takes a turn for the worse. In such ecological crunch times, food may become severely limited, and natural selection may favor the individuals that are the best foragers and food competitors. Evidence that lean times, droughts, and famines increase feeding competition have been reported for primates as diverse as mouse dwarf lemurs (Hladik, 1975), howlers (Milton, 1982), and vervet monkeys (Cheney et al., 1988).

Territories and Ranges   All mammals, including nonhuman primates, live in defined places called **home ranges** (Figure 7.47 on page 202). This area can be very limited—smaller than a football field in the case of some nocturnal strepsirhines—or many square kilometers in the case of some apes and monkeys. The range must contain all the resources needed by a nonhuman primate or a social group: water, food, shelter, and mates. Home ranges often overlap, either slightly or entirely. Parts of the home range that are used most intensively are called the **core area**. In some species, such as gorillas, home ranges overlap greatly, and groups encounter one another often. In other species, such as chimpanzee, community ranges overlap only slightly, and aggressive encounters occur in the overlap zone. In some species, the home range is defended against other members of the same species, in

home range   The spatial area used by a primate group.

core area   The part of a home range that is most intensively used.

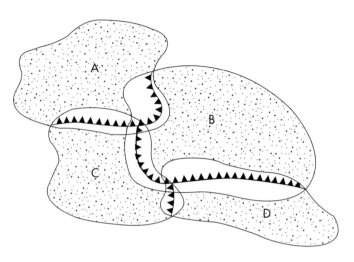

Boundary of home range, limits of animal A's normal movement

Area of exclusive territory, which conspecifics do not enter

Defended territorial boundary

FIGURE 7.47   Primates use their space in a variety of ways; home ranges, core areas, and territories.

which case we call it a **territory**. The defended portion of the home range usually is the part in which critical resources are located.

Territorial defense can take the form of vocalizing, such as the songs of gibbons. By setting up loudspeakers within, at the border of, and outside the territorial boundaries of gibbon pairs, John Mitani (1985) showed that gibbons use their songs as territorial markers. As Mitani predicted, gibbons that heard the calls of strange gibbons coming (via loudspeakers) from within their territory responded most vigorously, calling and approaching the site of the call in obvious territorial defensiveness. Territorial defense can also result from visual encounters along territorial borders, in which males, females, or both (depending on the species) intimidate and chase the potential intruders. Among many Old World monkeys, females rather than males engage in territorial disputes. In some species, territorial disputes may be settled through physical contact, including lethal contact in rare cases such as chimpanzees.

Why be territorial? Primatologists have spent years trying to understand the key resources nonhuman primate groups are willing to protect. Males seek to obtain and control females. In some mammals (ungulates, for instance), males try to hold territories because females are on those territories, and females may judge a male's quality by the size and quality of the territory he commands (Jarman, 1974). This is less true among nonhuman primates. We believe that nonhuman primates defend their home ranges when food resources are worth defending because of their high nutritional value or when males can control females through their defense of territory. But territories typically are defended only when it is energetically possible and worthwhile to do so. A slow-moving colobus monkey may not defend a patch of forest containing its favored leaves because the folivore may not be able to effectively monopolize its range, and the leaves may not be nutritious enough to warrant defending anyway.

Mate defense territoriality is a different equation. Females in many nonhuman primate species use their habitat to maximize their intake of food for themselves and their offspring. As we saw in Chapter 5, males are concerned mainly with where females are. So what might appear to be male defense of a territory for the sake of protecting a relished fruit tree may in fact be territorial defense aimed at keeping males from other groups away from the male's females. This is dramati-

territory   The part of a home range that is defended against other members of the same species.

cally the case in chimpanzees, in which male patrols capture young, fertile females near territorial boundaries, and males attack intruders who may be intent on doing the same in the residents' community.

Predation　Nonhuman primates in the wild face the difficult challenge of finding food while avoiding attacks by predators. Failing to find food on a given afternoon will leave a monkey hungry the next day, but failing to avoid an attack by an eagle or leopard will leave it dead or injured. So we should expect that nonhuman primates have evolved behavioral defenses against predators. But actually observing predation is difficult because the predators are stealthy and usually nocturnal and solitary (Figure 7.48). Most often a member of a nonhuman primate group being studied disappears one day, and the researcher has no idea whether disease, accidental death, or a predator was responsible.

Despite a lack of field observations, we can make a few generalizations about predation. First, small-bodied nonhuman primates are more vulnerable to predation than larger species. In Madagascar, owls have been reported to kill up to one-quarter of the mouse lemur population each year (Goodman et al., 1993). Even a much lower predation rate could be a major source of mortality in a population of monkeys. Second, many nonhuman primate species exhibit behaviors that appear to have evolved in response to the threat of predation. Alarm calls are often given when a predator approaches, and experimental studies using loudspeakers to play the calls of leopards and eagles have shown that monkeys respond in a variety of ways. Vervet monkeys studied in Amboseli National Park, Kenya, by Dorothy Cheney and Robert Seyfarth (1991) give alarm calls that vary depending on the type of predator spotted; different calls are given for eagles, leopards, and pythons. Red colobus monkeys studied by Ronald Noë and colleagues in the Taï Forest of Ivory Coast responded to the calls of wild chimpanzees by moving toward other monkey species nearby; the chimpanzee calls seemed to be acting as early warning systems that the colobus could capitalize on (Noë and Bshary, 1997).

One of the few cases in which we can directly observe predation on nonhuman primates is in African forests in which chimpanzees prey on other nonhuman primates. We saw earlier that chimpanzees are avid meat-eaters, and red colobus monkeys are their most frequent prey. Where chimpanzees are accustomed to being

FIGURE 7.48　Primates face a wide variety of predators in the wild, including birds of prey.

watched by human observers, both their hunting behavior and its impact on red colobus can be studied in detail. In Gombe National Park, Tanzania, chimpanzees kill 18% of the red colobus population living in their home range in some years (in other years predation is much lighter; Stanford, 1998a). Red colobus living in larger groups have a lower individual risk of being captured by a chimpanzee, and red colobus groups containing many adult males are at less risk than groups with only a few males. This is the case because adult male colobus mount a fierce counterattack when chimpanzees attack them. The counterattack is more likely to succeed in driving off the chimpanzees when there are five or more male colobus defending.

Finally, the pattern of predation on the colobus depended very much on where the colobus lived relative to the border of the territory of the chimpanzee community. In the chimpanzees' core area, predation on colobus monkeys was intense, and as a consequence groups were small and had few immature members (Gombe chimpanzees kill mainly young colobus monkeys). Toward the periphery of the chimpanzees' community territory, hunting was much less common. Chimpanzee predation was overall such a major source of colobus mortality that the colobus population would have been in serious decline at Gombe were it not for the fact that in some years predation was infrequent.

PRIMATE COMMUNITIES

If you were to walk through some tropical forests, you would see not one but many species of primates. In the Congo Basin of central Africa or the Amazon Basin of Peru, it's possible to see more than a dozen primate species in a single acre of forest. If you were to take a walk through the same forest at night, you would see a different, nocturnal community of primates. With so many closely related and often morphologically similar primates sharing the same forest, why isn't there more intense competition between them for food and other resources? The answer is that there is or was competition in the evolutionary past of the species. Ecological theory predicts that when two or more organisms with very similar needs are sympatric, sharing the same space, they will diverge from one another in some critical aspect of their *niche*, or ecological role. For example, two monkeys that seem to eat the same foods will be found to eat different diets when food is scarce. One species might forage high in trees, whereas the other finds its food on the ground. Without such *niche separation*, species would drive each other into extinction far more often than they are observed to.

For example, in a study of two lemur species in Beza-Mahafaly Reserve in Madagascar, Nayuta Yamashita found that Verreaux's sifakas ate a more folivorous diet than sympatric ring-tailed lemurs did in the same habitat. The sifakas have dental adaptations to a tough, fibrous diet, which may allow them to coexist with more frugivorous species such as the ring-tailed lemurs (Yamashita, 2002). In Ranomafana National Park, also in Madagascar, Chia Tan found that three closely related bamboo lemurs (of the genus *Hapalemur*) shared the same forest space, and all ate bamboo (which accounted for at least 88% of the annual diet of all three) (Figure 7.49). Given what we said earlier about the impossibility of multiple species living on the same diet, how could these three lemurs coexist without driving each other into extinction? Tan found that one species ate mainly the tender young shoots of the bamboo, whereas the other two species ate different bamboo species during some seasons. In this way the three species partitioned their food resources (Tan, 1999).

Niche divergence occurs among all primates that are sympatric, and such divergence often is evident only during ecological crunch times. What's more, it can be very difficult to demonstrate feeding competition in the wild—simply overlapping strongly with another species' ecology is not evidence that the two species

FIGURE 7.49 Ranomafana National Park, Madagascar, home to multiple species of lemurs that divide up their forest resources.

compete—so field studies more often record the nature of ecological overlap than the occurrence of ecological competition. Gorillas and chimpanzees share forests across central Africa, and both species prefer a diet heavy in ripe fruit. But during lean seasons, gorillas fall back on fibrous plants as their staple, while chimpanzees continue to forage widely for fruit. Although the diets of the two ape species overlap extensively, direct contest competition over food is rare (Stanford and Nkurunungi, 2003).

Some primates form *polyspecific groups,* made up of two, three, or more species that travel and feed together for part or all of each day. These have been studied both in the Old World tropics and also the New World (Terborgh, 1983). The antipredator benefits of foraging in such a group are obvious; more eyes on the lookout mean safer and better foraging. Feeding competition is lessened by the fact that the participating species usually have key differences in some aspect of their diet or feeding strategies. African guenons, for example, have a strong tendency to form such associations (Gautier-Hion et al., 1983).

Marina Cords studied blue monkeys and red-tailed monkeys, two closely related guenons, in Kakamega forest of western Kenya. She found that neither blue nor red-tailed species seemed to benefit greatly or suffer feeding competition when feeding in the same tree (Cords, 1990). In West Africa, however, another guenon, the diana monkey, often is joined by red colobus. The latter appears to use the former as a sentinel, fleeing from predators when they hear the diana monkeys give alarm calls (Bshary and Noë, 1997). In Gombe National Park, Tanzania, the relationship between guenons and red colobus is the opposite: Red-tailed and blue monkeys use colobus as sentinels to warn them of approaching danger (Stanford, 1998a). The interactions between primate species can be as diverse as the primate species themselves, depending once again on the habitat and its ecology.

As you can see, primates are a highly diverse group of mammals that are subject to many of the same evolutionary and ecological principles that guide the lives of other mammals. However, nonhuman primates have two adaptations—sociality and large brains—that set them apart from nearly all other animals. In the next chapter, we will examine nonhuman primate social behavior and cognition to see what they tell us about human evolution.

SUMMARY

1. **What characteristics distinguish nonhuman primates from other mammals?**

   Primates share a suite of characteristics: grasping hand and opposable thumb, stereoscopic vision, single births, sociality, large brain–body size ratio, extended ontogeny, visually oriented daytime activity, nails instead of claws, and an enclosed bony eye orbit.

2. **What are the main hypotheses that account for the origin of the primates?**

   The arboreal hypothesis was the first theory put forward to explain primate origins. This centered on the role of stereo vision and the grasping hand in life in the trees. The leading alternative theory is the visual predation hypothesis, which Cartmill proposed based on the likely predatory behavior of the earliest nonhuman primates.

3. **Why is the diversity of lemurs on Madagascar today only a shadow of lemur diversity in the past?**

   The largest lemur species went extinct not long after human arrival on Madagascar about 1,500–2,000 years ago. The species found there today are mainly the smaller species, presumably less desirable as food and so less hunted.

4. **What is the taxonomic position of the tarsier?**

   The tarsier is a haplorhine, linking it to the anthropoid primates, but it retains many prosimian characters, such as a combination of nails and claws on its feet. Therefore, it may represent an evolutionary bridge between the prosimian and anthropoid primates.

5. **What is an ape?**

   An ape is an anthropoid primate with a suspensory shoulder anatomy that allows brachiation. Apes also lack tails, have large brains, and exhibit a highly elaborated degree of social complexity.

6. **Why is it a mistake to think of a tropical rain forest as a cornucopia of food available for wild nonhuman primates?**

   Plant foods in tropical forests are protected by a variety of adaptations, from high fiber content to bristles to chemical defenses. In addition, tropical forest trees often produce leaves and fruit at different times, making it difficult for nonhuman primates to predict when they can harvest the tree's products.

7. **What is the difference between a home range and a territory?**

   A home range is the area that a nonhuman primate or nonhuman primate group uses over a long period of time. A territory is the part of the home range that is defended against members of other groups of the same species. All, part, or none of the home range may be defended as a territory.

8. **Why would primates of different species associate together despite increased feeding competition?**

   Primates of different species may capitalize on the food-finding and predator detection abilities of other species, which may outweigh the disadvantages of being in a larger group.

CRITICAL THINKING QUESTIONS

1. We say that primates are the mostly highly social animals on Earth. But many animals, from fish to birds to hoofed mammals, live in enormous herds, flocks, or schools that are far larger than any primate group. What is difference between those sorts of groups and those in which nonhuman primates live?

2. Chimpanzees and bonobos are very similar anatomically but quite different behaviorally. Based on what you learned about species concepts in Chapter 5, should they be considered separate species or merely variants on a single species? Why?

3. Why should we consider the primate body plan to be a series of evolutionary compromises?

KEY TERMS

metatheria
prototheria
eutheria
strepsirhine
    (Strepsirhini)
haplorhine (Haplorhini)
prosimian
anthropoid
arboreal hypothesis
visual predation
    hypothesis
dental arcade
nocturnal
diurnal

neocortex
ontogeny
sociality
Playtrrhini
prehensile tail
polyandry
Catarrhini
estrus
hylobatid
    (Hylobatidae)
pongid
    (Pongidae)
hominid
    (Hominidae)

brachiation
frugivorous
fission–fusion
ecology
folivores
secondary compounds
phenology
activity budget
home range
core area
territory

SUGGESTED READING

Cheney, Dorothy, and Robert M. Seyfarth. (1991). *How Monkeys See the World*. University of Chicago Press, Chicago.

Goodall, Jane. (1986). *Chimpanzees of Gombe*. Harvard University Press, Cambridge, MA.

Stanford, Craig. (2001). *Significant Others*. Basic Books, New York.

Strier, Karen (2003). *Primate Behavioral Ecology*, 2nd editon. Boston, Allyn & Bacon.

Chapter 8

PRIMATE BEHAVIOR

THE FOLLOWING DAY I TRACKED GROUP 8 [a group of gorillas] into the saddle area west of Visoke and contacted them from a distance of about sixty feet. They gave me the calmest reception I had ever received from an unhabituated group. The first individual to acknowledge my presence was the young silverback, who strutted onto a rock and stared with compressed lips before going off to feed. I named him Pugnacious, Pug for short. He was followed by the extremely attractive blackback, who nipped off a leaf to fold between his lips for a few seconds before spitting it out, a common displacement activity known as symbolic feeding and indicative of mild unease. After whacking at some vegetation, the magnificent male swaggered out of sight into dense foliage, seemingly quite pleased with himself. I named him Samson. Next, the two young adults scampered into view and impishly flipped over on to their backs to stare at me from upside-down positions, giving the impression they were wearing lopsided grins. In time they were named Geezer and Peanuts. When the elderly female came into view, she gazed briefly at me in a totally uninterested manner before sitting down next to Peanuts and maneuvering her patchy rump almost into his face for grooming. I named her Coco because of her somewhat light chocolate-colored hair. Lastly, the old silverback came forward. In all my years of research I never met a silverback so dignified and commanding of respect. His silvering extended from the sides of his cheekbones, along neck and shoulders, enveloped his back and barrel, and continued down the sides of both thighs. Having little to go by in comparison, except for zoo gorillas, I estimated his age as approximately fifty years, possibly more. The nobility of his character compelled me to seek a name for him immediately. In Swahili, *rafiki* means "friend." Because friendship implies mutual respect and trust, the regal silverback became known as Rafiki.

—Dian Fossey, *Gorillas in the Mist* (1983)

Watching nonhuman primates is one thing; understanding their behavior is another. But observation of behavior is at the heart of the subfield of biological anthropology known as *primatology*, as pioneering researcher Dian Fossey understood.

Primates are intrinsically fascinating animals that serve as illustrations of evolutionary principles of natural selection, adaptive radiation, convergent evolution, and sexual selection. They also inform us about human evolution, offering a window onto how early humans may have behaved. In this chapter we will consider how biological anthropologists study nonhuman primates and their social evolution. We will see that evolutionary principles that you learned in Chapter 5, such as natural selection and sexual selection, play key roles in shaping primate behavior. You'll also examine the diversity of societies in which nonhuman primates may live and explore the reasons these societies evolve the way they did. And you will read about some of the current controversies over the form and function of primate social behavior.

STUDYING PRIMATES

As we saw in Chapter 7, *sociality* is the most fundamental primate behavioral adaptation (Figure 8.1). It is the hallmark of nearly all the anthropoid primates, and its study is an essential component of nearly all nonhuman primate behavior research. Primatologists want to learn why nonhuman primates are social. To do this they study the costs and benefits of group living and examine how the same evolutionary processes that promoted sociality in nonhuman primates may have promoted the emergence of humankind.

The rise of the modern approach to the study of nonhuman primate behavior coincided with major changes in the way primates were studied. The earliest field researchers spent only a few days or weeks watching nonhuman primates in the wild, and little effort was made to collect data systematically. Jane Goodall (1968) was the first researcher to immerse herself in the lives of the animals. She learned intimate details of their lives and followed her subjects year after year (Figure 8.2). What Goodall did in the early 1960s is now the norm for primatologists; graduate students typically spend 1–2 years living in the habitat of the primates for a doctoral thesis project. Many field studies of more than 10 years' duration have been carried out. In extended studies, multiple primate generations can be followed and individuals' lives more fully understood. Studies of nonhuman primate demography have revealed aspects of the evolution of life histories and the ways in which long-term patterns of mating success are related to reproductive success. Primatologists have also added new research tools to their arsenal: paternity tests using DNA from hair follicles, feces, or urine; studies of endocrine influences on behavior using hormones extracted from feces or urine; and studies of nonhuman primate communication using sophisticated sound recording equipment (Figure 8.3).

We can study nonhuman primates in several different settings, each of which strongly influences the sort of research that is possible. A **captive study** allows us to closely observe a nonhuman primate group every day—subjects won't hide in dense trees for hours on end—and individuals that have well-recorded life histories. We often study captive populations over many generations and know their kin network. We can also manipulate the study group; the researcher might move a new male into the social group in order to observe the effect on the rest of the group. This opportunity makes behavioral experiments possible that we cannot usually achieve in the field. The downside of studying nonhuman primates in captivity is obvious: The animals are kept in highly unnatural settings rather than the forests in which their behaviors evolved, and so we cannot expect to see natural patterns

FIGURE 8.1 Sociality is the most fundamental behavioral adaptation of the primates.

FIGURE 8.2 Jane Goodall pioneered the modern approach to studying primates in the wild, involving close-up observation of known individuals over many months.

FIGURE 8.3 Modern primate study sometimes involves high-tech methods. This golden lion tamarin is having a battery changed in its radio transmitter collar.

of behavior. Enforced proximity leads to higher levels of aggression, sex, and affiliation than we would see in the same animals in the wild. The artificial food supply also means we cannot conduct ecological studies. A valuable use of captive studies is to confirm and refine the results of studies done in the wild.

Some nonhuman primate studies are conducted in a more spacious **semi–free-ranging** environment. Very large enclosures, or even small islands, sometimes have nonhuman primate populations. Cayo Santiago, an islet off the coast of Puerto Rico onto which rhesus macaques from India were introduced in the 1930s, is one example. The animals in a semi–free-ranging setting can establish territories, form their own groups, and forage for food, even though they are in captivity. Because they are confined (though in a large area), we can easily study kinship and follow many generations of the animals. This setting is a compromise between the confines of captivity and an entirely natural field study.

A modern study of primate behavior called **field study**, is conducted in the habitat in which the species evolved. Only in the field can researchers see patterns of behavior that evolved in response to environmental variables (Figure 8.4). As we saw earlier, the interplay between genes and behavior depends on a third critical variable: the physical environment. Studies of nonhuman primates in the wild focus on various aspects of ecology, such as diet and its influence on grouping patterns and social behavior; *positional behavior,* the relationship between locomotor morphology and the physical environment; and social interactions within and between primate groups.

There are significant difficulties in studying nonhuman primates in the wild. First, the primatologist must accustom the animals to his or her presence. This is a slow process that can take months or even years. Only once habituated can the

semi–free-ranging Primate behavior study conducted in a large area that is enclosed or isolated in some way so the population is captive.

field study Primate behavior study conducted in the habitat in which the primate naturally occurs.

FIGURE 8.4 Field research on free-living primates allows primatologists to study patterns of behavior in the setting where the behavior evolved.

primates be identified as individuals and observed closely. However, habituation may also allow other people, including poachers intending to kill the animals, to approach. Therefore, habituation can be undertaken only in areas where the animals' lives will not be placed in danger should the scientists pack up their project and go home. And even well-habituated primates are difficult to watch because so much of their behavior takes place behind dense foliage and rocks or in tall trees. Some nonhuman primates have huge home ranges, and just locating the group every day can be a challenge. A year spent in the wild watching monkeys may produce a small fraction of the observation hours that a scientist could obtain in a zoo in one month. And the sort of manipulations of the social and physical environment that can be done easily in captivity, from diet changes to the taking of DNA samples, are rarely possible in the wild.

WHY ARE NONHUMAN PRIMATES SOCIAL?

Primatologists choose their study subjects according to the evolutionary principles they intend to investigate. As we saw in Chapter 7, one of the most fundamental primate adaptations is sociality, and the reasons for the diversity of societies among nonhuman primates is a major area of research. A primatologist wanting to understand how monogamy works in nonhuman primates, with an eye toward understanding the origins of monogamy in human societies, might study a monogamous primate such as the gibbon. The gibbon certainly is an animal of great intrinsic beauty and interest, but to a primatologist it is also an illustration of how natural and sexual selection operate in the wild.

We are limited in our ability to extrapolate likely patterns of behavior in ancient primates, including hominids, by the small number of nonhuman primates species living. Not including the largely solitary strepsirhines, we have perhaps 150 species from which to reconstruct likely patterns of the evolution of primate social behavior. By contrast, biologists seeking to understand the evolution of bird social behavior have more than 9,000 species from which to draw examples of how adaptation and natural selection work. Nevertheless, we have made much progress in recent years in understanding the evolutionary and ecological influences on sociality.

THE PARADOX OF SOCIALITY

Nonhuman primates, like all other social mammals, tend to behave in ways that maximize their individual fitness. But this creates a paradox: Why would any animal live in a group if the bottom line evolutionarily is individual mating success? Group living is an anthropoid adaptation, and it may provide the individual monkey or ape with access to three basic necessities: mates, food and, protection from predators. Each of these benefits has, however, a significant downside.

Access to Mates   Access to multiple potential mates is an obvious benefit of living in a group rather than in pairs or alone. Nonhuman primates exhibit a variety of grouping patterns, but in each mating system male and female goals are the same: enhancing their reproductive success. The behavioral strategies each sex uses to achieve this goal, however, differ markedly.

Group life may provide access to mates, but it also means that males must compete for mating. Among nonhuman primates that live in large social groups, enormous energy and time are consumed in the quest for mating success, and many males lose out. When access to a female is at stake, male baboons are more willing to engage in highly aggressive behavior toward one another, inflicting injury (Figure 8.5). Males also form alliances when females are ovulating and sexually receptive, and if a male is not in an alliance his ability to obtain matings may suffer.

(a)

(b)

FIGURE 8.5 (a) Male competition can be fierce. (b) This male baboon has bite wounds suffered in competition with other males.

The intensity of male–male competition, and the importance of female choice of male traits, is also reflected in the level of sexual dimorphism we see among primates. Species in which males compete aggressively for females tend to feature high degrees of sexual dimorphism because male size and strength help to determine mating success. Species exhibiting sexual dimorphism in body size also tend to live in **polygynous** groups, which have multiple females living with either one or multiple males. Monogamous and solitary species tend to be less dimorphic. In baboons, for instance, males compete fiercely with other males for mating opportunities and are about 30% larger and heavier than females. Gibbons, on the other hand, live in monogamous pair bonds and are not dimorphic with respect to body size (Figure 8.6). There are exceptions to this pattern, however, such as the highly dimorphic but largely solitary orangutan.

polygynous Mating system consisting of at least one male and more than one female.

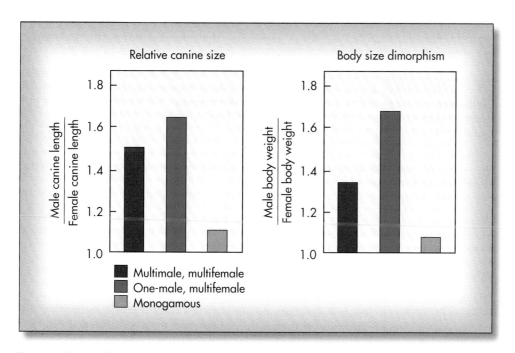

FIGURE 8.6 The most polygynous primates live in groups with many more females than males. In such species the degree of sexual dimorphism tends to be pronounced.

Food   Exploiting the food-finding abilities of other group members to find food yourself is one benefit of group life. But the feeding and foraging benefits of living in a social group are offset by the need to compete for food with group mates once food is found. If a monkey is led to a bonanza of fruit by others in the group, it must then compete with its group mates. Much evidence supports the notion that feeding competition strongly affects group life in nonhuman primates. Females are particularly dependent on the availability of food resources in their habitat because they must nourish themselves adequately to bear the costs of reproduction. When females live in large groups, they often form **matrilineal** clusters in which mothers, daughters, and other female relatives socialize with each other more than they do with nonrelatives.

Avoiding Predators   As we saw in Chapter 7, many species of predatory animals hunt nonhuman primates. In tropical forests, attacks by birds of prey, big cats, large snakes, and humans are all potential causes of mortality. Predation can have a major impact on nonhuman primate populations, even when it occurs rarely. We should therefore expect evolved responses to predation in any nonhuman primate species prone to being hunted. However, little direct evidence of predation exists because of the difficulty of observing predation. Predators themselves tend to be silent, stealthy, and often nocturnal, so a primatologist records only the sudden disappearance of one of his study subjects from its group. Whether the disappearance resulted from disease, migration, infanticide, or predation often is unclear.

There is abundant indirect evidence, however, that group living helps nonhuman primates avoid predators. In larger groups, there are more eyes to act as sentinels, warning group members about danger approaching. Michelle Sauther has studied the response to predation risk by small and large groups of ring-tailed lemurs in Beza Mahafaly Reserve in southern Madagascar. She found that lemurs in small groups avoided foraging on the ground in areas where predator pressure was intense. Therefore, those animals found less food. On the other hand, small groups tended to associate with other lemur species when feeding and during the birth season, when highly vulnerable infants were present. Sauther reasoned that small ring-tailed lemur groups compensate for their lack of numbers by combining with other species. Larger groups entered new and unknown areas of the forest and therefore encountered predators more often than smaller groups did and reaped more food. Sauther (2002) showed that lemurs face tradeoffs between predation risk and food intake that vary according to social factors such as group size.

In some nonhuman primate species, social groups actually mob predators, counterattacking in the hope of persuading the predator that hunting them is not worth the trouble or risk of injury. Terrence Gleason and Marilyn Norconk (2002) found that among the small South American white-faced saki, smaller predators (small hawks, cats, and snakes) evoked a mobbing response. Faced with larger, more dangerous predators such as eagles, the monkeys retreated quickly into dense thickets and froze to avoid detection.

Simply being in a large group means that if a predator strikes, one's individual chances of being the victim are lowered. Although being in a large group may be an effective way to detect predators, it may also make the group itself more easily detected because large groups are noisy and visible.

Most nonhuman primate species have an alarm call of some sort that they use to warn group members of approaching danger. This suggests that predation is a strong evolutionary pressure molding their behavior. Nonhuman primates also tend to be very vigilant, scanning the ground and trees around them continually while feeding. Many studies of primates and other mammals have shown that animals of many species spend less time scanning their surroundings when they live in larger groups, which suggests a greater margin of safety when more eyes are present to look for danger.

matrilineal   Pattern of female kinship in a primate social group.

TYPES OF NONHUMAN PRIMATE SOCIETIES

Nonhuman primates number only 250 species but exhibit great diversity in grouping patterns. We call the type of group in which nonhuman primates live their **social system**. Earlier generations of primatologists viewed social groups as male-centered; they believed that females wanted to live with or near males, and so males determined the form that social systems took. However, the consensus today is that females have evolved strategies, behavioral and ecological, to cope with the need to balance limited food supplies while avoiding predators with the demands of mating and rearing offspring. Males then use their habitats in such a way as to maximize their access to females. This section outlines the types of nonhuman primate social systems.

Solitary   Most prosimians live in much the same social system that we believe the earliest primates did. They are largely solitary. Females occupy individual territories along with their dependent offspring, which they defend by scent-marking objects (Figure 8.7). Of course, no mammal is truly solitary; it must locate mates during the breeding season. Males occupy territories that overlap a number of female territories; they attempt to maintain exclusive mating access to all these females and keep transient males away. Males use scent-marking and a variety of calls to communicate with one another and to warn intruders to stay out. This social system characterizes many of the strepsirhines, especially the nocturnal galagos and lorises.

When females live solitary lives, males must choose whether to try to defend them from all other males or to share access to them with other males. Most solitary nonhuman primate species feature males that attempt to maintain exclusive access, as is the case in monogamy.

Monogamy   **Monogamy** describes the relationship between a male and female living in a pair bond for an extended period of time, perhaps years (Figure 8.7). Recent studies have shown that our notion of monogamy needs some adjusting because members of pair bonds sometimes mate secretly outside the pair bond as well. In some cases, a pair of gibbons may live as a socially monogamous pair bond, but both male and female secretively mate with other gibbons. Social monogamy thus is not necessarily strict reproductive monogamy.

social system   The grouping pattern in which a primate species lives, including its size and composition evolved in response to natural and sexual selection pressures.

monogamy   A mating bond; primates can be socially monogamous but still mate occasionally outside the pair bond.

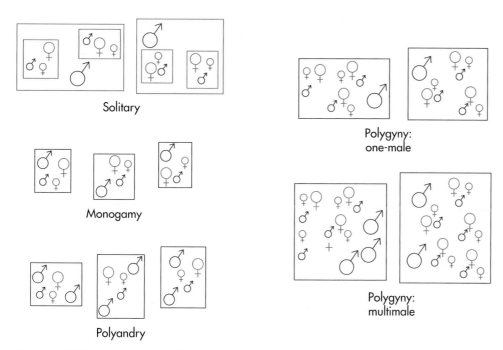

FIGURE 8.7   A taxonomy of primate social systems. Larger symbols indicate adults.

polygynandrous Primate social system consisting of multiple males and multiple females.

Monogamy is best understood as a female reproductive strategy. Monogamous female primates establish and hold territories, and on each territory a single male attaches himself to the resident female. The female therefore tolerates the presence of a male. The male may provide some essential services to the female, such as aiding in territorial and food defense or protecting the female's offspring from infanticide by marauding males. In a few species, males actually aid in the rearing of infants by carrying young and shielding them from harm. In exchange for this service, they receive a high degree of certainty that they fathered the offspring (though not absolute certainty, as females are prone to sneaking off to mate with other males).

Because males in monogamous pairs don't appear to compete as directly with other males as those in social groups need to, we expect that sexually selected aspects of male competition, such as large canines or big body size, would be deemphasized. And we find this to be the case. For instance, gibbons exhibit little sexual dimorphism except in hair color.

Polygyny The majority of anthropoid nonhuman primate species are *polygynous;* they live in groups composed of one or more males and more than one female (Figure 8.7). Groups composed of multiple males and multiple females often are called **polygynandrous** (literally, "many males and many females"). Of course, many animals, from geese to deer, live in large social groups comprising both males and females. What characterizes nonhuman primate polygyny is the complexity of social interactions. In a few species, sociality has accompanied the evolution of brains capable of remembering a long history of interactions with group mates—the debts and favors an animal owes and is owed by others—and of strategizing accordingly.

The complexity of social interactions in nonhuman primate groups is influenced by the social system. A male in a multiple-male group must by necessity use a far more complex set of tactics to obtain mates than a male living in a group in which he is the only male or living monogamously with just one female.

One-Male Polygyny *One-male polygynous groups* are what primatologists used to call harems. One male lives with as many females as he can monopolize (Figure 8.8). The term *harem* implies male control over females and is obsolete because it dates from a time when primatologists did not appreciate the role that females play in the mating system. In some cases one-male groups are driven by choices made by females, not males. For example, Robin Dunbar showed that in the multitiered social system of the gelada baboon, females bond to one another, and the male, despite all appearances of being the central hub of the social system, is simply hoping to be accepted by "his" females (Dunbar, 1983). Among mountain gorillas, half of all groups are one-male. But females often transfer between groups, and resident silverbacks appear to regard other males with fear and anxiety mainly because of the risk that their own females may emigrate for a new silverback in a different group.

When one-male polygynous groups exist, males who are not able to obtain females usually live as extragroup males, either alone or in all-male "bachelor" groups. In some species, these all-male groups attack one-male groups and attempt to evict the resident male from his females (Figure 8.9) (Box 8.1 on page 218).

In some one-male group species, there are occasional influxes of males from outside the group, particularly if the species has a well-defined breeding season. The resident male then finds it impossible to restrict access to the group's females, and the females may have an active interest in seeking matings with the extragroup males. Such influxes occur seasonally in blue monkeys (Rowell, 1988), Hanuman langurs (Boories, et al. 1999), ring-tailed lemurs (Sussman, 1992), and sifakas (Richard, 1992). These events may contribute to the formation of multimale groups.

FIGURE 8.8 A group of capped langurs.

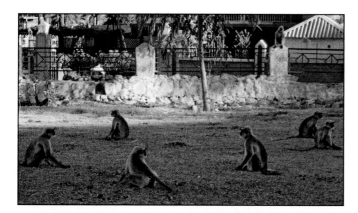

Figure 8.9 In one-male group species, extra males typically reside in all-male "bachelor" groups. These are Hanuman langurs.

Multimale Polygyny A male nonhuman primate would like to have as many females to himself as he can monopolize. The downside of this is that he may have to constantly fend off intruding males who want to mate with his females. As the number of females in a one-male group increases, it becomes impossible for a male to prevent other males from joining the group. A better option for him may be to allow other males to enter the group but continue to obtain the majority of matings with the females by being socially dominant. So in many species, we see multimale, multifemale polygynous groups.

Instead of competing for sole access to females, males in multimale groups may compete for priority of access. Priority often takes the form of a **dominance hierarchy**, in which a top-ranking, *alpha male* allows other males access to the females in the group but may attempt to exclude his rivals when females are in estrus and may conceive. In this way he strikes a balance between the goal of maximizing mating success and the burden of spending all his time and energy fending off other males. In species living in multimale groups, females are not typically all in estrus at the same time. When one female enters estrus, she becomes a focus of competition among the group males. That such competition is far more intense than among monogamous primates is reflected in polygynous primates' canine tooth size and body size sexual dimorphism, both of which contribute to male success in mate competition, and even the size of the males' testes, which may allow him to produce more sperm than other males to impregnate a female.

In some multimale groups, intense mating competition occurs when the species breeds seasonally. This is because the high-ranking males are unable to restrict access to all the females at the same time. In squirrel monkeys (*Saimiri* spp.), for example, males undergo dramatic physiological changes during the mating season, bulking up in order to compete successfully with other males in the group. The largest male tends to be the most dominant for that mating season and also has the highest reproductive success (Boinski, 1987).

Some nonhuman primate species maintain both one-male and multimale groups in the same population. Hanuman langur monkeys live across the Indian subcontinent in populations that can be mainly one-male or multimale. Why this variation occurs is unclear. Primatologists have tried to explain it as a response to the local physical environment, local demographic trends, or the number of females and the overall population density (Newton, 1987; Sommer, 1994). In any case, populations featuring a preponderance of one-male groups also tend to exhibit higher levels of intergroup aggression and especially a tendency for strange males to attempt group takeovers of existing groups, with accompanying **infanticide** of the group's infants (Box 8.1).

A few polygynous species organize themselves in multitiered social systems. In northeastern Africa, both hamadryas baboons and gelada baboons live in small

dominance hierarchy Ranking of individual primates in a group that reflects their ability to displace, intimidate, or defeat group mates in contests.

infanticide The killing of infants, either by members of the infant's group or by a member of a rival group.

BOX 8.1 The Infanticide Wars

Infanticide is the killing of infants. Scientists have observed infanticide in many different animal species, from birds to monkeys to humans. Most of the debate among scientists has centered around infants that are killed by a male other than the biological father.

Scientists once believed that the ultimate goal of animals living in a social group was the attainment of group harmony. Events that disrupt the harmony, such as fights or sexual jealousy, were thought to disrupt the balance of the group in a negative way. But the rise of Darwinian theory to explain social behavior changed that. Scientists recognized that individuals seek to reproduce themselves, often at the expense of other, unrelated individuals.

In the early 1970s Sarah Blaffer Hrdy was planning a doctoral thesis on Hanuman langur monkeys, a large and graceful monkey ubiquitous across the Indian subcontinent (Figure A). Hrdy had heard

FIGURE A Infanticide in nonhuman primates has been best-documented in Hanuman langurs.

reports from the arid western regions of India that langurs living at high population density committed infanticide. She set off to investigate, settling in Mount Abu, a town nestled among the red hills of southernmost Rajasthan.

At Abu and elsewhere, langurs live in two types of social groups: one-male and multimale. One-male groups predominate at Abu, and in this social setting the lone resident male becomes a target for attack by bands of males that lack a group of females of their own. As it turned out, some of the Abu langurs were killing infants, and they did not seem to be acting pathologically. Instead, Hrdy observed bands of males invading established social groups, ousting the resident male, and in some cases killing infants sired by him. She observed four infanticides and strongly suspected numerous others over a 5-year period.

Hrdy viewed the killings in a Darwinian light. Instead of pathological reactions to overcrowding or stress, Hrdy saw infanticide as a reproductive strategy by otherwise bachelor males. By ousting a resident male and then fending off other competitors, a marauding male langur reaped a sudden windfall of mating opportunities with the group's females, except that some or all of the females were preoccupied, reproductively speaking, because they were pregnant by the previous resident male or were nursing his infants. In either case, the females would not be cycling, rendering them unavailable for a new male eager to sire his own progeny. Hrdy reasoned that if the tendency toward infanticide were inherited, males who engaged in the behavior would have greater reproductive success

than other, noninfanticidal ones. This suggested that infant killing was an adaptive strategy evolved through sexual selection to promote a male's genes, at the expense of other males. Female langurs who preferred noninfanticidal males as mates lost in the evolutionary arms race because by failing to kill rivals' offspring, their sons would leave fewer descendants.

The results of Hrdy's long-term field research at Abu appeared in her 1977 book *The Langurs of Abu: Female and Male Strategies of Reproduction*. The reaction from the scientific community was swift and angry. Many primatologists initially denied that the infanticides she reported had occurred at all. When it became clear that the infant killing had occurred in this and other populations of langurs, the critics argued against its evolutionary relevance. The critics noted that most reported cases of infanticide were only circumstantial; the prime evidence often was an infant found dead with bite wounds shortly after a group takeover. Critics charged that the explanation for langur infanticide at Abu was social pathology, not reproductive strategy (Curtin and Dolhinow, 1978). Perhaps the high langur population density and level of human disturbance in and around Abu had made it impossible for males to take over new groups in a gradual, nonaggressive fashion (Figure B). Instead, in the melee of male–male encounters, aggression directed at other males and at females sometimes injured or killed infants accidentally.

The debate over langur infanticide continued to rage as other researchers produced field data supporting the re-

one-male groups. But these one-male units join other one-male units to form larger bands, and these bands sometimes merge to form troops. In both species, enormous herds sometimes form, especially at sleeping sites in the evening, made up of many one-male groups (Kummer, 1968; Dunbar, 1983). This unusual social system probably results in part from phylogeny—inherited patterns of social behavior—and in part from local ecology (sleeping in large groups may help protect individuals from

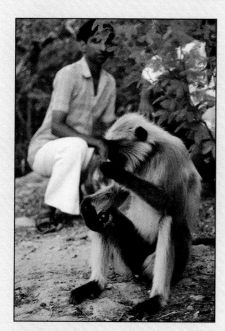

FIGURE B Some scientists believed that langur infanticide was influenced by human disturbance.

productive strategy theory. Primatologist Volker Sommer studied langurs living in the arid scrubland of Jodhpur, Rajasthan, in collaboration with an Indian team led by S. M. Mohnot (Figure C). Between 1969 and 1985 they documented 14 cases of infanticide, plus 20 other suspected killings and 14 nonfatal attacks on infants. They also showed that the pattern of aggression was consistent with the sexual selection hypothesis. Females whose babies were killed by incoming males began to cycle again significantly sooner than those whose infants survived, thus rewarding a marauding male with procreative opportunities months earlier than he would have gotten by waiting for the infants to mature (Sommer, 1994).

Elsewhere in India, zoologist Paul Newton documented infanticide in a pristine forested region in Kanha National Park. In Kanha, langurs live in a natural state, preyed upon by tiger and leopard while foraging among Kanha's rich wildlife diversity. Newton demonstrated that infanticide and heightened male aggression were not correlated with either langur or human population density, refuting the idea that infant killing was the outcome of monkeys living at high density in human-disturbed environments (Newton, 1987). More recently, a team of researchers led by primatologist Carola Borries and colleagues (1999) conducted paternity analysis using DNA from langur feces on a population of the monkeys from southern Nepal. They showed that in all cases, the infanticidal males were not the fathers of the infants they killed.

Meanwhile, reports of infanticide mounted for a wide range of species. David Watts (1989) showed that among the mountain gorillas of the Virunga Volcanoes, infanticide by silverback males is a leading cause of infant mortality. In species as different as marmosets and macaques, the killing of infants was witnessed, often in scenarios that were consistent with the Darwinian model.

For the past two decades, researchers have produced increasingly strong evidence that infanticide among social animals often is carried out strategically in accordance with Darwinian predictions. Opponents of the adaptationist approach argue that unless a gene or complex of genes can be found that causes infanticidal behavior, we should not speak of infant killing as an evolved trait.

Although there are a few examples of direct gene–behavior relationships (some captive-bred strains of mice commit infanticide whereas other strains do not), higher social animals are too complex genetically and behaviorally for simple gene–behavior links to be made. No doubt infanticide occurs in a variety of scenarios and for a variety of reasons, and not all episodes of infanticide can be linked to reproductive benefits to the infant killer. However, the weight of current evidence lends support to the reproductive strategy theory.

FIGURE C Primatologist Volker Sommer and his colleagues showed that langur infanticide had adaptive value and is likely an evolved reproductive strategy.

attacks by predators such as leopards). A parallel to this social system may be found among the Asian snub-nosed monkeys (genus *Rhinopithecus*). Chinese golden snub-nosed monkeys forage in groups of up to 300 animals, but within this group there are well-defined smaller units, each controlled by only one or a few males (Kirkpatrick, 1998). The groups forage in pine forests and on the ground, feeding heavily on lichens and mosses, which are abundant and evenly distributed. Such a

FIGURE 8.10 Chimpanzees and a few other primates live in fission-fusion polygynous communities.

widespread resource may enable the formation of such enormous groups, within which individual males compete for access to smaller numbers of females.

Fission–Fusion Polygyny One additional form of polygyny is perhaps the most complex social system found in nonhuman primates. A few species do not live in cohesive groups; instead, temporary associations of individuals come together and split up repeatedly (Figure 8.10). This is called **fission-fusion polygyny**, and it is seen in species as different as chimpanzees, bonobos, and spider monkeys. Instead of forming a well-defined stable group, populations divide into communities. These communities have distinct home ranges and community membership, within which the community members join and part with one another unpredictably in temporary foraging units called parties. The same chimpanzee may be in a party of 2 at dawn, of 10 an hour later, and of 30 later in the day. The only stable unit in the social system is a female and her young offspring. Males often travel together, forming coalitions among themselves.

Fission–fusion polygyny is believed to be an evolved response to reliance on ripe fruit in the diet. Because of the patchy and seasonal distribution of fruits in a tropical forest and the daily variation in fruit availability, foraging for food in large cohesive groups would incite intense competition for resources. Females forage on their own to optimize their access to fruit, and males attempt to control access to females by forming bonds with one another.

Polyandry When one female lives in a reproductive or social unit with multiple males, we say the social system is polyandrous (Figure 8.7). **Polyandry** is quite rare in nonhuman primates; it is better known in birds, where it has demonstrated key rules of sexual selection. Among nonhuman primates, only a few species of marmosets and tamarins in New World tropical forests exhibit this social system, and it remains poorly understood. In some species of these monkeys, males bond together and help females to rear offspring. This is probably a reproductive strategy by males. Marmosets and tamarins are very small (< 1 kg) monkeys and are vulnerable to a wide range of predators. Females boost their reproductive output by producing twins, but these twins weigh an extraordinary 20% of the mother's body weight. Males assist in infant caregiving by carrying babies and may help in antipredator defense as well. Males may opt to assist a female for the opportunity to achieve reproductive success; if two males mate with the same female, each has a 50% chance of being the father of the twins.

Primatologist Paul Garber has shown that the presence of multiple males increases a female's overall reproductive success as well, a compelling argument for males to engage in this sort of cooperative breeding (Garber, 1997). However, an-

fission-fusion (polygyny) Type of primate polygyny in which animals travel in foraging parties of varying sizes instead of a cohesive group.

polyandry Mating system in which one female mates with multiple males.

other field study by Leslie Digby has shown that among the two or more males in a marmoset group, one tends to be socially dominant and to sire most of the infants (Digby, 1995). In other words, marmosets and tamarins are perhaps best considered to be socially polyandrous but reproductively monogamous.

THE EVOLUTION OF PRIMATE SOCIAL BEHAVIOR

We can understand and study behavior at different levels. All behaviors we see in the wild have immediate causes: hunger, fear, sexual urges, and the like. The immediate, or *proximate*, causes involve the hormonal, physiological reasons for the animal to act. At the same time, behaviors reflect deeper, evolved tendencies that have been shaped over millions of years of natural and sexual selection to promote reproductive success. A baboon mates because of immediate impulses that are both hormonal and social. But ultimately, the urge to mate reflects deeper, evolved strategies that arise through natural selection to enhance the baboon's odds of reproduction. In Chapter 5 you saw how these evolutionary forces work on an organism's phenotype. In this chapter you will examine how the same forces shape primate behavior as a phenotype.

The value of an evolutionary approach to nonhuman primate behavior and ecology is that it allows us to test hypotheses. Using an evolutionary framework, we can study mating as one of many behaviors that has fitness consequences. The pattern of mating may be related to everything from dominance relationships and coalitionary networks to female physiology, which may in turn reveal something important about the evolution of the social system. In other words, behavior can be seen as an adaptation, one aspect of the primate's phenotype. Although the genetic basis for a specific trait remains largely unknown, we can study the consequences of the behavior. For example, if being aggressive promotes reproductive success for a baboon compared with less aggressive baboons in the group, we may infer that aggression is subject to evolutionary forces.

SOCIAL BEHAVIOR AND REPRODUCTIVE ASYMMETRY

The reproductive asymmetry between males and females plays a key role in our understanding of the evolution of nonhuman primate social strategies. Females have a lower reproductive potential and lower variance in reproductive output than males. Females invest far more energy and time in offspring, during both gestation and offspring-rearing, than males do. In accordance with Darwinian sexual selection theory (Chapter 5), females tend to be competed for by males, rather than the other way around. As a result, we expect females of all social mammals to prioritize obtaining adequate food supplies for themselves and their offspring. Females do not need to be very concerned about finding a male; because of their lower reproductive potential, they will always be the sought-out sex, and males will find them. Because the availability of females is the single factor that most limits a male's opportunity to achieve reproductive success, we expect that males will go where females go and will map themselves onto the landscape in accordance with the distribution of females.

The form the social system takes therefore depends on the way females distribute themselves. The social system of nonhuman primate species in which females form the core of the group is called **female philopatry**. This means that females do not migrate at maturity; they stay in the group of their birth to reproduce and rear offspring. In such groups, males typically migrate. Females in female philopatric groups often form tight bonds, based partly on the likelihood of their kinship. Such matrilines of mother, daughters, grandmother, and so on can form the core of the group. In **male philopatry** males remain in their natal home range throughout life, and females migrate. The two types of social systems are closely connected to other important aspects of behavior, so each bears closer examination.

female philopatry Primate social system in which females remain and breed in the group of their birth, whereas males emigrate.

male philopatry Primate social system in which males remain and breed in the group of their birth, whereas females emigrate.

BOX 8.2   Are Chimpanzees from Mars and Bonobos from Venus?

Jane Goodall shocked the scientific world in 1961 when she reported that chimpanzees relish meat and hunt other mammals eagerly; they are not the vegetarian pacifists they had always been thought to be. As observations in the wild accumulated, it became clear that there is a brutal side to chimpanzees (Figure A).

Males strive to ascend a rigid dominance hierarchy, and upon reaching high rank they wield their political power with Machiavellian cunning. They patrol the perimeter of their territory, attacking and sometimes killing their unwary neighbors (Goodall, 1986).

FIGURE A Chimpanzees are far better studied than bonobos.

Chimpanzees are also efficient predators, consuming hundreds of prey animals including monkeys, antelope, and wild pigs at some study sites. Colobus monkeys are attacked by hunting parties of chimpanzees, and the male colobus defend their groups by courageously counterattacking the ape marauders. Nearly all kills are made by males, and after a successful hunt the meat is controlled by the high-ranking males in the hunting party.

Only since the mid-1980s has the closely related bonobo become well known to science (Figure B). Studies of bonobo behavior have revealed a society contrasting sharply with the hierarchical nature of chimpanzee society. Bonobo social life is marked by female cooperation, sex as social communication, and alliance formation rather than aggression. Female bonobos band together in coalitions to dominate males, avoiding the sort of domination and sexual coercion that male chimpanzees routinely inflict on females. Such coalitions among females are nearly unknown in chimpanzees (Parish, 1996).

Bonobos often are said to be the "Make love, not war" ape. They mate in more positions, seemingly for recreation as much as procreation, than any mammal other than humans. They engage in same-sex pairings, in which two females rub their genital swellings together ("GG rubbing"). This behavior eases tensions between individuals and may allow them to feed near one another without undue stress. This female bonding is absent in chimpanzee society.

An even more striking difference between female chimpanzees and female bonobos exists in reproduction. Females

of nearly all mammalian species are reproductively active only during a constricted time period surrounding ovulation. This estrus period characterizes all the higher primates except humans (see Chapter 7). Females of our species, though more likely to conceive around the time of ovulation, are free of the bonds of a strictly defined period of "heat." As a result, sex serves not only for procreation but also as a mechanism of social communication and reinforcement of long-term pair bonds. This release from the constraints of estrus means that the timing of ovulation is no longer advertised to males and is thought to have been a pivotal event in the evolution of early human society.

Bonobo females often are said to be the only mammals other than humans to be released from the bonds of estrus (de Waal and Lanting, 1997). They maintain their sexual swellings for a much longer portion of their menstrual cycles than chimpanzees do and therefore mate nearly throughout the cycle, as humans do. Being released from estrus, bonobos have come to use sex as much for communicating with males as for conceiving offspring, as in our own species.

In conflict as in mating, bonobos and chimpanzees appear to be strikingly different. Bonobo researcher Takayoshi Kano (1992) observed that when two bonobo communities meet at a range boundary, not only is there no lethal aggression, but there may be socializing and even sex between females and the enemy community's males.

In hunting and meat-eating, which chimpanzees so relish, we see another

When female kin live together, they share a strong incentive to cooperate or at least to limit their competition over food resources. Studies have shown that in female philopatric groups, territorial defense is done mainly by females, and the degree of affiliation among females is far greater than among females in male philopatric species. For instance, in Gombe National Park, Tanzania, female baboons, which are female philopatric, spend much time sitting together and grooming one another. In the same forest, female chimpanzees, which are male philopatric, rarely engage in social grooming or contact (Figure 8.11 on page 224). Competition among females can be fierce, with nutrients and calories for bearing

FIGURE B Bonobo females form close alliances, maintained through sex, that are lacking in chimpanzees.

apparent contrast between the two apes. Bonobos capture baby monkeys and then use them as dolls or playthings for hours, only to release the monkey unharmed (though worse for the wear) without eating them, as a chimpanzee would (Sabater-Pi et al., 1993).

The close genetic kinship between these apes and humans and the behavioral differences between them have led anthropologists to debate which species is the better model for understanding the evolution of human behavior. Were our ancestors violent, meat-eating male-dominated creatures or more gentle, female-bonded vegetarians?

While this debate rages, some researchers have pointed out that the differences between chimpanzees and bonobos may not be as stark as they are usually depicted. Many stark behavioral contrasts reported between chimps and bonobos have been based on comparisons between wild chimpanzees and captive bonobos (Stanford, 1998b). Animals in captive settings are well known for their tendency to display greater frequencies of the whole gamut of social behavior, from fighting to

sex, than do their wild counterparts. Therefore, their behavior patterns do not necessarily reflect those that evolved for living in an African forest.

Although wild bonobos are far less studied than chimps, we know about naturalistic patterns of bonobo behavior from two long-term study sites in the Democratic Republic of the Congo: Wamba, the site directed by Kano, and Lomako, which has been occupied by two separate research teams including scientists from the United States and Germany. Field data show that in two important respects, female bonobos are not more sexual than their chimpanzee counterparts. First, the frequency of copulating, in which captive bonobos show a markedly higher rate than wild chimpanzees, is no different between wild bonobos and wild chimpanzees (Stanford, 1998b). Second, the idea that bonobo females are released from estrus is derived from data on the duration of sexual swelling taken mainly from bonobos in captivity. In captivity, female bonobos maintain their sexual swelling for up to 23 days, nearly half of their 49-day (captive) cycle. This dwarfs the receptive period of wild fe-

male chimpanzees, who swell for about 10 days of their 37-day cycle. However, this comparison changes completely if we consider wild bonobos rather than captive specimens, whose excellent nutrition may enhance the reproductive system. Wild bonobos from Wamba are swollen for only 13 days of a 33-day cycle, numbers that are much closer to those of wild chimpanzees than they are to captives of their own species. A report of captive bonobos in Belgium shows that even in captivity bonobos do not necessarily have longer swelling durations than chimpanzees (Vervaecke et al., 1999).

Meat-eating, though certainly less common than among chimpanzees, may be quite common among bonobos as well, but it has been underrated because little field research has been done on this ape. German researchers Gottfried Hohmann and Barbara Fruth (1993) have observed extensive meat-eating and meat-sharing by bonobos at Lomako, but most chimpologists still call the bonobo the "vegetarian" great ape.

Finally, the idea that bonobos are somehow more closely linked to humans has been based on the claim that they walk upright more often than chimpanzees do (Kano, 1992). But this may also be a myth: In a recent study that compared bipedal walking captive bonobos and captive chimpanzees, Elaine Videan and William McGrew (2001) found that bonobos were no more bipedal than chimpanzees.

Before we tar ourselves with the legacy of the male-chauvinist, carnivorous, warring chimpanzees or congratulate ourselves for leaning toward the sisterhood-is-powerful bonobos, we would do well to consider how our depiction of primate societies sometimes becomes intertwined with our own political views.

and rearing offspring at stake. But on the whole, females in female philopatric societies—such as most macaques, baboons, and numerous other Old World monkey taxa—socialize in ways that females in male philopatric species do not.

When females feed on widely scattered resources, as species exhibiting the fission–fusion social system seem to, males may not be able to maintain access to them. In such a situation, male bonds may be the most effective way of controlling females. This may explain the fact that chimpanzees, bonobos, some spider monkeys, and a few other species are male-bonded. These bonds are based partly on male kinship because remaining in the natal group means that a male ends up

(a)

(b)

FIGURE 8.11　(a) Savanna baboons live in female-philopatric groups, among which males migrate. (b) Chimpanzees live in male-philopatric communities, among which females migrate.

living next to his cousins, brothers, and other male kin. Closely allied males, whether relatives or not, can coerce females for mating purposes, and control access to fruit trees that other male cohorts might want to enter. So male-bonded primate societies offer some major nutritional and reproductive benefits to males and uncertain benefits to females. The benefits to males are believed to be sufficient to keep males on their natal home range. Females tend to be the sex that emigrates (because one sex or the other presumably must emigrate to avoid inbreeding problems).

Females in male philopatric societies, on the other hand, may not show a high degree of affiliation, perhaps because of their lack of kinship (Figure 8.12). In chimpanzee society, females rarely groom one another, and they often engage in competitive aggression, including infanticidal aggression in which a female may attempt to kill the offspring of another female. Bonobos are an exception to this pattern in that immigrant females in a community, though unrelated, establish close bonds with one another. These bonds are used to protect females from harassment by males.

The form of the social system cannot be entirely explained by the behavior of females, however. Some researchers have linked the number of males in a primate group to other factors, such as the intensity of the risk of predation. In separate studies, Carel van Schaik and Marc Hörstermann (1994) and John Mitani and colleagues (1996) hypothesized that the number of males in a primate group, though subject to multiple factors, depends most strongly on the number of females and also on the presence of predators in the species' habitat.

MALE REPRODUCTIVE STRATEGIES

Within a primate society, both males and females seek the same goal: reproductive success, or fitness. The ways each sex tries to enhance its fitness differ dramatically, however. A male baboon should be expected to fight with other male baboons over females if fighting improves his opportunities to place his genes into the next generation. If fighting and aggression were counterproductive, we should expect to see male baboons achieving mating success some other way. In practice, however, strategies for achieving reproductive success are much more complex than just being aggressive or nonaggressive. Males rarely engage in paternal care, and in most species their relationship with offspring is neutral or even harmful. Their direct contribution to their offspring's health and welfare often is only their genes. In the few species in which males provide parental caregiving, such as marmosets and tamarins, the selection pressures on males

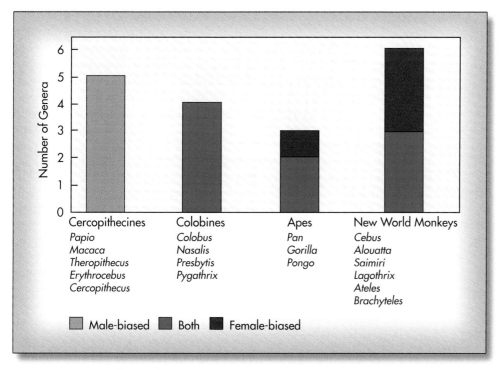

FIGURE 8.12 Male and female philopatry. The internal dynamics of primate societies differ greatly depending on which sex emigrates from the group at sexual maturity.

may be very different from those on, say, a male baboon. The degree of parental investment is a key factor in shaping the evolution of the social system.

Dominance   One important way males and females achieve reproductive success is by establishing dominance relationships with other members of the same sex. Once he enters a new group, a male must compete directly with the resident males over the group's females. Although this is sometimes done by fighting, competition often is settled through the establishment of dominance hierarchies, in which high-ranking and low-ranking males sort out their relationship through a series of contests that leaves the lower-ranking animal unlikely to challenge the more dominant one.

Dominance relationships among males are established early in life, as males play together and some assert themselves over others. Of course, males that later emigrate from their home group cannot assume high rank in a new group, at least initially. Males growing up in male philopatric groups may face a different dilemma. To achieve high rank they must demonstrate to males that they have grown up and that they are now a force to be reckoned with. In chimpanzee society, all the adult males in the community are dominant to all the females. An adolescent male climbs the dominance hierarchy by first taking on and dominating (fighting with or supplanting at fruit trees) each of the adult females. Once he has risen to the top of the female hierarchy, he will begin to challenge the lowest-ranking males, and so on until he has risen as high as he will go. These challenges illustrate the political nature of life among nonhuman primates.

However, males are not the dominant sex in all primates species. Among many lemur species, females are dominant to all males, displacing them at food sources and choosing newly immigrated males to mate with (Erhardt and Overdorff, 1998). Male lemurs do not engage in the sort of complicated dominance interactions that we see in anthropoid primates, perhaps because much of the social intercourse of the group is strongly controlled by high-ranking females.

Dominance relationships in nonhuman primate males are far more complicated than the image you may have of a pecking order. In fact, rarely do the males of a polygynous group sort themselves into a neatly linear hierarchy (Figure 8.13). Far more commonly, dominance relationships take a flexible, multifaceted form in which Monkey A is dominant to Monkey B, except when Monkey B is in the company of Monkey C, in which case B and C are dominant to Monkey A. In a classic study of a captive chimpanzee colony at the Arnhem Zoo in the Netherlands, Frans de Waal (1982) described the triangular nature of many chimpanzee dominance interactions, in which Chimp C was able to assert himself while Chimp A was busy dealing with Chimp B. These sorts of fast-paced, often subtle interactions in nonhuman primate groups are challenging for primate researchers to observe but crucial in explaining the role that cognition and social complexity play in nonhuman primate societies.

Why males should strive to become dominant has always been perplexing. The long-standing assumption was that high-ranking males were able to obtain a higher proportion of matings with females, so dominance was part of the overall male reproductive strategy. But field studies have returned mixed results with respect to the correlation between dominance and reproductive success. For example, in the 1970s Glenn Hausfater (1975) reported that dominant male savanna baboons (*Papio anubis*) had greater mating success than lower-ranking animals, which they achieved by monopolizing females during their peak ovulatory periods. But studying the same species, primatologist Barbara Smuts (1985) found no such correlation. In fact, low-ranking males enjoyed greater mating success than the alpha. And we know that high-ranking males often have higher levels of cortisol, the hormone that is associated with stress-related diseases in many primates including humans, which may be necessary to keep them continuously primed to function as the most powerful male in the group. So the benefit to a male of achieving high rank is presumed to be reproductive, but the evidence is ambiguous.

FEMALE REPRODUCTIVE STRATEGIES

Females invest much more time and energy in reproduction than males do, and their reproductive strategies reflect this. Instead of competing for males, female nonhuman primates typically are competed over. But females do not mate with whichever male is the winner of the competition. Sexual selection theory predicts that females should choose their mates carefully because a given mating may result in years of investment in gestation, lactation, and offspring-rearing (Figure 8.14). A nonhuman primate must undergo years of socialization to learn how to behave successfully as an adult, and this socialization is closely connected to the development and growth of its brain. During the socialization period the maturing offspring is utterly dependent, physically and psychologically, on its mother. And we know from Jeanne Altmann's (1980) long-term study of mother and infant baboons that when they are carrying fetuses or young in-

FIGURE 8.13 Dominance relationships among individuals play an important role in many primate societies.

FIGURE 8.14 Despite the traditional focus on males, females actively choose mates and are the driving force in the reproductive process.

fants, females suffer high mortality rates, presumably because they are less able to escape predators and more likely to suffer nutritional stress, leading to disease.

As we have seen, female choice of mates drives the appearance and behavior of the males of many social animals. However, what we call female choice is a bit unclear. Meredith Small (1989) has pointed out that female primates are clearly choosy about their mates. Depending on the species, they prefer males based on body size, color, aggressive behavior, nonaggressive (caregiving) behavior, and familiarity. But choosiness is not the same thing as evolved mate choice. Is there evidence of mate choice in nonhuman primates? Barbara Smuts's savanna baboons, among whom males who were the most protective and nurturing allies of females received the most matings, are one example (Smuts, 1985).

Role of Dominance   Although dominance rank usually is not as important to female primates as it is to males, dominance may nonetheless have important consequences for female reproductive success. A study of the relationship between dominance and reproductive success among Gombe chimpanzees showed that there was a small but significant influence of rank on the number of surviving offspring a mother bore (Figure 8.15 on page 228). The daughters of high-ranking females also matured slightly more rapidly than did those of low-ranking females (Pusey et al., 1997). And as we have seen, females form matrilineal kin groups in Old World monkeys such as baboons, macaques, and langurs, within which a female's status may influence her reproductive success.

Primatologists think females choose dominant males more often than low-ranking males because dominant animals are so often in better health, with priority of access to food. The offspring of dominant animals also tend to grow up to be high-ranking; we can't say whether this reflects a genetic predisposition to become dominant or is the proximate result of having a mother who is dominant herself and whose alliance network and socialization perpetuate high status.

Sexual Receptivity Signals   Female primates use sexual signals to promote their reproductive success. These signals can be behavioral, anatomical, or physiological. Such signals are intended to advertise a female's **sexual receptivity**, or willingness to mate. They also make a female more attractive to males. Some nonhuman primates use body posture to indicate receptivity; female Hanuman langurs arch their tails over backs and shake their heads side to side to indicate willingness to mate. Females of many other species simply move in front of a male and present

sexual receptivity   Willingness and ability of a female to mate, also defined as fertility.

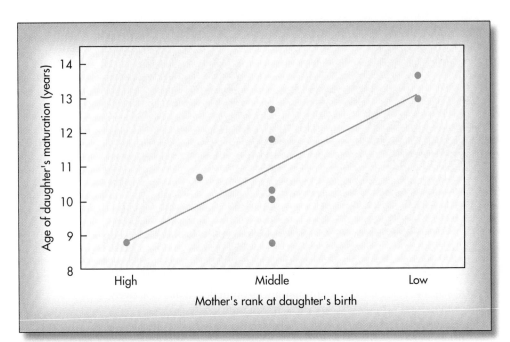

FIGURE 8.15 In some species, dominant females have more surviving offspring that mature earlier indicating an adaptive value for high social status.

their rumps as a solicitation for mating. As we saw in Chapter 7, behaviors associated with such a willingness to mate constitute *estrus*.

Nearly all female mammals are fertile during only a restricted part of each reproductive cycle. The time around ovulation often produces changes in female appearance and behavior that incite males to compete to mate with them. Only during this time are females likely to conceive, and only then are they willing to mate. Around the time of ovulation, the rump of a female primate may change color, produce a fluid-filled swelling, or emit odors, any of which signal males in the vicinity that she is ready and willing to mate (Figure 8.16). Although it was long thought that such female features existed for the convenience of males, we now realize that females evolved these traits to aid their own reproductive strategy. Because females choose their mates, using vivid sexual signals to excite males is a good way to persuade them to compete with one another. This competition may allow a female to assess the quality of her potential mates.

Sexual swellings have evolved independently at least three times in the primate order, always in species living in multimale polygynous groups. Female baboons possess enormous fluid-filled swellings during a brief portion of their monthly cycle, and some colobine monkeys exhibit subtle versions of swellings too. Among

FIGURE 8.16 Sexual swellings are one way for females to advertise their mating availability, thereby inducing male competition for them.

the great apes, female chimpanzees and bonobos exhibit swellings for about one-quarter of their monthly cycles. In chimpanzees, a female swells for approximately 10 days of a 37-day menstrual cycle, and ovulation occurs near the end of the swelling period, after which the swelling rapidly deflates. The swelling doesn't always signal ovulation, however; even females that are pregnant or nursing babies swell, although less regularly. Males may be able to distinguish "real" swellings from nonovulatory ones by sight or smell.

The adaptive function of sexual swellings and other such signals of fertility lies in the information it conveys to males. They may confuse paternity, in that many males are attracted to the swollen female, who mates with as many males as possible during this brief period. This leaves each male in the group with a chance of being the father of the ensuing offspring and may discourage them all from being aggressive toward the infant or its mother. Alternatively, the swelling may increase the investment a male makes in the female and her offspring by establishing paternity. This would work best if the female mates only with one male during her peak period of ovulation (Hrdy and Whitten, 1987).

RECONSTRUCTING THE EVOLUTION OF PRIMATE SOCIETIES

In the early years of modern nonhuman primate behavior study, many primatologists believed the form a primate social system took followed fairly simple ecological rules. They created taxonomies of social systems in relation to the species' natural habitat. For instance, because a number of distantly related primate species ate a fruit diet and lived in polygynous groups, it was thought that frugivory and polygyny were linked. Monogamy was also thought to be linked to fruit-eating and territoriality because gibbons exhibit both. But as more and more nonhuman primate field studies were carried out, it became clear that such pigeonholes were simplistic.

Today, primatologists use increasingly quantitative models and large numbers of field studies of nonhuman primates and their ecology to understand the workings of primate social systems. However, primate social systems are molded by the evolutionary history of each species. This makes interpreting the effect of natural selection difficult because for many primates the environment that molded their evolution may not be the one they currently occupy. Anthony Di Fiore and Drew Rendall (1994) used statistical models of primate family trees to show that the evolutionary history of a primate lineage plays a major role in determining what the social system looks like today. Unfortunately, in most cases we can only guess about the way in which this evolution happened.

Primate ecologists differ on which influences—feeding competition, mate competition, or predation—are the most important in shaping primate societies. In the 1980s, several theorists attempted to explain primate societies based on the importance of intragroup and intergroup competition. Carel van Schaik surveyed a range of primate societies and found that female reproductive success was lower in larger groups suggesting that intragroup feeding competition was important. This implied that group living was overall a negative influence on sociality and led him and his colleagues to devise a number of innovative tests for other possible influences on why nonhuman primates should be social. They concluded that depending on the taxon, predation and infanticide were extremely important influences that molded sociality in nonhuman primates (van Schaik and van Hooff, 1983; van Schaik and Höstermann, 1994).

Meanwhile, Richard Wrangham proposed a model for why primates formed male philopatric or female philopatric groups. He pointed out that, as we saw in discussing sexual selection, females are the ecological sex in that their reproductive success is so closely tied to their ability to find and defend food. He proposed

	Rank order of competitive abilities	Individuals occupying feeding sites	Individuals excluded
No cooperation	A > B > C > D	A B	C,D
Cooperation between C and D	(C > D) > A > B	C D	A,B
Cooperation between A and B, C and D	(A > B) > (C > D)	A B	C,D

FIGURE 8.17 Richard Wrangham's 'female-bonded' theory of intergroup competition was highly influential in our understanding of the evolution of primate societies.

that the key to solving the paradox of female sociality—that female primates live with group mates that limit their food intake—was the kinship patterns in female philopatric groups. Where females live together, they tend to be relatives, and this kinship mitigates the high cost of intragroup feeding competition. Wrangham (1980) proposed that kin groups of females may jointly defend key feeding trees (Figure 8.17). Because larger groups could successfully control more fruit in bigger trees, there would be a strong benefit for females to live together in large groups.

As mentioned earlier, feeding competition, mate competition, and predation often are interrelated. We can see their relationship clearly in a study by Charles Janson and Michele Goldsmith. They analyzed the relationship between group size and ranging among diverse primate species and found that larger groups tend to travel further. Janson and Goldsmith (1995) argued that this occurs because each group member must travel a bit further to find food when surrounded by more competitors. In an earlier study, Janson (1985) had shown that capuchin monkeys vie for a position near the center of a foraging group, probably to be able to obtain the best food while avoiding the most predators. In the group center there are more eyes to detect the approach of a predator. Craig Stanford (1998a) found that red colobus monkeys living in larger groups were less vulnerable to predators, even though larger groups were more often detected by predators. This was true probably because in a larger group, the odds of an individual monkey being killed are lower. But feeding competition was higher in larger groups too. So there were survival advantages and disadvantages in both large and small groups for both obtaining food and avoiding predators. As in many other primate examples, group life is all about costs and benefits and tradeoffs between different behavior options.

In Chapters 7 and 8, you have seen how the lives of nonhuman primates inform us about ourselves and our ancestry. In this chapter we examined social behavior, but social behavior and ecology cannot be fully separated from each other. Primate social behavior has been molded by natural selection, with the environment as the filter. These same natural forces shaped human ancestry, human anatomy, and perhaps aspects of human behavior. Now that you have seen the context for the roots of human evolution, it's time to turn in Chapter 9 to the fossil record and what it tells us about the context of primate evolution.

SUMMARY

1. **What are the three major influences on the evolution of nonhuman primate sociality?**

   All wild primates must find mates, find food, and avoid predators in order to survive and reproduce.

2. **What are the major types of nonhuman primate grouping patterns?**

   Nonhuman primates may live solitarily, monogamously, or in polygynous groups that can be one-male, multimale, or fission–fusion, or they can be polyandrous.

3. **Why are social systems and mating systems not always the same?**

   A primate may live in a particular grouping pattern but mate outside that pattern. For instance, a gibbon may live in a socially monogamous pair bond but mate secretly with gibbons other than his or her mate.

4. **What do we mean by the reproductive asymmetry between males and females?**

   Females have a lower reproductive potential than males, which makes them the object of male competition in most species. Because females invest so much more time and energy in reproduction, they tend to be more discriminating in choosing a mate.

5. **What is the basis of female mate choice in nonhuman primates?**

   We know that female primates are choosy when it comes to selecting a mate. We believe that aspects of this choice are under evolutionary pressure. Females may choose males on the basis of size, strength, or aggressiveness. But they may also choose males for their caregiving behavior and their lack of aggression toward them. We believe females seek genetic quality in a mate; how they discover this in potential mates is an area of intense research.

6. **Do dominant males always enjoy high mating success?**

   Dominance and mating success often are associated, but the equation is complicated. Dominant males may have high social status but low mating success, or vice versa. Low-ranking or adolescent males may compensate for their low dominance rank by mating covertly with females.

7. **What is the likely function of sexual swellings during estrus?**

   Sexual swellings are female reproductive adaptations. They may allow a female to confuse a mate as to paternity of her offspring by attracting many males to mate with her. This may discourage males from later aggression toward her infant.

8. **What key ecological factor affecting sociality do the van Schaik and Wrangham models have in common?**

   Both van Schaik and Wrangham theorize that feeding competition is the key ecological influence on sociality, although van Schaik emphasizes competition within the group, whereas Wrangham emphasizes competition between groups.

CRITICAL THINKING QUESTIONS

1. If primate behavior tells us much about human origins because primates are big-brained and socially complex, then what other animals unrelated to primates might be informative about the origins of human social behavior?

2. Why would male primates spend their lives striving to rise in dominance rank if being high-ranking does not guarantee high mating success?

3. Nonhuman primates are but one type of animal living in tropical forests. Do you think that they have had a major impact on the evolution of tropical forests? Why or why not?

KEY TERMS

captive study	social system	polyandry
semi–free-ranging	monogamy	female philopatry
field study	polygynandrous	male philopatry
polygynous	dominance hierarchy	infanticide
matrilineal	fission–fusion polygyny	sexual receptivity

SUGGESTED READING

de Waal, Frans B.M. (1982). *Chimpanzee Politics*. Johns Hopkins University Press, Baltimore.

Hrdy, Sarah B. (1999). *Mother Nature*. Pantheon Books, New York.

McGrew, W.C., Linda F. Marchant, and Toshisada Nishida (editors). 1996. *Great Ape Societies*. Cambridge University Press, Cambridge.

Wrangham, Richard, and Dale Peterson (1996). *Demonic Males*. Boston: Houghton Mifflin.

PART IV
THE FOSSIL RECORD

Chapter 9
FOSSILS IN GEOLOGICAL CONTEXT

AS THE SUN DROPS TOWARD THE HORIZON over a remote African badland, a sunburnt geologist sets down his rock hammer, takes a swig of lukewarm water from his canteen, and mops the sweat from his forehead with a bandanna. He has just finished collecting chunks of volcanic ash from layers above and below the place where fossils of a primitive human ancestor had been recovered earlier that field season. Physical exhaustion and the excitement of anticipation make his hand shake slightly as he drops the chunks into plastic bags. He carefully seals the bags and records his location. With the samples stowed safely in his backpack, the scientist scrambles down the slope and makes the long hike back to base camp.

Back in his laboratory a few weeks later, portions of each rock sample are broken up in a mortar and pestle. The scientist peers through a microscope, picking through the sample of volcanic ash with steel forceps, carefully selecting fresh feldspar crystals. He cleans the crystals in an acid solution and then places each into the recess of a sample chamber. The chamber is sealed and sent to a nuclear reactor for irradiation, and the scientist moves on to other projects. A month or so later, the chamber returns marked with a radioactive warning label. After a cooling off period it will be placed in the way of a laser beam, and each crystal in turn will vaporize slightly, then bubble and melt. A key piece of equipment, a mass spectrometer, begins to analyze the isotopes in the gas released from the melting crystal. The scientist checks the results and sits down to begin his calculations.

After several months of experiments and calculations, checking and rechecking, the scientist picks up the telephone. As he listens to the ringing on the other end, he smiles wryly. It is always interesting to hear a colleague react to just how ancient a new discovery is.

Techniques developed over the last 50 years allow scientists such as this geochronologist to provide a more accurate context for understanding our evolutionary past. To understand our evolution we study **fossils**. As the preserved remnants of once-living things, fossils provide information about past life. **Paleontology**, a field that takes its name from the Greek words for "old" (*paleos*) and "existence" (*ontos*), is devoted to gleaning all the information that can be extracted from fossils. This information includes how ancient the fossil is, what kind of organism it represents, and the ecological adaptations of the organism, such as its diet and locomotion We must also know about how that fossil came to be preserved where it was and how the preservation process affected the fossil. A fossil without its context is almost useless because we have no way of assessing how old it is, what kind of environment it lived in, or what other animals it might have lived and competed with.

In this chapter we will set the stage for answering these questions by looking closely at the field of **geology**, the study of the Earth, to understand the preservation, age, and environment in which primate fossils are found. Because the evolutionary history of humans and our primate relatives is a story that unfolds through time, geological principles are fundamentally important to the study of human evolution. We will see how materials fossilize and look at what we can learn from both the fossils themselves and the surroundings in which they are found. We'll introduce and compare some of the most important dating methods in use today and the context in which each is most valuable. Finally, we'll explore conditions on Earth during the Cenozoic era, the time period in which primates evolved.

HOW TO BECOME A FOSSIL

You might think that fossils are abundant. After all, every organism eventually dies, and natural history museums are filled with fossils of dinosaurs and other prehistoric creatures. In reality, very few living things become fossils. This is a good thing because it means that the tissues of most plants and animals are instead recycled and used by new organisms in the ongoing carbon cycle of the Earth. The nutrients they contain might be lost forever if every organism that died became a fossil. Not only does a minute fraction of living things become preserved as fossils, but only an exceedingly small proportion of the fossils that are preserved end up being discovered, collected, and studied. Not surprisingly, therefore, the fossil record is not entirely representative of the composition of past biological communities (Behrensmeyer and Hill, 1980). Instead, the fossil record preserves some organisms in abundance, whereas others are seldom preserved.

Taphonomy, the study of what happens to remains from death to discovery, reveals some of the factors that determine whether an organism becomes a fossil (Shipman, 1981). These include both biological and geological processes. Death might come to a human ancestor or any other animal in a number of ways, such as injury, disease, or predation (Figure 9.1). In many instances, the agent of death may leave marks on the skeleton, such as the bite marks of a predator. After death, the carcass begins to decompose when living tissues are no longer maintained by the organism and as numerous microbes, such as bacteria and mold, and carrion-eating insects accelerate decay. While this is happening, scavengers may ravage the carcass, consuming its soft tissues and perhaps even chomping on the bones of the skeleton, especially the soft articular ends of bones that form our joints. Eventually, only the most durable tissues remain, especially the densely constructed cortical bone at the middle of the long bones, the jaws, and the teeth (Brain, 1981). Even these durable remains can disappear, recycled into the earth's carbon system, through various means including erosion and trampling.

However, to become a fossil, part of the organism must be preserved by burial, a natural process in which the carcass or part of it is covered with sediment. Burial interrupts the biological phase of decomposition, protecting the skeleton from further ravaging and trampling by biological organisms. Because sediments such as sand, silt, mud, and gravel usually are carried by water, burial often occurs in the floodplains of rivers, along the shores of lakes, and in swamps where uplift, erosion, and sedimentation are occurring. In other circumstances, sediment such as dust and volcanic ash carried by the wind sweeps over the remains. Once buried, skeletal remains may be preserved in a variety of ways. Usually they absorb minerals from the surrounding soil or ground water that eventually replace the

fossils The preserved remnants of once-living things, often buried in the ground.

paleontology The study of extinct organisms, based on their fossilized remains.

geology The study of the Earth.

taphonomy The study of what happens to the remains of an animal from the time of death to the time of discovery.

FIGURE 9.1 Fossils are formed after an animal dies, decomposes, and is covered in sediment. Minerals in ground water replace bone mineral turning bone into stone which may later be discovered if the surrounding rock erodes away.

organism's original inorganic tissues. The result is *petrifaction* the process of being turned stone.

Fossilized remains usually preserve only the most durable tissues of the body, such as teeth and bones, and just as the inorganic component is replaced by minerals in ground water, eventually the organic component of the skeleton (collagen) degrades and is lost (Figure 9.1). On occasion, however, soft parts such as skin or hair may be preserved. In very exceptional circumstances, the original tissues of an organism are preserved largely intact, as when animals' bodies are frozen, such as the well-known mammoths of Siberia, or when ancient people are naturally mummified. Finally, *trace fossils* such as the tracks left by animals may provide impressions of their activities, and *coprolites*, or fossilized feces, also tell us about the presence of past animals (Figure 9.2).

We understand today that fossils found in rock represent once-living organisms that were buried by sediment and subsequently turned to rock. In the past, the way a solid (a fossil) could end up in another solid (the rock) was a conundrum, and fossils were thought to be of perhaps supernatural origin. In 1669, Danish geologist Nicolas Steno (1638–1686) offered the solution to the problem in his *Forerunner to a Dissertation on a Solid Naturally Occurring in Another Solid*, in which he explained how this phenomenon could occur naturally. This was one of the turning points in our understanding of paleontology and geology.

THE IMPORTANCE OF CONTEXT

As we mentioned previously, a fossil without its context is useless, except perhaps as a pretty object on the mantlepiece. In this section we review the important principles used in geology to understand the position of a fossil in its rock layers and of different fossil sites relative to each other.

STRATIGRAPHY

Imagine driving through a road cut, where you see what looks like layers or bands of rock. These are **strata**, literally "layers" in Latin. In some road cuts these layers are basically horizontal, but in others they may be more vertical or even quite deformed (Figure 9.3). **Stratigraphy** is the study of the distribution of these layers. In 1830 Charles Lyell, whose work influenced Darwin (see Chapter 2), synthesized a number of accepted geological principles including the principles of stratigraphy. The principles of geology rely in large part on the concept of *uniformitarianism*, originally developed by James Hutton, a Scottish geologist, in 1785 and further promoted in Lyell's book. Uniformitariansim suggests that

strata Layers of rock.

stratigraphy The study of the order of rock layers and the sequence of events they reflect.

FIGURE 9.2 Past life is preserved in many forms. (a) Soft tissues may be mummified or preserved in amber. (b) Whole skeletons or their parts may be fossilized in rock. From these various clues paleontologists piece together the evolutionary history of the animals preserved.

(a)   (b)

(a)

(b)

FIGURE 9.3 Rock layers (strata) usually look like the layers in a cake (a), but geological processes such as earthquakes and mountain building can deform these once horizontal layers (© Carr Clifton). (b) The paleoanthropologist must understand these deformations in order to figure out which strata a fossil comes from and how old it is.

processes operating today are also those that operated in the past and thus they can explain the fossil and geological record. The principles of stratigraphy include four that are critical to an understanding of the context of a fossil: original horizontality, superposition, cross-cutting relationships, and faunal succession.

The *principle of original horizontality,* formulated by Nicolas Steno, says that layers of rock (strata) are laid down parallel to the earth's gravitational field and thus horizontal to the earth's surface, at least originally. All the deformations and upendings that you see in road cuts are caused by later activity such as earthquakes and volcanic eruptions (Figure 9.4 on page 238).

Building on the principle of original horizontality is the principle of superposition, also proposed by Steno and summarized by Lyell. The *principle of superposition* (Figure 9.4) states that, with all other factors equal, older layers are laid down first and then covered by younger (overlying) layers. Thus older sediments are on the bottom, and the fossils found in them are older than those found above. However, stratigraphy is not always so straightforward, and in the late 1700s James Hutton added the *principle of cross-cutting relationships*, which says simply that a geological feature must exist before another feature can cut across or through it and that the thing that is cut is older than the thing cutting through it (Figure 9.4), just as the layers of a cake must exist before you can stick a candle into them.

Finally, the *principle of faunal succession,* first proposed in 1815 by William Smith, whose nickname was "Strata" because of his passion for stratigraphy, addresses the changes or succession of fauna (animals) through layers. Smith recognized not only that deeper fauna is older but also that there are predictable sequences of fauna through strata, that successive layers contain certain types of faunal communities and types of fossils that follow one another in predictable patterns through the strata (Figure 9.5 on page 239). Certain of these animals that typify a layer are called index fossils. Furthermore, Smith noted that once a type of fossil leaves a

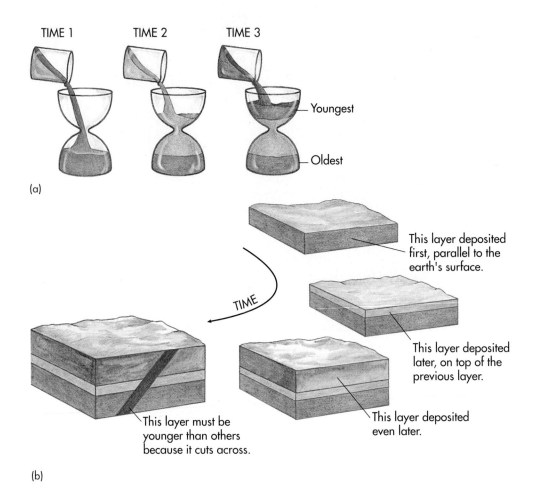

TIME 1   TIME 2   TIME 3

— Youngest

— Oldest

(a)

TIME

This layer deposited
first, parallel to the
earth's surface.

This layer deposited
later, on top of the
previous layer.

This layer must be
younger than others
because it cuts across.

This layer deposited
even later.

(b)

FIGURE 9.4 (a) The principles of stratigraphy help us understand the relative age of rock layers. (b) Layers are deposited parallel to the Earth's surface (horizontality). Younger layers are deposited on top of older layers (superposition). A layer that cuts across others is younger than those it cuts (cross-cutting relationships).

section, it does not reappear higher in the section. With the benefit of Darwin's work, we understand this to mean that once a type of animal goes extinct, it does not reappear later (and so cannot be fossilized in younger sediments). Smith's observations were made on invertebrates but apply equally well to vertebrates.

Using the principles of stratigraphy, as we shall see when we discuss dating techniques, we can determine which strata are older and younger. Comparisons between sites can provide a sequence of rocks from older to younger for both areas. By comparing the stratigraphy of sites from around the world, especially for marine sediments that are very continuous, geologists have assembled a great geological column from the very oldest to the very youngest rocks on Earth. This geological column, with age estimates provided by dating techniques discussed later in this chapter, is called the geologic time scale.

THE GEOLOGIC TIME SCALE

geologic time scale (GTS)
The categories of time into which Earth's history is usually divided by geologists and paleontologists: eras, periods, epochs.

The **geologic time scale (GTS)** is divided into nested sets of time. From most inclusive to least inclusive these are eons, eras, periods, and epochs (Figure 9.6 on page 240). The earth itself is approximately 4.5 billion years old, and the GTS covers this entire time, although human and primate evolution occurs only in the Cenozoic Era, or about the last 65 million years.

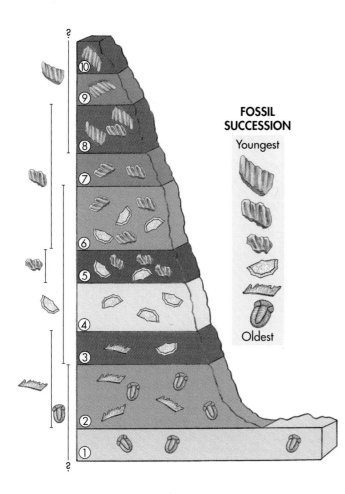

FOSSIL SUCCESSION

Youngest

Oldest

FIGURE 9.5 The principle of faunal succession uses animal fossils to tell relative time.

The scale is divided into two eons, the Precambrian and Phanerozoic. The Precambrian dates from 4.5 billion to 543 million years ago and is divided into three eras: the Hadean, Archaen, and Proterozoic. The Phanerozoic Eon dates from 543 million years ago to the present and is divided into three eras; from oldest to youngest they are the Paleozoic, Mesozoic, and Cenozoic. "Zoic" in each of these names refers to the presence of animals.

Although we will spend the next several chapters discussing the fossil record of only the last 65 million years (the Cenozoic Era), take a moment to consider the enormity of time represented by the entire history of the earth, 4.5 billion years (Figure 9.6). Primates are present for a little less than 1.5% of that tremendous span, and humans and our closest ancestors are present for only about 0.1% of that time. To put this in perspective, think about your 7 day spring break and the time you allot to different activities. On this scale, the Primates have existed for about 2.4 hours, and the human lineage has existed for about 11 minutes and 20 seconds. Hopefully that's less time than you allot to your least favorite spring break activities like homework!

Mammals arose in the Mesozoic Era; *Mesozoic* literally means "middle age of animals," but the era is often called the 'age of reptiles' because of the abundance of dinosaurs (Figure 9.7 on page 242). The Mesozoic spans 248–65 million years ago and has three periods: the Triassic, Jurassic, and Cretaceous. The Cenozoic, or recent age of animals, spans from 65 million years ago to present and has two periods: the Tertiary and Quaternary. The Tertiary Period, from 65 to 1.8 million years ago spans five epochs: the Paleocene (65–54.8 million years ago), Eocene

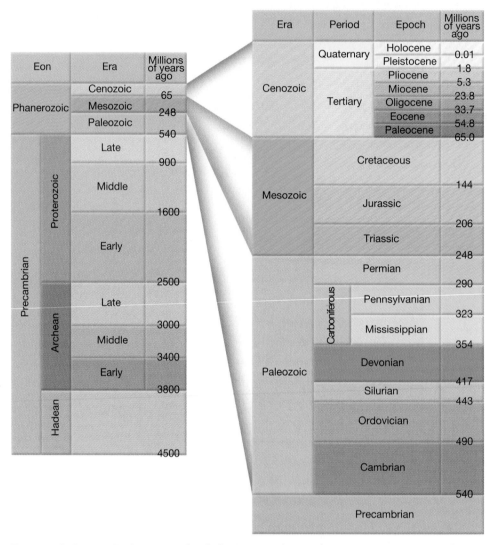

FIGURE 9.6 Earth's history is divided into nested sets of time—eons, eras, periods, and epochs—and called the Geologic Time Scale.

(54.8–33.7 million years ago), Oligocene (33.7–23.8 million years ago), Miocene (23.8–5.3 million years ago), and Pliocene (5.3–1.8 million years ago). The Quaternary period from 1.8 million years ago to present, spans two epochs: the Pleistocene (1.8 million years ago to 10 thousand years ago) and Holocene (10 thousand years ago to present). We live in the Holocene Epoch of the Quaternary Period of the Cenozoic Era of the Phanerozoic Eon.

The lengths of epochs, periods, and eras are not standard in the GTS. Boundaries are placed at points in the time scale where large shifts are evident in the geological column. For example, the boundary between the Cretaceous Period of the Mesozoic and the Tertiary Period of the Cenozoic Era (or the Cretaceous/Tertiary [K–T] boundary) records a great change in animal taxa: the drastic decrease of dinosaur species and increasing number of mammals (Figure 9.7). The boundary between the Pliocene and Pleistocene Epoch at 1.8 million years ago was originally placed to reflect the onset of more severe glaciation events in the Pleistocene, and some geologists would like to move this boundary earlier in time (to 2.5 million years ago) to reflect evidence for glaciations becoming severe at that time.

HOW OLD IS IT?

How do we determine where in the geologic time scale a site and the fossils within it fall? A vital first step in determining the antiquity of fossil remains is learning their **provenience**, the precise location from which the fossils come. After we have established provenience, preferably by recovering the fossil through careful excavation or prospecting but sometimes by geochemical comparisons between fossils and sites, we can apply a wide variety of techniques to estimating the age of fossil remains. These techniques fall into three main categories depending on the underlying method used. Relative dating techniques use concepts of stratigraphy to establish relative ages between localities and fossils found in these localities. Calibrated relative dating techniques compare a relative technique to an absolute time scale. Chronometric (or "absolute") dating techniques use an absolute clock, such as radioactivity, to produce an age estimate in years before present. Collectively, the field of geology devoted to studying time in the fossil record is *geochronology*. We review some of the major methods of this field in the next section.

RELATIVE DATING TECHNIQUES

Relative dating techniques tell us how old something is in relation to something else without applying an actual chronological age. If you say you have an older brother, we know your relative ages even though we do not know whether the two of you are 6 and 16 years old, 19 and 25, or 60 and 65. Almost all relative dating techniques rely on the geological principles of stratigraphy discussed earlier. These techniques include lithostratigraphy, biostratigraphy, tephrostratigraphy, and chemical methods.

Lithostratigraphy Using the characteristics of the rock layers themselves to correlate across regions is called **lithostratigraphy** (*litho* refers to rock). For example, if millions of years ago a layer of limestone was formed by an inland sea that extended over a large area of West Virginia, across Pennsylvania, and into New York, then we would expect to see the limestone layer in all these areas even if they exhibit different sequences of rock layers above and below the limestone. Therefore, the limestone layer allows us to correlate the widely separated sequences of rock layers (Figure 9.8 on page 244).

Tephrostratigraphy An increasingly important variant of lithostratigraphy is **tephrostratigraphy**, the identification of a volcanic ash by its chemical fingerprint of major, minor, and trace elements (Feibel, 1999). Chemical similarities allow us to correlate volcanic ashes (*tephra*) with each other, demonstrating time equivalence even in widely separated sites. This technique has been used with great success in the Turkana Basin of northern Kenya and southern Ethiopia, where researchers have made many important discoveries of ancestral human fossils.

Biostratigraphy Using Smith's principle of faunal succession (Figure 9.5), we can use the biological organisms found in rocks to correlate age between sites and across regions and thus to provide age estimates for fossils found at those sites. Making correlations based on biological organisms is called **biostratigraphy**. Organisms that are geographically widespread and vary anatomically through short time periods are the best biostratigraphic markers. Biostratigraphic markers that appear and disappear (go extinct) at roughly the same chronological time in all regions are most useful.

Rodents often are good biostratigraphic indicators of age. For example, the presence of certain rodent taxa that went extinct in the early Pleistocene has been used to estimate the age of Dmanisi, in the Republic of Georgia, the site of some of the earliest hominids outside Africa (see Chapter 13). In East Africa during the Plio-Pleistocene, the changes in pig taxa are systematic enough to also

provenience The origin or original source (as of a fossil).

relative dating techniques Dating techniques that establish the age of a fossil only in comparison to other materials found above and below it.

lithostratigraphy The study of geologic deposits and their formation, stratigraphic relationships, and relative time relationships based on their lithologic (rock) properties.

tephrostratigraphy A form of lithostratigraphy in which the chemical fingerprint of a volcanic ash is used to correlate across regions.

biostratigraphy Relative dating technique using comparison of fossils from different stratigraphic sequences to estimate which layers are older and which are younger.

Figure 9.7 KEY CHANGES IN EVOLUTION

The Earth's history spans 4.5 billion years. Geologists and paleontologists have pieced together the history of the Earth by correlating rock strata and examining the fossils within those rocks. Most of Earth's history is lifeless. Primates arise only about 65 million years ago, and the human lineage only 6 million years ago. Understanding primates in their geological context is critical to understanding their adaptations and evolution. Although the time line is drawn in equal epochs, vastly more time is represented by the Hadean, Archean, and Proterozoic (about 4 billion years) than by all of the later periods, which span only the last 540 million years.

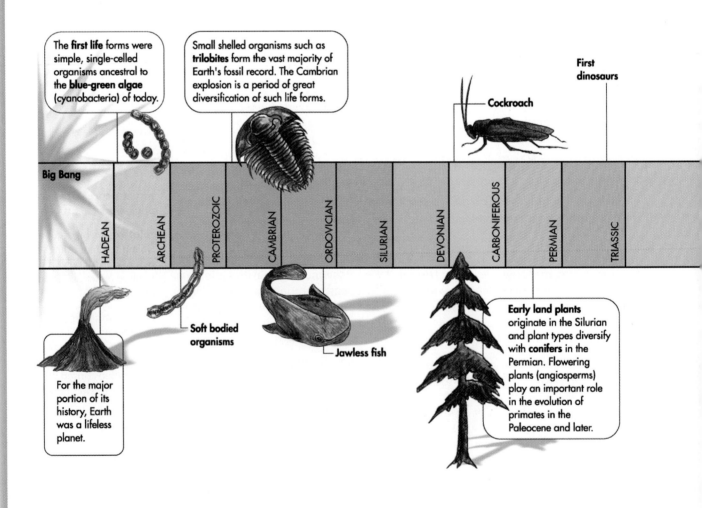

The **first life** forms were simple, single-celled organisms ancestral to the **blue-green algae** (cyanobacteria) of today.

Small shelled organisms such as **trilobites** form the vast majority of Earth's fossil record. The Cambrian explosion is a period of great diversification of such life forms.

First dinosaurs

Cockroach

Big Bang

HADEAN ARCHEAN PROTEROZOIC CAMBRIAN ORDOVICIAN SILURIAN DEVONIAN CARBONIFEROUS PERMIAN TRIASSIC

Soft bodied organisms

Jawless fish

For the major portion of its history, Earth was a lifeless planet.

Early land plants originate in the Silurian and plant types diversify with **conifers** in the Permian. Flowering plants (angiosperms) play an important role in the evolution of primates in the Paleocene and later.

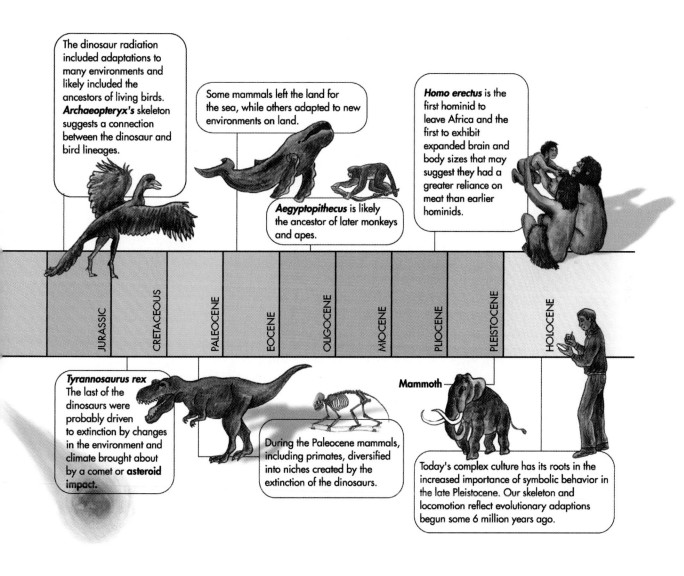

The dinosaur radiation included adaptations to many environments and likely included the ancestors of living birds. *Archaeopteryx's* skeleton suggests a connection between the dinosaur and bird lineages.

Some mammals left the land for the sea, while others adapted to new environments on land.

Homo erectus is the first hominid to leave Africa and the first to exhibit expanded brain and body sizes that may suggest they had a greater reliance on meat than earlier hominids.

Aegyptopithecus is likely the ancestor of later monkeys and apes.

JURASSIC

CRETACEOUS

PALEOCENE

EOCENE

OLIGOCENE

MIOCENE

PLIOCENE

PLEISTOCENE

HOLOCENE

Tyrannosaurus rex The last of the dinosaurs were probably driven to extinction by changes in the environment and climate brought about by a comet or **asteroid impact.**

During the Paleocene mammals, including primates, diversified into niches created by the extinction of the dinosaurs.

Mammoth

Today's complex culture has its roots in the increased importance of symbolic behavior in the late Pleistocene. Our skeleton and locomotion reflect evolutionary adaptions begun some 6 million years ago.

FIGURE 9.8 Lithostratigraphy uses the correlation of rock units to estimate the relative age of different areas. The overlapping rock units for U.S. parks show that the Grand Canyon contains strata that are mostly older than those at Zion National Park and that Bryce Canyon National Park is the youngest.

calibrated relative dating techniques Techniques that can be correlated to an absolute chronology.

geomagnetic polarity time scale (GPTS) Time scale composed of the sequence of paleomagnetic orientations of sediments through time.

paleomagnetism The magnetic polarity recorded in ancient sediments. Reversed or normal direction is used to correlate with the geomagnetic polarity time scale to infer an age for a site.

be good indicators of relative age. The presence of certain taxa, such as pigs or rodents, tells you only how old the site is relative to other sites with similar or different animals. An absolute age (that is, an age in years, such as 1.6 million years old) can be assigned only because at other sites with these index fossils there are also associated absolute ages. So in the case of the Dmanisi site the age must be older than 1.6 million years ago because, based on sites with absolute ages in Europe, the rodents present at Dmanisi are known to have gone extinct by that time.

Chemical Techniques within Sites A few chemical techniques are useful for identifying the relative age of different fossils from the same site. These techniques include the analysis of the fluorine, uranium, and nitrogen content of the fossils themselves. Such techniques become important when the association between different fossils or between the fossils and their sediments is in question, as in the Piltdown hoax, in which chemical techniques proved that the human fossils were fakes (Box 9.1 on page 246). As bones and teeth lie buried in sediment, they take up fluorine and other elements from the soil, roughly in proportion to the amount of time they have been buried (Oakley, 1963). How much of these elements is available is very dependent on the local environment, so the techniques are not useful between sites. However, two bones buried in the same sediments for the same amount of time should have similar chemical signatures. Thus these methods test associations within sites.

CALIBRATED RELATIVE DATING TECHNIQUES

Calibrated relative dating techniques include regular or somewhat regular processes that can be calibrated to a chronological scale if certain conditions are known. Such techniques include obsidian hydration, amino acid racemization, and paleomagnetism. Given the time scale of interest, we discuss only the latter in this section.

Geomagnetic Polarity   Although we take for granted the current position of the Earth's north and south magnetic poles, the polarity of the Earth's magnetic field has alternated through geologic time (Brown, 1992). Currents in the Earth's outer core create this magnetism, and as they change, the Earth's polarity may flip. At times in the past, magnetic north has been the opposite or reverse of today, that is, in the South Pole. Such reversals occur quickly, perhaps over thousands of years, and do not last for set periods of time. As rocks are formed, their magnetic minerals orient themselves toward magnetic north. Rocks laid down today would have a polarity, or orientation, similar to today's magnetic field. Such polarities are called *normal*. Rocks formed under a reversed field have a *reversed polarity*. Geologists use these facts to assist in the dating of stratigraphic units.

Paleomagnetists have assembled a **geomagnetic polarity time scale (GPTS)** that records the orientation of sediments from different intervals (Figure 9.9). The time scale is based on a sequence of changes in the magnetism of ancient layers, or **paleomagnetism,** that has been pieced together, mainly from sediments that have

FIGURE 9.9   The geomagnetic polarity time scale shows how the Earth's magnetic pole has changed through geologic time. Red bands indicate periods of reversed polarity and white bands indicate normal polarity.

(a)

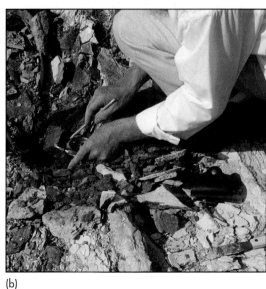

(b)

FIGURE 9.10   (a) At Sangiran, Java, scientists collect rock samples to measure the polarity of the sediments around the time *Homo erectus* fossils were deposited. (b) In the field the scientists use a compass to record the direction of present-day magnetic north which is marked directly on the rock. The polarity of the minerals in the rock itself will be measured later in the lab.

BOX 9.1   The Piltdown Hoax

Sometimes in the history of science, preconceptions about the way life should be get in the way of how they really are. The most vivid and embarrassing example of this in the history of paleoanthropology is Piltdown Man (Figure A). From 1908 to 1913, a number of fossil fragments were uncovered in a gravel pit at Piltdown Common, near the village of Uckfield in southern England, that appeared to show that the cradle of humankind was in the United Kingdom.

A laborer who was quarrying gravel at the site made the first find when his pickaxe struck a human skull fragment. He turned his discovery over to Charles Dawson, a local attorney and amateur geologist, who launched an intensive search at the site for more fossils. Dawson did not find more fragments, but over the next 3 years he discovered fossil bits of other creatures such as hippos and rhinos during visits to Piltdown. In 1911, Dawson contacted Arthur Smith Woodward of the Natural History Museum in London and reported that he had uncovered an ancient human skull (Figure B). Woodward visited Piltdown and saw the fossils that spring, along with a young priest and amateur prehistorian, Teilhard de Chardin (later to achieve fame as a philosopher of theology), and was impressed. During ensuing excavations, Dawson and Woodward re-

trieved more primitive human fossils and fossils of an assortment of long-extinct mammals. The key finds were the original skull, with an estimated cranial capacity smaller than that of a Neandertal but in other respects quite modern looking, and a large mandible with teeth that were decidedly apelike (Spencer, 1990).

The anatomy of "Piltdown Man" might have tipped off experts immediately that it was a fake. Piltdown possessed a large, human-like braincase, with primitive ape-like teeth and jaws. Today, we know that the earliest humans possessed the opposite suite of traits: a small, ape-like brain with bipedal lower anatomy (see Chapter 12)

However, when Piltdown Man was announced to the world in 1912, at the same prehistory conference in which two far better-documented fossil humans, Neandertal and Java Man (*Homo erectus*), were disputed and even dropped from the human family tree by some prominent scientists, the leading scientists of the Western world believed firmly that the first humans lived in Europe and were large brained. European scholars waged nationalistic verbal battles over whether the earliest humans would be found in Britain, France, or Germany. Although a few scientists advocated East Asia as the cradle of humankind, no one could imagine big-brained progenitors of our species being

FIGURE A   The Piltdown hoax was exposed by fluorine analysis, a relative dating technique that can test whether two bones have come from the same paleontological site. The mandible and skull fragment were shown to have different fluorine compositions.

Africans. That, together with the abundant other fossil European mammals with which the hominid remains were found, contributed to the acceptance of Piltdown as the first European, something of which the British scientific establishment was quite proud.

spread outward from midoceanic ridges at the bottom of the sea (Cande and Kent, 1995). The GPTS is divided into long intervals of similar polarity (normal or reversed) called chrons. Within these chrons there are often short periods of opposite polarity called subchrons. The GPTS extends back into the Jurassic period, but here we are most concerned with the last four chrons, the Gauss (reversed, 4.2–3.5 million years ago), Gilbert (normal, 2.6–3.5 million years ago), Matuyama (reversed, 2.6 million years ago–780,000), and Brunhes (normal, 780 thousand–present), and some of their subchrons. The present-day interval is the Brunhes Chron, which began about 780,000 years ago.

Paleomagnetists can use the polarity of sediments to assess site ages. First, they collect multiple samples from the site, being sure to indicate the direction of present-day north (Figure 9.10 on page 245), and measure the rock's polarity in the laboratory. Their analyses must carefully consider whether secondary overprints of polarity exist in the sample. Certain conditions such as weathering, heating, or lightning strikes can cause either the formation of new minerals with new

Yet as new human fossil finds began to accumulate in the 1920's and 1930s, all presented a view of human prehistory different from that offered by Piltdown's advocates. Instead of a large braincase and apelike jaw, most of the new fossils displayed the opposite. Beginning in 1950, British scientists conducted chemical tests on the fossil and found that the level of fluorine in the skull did not match that of the mandible; Piltdown was indeed a fraud. Piltdown Man was really a nearly modern human skull, artfully stained to appear ancient, with an associated orangutan mandible whose teeth had been filed down to appear more human (the file's scratches were clearly visible under a microscope). The mandible's connecting points with the skull had been carefully broken off to disguise the fact that the two did not belong together.

Once the hoax had been exposed, the question of course became, Who did it? All eyes turned initially to Dawson himself; who better to discover a new "fossil" than the person who planted it in the soil? But the question of motivation arose. As an amateur, Dawson seems unlikely to have chosen to self-aggrandize by planting a fake fossil if his passion was for finding real ones. Teilhard de Chardin, an avid archaeologist but also religiously passionate enough to be a skeptic about human fossils, has long been seen as one potential perpetrator. Keith or his colleague Grafton Elliot Smith also have been suspected at times because of attention a fossil such as Piltdown could bring to their

FIGURE B   Anatomists disagreed on the importance of the find.

careers. Some armchair detectives have even accused Sir Arthur Conan Doyle, writer of the Sherlock Holmes mysteries. Doyle, a physician who abandoned his practice to become a very successful novelist, fancied himself a serious scientist who used his medical know-how in spinning his tales. Failing to receive the respect of British scientific establishment, he might have set out to embarrass their august ranks with an ingenious practical joke.

The mystery remained unsolved for decades until a cleaning of the attic of the Natural History Museum in London in the 1980s, revealed a trunk with the initials of a former museum clerk named Martin Hinton. Inside they found an assortment of hippo and elephant teeth, all stained to the exact color of the Piltdown fossils. They also found human teeth that had been stained in different ways, as though by someone practicing the best way to fake an ancient appearance.

Hinton had two possible motives. First, he had a financial dispute with one of the curators of the museum and may have wanted to embarrass the museum officials by luring them into boastful claims about a fake ancestor (Gardiner, 2003). Secondly, Hinton was also an avowed anti-Darwinian, preferring Lamarck's debunked views even at the time of the Piltdown discoveries.

It is not clear how Hinton would have planted the fossils in the quarry for Dawson to find unless Dawson (who had a history of "discovering" historical artifacts that turned out to be frauds) was a co-conspirator. It appears that Hinton and Dawson were the likely perpetrators of one of science's greatest hoaxes.

polarities or the resetting of the polarity of existing minerals to reflect the polarity at the time the condition occurred, not the polarity at the origin of the rock. Often these overprints can be removed, but if they are not considered they can lead to an erroneous conclusion regarding polarity and ultimately age (Box 9.2 on page 248).

After overprint removal, paleomagnetists observe the sequence of polarities and compare it with the GPTS. Because paleontological localities do not often contain long stratigraphic sequences and can be only either reversed or normal, there is likely to be more than one match between the GPTS and the site polarity. This means that we must use other means, usually either chronometric ages or index fossils, to constrain or calibrate the possible ages provided by the GPTS. However, paleomagnetic analyses can be critical tests of absolute chronologies because the GPTS provides an expectation of rock polarity at any given chronological age. For example, the site of Dmanisi mentioned previously yielded hominid fossils in association with rodents known from other localities to have gone extinct at 1.6 million years ago. They also overlay a basalt dated to 1.8 million years ago. The GPTS

BOX 9.2 Dating Controversies

Although modern radiometric dating techniques provide some of the most rigorously scientific data available to biological anthropologists, the resulting age estimations often are highly controversial. A number of variables introduce uncertainty into our attempts to estimate the age of fossils. One vexing problem is the absence of material suitable for chronometric dating. A number of chronometric dating techniques (including potassium–argon, argon–argon, uranium series, and fission track) date the geological context and not the fossils themselves. Consequently, an age determination for a fossil is doubtful unless there is a secure understanding of the relationship between the fossil and its geological context. Biostratigraphic and tephrostratigraphic correlation provide an important means of testing the validity of chronometric age estimations and have pointed out simple errors in radiometric dates on a number of occasions.

An example of one such instance that comes from Pliocene deposits of Ethiopia illustrates this point and shows how all available dating information ultimately yields resolution of the ages of a fossil locality. The Hadar Formation in the Afar Triangle of Ethiopia provides the most complete paleontological evidence currently available for human ancestors between 3 and 4 million years ago (Box 12.1). Geochronologists using the argon–argon technique estimated an age of 3.8 million years before present on a basalt in the Hadar sequence, suggesting that many of the Hadar hominids were more ancient than the same species from the 3.5- to 3.7 million years old site of Laetoli in Tanzania (Walter and Aronson, 1982). In contrast, tephrostratigraphic correlation between Hadar and the Turkana Basin, in Kenya, indicated that these same Hadar hominids should be younger than 3.4 million years old (Brown, 1983). Detailed biostratigraphic comparisons concurred, revealing that the assortment of fossil mammals from Hadar is most comparable to those from deposits dating from approximately 3.4 – 3.0 million years ago in the Lower Omo River Valley of Ethiopia (White

et al., 1984) (Figure A). The radiometric and other age estimates differed by 400,000 to perhaps 800,000 years. This discrepancy led to a closer inspection of all of the age indicators. Ultimately, it was discovered that simple arithmetic errors had contributed to the 3.8 million years age estimate for the Hadar basalt. The corrected age more nearly matched the other estimates; scientists concluded that the important sample of early human ancestors from Hadar dated to the 3.0- to 3.4 million year time period rather than to 3.8 million years before present as once claimed. Without the use of several

lines of evidence, the true age of the locality might not have been resolved.

Dating controversies will continue to exist, but securely establishing provenience and applying multiple methods of age estimation should almost always lead us to the correct determination of antiquity.

FIGURE A (a) Scientists use the chemical signature of sediments from volcanic eruptions to correlate across large areas. (b) Correlations among east African hominid sites. The absolute ages are provided by argon-argon or potassium argon techniques.

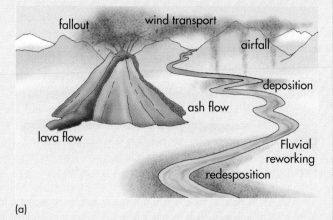

(a)

Age (Mya)	KENYA AND ETHIOPIA	ETHIOPIAN RIFT	NORTHERN TANZANIA	
2.0			**Laetoli**	
	Turkana Basin		Naibadad Beds	2.26 ± 0.06
			Ogol Lavas	2.41 ± 0.12
	Burgi — 2.68 ± 0.03	**Hadar**		
		BKT-2 — 2.88 ± 0.08		
3.0	Tuff B-10 2.95 ± 0.05	Kada Hadar		
	Toroto 3.32 ± 0.02			
	Tulu Bor	Sidi Hakoma	Laetolil Tuff 8	3.46 ± 0.12
				3.56 ± 0.20
			Base, Laetolil Upper Unit	3.76 ± 0.03
4.0				
				4.32 ± 0.05

(b)

(a)

(b)

FIGURE 9.11 (a) The site of Dmanisi, in the Republic of Georgia, has produced some of the earliest *H. erectus* outside of Africa. (b) The basalt below the hominids is dated to 1.8 mya using argon-argon techniques, and the geomagnetic polarity of the sediments is recorded by plusses and minuses on the wall of the excavation. The fossils come from reversed polarity sediments.

would predict that if the fossils dated from 1.8 million years ago, they should be found in sediments of normal polarity because they would have been deposited during the Olduvai Subchron of the Matuyama, a normal subchron that lasts from about 1.95 to 1.79 million years ago. Alternatively, sediments dated from 1.79 million years and younger postdate the Olduvai Subchron and are found in reversed-polarity deposits. Systematic evaluation of the polarity of the Dmanisi deposits found that the basalt was of normal polarity, coinciding with its chronometric age, and that the hominids and rodents were recovered in reversed-polarity deposits, confirming that they must be younger than 1.79 million years (Figure 9.11).

CHRONOMETRIC DATING TECHNIQUES

Unlike relative dating methods, **chronometric dating techniques** provide a chronological age estimate of the antiquity of an object in years before the present. These methods rely on having a clock of some sort to measure time. Such clocks include annual growth rings on trees and the recording of annual cycles of glacial retreat, which date very recent events. Radioactive clocks date more distant events,

chronometric dating techniques Techniques that estimate the age of an object in absolute terms through the use of a natural clock such as radioactive decay or tree ring growth.

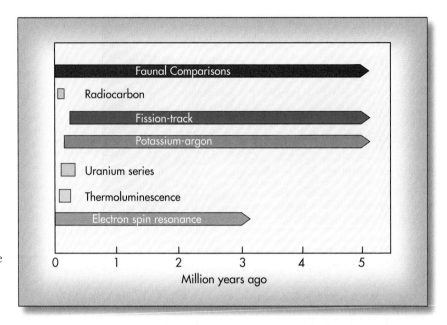

FIGURE 9.12 The relative age ranges of different dating techniques depend upon the half-life of the system used.

depending on the isotope used. The most famous of the radioactive decay clocks is Carbon-14 (^{14}C, or radiocarbon); other important techniques include potassium–argon (K–Ar), argon–argon ($^{40}Ar/^{39}Ar$), and uranium series (U-series) dating.

Other chronometric methods measure not the amount of radioactivity lost since formation but the amount gained from the environment since deposition. These include the electron trap techniques electron spin resonance (ESR), optical stimulated luminescence (OSL), and thermoluminescence (TL). Because we are concerned primarily with providing age estimates over the past 65 million years to perhaps as recently as 100 or 50 thousand years ago, we focus here on the clocks appropriate for this time scale. Figure 9.12 illustrates the relative age ranges of the different chronometric techniques discussed in this chapter, and Table 9.1 compares the materials dated.

TABLE 9.1	Comparison of Chronometric Techniques	
TECHNIQUE	AGE RANGE	MATERIALS DATED
K–Ar	10,000–4.5 billion years	K-bearing minerals and glass
$^{40}Ar/^{39}Ar$	Same as for K–Ar	K-bearing minerals (can date single grains)
Fission track	Tens of millions of years	Uranium-bearing, noncrystalline minerals, zircon, apatite, and glasses
Uranium series	Thousands to 500,000 years	Uranium-bearing minerals, $CaCo_3$, flowstones, corals, shells, teeth
Radiocarbon	<40,000 years	Organic materials such as wood, bone, shell
TL	100–500,000 years depending on material	Quartz, feldspars, pottery, tools
OSL	1,000–400,000 years	As above
ESR	Typically to 500,000 years and possibly to a few million years depending on material	Uranium-bearing materials and either closed or open systems in which uranium has been taken up from external sources

Radiometric Dating   **Radiometric dating** relies on the natural, clocklike decay of unstable isotopes of an element to more stable forms. *Elements* are chemically irreducible categories of matter such as carbon (C), hydrogen (H), and oxygen (O) that form the building blocks of all other matter, such as molecules of water (H_2O) and carbon monoxide (CO). Elements often occur in nature in more than one form, differing slightly on the basis of their atomic weights, which reflects the number of neutrons and protons in the nucleus. These different forms are called **isotopes**. For example, there are three isotopes of carbon, ^{12}C, ^{13}C, and ^{14}C, each with six protons (positively charged) but with six, seven, and eight neutrons (neutral particles), respectively (Figure 9.13). Although ^{12}C and ^{13}C are stable (they do not naturally decay), the extra neutron of ^{14}C makes it unstable or prone to decay. The rate at which this radioactive decay takes place is constant, and the **half-life** of the isotope is the amount of time it takes for one-half of the original amount to decay. To determine the age of a sample we measure the amount of **parent isotope**, the original radioactive isotope the sample started with, and the amount of **daughter isotope (product)** in the sample, which is the isotope formed by radioactive decay of the parent isotope. The total of these two is the amount of total parent that existed before radioactive decay started. The amount of daughter as a percentage of total parent tells you the number of half-lives expended. Knowing the length of the half-life yields an age (number of half-lives × length of half-life = age estimate). For example, the half-life of ^{14}C is about 5,730 years; if we know that two half-lives have passed in our sample, then we know that the sample is 11,460 years old. In this section we review the radiometric techniques most commonly used in paleoanthropology, beginning with those that measure samples of the oldest geological age.

   Potassium–argon (K–Ar) dating was first developed as a dating technique in the 1960s (Evernden and Curtis, 1965). The system measures the decay of the isotope ^{40}K (potassium) to ^{40}Ar (argon) and requires potassium-bearing minerals, such as feldspars, to work. Unlike the short half-life of ^{14}C, the decay from potassium to argon has a half-life of 1.3 billion years, making its effective range quite extensive (Deino et al., 1998). This decay series has been used to date some of the oldest rocks on Earth and has also dated events as recent as the eruption of Mt. Vesuvius in Italy in A.D. 79. K–Ar dating is useful in dating the timing of the eruption of volcanic sediments because heating during the eruption drives off all argon gases, and at the time the volcanic material cools, the clock is effectively set to zero (there is no argon and only potassium in the system).

   Thus the method dates the timing of the formation of the volcanic rocks. Fortunately, there are many situations in which fossil hominids are in sediments

radiometric dating
Chronometric techniques that use radioactive decay of isotopes to estimate age.

isotopes   Variant forms of an element that differ based on their atomic weights and numbers of neutrons in the nucleus. Both stable and unstable (radioactive) isotopes exist in nature.

half-life   The time it takes for half of the original amount of an unstable isotope of an element to decay into more stable forms.

parent isotope   The original radioactive isotope in a sample.

daughter isotope (product)
The isotope that is produced as the result of radioactive decay of the parent isotope.

potassium–argon (K–Ar) dating
Radiometric technique using the decay of ^{40}K to ^{40}Ar in potassium-bearing rocks; estimates the age of sediments in which fossils are found.

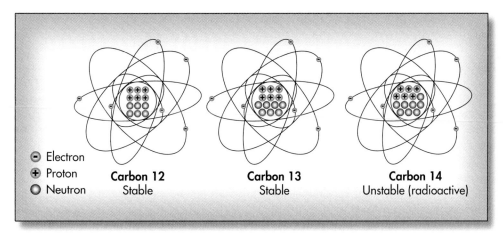

Electron
Proton
Neutron
Carbon 12
Stable
Carbon 13
Stable
Carbon 14
Unstable (radioactive)

FIGURE 9.13   Isotopes may be stable or radioactive depending on the arrangement and number of neutrons in the nucleus. Carbon 14 is heavier than Carbon 12 or 13 because it has more neutrons, and it is radioactive (or unstable) for the same reason.

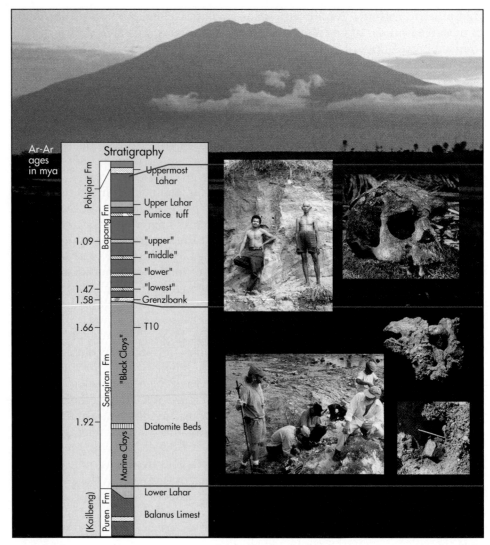

FIGURE 9.14 The argon–argon method is useful for dating volcanic sediments such as those at the Sangiran Dome region of Java that has yielded many *Homo erectus* fossils. Geologists have used lithostratigraphy to define the stratigraphy of the region. Argon–argon on tuffs in the section provide ages for the fossils and magnetic polarity provides confirmation.

sandwiched between volcanic sediments, so we can estimate the fossil ages by their association with the age of the volcanics (Figure 9.14).

However, K–Ar as a technique has some limitations. Potassium exists as a solid, and argon is a noble gas. So, measuring the relative amounts of these entails using two different samples of the same rock, measuring potassium as a solid in one sample and argon as a gas from the other. This assumes that all parts of a rock are homogeneous and that each sample is measured without error, assumptions that are often incorrect. Furthermore, it entails the use of whole rock samples, which increases the risk of contamination from trapped argon or argon loss. Extra argon not produced by decay of potassium makes a rock appear too old because the amount of daughter product is artificially large, whereas losing argon artificially lowers the amount of daughter product, making the rock appear too young.

Argon–argon (^{40}Ar/^{39}Ar) dating is a refinement of the K–Ar method that allows the use of smaller samples, sometimes even a single crystal, and greater control over the measurements and possible sources of sample error. ^{40}Ar/^{39}Ar uses a trick to measure ^{40}K by a proxy gas, ^{39}Ar, thus allowing measurement of both parent and

argon–argon (^{40}Ar/^{39}Ar)
Radiometric technique modified from K–Ar that measures ^{40}K by proxy using ^{39}Ar. Allows measurement of smaller samples with less error.

daughter in a single sample. So in the ^{40}Ar/^{39}Ar method both isotopes of argon are measured as gases, eliminating the limitations we saw in K–Ar. The ratio of ^{40}Ar to ^{39}Ar is the percentage of parent that has decayed (^{40}Ar = the amount of daughter product, ^{39}Ar = proxy for the amount of total parent originally in the system), and with this and the known half-life an age can be calculated.

An advantage of measuring both parent and daughter products as gases is that we can use smaller samples. This means that crystals can be picked for freshness, making less likely the possibility of argon loss caused by weathering. And it is possible to measure many different crystals from a rock instead of averaging them all for a whole rock sample. This means that you can be sure whether your crystals represent a single age population or whether they include older, reworked crystals (thus yielding too old an age). Thus our confidence in the age increases.

K–Ar and the ^{40}Ar/^{39}Ar methods have been widely used in paleoanthropology for dating volcanic sediments associated with hominids in Africa, Georgia, and Indonesia. In the late 1960s early K–Ar dates suggested that hominids had left Africa and migrated to Indonesia by about 1.9 million years ago, a remarkably early age given the conventional wisdom of the time. Because most of the volcanic rocks in Indonesia are very low in potassium, it was not until 1994 and the application of the more accurate ^{40}Ar/^{39}Ar method that these early ages were confirmed and expanded upon, and it is now generally accepted that *Homo erectus* dispersed to Indonesia by at least 1.6 million years ago (see Chapter 13).

Fission track dating provides age estimates for volcanic glasses, tektites (glasses formed by meteoritic impacts on the earth), and zircons that contain uranium. Only these noncrystalline materials can be dated with fission track techniques because the method relies on counting the small tracks produced each time an atom of ^{238}U decays by fission (hence its name). The technique involves etching the surface and counting the tracks (a proxy for the daughter product) of the sample, then irradiating the sample and measuring the number of additional tracks made by the fission of the nonradioactive ^{235}U. Because the ratio of ^{238}U to ^{235}U is known, the tracks from ^{235}U are a proxy for the original amount of parent isotope. Fission track dating provides a viable age range from about 100 years to the oldest rocks on Earth, although it is not as reliable for very young (<100,000 years) or very old samples. The low density of tracks makes it difficult to date very young samples, and old samples have too many tracks to count accurately. In addition, a number of processes can cause undercounts (and artificially young ages), so, particularly in glasses, fission track ages should always be considered minimum ages. In fact, fission track often is used as an ancillary to other chronometric techniques.

The fission track method is perhaps most famous for establishing the age of the Australasian tektite field, a series of glasses formed by the impact of a meteor in Australasia about 780 thousand years ago. Not only has fission track dating been used to date these tektites, but in the Nihewan Basin in China tektites are found in association with early evidence of stone tool manufacture. Thus their age, as established by fission track dating, makes them among the earliest stone tools in China.

Uranium series (U-series) techniques use the decay chain of ^{238}U, ^{235}U, and ^{232}Th, all of which decay to stable lead isotopes, to provide age estimates for calcium carbonates, such as flowstones precipitated in caves, shells of invertebrates, and sometimes teeth. Intermediate steps in the decay chain produce isotopes with very different half-lives, and the technique takes advantage of disequilibrium between the ratios of the various parent and daughter products to estimate an age (Figure 9.15 on page 254) rather than relying on the single parent to daughter decay of a system such as K–Ar. Because uranium is soluble in water but its daughter products (thorium, protactinium, and lead) are not, at the time of formation of the shell or flowstone (T_0), no daughter products are present. Once formed, the daughter products produced by the radioactive decay of each step in the decay chain are trapped in the crystal lattice of the flowstone (or shell) and can be measured to provide an age estimate.

fission track dating
Radiometric technique for dating noncrystalline materials using the decay of ^{238}Ur and counting the tracks that are produced by this fission. Estimates the age of sediments in which fossils are found.

uranium series (U-series) techniques Radiometric techniques using the decay of uranium to estimate an age for calcium carbonates including flowstones, shells, and teeth.

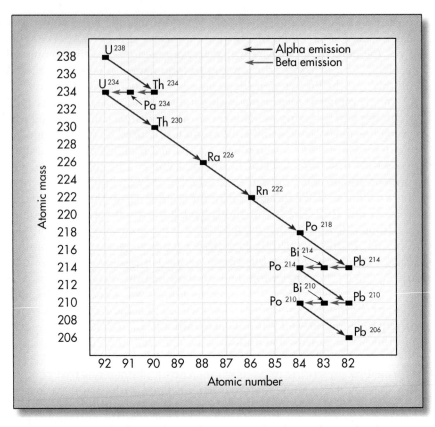

FIGURE 9.15   The figure shows the steps in the decay chain of radioactive Uranium 238 to stable Lead (Pb) 206. The daughter products along this decay chain, such as Thorium (Th) 234 and 230, each have half lives of different length. The Uranium series method uses ratios among these daughter products to estimate age.

In the case of shell, calcium carbonates in caves, and bone or tooth, the portion of the decay chain we measure is the ^{230}Th/^{234}U ratio, which can date samples from about five thousand to 500 thousand years ago. Other portions of the decay chain may allow older age estimates (McDermott et al., 1993). Uranium series techniques usually date strata associated with a fossil, not the fossil itself. Associations therefore are critical to providing the correct age estimate for a fossil, and because cave stratigraphy often is complex, these associations may not be accurate.

It may be possible to date a fossil directly with uranium series techniques, but the method is more complicated. Uranium does not naturally occur in either tooth or bone but is introduced to the system when these structures are buried in sediments. Remember that uranium is soluble in water, so uranium from ground water can migrate into the crystal lattice of, say, a tooth and from there begin its production of decay products. However, we can't always tell how quickly inmigration of uranium occurs, and modeling this uptake is critical to age assessment. Outmigration of parent or daughter may also occur; tooth and bone are not closed systems, making age difficult to determine. In general, tooth enamel is considered preferable for dating because of its tighter crystal lattice and, presumably, its lower susceptibility to migration of uranium. Despite these pitfalls, uranium series techniques have been critical for estimating ages for hominid sites, particularly those outside the range of radiocarbon and those in areas lacking volcanic rocks, such as China. Uranium series techniques on both flowstones and teeth at Chinese hominid sites have established ages for the famous Peking Man site that suggest a time range between about 250,000 and 600,000 years ago. (see Chapter 13).

Radiocarbon dating is the primary technique for estimating the antiquity of organic items from the latest Pleistocene through the present, including primate and human fossils as well as artifacts from archaeological sites. All living organisms are composed of molecules that contain carbon. Recall that three isotopes of carbon, ^{12}C, ^{13}C, and ^{14}C, exist in the atmosphere, only one of which, ^{14}C, is radioactive. As plants photosynthesize carbon dioxide they take up these isotopes at atmospheric levels. Animals that eat plants then take up carbon, and so do animals that eat other animals. Uptake of carbon ceases at the death of the organism. At this point (T_0), the atoms of ^{14}C begin to decay and are not replenished by additional ^{14}C from the atmosphere. We estimate age in the usual way by comparing the amount of daughter product (in this case ^{14}N) with the amount of original parent in the material and multiplying this percentage by the half-life.

The decay rate of ^{14}C is well understood, with a half-life of 5,730 years (Taylor, 2000). Because this half-life is so short, the radiocarbon technique is useful for organic remains from the last 30,000–40,000 years. So little of the original ^{14}C remains after this time (less than 1%) that counting errors preclude greater age estimates. In some cases, we can improve precision by measuring samples using accelerator mass spectrometry, but even then objects older than 40,000 years are beyond the reach of this technique. The limited age range of the ^{14}C technique limits its paleoanthropological applications to the latest part of the Neandertal lineage and their overlap with anatomically modern humans.

Electron Trap Techniques   **Electron trap techniques**, which include electron spin resonance, thermoluminescence, and optical stimulated luminescence, rely not on the decay of radioactive isotopes in a specimen but on the effect that exposure to radioactivity has on the specimen. Only crystalline materials can be dated with these methods.

When materials are exposed to naturally occurring radiation, some of their electrons become excited and separate from the parent atom. In a crystal lattice, these excited electrons may become trapped in defects or open spaces of the lattice rather than returning to their original location around the parent atom. If the *dose rate*, that is, the amount of radiation to which an object is exposed over a given period of time, is constant, then the number of trapped electrons will be proportional to the age of the material (age = total dose/annual dose rate, or the length of time since the electron traps were all empty). This radiation comes mostly from ^{238}U, ^{230}U, and ^{40}K, the most abundant radioisotopes. Although the dose rate varies by locality, we assume it to be constant over time at a given locality. We measure annual dose rate over the course of a year at the locality where the specimen was recovered. We measure total dose of the specimen in different ways for different electron trap techniques, as we'll see next.

Thermoluminescence (TL) measures the number of trapped electrons by measuring the amount of light given off when they are released. TL is useful on materials that had their traps emptied by being heated at a given time in the past. TL is particularly useful in dating pottery that was fired or stone tools that were heated in a campfire. As these items lie buried in the ground, they begin to accumulate trapped electrons again. In the lab we reheat these materials and then measure these newly trapped electrons by the amount of light emitted when they are heated. TL can date things over hundreds of thousands of years but is most typically used in the range of the past 100,000 years, which is older than ^{14}C can measure. TL on burnt flints has been important in establishing that the Near Eastern Neandertal sites of Amud and Kebara are young (about 45,000–60,000 years) compared with those of modern humans in the same region (about 100,000 years), whereas those at Tabūn, Israel, are older (about 100,000–150,000 years)

radiocarbon dating   Radiometric technique that uses the decay of ^{14}C in organic remains such as wood and bone to estimate the time since death of the organism.

electron trap techniques   Radiometric techniques that measure the accumulation of electrons in traps in the crystal lattice of a specimen.

thermoluminescence (TL)   Electron trap technique that uses heat to measure the amount of radioactivity accumulated by a specimen such as a stone tool since its last heating.

FIGURE 9.16 In the caves of the Mt. Carmel region of Israel, electronic spin resonance, uranium series techniques, and thermoluminescence have shown that modern humans and Neandertals alternated their use of the region.

(Figure 9.16). These dates suggest that Neandertals and modern humans alternated their use of the region over time, perhaps in response to climatic conditions in the region (see Chapter 14).

Optically stimulated luminescence (OSL) dates materials whose traps were emptied by bleaching from sunlight. Thus OSL dates the age of burial of an item, usually by sediment. We reexpose the materials to light of a known wavelength and measure the resulting luminescence, hence the name of the technique. Many measures from a sample are needed, and caution is necessary because incomplete emptying of traps yields ages far too old. The age range that OSL can measure is similar to that of TL. The method has been used successfully to investigate the initial colonization of Australia.

Electron spin resonance (ESR) requires a material to decompose with heat; it has been most successfully applied to tooth enamel. The tooth is powdered and exposed to microwaves. The trapped electrons resonate as they absorb the microwaves, and the extent of this resonance has been shown to be proportional to the total dose of the specimen.

However, there is an added step in measuring teeth. Not only must we measure the number of trapped electrons, but we must model the way uranium is introduced into the tooth in the first place. Because the mineral of tooth enamel (hydroxyapatite) contains no radioactivity at death and accumulates it all after burial, we must adjust the total rate for the way in which radioactive uranium is taken up by the tooth. The early uptake (EU) model estimates dose rate under the assumption that all the uranium uptake occurs soon after burial. The linear uptake (LU) model assumes uranium uptake occurs continuously through time. The choice of model can greatly affect the age estimates. The age range of ESR is about the same as that for the uranium series techniques, and the two are often used together if U-series is being conducted on tooth rather than on flowstone. For example, ESR analyses have been critical in corroborating the early age of the Tabun Neandertals (about 100,000–150,000 years) and of the Skhul and Qafzeh modern human sites (about 100,000 years) in the Near East (Stringer et al., 1989; Grun et al., 1991) (Figure 9.16). In conjunction with uranium series and TL analyses, these data suggest that modern humans occupied the Near East early but that the region was occupied by Neandertals both earlier and later in time (see Chapters 14 and 15).

optically stimulated luminescence (OSL) Electron trap technique that uses light to measure the amount of radioactivity accumulated by crystals in sediments (such as sand grains) since burial.

electron spin resonance (ESR) Electron trap technique that measures the total amount of radioactivity accumulated by a specimen such as tooth or bone since burial.

THE EARTH IN THE CENOZOIC

Having established the various ways we might assess the age of a paleontological site and the fossils within it, we now turn to other issues of understanding the context in which fossil primates are found. Most importantly we will look at the position of the major land masses during the Cenozoic, which has implications for how animals moved from one place to another and at the various methods scientists use to reconstruct the habitat that animals once lived in.

CONTINENTS AND LAND MASSES

As you may be aware, the continents have not always been in their current locations. Approximately 200 million years ago the earth was divided into two major land masses that we now call Laurasia and Gondwanaland. Laurasia was composed of most of present-day North America and Asia, and Gondwanaland included Africa and South America (Figure 9.17). By 50 million years ago North America and Asia were beginning to spread apart, and both South America and Africa had separated from one another and from the other continents. Africa eventually became connected to Asia via the Near East, North America and Asia were separated by a chain of islands (but remained connected during low sea levels), and South America was an island continent until well into the Pliocene (~ 3.5 million years ago), when the Central American land bridge connected it to North America. As we will see in Chapter 10, these movements are critical for understanding early primate evolution, particularly the distribution of the Eocene primates and the conundrum of the origin of the South American primates (which appeared while that continent was still an island). Once the continents were in their present positions, the onset of severe glacial events in the late Piocene and Pleistocene periodically lowered sea levels, exposing additional land and sometimes resulting, as is the case between continental Asia and Indonesia, in land bridges between otherwise isolated areas (see Chapter 13).

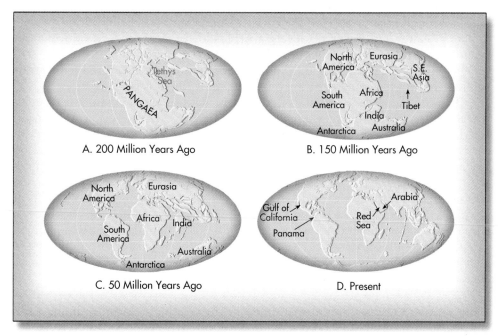

FIGURE 9.17 The continents were not always in their present positions. The position of the continents is important for understanding movements of primates in the past.

HOW COLD WAS IT?

Familiarity with an animal's environment is critical to understanding its survival and, in the long run, its evolution or extinction. As we saw in Chapter 2, conditions in the environment naturally select individuals most suited to them, and because of their favored traits, these individuals reproduce more than others in the population. Understanding past environmental conditions is critical, if complicated. We can reconstruct environmental conditions from several kinds of geological and biological evidence that we refer to here as environmental proxies. For our purposes we consider proxies for reconstruction of temperature, sea levels, and animal and plant communities. Each of these proxies can help us reconstruct local environments from the record at a particular paleontological or archaeological site. We can aggregate these proxies from different sites over time and across space to infer what the global environment was like and how it changed through time.

Oxygen Isotopes, Temperature, and Sea Level   Perhaps the best-known climate proxies are oxygen-isotope curves that rely on the past ratio of stable oxygen isotopes as a proxy for global temperature and sea level. The process works like this. Two stable isotopes of oxygen, ^{16}O and ^{18}O, differ in weight, with ^{18}O being the heavier of the two. These isotopes exist as oxygen in water molecules and other compounds. In water they are incorporated into the shells of marine invertebrates that are composed of calcium carbonates. Water molecules formed of the lighter isotope tend to float nearer the ocean surface, whereas water molecules formed of the heavier isotope tends to sink; therefore, the lighter isotope of oxygen tends to evaporate from ocean surfaces sooner than does ^{18}O. During cold periods, when ^{16}O evaporates from the ocean it is not returned to the world's water reserves via rain but is instead locked up in ice at the poles and northern latitudes. Consequently, sea levels are lower during cold periods and contain a greater percentage of ^{18}O than during warmer periods. Therefore, the $^{18}O/^{16}O$ ratio increases in sea water during cold periods and in the shells of the animals formed in them at that time.

Geologists studying marine cores measure the $^{18}O/^{16}O$ ratio of these marine shells through time to develop the oxygen isotope curves. Higher ratios indicate colder climates and lower sea levels, whereas lower ratios indicate warmer climates and higher sea levels. We can also use the oxygen isotope ratios in lake sediments to infer local climate, and some scientists have even measured these ratios in human teeth to estimate the temperatures those humans lived in.

The Plio-Pleistocene is characterized by oscillations in temperature from colder (glacial) to milder (interglacial) periods (Figure 9.18). The oxygen isotope stages of glacial and interglacial events are numbered, starting from the most recent. Interglacial periods receive odd numbers because we are in an interglacial period today, which is labeled oxygen isotope stage 1; glacial periods receive even numbers. On a finer scale, oxygen isotope curves have been important for reconstructing climate patterns in the mid- and late Pleistocene and correlating the movements of Neandertals and modern humans in relation to climate change (as we'll see in Chapter 14). Remember that microclimates still exist within these patterns—for example, think of the differences in climate between the beach and the mountains—but global climatic proxies can help us understand what kinds of conditions animals lived in during the past.

Paleosols and Loess   Soil formation occurs by weathering of surrounding sediments, and soil structure reflects conditions in the environment at the time the soil was formed. For this reason we can use **paleosol**, or ancient soil, to understand the environmental conditions that existed for ancient plants and plant-eating animals. For example, differences between paleosols can differentiate between more tem-

paleosol   Ancient soil.

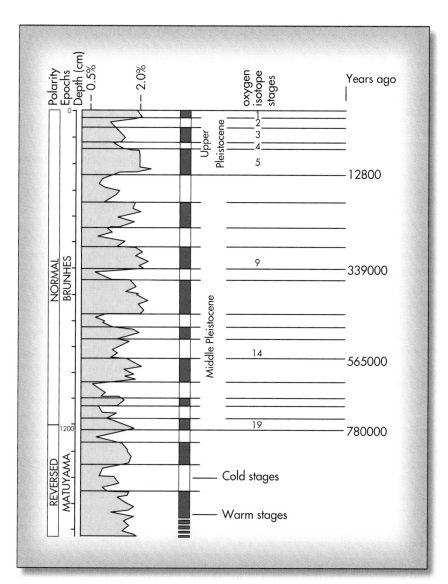

FIGURE 9.18 The oxygen isotope curve illustrates the ratio between oxygen[16] and oxygen[18]. More of the heavy isotope indicates colder periods (even numbered stages), more of the lighter indicates warmer periods (interglacials, odd-numbered).

perate humid conditions and dryer colder conditions. Paleosols can also correlate strata between sites. In addition to paleosols, we can also use windblown sediments in both stratigraphy and paleoclimate reconstruction. The most important of these sediments to paleoanthropology are the loess sequences (windblown silt) in Asia. Asian loess indicates drier conditions than other loess in the world and is often interstratified with paleosols that provide additional paleoclimatic and environmental information (Lowe and Walker, 1997).

Vegetation Plant macrofossils (or other traces such as root casts) may be preserved at some sites. Local plants often are preserved in bog or peat environments, but plants and plant imprints may also fossilize in very fine-grained sediments. The sediments that yield the winged dinosaurs of Liaoning, China, for example, also preserve early examples of flowering plants (angiosperms). And leaves from Eocene fossil floras share features in common with leaves from tropical and subtropical trees today.

Such evidence of the vegetation at paleontological sites can be used to compare the environments that animals once lived in with those of today. For example, using fossilized sediments and vegetation data from ancient riverside habitats

Jeanne Sept compared the plant diversity in modern East African *gallery forests,* those that grow alongside streams, with that in the Pliocene (Sept, 2001). By so doing she was able to make a vegetation map of the "edible landscape" available to early human ancestors called australopithecines (see Chapter 12) and to conclude that, based on available resources, closely related hominids could have coexisted mainly if one species was an omnivore.

The recovery of fossil pollens can also tell us about the presence of certain kinds of plants in an area. We must be careful when determining how pollens got into the site, however. For example, windblown pollens may have traveled a great distance, so their presence at a locality may indicate a certain plant within some particular distance of the locality, but not precisely at the locality. Mixed pollen samples therefore may be particularly prevalent in patchy environments as well. Also, contamination by modern pollens may be difficult to differentiate. As we shall see in Chapter 14, the Neandertal site of Shanidar has been purported to show a burial ritual with a Neandertal interred on a blanket of flowers (based on the plentiful pollen around the skeleton). But it is more likely that modern pollens were introduced to the site, either as the archaeologists excavated or as the wind blew over local plants.

Another direct means of assessing plant resources is the presence of **phytoliths,** opaline silica bodies secreted by some plants, especially grasses, whose shape is often characteristic of that plant. Fine, wet screening of sediments is needed to retrieve these small items. The presence of phytoliths has been important in the reconstruction of available plants and diet of the Miocene ape *Sivapithecus* (see Chapter 10) and has been used to interpret the uses of some stone tools.

Stable Carbon Isotope Ratios *Stable carbon isotope ratios* are also a useful tool in climatic and environmental reconstructions; they are used to reconstruct the types of vegetation in a region. We can use carbon isotopes to differentiate between plants using different photosynthetic pathways. Plants use three basic means to photosynthesize. The most common is the C3 pathway, so called because plants that use it make a three-carbon compound during the first stage of photosynthesis. Trees and shrubs are mostly C3 plants, as are most of the world's plants.

The second pathway, called C4, is so called because the plants that use it make a four-carbon compound during photosynthesis. It is thought that this pathway evolved in response to low levels of carbon dioxide in the environment over the past 50 million years. Tropical grasses are almost all C4 plants, although a few, especially those from shaded or closed canopy environments, are C3 plants. However, fewer than 1% of the earth's plants are C4 plants.

Finally, CAM (Crassulacean acid metabolism) plants exist in areas where preventing water loss is critical. CAM plants use a C4 pathway at night, and as a result of their more complicated pathway they tend to lose less carbon during photosynthesis. About 4% of the world's plants are CAM plants, including cacti and agave (the plant from which tequila is made).

Because of their different pathways for photosynthesis, different types of plants retain different amounts of the carbon isotopes. C3 plants tend to have less ^{13}C and hence lower $^{13}C/^{12}C$ ratios. C4 plants have more ^{13}C. By evaluating these ratios we can tell whether there was an abundance of C3, C4, or CAM plants. Fortuitously, $^{13}C/^{12}C$ ratios are produced during analyses for ^{14}C dating.

By looking at these ratios of stable carbon isotopes in the teeth of fossil animals, we can infer the type of vegetation the animals ate and the type of vegetation present in the area. By looking at these ratios in various animal taxa in an area or through time, we can begin to build a vegetation map. For example, fossil horse teeth have been used to look at the distribution of grass types throughout the world

phytoliths Silica bodies produced by some plants, especially grasses, that can be used to indicate the presence of certain types of vegetation at a fossil site.

during the Pleistocene (McFadden et al., 1999). This work suggests that Pleistocene vegetation gradients varied by latitude, as they do today.

We can also look at the stable carbon isotope ratios in paleosols because the organic carbon found in soils comes from local plants. Analyzing paleosols in this way has been important in reconstructing environments in Africa during hominid evolution, particularly because the abundance of C3 and C4 grasses varies between open (savanna) environments and shaded or wooded environments (Figure 9.19). As we shall see in Chapters 11–15, knowing the kind of environment hominids originated in is critical to many explanations for how and why bipedality evolved in hominids. We used to think bipedality arose in an open savanna environment, perhaps implicating heat stress or other selective factors in its origin. However, we are learning that many of the early hominid environments were more wooded, suggesting that another selective factor was at work; perhaps bipedality was an efficient means of crossing short distances between food patches while also carrying food.

Animal Communities   Although some types of animals seem to be able to live just about anywhere, most have preferred types of habitats. Hippos and crocodiles live near water sources, and the presence of monkeys usually indicates wooded areas. Animals that are adapted to running long distances over open terrain tend to have longer, slighter limbs; those adapted to life in forested areas often tend to have shorter limbs. Based on comparisons with the adaptations in living animals of known habitat preference, paleontologists infer the climatic and environmental preferences of past animals associated with hominid sites and thus the paleoenviromental conditions in which hominids lived.

These types of analyses focus on all the animals found at a particular site during a particular time interval, not just on a single species. This is important because the relative abundance of animals can tell you more about an environment than can the presence of a single species. As with pollen analysis, paleontologists must be careful to consider how the animals were introduced to the site. Does the site represent a single community at a single time or a single community through time? Could the site be sampling animals from different areas? For example, running water might wash in animals from different areas that didn't inhabit the same

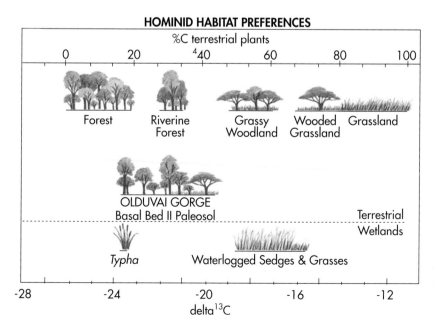

FIGURE 9.19 Habitat reconstruction is possible based on the kinds of plants present at past sites. The kinds of plants present are reflected in the ratios of stable carbon isotopes in soils, fossils and fossil carbonates.

environmental zone. Therefore, we must carefully assess the taphonomic processes at work on an assemblage.

Once this has been done, the work focuses on trying to reconstruct the ecological community of animals that lived at the site and their diversity. Paleontologists consider the dietary and locomotor adaptations of the animal. Locomotor categories might include whether the animal in question is terrestrial, arboreal, a combination of the two, aquatic, or a burrower or digger. Trophic level categories describe whether the animal is a browser (eats leaves), grazer (eats grass), frugivore (eats fruit, in combination with other foods), carnivore (eats meat and of what source or in combination with what other foods), or omnivore. Combining this information from all the animals of the site gives a good impression of the kind of habitat (trees, water, open areas, and so on) and food (grasses, trees, insects, and so on) that was available. This gives a pretty clear idea of what kind of habitat hominids were living in. For example, Kaye Reed examined the anatomical adaptations of different species of fossil antelopes found in early hominid sites (Figure 9.20). She found that the likely habitat in which most early australopithecines lived was wooded regions interspersed with lakes and rivers. Later in the fossil record, again with antelope taxa as markers, the robust australopithecines appeared to prefer habitats that included swamps and marshes (Reed, 1997). These kinds of reconstructions of animal communities have been critical for reconstructing paleoenvironments of the Plio-Pleistocene hominids in Africa and elsewhere (see Chapters 12–15).

OVERVIEW OF CLIMATIC CHANGES DURING THE CENOZOIC

Based on the kinds of studies just described, scientists have drawn a general picture of the climate during the evolution of the Primate order. In this section we provide an overview of climate changes through the Cenozoic, and in each of the succeeding chapters we will discuss how specific climatic changes affected the evolution of human and nonhuman primates. Recall that climate and environment are the source of important selective pressures that influence the evolution of all animal groups. Figure 9.21 provides a graphic overview of temperature changes throughout the Cenozoic.

Paleocene to Miocene Climate   The story of Cenozoic climate change is generally one of cooling and drying. The Cenozoic began much, much warmer than it is today. Furthermore, there was less difference between temperatures at the equator and the North and South Pole than we currently experience. Thus, when pri-

FIGURE 9.20   Antelope species have specific habitat preferences. These wildebeest prefer more open areas, other species prefer more wooded areas. Identifying the kinds of fossil antelope at hominid sites suggests the kind of environment that existed at that site in the past.

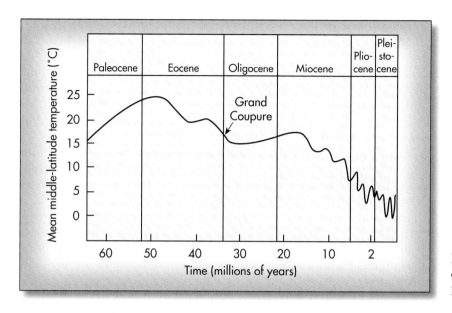

FIGURE 9.21 Climate has cooled substantially during primate evolution.

mates first arose, not only were they equatorial and subequatorial animals, as they largely are today, but they existed in abundance fairly far north and south. Although it was warmer than today, there was some climatic fluctuation during each epoch. As the era proceeded, the climate cooled and dried but still fluctuated somewhat.

The Paleocene and early Eocene were by far the warmest epochs of the Cenozoic. During the Eocene there was a precipitous drop in global temperature until finally, at about the Eocene/Oligocene boundary (around 36 Million years ago), there was a decided cold snap that resulted in large-scale extinction and replacement of many species. This "turnover" is often called the *Grande Coupure* (or big cut) because of the large number of taxa that went extinct. The early Oligocene continued to see decreases in temperature, and then late in the Oligocene temperature rose a bit, returning to the levels at the beginning of the epoch (so it was still quite cold compared with most of the Eocene but warm by modern standards). It is likely that the lowest temperatures in the Oligocene (at the start, and then again around 31 and 24 million years ago) were associated with short glacial periods. These temperature changes may have been caused by the movement of continents and the resulting changes in ocean and wind currents that alter climate patterns.

From the end of the Oligocene to about the middle of the Miocene temperature rose again gradually, although it remained well below levels of the Eocene. About the middle of the Miocene, perhaps 15 million years ago, another abrupt cooling and drying trend occurred, this time driving temperatures well below any previously experienced in the Cenozoic. This severe cooling probably was related to the appearance of a permanent Antarctic ice sheet at the South Pole. The evolution of the Antarctic ice sheet removed much water from the oceans, resulting in the so-called Messinian event or crisis in which the Mediterranean ran dry, leaving a great salt lake. As we will see in Chapter 10, these changes in climate often are correlated with the origin, extinction, or diversification of primate groups.

Pliocene to Early Pleistocene Climate   During the early Pliocene temperatures increased and the Mediterranean Sea refilled, but shortly thereafter cooling began again. Ice sheets at both poles became permanent features throughout the Pliocene. Cyclic glaciation set in only about 3 million years ago but did not become more intense until 2.5 million years ago and then became even more intense in the Pleistocene. Most of the paleoclimatic reconstructions that we are concerned with for human evolution are for the continent of Africa because until a little less than 2 million years ago, our ancestors were entirely restricted to that continent.

Elizabeth Vrba studied paleoclimatic fluctuations in order to understand the changes in plants and animals through time in the Pliocene, which is important evidence of the context of human evolution. She asks why some lineages of animals have flourished and diversified in the course of mammalian evolution but others have not. Vrba (1996) argues that there is evidence in the climate data from Earth's history to suggest that physical environmental factors (long-term trends in rainfall and temperature) were more important than biological factors (predators, for example) in East Africa. In the pattern of climate fluctuations over the past 5–10 million years, she sees the context for natural selection pressures that would have altered the abundance and distribution of forests and grassland. These changes in East African ecosystems in turn changed the communities of plants and animals that lived there. Using ungulates (antelopes, zebras, and the like) as index species, she found that climatic changes that occurred as pulses, or punctuated events, wrought major changes in the community of large animals.

In another study, René Bobe, Anna K. Behrensmeyer, and colleagues found that changes in the abundance of various mammalian taxa, from rodents to ungulates, changed over time between 4 and 2 million years ago in the Omo region of Ethiopia. The period of greatest variability in the fossil record (that is, when we see the most shifts in the occurrence of different species of mammals) coincided with the first appearance of the genus *Homo* in the fossil record. A later period of climatic fluctuation that was tied to changes in mammal species diversity was also linked to the appearance of early stone tools, and a still later fluctuation period was linked to the apparent extinction of some australopithecine taxa. This interesting correlated pattern of periodic fluctuations in African climate, changes in the fauna, and key events in human prehistory has led Rick Potts to argue that humans are adapted to such periods of instability and that our intelligence and adaptability may have been honed as a result of it.

Early to Late Pleistocene Climate   As mentioned earlier, around 2.5 million years ago glacial cycles began to become more severe. We know the extent of the glaciation based on the oxygen isotope curves. The glaciation was so severe that it lowered sea levels enough to connect island Southeast Asia to mainland Asia for the first time. This was important as hominids started to move out of Africa. Starting about 1.8 million years ago, a series of glacial events intermittently lowered sea levels enough to connect mainland and Southeast Asia, allowing fauna and hominids to cross back and forth between the two at times and to be isolated from one another at other times (see Chapter 13).

One of the results of this increasing cold and glacial cycling is that latitudinal variation in climate became quite significant (remember that temperature varied little from north to south early in primate evolution). As hominids began to move out of Africa around 1.8 million years ago and into western Asia and ultimately the northerly latitudes of Europe (~800,000), climatic conditions in some instances were quite harsh. This harsh climate appears to have kept hominids from moving too far north permanently until they had sufficient cultural means of mitigating the conditions. Not until Neandertals and their ancestors was there permanent settlement in Europe (see Chapters 14 and 15).

Understanding the context in which fossils are formed and found is critical to identifying their age and the natural selective factors that influence their evolution. Here we have set the foundation for understanding the geological age and environmental context of fossil primates. In Chapter 10 we embark on the evolutionary journey of the Primates as written in the fossil record.

SUMMARY

1. **Why is the fossil record so fragmentary?**

   The fossil record is fragmentary because only a tiny fraction of Earth's creatures die in a circumstance in which they may be fossilized, and then only a tiny fraction of those are ever found by paleontologists.

2. **What is taphonomy?**

   Taphonomy is the study of what happens to remains from the death of the organism until the discovery of the fossils.

3. **What is the difference between relative and chronometric dating techniques?**

   Chronometric dating techniques provide a fairly precise date for a fossil, based on measurement of some natural clock, often the radioactive decay of an element such as potassium (K) or carbon (C) in either the rock in which the fossil is found or in the fossil itself. Relative dating techniques provide only an estimate of whether a fossil is older or younger than other materials found above and below it at the same site or in sediments at other sites.

4. **Why does ^{14}C usually date younger sites than K–Ar?**

   Because of the short half-life of radiocarbon, too little of the radioactive isotope remains after about 30,000–40,000 years to be accurately measured. K has a longer half-life and thus can estimate age over longer time periods. In special circumstances we can also use it to determine the age of younger fossils.

5. **How do oxygen isotopes tell us about past climate?**

   Two stable isotopes of oxygen, ^{16}O and ^{18}O, differ in weight, with ^{18}O the heavier of the two. In water they are incorporated into the shells of marine invertebrates that are composed of calcium carbonates. During cold periods, when ^{16}O evaporates from the ocean it is not returned to the world's water reserves via rain but is instead locked up in ice at the poles and northern latitudes. Consequently, sea levels are lower and contain a greater percentage of ^{18}O than normal. The $^{18}O/^{16}O$ ratio increases. Higher ratios indicate colder climates and lower sea levels, whereas lower ratios indicate warmer climates and higher sea levels.

6. **How do scientists think climate changed from the Paleocene to present, and on what do they base their evidence?**

   Past climate reconstructions are based on geological and biological data including oxygen isotope curves, fossil soils, fossil animals, fossil plants, and pollens. These reconstructions suggest that temperatures were warmer and moister in the past and have cooled and dried over the Cenozoic. There were marked cooling events at the Eocene/Oligocene boundary and the onset of severe glaciation in the late Pliocene and Pleistocene.

CRITICAL THINKING QUESTIONS

1. Given how few of Earth's creatures end up as fossils, do you think we will continue finding new and important fossils, or have we already found most of those fossils that exist?

2. Given the different techniques to reconstruct climate and environment, if you were leading a paleontological project, how would you design your research program to figure out the context in which the fossils from your site came?

3. Imagine that you find a fossil hominid with some animal bones. How would you go about determining whether the animals and the hominids were deposited at the same time (were the same age)? Do you think that you could be mistaken, and what factors might make determining the age of the fossils difficult?

KEY TERMS

fossils
paleontology
geology
taphonomy
strata
stratigraphy
geologic time scale
   (GTS)
provenience
relative dating
   techniques
lithostratigraphy
tephrostratigraphy
biostratigraphy
calibrated relative
   dating techniques

geomagnetic polarity
   time scale (GPTS)
paleomagnetism
chronometric (absolute)
   dating techniques
radiometric dating
isotope
half-life
parent isotope
daughter isotope
   (product)
potassium–argon (K–Ar)
   dating
argon–argon (^{40}Ar/^{39}Ar)
   dating
fission track dating

uranium series (U-series)
   techniques
radiocarbon dating
electron trap techniques
dose rate
thermoluminescence
   (TL)
optical stimulated
   luminescence (OSL)
electron spin resonance
   (ESR)
paleosol
phytoliths

SUGGESTED READING

Cutler, Alan. (2003). *The Seashell on the Mountaintop*. Plume, Penguin Group, New York, NY.

Lowe, John J., and Walker, Mike, J. C. (1997). *Reconstructing Quaternary Environments*, 2nd edition. Prentice Hall, Englewood Cliffs, NJ.

Repcheck, Jack. (2003). *The Man who Found Time: James Hutton and the Discovery of the Earth's Antiquity*. Perseus Publishing, New York, NY.

Shipman, Pat. (1981). *Life History of a Fossil*. Harvard University Press, Cambridge, MA.

Tarbuck, Edward J., and Frederick K. Lutgens. (2004). *Earth: An Introduction to Physical Geology*, 8th edition. Prentice Hall, Englewood Cliffs, NJ.

Taylor, R. E., and Aitken, M. J. (1998). *Chronometric Dating in Archaeology*. Kluwer, Dordrecht, The Netherlands.

Chapter 10

ORIGIN OF PRIMATES

"DOOM WAS COMING OUT OF THE SKY in the form of an enormous comet or asteroid—we are still not sure which it was. Probably 10 km across, traveling tens of kilometers a second, its energy of motion had the destructive capability of a hundred million hydrogen bombs" (p. 5).

"It is worth pondering the realization that each of us is descended from unknown ancestors who were alive on that day when the fatal rock fell from the sky. They survived and the dinosaurs did not, and that is the reason why we are here now—as individuals and as a species. That one terrible day undid the benefits which 150 million years of natural selection had conferred upon the dinosaurs, making them ever fitter to be the large land animals of Earth. Evolution had not equipped them to survive the environmental disasters inflicted by a huge impact and when the holocaust was over, they were gone.

Evolution had not provided impact resistance for the mammals either, but somehow they did survive. No one knows why, but it must have helped that they were smaller and therefore much more numerous than the dinosaurs, so that there was a better statistical chance that some would live.

When the environmental disruptions from the impact had waned and the mammal survivors emerged into a new world they must have faced great dangers and great opportunities"—W. Alvarez, *T. rex and the Crater of Doom* (1997:130)

As the vignette suggests, geological forces have a critical impact in developing new opportunities for mammalian evolution, including primate evolution. In Chapter 9 we set the foundation for understanding the context in which animals evolved, based on the geological clues gathered from paleontological sites. We now turn to the primate fossil record itself. Throughout this chapter, keep in mind that living primates evolved from fossil primates. Our task is to try to figure out what kind of primate each fossil group represents and then, by looking at the context in which the fossils are found and the characters they exhibit, to consider what kinds of selective pressures led to their evolution. By doing this we will understand more of the process by which living primates came to be, and we will move well on our way toward understanding our own origins.

To help in this task you will want to refer to the family tree of living primates in Chapter 7 (Figure 7.9) and review the bony characteristics that allow us to recognize animals at different levels of that tree. You will also want to refer back to the geological time scale in Chapter 9 (Figure 9.6). As we examine the primate fossil record, compare the skeletal characters of the fossils with the characters that differentiate primates from other mammals and groups of primates from one another. On the basis of these anatomical characters, decide where on the tree you think the fossils fit and think about what the characters tell you about the selective pressures that might have molded these species. You may find it useful to make yourself a giant primate chart of living taxa and a small card for each fossil group listing its anatomical characters. Tack your chart on a bulletin board or your fridge and then attach the fossil cards at the appropriate place on the living hierarchy.

In this chapter we review what we know about the origin of the Primate order and the major nonhuman primate groups from the Paleocene through the Miocene epoch. We begin with fossils that are only questionably associated with primates and consider the strepsirhine–haplorhine split, the origin of Old World and New World monkeys, and finally the origin of the apes. In each case we focus on the anatomical characters of the fossils and the ecological circumstances in which they evolved, and we discuss possible scenarios for what this evidence tells us about the natural selective factors that favored the origin of each group. We conclude the chapter with a review of what the molecular data tell us about the timing of primate evolution and the genetic changes that led to the origin of the human lineage, setting the stage for the next five chapters, which review the human fossil record.

THE MESOZOIC AND BEYOND

Our review of the primate fossil record begins in the Mesozoic Era (225–65 million years ago) because the origin of primates is tied first to the origin of mammals, a process that begins in an era dominated by dinosaurs. During this era critical ecological changes provided opportunities for small, insect-eating mammals from which primates evolved.

Dawn of the Age of Mammals

The mammals of the Mesozoic Era were small, secretive creatures, overshadowed both in our imaginations and in reality by their contemporaries, the dinosaurs. The mammals that first appeared during the late Triassic Period most closely resembled the living monotremes, such as the echidna and platypus. In the Jurassic Period the first marsupial and placental mammals appeared, and both diversified greatly during the final period of the Mesozoic, the Cretaceous.

Diversification of the mammals in the middle to late Cretaceous was almost certainly a result of profound diversification of *angiosperms,* or flowering plants, at the end of the Mesozoic that heralded the beginning of one of the most important ecological interactions in modern ecosystems: pollination of flowering plants by insects. To disperse their pollen, flowering plants evolved showy blossoms and sweet nectar to entice insects. The presence of abundant insects buzzing around flowers probably attracted vertebrates, including birds and mammals. As we saw in Chapter 7, flowering plants also lure birds and mammals into dispersing their seeds by producing sweet and colorful fruit. And as we shall see shortly, early primate ancestors also ate these insects.

The Crater of Doom: What Happened at the K–T Boundary?

At the end of the Mesozoic, drastic environmental changes, probably arising from an asteroid or comet crashing into the surface of the Earth, caused or contributed to the extinction of the dinosaurs and generated opportunities for mammals (Alvarez et al., 1980). Evidence of such an impact comes from a giant crater called Chicxulub in the Yucatán Peninsula.

The impact probably caused an all-consuming firestorm and a number of tidal waves, all followed by abrupt global cooling. It is thought that this combination of fire and cold killed off much of the terrestrial plant life at that time, which caused the extinction of herbivorous dinosaurs and then also of the carnivorous dinosaurs that preyed on them.

The ensuing environmental and ecological circumstances, including the absence of large prey animals, favored small, insect-eating mammals over the larger dinosaurs. Some of the primitive mammals of the Mesozoic, such as *multituberculates,* persisted into the Paleocene, the earliest Cenozoic epoch, but for the most part there is a comprehensive replacement of mammals at the K–T boundary. Many of these new mammals are archaic forms that are not traceable to living groups. Such is the case with the possible ancestors of the primates.

AFTER THE CRATER OF DOOM: CHANGES IN THE PALEOCENE

During the Paleocene Epoch, many archaic groups of mammals arose that are not precisely like any living group. Among these groups are the ancestors of living mammalian orders, including primates. There is some controversy as to the precise evolutionary relationship between primates and a Paleocene group called the plesiadapiforms (Figure 10.1). For this reason we call the plesiadapiforms questionable primates.

QUESTIONABLE PRIMATES: THE PLESIADAPIFORMS

plesiadapiforms Mammalian order or suborder of mammals that may be ancestral to later Primates, characterized by some but not all of the primate trends.

Among the new arrivals at the beginning of the Paleocene are primate-like mammals, the **plesiadapiforms,** either a separate order of mammals or a suborder of the primates, on equal footing with strepsirhines and haplorhines (see Chapter 7). Known

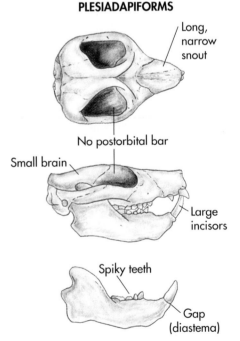

PLESIADAPIFORMS

Long, narrow snout

No postorbital bar

Small brain

Large incisors

Spiky teeth

Gap (diastema)

Claws, not nails

FIGURE 10.1 The plesiadapiforms may have been primates but they lacked certain features, such as a postorbital bar and nails, common to living primates. Note also their small brain and long nose.

mainly from North America, the plesiadapiforms have also been discovered in Europe and in China and range from the early Paleocene to the late Eocene.

Much controversy has swirled around whether the plesiadapiforms were true primates (Szalay, 1975) or representatives of another closely related order of mammals such as the Scandentia (tree shrews), Dermoptera (colugos or "flying lemurs"), or Chiroptera (bats). In recent years, there has been a tendency to exclude some or all of the plesiadapiforms from the order Primates (Rasmussen, 2002), but new fossil evidence indicates that at least some of these archaic forms were true primates that diverged before the last common ancestor of living species (Bloch and Silcox, 2001). And, as we shall see at the end of this chapter, genetic evidence suggests that at about the time of *Purgatorius* (63 million years ago) the primate lineage arose.

Paleontologists use the form of teeth and bones to decide to which group a fossil belongs, so to be identified as primates, fossils must show the primate trends in anatomy. The controversy with the plesiadapiforms arises because in many ways they were more primitive than any living primate. They had small brains, a **prognathic face** that projected well in front of their braincase, and small eye sockets positioned on the sides rather than the front of their face. They lacked a **postorbital bar**, a bony ring encircling the eye, a key feature of primates that indicates the importance of vision to the order. Many plesiadapiforms possessed large, rodent-like lower incisors that were separated from the premolars by a large **diastema**, or gap between their anterior teeth Some had claws (rather than nails) and lacked an opposable big toe. In all these ways plesiadapiforms do not look like primates.

Only jaws and teeth are known for the earliest representative of the plesiadapiforms, *Purgatorius,* so named for its type locality in Purgatory Hills, Montana (Buckley, 1997). Compared with other mammals from the very earliest Cenozoic, the molar teeth of *Purgatorius* are less specialized; they have somewhat less spiky cusps, suggesting a diet of both insects (the spikes help break into the insect shell) and fruit. The dental formula (see Chapter 7) of *Purgatorius* is 3:1:4:3, meaning that the genus is generalized enough to have given rise to the first clear primates that appear in the fossil record of the Eocene.

From an ancestor such as *Purgatorius,* an *adaptive radiation* (see Chapter 2) of plesiadapiforms evolved, ranging from the very tiny, mouse-sized forms (approximately 0.70 lb. (20 g) to creatures that are about the size of a small monkey 11 lb. (5 kg). These include the genus *Plesiadapis,* a rodent-like animal from the early Paleocene and Eocene of Europe and North America that seems to have moved slowly along tree branches and perhaps traveled on the ground as well, and the paromomyidae, a family of plesiadapiforms that lived from the middle Paleocene until the late Eocene of Europe and North America, which may have fed on sap and gum that flowed from places that these animals had gouged in tree bark.

The plesiadapiform radiation reveals clearly that very early primates (or primate-like mammals) were anatomically more primitive than living primates in almost all respects, although some families were also quite specialized. Some of the more generalized forms may have been ancestors of the primates alone or of primates and other closely related mammals (such as tree shrews, colugos, and bats). The more specialized forms probably were side branches that went extinct without issue. Although some plesiadapiforms persisted into the Eocene, they failed to compete with two new kinds of mammals that made their appearance at the beginning of the Eocene: rodents and the first "primates of modern aspect."

WHY PRIMATES?

As we saw in previous chapters, environmental conditions shape the characteristics of a group by favoring individuals who exhibit certain traits and selecting against individuals without those traits (see Chapter 2). So what environmental change or problem favored the origin of the primate trends? The Paleocene was

prognathic face Projection of the face well in front of the braincase.

postorbital bar A bony ring encircling the lateral side of the eye but not forming a complete cup around the eye globe.

diastema Gap between anterior teeth.

FIGURE 10.2 Adapoids (a, b) and omomyoids (a, c) are the first 'true' primates. Both have a postorbital bar. Omomyoids have shorter snouts and include *Necrolemur antiquus*.

warmer than today and was a period of recovery from the giant impact described earlier. In the Paleocene flowering plants evolved, insects increased in number and diversity as pollinators for these plants, and the plants evolved visual cues to lure these insects (see Chapter 9). The plesiadapiform fossils suggest that primate ancestors took advantage of these changing resources by eating insects (remember the spiky teeth of the plesiadapids that are good for crunching the hard bodies of insects) and possibly fruit from new plants (remember also that the teeth of *Purgatorius* are slightly less spiky than rodents of the Cretaceous, better for mashing fruit). We know that living primates emphasize vision over olfaction and have tactile pads on their fingers, not hard pads and claws (see Chapter 7).

In the past scientists thought that primates evolved these features in response to life in the trees rather than on the ground. However, the fossil record of early proto-primates such as the plesiadapiforms has helped us to understand that early primate forebears probably were *visual predators* dependent on sighting and catching insects to survive rather than clambering on branches for fruit (see Chapter 7 for a review of this hypothesis). As we move into the Eocene, we will see the first true primates and the many ways in which they expand on this early primate adaptation.

EARLY PRIMATES OF THE EOCENE

Climate warmed significantly at the beginning of the Eocene, around 54 million years ago (Figure 9.21), resulting in the replacement of the archaic mammals of the Paleocene by the first representatives of a number of modern orders of placental mammals, including Rodentia (mice, squirrels, beavers, and so on), Artiodactyla (even-toed ungulates or hooved animals such as deer, camels, antelopes, hippopotami, and pigs), Perissodactyla (odd-toed ungulates such as horses, rhinoceros, and tapirs), and of course Primates.

The fossil record of the Eocene reveals the first true primates, those that possess the bony characters by which we identify living primates (Figure 10.2). We also see the origin of the strepsirhine–haplorhine split during this epoch. The two main superfamilies of Eocene primates, the Adapoidea and Omomyoidea, appeared at the beginning of the Eocene. They flourished during the Eocene of Europe, North America, North Africa, the Middle East, and Asia but declined during the Oligocene (Covert, 2002).

We recognize these fossils as true primates because, unlike the plesiadapiforms, they possess the full suite of primate trends. In particular, they possess slightly larger brains than plesiadapiforms, eye sockets positioned on the front of the face (allowing stereoscopic vision and depth perception), a complete postorbital bar for greater protection of the eye, an opposable big toe, and nails (rather than claws) at the ends of their fingers and toes. At the same time, the reduction of their snouts and whiskers suggests that smell was less important for locating food than was sight (Figure 10.2). Based on other anatomical evidence discussed in this chapter, we think the adapoids and omomyoids gave rise to the lineages that became the living strepsirhines (lemurs and lorises) and haplorhines (tarsiers, monkeys, and apes), respectively.

ADAPOIDS (STREPSIRHINE ANCESTORS)

Adapoids resemble modern strepsirhines mainly in primitive ways, and most lack the features of modern primates such as the tooth comb. Therefore, the adapoids are best considered the most primitive known group of early modern primates, that probably gave rise to strepsirhines before the evolutionary divergence of lemurs and lorises (Figure 10.3 on page 274). This interpretation is consistent with the molecular evidence that suggests lemurs and lorises diverged around 45 million years ago (later than the first appearance of the adapoids) but that strepsirhines and haplorhines had already split by about 58 million years ago. The **adapoids** were mostly small- to medium-sized and weighed approximately 3.5 oz. to 15 lb. (100 g to 6.9 kg). They were slow-moving arboreal quadrupeds that were active by day and probably ate fruit and leaves (Figure 10.2).

The highly successful superfamily Adapoidea is usually divided into three families: the Notharctidae, Adapidae, and Sivaladapidae (Fleagle, 1998). Although they occur in both North America and Europe, adapoids are most abundant in the Old World. Fossils of genera such as *Northarctus* and *Adapis* show long broad snouts with teeth that suggest some may have eaten a fibrous diet. Their eyes indicate some were probably nocturnal, others diurnal. Their postcrania indicate a diverse range of locomotion from leaping to quadrupedal climbing.

Although some of the adapoids are likely to be ancestral to living strepsirhines (lemurs and lorises), and early representatives of the lorises and galagos have been discovered in Eocene deposits of North and East Africa (Le Gros Clark and Thomas, 1952; Seiffert et al., 2003), the fossil record of true lemurs is confined

adapoids Family of mostly Eocene primates, probably ancestral to all strepsirhines.

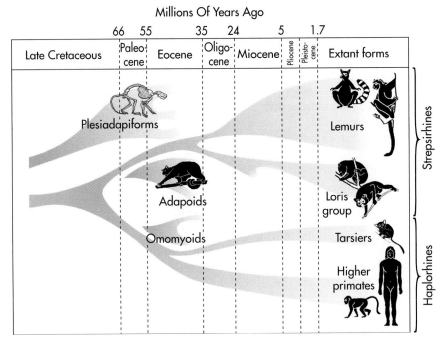

Millions Of Years Ago

FIGURE 10.3 Possible relationships between fossil and living primates: Plesiadapiforms may or may not be primates. Adapoids are probably ancestral to living strepsirhines, and omomyoids to living haplorines.

to the Holocene of Madagascar. This record of lemur diversity before human occupation of the islands provides a good example of an adaptive radiation and devastating documentation of the calamitous impact that humans can have on ecosystems (Box 10.1).

OMOMYOIDS (HAPLORHINE ANCESTORS)

Omomyoids are best regarded as Eocene primates that had recently diverged from the adapoids and may have given rise to the common ancestor of both tarsiers and anthropoids (Figure 10.3). This view is consistent with the molecular evidence that suggests that the strepsirhine–haplorhine split occurred around 58 million years ago and with the anatomical evidence.

The omomyoids were even more diverse than the adapoids. Omomyoids were smaller-bodied primates 1 oz. to 5 lbs. (30 g to 2.2 kg) that ate diets of insects and fruit and had larger orbits, probably for a nocturnal lifestyle. Their limb bones probably were evolved for active arboreal quadrupedalism and leaping, like those of living mouse lemurs and galagos (Godinot and Dagosto, 1983). Although they occur in both Europe and North America, omomyoids are more abundant in North America. The best known genus of the Omomyidae is the tiny *Necrolemur* (Figure 10.2) whose skull clearly shows the short face and large eye sockets typical of nocturnal and insectivorous strepsirhines, such as galagos and mouse lemurs. A galago-like mode of vertical clinging and leaping locomotion is indicated by the anatomy of omomyid hind limb and ankle bones.

Previously, the omomyoids had been widely regarded as the ancestors of tarsiers. However, although both cranial and postcranial evidence point to a link between omomyoids and haplorhines (the suborder that allies tarsiers with anthropoids), omomyoids differ from tarsiers. Omomyoid eye sockets are not nearly as large as those of tarsiers, and their ankles do not possess the unique tarsier features for exceptional leaping. These differences suggest that omomyoids may have been ancestral to all haplorhines rather than only to tarsiers.

omomyoids Family of mostly Eocene primates probably ancestral to all haplorhines.

Box 10.1 Subfossil Lemurs of Madagascar

Among living strepsirhines there are more families, genera, and species of lemurs from Madagascar than there are lorises and galagos combined. Moreover, unlike the entirely arboreal, nocturnal, and solitary lifestyles of the lorises and galagos, the lemurs include one species that is semiterrestrial, a few species that are diurnal, and some that live in social groups composed of several individuals.

But the diversity of living lemurs is only a shadow of their actual radiation (Figure A). Cave deposits from the late Pleistocene and Holocene of Madagascar have yielded skeletons of a bewildering array of giant lemurs (Godfrey and Jungers, 2002). There were at least sixteen species of these subfossil lemurs (their remains are so recent that the bones have not yet fossilized). A 22 lb. (10 kg) subfossil aye-aye, *Daubentonia robusta*, is about five times larger than the living aye-aye. However, the most astonishing subfossil lemurs are three species of the Lepilemuridae, the family that includes the living sportive lemurs, and ten species of the Indriidae, the family that includes the living sifaka and indri.

In terms of their feeding ecology, the living lepilemurids are an anomaly; they eat leaves but are much smaller than all other folivorous primates. As we learned in Chapter 7, mature leaves are a challenging food source that often include toxins and structural carbohydrates that are difficult to digest. Weighing in at only 17 oz. (500 g), *Lepilemur* (the living sportive lemur) is so small that it is difficult for its gut to break down the cellulose and toxins in leaves. For this reason, the living sportive lemurs occasionally resort to reingesting their feces to give their digestive systems another chance to break down the leaves. But just a few thousand years ago, the sportive lemurs were much larger creatures called koala lemurs (Godfrey and Jungers, 2002).

At the other end of the spectrum the huge *Megaladapis* a subfossil lepilemurid, weighed 165 lb. (75 kg), about as much as a female orangutan. Like the living sportive lemurs, *Megaladapis* ate leaves. The postcranial skeleton of *Megaladapis*, especially its enormous hands and feet, indicates that it was mainly a slow, tree-climber that moved along vertical branches as it foraged for leaves.

A few thousand years ago the indriids included representatives unlike any living lemur. One group of subfossil indriids, known as the monkey lemurs (Godfrey and Jungers, 2002), came down from the trees and adopted a macaque- or baboon-like lifestyle, foraging for food on the ground. The most specialized monkey lemur is *Hadropithecus*, a 55 to 65 lb. (25 to 30 kg) form with a short, robustly built face that appears to have evolved for processing grass and seeds.

Another group of subfossil indriids are the sloth lemurs, including *Palaeopropithecus*. The sloth lemurs were arboreal primates that like the sloths of South America, suspended themselves beneath horizontal tree limbs with enormous, hooklike hands and feet. Specialized folivores, they moved slowly through the forests of Madagascar, munching on leaves. One sloth lemur, *Archaeoindris*, is estimated to have weighed approximately 441 lb. (200 kg), about the same as a silverback male gorilla!

The subfossil lemurs reveal a great many things about how competition and predation limit strepsirhine diversity. In continental Africa and tropical Asia, most are small, cryptic creatures that are nocturnal, and arboreal. On Madagascar, conditions were different; there was no competition from monkeys and apes or from many other herbivorous mammals, such as antelopes and pigs and there were fewer predators. Unfettered by competition and predation, the lemurs exploited lifestyles that we don't normally associate with strepsirhines including diurnal activity patterns, suspensory and terrestrial locomotion specialized leafeating and large body size.

Without the bony record we would have no idea of the previous diversity of lemurs on Madagascar or the devastating role of humans in their demise. Most lemurs appear to have gone extinct about 2,000 years ago. Radiocarbon dates and anecdotal reports suggest that some subfossil lemurs persisted until just a few hundred years ago. Their extinction seems to be related in large part to the activities of people, including predation and deforestation.

FIGURE A The subfossil lemurs of Madagascar filled a variety of niches occupied elsewhere by monkeys, as shown in this artist's rendition.

FIGURE 10.4 The skulls of living haplorhines differ from those of strepsirhines by having enlarged brains, an enclosed orbit, and fused frontals and mandibles.

CONTINENTAL DRIFT AND EOCENE PRIMATES

The geographic distribution of the adapoids and omomyoids in North America and Europe is understandable if you recall from Chapter 9 the position of the continents between 54 and 34 million years ago. Europe and North America were joined by a broad band of land, and there was little difference in climate from north to south or east to west (see Figure 9.22). Thus the distribution of primates from North America to Europe makes sense given that they could have freely walked (or leaped or scampered) between the two.

SELECTIVE PRESSURES FAVORING THE STREPSIRHINE–HAPLORHINE SPLIT

Adapoids and omomyoids seem to represent the origin of the split between strepsirhines and haplorhines, with adapoids probably giving rise to the former and omomyoids to the latter. Again we may ask what aspects of the environment might have driven their evolution. In the Eocene in particular, what selective pressures may have favored the divergence of strepsirhine and haplorhine lineages? We know from molecular data that the groups diverged around 58 million years ago, but anatomically they are similar in some aspects throughout the Eocene epoch. Clues from anatomy such as relative snout length and the shape of their teeth suggest that adapoids and omomyoids (that is early strepsirhines and haplorhines) divided up the available food resources, thus avoiding competition. Adapoids ate leaves and relied more on their sense of smell (remember their longer snouts). Omomyoids focused on fruit and insects and had a shorter snout. From these original differences, the haplorhines eventually diverged quite far from the original primate niche.

EVOLUTION OF HIGHER PRIMATES

Representatives of the higher primates (monkeys and apes, including humans) first appeared in the late Eocene and early Oligocene epochs, after the strepsirhine–haplorhine split. The earliest higher primates are generalized monkeys that probably gave rise to all later higher primates. Early apes appeared in the Miocene and were also more generalized than their living descendants and more diverse. The initially diverse apes decreased in abundance through time, while the monkeys became more abundant.

THE FIRST MONKEYS?

As you will recall from Chapter 9, the marked cooling and drying of the climate at the end of the Eocene resulted in a large-scale faunal turnover called the Grande Coupure. Like all large-scale climatic changes, the Grande Coupure created both challenges and opportunities for the animal populations alive at the time. In response, the adapoids and omomyoids nearly vanished from North America and Europe, as did many other mammalian taxa. Likewise, animals that we recognize as monkeys first appeared in the Oligocene. Remember from Chapter 7 that all higher primates (monkeys, apes, and humans) share certain anatomical characters, including greater enclosure of the orbits, smaller snouts, fewer teeth, a fused frontal bone and a fused mandible, and larger body size (Figure 10.4). These anatomical changes signal changes in the foraging habits of these primates, probably catalyzed by the changing environmental conditions. The molecular evidence tells us that the first monkeys occurred between 58 and 40 million years ago, after the split between tarsiers and anthropoids occurred and before New World and Old World monkeys diverged.

The fossil record provides two windows into the origin of anthropoids. One is in the Eocene of China, the other in North Africa and the Middle East. A strong candidate for ancestor of the earliest anthropoids was recently found at Shanghuang in Jiangsu Province, China, and dated to the middle Eocene (Beard et al., 1994). This tarsier-sized about 3.5 oz. (100 g) animal was named *Eosimias* and placed in its own family, the Eosimiidae. Some details of the anatomy of the jaws, teeth, and ankle bones suggest that the Eosimiidae are at the very base of the anthropoid radiation, before its diversification into platyrrhines (New World monkeys) and catarrhines (Old World monkeys, apes, and humans).

Much of what we know about the evolution of higher primates in the late Eocene and early Oligocene comes from research done under the direction of Elwyn Simons at the Fayum depression in Egypt. Although the Fayum region is in the arid and inhospitable Sahara Desert today, during the Eocene and Oligocene it was a lushly forested area surrounding a large river system that supported a great diversity of tropical fauna and flora (Figure 10.5 on page 278). Scientists have found several genera of small (approximately 17 oz. to 2.2 lb. or 500 to 1,000 g) early anthropoids in the Fayum deposits. Currently, we know these forms only from fragmentary jaws, teeth, and isolated postcranial elements. As with the Eosimiidae of China, these early forms from the Fayum combine primitive (in this case adapoid) features and anthropoid-like features.

It is not until the end of the Eocene and the early Oligocene that we find clear anthropoids in the fossil record. There are three families of these early anthropoids, all known best from the Fayum depression: the Parapithecidae, the Oligopithecidae, and the Propliopithecidae. Like modern higher primates, these early anthropoids possessed advanced features of the skull and jaws, including a fused frontal bone, a fused lower jaw, and postorbital closure, that distinguish them from strepsirhines (Figures 10.4 and 10.5).

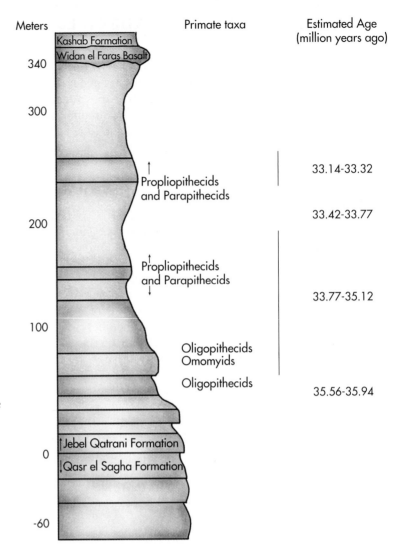

Meters

Kashab Formation
Widan el Faras Basalt

340

300

↑
Propliopithecids
and Parapithecids

200

↑
Propliopithecids
and Parapithecids
↓

100

Oligopithecids
Omomyids

Oligopithecids

Jebel Qatrani Formation

0

Qasr el Sagha Formation

-60

Primate taxa

Estimated Age
(million years ago)

33.14-33.32

33.42-33.77

33.77-35.12

35.56-35.94

FIGURE 10.5 Stratigraphic section of the Fayum shows the relative age of early anthropoids fossils. The primates include the potential ancestor for all anthropoids (*Apidium*, A. Parapithecid) and the potential ancestor for all Old World monkeys and apes (*Aegyptopithecus*, A. Propliopithecid).

The Parapithecidae is a diverse group of early anthropoids that includes the genus *Apidium* (Figure 10.6). In life, *Apidium* probably resembled the South American squirrel monkey, weighing approximately 2.2 lb. (1 kg), leaping and running among tree branches on all fours, and eating seeds and fruit (Fleagle and Kay, 1987). Like living New World monkeys, *Apidium* possessed three premolars in each quadrant of its jaws, suggesting that it predated the split between New World monkeys (with three premolars) and Old World monkeys (with two premolars).

The Oligopithecidae, including *Oligopithecus* and *Catopithecus*, were small weighing 1.8 to 3.3 lb. (800–1,500 g) quadrupedal monkeys that lived in the trees and probably ate insects and fruit (Simons, 1995). This group combined primitive, strepsirhine-like molars with the earliest known record of more advanced features such as a fused frontal bone and postorbital closure.

The Propliopithecidae (Figure 10.7 on page 280) were the largest weighing 13 to 15 lb. (6 to 7 kg) and most advanced of the early anthropoids from the Fayum, exemplified by the genus *Aegyptopithecus* (Simons, 1987). In life, *Aegyptopithecus* may have looked something like the living howler monkey of South America, slowly moving from branch to branch in search of leaves. Unlike the parapithecids, both the oligopithecids and the propliopithecids had the 2:1:2:3 dental formula of living Old World higher primates.

(b)

FIGURE 10.6 (a) *Apidium* may be ancestral to all later higher primates and is reconstructed as looking like a small-bodied monkey. (b) The genus has the skeleton of an arboreal quadruped and a 2:1:3:3 dental formula.

The early anthropoids of the Fayum reveal a radiation of early monkeys, some of which (*Apidium*) may have been ancestral to all later anthropoids, whereas others (*Aegyptopithecus*) may have been early representatives of the Old World higher primates, before the divergence of Old World monkeys, apes, and humans (Figure 10.8 on page 281).

NEW WORLD MONKEYS

The molecular evidence suggests that New World and Old World monkeys diverged around 40 million years ago, but the earliest fossil record of monkeys in South America comes from the late Oligocene (about 25–30 million years ago). The earliest South American genus is the enigmatic *Branisella,* known from deposits in Bolivia (Fleagle and Tejedor, 2002).

How monkeys got to South America is still something of a mystery. As we learned in Chapter 9, South America was an island continent during the early part of the Cenozoic; the connection to Central and North America, via the Panamanian Isthmus, was established less than 5 million years ago by sea level changes (see Figure 9.21).

Controversy surrounds the question of whether the New World monkeys originated from an advanced stock of Eocene strepsirhines in North America or from the most primitive anthropoids of Africa. Perhaps New World monkeys are descended from North American Eocene primates that migrated south across open waterways between islands. New World monkeys therefore would have evolved in

(a)

FIGURE 10.7
(a) *Aegyptopithecus* may be ancestral to catarrhines and has full postorbital closure and two premolars. (b) *Aegyptopithecus* has the skeleton of an arboreal quadruped.

(b)

parallel with Old World monkeys and would be only distantly related to them. Alternatively, New World monkeys have three premolars rather than the two seen in all catarrhines, linking them to *Apidium*, a fossil monkey from Egypt. In the late Eocene and early Oligocene, the Atlantic Ocean would have been far less of a geographic barrier to dispersal from the Old World because it was not as wide as it is today. In addition, the molecular evidence argues that the two groups split recently, about 40 million years ago. Because of these anatomical and molecular links, most scientists currently support a model that supposes an *Apidium*-like

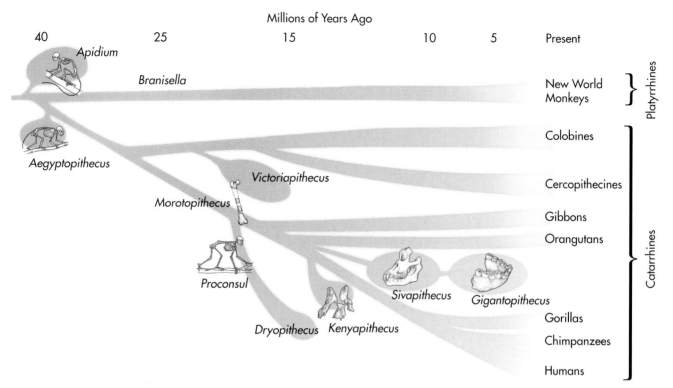

FIGURE 10.8 Proposed relationships between living and fossil platyrrhines and catarrhines.

ancestor "rafting over" from Africa to South America during the late Eocene or early Oligocene (Hartwig, 1994). We know that during floods animals get isolated on floating mats (natural or vegetative) and are carried to sea (Figure 10.9). Early monkeys could have reached the New World in this way.

However they got there, in the early and middle Miocene we see an increasingly rich fossil record of New World monkeys. This record shows diversification into the five major subfamilies of living New World monkeys: Cebinae, Aotinae, Pitheciinae, Atelinae, and Callitrichinae (Rosenberger, 2002).

OLD WORLD MONKEYS

According to DNA comparisons, Old World monkeys and apes shared a common ancestor about 25 million years ago. The fossil record tells us that ancestor had anatomical features shared by both monkeys and apes, such as a bony ear tube and presence of two rather than three premolars, but lacked characters unique to each group, such as the bilophodont molars characteristic of modern Old World monkeys and the suspensory shoulder characteristic of modern apes.

The earliest fossil evidence of a lineage leading just to Old World monkeys comes from the 19-million-year-old site of Napak in Uganda. This monkey represents an early radiation of the family Victoriapithecidae that predates the split between the subfamilies of the modern leaf-eating Colobinae and fruit-eating Cercopithecinae and may be a good candidate for the common ancestor of all later Old World monkeys (Benefit, 1999). The Victoriapithecidae lived in the early to middle Miocene of eastern and northern Africa, but they are best known from thousands of specimens of the species *Victoriapithecus macinessi* from 15-million-year-old deposits at Maboko Island in Kenya (Benefit and McCrossin, 2002).

FIGURE 10.9 Monkeys may have reached South America by floating on natural mats, as this dog took advantage of the floating box during recent floods.

Victoriapithecus was a vervet-sized monkey weighing between 6.6 and 11 lb. (3 and 5 kg). Its limb remains indicate that it used a semiterrestrial pattern of locomotion, making it one of the oldest and smallest anthropoid primates to make the shift to life on the ground. Its snout was moderately long, like a macaque's, but its braincase was longer and lower than in modern monkeys, and it possessed a strong sagittal crest not seen in living forms (Figure 10.10). Its low molar cusps and broad upper incisors indicate that *Victoriapithecus* probably ate hard fruits and seeds. Their ability to exploit hard foods on the ground and in the trees appears to have been a very successful adaptation for the Miocene monkeys. Nonetheless, they disappeared from the fossil record approximately 12 million years ago, replaced by the true Colobines and Cercopithecines.

The molecular evidence suggests that within the Old World monkeys, the cercopithecine and colobine split dates to between about 14 and 16 million years ago. The first true cercopithecines (*Macaca* sp.) appear in the fossil record of North Africa about 11 million years ago (Delson, 1980), and the first true colobines appear in Kenya at about the same time period. Soon after their first appearance, colobine monkeys expanded their ranges in Eurasia. Although cercopithecines may have delayed their migration into Eurasia, they are represented by numerous Pleistocene Asian macaques.

The Plio-Pleistocene radiation of African Old World monkeys is based on fossils collected at numerous sites that are more famous for their hominid remains, such as Koobi Fora, Kenya (see Chapters 12 and 13). These monkeys were more diverse in terms of their body size, locomotion, and dietary habits than monkeys are today. They also appear to have formed distinct communities in eastern and southern areas of Africa. For example, there were many medium- and large-sized colobine species in the Plio-Pleistocene of eastern Africa, where some were adapted for life in the trees and others apparently lived on the ground. Eastern Africa was dominated by a variety of *Theropithecus* baboons that shared a dentition similar to that of the modern gelada baboon, presumably for eating grasses, but otherwise differed significantly from their modern counterparts in their postcranial anatomy and size.

FIGURE 10.10 The most complete *Victoriapithecus* skull from Maboko Island, Kenya, is a likely ancestor for Old World monkeys. *Victoriapithecus* had complete postorbital closure, and partially bilophodont molars.

WHAT FAVORED THE ORIGIN OF ANTHROPOIDS?

During the Oligocene we see the origin and diversification of true anthropoids. What conditions drove their evolution? We know from the climatic evidence that temperature continued to cool during the Oligocene. We know from the fossil evidence that some of the early monkeys, such as *Victoriapithecus*, were eating tough objects and that their bodies were growing bigger. We also know that their skulls were changing, the mandible becoming a single bony unit, as did the frontal bone, and the orbits becoming completely enclosed by bone. This evidence seems to suggest that the early monkeys were successful because they were able to chew a tougher diet and better protect their eyes.

Although these may seem like unrelated abilities, it turns out that they are not. A fused mandible transfers force from one side of the tooth row to the other more effectively than an unfused mandible. Perhaps chewing on a harder diet favored animals with fused or partially fused mandibles. These changes might have allowed the ingestion of more food and the eventual development of larger body size. Orbital closure may also be related to chewing, although this is more debatable. One of the main chewing muscles, the temporalis muscle, is located just behind the eye on the side of the skull. If you place your finger on your temple and clench your teeth you will feel your temporalis muscle contract. Your eye is protected from that contraction (and expansion) of the muscle by the bone plate that sits between the muscle and your eyeball. In strepsirhines, however, that muscle can bulge into the orbital area, deforming the globe of the eye and causing vision to blur momentarily. An anthropoid might thus be favored if it had a bone cup around its eye. On the other hand, some scientists argue that the postorbital closure of anthropoids arose as a consequence of the greater orbital frontality seen in anthropoids. Both hypotheses recognize the increasing importance of stereoscopic vision to anthropoid survival. The Old World monkeys took this initial adaptation and enhanced it with adaptations for a more folivorous diet.

THE EARLIEST APES

Living ape species are few in number and limited to just four genera: *Hylobates* (the gibbons and Siamangs), *Pongo* (the orangutan), *Gorilla* (the gorilla), and *Pan* (the bonobo and the common chimpanzee). However, the fossil record of hominoid primates reveals a surprisingly diverse succession of adaptive radiations. This ape fossil record is characterized first by the appearance of **dental apes**, animals with apelike teeth but monkey-like postcranial skeletons.

Molecular evidence suggests that the monkey and ape lineages diverged about 25 million years ago. Fossil apes first appeared during the Early Miocene, approximately 23 to 16 million years ago. At that time, hominoids were almost totally restricted to Africa, where they are well known from sites in Kenya, Uganda, Ethiopia, and Namibia (Figure 10.11 on page 284). Unlike today, the early Miocene of Africa probably was covered by uninterrupted expanses of forest and moist woodland. The uplifting and rifting that dominate eastern Africa today had not yet occurred, nor had the climatic divisions of arid and wet zones.

On this forested continent lived dozens of genera of early apes with very monkey-like postcranial skeletons. In fact, we might call them dental apes to show that we recognize them as apes based only on their dental anatomy. You'll remember from Chapter 7 that Old World monkeys possess specialized, high-crested bilophodont molars for shearing leaves, but all apes possess molars with five rounded cusps, connected by a pattern of Y-shaped fissures or grooves (Figure 10.12 on page 284). This "Y-5" molar pattern is seen in even the most primitive apes. The dental apes were small-bodied compared with modern apes, they lacked a suspensory shoulder for brachiating, and they walked in plantigrade fashion, that is, on the soles of their feet rather than on their knuckles.

dental apes Early apes exhibiting Y-5 molar patterns but monkey-like postcranial skeletons.

FIGURE 10.11 Miocene apes were found throughout Europe, continental Asia and Africa. Important east African localities are plotted on the inset map.

The best known of the early dental apes is the genus *Proconsul* (Figure 10.13), which lived in Africa about 18 to 20 million years ago. There are at least three *Proconsul species*, ranging in size from approximately 33 to 110 lb. (15 to 50 kg) (Walker and Teaford, 1989). *Proconsul* was discovered in the 1920s in East Africa and was named Consul, after performing chimpanzees of that era. *Proconsul* teeth are apelike, with a Y-5 molar pattern, and aspects of the limb skeleton show a more monkey-like locomotor adaptation for running. In addition, *Proconsul* appears to have possessed a long and flexible torso, like that of quadrupedal

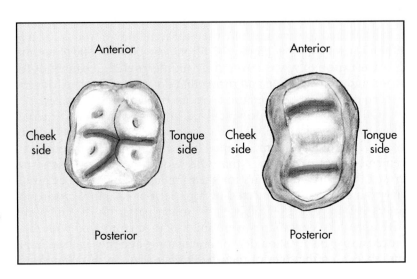

FIGURE 10.12 The Y-5 molar pattern (left) characterizes the ape whereas bilophodont molar (right) characterizes the Old World monkey. Both indicate a 2:1:3:3 dental formula.

FIGURE 10.13 The dental ape *Proconsul* has an ape-like dentition but monkey-like skeleton.

monkeys, rather than the short and stable back of living suspensory apes and perhaps a tail (Ward, 1997).

Until recently, *Proconsul* was thought to be the last common ancestor of great apes and hominids, but *Morotopithecus bishopi* may be a better candidate. In 1997, paleoanthropologists Daniel Gebo and Laura MacLatchy named a new species of Miocene ape, *Morotopithecus bishopi*, from the 20.6-million-year-old site of Moroto in Uganda based on fossils that had been collected in the 1960s and 1990s. *Morotopithecus* exhibits primitive conditions of the upper jaws that indicate a basal position within the hominoid radiation, but portions of the backbone and the shoulder girdle suggest that, unlike *Proconsul, Morotopithecus* possessed the short and stiff back and suspensory shoulder anatomy of the modern brachiating (arm-swinging) apes (MacLatchy et al., 2000). *Morotopithecus* was one of the earliest and largest hominoids from this time period (Gebo et al., 1997).

Around 17 million years ago there appeared the first evidence of a land connection between Africa and Eurasia, created mainly by the northern movement of the plate on which Africa rests. This connection allowed hominoid primates to migrate outside Africa for the first time, and small, gibbon-like forms appeared in China (Harrison and Gu, 1999).

Sweeping environmental changes transformed the world during the middle Miocene, and the first fossil apes that show both cranial and postcranial characteristics linking them to living African apes appeared in the fossil record. Previously, Africa had been moist and forested, but fauna and flora from middle Miocene sites such as Maboko Island and Fort Ternan in Kenya indicate that these areas were dry and the vegetation was open, with dry woodland and even grassland emerging as the dominant environment. The molecular evidence suggests that around this time (14 million years ago) the African great ape and human lineage diverged from the Asian great ape lineage (the orangutans). The skeleton of one middle Miocene hominoid, *Kenyapithecus* (Leakey, 1962), shows that it practiced a primitive form of knuckle-walking, the distinctive pattern of locomotion shared by living gorillas and chimpanzees. This ape was the first to descend from the trees to the ground (McCrossin et al., 1998). One species in particular, *Kenyapithecus wickeri*, may be closely allied with the lineage leading to the hominids.

During the Middle and Late Miocene (approximately 11 to 5 million years ago), large-bodied hominoids diversified and dispersed into Europe and Asia. G. E. Lewis, a graduate student at Yale University, discovered the fossilized remains of a primitive apelike hominoid in the hills of British India, in what is today Pakistan. Lewis named the 15-million-year-old partial mandible with thick-enameled teeth *Ramapithecus* in honor of the hero of the Hindu epic *The*

Ramayana (it has since been reclassified as *Sivapithecus*). The specimen then sat ignored in a drawer in the Peabody Museum at Yale for 30 years until, in the early 1960s, paleoanthropologist Elwyn Simons undertook a new study of the mandible with his student David Pilbeam. Simons and Pilbeam concluded that *Ramapithecus* was a direct ancestor of modern humans. The debate over the place of *Ramapithecus* in the hominoid phylogeny continued for more than a decade, and in some older textbooks *Ramapithecus* is depicted as walking upright, and even carrying primitive tools. However, at 15 million years *Ramapithecus* predates the split between humans and other apes and therefore may represent either the ancestor of all later great apes or simply an extinct ape side branch.

Sivapithecus (after the Hindu figure Siva) is known from the late Miocene of the foothills of the Himalaya Mountains in northern India and Pakistan. Cranial and dental remains of *Sivapithecus* exhibit several similarities to the orangutan. The eye orbits are long and oval and separated from each other by a tall and narrow septum. Also, in side view the face is strongly "dished," or concave, except for the portion of the upper jaw that holds the incisors, which is convex (Figure 10.14). Taken together, these features indicate an evolutionary relationship between *Sivapithecus* and modern orangutans (Pilbeam, 1982). In other ways, however, *Sivapithecus* is distinct from the orangutan; the chewing surfaces of its molar teeth, although possessing a thick coat of enamel, are smooth and differ from the strongly *crenulated* (wrinkled) enamel of the orangutan, and the postcranial remains of *Sivapithecus* indicate arboreal quadrupedalism rather than the quadrumanous ("four-handed") clambering seen in orangutans. Therefore, *Sivapithecus* is a relative of the modern orangutan but not its unique ancestor.

At about the same time that *Sivapithecus* lived, a huge new ape arose in the same geographic region. In the 1930s, German paleontologist Ralph von Koenigswald searched for fossils in drugstores as well as the field because bones and teeth often are used in traditional East Asian medicine. In 1935, in drugstores in Hong Kong and the Philippines, he found enormous primate molars. He named the previously unknown creature to whom they belonged *Gigantopithecus* (von Koenigswald, 1952). *Gigantopithecus* is known mostly from jaws and teeth. Although an early form of this genus occurred in the late Miocene, it is better known from the early and middle Pleistocene of China and Vietnam, where it grew to an enormous size, perhaps as large as 660 lb. (300 kg), and coexisted with *Homo erectus* (Figure 10.15). *Gigantopithecus* was thus the largest primate that ever lived. Some scholars speculate that legends of the sasquatch in North America and the yeti in Asia may have begun long ago when *Gigantopithecus* walked the earth. Most authorities view *Gigantopithecus* as a distant relative of *Sivapithecus*. Based on its large size and molar anatomy, *Gigantopithecus* probably ate a tough, fibrous diet, perhaps even bamboo.

(a)   (b)

FIGURE 10.14   (a) *Sivapithecus* is a Miocene ape (middle) with anatomical similarities to orangutans (left) rather than chimpanzees (right). (b) Siwaliks, Pakistan, where *Sivapithecus* was found.

Ouranopithecus was a very large 242 lb. (110 kg) hominoid from the late Miocene (10 million years ago) of Greece (deBonis and Koufos, 1993). Unlike *Sivapithecus* and orangutans, *Ouranopithecus* possessed a massive browridge and a wide space between the eye sockets, thus superficially resembling a gorilla. Some researchers have argued that *Ouranopithecus* is an ancestor of both African great apes and hominids. However, details of its face, jaws, and teeth indicate that *Ouranopithecus* lacks aspects of cranial anatomy that are shared, derived features of both African great apes and humans (Benefit and McCrossin, 1995).

Another late Miocene ape from Europe is *Dryopithecus*, long known from isolated jaws, teeth, and an upper arm bone. Recent discoveries of a skull and skeleton at Can Llobateres in Spain have greatly improved our understanding of this 8- to 12-million-year-old form. Although it was large-bodied 44–77 lb. (20–35 kg), *Dryopithecus* does not share derived features with either Asian or African great apes. Instead, *Dryopithecus* possesses a primitive anatomy reminiscent of both *Proconsul* and gibbons. Additional fossils from Rudabanya in Hungary reinforce the interpretation that *Dryopithecus* is a late-surviving, primitive Miocene ape.

In many ways the most peculiar and vexing of the European hominoids is *Oreopithecus,* from the late Miocene of Italy. An almost complete but very flattened skeleton of *Oreopithecus* about 66 lb. (33 kg) was found in coal deposits that had developed in a swampy environment between 7 and 8 million years ago. Paleontologists Meike Köhler and Salvador Moyà-Solà consider *Oreopithecus* to have been a biped, based on their reconstruction of the creature's feet and ankles, but not a biped like us. They argue that its feet were shaped almost like tripods in life, with a divergent big toe and four other toes that were aligned in nearly the opposite direction. The researchers do not argue that *Oreopithecus* was a direct hominid ancestor; instead, they believe the species evolved in the isolated habitat of a Mediterranean island that lacked predators, leading to adoption of a strange and awkward way of walking. However, other researchers argue that a more accurate reconstruction of *Oreopithecus* indicates monkey-like quadrupedalism. The teeth of *Oreopithecus* are also distinctive, featuring unique molar cusps and crests. These features suggest that *Oreopithecus* ate leaves. Overall, therefore, *Oreopithecus* appears to have been a unique lineage in the ape and human family tree, and one that left no living descendants.

Although we have identified many ape taxa from the Miocene, we have little or no fossil evidence for the lineages that led directly to gorillas, chimpanzees, and bonobos. One possible exception is *Samburupithecus*, a poorly known fossil ape from the late Miocene (approximately 8–9 million years ago) of Kenya (Ishida and Pickford, 1997). In some respects, the upper molars of *Samburupithecus* are reminiscent of those of a gorilla. The dearth of fossils is related in part to the tropical forests in which apes live, moist places where biological processes often lead to the complete destruction of the skeleton.

The Miocene hominoids provide a picture of the ape and human family tree before it was so drastically pruned back to just the few branches that exist today (see Figure 10.8). Some genera, such as *Proconsul*, were early representatives of the superfamily that diversified before the common ancestor of living forms. One Miocene hominoid, *Sivapithecus*, appears to be allied to the modern Asian great ape lineage, the orangutan. Other late Miocene Eurasian hominoids, such as *Dryopithecus* and *Oreopithecus*, now appear to be side branches that left no modern descendants. Finally, a few genera, including *Kenyapithecus* and *Samburupithecus*, appear to be members of the African ape and human clade that diversified before the last common ancestor of gorillas, chimpanzees, and humans. The environmental conditions that favored the divergence of this lineage from that of the monkeys and that later so severely pruned its diversity are reviewed in the next two sections.

(a)

(b)

FIGURE 10.15
(a) Reconstruction of *Gigantopithecus,* a fossil ape, towers over artist Bill Munns.
(b) The enormous mandible of *Gigantopithecus* dwarfs a modern human mandible.

SELECTION PRESSURES AND THE DIVERGENCE OF MONKEYS AND APES

Monkeys and apes differ in specific anatomical ways related to their form of locomotion, so the origin of hominoids probably is related in part to this shift in locomotor pattern. Monkeys have bodies shaped like your dog or cat: The thorax is narrow from side to side but deep from back to front. Apes are the opposite, having wide but not very deep thoraxes. This change is thought to be related to the origin of a particular kind of locomotion called *brachiation* that is used by living lesser apes (gibbons and siamangs) and probably by the common ancestor of all apes. Because it is advantageous for a brachiator to have an arm positioned well lateral of the midline, apes evolved a wide thorax (and longer clavicles, or collarbones). And because the arm is often over head, the humeral head is round and the shape of the scapula is changed; it is rotated onto the animal's back from the side and elongated in the direction of the head and tail (Figure 10.16).

The apes appear to have evolved their specialized locomotor capacity in the early middle Miocene (remember *Morotopithecus*), when forests were widespread. Later the African apes modified this brachiating anatomy for knuckle-walking so that in the middle Miocene, when body size increased and apes became more terrestrial, we see evidence of knuckle-walking anatomy (remember *Kenyapithecus*). The Asian apes eventually become quadrumanous after *Sivapithecus*.

So part of the origin of the living hominoid pattern is related to shifts in climate and the relative abundance of forested and unforested areas. However, you will recall that the first distinctive evidence of apes in the fossil record is from the dentition and the groups we called dental apes. The shape of these dentitions suggests that the initial change in the ape lineage was a dietary shift, probably to eating more fruits. During the Miocene we see the drying and cooling of the environment and the breaking up of habitats into smaller wooded areas and patchy grasslands. And in this changing environment we see a differentiation between monkey and ape lineages, with monkeys focusing increasingly on more leafy diets and early apes focusing more on fruits. Later apes, such as the gorilla, return to a fibrous diet, modifying the original ape niche.

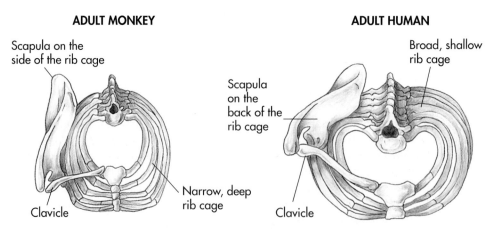

FIGURE 10.16 The thorax of apes including humans reflects our brachiating ancestry and is broad but shallow in contrast to the narrower, deeper chest of the monkey.

THE MONKEY'S TALE: WHAT HAPPENED TO PRIMATE DIVERSITY IN THE MIOCENE?

From the beginning to about the middle of the Miocene, fossil apes were abundant and monkeys fairly rare. But after the mid-Miocene it is a monkey's world, with apes decreasing in both diversity and number of taxa. Why this shift?

Recall the climatic changes of the Miocene, when the world got drier and colder. Forests dried up, grasslands and wooded grasslands became more abundant, new niches became available. Animals that once lived in the forest had a few possible routes to survive: Stick with the same old pattern but reduce numbers of individuals (after all, the forested areas were smaller) or strike out into a new area with new resources necessitating new adaptations. Animals that reproduce more quickly (that is, those that are **r-selected**, with each female having many offspring during her lifetime at short interbirth intervals and making less maternal investment per offspring) could colonize areas faster and rebound from population declines more quickly and thoroughly. Although monkeys reproduce more slowly than many nonprimates, they reproduce more quickly than apes and so had an advantage in colonizing new areas. (Apes are strongly **k-selected**, exhibiting the opposite reproductive characteristics of r-selected animals.) In addition, the shape of the monkey thorax and limbs is more conducive to evolution of quick terrestrial locomotion. These attributes seem to have favored the monkeys over the apes during the late Miocene. In contrast, the apes seem to have stuck with their shrinking, forested homes. Their numbers decreased along with their habitat and continue to do so today. Only one group of apes seems to have overcome the issues of locomotion and reproduction to move into new, more open habitats. This lineage eventually evolved into humans (Figure 10.17 on page 290).

MOLECULAR EVOLUTION IN PRIMATES

Throughout the chapter we have presented the picture of primate evolution that can be drawn from fossil remains and augmented it with estimated divergence times based on molecular evidence. In Chapter 3 we discussed several methods by which molecules can be used to inform evolutionary studies—to figure out phylogenetic relationships among species. We use some of these methods (immunological method, DNA hybridization) to indirectly compare the structure of molecules, and we use other, direct methods, such as DNA sequencing, to compare differences in the base pair composition of genes or noncoding portions of the genome between different species.

A *molecular phylogeny* is a tree of relatedness among species, or larger taxonomic groupings, based on a gene or protein (such a tree can also be constructed by pooling information from more than one gene (see Chapter 6). The structure of the tree provides a visual summary of how similar or dissimilar a given molecule is in any two or more of the taxa represented on the tree. Constructing a tree from molecular data can be a statistically complex operation. If the taxa are very different and have not shared a recent common ancestor, then the molecular differences probably are profound, and making a phylogenetic tree is not that difficult. However, scientists are not as interested in the obvious cases as they are in the evolutionary relationships between three or four closely related taxa whose lineages split from one another over a short period of time several million years ago or the genetic relationships among populations within a species.

In 1967, a key advance in molecular phylogenetics occurred when anthropologist Vincent Sarich and biochemist Allan Wilson demonstrated that it was possible to use molecular relationships between species to determine divergence

r-selected Reproductive strategy in which females have many offspring, interbirth intervals are short, and maternal investment per offspring is low.

k-selected Reproductive strategy in which fewer offspring are produced per female, interbirth intervals are long, and maternal investment is high.

Figure 10.17 PRIMATE EVOLUTION

Primates or primate ancestors appear around 63 million years ago and diversify into niches created by the extinction of the dinosaurs but do not show most of the anatomical characters of living primates. Strepsirhine and haplorhine lineages appear in the early Eocene. The first monkeys with postorbital closure appear in the Oligocene. Apes diversify in the Miocene but are rare by the Pliocene.

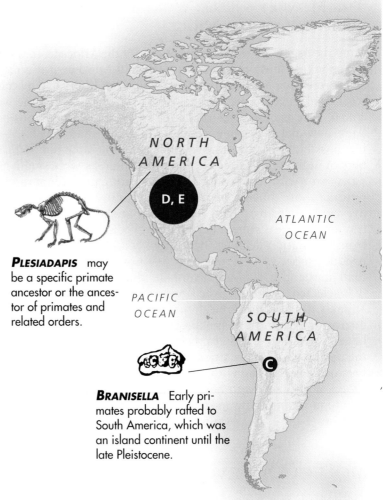

NORTH AMERICA

D, E

ATLANTIC OCEAN

PACIFIC OCEAN

SOUTH AMERICA

C

PLESIADAPIS may be a specific primate ancestor or the ancestor of primates and related orders.

BRANISELLA Early primates probably rafted to South America, which was an island continent until the late Pleistocene.

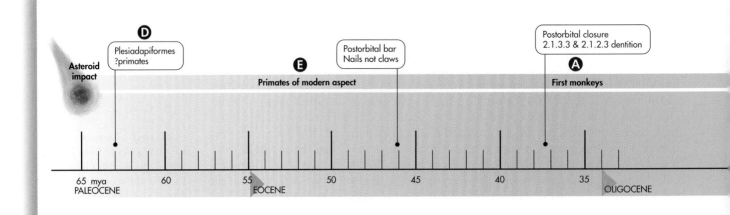

D Plesiadapiformes ?primates

Asteroid impact

E Primates of modern aspect

Postorbital bar Nails not claws

Postorbital closure 2.1.3.3 & 2.1.2.3 dentition

A First monkeys

65 mya PALEOCENE   60   55 EOCENE   50   45   40   35   OLIGOCENE

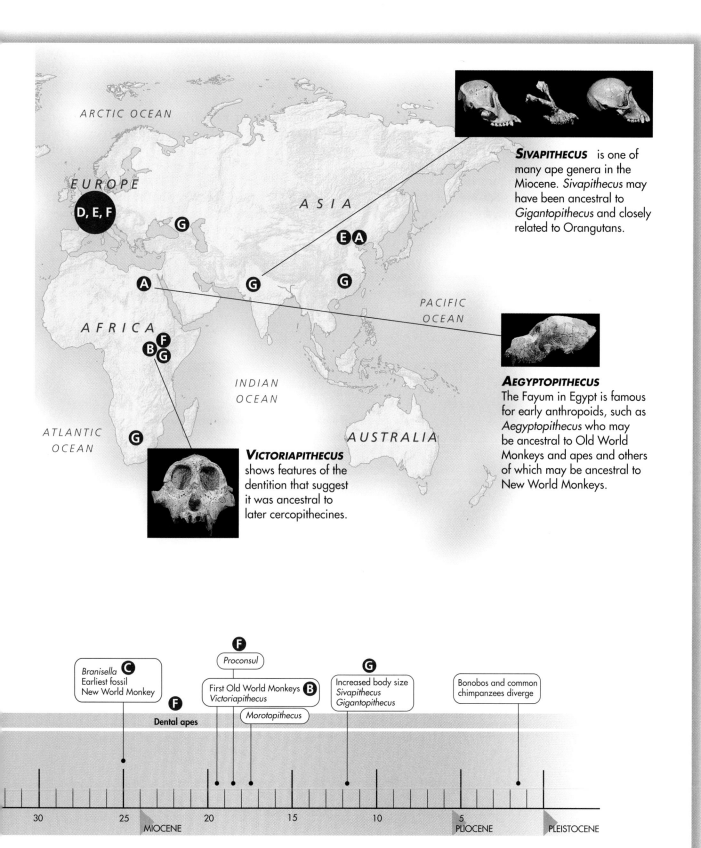

SIVAPITHECUS is one of many ape genera in the Miocene. *Sivapithecus* may have been ancestral to *Gigantopithecus* and closely related to Orangutans.

AEGYPTOPITHECUS
The Fayum in Egypt is famous for early anthropoids, such as *Aegyptopithecus* who may be ancestral to Old World Monkeys and apes and others of which may be ancestral to New World Monkeys.

VICTORIAPITHECUS shows features of the dentition that suggest it was ancestral to later cercopithecines.

ARCTIC OCEAN

EUROPE

ASIA

AFRICA

PACIFIC OCEAN

ATLANTIC OCEAN

INDIAN OCEAN

AUSTRALIA

Branisella
Earliest fossil
New World Monkey **C**

Proconsul **F**

First Old World Monkeys **B**
Victoriapithecus

Morotopithecus

Dental apes **F**

Increased body size **G**
Sivapithecus
Gigantopithecus

Bonobos and common chimpanzees diverge

30   25   20   15   10   5
          MIOCENE   PLIOCENE   PLEISTOCENE

dates in the past; in other words, there existed a **molecular clock**, or a systematic accumulation of genetic differences through time that, if measured, could be used to estimate the amount of time since two groups shared a last common ancestor.

A molecular clock needs two things in order to work. First, the clock must be *calibrated* with a date from the fossil record that corresponds to one of the nodes in the tree. The date for this one node can be used to determine the rate of change in the molecule, which then allows us to date each node in the tree (Figure 10.18).

Second, there must be a demonstration of *rate constancy* in the molecule that is used to make the tree: A molecular clock can work only if the molecule is changing at a similar rate in each branch or lineage represented in a phylogeny. Sarich and Wilson proposed a way to demonstrate rate constancy for any protein or gene. For example, say we want to use DNA hybridization data to make a phylogeny of the living primates. How can we demonstrate that the rate of change of DNA within primates is similar in all primate groups? Sarich and Wilson proposed a

molecular clock A systematic accumulation of genetic change that can be used to estimate the time of divergence between two groups if relative rates are constant and a calibration point from the fossil record is available.

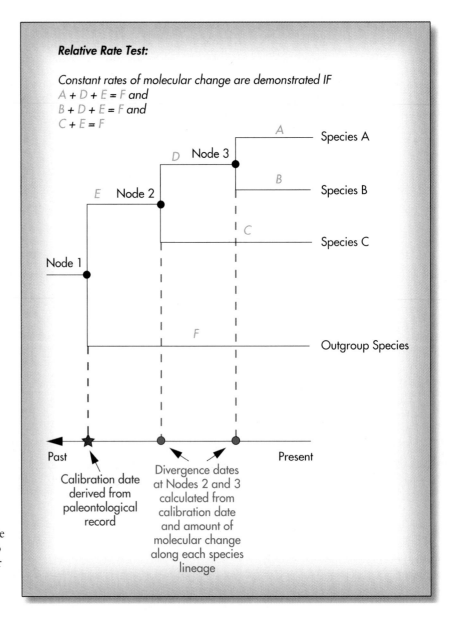

FIGURE 10.18 Relative rate test, calibrating the molecular clock, and calculating divergence dates. Letters *A-F* correspond to amounts of molecular change or molecular distance along each lineage.

relative rate test, or a comparison of the amount of genetic difference between each primate species of interest and a member of an *outgroup,* such as a dog. If the DNA of each primate is equally different from a dog's DNA, then there must be rate constancy within primates; if there had been a slowdown in the rate of change on one lineage, then that lineage would have shown fewer differences from the outgroup DNA than the others did. Relative rate tests can be used to account for variability in the rates of change of genes in different lineages, if they are present.

Not all genetic systems can be used as molecular clocks because some systems are influenced by natural selection, lineage-specific rate changes, and other factors that make them inappropriate for timing evolutionary events. On the other hand, several different proteins, genes, and noncoding regions of DNA have proven to be useful as molecular clocks, and researchers have used them to shed new light on evolutionary relationships between all forms of life on Earth. Molecular phylogenies sometimes have been controversial, especially when they do not agree with phylogenies determined by traditional anatomical and paleontological methods. However, only one history is being reconstructed and ultimately molecular and paleontological phylogenies must agree with each other.

A PRIMATE MOLECULAR PHYLOGENY

Over the years, several molecular phylogenies of the primates have been proposed. In 1998, Morris Goodman, a pioneer of molecular anthropology, published a comprehensive phylogeny of primates based primarily on evolution in the *beta-globin* gene cluster on chromosome 11 (in humans) (Goodman et al., 1998; Goodman, 1999). Beta-globin is one of the polypeptide chains that make up hemoglobin. Although there appears to be variability in the rate of change of beta-globin genes along some primate lineages, Goodman and his colleagues corrected for these rate variations using a "local molecular clock" model. Goodman's phylogeny is based on beta-globin gene sequences from more than 60 primate species, calibrated with several dates from the fossil record (Figure 10.19 on page 294).

We have referred to these divergence time estimates in earlier sections and bring them together here as an overview of the timing of primate evolution. Goodman's phylogeny places the *last common ancestor* (LCA) of all primates at 63 million years ago. It is at this point that we get the deepest split within primates, that between the strepsirhines and the haplorhines. Within the strepsirhines, there was a split between the lemurs and lorises 45 million years ago. Within the haplorhines the tarsiers branched off from the anthropoid lineage at 58 million years ago, and the major split within the anthropoids, that between the platyrhines and the catarrhines, occurred 40 million years ago. Within the catarrhines, the division between the cercopithecoids and the apes occurred 25 million years ago, just at the beginning of the Miocene. Within the Old World monkeys, cercopithecines and colobines split about 16 million years ago. Within the apes, lesser apes (gibbons and siamangs) split about 17 million years ago from the great apes. African and Asian great apes split around 14 million years ago, gorillas splits from the chimp–human clade about 8 million years ago, and human and chimp lineages split about 6 million years ago. Chimps and bonobos split about 2.2 million years ago.

In terms of the largest branches and major nodes, this molecular phylogeny, which relies on multiple calibrations from the fossil record, fairly accurately represents current ideas about the major phylogenetic events in primate evolution. However, controversy still remains regarding the synthesis of fossil and molecular data in determining primate phylogenetics of closely related groups of primate species (Stewart and Disotell, 1998). The first major debate involving molecular

relative rate test A means of determining whether molecular evolution has been occurring at a constant rate in two lineages by comparing whether these lineages are equidistant from an outgroup.

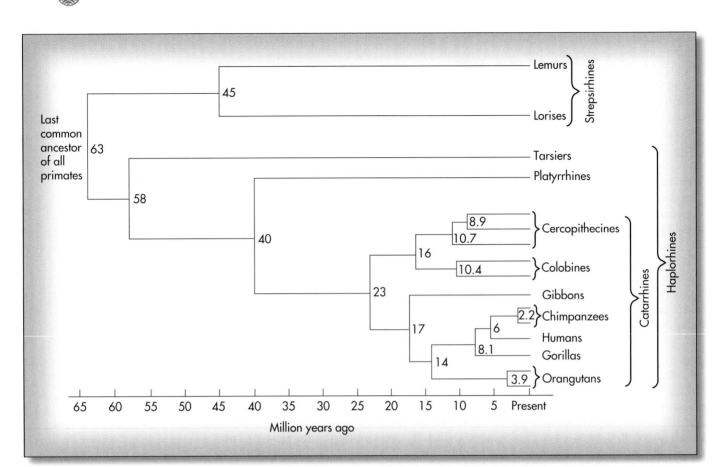

FIGURE 10.19 Relationships and dates of divergence of living primate groups based on molecular and DNA comparisons (Data from Goodman, M., 1999).

phylogenetics in understanding primate evolution was focused around the dating of the human split from the great apes and the implications for that date on interpretations of the fossil record and the timing of hominid origins.

MOLECULAR PHYLOGENY AND HUMAN ORIGINS

In 1967, when Sarich and Wilson provided the first application of the molecular clock in primate phylogenetics, the prevailing view was that the origins of hominid and pongid lineages dated back to the first half of the Miocene, maybe even earlier. *Ramapithecus* was considered the earliest hominid represented in the fossil record, an assignment based entirely on characteristics of the teeth and jaw. This implied that the hominid line originated about 15 million years ago. In addition, specific Miocene ape species were considered the likely direct ancestors of the chimpanzees, gorillas, and gibbons. Recall from our earlier discussions that the current view recognizes no direct fossil record for the living African apes.

Using a phylogeny based on the protein *albumin* (immunological method) and calibrating the tree using a date of about 30 million years ago for the separation of apes from the other catarrhines, Sarich and Wilson determined a date for the origins of hominids of 5 million years ago, some 10 million years younger than *Ramapithecus*. At this node in the tree, humans shared a common ancestor with both the African apes, the gorilla and the chimpanzee. In other words, Sarich and Wilson suggested that we were more closely related to the African apes (and they to us) than we were to the other great ape, the orangutan, which branched off earlier in the Miocene. *Ramapithecus* could not be the exclusive hominid, chimpanzee, or gorilla ancestor because those lineages did not even exist at that time. For several years, this claim was hotly debated, but it has been substantiated by later molecular and paleontological research. The molecular dates also led to the reexamination of the anatomical features used to link *Ramapithecus* with hominids and the recognition that many of these were either artifacts of the reconstruction process or characters (such as thick enamel) that we have more recently learned have arisen multiple times in evolutionary history.

Over the years, much genetic research has focused on resolving the chimp–human–gorilla trichotomy that Sarich and Wilson's albumin system did not have the resolving power to separate. In 1997, Maryellen Ruvolo performed a combined analysis of DNA sequence data from fourteen different loci that had been analyzed in humans, chimpanzees, and gorillas. She concluded, "It is overwhelmingly likely that *Homo* and *Pan* are most closely related, with *Gorilla* as a sister group on the hominoid species tree" (p. 261). In other words, chimps and humans are more closely related to each other than either is to the gorilla, despite strong anatomical similarities between chimps and gorillas. This division is also favored in the Goodman phylogeny. Given the molecular consensus on this issue and the current understanding of the hominid fossil record, it is safe to say that any claims for a hominid ancestor older than about 6 million years will be regarded with a healthy amount of skepticism by both molecular geneticists and paleontologists.

GENE FUNCTION AND HUMAN ORIGINS

In the kinds of phylogenetic studies discussed earlier, the function of the gene or protein used to construct a phylogeny is not a concern: The molecule is just a tool used to accomplish the goal of uncovering evolutionary relationships. As molecular and phylogenetic methods have become more sophisticated, however, researchers have tried to interpret the functions of genes and their phylogenetic histories in the broader evolutionary contexts of speciation and adaptation.

One recent example involves the evolutionary history of the gene for the protein *myosin* (Stedman et al., 2004), which is an important component of muscle. Different forms of myosin are found in different muscles, depending on the function of the muscle. Hansell Stedman and colleagues looked at a form of myosin (called MYH16) that is expressed in the jaw muscles of humans, apes, and monkeys. They found that humans have a unique mutation in this protein that prevents the accumulation of MYH16 in jaw muscles. Stedman and colleagues argued that this mutation may have been selected for during hominid evolution and that it accounts for the small size of human jaw muscles compared with those of other primates. Other scientists argue that the mutation was allowed to persist in the human lineage because smaller jaw muscles proved to be no disadvantage to hominids that were foraging on a soft diet; that is, the persistence of the mutation was a result of a foraging shift, not the cause of one.

A different view of the importance of functional changes in molecular evolution comes from an analysis not of a single gene but of hundreds of genes. A recent study comparing chimpanzee chromosome 22 with its human counterpart, chromosome 21, has shed light on the general nature of molecular evolution between the two species (Watanabe et al., 2004). The researchers found that compared with the human chromosome, 1.44% of the chimpanzee chromosome had single-base substitutions. In addition, there were more than 68,000 insertions and deletions. Most significantly from a functional standpoint, 83% of the 231 genes that code for proteins were found to have differences that led to substitutions at the amino acid level. Many of these changes affected proteins with important functions, such as those involved in the immune response to specific diseases and in heart development and in regulatory regions surrounding structural genes. The number of potentially important functional differences between chimpanzees and humans was greater than expected. Although many scientists and writers have stated that there is only a 2% (or 5%) difference between human and chimpanzee total DNA, this new study shows that changes in only 1.44% of the bases in a single chromosome can have a major functional impact.

The fossil record of primate evolution provides a full view of the history of primate relationships, adaptations, and ecology. In addition to documenting the evolutionary history of nonhuman primates, this record sets the stage for the emergence of the lineage that ultimately led to humans. In the next five chapters we explore the fossil record for hominid evolution and the selective pressures that shaped the evolution of our ancestors.

SUMMARY

1. **Were plesiadapids the first primates?**

   This depends on which authority you ask. After their discovery, plesiadapids were considered to be primates. This view faded after many researchers noted their lack of modern primate anatomical traits. They occur about the right time, according to molecular data to be primate ancestors, but they may be just primate-like mammals. In recent years, however, researchers have begun to reconsider the role of plesiadapiforms in primate evolution.

2. **How are adapoids and omomyoids similar, and how do they differ?**

   Both existed in Europe and North America, although adapoids were more prevalent in Europe and omomyoids in North America. Adapoids had longer snouts and smaller eyes and probably ate leaves. They are the likely ancestors of strepsirhines. Omomyoids had shorter snouts and larger eyes and probably ate fruit and insects. They are the likely ancestors of haplorhines.

3. **What is the significance of *Apidium* for reconstructing the primate phylogeny?**

   The significance of *Apidium* is its dental formula: 2:1:3:3. This is the same as that of New World monkeys and is the primary link between Old and New World fossil monkeys. *Apidium* supports the hypothesis that New World monkeys are descendants of fossil Old World monkeys that rafted across the then-smaller Atlantic Ocean in the late Eocene.

4. **Why were the earliest apes not easily identified as such?**

   The earliest apes did not possess the anatomical features of living apes such as a suspensory shoulder and knuckle-walking hands. They can be identified as apes based on their molar teeth, which feature the same Y-5 configuration of cusps and fissures as those of all living apes. For this reason we call these primitive hominoids the dental apes.

5. **How do molecular phylogenies help us to understand primate evolution?**

   Molecular phylogenies provide an estimate of the relationships and dates of divergence of living primate taxa that we can use to augment information from the fossil record. However, divergence dates are calibrated by the fossil record.

CRITICAL THINKING QUESTIONS

1. How would the rise of rodents in the Eocene have contributed to the demise of the plesiadapids? What evolutionary principles can be applied here?

2. When we had only anatomical comparisons to rely on, we could not learn whether New World monkeys were descended from Old World monkeys or from early Eocene primates in North America. Now, with the rise of genetic dating, the answer is still unclear. What do you think this tells us about the limitations of genetic techniques for resolving problems of primate phylogenetics?

3. Discuss the possible selective pressures involved in the origin of primates, strepsirhines, and anthropoids. Can you think of other possible scenarios for the origins of these groups?

KEY TERMS

plesiadapiforms
prognathic face
postorbital bar
diastema

adapoids
omomyoids
dental apes
r-selected

k-selected
molecular clock
relative rate test

SUGGESTED READING

Alvarez, Walter (1997). *T. rex and the Crater of Doom.* Princeton University Press, Princeton, NJ.

Beard, Christopher K. (2004). *The Hunt for the Dawn Monkey: Unearthing the Origins of Monkeys, Apes, and Humans.* University of California Press, San Francisco.

Fleagle, John G. (1998). *Primate Adaptation and Evolution,* 2nd edition. Academic Press, San Diego, CA.

Chapter 11

BECOMING HUMAN:
The Ape–Hominid Transition

AS THE SUN ROSE OVER THE TREETOPS, the young australopithecine opened her eyes reluctantly, rolled over in her leafy nest, and yawned. By the time the sun had moved fully above the horizon she was climbing out of the tree and shimmying down the trunk. Watching her do this, you might easily have mistaken her for a chimpanzee. But as she reached the ground and stepped away from the tree, she assumed an upright posture. She walked purposefully on two legs across a clearing to some fruit trees. There she joined a small cluster of others like her, some of them perched in branches, others collecting fruits that had fallen to the ground. She sniffed a fruit for ripeness and popped it in her mouth. She looked over at the alpha male of the group, an imposing creature much bigger than she was with large canine teeth, a prominent brow ridge above his eyes, and a muscular body carried about on equally muscular legs.

As the day warmed up, the group headed toward some low, densely forested hills a kilometer away. There were patches of grassland amid the expanse of forest, but they stuck to the comforting safety of the trees. Only last month, in this same spot, a young female had been ambushed by a lion. She had screamed in fear and tried to escape to the safety of the tree, and the males came to her aid, but too late: The lion had caught and eaten her.

Although predators were a constant worry, so too was the possibility that when they reached their objective a neighboring group of their own species would have gotten there first. The battles that raged between the two adjacent groups were as terrifying for them as any lion, and many family members and allies had been brutally injured. Today they reached the trees without competition and settled in for a meal of ripe fruits.

We will never know exactly how the earliest humans looked or behaved. But biological anthropologists have a number of intellectual tools that help them reconstruct the likeliest path from an ape ancestor to a hominid. Anatomically inclined anthropologists analyze the functional shifts involved in changing a four-legged ape into a two-legged human. After all, the fossil record for human origins is the only direct physical evidence of our ancestry that we will ever have. Behavior experts attempt to extrapolate likely patterns of behavior for the earliest humans or at least define the likely range of behaviors that might have been present in the last common ancestor of apes and humans from comparative studies of living nonhuman primates. And genetic studies have helped unravel the mystery of our divergence from the apes and have become increasingly central to our understanding of our own relationship to extinct species in our lineage.

Recall from Chapter 7 the adaptations that characterize living African apes, our closest relatives. These adaptations include a large brain-to-body size ratio and extended ontogeny compared with monkeys, traits related to knuckle-walking, and traits related to a brachiator ancestor, including thorax shape, a highly mobile shoulder, and the absence of a tail. In a remarkable adaptive shift at the end of the Miocene, this combination of traits gave way to a new suite of traits in a new family, the Hominidae. (Hominids include humans and our extinct ancestors after the split from the last common ancestor with chimps.)

Initially, the most noticeable anatomical development in the hominids is in locomotion; bipedality, along with slightly smaller canine teeth was among the earliest adaptations. The dramatic expansion of the brain that characterize living humans came millions of years later. The appearance of cultural traditions such as stone tool use probably was just a difference in degree at first, rather than kind, from the ape–human common ancestor. Because the fundamental adaptation was the shift to upright postures, this is where we begin to try to understand how and why one lineage of Miocene apes evolved into the earliest hominids.

This chapter is about the quest to understand the origin of the earliest humans. First we review the basic anatomical changes that natural selection produced in the bipedal skeleton. Once we understand how anatomy changed, we explore scenarios for why a bipedal primate might have evolved. Many of the time-honored assumptions about human origins have been questioned or challenged in recent years, and we review some of the controversy. Then we examine the behavioral changes that mark the transition from an apelike ancestor to a human lineage, specifically those related to the evolution of the brain and intelligence. This focus on the anatomical and behavioral changes that occur at the transition from ape to human sets the stage for the next four chapters, which look in detail at the fossil record for hominid evolution.

BECOMING A BIPED

Walking upright is an extremely rare way to move about (Figure 11.1). In the entire history of life on Earth, truly bipedal posture and walking have appeared in just a few lineages. Only among the dinosaurs—where creatures such as *T. rex* and its two-legged kin proliferated over eons—and in hominids did bipedalism become a widespread adaptation. Of some 4,000 living mammals, only humans are habitual bipeds today.

Although we tend to think that there was a natural progression from four-legged walking to a transitional state to fully upright posture, the example of the dinosaurs shows us that this is not necessarily the case. All dinosaurs evolved from a small bipedal species, which gave rise to the gigantic quadrupeds and bipeds. So among dinosaurs, two-legged posture was simply a primitive adaptation that allowed some forms to exploit new resources. Although we are more efficient bipeds than our earliest hominid ancestors, it is quite possible that early in human evolution, bipedality was an experiment that natural selection favored in different ways for different ecological reasons (Figure 11.2).

  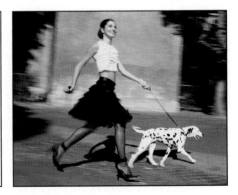

FIGURE 11.1 Habitual bipedality is a relatively rare occurance and the striding bipedalism of hominids required particular anatomical adaptations not found in quadrupeds.

THE FAR SIDE®   BY GARY LARSON

"And now there go the Wilsons! ... Seems like
everyone's evolving except us!"

FIGURE 11.2

Bipedalism is extraordinarily different from other ways that primates use for
getting around (Figure 11.3). A number of other primates, from sifakas to chimpanzees, stand upright occasionally while walking or feeding. However, hominids
not only exhibit the behavior of upright walking but also possess extensive morphological adaptations to it.

ANATOMICAL CHANGES

The shift from quadrupedal to bipedal locomotion poses several problems. Critical among these is the issue of balancing the body's weight over two limbs (while
standing) and often over one limb (while walking) (Figure 11.4 on page 302).
Think of the quadruped as a four-legged table: The center of gravity falls in the area
between the four legs, and the body weight is distributed equally over all four
limbs (while standing). Remove one leg and it is still possible to balance the table's
weight by shifting it to the area between the three legs. But take away two legs and
the task becomes extremely difficult. When an animal that evolved to walk on four
legs walks on its two hind limbs instead, it compensates for this lack of support
by constantly moving its weight between the remaining limbs. Imagine your dog
dancing on its hind limbs for a treat, constantly in motion forward and backward
(trying to move under that center of gravity) and standing only briefly, tiring quickly from the constant muscular work. But when you stand, your body weight falls
naturally between your two feet–no dancing required (although you can if you
like). And when you walk, your foot naturally falls directly under your center of
gravity without you even having to try. This greater efficiency means that while
standing at rest, you burn only a few more calories than you would lying down.
The reasons for these differences lie in the structural changes in our skeleton that
directly affect the skull, spine, pelvis, leg, and foot.

The Vertebral Column and Skull   The spine, or **vertebral column**, is made up
of a series of vertebrae from the neck (**cervical vertebrae**), thorax (**thoracic vertebrae**), lower back (**lumbar vertebrae**), and pelvic (**sacrum** and **coccyx**) regions

vertebral column   The column of
bones, and cartilaginous disks, that
houses the spinal cord and provides
structural support and flexibility to
the body.

cervical vertebrae   The seven
neck vertebrae.

thoracic vertebrae   The twelve
vertebrae of the thorax that hold the
ribs.

FIGURE 11.3   Some nonhuman
primates can walk bipedally for
short periods of time but lack key
bipedal adaptations.

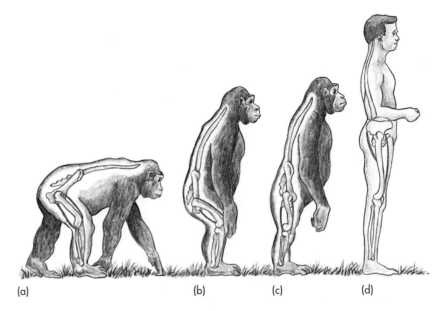

FIGURE 11.4 Becoming a biped changes the way an animal balances. The quadruped's center of gravity goes right through its back to the ground, balancing its weight over four legs (a). If the quadruped stands on two legs it either must bend its knees (b) or fall forward (c). A habitual biped has structural changes in the skeleton so that the center of gravity falls between the two feet when standing with legs extended (d). (After Wolpoff, 1999).

(a)   (b)   (c)   (d)

(Figure 11.5; Appendix B). The quadruped has a gently C-shaped curve that makes the thoracic region of the spine slightly convex. The biped has an S-shaped spine made by adding two secondary and opposing curvatures (in the cervical and lumbar regions) to the C-shape curvature of the quadruped. If you stand a quadruped up on its back legs, the C-shape of its spine tends to put the center of gravity in front of its feet, causing the animal to fall forward (or dance to avoid falling). The secondary curvatures in the bipedal spine compensate for that C-curve and bring the center of gravity back closer to the hips, ultimately resting over the biped's two feet.

The weight of the biped is borne down the spine to the sacrum, where it passes to the hips and from there through the two legs. The amount of weight increases as you go down the spine, so the vertebrae of a biped get increasingly large as you approach the lumbar region. In contrast, weight-bearing doesn't increase along the quadruped's spine, and the vertebral bodies are of nearly equal size in different regions of the spine. These differences can have adverse effects on the biped's body. Lower back problems, especially among pregnant women, are among the most common medical ailments today; these problems are a result of the changes wrought in our ancestral skeleton.

The vertebral column is also oriented differently to the head of the biped, coming out from the bottom rather than the back of the skull. So the junction of the

lumbar vertebrae The five vertebrae of the lower back.

sacrum The fused vertebrae that form the back of the pelvis.

coccyx The fused tail vertebrae that are very small in humans and apes.

FIGURE 11.5 The spine of a biped has two additional curves in it at the neck and lower back to move the center of gravity over two feet. The ape (quadruped) had a C-shaped spine.

Human

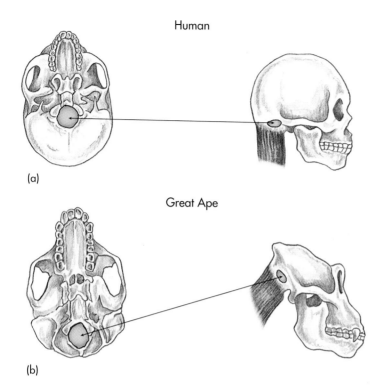

(a)

Great Ape

(b)

FIGURE 11.6 (a) The spine meets the skull from below in a biped, so the foramen magnum is directly beneath the skull and the neck muscles run down from the skull. (b) In the ape the spine meets the skull from the back so the foramen magnum is positioned posteriorly and the neck muscles also run posteriorly from the skull.

spinal cord and the brain, which occurs through a hole called the **foramen magnum** in the occipital bone, is positioned underneath the skull in bipeds but toward the back of the skull in quadrupeds (Figure 11.6 and Appendix B). In addition to the foramen magnum, another indicator of the angle at which an animal holds its body in life is the form of the **nuchal plane**, the flattened bony area of the occipital to the rear of the foramen magnum that provides surface area for the attachment of neck muscles. In modern humans the nuchal plane is a horizontally flat region on the bottom of the skull, facing directly downward. In a quadruped, however, the nuchal plane faces rearward. In apes the nuchal plane's angle is somewhere between the human and quadruped condition. So the occipital bone is a clue for paleoanthropologists about the way in which a fossil may have stood and walked.

The Pelvis and Birth Canal   When you walk, you spend a significant amount of time on one leg. This entails keeping your center of gravity over that one support and not falling off to the unsupported side. Quadrupeds such as chimps accomplish this by throwing their weight over the supporting limb when they walk bipedally, resulting in a rocking from side to side that wastes a lot of energy. The skeleton of habitual bipeds such as hominids is rearranged to counter this shift automatically, and many of these changes occur in the pelvis. The bony pelvis consists of two **innominate bones (os coxae)**, each of which is composed of three bones (the **ischium, ilium,** and **pubis**) that fuse during adolescence and the sacrum, part of the vertebral column (Figure 11.7 on page 304 and Appendix B). The ischium is the bone you sit on. The ilium is the bone you feel when you put your hands on your hips. And the pubis is the bony portion of the pelvis in the pubic region.

The pelvis of a biped is basin-shaped with a short, broad ilium that runs from the posterior to the anterior of the animal. The quadruped ilium is long and flat and situated on the back of the animal. The basin shape supports abdominal organs that tend to be pulled downward by gravity, and it places important locomotor and postural muscles in a better mechanical position. Most important are the anterior **gluteal muscles** (gluteus minimus and medius), which attach to the ilium and are rotated around to the front and side of the biped. In this position they connect the ilium to the top of the femur (thigh bone), and when you stand on one limb

foramen magnum Hole in the occipital bone through which the spinal cord connects to the brain.

nuchal plane Flattened bony area of the occipital posterior to the foramen magnum, to which neck muscles attach.

innominate bones (os coxae) The pair of bones that compose the lateral parts of the pelvis; each innominate is made up of 3 bones that fuse during adolescence.

ischium Portion of the innominate bone that forms the bony underpinning of the rump.

ilium The blade of the innominate to which gluteal muscles attach.

pubis Portion of the innominate that forms the anterior part of the birth canal.

gluteal muscles Gluteus maximus, medius, and minimus, the muscles of walking, which have undergone radical realignment in habitual bipeds.

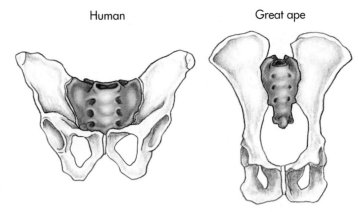

Human   Great ape

FIGURE 11.7 To maintain balance the bipedal pelvis has a foreshortened ilium and is broader and bowl-shaped. The quadrupedal pelvis has a long ilium positioned on the back, not the side, of the animal.

they contract, pulling the ilium (and the rest of your trunk) toward the support side, so your center of gravity balances over the single foot. The gluteus maximus runs from the back of the ilium to the back of the femur, and when it contracts it keeps your pelvis (and you) from tipping forward in front of your feet (Figure 11.8 and Figure 11.4). The shortening and broading of the ilium also results in the hip joint (**acetabulum**) being closer to the sacroiliac joint. This is good for balance but narrows the birth canal, a problem with which later hominids including ourselves will have to contend.

Efficient bipedalism requires a narrow pelvis, but that need must be balanced against the need for a birth canal wide enough for the large shoulders of an ape infant. Early in hominid history selection for birth canal size probably widened the pelvis from side to side by widening the sacrum. Later, as brain size increased, the baby was also required to rotate during delivery (see Chapter 17). Chimpanzee or gorilla babies emerge from the mother's body face up, but human babies emerge face down. Paleoanthropologists are unsure about exactly when this shift occurred, but its evolution was crucial to successful birthing in later, larger-brained hominids. The evolutionary drawback of this new anatomy was that it left the mother unable to assist in the birth of her own child. Karen Rosenberg and Wenda Trevathan (1996) see the constraints of bipedalism as an evolutionary incentive for the development of socially assisted birthing, in which females aid one another in achieving successful births.

acetabulum The cup-shaped joint formed by the ilium, ischium, and pubis at which the head of the femur attaches to the pelvis.

Gluteus medius
Gluteus minimus
Gluteus maximus

Gluteus medius
Gluteus minimus
Gluteus maximus

FIGURE 11.8 The gluteal muscles are repositioned in the biped and aid in support.

Chimpanzee *Australopithecus* Human

FIGURE 11.9 To keep the foot under the center of gravity, the biped leg is angled from hip to knee. The quadruped leg is not.

The Leg The broad pelvis places the top of the femur far to the side of the biped, but remember that when you walk your foot must fall directly below your center of gravity. A straight femur, such as that seen in a quadruped, would result in a foot far to the side of the center of gravity. The solution is to angle the femur from the hip into the knee; this places the foot below the center of gravity (Figure 11.9 and Figure 11.4). However, it creates problems for the knee because the musculature attached to the femur is also acting at an angle. When the animal flexes its muscles on the front of the femur in an effort to extend the knee, the muscles pull both superiorly (up) and laterally (out). The patella (knee cap) sits in the tendon of this muscle and is likewise displaced outward. To avoid dislocating the patella in a biped, the groove on the femur that the patella sits in is deep, and the outside edge or lip is enlarged. In addition, to help support the excess body weight going through each limb, the bottom of the femur (**femoral condyles**) is enlarged. The top of the tibia or shin bone reflects similar changes.

Although relatively short in early hominids, the leg lengthened relative to trunk length during human evolution. This increased stride length and efficiency in walking. Imagine a Great Dane and a Chihuahua walking side by side and the greater number of steps the shorter-legged dog takes compared with the longer strides of the Great Dane. The leg attained modern human proportions with the origin of *Homo erectus*.

The Foot The foot skeleton is composed of three types of bones: **tarsals**, which form the heel and ankle region; **metatarsals**; and **phalanges** (the toes) (Figure 11.10 on page 306). In bipedal walking, the heel strikes first, followed by the rest of the foot. The main propulsive force comes at toe-off, when the big toe pushes off from the ground and the toes bend strongly backward (dorsiflex). To accommodate toe-off and dorsiflexion, the big toe moves in line with the other toes and becomes much, much larger than the other toes, and all the phalanges shorten and change joint orientation. Imagine the advantage to the biped of shorter toes; it is rather like the difference between walking in floppy clown shoes and wearing shoes with regular-sized toes.

A biped's foot is stouter and has arches that accommodate the great weight put through the two feet. The tarsal bones and big toe are robust and bound tightly together by ligaments, providing stability but decreasing overall manipulability of the foot. The foot has two structural arches: a transverse arch running from medial to lateral that is formed by the wedge-shaped tarsals, much like a stone architectural arch, and a longitudinal arch running the length of the foot and formed by the metatarsals and tarsals. The arches are shock absorbers which store and

femoral condyles The enlarged inferior end of the femur that forms the top of the knee joint.

tarsals Foot bones that form the ankle and arches of the foot.

metatarsals Five foot bones that join the tarsals to the toes and form a portion of the longitudinal arch of the foot.

phalanges Bones that form the fingers and toes.

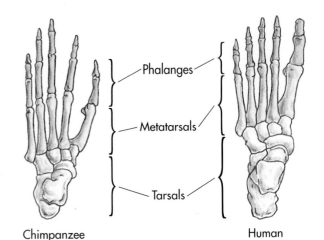

FIGURE 11.10 The biped's foot bears more weight than the quadrupeds and so the bones are stouter. The big toe is especially big and in line with the others, and the phalanges are shorter and less curved.

Phalanges

Metatarsals

Tarsals

Chimpanzee   Human

return some of the energy to the walking biped. Arches help to reduce the incidence of fatigue fractures to the lower leg.

The Arm   One advantage of walking on two legs is that it frees the arms to do other things. Carrying objects and tool making are two activities often associated with the hominid lineage (although, as we shall see, they are not exclusive associations). Throughout hominid evolution the arm and hand skeleton have changed as a result of their release from locomotor activities and their new use, particularly in tool making. Although early hominids have relatively long arms, through hominid evolution the arms shortened relative to trunk length, and arm strength decreased because it was no longer weight bearing. The thumb became opposable and the phalanges shortened. The arm assumed modern human proportions around the time of the origin of *Homo erectus*.

CONSTRUCTING THE BIPEDAL BODY PLAN

It is easy to make the mistake of thinking that once the shift from quadrupedalism to bipedalism began, it was somehow preordained that an efficient biped would result. But remember that such master plans do not exist in evolution: all the anatomical changes we've discussed occurred like the construction of a mosaic, with interlocking pieces driven by natural selection in every generation. Natural selection drove the evolution of bipedalism because in each subsequent generation once the shift began, each transitional stage conferred survival and reproductive benefits on individuals. The mental image of a shuffling prehominid that was neither efficient quadruped nor biped is certainly wrong. Instead, in each generation the emerging biped must have been very good at surviving and reproducing, or else natural selection would not have pushed the process further. This strongly suggests that bipedalism arose in a variety of forms and functions, some of which may have died out while others succeeded. Ultimately, one lineage of bipeds—our own—succeeded, and we are the product of that lengthy process.

LOCOMOTION OF THE LAST COMMON ANCESTOR

Because African apes and humans differ so dramatically in their anatomical adaptations to locomotion, identifying our ancestors in the fossil record is easy. We just look for the anatomical adaptations to bipedalism. However, scientists disagree as to the most logical precursor of bipedalism. Did the last common ancestor (LCA) of African apes and humans knuckle-walk? Or were they adapted to life in the trees? Sir Arthur Keith (1923) raised the possibility that humans were descended from arboreal apes. In this view, the LCA of apes and humans was arboreal, not a knuckle-walker (Figure 11.11a). Alternatively, although a deeper arboreal ancestor is accepted, other researchers argue that the LCA of chimps and humans was a knucklewalker (Gebo, 1996; Figure 11.11b).

WHY BIPEDS?

Bipedalism is the basic adaptation of the hominid line, and by now you should be wondering what selective pressures favored bipeds. Why did bipedalism evolve? Many scenarios have been proposed (Figure 11.12 on page 308), most of which have a fatal flaw. For purposes of explanation, we can categorize bipedalism scenarios as those related to energetics, ecology, diet, and sexual selection. Some of the scenarios overlap.

Energetic Efficiency   Peter Rodman and Henry McHenry (1980) demonstrated that bipedal walking is a more efficient way of traveling than walking on all fours, at least if we compare human and chimpanzee walking. Rodman and McHenry pointed out that although humans do not necessarily walk more efficiently than all quadrupeds, they certainly walk more efficiently than knuckle-walking apes. In other words, if hominids evolved from knuckle-walking apes,

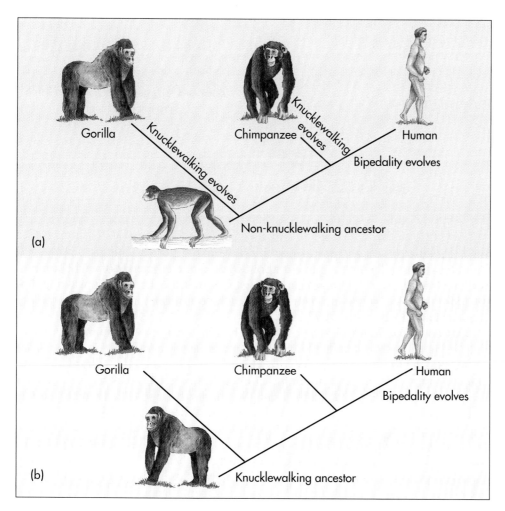

FIGURE 11.11   (a) If the last common ancestor of gorillas, chimpanzees, and humans was not a knucklewalker, then knucklewalking would have evolved independently in both the chimpanzee and gorilla lineages and the ancestral condition for humans is not knucklewalking. (b) Alternatively, if the last common ancestor of gorillas, chimpanzees, and humans was not a knucklewalker, then the ancestral condition for humans is knucklewalking.

Carrying tools, food, or infants

Ecological influences: traveling between trees
or seeing over tall grass

Feeding on grasses or from bushes

Provisioning family

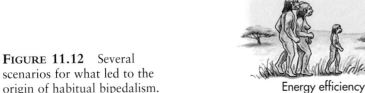

Energy efficiency

FIGURE 11.12 Several scenarios for what led to the origin of habitual bipedalism.

then the shift to upright posture would have made perfect energetic sense. Although there is still some argument about the relative efficiency of early hominid walking (see Chapter 12), most energetic analyses indicate that bipedal walking (but not running) is a more efficient means of locomotion than knuckle-walking (Leonard and Robertson, 1997).

A second way in which the body plan of a biped may have been more efficient than its ape ancestor is in its ability to dissipate heat. Dean Falk and Glenn Conroy (1983, 1990) studied the way in which fossil hominid skulls drained blood and suggest that successful hominids in open (unforested) areas had a means of draining blood that also cooled the brain. We discuss their so-called radiator model of bipedal origins in Box 11.1. In addition, Pete Wheeler (1991) has shown that bipeds dissipate heat faster than quadrupeds because they stand slightly taller above the ground, and when exposed to midday sun they present less surface area to be heated. However, although hominids may have been better at dissipating heat from their bodies and brains than was the LCA, it seems unlikely that hominids arose because of these qualities rather than benefiting from them once bipedality was favored for other reasons.

Box 11.1   Overheated Radiator?

Dogs pant when they're hot, slobbering all over your carpet. We sweat, sometimes profusely. A baseball pitcher can lose 10 pounds of body fluid while putting in nine innings on a hot July afternoon. People who lose the ability to sweat (New York Yankee great Whitey Ford had this medical problem late in his career) are in grave danger of lethal overheating. When early humans began to walk upright, their walking no doubt took them out of the forest and into blazing tropical sunshine. Like any other warm-blooded animal, they must have had a way of cooling themselves.

A four-legged animal walking in the hot equatorial sun exposes the expanse of its broad back to the sun, a sure recipe for hyperthermia without some adaptation for rapid, effective heat loss. Many mammals use a complex system of transferring heat from the blood of the arteries being pumped from the heart to the cooler blood of the veins as it returns to the heart.

Humans don't possess this system. But, as Pete Wheeler noted, two-legged walkers are in a better position, literally: The sun strikes only the top of their head and shoulders (Figure A). Even the slight height difference between a quadruped's head and that of a biped puts us in significantly cooler air because wind speed is higher and the temperature is cooler than near the ground. Being naked rather than hairy helps too, because hair traps heat.

But standing tall created a new heating problem: the need to get blood up to the head, counter to the force of gravity. Most animals that constantly shift from horizontal to vertical orientations have evolved circulatory system features that combat the pull of gravity. When snakes climb up-

FIGURE A   At midday, the sun only strikes the head and shoulders of this Masai.

ward, the pattern of blood flow to the head is radically altered by circulatory adaptations, including a forward-positioned heart, designed to keep blood flowing. When a giraffe leans its elegant neck down to a waterhole and then raises it again, special valves, tissue wraps, and pumps prevent blood from pooling in the lower body and boost it up to the head.

When you lie down, blood flowing to the heart drains away from your skull through your neck's jugular veins. But when you stand up, the blood seeks a different escape route through a vast network of veins surrounding the spinal cord. Called the vertebral plexus, this network extends from the skull down to the base of your spine. It diverts blood into the smallest vessels, boosting the blood's flow rate and its capacity to move about the body.

Anthropologists Dean Falk and Glenn Conroy applied this knowledge to the human fossil record and found two differ-

ent methods of draining blood in different fossil lineages. They reasoned that the routing of the circulatory system provides keys to the lives and habitats of earliest humans. When the shift to bipedalism happened, it must have been accompanied by a change in the way blood was moved up and down the now-vertical column of the body.

Brains in particular need to be kept cool; overheating poses a greater risk to the brain than to other parts of the body. Falk (1990) suggested that the vertebral plexus evolved to cool down a rapidly expanding brain as emerging humans moved out onto the open, sun-soaked grassland. The idea is provocative: the circulatory system as a radiator designed to keep a growing brain cool, enabling more and more brain expansion in one lineage but not in another. If Falk is right, there were two ways to drain blood from the human skull in prehistory. One option was taken by the early hominids that were direct forerunners of modern people. Another was used by other lineages that went extinct without any descendants. It can thus be used as a test of which species of our ancestors were our direct forbears.

The hypothesis is not without detractors. Both ways of draining the blood can be found in modern people, suggesting that variation between individuals in prehistory may be more important than species-wide differences. And the correlation between species with "radiator" skulls and open-country habitats is not perfect. But as a prime mover hypothesis, the idea has generated a great deal of valuable discussion. (Adapted from Stanford, 2003).

Ecological Influences   Ecological models for the origin of bipedalism focus on the role of the changing environment of East Africa between 5 and 8 million years ago that may have placed a premium on the ability to walk upright. As we learned in Chapter 9, Africa experienced a major drying and cooling trend in the late Miocene that led to the expansion of grassland and a decrease in the amount of forest. This trend culminated in the widespread savannas we find in East Africa today. Some scientists argue that increased grassland caused a wider scattering of the food trees protohominids needed for their meals, so they had to forage over longer distances across more open country. With increased travel across open country, natural selection may have driven the evolution of a more energy-efficient mode of transport, namely bipedalism (Box 11.2).

Many researchers have observed that, particularly in grasslands, standing upright would have offered greater ability to see over tall grass or to scan for potential predators. Gaining a better view of one's surroundings by walking upright has long been advocated as the selective advantage necessary to drive the evolution of bipedalism. But other researchers ask why the enormous changes to the anatomy that allow habitual bipedalism would have taken place, when a brief look over tall grass now and then might have been just as effective without these fundamental anatomical changes.

Dietary Scenarios Most of the models that seek to explain the origins of bipedalism invoke its behavioral advantages. The most persuasive and influential of the dietary models may be the idea that a lineage of fossil apes became bipedal because of the value of standing upright for feeding in fruit trees. In the 1970s and 1980s, Russell Tuttle (1981) developed the idea that the earliest stages of bipedalism may have taken place in the trees, based on his observations of gibbons walking bipedally on tree limbs. About the same time, Clifford Jolly (1970) proposed models of the evolution of upright walking based on observations of the short-distance shuffling that some baboons do while feeding on seeds scattered in African grasslands. In the 1990s, Kevin Hunt proposed that the value of standing upright, both on the forest floor and on tree limbs, was that it made the plucking of small fruits such as figs more efficient. Craig Stanford (2002) also observed chimpanzee bipedal feeding, which occurred mainly on the largest limbs of large fruit trees. The chimpanzees stood on two legs for only a few seconds at a time and for only a few minutes a day. Although differing in detail, these researchers all envision a protohominid that became increasingly bipedal for the feeding advantages that this posture offered, eventually becoming a habitual biped. Whether such feeding benefits would have made the conversion to full-time bipedalism likely is a question that has not yet been answered.

Others have argued that bipedality, group size, and body size increased in response to not only the greater patchiness of food resources and the need to walk across open areas to access food but also to the greater risk of being eaten while crossing those areas, as we saw in the vignette. In this case, safety in numbers applies to animals crossing savannas, so Lynn Isbell and Truman Young (1996) suggested that one possible response to the increasing patchiness of forests was to increase group size and body size and adopt efficient bipedal locomotion. Isbell and Young saw this as the route taken by early hominids. An alternative route is to stay in forested areas and keep group size small when foraging but to re-merge groups for mating and other behaviors. Isbell and Young suggested this was the route taken by the chimpanzee lineage, leading to their fusion–fission group form (see Chapter 7).

Sexual Selection and Mating Strategies The most prominent of the bipedalism scenarios that advocate a mating benefit is the Lovejoy model, which we discuss in detail in Box 11.2. But other researchers have proposed that bipedalism arose because it conferred mating benefits on protohominids that were upright. Nina Jablonski and George Chaplin (1993) argued that bipedalism would have been beneficial to males engaging in social displays. Male chimpanzees often stand upright briefly when they assert their dominance over other males during charging displays; upright posture presumably makes a charging male look more impressive. Jablonski and Chaplin proposed that the benefits of walking upright lie in the ability of males to look impressive and therefore get more matings with females by being bipedal. But it is unclear why this benefit would lead to habitual bipedalism and all the accompanying anatomical alterations rather than just a temporary behavioral tactic.

Box 11.2   What Did Love Have to Do with It?

Perhaps the most talked-about scenario to explain the origins of the human mating system in the past two decades is one that incorporates food-carrying, monogamy, and the evolution of the human female reproductive signaling. C. Owen Lovejoy began with a well-established premise, the diversity of types of fossil apes had been declining since well before the emergence of the hominids. At one time, as we've seen, the tropical forests of the Earth were dominated by a rich diversity of apes, comparable to what we see today among monkeys. The four living great ape species are but a pale remnant of their former species-rich glory. Why?

Lovejoy claimed that this reduction occurred because of the woefully slow reproductive rate of the great apes. None of these animals give birth as often as the 2-year interval in many human societies; the interval between successive gorilla births is about 4 years, 4–5 years for chimpanzees and bonobos, and as many as 7 years for orangutans. If a female orangutan has her first baby at age 16 and her last at age 36 (typical in the wild), she has time to bear and rear only about three babies (a mother baboon or rhesus monkey more than doubles that rate). Monkeys simply outbreed apes.

More important, to Lovejoy, the entire human lineage, as an offshoot of an ancient ape lineage, would have gone the same dismal reproductive route unless natural selection molded adaptations that allowed our direct ancestors to compete successfully with monkeys. This breed-or-die dilemma came at the same time, about 5 million years ago, that the great tropical forests in East Africa were breaking up into a quilt of forest and grassland as the climate became drier.

Into this circumstance walked the earliest hominids. Lovejoy has advocated high-

ly refined bipedalism in even the earliest bipeds (see Chapter 12) and saw the emergence of bipedal gait as an adaptation to crossing wide patches of savanna in search of fruit and perhaps also increasing amounts of meat in the diet. He pointed out that most of the supposedly uniquely human traits are not so unique. Other primates have opposable thumbs and many of the other anatomical traits we once thought to be solely human features. Tool use began much later than the rise of bipedalism. According to Lovejoy, the one trait that most crucially set our first ancestors off from their simian cousins was female reproductive physiology.

The pink sexual swellings that protrude from the rear ends of female chimpanzees are vivid billboards of sexual availability, advertising that the bearer is either ovulating or otherwise eager for a male's attention. Swellings are notably absent in women. Lovejoy saw a possible link between the fact that we no longer advertise ovulation and the other traits that were emerging as humanity evolved. Female protohominids, he suggested, had to cope with a patchy environment, widely dispersed food, and males eager to mate with as many females as they could. This is not a winning game plan for a female, being abandoned for all but a few fertile days of each monthly cycle. But if the female protohominid concealed her reproductive state by losing that attention-getting swelling, a male would have a far greater incentive to hang around, perhaps even offering his services in the form of food provisioning.

This is where Lovejoy saw the tie-in with bipedalism. As forests contracted, males had to walk further to find food to carry back to the females they were covetously guarding from the attentions of other males. Two-leggedness raised the energy efficien-

cy of walking and enabled the male to carry food in his arms. Back at home, the female's physiology, fortified by the extra nutrition she received from her now-attentive mate, could produce more offspring. The interval between births shortened, and the emerging hominids not only staved off extinction but also invaded a new grassland niche.

Lovejoy's model ties together information about ancient climate, anatomy, and reproductive physiology with speculation about behaviors such as carrying, fruit eating, and human mating systems. But many experts saw the model as riddled with holes. We now think critical stages of human evolution took place in the forest, not on the savanna, although that may not entirely refute the model. And contrary to Lovejoy's assumption that the ancestor of chimpanzees and humans had a huge sexual swelling that our own ancestors lost, there is every reason to think that chimpanzees and bonobos have evolved huge sexual swellings rather than our having lost them. Lovejoy's scenario also assumes that the ancestral, "natural" mating system of humanity was monogamy. Much evidence points to ancestral hominids having a polygamous mating system much like that of modern chimpanzees, including fossil evidence showing a large amount of sexual dimorphism in early hominids, a trait usually associated with polygyous mating structures (see Chapters 7 and 12) although recent work by Lovejoy may revise dimorphism estimates.

Nonetheless, Lovejoy's model attracted a great deal of attention because of its creativity and because it was a compelling story. Other hypotheses perhaps more fundamentally sound but lacking in the narrative qualities that Lovejoy used, fell by the wayside during the same decades that Lovejoy's continued to be debated. (Adapted from Stanford, 2003).

THE TRANSITION TO HUMAN BEHAVIOR

We have now considered the fundamental anatomical change that marked the rise of the hominids: the appearance of a wholly new posture and mode of travel 5–6 million years ago in East Africa. Now we must examine how the behavior of those emerging hominids changed. This is a much more difficult, speculative task than reconstructing the morphological changes because behavior does not fossilize in the way that bones do. Or does it?

Although the behavior of extinct primates is not preserved in their fossilized remains, we can make strong inferences about how they behaved in life because we have every reason to assume that primates living in the past followed the same guiding principles of natural selection and sexual selection that primates follow today. The inference that the present reflects the past allows us to reconstruct diets, modes of locomotion, and other aspects of primate lives that inform us about the ways extinct hominids behaved.

As we saw in Chapter 7, primates possess traits that few other mammals have. Foremost among these are intelligence and social complexity. Any attempt to use the behavior of living primates to understand the behavior of extinct primates, including hominids, has these two traits as central features. The most primitive primates, the strepsirhines such as lorises and galagos, resemble ancient primates you saw in Chapter 10 and also resemble lower mammals rather than haplorhine primates in many ways. These nocturnal strepsirhines are generally solitary, lacking in advanced social complexity. Of course, intelligence and social complexity have evolved in nonprimate lineages too, from dolphins to elephants. But given the phylogenetic relationship between humans and nonhuman primates, we look to the higher primates first when we want to reconstruct aspects of the behavior of our ancestors. We are therefore using the principle of homology, as discussed in Chapter 2, that shared ancestry allows us to infer how we once used to be.

PRIMATE INTELLIGENCE: WHY ARE HUMANS SO SMART?

If the fundamental hominid adaptation was bipedalism, the fundamental primate adaptation that reaches its zenith in humans is intelligence. Although many large mammals, such as elephants and whales, have brains larger in absolute size, no mammalian group rivals the higher primates for the ratio of brain to body size. Because a huge output of caloric energy is needed to grow a large brain, we can be sure there were benefits to the evolution of intelligence that drove brain size and reorganization forward in each successive generation. Although we all agree that big brains are a defining feature of humankind and that their existence suggests they must have conferred a survival advantage to hominids, how exactly big brains facilitated survival is still unknown.

Scholars have disagreed for years about how to define intelligence. The term "intelligent" has very little precise meaning when we speak of animal behavior in particular; does it refer to learning, memory, or some other cognitive factor? Psychologist Richard Byrne (1995), one of the leading researchers in the area of primate intelligence, considers problem-solving capacity to be a measure of intelligence. Problem-solving cognition allows primates to respond effectively to novel situations. Every day, all primates past and present must navigate their way through an environment, both physical and social, that tests their ability to survive and reproduce. Primate intelligence, Byrne and others believe, is the way natural selection chose to promote those skills. We will consider three competing schools of thought for the origins and evolution of primate intelligence: technical, ecological, and social.

Technical Intelligence and Tool Use   **Technical intelligence** is the ability of some nonhuman primates to use cognitive skills to extract food and other resources from their natural environment by modifying that environment. Because we regard the advent of tool use to be a major hallmark of the rise of human intellect, anthropologists feel tool use by other primates offers intriguing clues about the evolution of intelligence and of culture. As we will see in Chapter 13, human tool use dates back at least 2.5 million years. Before that time, however, our most prim-

technical intelligence Hominid intelligence and brain size increase modeled as a result of tool use and extractive foraging.

itive ancestors no doubt fashioned and used tools in much the same way that some great apes do today (Figure 11.13).

Consider these three examples:

- A chimpanzee in Tanzania pauses in her daily journeys to pluck a twig from a bush. She strips the leaves from the twig, then inserts it between her lips and walks on. A hundred meters ahead she arrives at an enormous termite mound, standing 2 meters high and extending an equal distance underground. Inside, millions of the small insects live in a colony, using tunnels that extend to the surface. The chimp scratches the dirt away from the entrance to one of the tunnels and extends her probe into it. Solider termites rush to defend their nest, grabbing the twig with their mandibles. Smaller worker termites also swarm onto the stick. The chimpanzee delicately draws the probe from the tunnel and runs it between her lips, crunching the meaty soldiers along with hundreds of workers. In 30 minutes, the chimpanzee eats thousands of termites.

- In the same forest, another chimpanzee is climbing in an old tree when he sees a small hole in the trunk. Poking his finger into the hole, he flushes a woodpecker. After repeated attempts to reach some unseen object with his fingers, he descends to the ground and locates a strong stick. Returning to the woodpecker hole, he inserts the stick deep into the cavity several times, each time inspecting the end of the stick as he withdraws it. Finally, the end of the stick emerges from the hole dripping with liquid: runny egg yolk. The chimp licks the egg yolk from the stick and continues to probe the hole with the tool, breaking the eggs inside and lapping the contents from the stick.

- Two thousand miles west, in Côte d'Ivoire, another chimpanzee carefully places a nut into a shallow depression between the roots of a huge tree. She then wields a rock in her fist, pounding the nut time and again, replacing it in her makeshift anvil when it pops out. After several whacks, the nut breaks open, and she reaps a meal rich in protein and fat.

Each of these incidents is an example of tool manufacture and use for extractive foraging. Not all tool-using primates make their own tools. Indeed, chimpanzees are the most technological of all nonhuman primates by a wide margin. But other primates use simple tools. Capuchin monkeys in Central and South America use sticks to help them gain access to insects and other food items hidden within plants and to break open nuts. Orangutans use simple sticks as probes in tree cavities in much the same way that chimpanzees fish for termites.

FIGURE 11.13 Technical intelligence, tool use, and culture may have spurred our intellectual development and favored the origin of our large brains.

Chimpanzee tools fall into four broad categories: probes to extract insects and other food items, hammers to crack open nuts, sponges to soak up liquids, and branches wielded as weapons against prey or other chimpanzees. Tool use varies widely between different chimpanzee populations across Africa. In general, stick probe tools are more commonly found in eastern Africa, and stone hammers are more commonly found in western Africa. However, there is a great deal of variation in the distribution of tool cultures.

William McGrew (1992) has done extensive research on patterns of tool use by wild chimpanzees and what they may mean for the advent of human culture. Defining culture as the learned traditions of a group, McGrew considered whether the differences in tool cultures across Africa are the result of genetic differences among chimpanzee populations, environmental differences among the sites, or cultural traditions that differ between sites. He concluded that cultural traditions best explained the diversity of tool cultures. Although there has been genetic differentiation among African chimpanzee populations, there is no reason to expect that individual tool-using behaviors would be under genetic control, just as cultural traits particular to individual cultures have no basis in genes. The environmental explanation fails because in many cases the same resources are available in different forests, yet chimpanzee cultures differ across those forests. For example, Gombe National Park is a rock-strewn landscape, yet Gombe chimpanzees do not use rocks as tools. By contrast, the lowland rain forests of western Africa, where chimpanzees use stone tools, have few rocks, and the apes must search for the tools they need. There are also sex differences in chimpanzee tool use. Females at Gombe are more avid termite foragers throughout the year, whereas males tend to fish for termites seasonally (McGrew, 1992). This contrasts with the effort put into acquiring the meat of other mammals, in which males predominate.

Tools are an obvious element of cultural variation among chimpanzees, but they are not the only examples of culture. In a study of the diversity of chimpanzee cultural traditions across several long-term study sites. The authors documented thirty-eight cultural features—not only tool use but also styles of grooming and other behaviors—that occurred consistently across populations and appeared not to be environmentally determined (Whiten et al 1999).

The ability to use tools entails some sophisticated cognitive skills. One must be able to use foresight, plan, and be flexible enough to apply the tool to a variety of similar contexts. The invention of the tool may have been the work of a distant ancestor, but in each generation offspring must observe the style and technique of tool use in order to master it. Many scientists think that tool use, production, and transmission over generations indicate just this level of sophisticated cognitive skill in primates. However, as you will see later in this chapter, other scientists disagree.

As important as the use of tools would have been for early humans, there is at least one good reason that technical intelligence probably was not the impetus for hominid origins. The earliest bipeds arose between 5 and 6 million years ago, but the first stone tools did not appear in the fossil record until 2.5 million years ago. Tool use therefore is unlikely to have played a major role in the origins of bipedal locomotion. And brain size, which Darwin believed was in a feedback loop with bipedalism and tool use, did not expand dramatically until about 300,000 years ago, with the rise of modern people. Until that time brain expansion was incremental, and it may have been scaled to gradual evolutionary increases in body size (see Chapter 16).

Ecological Intelligence   Models of **ecological intelligence** suggest that the key impetus for the expansion of the brain was the selective advantage of being able to navigate and find food in a highly complex environment. A tropical forest, with its patchy and temporary availability and distribution of fruit, placed a premium on the evolution of large brains, especially in frugivorous species, which had to remember food locations and be able to navigate between them. Although

ecological intelligence
Hominid intelligence and brain size increase theorized as a result of benefits of navigating and foraging in a complex tropical forest ecosystem.

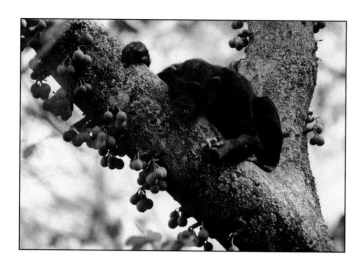

FIGURE 11.14 The complexity of a tropical forest may have favored the evolution of primate intelligence.

many animals forage in ways that optimize their chances of stumbling onto good food patches—hummingbirds and bumblebees fly optimized routes in fields of wildflowers, for example—primates possess mental maps of the landscape they live in.

Evidence exists that highly frugivorous anthropoid primates may have larger brain-to-body size ratios than folivorous species (Milton, 1981). In African forests, chimpanzees travel from tree to tree, feeding all day long. Many fruit species, such as figs, ripen unpredictably, but a party of chimpanzees usually will be at the tree as soon as ripe fruits appear. This suggests that the apes are monitoring the fruiting status of trees as they forage and remember which trees are worth waiting for (Figure 11.14). Paul Garber (1989) studied callitrichid monkey food-finding abilities in South American rain forests and found that even these little monkeys have the ability to recall the locations of hundreds of potential food trees. We know that nonhuman primates can hold fairly sophisticated information about food items in their heads. Marc Hauser and colleagues (2001) showed that rhesus macaques can count up to three food items, a skill that might be useful when foraging. Charles Menzel (1991) has studied the ability of monkeys to locate food, for which they appear to use a cognitive map that keys on familiar food items.

If environmental complexity accounted for the increase in brain size that began with the emergence of the hominids, then the expansion of savanna that occurred in the late Miocene might have been the driving force. As forests became more fragmented, the patchiness of the habitat increased, and emerging hominids with the capacity to navigate through it had a selective advantage.

The ecological intelligence school, which enjoyed much support in the 1980s, has become less accepted in recent years. First, some scholars have pointed out that many very small-brained animals navigate and forage in the same highly complex environment in which primates were thought to benefit from their large brains. There is no evidence that other small mammals such as squirrels are less efficient foragers than primates. In addition, the premise of the ecological complexity argument for hominization, that hominids arose in fragmented forest with patches of open grass, has been questioned in recent years. As we shall see in the coming chapters, some of the earliest fossil human discoveries have come from sites that appear to have been forest, not savanna, in the late Miocene and Pliocene.

Social Intelligence The prevailing view among scientists today is that the brain size increase that occurred in great apes and was extended into hominids resulted from the premium that natural selection placed on individuals that were socially clever. This theory, often called **social intelligence** or Machiavellian intelligence, argues that the primary evolutionary benefit of large brain size was that it allowed

social intelligence Hominid intelligence and brain size increase theorized as a result of benefits of being politically or socially clever when living with others; sometimes called Machiavellian intelligence.

apes and hominids to cope with and even exploit increasingly complex social relations. In large social groups, each individual must remember the network of alliances, rivalries, debts, and credits that exist among group members. This is not so different from the politics of our own day-to-day lives. Frans de Waal (1982) has observed that chimpanzees seem to engage in a "service economy" in which they barter alliances and other forms of support with one another.

The individuals best able to exploit this web of social relationships would have reaped more mating success than their group mates. Richard Byrne and Andrew Whiten (1988a, b) point out that the ability to subtly manipulate others is a fundamental aspect of group life. Robin Dunbar (1992) argues that as average group size increased, the cerebrum, or neocortex, of the primate brain increased in size to handle the additional input of social information, in much the same way that a switchboard would be enlarged to handle added telephone traffic. This effect holds true even when we take into account the evolved patterns of social grouping. Dunbar observes that small-brained primates, such as strepsirhines, typically live alone or in smaller groups than do most monkeys and apes.

Richard Byrne and Andrew Whiten (1988b) collected examples of potential lying in nonhuman primates and concluded that this behavior showed an evolutionary trend, one that was more widespread in higher primates. Great apes seem to be skilled at deceiving one another, whereas lemurs rarely if ever engage in tactical deception. Cheney and Seyfarth found that vervet monkeys engage in *tactical deception,* or lying. In Cheney and Seyfarth's study, a vervet gave a predator alarm call as the group fed in a desired fruit tree. As other group members fled from the "predator," the call-giver capitalized on its lie by feeding aggressively in their absence. Great apes are characterized by their clever use of deception to get what they want. Craig Stanford once watched a low-ranking Gombe male chimpanzee named Beethoven mate with a female, despite the presence of the alpha male Wilkie, by using tactical deception. As a party of chimpanzees sat in a forest clearing, Beethoven did a charging display through the middle of the group. Because Beethoven was a low-ranking male, this was taken by the alpha Wilkie as an act of insubordination. As Beethoven charged past Wilkie and into dense thickets, Wilkie pursued and launched into his own display. With Wilkie absorbed in his display of dominance, Beethoven furtively made his way back to the clearing and mated with an eagerly awaiting female.

Why do primate researchers think that deception is at the heart of understanding the roots of human cognition? The reason lies in the nature of intentional deception. In order to lie to someone, you must possess a **theory of mind**. That is, you must be able to place yourself in the mind of another, to understand the other's mental states. The ability to lie, to imitate, and to teach all rely on the assumption that the object of your actions thinks as you do. Whether nonhuman primates possess a human-like theory of mind is a subject of intense debate. Small children develop a theory of mind as they grow up, but not until they are past the age of about 2 years. Of course, to some extent the ability to impute mental states to others around you is a fundamental prerequisite to living in a complex social group. Among primates social dynamics are complex enough that a theory of mind becomes a critical issue.

Here's an example of why it is difficult to determine whether primates have a theory of mind. Michael Tomasello set out to determine whether a chimpanzee could imitate the way a person performs a task requiring forethought and planning. He set up an experiment in which one could reach a ball at the end of a table only by inserting a rake through a grate from the opposite end and using the rake to drag the ball (Figure 11.15). When a small child observed this, it took the child only one trial to learn how to get the ball using the rake, and the child perfectly imitated the researcher's demonstration. The chimpanzee also was able to get the ball after watching a single trial. However, the chimp devised its own method of using the rake to obtain the ball, not the style the researcher had demonstrated. Tomasello

theory of mind Ability to place oneself into the mind of others; necessary for possessing an awareness of the knowledge or cognitive ability of others and for imitating or teaching others.

Figure 11.15   Both humans and apes engage in learned imitative behavior readily.

concluded from this that the chimpanzee failed to imitate the process—even though it could achieve the same result—because it lacked a theory of mind that is necessary for true imitation. Tomasello labeled what the chimpanzee did *emulation:* achieving the goal without understanding the importance of imitating the process. Tomasello and a number of other researchers doubt that chimpanzees possess a theory of mind. But their critics point out that the rake–ball test is conducted in a context highly familiar to many children and utterly unnatural to any chimpanzee. This is a persistent problem for laboratory studies of great apes, primates that evolved cognitive abilities in response to the ecological and social pressures of tropical forest environments, not captive settings. Most laboratories provide severely impoverished social learning environments for their study subjects relative to what children growing up in families experience.

The problem with the social intelligence model as an explanation for the evolution of intelligence among apes and humans is twofold. First, if increasing social complexity went hand in hand with increasing brain size, then why is the brain-to-body size ratio of early hominids only modestly larger than that of great apes? Second, other animals with much more modest brain size, such as wolves, nevertheless exhibit social dynamics as complex as those seen in nearly all nonhuman primates. At the same time, one of the biggest-brained primates, the orangutan, does not live in large complex groups. In fact, orangutans don't live in groups at all, casting doubt on the ability of the social intelligence school to fully explain the rise of hominid intelligence.

What Made Humans Human?

Although there is no single explanation for the behavioral shift from apes to humans, we can be sure of a few facts. First, the anatomical shift from quadrupedalism came after a behavioral shift began. Whether for feeding or carrying or any other reason, natural selection favored individuals possessing slight anatomical differences that made them better bipeds.

Second, the transition to bipedality happened only because at every stage of the process, natural selection favored the form the evolving prehominid took. At each intermediate stage of the evolution of bipedalism, and of neocortical brain size, the emerging hominid had to be very good at what it did or bipedalism and increasing brain size would not have been the result. We can be sure that the earliest hominids were agile, powerful creatures, combining elements of ape and human behavior and morphology. Even if they were not as efficient at walking upright as modern people are, they were without doubt highly effective foragers.

Third, although we have focused on both bipedalism and intelligence in this chapter, at the earliest stages of hominid evolution brain neocortex size and intelligence were quite apelike. Paleoanthropologists debate exactly when hominids became more like people than like apes, but certainly the very earliest hominids (and also the australopithecines we will discuss in Chapter 12) were still quite primitive. Terry Deacon (1990) points out that the notion of linear progression in brain size from the most primitive to the brainiest primates is largely a fiction. Deacon's research on primate brains showed that a good deal of the variation in brain-to-body size ratio in the Primate order results from body size differences between taxa, with the brain being scaled in size accordingly, rather than from natural selection operating directly on brain size itself. The bigger-is-naturally-better notion may be the product of outdated thinking about the evolution of intelligence, natural selection will select for a bigger brain only if other, less costly solutions are not available.

We have now examined several models that seek to explain why primates are intelligent. Earlier in the chapter we considered some models to explain the origin of bipedalism. From this foundation we turn in the next several chapters to the hard evidence for human evolution, the fossils themselves.

SUMMARY

1. **What effect did the shift to bipedal posture have on human birth?**

   The requirements of habitual bipedal posture select for a narrow pelvis, but this need must be balanced by the need to accommodate wide shoulders and eventually large human brain sizes. The shape of the human pelvis reflects this balance, as does the rotational means of giving birth, in which the baby rotates in the birth canal.

2. **How does the foot skeleton differ between a biped and a knuckle-walker?**

   The foot of a biped has more robust bones for greater weight bearing, which are more tightly bound together by ligaments (less flexible). The big toe is enlarged and in line with the other toes, all of which are shortened. The tarsals form two arches that serve as shock absorbers.

3. **What is the "Radiator" model?**

   This model suggests that hominids evolved a special blood drainage system that facilitated cooling of their enlarged brains as they walked on the savanna.

4. **What is ecological intelligence?**

   Ecological intelligence models suggest that the key impetus for the expansion of the hominid brain was the selective advantage of being able to navigate and find food in a highly complex environment.

5. **What is a theory of mind?**

   To have a theory of mind is to have the ability to place yourself in the mind of another, to be able to understand the other's mental states. The ability to lie, to imitate, and to teach relies on the assumption that the object of your actions thinks as you do.

CRITICAL THINKING QUESTIONS

1. Evolution by natural selection is all about tradeoffs: One trait is enhanced, but another connected trait is compromised as a result. What were some of the tradeoffs that accompanied the evolution of bipedal posture?

2. Many scenarios have been put forward to explain the origin of bipedalism. Which one do you favor and why? Are there elements to a successful model, apart from the factual evidence, that may explain why it is accepted and others are not?

3. You've read about the three leading schools of thought to explain the rise of intelligence: technical, ecological, and social. But are these mutually exclusive? Explain why or why not.

4. Do you think human cognitive abilities are an extension of those of nonhuman primates? Or have humans made an evolutionary break from our primate past in some way? If so, in what way?

KEY TERMS

vertebral column
cervical
thoracic
lumbar
sacrum
coccyx
foramen magnum
nuchal plane

innominate bones
  (os coxae)
ischium
ilium
pubis
gluteal muscles
acetabulum
femoral condyles

tarsals
metatarsals
phalanges
technical intelligence
ecological intelligence
social intelligence
theory of mind

SUGGESTED READING

Byrne, Richard W. (1995). *The Thinking Ape*. Oxford University Press, Oxford.

Meldrum, Jeff E., and Hilton, Charles E. (2004). *From Biped to Strider: The Emergence of Modern Human Walking, Running, and Resource Transport*. Kluwer, Dordrecht, the Netherlands.

Savage-Rumbaugh, Sue, and Lewin, Roger (1996). *Kanzi: The Ape at the Brink of the Human Mind*. Wiley-Liss, New York.

Stanford, Craig B. (2003). *Upright*. Houghton Mifflin, Boston.

Chapter 12

EARLY HOMINIDS

THE SKY WAS HAZY AS THE SUN began to lower in the distance. The small hominids coughed slightly as they breathed the dusty air, the result of a burping volcanic eruption earlier in the day. A light rain began falling, dampening the ash layer that covered the ground like a dusting of snow and leaving small impressions as it did. They looked around furtively for a stand of trees and began moving toward them. Night would fall sooner than usual given the volcanic haze, and predators were sure to be on the move. Two hominids walking side by side were followed by a third as they moved toward the relative safety of the trees. Other animals moved about as well, disturbing the pristine ash fall. Gazing back over her shoulder briefly a young hominid watched the tracks they made, tracks similar to those you and I would make on a wet sand beach. She worried slightly that this strange new trail would give them away. Little did she know how permanent the trail would be, with the ash drying to a hard cement and future explosions soon covering the lot, protecting her resting place and immortalizing her journey.

Millions of years later in the 1970s, a team of paleontologists led by Mary Leakey was unwinding by playing Frisbee at Laetoli in northern Tanzania, not far from Olduvai Gorge. There, Paul Abell, a geochemist with the group, found the first evidence of the fossilized footprint trail that would ultimately yield the long-buried prints of those early hominids, probably *Australopithecus afarensis*. The tracks were well preserved and dated to about 3.6–3.7 million years ago. They told of a small but capable biped weighing 77–88 pounds and walking toward something.

The footprint trail made by this small group of hominids in the early Pliocene provides scientists with clues about the anatomy and behavior of our earliest ancestors. In this chapter we examine the fossil record for early hominids, beginning around 7 million years ago. We explore the adaptations of the very earliest hominids and how we recognize their fossils as such. Then we explore the radiation of the genus *Australopithecus*, whose species exhibit a diverse array of dietary adaptations and favored habitats. One species of the genus is likely to have given rise to our genus, *Homo*. At the end of the chapter we consider who the likely candidates are for the last common ancestor of *Homo* and set the stage for Chapters 13–15, in which we explore the evolution of our own genus.

WILL YOU KNOW A HOMINID WHEN YOU SEE ONE?

Hominids are the family of primates that includes humans and our ancestors since diverging from the last common ancestor with chimpanzees, about 6 million years ago. (Currently, there is a debate over the best name for this group; the traditional classification we use calls them hominids, but classifications based on molecular evidence call them *hominins* [Box 12.1 on page 322].) However, recognizing a hominid in the fossil record may not be easy because all we have to work with are fossilized skeletal remains. A fundamental adaptation in the hominid lineage is bipedality and

Box 12.1   A Rose by Any Other Name: Hominids versus Hominins

As you learned in Chapter 7, in the traditional classification system of the primates based on morphological characteristics the superfamily Hominoidea contains three families: the Hominidae, Pongidae, and Hylobatidae (Figure A). In this system the Hominidae, or hominids, are humans and our extinct ancestors, the Pongidae includes the great apes, and the Hylobatidae are the lesser apes. This system reflects how startlingly different we as bipeds are from our closest quadrupedal relatives. However, genetic distances suggest a slightly different classification system. Recall from Chapter 10 that humans and chimpanzees are more closely related to one another genetically than either is to gorillas. Therefore, humans and chimps should be grouped together, despite their morphological differences.

A new classification system that reflects these genetic distances is growing in scientific popularity. In this grouping the superfamily Hominoidea still includes three families: Hominidae, Pongidae, and Hylobatidae. However, two of these families include different animals than in the traditional classification. The Pongidae now includes only the orangutan. The Hominidae now includes humans and our extinct ancestors as well as the African apes and their ancestors, that is, everything since the last common ancestor with orangutans. Within the family Hominidae are two subfamilies that separate gorillas (Gorillinae) from chimpanzees and humans (Homininae). And within the subfamily Homininae humans and our

ancestors are in the tribe Hominini, or hominins for short. In this book we use the more traditional classification system and call humans and our exclusive ancestors

hominids because this is the way that most of the current literature is constructed. But you should be aware that the use of *hominins* is on the rise.

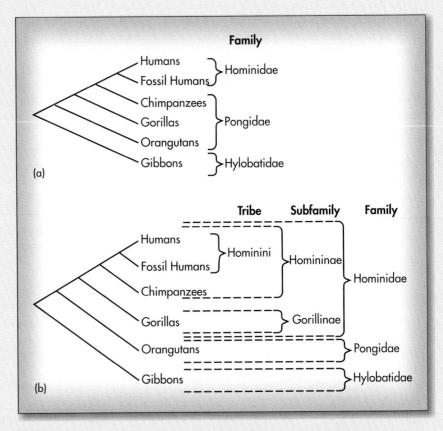

FIGURE A Taxonomic classification of hominins versus hominids. (a) A traditional classification system recognizes only humans and our fossil ancestors in the family hominidae which we refer to as hominids. (b) A classification system that reflects molecular relationships groups chimpanzees and humans together at the subfamily level in the homininae and humans and our ancestors in the tribe hominini, or hominins.

in Chapter 11 we discussed the anatomical characters that distinguish bipeds (humans) from quadrupeds (apes). We can use these features to recognize the fossilized remains of bipeds and hence hominids.

Another set of features of the skull and dentition that are not related to bipedality also differ between humans and apes. We infer that a fossil that possesses the human condition of these traits, or an intermediate condition tending toward the human condition, is a hominid. For example, the modern human dental arcade is shaped differently than an ape's. The human tooth row forms a rounded, parabolic arch reflecting the smaller anterior teeth (canines and incisors) and posterior teeth

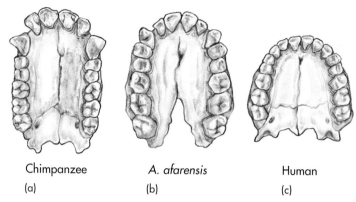

Chimpanzee
(a)

A. afarensis
(b)

Human
(c)

FIGURE 12.1 (a) Chimpanzees and other great apes have large incisors and projecting canines, a diastema, and U-shaped dental arcades caused by parallel rows of cheek teeth. (b) Early hominids like *A. afarensis* have relatively smaller canines, little or no diastema and a less U-shaped arcade with a still shallow palate. (c) Modern humans have very small canines, no diastema and a parabolic dental arcade.

(premolars and molars). The dental arcade of a primate with large canines, such as an ape or baboon, is broader in front (Figure 12.1) and U-shaped, with the teeth behind the canines forming two parallel rows. Early hominids tend to have somewhat smaller anterior dentition than such primates, but the arcade remains relatively U-shaped. In addition to changing the shape of the dental arcade, large anterior teeth also contribute to greater *facial prognathism*, the degree to which the face projects in front of the braincase. Like that of apes, the face of most early hominids is relatively prognathic.

The sizes and shapes of the teeth also differ between apes and humans. Lower vertebrates such as lizards and fish tend to have a **homodont** dentition, teeth that all look alike and serve essentially the same purpose: grabbing and bolting down food. Mammals are distinct in possessing a **heterodont** dentition; they have an array of different types of teeth in the mouth, each with a different function. The typical pattern in living primates is two incisors, one canine, two or three premolars, and three molars in each quadrant. As we saw in Chapter 7, the form and function of these four types of teeth differ depending on the primate group.

One aspect of the dental pattern that paleoanthropologists use to differentiate fossil apes from fossil hominids is the **CP$_3$, or sectorial premolar,** complex (Figure 12.2 on page 324). In a monkey or ape, the enormous canines of the upper jaw (the maxilla) must fit into a space or *diastema* in the tooth row of the lower jaw (the mandible) where they slide past the third premolar, hence the name *CP$_3$* for the area. (This premolar is called P$_3$, even though in an ape it is the first premolar in the tooth row, because the first and second premolars were lost during evolution). The back of the upper canine is sharpened, or honed, by the bladelike or sectorial P$_3$. As canines shorten during evolution, the blade on P$_3$ disappears and the tooth changes from having one cusp to having two. The very earliest **australopithecines** show some reduction of the canine, the absence or reduction of a diastema, and at least partial loss of the CP$_3$ honing complex, including the presence of a two-cusped P$_3$.

Another aspect of the teeth that differs between humans and apes is the thickness of the enamel, the white outer coating of our teeth. Living African ape enamel is thin, but our enamel is thick. All but the earliest hominids have somewhat thicker enamel than those apes, and this character has often been used to identify hominids. However, thicker enamel probably arose several different times during human evolution as an adaptation to the kinds of foods a group was eating,

homodont Having teeth that are uniform in form, shape, and function.

heterodont Tooth array in which different teeth have different forms and functions.

CP$_3$ complex Combination of canine and first premolar teeth that form a self-sharpening apparatus.

australopithecines The common name for members of the genus *Australopithecus*.

FIGURE 12.2
(a) A canine/premolar or CP_3 honing complex consists of a large, projecting upper canine passing across the bladelike edge of the lower premolar. Hominids lose this complex as the anterior teeth decrease in size. (b) Monkeys and apes such as this chimpanzee can be recognized in the fossil record by the anatomy of their teeth.

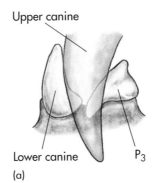

Upper canine

Lower canine P_3

(a)

(b)

so just the presence of thick enamel does not guarantee that we are looking at a hominid tooth.

Apes and humans also differ in brain size, cranial proportions, and cranial cresting. Although early hominids possessed essentially ape-sized brains, throughout hominid evolution brain size increases while facial size decreases. This change in proportions reflects both a deemphasis of the masticatory (chewing) system and an emphasis on brain size and probably intelligence (see Chapter 16). In early hominids this de-emphasis results in the loss of **cranial crests** in one lineage and as a result a more rounded braincase. The decrease in facial size also reflects the change in the size and shape of the teeth described previously.

So fossil hominids, including human ancestors since the split from the chimpanzee lineage, can be recognized by anatomical characters related to bipedality and by reduction of the canine teeth and CP_3 complex and changes in palate shape. The very earliest of the hominids show these features to only a very slight degree and therefore are often difficult to differentiate from fossil apes. Other changes that we associate with humans, such as our very large brain and extremely small face and jaws, appear only later in human evolution.

THE FIRST HOMINIDS?

The majority of the fossil evidence of the earliest hominids has come from the Great Rift Valley of East Africa, a broad expanse that runs north to south from the Horn of Africa at the Red Sea southward to Zambia (Figure 12.3). This ancient rift system is the result of tectonic activity, and the valley contains a string of lakes—Lake Victoria, Lake Turkana, Lake Tanganyika, and Lake Malawi, among others—that are often called the Great Lakes of Africa and a series of ancient volcanoes. The Rift Valley's tectonic history resulted in the creation and disappearance of lakes and streams during hominid evolution. These waterways provided likely habitats for species of early hominids, and the volcanic sediments allow radiometric assessment of fossil ages.

During the later Miocene from 10–5.5 million years ago and early Pliocene (5.5–4 million years ago) at least one lineage of apes made the adaptive shift to a terrestrial niche and became increasingly bipedal. As we learned in Chapters 9 and 11, the shift to bipedality came about partly in response to major climatic changes that were occurring in equatorial Africa in the late Miocene. This shift was accompanied by anatomical changes to the pelvis, spinal column and other body systems of hominids.

Molecular evidence suggests that the first signs of hominization should appear in lineages of late Miocene apes. Unfortunately, between 10 and 6 million years ago, the fossil record for the roots of the Hominidae is poorly represented. Between 7 and 4.4 million years ago, we have several candidates for the site of the earliest hominid remains, but all or some of them may represent fossil apes rather than hom-

cranial crests Bony ridges on the skull to which muscles attach.

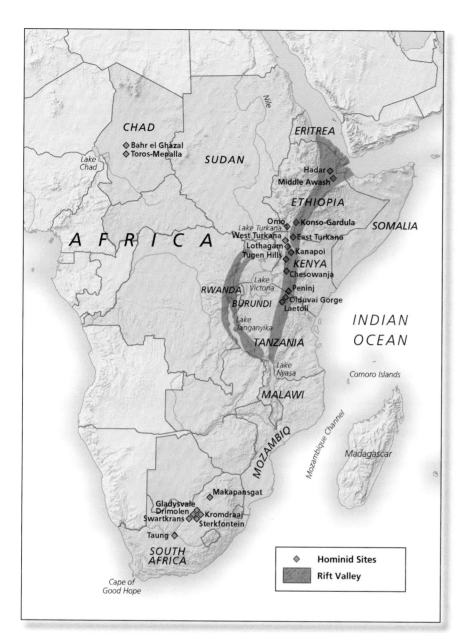

FIGURE 12.3 Geographic distribution of early hominids. Hominids are limited to the continent of Africa until about 1.7 million years ago. Some of the important sites for australopithecine and other early hominid fossils are located on the map. Although most known sites are in Eastern and Southern Africa, *Australopithecus* likely inhabited most of the African continent.

inids. Some of these sites (Lothagam, Tabarin, Djurab, and Tugen Hills) have produced evidence too fragmentary for an unambiguous answer. The others (Aramis and several Middle Awash sites) have produced a plethora of remains, but the analysis of the material is still in progress (Table 12.1 on page 326). Two recently discovered fossils from 7 to 6 million years ago may be the very earliest hominid remains known. However, both have generated much debate, and whether they are primitive hominids or fossil apes remains to be determined.

SAHELANTHROPUS TCHADENSIS (7.0–6.0 MYA)

A French expedition led by Michel Brunet discovered a fossilized skull, which the team nicknamed Toumai ("hope of life"), in the sands of the Djurab Desert in northern Chad in 2001 (Figure 12.4 on page 326). Formally named *Sahelanthropus tchadensis* ("the Sahara hominid from Chad"), the fossil was estimated to be between 5.2 and 7 million years old based on biostratigraphic correlations with East African sites, with 6–7 million years considered most likely by

TABLE 12.1	Candidates for the Earliest Hominid (all could be fossil apes)	
SITE	MYA*	SPECIES
Toros-Menalla, Chad	7.0–5.2	*Sahelanthropus tchadensis*
Tugen Hills, Kenya	6.0	*Orrorin tugenensis*
Middle Awash, Ethiopia	5.8–5.2	*Ardipithecus kadabba*
Lothagam, Kenya	5.8	??
Tabarin, Kenya	5.0	??
Aramis, Ethiopia	4.4	*Ardipithecus ramidus*
*MYA = millions of years ago		

Brunet. This age would make it the oldest member of the Hominidae. Toumai would also be the oldest hominid remains found west of the Great Rift Valley of East Africa; a jaw fragment assigned to *Australopithecus bahrelghazali*, also found by Brunet, dates to about 3 million years ago and is the only other hominid from Chad. The site where Toumai was found was a dry, lightly forested area near a lakeshore in the late Miocene, when *S. tchadensis* lived.

The Toumai fossil consists of a fairly complete skull, mandibular fragments, and isolated teeth. Surprisingly, the face is less prognathic than expected for an early hominid. Other characters that argue for Toumai being a hominid are a large browridge, somewhat smaller canine teeth, a non-functional CP_3 honing complex, no diastema, a horizontal nuchal plane, and possibly an anteriorly placed foramen magnum, which may indicate bipedality. However, Toumai also exhibits a number of apelike characters, including small brain size (cranial capacity is 320–380 cc), a U-shaped dental arcade, and somewhat thin enamel (but intermediate between chimps and *Australopithecus*). Milford Wolpoff, Brigitte Senut, and Martin Pickford (2002) have argued that deformation of the cranium makes assessing some features difficult and that Toumai's nuchal region indicates it was a quadruped. They further suggest that large female apes (such as gorillas) can have small canine teeth and that for these reasons Toumai is an ape, not a hominid. Alternatively, some of those who accept the hominid status of Toumai prefer to place it in the genus *Ardipithecus*, thus making it closely related to the somewhat later hominids from Ethiopia. In either case, Toumai is profoundly important because it fills key gaps in the fossil record in the 6 to 7-million-year age range and pushes the distribution of fossil hominids far to the west of the Rift Valley.

FIGURE 12.4 The skull of *Sahelanthropus tchadensis* is argued to be the earliest of the hominids and one of only two species known from western Africa. The significance of the specimen is still hotly debated given its recent discovery.

FIGURE 12.5 Brigitte Senut and Martin Pickford with the postcranial remains of *Orrorin tugenensis*. Discovered in 2000, "Millenium Man" may be among the oldest of the hominids, although its taxonomic position is still debated.

ORRORIN TUGENENSIS (6.0 MYA)

In 2001, paleoanthropologists Martin Pickford and Brigitte Senut announced the discovery of "Millennium Man" (Pickford and Senut 2001), so named because the discovery was made in the year 2000. The approximately 6-million-year-old fossils were found in the Lukeino formation of the Tugen Hills of Kenya and consist of fragmentary cranial and postcranial remains, most importantly multiple femoral (thigh bone) fragments (Figure 12.5). Pickford and Senut thought that the new fossils were so different from other known hominids that they chose a new genus name, *Orrorin tugenensis* ("hominid from the Tugen Hills"). They argue that *Orrorin* is a hominid because of a suite of postcranial characters that indicate it was a biped. The interpretation of bipedality has been doubted, however, because the anatomy of the femur and the arm are not conclusive indicators of bipedality. The remains do indeed indicate a larger body size than expected for a late Miocene ape and internal femur anatomy may support bipedality (Galik et al 2004). Also linking *Orrorin* to the hominids is the fact that the small teeth possess thick enamel. However, the upper canine is large and perhaps more apelike. Because we typically define hominids based on bipedal anatomy, more fossilized remains will be needed before we can make a final determination about the place of *Orrorin tugenensis* in the hominoid family tree.

ARDIPITHECUS RAMIDUS (4.4 MYA) AND ARDIPITHECUS KADABBA (5.8–5.2 MYA)

In 1994, an international team led by Tim White, Berhane Asfaw and Gen Suwa, announced the discovery of fossilized remains of a very primitive hominid in the northeastern part of Ethiopia near the Red Sea (Figure 12.6). In the Middle Awash

Pan troglodytes ♀   *A. kadabba*

FIGURE 12.6 *Ardipithecus kadabba* has large canine teeth that are only slightly smaller than those of living apes. The oldest of the Ethiopian hominids at 5.7 million years old, *A. kadabba* was ancestral to the 4.4 million-year-old *A. ramidus* and perhaps the rest of the hominid lineage.

The Afar triangle (Figure A) is among the most famous fossil-bearing regions, not because of the sheer quantity of fossils; the Gobi Desert of Mongolia has produced far more dinosaurs, for example. But because, the Afar has produced the most extensive record of human evolution from the earliest days of the Hominidae until the dawn of modern people.

Today the Afar in northeastern Ethiopia is a dry, dusty badlands region of baking hot days, chilly nights, and a stark, otherworldly landscape. But between 6 and 2 million years ago, the Afar was a fertile valley, the delta of a great river called the Awash, which flowed through the region en route to the sea. It is in and around the Awash that the most exciting finds have been made. One of the world's most active volcanic areas, including the enormous volcano Erta Ale, rings the northern edge of the Afar, and the sea borders its other side.

In 1972, Maurice Taieb led Donald Johanson to an unexplored site in the Afar called Hadar (from *Ahda'ar*, or "treaty stream" in the local Afar language). This 20-km² region holds an exquisitely preserved record of hominid evolution.

In late 1973 Johanson made the first major discovery, the fossil knee of an unknown primitive hominid that was later dated to 3.0 million years ago. In late 1974, during a follow-up expedition to Hadar, the team discovered more fossils, including the now-famous Lucy. Then in 1975, Johanson's team unearthed the

FIGURE A

"First Family," an entire group of Lucy's species, *Australopithecus afarensis*. In the three decades since, *A. afarensis* has become the best known of the early hominids.

A. afarensis is far from the only early human species from the region. Not far from Hadar, the international Middle Awash team including Tim White, Berhane Asfaw, Giday WoldeGabriel, and Gen Suwa discovered new hominids in the early 1990s and 2000s. *Ardipithecus ramidus* and *A. kadabba* lived in the then forested Afar 1.5 to 3 million years before *Australopithecus afarensis* roamed there.

More recent hominids and their artifacts have also been found in the Afar. In the late 1990s, the Middle Awash team found the earliest evidence of hominid meat-eating and butchery at Bouri, only 40 miles from Hadar. The fossilized remains of a 2.5-million-year-old hominid, named *Australopithecus garhi*, were found just a short distance from butchered antelope remains.

In 2000–2001, Ethiopian paleoanthropologist Sileshi Semaw's team found the oldest known stone tools at Gona, dated to about 2.6 million years ago (see Chapter 13). The team also found a nearly complete cranium from a 1.5 to 2.0-million-year-old hominid of the genus *Homo*, and numerous other hominid remains. More recently, a nearby site, Dana Aoule, has yielded stone tools that may be even older than those from Gona. From younger levels of the geological strata have come hand axes and remains of *Homo erectus* from 1.5 to 1.0 million years ago, as well as the famous Bodo specimen of a hominid that appears transitional between *Homo erectus* and more modern *H. sapiens* (see Chapters 13 and 14).

Most recently, the Afar was in the news after the discovery of a 160,000-year-old specimen of very early modern humans, from Herto (see Chapter 15). Discovered in 1997 by the Middle Awash team, the skulls from Herto form the recent end of an amazing spectrum of human use of the Afar region extending from the dawn of humankind to the near present.

region of an ancient river delta called the Afar Triangle the group collected fossils at a site called Aramis (Box 12.2). In the late Miocene and early Pliocene, Aramis had been a dense forest inhabited by ancestors of modern colobine monkeys and forest antelopes. This is very interesting because we expected to find the earliest hominids living in open savanna habitat, not closed forests similar to those in which apes live today (see Chapter 11).

The group first placed the 4.4 million year old fossils in the genus *Australopithecus* but noted that it was certainly more primitive than other *Australopithecus* species, that its locomotor pattern was in question, and that it could be a sister taxon of other hominids. This suggestion, and the fact that the specimen had some more primitive traits than *Australopithecus*, including thinner enamel and less postcanine enlargement **megadontia**, led the Middle Awash team to reassign the team species to a new genus, *Ardipithecus*.

Ardipithecus ramidus ("ground-living root hominid") is a primitive hominid. The initial announcement was based on isolated teeth, cranial fragments, and partial postcrania, some of subadults. The Middle Awash group argued for hominid status on the basis of a somewhat smaller canine and the anterior position of the foramen magnum, which may indicate bipedality. The researchers noted that the arm anatomy has aspects seen in both bipeds and quadrupeds, and they could not give a definitive answer to the question of locomotor pattern. In addition, the molars are apelike in size and have intermediate enamel thickness between apes and humans.

The bipedal nature and hominid status of *A. ramidus* are still questioned by some scientists. For now, there seems to be more certainty that *A. ramidus* was a biped and therefore a more likely candidate for the stem hominid than either *Orrorin* or *Sahelanthropus*. However, the possibility remains that *A. ramidus* may not be directly ancestral to later hominids.

In 2004, the same team that discovered *A. ramidus* announced new specimens they considered minor (subspecific) variants of *A. ramidus* that had lived much earlier, around 5.7–5.8 million years ago. On the basis of a more apelike dentition, the researchers have proposed elevating the former variant of *A. ramidus* called *A. r. kadabba* to its own species, *Ardipithecus kadabba*. These finds by Yohannes Haile-Selassie and colleagues have expanded our understanding of the range of variation in *A. ramidus*, and their anatomy and age suggest to some that the genera *Orrorin* and *Sahelanthropus* should be lumped into the genus *Ardipithecus* (Haile-Selassie et al., 2004). All early hominids would be defined by absence of a functional CP_3 honing complex.

AUSTRALOPITHECUS AND KIN

The identity of the first hominids is as contested as that of the earliest primates (see Chapter 10). Recognizing the very earliest members of a group is difficult for two reasons: The fossil record is fragmentary, so the evidence is incomplete, and the more ancient the ancestor, the more apelike the fossil. So it will be very hard to differentiate an early hominid from an ape, for example. The first hominids discussed previously fall in this nebulous position.

However, most of the early members of the hominidae do not suffer from this ambiguity and are assigned to the genus *Australopithecus*. The name *Australopithecus*, meaning "southern ape," was coined by Raymond Dart in the 1920s for the very first specimen of the genus ever discovered. Since that time discoveries of australopithecines have revealed an adaptive radiation of early hominids that filled a variety of habitat types in eastern, southern, and central Africa and are now known to have lived from 4.2 to about 1.0 million years ago. The genus *Australopithecus* can be usefully thought about as species of bipedal apes that are characterized by being small bodied (64–100 pounds) and small brained (340–500 cc), with moderately prognathic faces and a mosaic of primitive and derived craniodental anatomy (Figure 12.7 on page 330).

Scientists disagree a bit over the composition of the genus; the newly described genus *Kenyanthropus* has been proposed for one species that other scientists include in *Australopithecus*, and many researchers assign *A. robustus* and *A. boisei* to the genus *Paranthropus*. As we discover new specimens and new taxa, we will no doubt expand both the geographic distribution and the time span for this group and raise additional questions about their origins and descendants (Figure 12.8 on page 332).

megadontia Enlarged teeth.

Australopithecus afarensis (about 29 to 44 kg)

Australopithecus africanus (30-40 kg)

Homo sapiens (50 to 90 kg)

FIGURE 12.7 Comparison of hominid skeletons. The australopithecines (left and center) were short bipedal primates with relatively long arms and short legs. Compared to modern humans (right) the australopithecine torso was broad and funnel shaped.

AUSTRALOPITHECUS ANAMENSIS (4.2–3.9 MYA)

Around 4 million years ago several similar forms appeared roughly simultaneously. The oldest and most primitive of these is *Australopithecus anamensis* (Figure 12.9 on page 334). Announced in 1995, *A. anamensis* ("southern ape of the lake") was discovered by a team led by Meave Leakey. At separate sites near Lake Turkana, Kanapoi, and Allia Bay, Leakey's team found a portion of tibia, some teeth, and a partial mandible of a hominid. The researchers ultimately uncovered dozens of bone fragments, dating to 4.2–3.9 million years ago. Other remains, discovered in 1965 by a Harvard University excavation, have also been assigned to this species.

A. anamensis provides the earliest incontrovertible evidence of bipedality. In particular, the tibia has thickened bone at its proximal and distal ends, where bipeds place stress on their lower legs. Furthermore, the tibial plateau, where the tibia meets the femur, is enlarged as the result of the greater weight-bearing seen in the bipedal lower limb.

The *A. anamensis* teeth and jaws are more primitive than those of later hominids but more derived than those of early hominids such as *Ardipithecus*. The dental arcade is U-shaped, with parallel sides and large anterior teeth, and the palate is shallow, all features that are more apelike than human. Although the canine is smaller than in *Ardipithecus*, the root of the canine is longer and more robust in *A. anamensis* than in *Australopithecus afarensis* and there is a distinct CP_3 complex, but the molars of *A. anamensis* are shorter and broader. As in later australopithecines, the molar enamel of *A. anamensis* is distinctly thicker than in the more primitive *Ardipithecus ramidus*, all characters that make *A. anamensis* a hominid.

In many respects, the fossils of *A. anamensis* strongly resemble those of *A. afarensis*, and some researchers think the two species should be considered one and the same. However, in general *A. anamensis* is more primitive than *A. afarensis*, and this led Leakey's team to assign the fossils to a new hominid species. Leakey argues that although *A. anamensis* shares many anatomical traits with later australopithecines, it differs from them in aspects of the mandible and dentition that indicate it is probably ancestral to them.

Associated fossils of fish and aquatic animals indicate that both Allia Bay and Kanapoi were streamside forests in the early Pliocene, when *A. anamensis* roamed the area. The context in which the hominids lived is critical to our thinking about the selective pressures favoring bipedality. It was once thought that hominids evolved on savannas, but evidence such as that from Kanapoi and Allia Bay suggests that at least some early bipeds occupied forested areas.

AUSTRALOPITHECUS AFARENSIS (3.9–2.9 MYA)

Australopithecus afarensis was named as a result of the 1974 discovery of the famed specimen Lucy (named after the Beatles song "Lucy in the Sky with Diamonds"), by a team led by Donald Johanson working at Hadar, in the Awash Valley of the Afar triangle of Ethiopia (see Box 12.2). The discovery of the diminutive A.L. 288-1 (Lucy's museum catalog number) was extraordinary for two reasons. First, her anatomy is more primitive than that of any hominid discovered up to that time, and it includes a clear mosaic of human-like and apelike features. She stood a little over a meter tall and possessed a cranial vault suggesting a modest brain size about equal to that of an adult chimpanzee. Second, her skeleton is more complete than that of nearly any other fossil human. Although more primitive hominids have been discovered since, none is nearly so well studied, and *A. afarensis* has remained the benchmark by which the anatomy of all other early hominids is interpreted. In addition to Lucy, thousands of finds of *A. afarensis* have been made in the Afar in the past 30 years, as well as at other East African localities. In fact, the **type specimen** of the species, the specimen that according to the laws of zoological nomenclature serves as the original anatomical reference for the species, is the LH 4 mandible from Laetoli, Tanzania.

There are several key anatomical features of *A. afarensis* (Figure 12.10 on page 334). The cranium and teeth of *A. afarensis* are intermediate in appearance between those of a living ape and a modern human. The cranial capacity is small but slightly larger than that of earlier hominids and living apes (range 350–500 cc). A complete skull recovered by Bill Kimbel and Don Johanson shows that the *A. afarensis* face was prognathic, but not as much as in the living apes, and the cranial base was relatively flat, similar to that of living apes (Figure 12.11 on page 335) (Kimbel et al. 2004). Cranial cresting including both a **sagittal crest** (for the temporalis muscle) and a **compound temporonuchal crest** (formed where the neck muscles approach the temporalis muscles) are present, especially in presumed males. These crests tell us that *A. afarensis* still placed a premium on chewing. The dental arcade is U-shaped, with large anterior teeth, parallel rows of cheek teeth, and a shallow palate, all primitive, apelike traits. But as expected of a hominid, the canine teeth are much smaller than those of a chimpanzee or of the earlier hominids *Ardipithecus* and *A. anamensis* but larger than those of more recent hominids or other *Australopithecus* species. With smaller canine teeth, no CP_3 honing complex is present in *A. afarensis*, and many specimens have P_3s with two cusps. The molar and premolar teeth are modest compared with those of later *Australopithecus* but much larger than those of the earliest hominids and *A. anamensis*.

In its postcranial skeleton, *A. afarensis* is clearly an accomplished biped. *A. afarensis* possesses a pelvis, with short, broad iliac blades that curve around the side of the animal, forming the attachment area for the gluteal muscles, which aid in bipedal walking (see also Chapter 11). The femur is angled in toward the knee to keep the foot under the center of gravity, the condyles on the lower end of the femur are enlarged, and the groove for the patella is deepened. The tibia is

type specimen According to the laws of zoological nomenclature, the anatomical reference specimen for the species definition.

sagittal crest Bony crest running lengthwise down the center of the cranium on the parietal bones; for the attachment of the temporalis muscles.

compound temporonuchal crest Bony crest at the back of the skull formed when an enlarged temporalis muscle approaches enlarged neck (nuchal) muscles, present in apes and *A. afarensis*.

Figure 12.7 EARLY HOMINID EVOLUTION

The earliest hominids appeared around 6 million years ago in western and eastern Africa. About 4 million years ago *Australopithecus*, a bipedal genus characterized by small brains, large jaws, and small body size arose. *Australopithecus* is probably the first stone tool maker, and one species is likely to have given rise to *Homo*.

Several species of the genus overlapped with one another in time and space, probably avoiding competition by relying on slightly different food resources. In one lineage, the robust australopithecines (*A. aethiopicus, A. robustus and A. boisei*), several species evolved massive jaws, molar teeth, and cranial skeletons optimized for producing large chewing forces. These hominids probably relied on hard to open food items during times of nutritional stress.

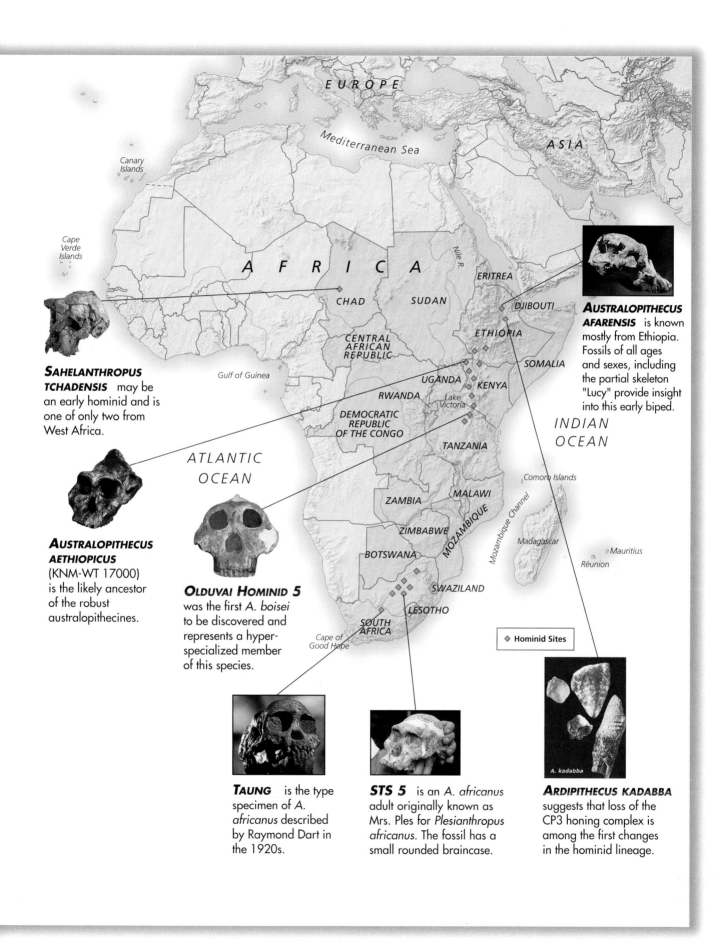

EUROPE

Mediterranean Sea

ASIA

Canary
Islands

Cape
Verde
Islands

AFRICA

Nile R.

CHAD

SUDAN

ERITREA

DJIBOUTI

ETHIOPIA

CENTRAL
AFRICAN
REPUBLIC

SOMALIA

Gulf of Guinea

UGANDA

KENYA

RWANDA

Lake
Victoria

DEMOCRATIC
REPUBLIC
OF THE CONGO

INDIAN
OCEAN

ATLANTIC
OCEAN

TANZANIA

Comoro Islands

ZAMBIA

MALAWI

Madagascar

Mozambique Channel

Mauritius

Réunion

ZIMBABWE

MOZAMBIQUE

BOTSWANA

SWAZILAND

LESOTHO

SOUTH
AFRICA

Cape of
Good Hope

Hominid Sites

SAHELANTHROPUS TCHADENSIS may be an early hominid and is one of only two from West Africa.

AUSTRALOPITHECUS AETHIOPICUS (KNM-WT 17000) is the likely ancestor of the robust australopithecines.

OLDUVAI HOMINID 5 was the first *A. boisei* to be discovered and represents a hyper-specialized member of this species.

AUSTRALOPITHECUS AFARENSIS is known mostly from Ethiopia. Fossils of all ages and sexes, including the partial skeleton "Lucy" provide insight into this early biped.

TAUNG is the type specimen of *A. africanus* described by Raymond Dart in the 1920s.

STS 5 is an *A. africanus* adult originally known as Mrs. Ples for *Plesianthropus africanus*. The fossil has a small rounded braincase.

A. kadabba

ARDIPITHECUS KADABBA suggests that loss of the CP3 honing complex is among the first changes in the hominid lineage.

333

FIGURE 12.9 The remains of *Australopithecus anamensis* from Kenya date to about 3.9 to 4.2 million years old.

modified to bear more weight, and the big toe is in line with the other toes. Indirect evidence of bipedal walking in *A. afarensis* comes from the Laetoli footprint track described at the start of this chapter that, on the basis of its age and location, is thought to have been made by *A. afarensis*. All these characters tell us that *A. afarensis* was a striding biped and clearly, therefore, a hominid.

The postcranial skeleton also differs from that of modern humans, however (see Figure 12.7). The thorax is more funnel shaped, similar to an ape's, perhaps indicating that *A. afarensis* had a large gut and a largely vegetal diet. *A. afarensis* arms are somewhat longer relative to leg length than in modern humans but their anatomy tells us that the arms were not used for walking. They also have more curved phalanges of both the toes and fingers; smaller, perhaps more flexible tarsal bones; and aspects of the shoulder and hip joints that may indicate some level of arboreality.

This mosaic pattern of postcranial anatomy indicating a successful biped that probably spent time in the trees as well has stirred debate about the type of bipedalism practiced by *A. afarensis*. Perhaps the pelvic and lower limb anatomy of *A. afarensis* indicate the species walked nearly as efficiently and gracefully as we do today (Johanson et al., 1982; Lovejoy, 1978, 1988). But anatomical aspects of the feet, toes, and lower limbs all seem to suggest some degree of adaptation to arboreality (Stern and Susman, 1983; Susman et al., 1984). It seems likely that on the ground *A. afarensis* moved on two legs. They may have retreated to the trees to escape from predators and to forage for fruits and leaves during the day and to sleep at night. Habitat reconstructions based on antelope remains found at *A. afarensis* sites suggest the hominids were living in woodlands rather than on open savannas (Chapter 9; Reed, 1997), which supports the idea that trees served as a refuge from predators or as sleeping areas for these small hominids.

It is likely that *A. afarensis* lived in groups, and because they were very sexually dimorphic, they probably were not monogamous. The largest adults from Hadar are, in some measures, nearly twice the size of the smallest *A. afarensis* (Lucy is one of the very smallest). This extensive range of variation has led some experts to suggest that *A. afarensis* is actually two species, not two sexes. However, the prevailing opinion is that *A. afarensis*, shows an extreme level of sexual dimorphism similar to that of modern orangutans (McHenry, 1991) (Table 12.2).

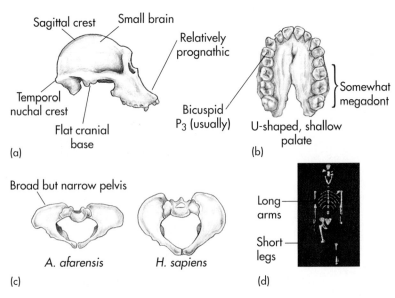

FIGURE 12.10 Key features of *Australopithecus afarensis* include (a) a small cranial capacity, and cranial crests (b) a shallow, U-shaped palate with reduced canine and (c, d) features of the postcranial skeleton that indicate habitual bipedality.

TABLE 12.2	Comparisons of *A. afarensis*, Great Ape, and Modern Humans	
	CRANIAL CAPACITY (CC)	SEXUAL DIMORPHISM (MALES *X* PERCENT HEAVIER)
A. afarensis	450	56%
Chimpanzee	400	15%
Gorilla	500	50%
Orangutan	400	Nearly 100%
Early genus *Homo*	600	63%
Modern human	1,400	15%

FIGURE 12.11 A complete cranium of *A. afarensis* from Hadar, Ethiopia shows a prognathic face and small braincase.

From this we infer that *A. afarensis* had a polygynous mating strategy because in living primates great sexual dimorphism usually is associated with multiple mates (see Chapter 7).

AUSTRALOPITHECUS BAHRELGHAZALI (3.5–3.0 MYA)

As we have seen, most early fossil hominids have come from eastern Africa, with two exceptions: the early hominid *Sahelanthropus tchadensis* and the later-living *Australopithecus bahrelghazali*. *A. bahrelghazali* ("the hominid from Antelope Creek"), announced in 1995, was the first of the West African hominids to be discovered by Michele Brunet. The species is known from a single fossil: the front of a mandible with seven teeth (Figure 12.12). Most researchers think that *A. bahrelghazali* is in fact a member of *A. afarensis* or at least that it is too fragmentary to define a new species around. Until additional fossils are known, the major importance of this find is its confirmation that hominids lived over much of the African continent, not only in Eastern Africa.

KENYANTHROPUS PLATYOPS (3.5 MYA)

Working on the arid western shore of Lake Turkana in northern Kenya, a place made famous by many other fossil finds, a team led by Meave Leakey discovered an early hominid dated to 3.5 million years ago (Leakey et al., 2001). Leakey and Fred Spoor thought the specimens, particularly a nearly complete but crushed cranium, were sufficiently different from members of the genus *Australopithecus* that they should be given a new genus name (Figure 12.13 on page 336). The researchers based their argument on the specimen's surprisingly flat face, a derived trait of later hominids rather than of *A. afarensis* and its kin, and its small molar teeth, a condition more primitive than the other australopithecines. They proposed the name *Kenyanthropus platyops* ("the flat-faced hominid from Kenya"). Some researchers, think *Kenyanthropus* should be considered just another species of *Australopithecus* or even a member of *A. afarensis*, although it differs from *A. afarensis*

FIGURE 12.12 The mandible of *A. bahrelghazali*. The first hominid found in western Africa, *A. bahrelghazali* dates to about 3.5 million years ago.

FIGURE 12.13 The cranium of *Kenyanthropus platyops* dates to about 2.5 million years ago in Kenya. The species takes its name from the very flat face.

not only in facial morphology but also in having other, more primitive cranial characters. Tim White thinks that the specimen was so deformed during fossilization that interpretation of *Kenyanthropus'* relationships to other hominids may be in error. Given the recency of the find, this question remains a point of contention.

Whether a distinct genus or a separate species, at 3.5 million years old, *Kenyanthropus* lived at the same time as *A. afarensis*. The presence of multiple taxa, or an adaptive radiation based on dietary differences, as Leakey's group suggests, means that one of these taxa is not a direct ancestor of modern people. It is not possible at this time to determine which is more closely linked to later hominids. But we now must acknowledge that the early days of the bipedal hominid radiation were more complex, and perhaps less linear, than we had realized.

AUSTRALOPITHECUS GARHI (2.5 MYA)

Another recent discovery of an australopithecine species has yielded possible information about how these creatures lived. The Middle Awash team discovered the skull fragments and other pieces of a previously unknown hominid at Bouri, not far from other hominid discoveries in the Middle Awash Valley in the Afar region of Ethiopia (Asfaw et al., 1999). These fossils date to approximately 2.5 million years ago. *Australopithecus garhi* ("the unexpected southern ape from the Afar") had a small brain (450 cc), a prominent prognathic face, large canines, and a sagittal crest (Figure 12.14). In most respects *A. garhi* is quite primitive anatomically,

FIGURE 12.14
Australopithecus garhi dates to about 2.5 million years ago in Ethiopia and was found in the same beds as early stone tools. It is slightly younger than and its cheek teeth are more robust than *A. afarensis*.

even for an australopithecine. Some workers argue that *A. garhi* may be better interpreted as a late surviving member of *A. afarensis*; remember that that species existed until about 2.9 million years ago in the same geographic area. Besides its age, *A. garhi* differs from *A. afarensis* only in a few anatomical characters, including having larger cheek teeth (molars and premolars) that diverge from one another near the back of the palate and a slightly larger canine. If the postcrania from a nearby site belong to this species, then, surprisingly, *A. garhi* has more human-like proportions between its arms and legs (because of a long femur) but apelike proportions between its upper arm (humerus) and forearm (radius and ulna). These proportions seem to differ from those of *A. afarensis,* which has a shorter lower limb.

Regardless of its taxonomic attribution, the proximity of *A. garhi* fossils to the earliest known stone tools is significant. At Bouri, and also at nearby Gona, archaeologists found stone tools in association with the fossilized remains of antelope and other likely prey species. These bones show cut marks and percussion marks, unmistakable evidence that early hominids had been using stone tools to butcher carcasses. We cannot say whether *A. garhi* was the butcher, but no other early hominid fossils have been found in the same strata. If supported by further field research, this would be the earliest evidence of tool use by an australopithecine. Although *A. gahri*'s role in later evolution cannot be resolved on the known morphology, the species ultimately could be ancestral to later *Homo*.

AUSTRALOPITHECUS AFRICANUS (3.5–<2.0 MYA)

With the exception of *Sahelanthropus tchadensis*, whose hominid status is uncertain, and *A. bahrelgazali*, we have thus far examined only hominids that occurred in East Africa. But southern Africa also saw a major radiation of hominid species during the Pliocene. In fact, the first australopithecine ever discovered, the Taung child, was discovered in southern Africa, which is why the genus is called *Australopithecus*, or "southern ape-man."

There are a few key differences between the study of fossils in southern and eastern Africa. Unlike the open-air sites of East Africa, most South African fossil sites are in cave and cliff deposits. Hominids and other animal remains are found in a mixture of ancient marine limestone and bone cemented into a **breccia**. The hominids did not live in the caves in which they were found, although the caves could easily be misinterpreted this way because natural processes can produce fossil deposits that look very much like they were created by humans. Careful taphonomic study of the caves and their included fossils reveals instead that the skeletal remains probably fell into the South African caves, which themselves are the result of dissolution of the bedrock by ground water (see Chapter 9). South African caves often appear as sinkholes in the ground, similar to those seen in parts of Florida, and often have trees growing along their rims (Figure 12.15 on page 338). Animals are thought to have fallen into these caves by accident or in some cases to have been introduced after having been killed by carnivores, such as leopards, which cache their kills in the branches of trees overhanging the sinks to protect them from larger carnivores (Figure 12.16 on page 339) (Brain, 1981).

There is another key difference between the East and South African fossil record. Volcanic ash that forms the matrix in which many East African fossils are embedded can be dated quite precisely using the ^{40}Ar/^{39}Ar techniques you read about in Chapter 9. However, South African deposits cannot be dated using the ^{40}Ar/^{39}Ar techniques. Although some uranium series dates have been attempted, paleontologists must rely mostly on geomagnetic polarity data and relative dating methods. They compare the fauna (biostratigraphy) and geology (lithostratigraphy) of rock strata containing human fossils with strata in other regions such as East Africa that contain similar fossil sequences but can be more precisely dated. This provides an estimate of the age of the deposits. However, the stratigraphy of the

breccia Cement-like matrix of fossilized rock and bone. Many important South African early humans have been found in breccias.

FIGURE 12.15 South African cave sites were formed by the dissolution and collapse of bedrock that later trapped sediments and animals, including hominids. (a) Initially bedrock is dissolved by groundwater, (b) when the water table lowers, there may be roof collapse into the chamber and stalagmite/stalactite formation, (c) with time the chamber may erode further, eventually connecting to the surface, and (d) vegetation including trees often grow near these wet openings and sediments and animals may fall into the chambers. (e) Over time other openings to the surface may form introducing new sediments and bones. (f) Erosion of the surface exposes the stratigraphy of these sediments, the relative ages of which are difficult to interpret because of their complex history.

South African caves is complex, so establishing the sequence of which fossil species lived contemporaneously with others sometimes is not possible.

In 1924, Raymond Dart, a young professor of anatomy in Johannesburg, South Africa, received a shipment of crates loaded with fossils collected from the Taung limestone quarry. One of the crates held a tiny partial skull, which Dart recognized as that of a very primitive hominid, and a juvenile at that (Figure 12.17). The face and teeth were attached to a fossilized impression of the interior of the skull as well, a so-called natural **endocast**. After carefully extracting the specimen from the limestone matrix, Dart realized that this endocast revealed the general appearance and size of the brain of the creature.

"The Taung Child" appeared to be a very young, apelike hominid who retained some baby teeth, which suggested an age of 5 or 6 years, based on modern human growth rates. This estimate of Taung's age at death has long been in debate because we can't be sure whether early hominids grew up along the same trajectory as modern people or as the great apes. These days, most researchers think that the answer is closer to an ape developmental rate and that the Taung child was about 2 or 3 years old at the time it died.

In an article for the British science journal *Nature,* Dart (1925) argued that Taung was a hominid, based on the position of the foramen magnum, which was almost directly centered on the underside of the cranium, as it would be in a biped (see Chapter 11). An authority on the brain, Dart devoted much space in the article to describing the features of the brain's surface that could be detected from the endocast, features that supported his contention that Taung was a direct link between the small-brained apes and larger-brained humans. Dart derided the place accorded to Piltdown man (see Box 9.1), which he thought had too apelike a jaw to be human, and also the *Homo erectus* skull dubbed Java Man (see Chapter 13).

endocast A replica (or cast) of the internal surface of the braincase that reflects the impressions made by the brain on the skull walls. Natural endocasts are formed by the filling of the braincase by sediments.

FIGURE 12.16 Some fossil remains of early hominids show evidence of carnivore bite marks similar to those made by lions and other carnivores suggesting that our early ancestors may have been hunted.

He concluded his paper by acknowledging Darwin's long-ago assertion that Africa, not Europe or Asia, was the birthplace of humanity.

The response of the British scientific establishment who still accepted Piltdown Man as evidence both of the big-brained nature of early humans and of Britain as the cradle of humankind, was predictable. In a series of letters to *Nature*, nearly all of the great minds of early twentieth-century paleoanthropology rejected the significance of the Taung discovery. The majority thought that Taung was merely a new variety of ape and implied that Dart (who had a reputation as a grandstander) had sought attention for himself in his bold assertions about the fossil.

Because of the controversy surrounding Taung and the entrenched view about Piltdown, it was not until nearly 1950 that *Australopithecus* was given its rightful place as a southern African forerunner of modern humans. Meanwhile, many other discoveries of fossils of the same species as Taung were being made. Most of these fossils have been dated to between 3.5 and 2.4 million years ago, with the possibility that some of the material may be much younger, possibly little more than 1 million years old.

The oldest *A. africanus* fossils come from Sterkfontein, Taung, Gladysvale, and Makapansgat (Figure 12.18 on page 340). Dart's colleague Robert Broom, a

FIGURE 12.17 The Taung child, the first of the australopithecines to be discovered, is the type specimen for *Australopithecus africanus*.

FIGURE 12.18   The site of Sterkfontein in South Africa is excavated for *Australopithecus* remains.

FIGURE 12.19   Francis Thackeray holding Sterkfontein 5, a presumed female *Australopithecus africanus*, that shows the rounded vault and moderate facial prognathism of that species.

Scottish-born doctor and amateur paleontologist, followed up on Dart's early claims for hominids in South Africa in the mid-1930s at the limestone quarry at Sterkfontein, near Johannesburg. In 1947, Broom discovered a partial skull of a presumed female *A. africanus* from Sterkfontein, dubbed "Mrs. Ples," short for the genus name "*Plesianthropus*" that he assigned to it (Figure 12.19). This discovery has been estimated to date to 2.6 million years ago and made it impossible for skeptics of Taung to insist that *A. africanus* might have only been an ape because the adult form represented by Mrs. Ples was clearly a bipedal hominid (Broom, 1947). Later, Phillip Tobias made important contributions in this area as well, and hundreds of *A. africanus* specimens of various ages and probably both sexes have been found since Broom's initial work. A nearly complete skeleton of *A. africanus* is being extracted from the deposits at Sterkfontein.

A. africanus is more derived than *A. afarensis* in several aspects of its cranial skeleton (Figure 12.20). Compared with *A. afarensis*, *A. africanus* has a larger braincase (about 450–550 cc, still quite small by modern standards), a rounded vault that lacks cranial crests and has fewer air cells in it, a less prognathic face, and a more flexed cranial base. The teeth of *A. africanus* are generalized and the molars more modestly proportioned than in later, more specialized australopithecines such as *A. robustus* and *A. boisei*. This has led to a classification into gracile australopithecines, including *A. africanus*, and robust

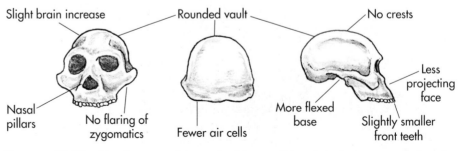

FIGURE 12.20   Key features of *Australopithecus africanus* include a rounded vault without cranial crests, a slightly flexed cranial base and moderate facial prognathism.

FIGURE 12.21 Olduvai Hominid 5 (OH 5) is a hyper-robust member of *Australopithecus boisei* discovered in Tanzania by Mary Leakey.

FIGURE 12.22 Key features of robust australopithecines include adaptations to heavy chewing such as a large sagittal crest and flaring zygomatics, a dished face and strongly flexed cranial base.

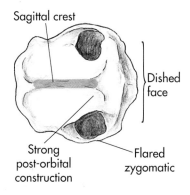

australopithecines for *A. robustus*, *A. boisei*, and *A. aethiopicus*. *A. africanus* has small anterior teeth, especially canines, compared with earlier hominids such as *A. afarensis* but larger anterior teeth than most of the later robust australopithecines. However, the molars of *A. africanus*, although clearly larger than in earlier forms, are smaller than the enormous molars of the robust australopithecines.

A. africanus was a small-bodied biped that possessed the broad and short iliac blade of the pelvis and structural adaptations in the spine, leg and foot that characterize habitual bipeds (see Chapter 11). Based on an extensive collection of postcranial remains, body size has been estimated at about 65–90 pounds for *A. africanus* (which is slightly smaller than the later robusts). *A. africanus* has the same general body plan as *A. afarensis*, with a more funnel-shaped thorax than in humans, although *A. africanus'* arms may be shorter (Figure 12.7).

The other animals found at *A. africanus* sites suggest that these hominids, like those in eastern Africa, were living in woodland and open woodland environments (Reed, 1997). These wooded areas may have provided some protection from predators. There are currently no earlier hominids in South Africa than *A. africanus*, but it is generally assumed that *A. africanus* evolved from a population of East African hominid, probably *A. afarensis*, that migrated to the south.

THE ROBUST AUSTRALOPITHECINES (OR PARANTHROPINES)

The robust australopithecines are a group of early hominids that, more clearly than any other group, appears to have been an evolutionary dead end because of their extreme anatomical specializations. The first robust was found in 1938 in South Africa by Robert Broom, and the East African species was first found by Mary Leakey at Olduvai Gorge, Tanzania, in 1959 (Figure 12.21).

The robust australopithecines are united by a suite of cranial features related to their feeding adaptation that make them extremely efficient at producing a lot of force at their molars (Figure 12.22). These cranial features often are thought of as an adaptation to **hard object feeding**, chewing tough food items such as hard-shelled nuts or fibrous vegetation. In fact, early fossils were nicknamed "nutcracker man" for this reason. To produce large bite forces, the **muscles of mastication** that produce chewing force are maximized in size and placement for mechanical efficiency. The robust australopithecine skull reflects these changes. One muscle, the temporalis, that sits on the side of the braincase lifts the mandible. (You can feel your own temporalis doing the work of chewing if you touch your temples while closing your jaw.) In the robusts, the temporalis is enlarged and moved forward, which is reflected in the presence of an anterior sagittal crest for its attachment, the presence of extreme **postorbital constriction** to accommodate its large size, and

hard object feeding Chewing tough, hard-to-break food items such as nuts or fibrous vegetation.

muscles of mastication The chewing muscles: masseter, temporalis, medial and lateral pterygoids.

postorbital constriction The pinching-in of the cranium just behind the orbits where the temporalis muscle sits. Little constriction indicates a large brain and small muscle; great constriction indicates a large muscle, as in the robust australopithecines.

zygomatic arch   The bony arch formed by the zygomatic (cheek) bone and the temporal bone of the skull.

the flaring of the **zygomatic arches** laterally to accommodate the bigger muscle (Figure 12.23). Another muscle, the masseter, sits on the outside of the jaw and also raises the mandible. (You can feel your masseter work if you put your fingers on the outside and rear of the jaw and clench your teeth.) The masseter is moved forward in robusts by placement of the zygomatic (cheek) bones to which it attaches forward over the teeth (resulting in a dished face in which the cheeks extend further forward than does the nose) and by flexing of the cranial base, which brings the face (and the teeth) up under the vault and chewing muscles. The mandible is large and deep, and the face is tall to counter these muscle forces. The molars and premolars are enormous, further indicating that at least at some times of the year these hominids relied on a diet that included tough objects. The premolars are like small molars and are referred to as molarized. In contrast, the anterior teeth are tiny, indicating the low degree of importance they had in the dietary habits of the robusts.

The robust australopithecine lineage thus has a suite of cranial adaptations related to chewing on tough foods. Scientists think that these adaptations allowed robust australopithecines to survive during times when not much food existed because they were specialized for eating a kind of food that other hominids could not eat. Most of the time robusts probably ate a lot of different things, but when food was scarce they relied on their "fallback food." Isotopic research on South African robusts shows that they were omnivores, probably eating some kind of animal protein (perhaps termites) at some times of the year. There is also evidence that they may have used bone tools to access this food, and they have been found with stone tools, as well, suggesting that they were fairly intelligent creatures. However, their reliance

FIGURE 12.23 Muscles of mastication in robust australopithecines. (a) The temporalis muscle (red) attaches to the sagittal crest and the mandible, and the masseter muscle (pink) attaches to the zygomatic bone which is moved directly over the molar teeth. (b) From above we can see that robust australopithecines had much greater muscle attachment area on their skulls than do modern humans (right).

on tough foods during times of resource scarcity seems to become more specialized through time. Eventually, this overspecialization would lead to their demise when food resources changed too dramatically and their fallback foods disappeared.

Habitat reconstructions based on the other animals found at robust australopithecine sites suggest that these hominids, like *A. africanus* and those in eastern Africa, were living in woodland and open woodland environments (Reed, 1997). However, some robusts seem also to have lived in slightly more open habitats but always to be associated with streams or waterways.

Some scientists think that the robust australopithecines are so different from other australopithecines that they should have their own genus, *Paranthropus*. The decision to define a new genus in the fossil record rests on the evidence that a sufficiently different adaptive plateau exists for a given group of species, in this case the robusts, than for other closely related species. Proponents of the use of *Paranthropus* argue that the masticatory features of the robusts are evidence of such an adaptive plateau. By using this separate genus name these scientists also are accepting that all the robust species are more closely related to one another than they are to species outside of *Paranthropus* and thus that they descend from a recent common ancestor. As we shall see, other scientists disagree as to how closely related the robust species are to one another, so in this book we take a conservative approach and include them in *Australopithecus*.

Australopithecus (P.) aethiopicus (2.7–2.5 mya)   There is no evidence that the robust australopithecines left any descendants, but there is some tantalizing evidence about their origin. In 1985, Alan Walker and Richard Leakey found the skull of a very primitive robust australopithecine that is a good candidate for the ancestor of both later robust species, *A. (P.) boisei* and *A. (P.) robustus*, and also shows some links to other early hominids (Walker et al., 1986). The fossil was discovered on the western shore of Lake Turkana, an area famous for many other fossil hominid finds. When unearthed, the fossil was stained black by minerals in the sediment and therefore was dubbed "the Black Skull" (Figure 12.24). The skull was originally assigned to *A. boisei* because it retains key traits derived in *A. (P.) boisei*. Because it retains primitive characters, some scientists prefer to call it *A. (P.) aethiopicus*.

A. (P.) aethiopicus shares the suite of masticatory characters described for the robust australopithecines but with some modifications and some more primitive characters as well. *A. (P.) aethiopicus* has a sagittal crest, dished face, flared zygomatics, and huge molars that both *A. (P.) boisei* and *A. (P.) robustus* possess, although the sagittal crest is positioned more posteriorly in *A. (P.) aethiopicus*

FIGURE 12.24 *Australopithecus aethiopicus*, called the black skull because of its manganese staining, is an early robust form dating to about 2.5 million years ago in Kenya.

(Figure 12.24). But *A. (P.) aethiopicus* also retains primitive traits from an earlier hominid, *A. afarensis*. *A. (P.) aethiopicus* differs from other robusts and is more similar to *A. afarensis* by being small-brained (about 400 cc), with a prognathic face, flat base, and large anterior teeth. There are no known postcranial remains of *A.(P.) aethiopicus*. At 2.5 million years old, *A. (P.) aethiopicus* is also slightly older than *A. (P.) boisei* but younger than *A. afarensis*. Many paleoanthropologists think that *A.(P.) aethiopicus* is primitive enough to be the evolutionary link between the early trunk of the hominid family tree and the specialized branch that led to the robust australopithecines (Figure 12.25). However, because *A. (P.) aethiopicus* and *A. (P.) boisei* uniquely share features (such as a heart-shaped foramen magnum) that differentiate them from *A. africanus* and *A. (P.) robustus*, some scholars still consider it possible that the East and South African robusts could represent two more distantly related lineages that have converged on a shared anatomy based on a similar dietary adaptation to hard object feeding, at least during fallback periods.

A. (P.) boisei (2.3–1.2 mya)   The culmination of the lineage that started with *A. (P.) aethiopicus* is *A. (P.) boisei* (Figure 12.21). In 1959, the skull that Mary Leakey found while working alone one day at Olduvai became the type specimen for a new genus and species, *Zinjanthropus boisei* ("hominid from Zinj [after a benefactor named] Boise"). It was later renamed *Australopithecus boisei* (Leakey, 1959).

Since 1959, East African sites in Kenya, Tanzania, and Ethiopia have yielded a plethora of *A. (P.) boisei* remains, both cranial and postcranial. Although the Leakeys did not know it at the time, Zinj represented the hyperspecialized end of this East African species of robusts. The species spans the time period from about 2.3 to about 1.2 million years ago, based mostly on radiometric ages. The brain size is about the same as that of the robusts from South Africa, and the postcranial skeleton is large, with an estimated body size between 75 and 110 pounds (McHenry, 1992, 1994).

The cranial skeleton of *A. (P.) boisei* reflects the suite of masticatory adaptations discussed previously and some features shared with *A. (P.) aethiopicus* but not shared with the South African forms; these include the shape of the nasal bones and browridge, and the absence of nasal pillars. However, an important fossil find from Konso, Ethiopia, shares the South African condition of some of these features, muddying the distinctions.

A. (P.) robustus (2.0–1.5 mya)   When Robert Broom discovered the first robust australopithecine in 1938 at Kromdraai in South Africa, most of the scientific com-

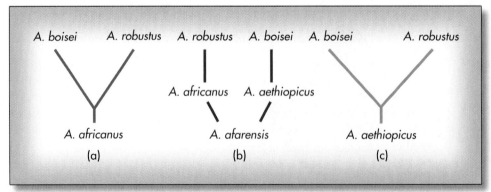

FIGURE 12.25 Some possible phylogenies for the robust australopithecines. (a) *A. africanus* may give rise to both *A. robustus* and *A. boisei*. (b) *A. afarensis* may give rise to two separate lineages, one of East African robusts the other of South African robusts. (c) Or *A. aethiopicus* may give rise to both *A. robustus* and *A. boisei*.

munity still doubted the presence of early hominids in Africa. However, Broom recognized that the forward location of the foramen magnum indicated a biped and thus a hominid rather than a robust ape skull (Figure 12.26). This was also a species quite different from the more gracile australopithecine fossil from Taung. The characters that led Broom to his conclusion are the suite of masticatory characters discussed previously. These characters led Broom to name the genus *Paranthropus* ("next to man"), and the species *robustus*. Later the Swartkrans remains were reassigned to genus *Australopithecus*.

FIGURE 12.26 *Australopithecus robustus* is a South African robust australopithecine first discovered in 1938.

P. robustus is known principally from Kromdraai, Swartkrans, and Drimolen, and based on biostratigraphy it dates to about 2.0–1.5 million years ago. Its cranial capacity is between 500 and 550 cc, and the postcranial skeleton indicates a body size of about 70–90 pounds (McHenry, 1993, 1994). *A. (P.) robustus* differ from their East African counterparts in several minor characters, including the shape of the nasals and browridge and the presence of bony pillars next to the nose.

In addition to hard-shelled tough foods, isotopic studies suggest that *A (P.) robustus* also ate substantial quantities of animal protein. (see Chapter 9 to read about the method). Andrew Sillen (1988) found that the ratio of isotopes of strontium and calcium in *A. (P.) robustus* fossils was consistent with what we would expect in a grassland inhabitant whose diet was composed at least partly of animal protein; *Australopithecus africanus* does not have such values. Julia Lee-Thorp and her colleagues (1994) suggested on the basis of carbon isotopic values that *A (P.) robustus* probably ate grass-eating insects such as termites. Supporting this idea are the wear patterns found on the ends of animal bones probably used by *A. (P.) robustus* as digging sticks (d'Errico et al., 2001). The researchers think that, unlike chimpanzees who improvise termite-collecting tools from blades of grass and twigs (see Chapter 11), the robust australopithecines used a more powerful bone tool to open up the massive mounds of hardened soil in which termites live.

UNDERSTANDING THE AUSTRALOPITHECINE RADIATION

Just as the Miocene period was a time of great diversification of the apes, the Pliocene was a time of adaptive radiation and diversification of the early hominids. We still do not know how large this radiation was, but continual discoveries of new taxa suggest that many more species of australopithecines and other hominids remain to be found.

Some of the increase in diversity in the Pliocene results from the "naming game," the splitting into two of species or genera formerly recognized as one. But most of the recently named new species are based on new fossil discoveries. As we have seen, the naming of *Kenyanthropus*, *A. bahrelgazali*, and *A. garhi* drew some criticism from scientists who consider them to be just another species of *Australopithecus* or members of previously named species. Additional finds and comparative studies should resolve these issues.

COHABITATION

It is difficult for us to imagine today that at various times in early prehistory, two or even three hominid species lived in the same regions of the African continent

TABLE 12.3	Examples of Potentially Contemporaneous Hominids by Region		
AGE (MYA)[*]	WEST AFRICA	EAST AFRICA	SOUTH AFRICA
~6	Sahelanthropus tchadensis	Orrorin tugenensis	
3.9		Australopithecus afarensis, A. anamensis	
3.5	A. bahrelghazali	A. afarensis, K. platyops	A. africanus
2.5		A. garhi, A. aethiopicus	A. africanus
2.5–2		A. boisei, A. garhi	A. africanus, A. robustus
2–1.5		A. boisei, Homo sp.	Homo sp., A. robustus

[*]MYA = millions of years ago

(Table 12.3). In some of these cases, two species occurred contemporaneously in the same habitat. When two or more species with similar diets and behaviors coexist in the same habitat, we predict that some key aspects of their biology will diverge as a result of competition. If this did not occur, then one species or the other probably would become rare or extinct in the face of head-to-head food competition with the other.

In the case of the australopithecines, taxa that appear to have shared the same habitat at the same time also show striking morphological differences. This suggests that natural selection molded them to avoid feeding competition.

One good way to understand the likely ecological relationship between sympatric early hominids is to look at how living great apes share a habitat. In Africa, there are many forests in which chimpanzees and gorillas coexist. Both apes travel on the ground to find food, but chimpanzees spend far more time feeding in trees than gorillas do. Both build nests each night, but gorilla nests usually are on the ground, and chimpanzee nests normally are high in trees. And although both species prefer fruit to all other forest foods, gorillas fall back on high-fiber leafy foods in lean seasons, whereas chimpanzees forage far and wide to continue eating fruits. In other words, although these two large-bodied apes are similar in many respects, there are key differences that probably are the result of their ancestors evolving together in African forests and that today allow them to coexist (Tutin, 1996; Stanford and Nkurunungi, 2003).

In addition to A.(P.) africanus and A. (P.) robustus in southern Africa, potential cases of sympatry in the hominid fossil include A. (P.) boisei (robust) and early genus Homo (gracile) in eastern Africa, A. garhi and A. (P.) aethiopicus in eastern Africa, and A. afarensis and K. platyops in eastern Africa. In all these cases it has been argued that anatomical differences between taxa reflect differences in dietary adaptations that suggest the hominids were partitioning the available resources, which allowed them to coexist.

TOOLS AND INTELLIGENCE

We used to think that only members of our own genus Homo were clever enough to make tools. Australopithecines were considered dim-witted in comparison and without tools. However, until the 1960s tool making was also unknown in the living great apes. Since, tool making is actually common in the great apes and even in some monkeys, although none make stone tools, we might expect that early hominids including australopithecines fashioned tools, perhaps out of organic materials, but did not necessarily make durable tools.

Dart, one of the few early proponents of australopithecine culture, proposed a so-called **osteodontokeratic culture** in which he envisioned early hominids using the bones, teeth, and horns of animals as tools (hence the name he gave the culture). Dart also considered the australopithecines to be bloodthirsty hominids. However, Dart's evidence for the tool culture was the accumulated remains found in South African cave sites, which more probably represent natural accumulations of bone rather than australopithecine toolkits. Although the osteodontokeratic culture has not held up under more recent scrutiny, Dart may have been one of the few scientists to be right in saying that australopithecines made and used tools.

The archaeological record for australopithecines is quite limited, but there is tantalizing evidence that these hominids were smarter than we think. The earliest evidence of tool use in the genus is the possible association between *A. garhi* and the butchered remains of animals about 2.5 million years ago in Ethiopia. At other sites in East and South Africa stone tools are found in the same beds and even at the same localities as the remains of robust australopithecines. No other hominid genera are known from these particular contexts, so this may indicate the production and use of stone tools by australopithecines.

Hand anatomy also gives us a small clue that the robust australopithecines may have been capable of tool production. The robusts share thumb anatomy that is similar to that of tool-making hominids such as ourselves and other members of the genus *Homo*, but earlier species of *Australopithecus* such as *A. afarensis* lack this anatomy. This may indicate that the robusts could make stone tools, although it does not tell us whether they did.

If tool production requires sophisticated cognitive skills, as argued in Chapter 11, then the australopithecines were at least as sophisticated as living great apes. However, it is not until around 2.5 million years ago, well into the australopithecine radiation, that we see the first use of stone tools. Thus the additional access to resources that these tools provide could not have been among the primary reasons that the genus arose. Indeed, as we discussed in Chapter 11, the benefits of bipedality as a foraging strategy appear to be the primary advantage that early hominids had over their quadrupedal relatives.

ANCESTORS AND DESCENDANTS

Based on the anatomy and timing of the known fossil australopithecines, there are several ways to envision the phylogenetic relationships among the early hominids we have examined in this chapter (Figure 12.27 on page 348). There is no single consensus model, and a number of plausible models exist. Based on anatomy, many scientists derive *A. afarensis* from the more primitive *A. anamensis* and then see *A. afarensis* as the base of the radiation of *A. africanus*, *A. garhi*, and *A. aethiopicus* and possibly the *Homo* lineage. Each of these lineages takes the *A. afarensis* anatomy in a slightly different direction depending on the environmental conditions for which it was selected. Many see *A. (P.) aethiopicus* giving rise to the robust radiation of *A. (P.) boisei* and *A. (P.) robustus*, whereas others derive the East African robusts from *A. (P.) aethiopicus* but the South African robusts from *A. africanus*. This splitting into South and East African lineages means that these scientists don't think the robusts shared a last common ancestor exclusive of other australopithecines and therefore are not part of a separate genus, *Paranthropus*. *A. africanus*, *A. afarensis*, and *A. garhi* have all been implicated as possible ancestors for the genus *Homo*; however, one thing that almost all scientists agree on is the idea that the robust australopithecines are too specialized to be ancestral to genus *Homo*. The key to a good potential ancestor is that it exists early enough to give rise to the later groups, is not more derived than those groups, and has characters that look as if they could give rise to later groups.

osteodontokeratic culture
A bone, tooth, and horn toolkit envisioned by Raymond Dart to be made by *Australopithecus*.

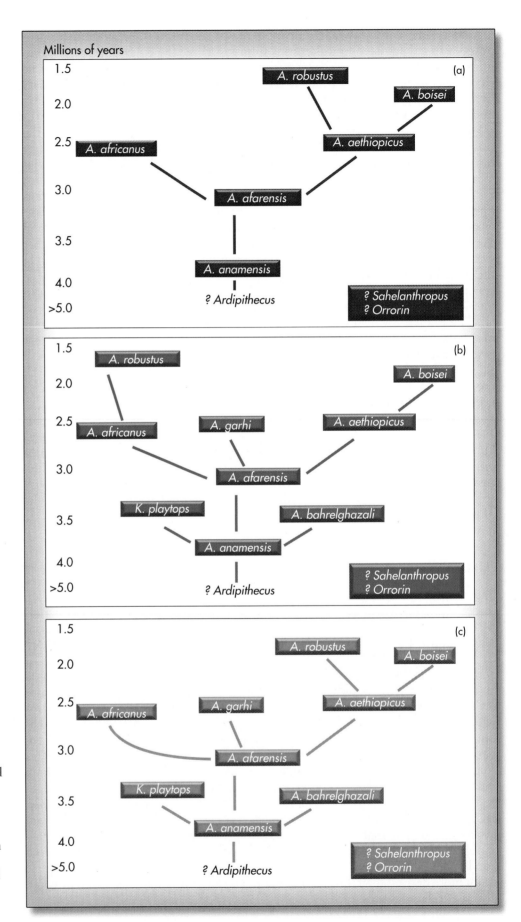

FIGURE 12.27 Three possible phylogenies for the australopithecines with *A. anamensis* as the stem ancestors and recognizing a small number of species and close relationships between (a) *A. robustus* and *A. boisei*, (b) a larger number of species and only distant relationship between *A. robustus* and *A. boisei*, or (c) a large number of species and a close relationship between *A. robustus* and *A. boisei*.

Because the fossil record is sparse, each new fossil discovery throws the tree into brief disarray, after which paleoanthropologists try to sort out the most likely phylogeny suggested by the sum of the evidence. This may seem as though scientists cannot agree but disagreement is a healthy feature of evolutionary science. Each new find tests previous hypotheses and produces new interpretations, new research, and new results that push the state of our understanding of human ancestry forward.

QUESTIONS FOR FUTURE PALEOANTHROPOLOGISTS

Despite all we have learned about the earliest hominids through the eight decades since Raymond Dart's time, the questions still far outnumber the answers.

How Many Species Were There? First and foremost, we don't know how extensive or diverse the early hominid radiation really was. In all likelihood there are more species, perhaps many more, waiting to be found. The rate of discovery of new hominid fossil taxa has increased in recent years; today a new species is described nearly every year.

How Large Was Their Geographic Distribution? So far the fossil record suggests that the earliest divergence of the australopithecines from ancient ape stock occurred in eastern Africa, probably in the Great Rift Valley. But the discovery of *Sahelanthropus* and *A. bahrelghazali* in Chad reminds us that very early hominids, or very hominid-like apes, also lived far outside East Africa. Conditions ideal for bone preservation, fossilization, and later discovery of ancient hominids are present in East Africa. Less ideal conditions and less intensive prospecting have limited the fossil yield from West Africa to date.

But we must remember the old adage that absence of evidence is not evidence of absence. The African continent is enormous, and there is no reason to believe that early hominids did not inhabit most of it. If early hominids radiated geographically across the warmer regions from east to west, as chimpanzees do today, there are vast areas and diverse habitats into which they may have radiated. If even a few of the australopithecine taxa were as versatile ecologically as chimpanzees, most of the African continent may have once been populated by early hominids. Their remains are yet to be discovered. However, there is, no evidence that early hominids ever occurred outside the African continent.

Did Only One Lineage Emerge from the Ancestral Ape Stock? There are two ways to interpret the earliest stages of hominid evolution. The first is the traditional view that between 5 and 7 million years ago, a single lineage of primitive apelike anthropoids evolved into hominids, and some species of this lineage eventually evolved into *Homo sapiens*. The alternative view is that early in hominid evolution, natural selection experimented with bipedal posture and locomotion and increased brain size, and there were multiple lineages of hominid-like apes in Africa. In this latter view, bipedalism was not the defining hallmark of hominids; more than one bipedal lineage arose, but only one eventually survived to become our direct ancestor. The defining characteristic of the hominids would thus remain unidentified but might include dental changes such as absence of a functional CP_3 honing complex. The degree of taxonomic diversity in the Pliocene will remain an intriguing and important question in decades to come as more and more fossils reinforce some views of the hominid phylogeny and contradict others.

As we have seen, the earliest hominids were a primitive lineage of very apelike creatures that enjoyed a diversification and wide distribution in Africa between about 6 and about 1 million years ago. Sometime around 2.5 million years ago, one lineage of the australopithecines gave rise to a new lineage with a slightly larger brain; genus *Homo*. Initially, *Homo* was not so anatomically different from australopithecines, but shifts in brain size, body shape, and perhaps technology gave it an advantage over *Australopithecus*. As we shall see in Chapters 13–15, although the exact point at which we should assign an early hominid to our own genus, *Homo*, is still debated, later shifts in foraging strategy and technology eventually led to modern people.

SUMMARY

1. **Why are the earliest hominids difficult to identify?**

   As you get closer to the LCA, hominid features appear more like the LCA making it difficult to distinguish early hominids from other apes.

2. **What are the several traits that define the australopithecines? Include both cranial and postcranial traits.**

   The genus *Australopithecus* is defined by being bipedal but of small body size, with a funnel-shaped thorax, small canines but postcanine megadontia, and small brains.

3. **What key anatomical traits define *A. afarensis*?**

   A. afarensis is characterized by a mosaic of primitive and derived characters, including bipedality, reduced canine size loss of the CP3 complex, and postcanine megadontia (derived) and small brain size, compound temporonuchal crest, flat cranial base, shallow, U-shaped palate, large anterior teeth, long arms, and curved phalanges (primitive).

4. **Why do we have precise dates on the ages of East African early hominid discoveries and only rough estimates of those in South Africa?**

   East African sites more often have volcanic rocks associated with them that can be dated using radiometric techniques such as argon–argon and potassium–argon. South African sites rely mainly on biostratigraphic age correlations.

5. **What key anatomical traits define the robust australopithecines?**

   The robust australopithecines share a suite of anatomical characters related to mastication. These include enormous postcanine megadontia and increased jaw size, enlarged chewing muscles (as reflected in a large sagittal crest, strong postorbital constriction and flaring zygomatics) and a dished face and flexed cranial base.

CRITICAL THINKING QUESTIONS

1. How many australopithecine species do you think are waiting to be discovered? How would you go about estimating how many more might exist?

2. If we discover an early hominid that exhibits great sexual dimorphism, such as the Hadar fossils, what are some of the inferences we can make about the social behavior of those creatures in life?

3. If gracile and robust australopithecines share the same habitat, why don't we see evidence of their hybridizing?

4. As recently as the late 1990s, we believed *A. afarensis* to be the stem of the hominid family. What happened to cast doubt on that view, and what does it tell us about the human family tree?

KEY TERMS

homodont
heterodont
CP$_3$ (sectorial premolar)
   complex
australopithecines
cranial crest
Great Rift Valley

megadontia
type specimen
sagittal crest
compound
   temporonuchal crest
breccia
endocast

hard object feeding
muscles of mastication
postorbital constriction
osteodontokeratic
   culture

SUGGESTED READINGS

Johanson, Donald, and Edey, Maitland (1981). *Lucy: The Beginnings of Humankind.* Simon & Schuster, New York.

Morell, Virginia (1995). *Ancestral Passions: The Leakey Family and the Quest for Humankind's Beginnings.* Simon & Schuster, New York.

Chapter 13

RISE OF THE GENUS *HOMO*

"F OR THE FOLLOWING FEW WEEKS, the excavating brought nearly nonstop excitement, but there was some meticulous scientific work behind the celebrations. . . . The bones kept coming, right up to the last moment, so we knew we would have to come back. Nearly everything we found was part of our skeleton. . . . When we closed down the site for the season, on September 21, 1984, we had found more of *Homo erectus*—the classic missing link—than anyone had ever seen. The next four field seasons laboring in the pit, as we came to call the enormous excavation, would see 1,500 cubic yards of rock and earth moved by hand. Our schoolboys, who worked with us faithfully year after year, grew from adolescents to young men while the Nariokotome boy, as we took to calling the specimen, grew from a fragment of skull to the most complete early hominid skeleton ever found."
—from *The Wisdom of the Bones,* by A. Walker and P. Shipman

The discovery of the skeleton of the Nariokotome boy, the remains of most of a *Homo erectus* skeleton, dramatically changed our understanding of early *Homo.* It showed us for the first time that the modern human proportions of long lower limbs and large body size existed as early as 1.5 million years ago. This finding suggests that the transition from the apelike body proportions of *Australopithecus* to modern human proportions occurred in the short time interval between 2.3 and 1.7 million years ago. What we know about the transition from *Australopithecus* to earliest *Homo* rests ultimately on the fossil record. And what we know of the fossil record, including the discovery of the Nariokotome boy, rests in equal parts on skill, perseverance, planning, and sheer luck. In fact, the early fossil record of genus *Homo* is remarkably sketchy in comparison to the australopithecine record, making the task of understanding the origin of the genus that much more difficult.

In this chapter we examine the early radiation of the genus *Homo,* from its beginnings in apelike African hominids to the first migrations out of Africa and into other parts of the Old World. First we consider the definition of the genus *Homo* and its earliest species. We discuss the appearance of *Homo erectus,* whose larger brain and body size may signal an adaptive shift in diet, who makes increasingly sophisticated tools, and who may use fire. Then we examine early tool technologies and subsistence. And finally we consider the debate over later stages of *H. erectus,* setting the stage for the discussion of other hominids outside Africa in Chapters 14 and 15.

DEFINING THE GENUS *HOMO*

The most primitive species assigned to genus *Homo* are not all that different from some australopithecines. Recall that the australopithecines were the earliest hominid radiation, featuring cranial capacities below 600 cc and a mosaic of apelike and human-like features. We used to think that even the earliest genus *Homo* were morphologically much more modern-looking than any australopithecine. However, recent discoveries have shown that some members of genus *Homo* had small brains and perhaps primitive postcranial skeletons. We also used to think that genus *Homo* was the sole

353

maker and user of stone tools. But in South Africa there are associations between stone tools and only *robust australopithecines,* and in East Africa there are similar and perhaps earlier associations between *Australopithecus garhi* and stone tools (although another hominid may have been the maker). So perhaps we can no longer consider the time-honored hallmark of genus *Homo,* stone tool making, to be unique to the genus.

Recall also that a genus name implies a certain adaptive strategy, so the switch from *Australopithecus* to *Homo* should tell you to expect to see a suite of adaptive differences between species in the two genera. In general, genus *Homo* differs from australopithecines by having a larger, more rounded braincase, a smaller, less projecting face, smaller teeth, and eventually a larger body and more efficient striding bipedalism. These features may be related to an adaptation that includes a shift in foraging strategy to a more animal-based diet, greater ranging, and greater food processing through tool use. However, early members of the genus *Homo* differ less strongly from australopithecines than later members and therefore are harder to distinguish from them.

There is much taxonomic debate over the application of names to the fossil record for genus *Homo.* Depending on the scientist, earliest *Homo* is conceived of either as a single, variable species (*H. habilis*) or as multiple, less variable species (usually *H. habilis, H. rudolfensis,* or *H. sp. nov,* referring to an unnamed new species of *Homo*). Similarly, *H. erectus* is seen as either a single species or two species, *H. ergaster* and *H. erectus,* and the presence of any of these taxa in Europe and the transition to modern humans is hotly debated. All this disagreement results in part from the paucity of the fossil record, differences in species concepts (lumpers versus splitters), and the inherent difficulty of applying a static classification system to the dynamic process of evolution.

EARLIEST GENUS *HOMO*

The great antiquity of the genus *Homo* was established at Olduvai Gorge in the 1960s by Louis and Mary Leakey. Their discovery of a nearly 2 million-year-old juvenile partial skull, Olduvai Hominid 7(OH 7), possessed a brain larger than

FIGURE 13.1 Key anatomical features of *Homo habilis* include reduced facial size, a parabolic palate, and some brain enlargement.

FIGURE 13.2 Crania of KNM-ER 1813 and 1470 differ enough that some scientists include them in two different species.

TABLE 13.1	Cranial Differences between Key Early *Homo* Fossils	
	KNM-ER 1813	KNM-ER 1470
Cranial capacity	510 cc	775 cc
Browridges	Moderate to Small	None
Face	Small	Large
Posterior tooth size	Small	Large

any known australopithecine and differed markedly from *Zinjanthropus boisei* (see Chapter 12). Louis Leakey, Philip Tobias, and John Napier included the new fossil in the genus *Homo* (Figure 13.1). They named the new species *Homo habilis,* or "the skilled human or handy man," referring to the use and manufacture of stone tools. Their announcement was met with initial skepticism; however, additional fossils from Olduvai including OH 16 and 24 and more recently OH 62 and 65, confirmed their initial diagnosis.

In the early 1970s at Koobi Fora on the eastern shore of Lake Turkana, Richard Leakey's team discovered a more intact skull of *H. habilis,* known by its National Museums of Kenya catalog number KNM-ER 1470 and believed to be approximately 1.8 million years old (Figure 13.2). KNM-ER 1470 has a large cranial capacity of 775 cc. Additional finds of *H. habilis* from Koobi Fora include KNM-ER 1805, 1813, and possibly 3732, which range in geological age from about 1.8 to 1.9 million years old and vary greatly in size (Figure 13.2).

Many scholars think that differences between the largest (1470) and smallest (1813) Koobi Fora crania are too great to fall within the variation of a single species (Table 13.1). In contrast to 1470, 1813 has a very different appearance, with a brain almost one-third smaller (only 510 cc), smaller teeth, and a differently proportioned face. To further complicate things, the smaller postcranial remains have longer upper limbs (a primitive trait) than do the larger specimens. Most who separate these fossils into two species place Olduvai Hominid 7, the type specimen and name-bearer of the species, with 1813, calling this *H. habilis,* while 1470 becomes the type specimen for *H. rudolfensis.* Other researchers think 1470 and 1813 may be a male and female, respectively, of the same hominid species.

Splitting early *Homo* into two species would mean that there were sympatric members of genus *Homo* living in East Africa between 1.5 and 2.0 million years ago along with sympatric australopithecines. It would be unclear which of the two species of early *Homo, H. habilis* or *H. rudolfensis,* gave rise to later species of *Homo* such as *H. erectus* and *H. sapiens.* Is the larger brain of 1470 a link to *H. erectus*? Or are the dental and facial similarities of the two a link between 1813 and *H. erectus*?

Although some of these specimens are bigger-brained than others, none show the extensive cranial and postcranial enlargement or adaptation for long stride length seen in *H. erectus*. Bernard Wood and Marc Collard (1999) suggested that the smallest-brained early *Homo* resembles larger-brained australopithecines and should be relegated to *Australopithecus* because of similarities that suggest they shared similar patterns of behavior and ecology. Wood and Collard particularly focus on differences in the postcranial skeleton between *H. erectus* and *H. habilis*. In this book we use *H. habilis* rather than *Australopithecus habilis*, but Wood and Collard have given important food for thought to researchers studying the emergence of the genus *Homo*.

EARLY TOOL USE

Oldowan　The tool industry characterized by simple, usually unifacial core and flake tools.

tool industry　A particular style or tradition of making stone tools.

core　The raw material source (a river cobble or a large flake) from which flakes are removed.

flake　The stone fragment struck from a core, thought to have been the primary tools of the Oldowan.

hammerstone　A stone used for striking cores to produce flakes or bones to expose marrow.

Whoever the first toolmaker was, stone tools occur in the record starting about 2.5 million years ago. The earliest tools are known as the **Oldowan** industry, so named for their first discovery at Olduvai Gorge in Tanzania. We refer to stone tools made in a particular way or tradition as a **tool industry** (Figure 13.3). Oldowan tools consist mainly of **cores**, lumps of stone, often river cobbles modified from the original rock by flaking pieces off it, and **flakes**, the small fragments taken from the core. Archaeologists used to think the core itself was the cutting tool, but new experimental evidence suggests the flakes were used as tools. The cores probably were used to produce flakes until they became too small and were discarded (Schick and Toth, 1993). Flakes can be extremely sharp and are effective at cutting through tough animal hides and removing meat from bones. Other Oldowan tools called **hammerstones** were used to crack open the bones of large animals to extract marrow and to remove flakes from cores. Oldowan tools are deceptively simple in appearance; if you held one you might not be sure whether it was human-made or naturally created. However, archaeologists, some of whom are proficient stone tool makers, can distinguish human manufacture patterns from natural breakage of stone.

Tool making was first and foremost an adaptation to the environment of the late Pliocene. Through the use of tools hominids could exploit animal resources,

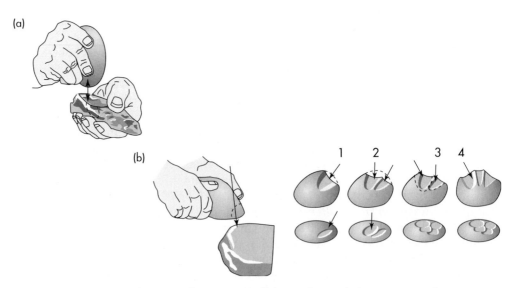

FIGURE 13.3　Oldowan tools are simple flake tools struck from a core using an (a) hammerstone or (b) an anvil technique. The flakes are useful for cutting through hides, meat, or plant material.

which became an increasingly important adaptive strategy for early humans. Based on the archaeological record, early *Homo* probably carried tools with them rather than constantly discarding or continually making them anew. This signifies the importance of tools in the foraging patterns of these hominids. Being bipedal (and therefore having their hands free) and larger-brained, these early hominids were far more capable than chimpanzees at tool production and use, from acquiring the raw materials, to making the tools, and finally to using them.

Archaeologists studying Oldowan tools and the bones associated with them think these tools were used primarily to remove meat from and crack open the bones of animals that were either hunted or scavenged. These butchery tools are found in abundance at some Oldowan sites in East Africa, including Olduvai, Koobi Fora, Gona, Lokalalei, and Kanjera. They are sometimes found in association with many fossilized animal bones, such as pigs, ungulates, elephants, carnivores, and even other primates. Taphonomic analysis (see Chapter 9) indicates that some of these accumulations were created by hominids and not simply by natural processes such as erosion, water movement, or the actions of carnivores. Some archaeologists have undertaken research on the behavior of carnivores such as hyenas and lions to understand how patterns of bone accumulation and modification by these meat-eaters differs from the likely actions of early hominids. A clumped pattern of distribution of the tools on the landscape strongly suggests that these are either sites of intensive food processing by hominids or places where tools were manufactured and then carried somewhere else to be used (Potts, 1988).

Archaeologists specializing in the study of stone tools have categorized the patterns of tool use at various Oldowan sites in East Africa. Some of these are believed to have been **butchering sites**: A variety of mammal bones, some with direct evidence of butchering such as cut and percussion marks, are found in association with stone tools. One such site at Olduvai Gorge contains the remains of a hippo with cut marks on its bones along with scores of flakes, suggesting the hippo had been butchered by early hominids. Some sites, where stone implements are found in great abundance, are **quarrying sites**, where hominids went to obtain the raw material for the tools. A third type of site is what the archaeologist Glynn Isaac (1978) called a **home base**. Isaac hypothesized that hominids repeatedly brought butchered carcasses back to a central place, possibly with a particular amenity such as a shade tree or a water source nearby, where they slept and ate in greater safety than at the site where the animal was killed. At such a home base, the hominids would have been manufacturing or refining tools as well. Some archaeologists are skeptical of this idea, arguing that natural processes such as movement of remains by water, wind, and animals, may account for what look like human-created bases of activity. Others believe that the accumulations may represent caches of material made by hominids for their later use rather than campsites. Some sites at Olduvai Gorge have been called home bases for their abundant accumulations.

We don't know for certain which early hominid made which tools because we don't find hominid fossils actually holding the tools. We can only infer tool use by the association between tools and hominid remains in the same excavations. Even this is dangerous, because antelope are the most abundant fossils found in association with stone tools, and we are quite sure the antelope are not the tool makers! Despite the enormous amount of evidence of meat eating, in the form of butchered bones, we don't know how often a group of early *Homo* might have actually eaten meat or how important meat (or marrow) was in their diet. Did a group of *H. habilis* butcher and consume one large mammal per week? Per month? Per century? Did all members of the group participate in this butchering activity and in the feast? How much did the incorporation of stone tool manufacture and annual consumption affect other aspects of early hominid behavior, ecology, physiology, and biology? It seems that after 2.5 million years ago, meat eating took on increasing importance, but the method of measuring that importance has been contentious.

butchering site A place where there is archaeological evidence of the butchering of carcasses by hominids. The evidence usually consists of tool cut marks on fossilized animal bones or the presence of the stone tools themselves.

quarrying site An archaeological site at which there is evidence that early hominids were obtaining the raw material to make stone tools.

home base Archaeological term for an area to which early hominids may have brought tools and carcasses and around which their activities were centered.

HUNTING AND SCAVENGING

The debate about the role of meat in the early human diet has a long and tumultuous history, beginning with Raymond Dart's recognition of an "osteodontokeratic" culture that he attributed to South African australopithecines' carnivorous diet (Dart, 1925; see Chapter 12). The earliest hominids almost certainly ate most of the same foods that modern apes eat: fruit, leaves, seeds, insects, and some animal prey. The first indisputable evidence of meat eating is stone tool use for carcass butchery (based on cut marks on fossilized bones of antelope), probably by earliest genus *Homo* but possibly also by *A. garhi*, at about 2.5 million years ago. Before this time, if emerging humans were making and using tools, they were using materials such as wood or unmodified bone that did not accumulate or preserve in the fossil record. And if they were eating meat or marrow without the assistance of stone tools, we have no visible archaeological record of it.

We would like to know whether our own lineage arose with the help of a hunting or scavenging way of life because each of these entails a different set of behavioral adaptations. There are currently three main models for how early hominids acquired carcasses. Did bands of early humans courageously attack and slaughter large and dangerous game (hunting), did they fight off large predators such as saber-tooth cats to gain access to significant amounts of meat (confrontational scavenging), or did they creep nervously up to decomposing, nearly stripped carcasses to glean a few scraps of meat and fat (passive scavenging)? Mostly, however, discussion focuses on differences between hunting and scavenging. As discussed in Chapter 18, in 1966 a perspective on human evolution known as "Man the Hunter" (see Box 18.1) was articulated in which men played the important role of obtaining the highest-quality nutrients and the calories that their households would use. It also implied that men had a natural right to occupy the glamour role of clever-minded forager, meat provider, and conqueror in human societies because hunting selected for intelligence. Many anthropologists took issue with this perspective, particularly because in some of the traditional societies that are most vaunted for the man's role in hunting, up to 85% of the protein obtained by a household came not from men but from women gathering foods such as nuts, tubers, and small animals (Tanner and Zihlman, 1976).

The reaction to "Man the Hunter" had the effect of swinging scientific research toward examining the possibility that *H. habilis* and kin were scavengers, not hunters, and that they were not necessarily the sole accumulators of fossil bone (Brain, 1981). At some fossil sites there was evidence that *H. habilis* had been butchering animal carcasses: Cut marks from their stone tools were visible on the fossilized bones of animals. When anthropologists Rick Potts (1988) and Pat Shipman (1986) studied the bones of animals from Oldowan sites, they found cut marks made by ancient, sharp-edged tools as well as tooth marks made by the gnawing of contemporaneous lions, hyenas, and leopards (Figure 13.4). When they examined these more closely, they saw that on some of the bones, the human-made cut marks were on top of the carnivore tooth marks, evidence that humans were cutting flesh from the bones *after* they had already been chewed by a predator. The implication was clear: On at least some occasions, hominids were scavengers rather than hunters.

To be a scavenger rather than a hunter affects every aspect of daily life. Instead of depending on an ability to chase down and kill elusive prey, a scavenger relies on finding the kills made by hunters and then somehow usurping some of the meat. Many scavengers, such as vultures and jackals, are tolerated by larger carnivores at a kill; would early hominids have been? Through the 1980s, archaeologists adopted new experimental approaches to understanding the role that the hominids may have played in those ecosystems (Box 13.1). These studies suggested that ample scavenging opportunities existed for hominids 2 million years ago.

FIGURE 13.4 Carnivores such as these wild dogs have skeletal adaptations for eating meat. In contrast, early *Homo* used stone tools to obtain meat and marrow.

Box 13.1 Understanding the Meat-Eating Past through the Present

In the 1970s and 1980s Glynn Isaac, an innovative experimental archaeologist who believed that the past could be better understood through direct analogies with the present, mentored a series of students who turned to the behavior and ecology of living carnivores to understand how early hominids might have used animal resources. Robert Blumenschine (1987) conducted field studies of lions, hyenas, and other African carnivores on the Serengeti. He found that early hominids would have had an ample supply of resources from carcasses left over after kills by lions and leopards, especially in woodlands located near streams where scavengers like hyenas are often delayed in finding the kills. In many modern ecosystems, even after a predator is done eating, the carcass provides rich sources of fat and protein in the form of bone marrow and brain that support a community of scavengers, a community that might have once included early hominids.

Blumenschine (1986) also studied how predators and scavengers both follow a customary sequence in which they rapidly devour the hindquarters, then the ribs and forelegs, followed by the bone marrow, and finally the contents of the head. This consumption sequence can be used as a signature in the fossil record to identify hunting and scavenging. Because scavengers eat the remains of what hunters leave behind, they should eat a disproportionate quantity of the last body parts with edible meat. Blumenschine argues these early hominids would not have needed to hunt because scavenging would have been a reliable enough source of calories and nutrients.

Archaeologist Curtis Marean (1989) thinks that early *Homo* could have occupied a scavenging niche simply by cleaning up after saber-toothed cats. Saber-tooths were among the top predators in many East African habitats 2 million years ago. Some were powerful, solitary hunters that could kill animals with much

more meat than they themselves could hope to eat or store, leaving a potential niche for a scavenging hominid to fill.

Nicholas Toth (Schick and Toth, 1993) was among the first to tackle another old problem in new ways when he learned to make stone tools. By studying stone tools found in archaeological sites such as Koobi Fora, Toth, an expert tool maker, was able to match his own style of tool making with what early hominids were doing. Toth and his assistants carved up the carcass of an elephant (which had died of natural causes in a zoo and was donated as a research subject) to test the cutting power of simple Oldowan tools They showed that using only the simple core and flake tools of the Oldowan industry, early humans could have sliced through the thick hide of large animals. Because it is unlikely that *H. habilis* and kin would have had the means to kill such large and dangerous animals, Toth's work supports the validity of the scavenging model of early human subsistence.

By the 1990s, field studies of meat eating by wild chimpanzees showed that even without tools, apes can capture and consume large quantities of small mammals (Boesch and Boesch, 1989; Stanford, 1998). John Yellen (1991) showed that modern hunter-gatherers consume large amounts of meat in the form of small mammals, none of which would leave any archaeological evidence had early hominids done the same. Archaeologists began to reinterpret the models for hominid scavenging behavior, arguing that aggressive, active carcass piracy was far more likely than passively locating dead animals that were already mostly consumed by primary predators (Bunn and Ezzo, 1993).

Perhaps the most sensible view is that *H. habilis* probably would have acquired animal resources in any form they could, through both hunting for small animals and scavenging carcasses. Modern foragers do the same. Cultural diversity in modern chimpanzee populations (see Chapter 11) suggests that some populations of early genus *Homo* could have hunted, whereas others may have preferred scavenging, and both strategies probably were included in a flexible behavioral repertoire. Early views of meat eating tended to emphasize a black-or-white approach, which is rarely the way that living creatures behave. Regardless of whether meat was obtained by hunting or scavenging, the archaeological record shows that hominid stone tool–assisted consumption of large animals began about 2.5 million years ago and gradually increased through time. The two innovations of stone tool manufacture and animal resource exploitation undoubtedly shaped much of subsequent human evolutionary history.

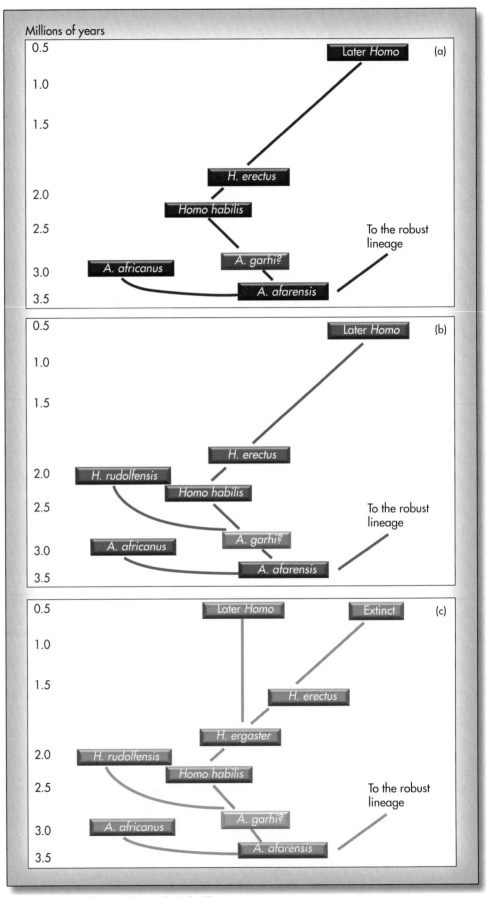

<FIG NUM="5" ID="FG.13.005">**FIGURE 13.5** Possible phylogenies for early

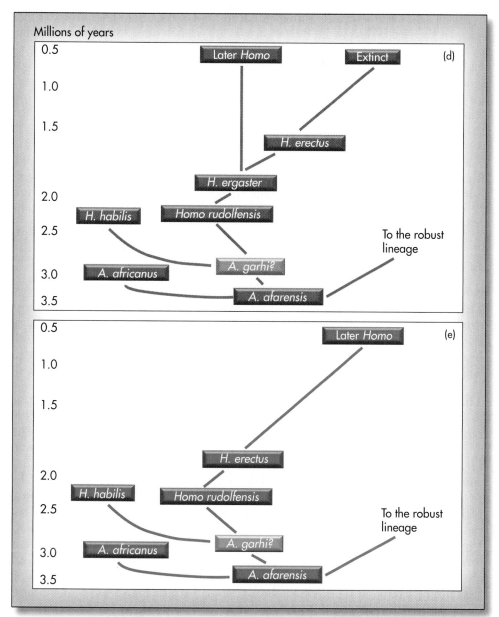

FIGURE 13.5 *(continued)*

WHO WAS *HOMO ERECTUS?*

Sometime around the Plio-Pleistocene boundary, about 1.8 million years ago, hominids underwent a major adaptive shift. This is reflected in the fossil record by body size increases and changes to the postcranial skeleton, such as lengthening of the femur, that indicate a more efficient gait, similar to that of modern humans. These changes may have been related to environmental and climatic changes during that time period. Remember, however, that while at least one hominid lineage was responding to these climate changes by adaptive shifts, another—the *robust australopithecines*—responded not by changing but by intensifying its previous adaptation to hard object feeding.

H. *erectus* appeared in Africa about 1.8 million years ago and was the first hominid to leave the continent (Figure 13.5). Until just a few years ago, the fossil evidence suggested that H. *erectus* did not leave until about about 1.0 million years ago. However, increasing evidence suggests that H. *erectus* was outside Africa by at least 1.7 million years ago, showing that our ancestors began migrating to other parts of the Old World while the taxon was still quite young. Some paleoanthropologists call these earliest *H. erectus* by another name, *Homo ergaster* (see Figure 13.5) (Wood and Collard, 1999). Whatever you call them, these hominids quickly left Africa. Fossils from the site of Dmanisi in the Republic of Georgia look like small-brained versions of early African *H. erectus,* and those from Sangiran in Indonesia look only a bit more derived. Why hominids left Africa when they did is a source of debate. What is certain is that dispersal probably was the result of multiple movements of small groups of hominids into new territories.

The last members of the species exist more than 1.5 million years later, being found in the late Pleistocene of Indonesia. These hominids overlap in time with hominids from other parts of the world, such as Europe and Africa, that seem to be transitional between *H. erectus* and either Neandertals or modern humans (Chapter 14).

ANATOMICAL FEATURES

Before we can discuss how they lived, why they left Africa, how they compare with earlier and later hominids, or even how they change through time, we must define what we mean by *H. erectus.* In general, *H. erectus* is a hominid species characterized by a somewhat larger body and brain and a uniquely shaped skull. In its postcranial features *H. erectus* shows the beginnings of a modern human body plan.

The Skull and Teeth　*H. erectus* crania are easily identified by their shape (Figure 13.6). The skull is thick-boned and robust, much longer than it is wide, relatively low and angular from the side, and pentagonal in rear view. The angularity of the skull is enhanced by a series of cranial superstructures, regional thickenings of bone along certain sutures and across certain bones. These include thickenings such as the prominent **supraorbital torus** or browridge on the frontal, a thickened **angular torus** on the back of the parietal, and the **occipital torus,** a ridge of bone that runs horizontally across the occipital. In addition, the forehead has a low, sloping or receding appearance and is often separated from the supraorbital torus by a gully or furrow. The pentagonal rear view is formed by other thickenings including those along sutures such as the **sagittal keel** along the sagittal suture that joins the two parietals and the **metopic keel** along the midline frontal at the site once occupied by the metopic suture of the infant. The pentagon is widest at its base; the sides slant inward from there to the lateral part of the parietal and then turn in to meet at the tip of the pentagon, which is formed by the sagittal keel.

H. erectus brain size ranges from approximately 700 cc to 1,200 cc, averaging about 900 cc (Figure 13.7 on page 364). Partly as a result of this expansion, the degree of *postorbital constriction* is less than in australopithecines but still marked compared with later forms. Early brain size increases in *H. erectus* may occur simply in proportion to body size increases in the species and real (that is, disproportionately large) brain size evolution may not occur until archaic *H. sapiens,* just a few hundred thousand years ago. Of course, not only sheer volume but also organization of the brain are key factors in determining the cognitive ability of a species. Certainly in absolute brain size, *H. erectus* was less cognitively endowed than modern humans. However, the brain size of *H. erectus* also shows regional and evolutionary variation (Table 13.2), indicating progressive but slow increase in the lineage through time (Antón and Swisher, 2001; Leigh, 1992). Brain size increases by about 160 cc per million years in *H. erectus* but by about 800 cc per million years from archaic *H. Sapiens* to modern humans (Figure 13.8 on page 364).

supraorbital torus　Thickened ridge of bone above the eye orbits of the skull; a browridge.

angular torus　A thickened ridge of bone at the posterior angle of the parietal bone.

occipital torus　A thickened horizontal ridge of bone on the occipital bone at the rear of the cranium.

sagittal keel　Longitudinal ridge or thickening of bone on the sagittal suture not associated with any muscle attachment.

metopic keel　Longitudinal ridge or thickening of bone along the midline of the frontal bone.

TABLE 13.2	Cranial Capacities for *Homo erectus*	
REGION	RANGE (CC)
Africa	700–1,067
Indonesia	800–1,250
China	855–1,225

LATERAL VIEW

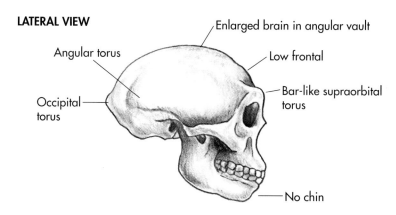

Angular torus

Occipital torus

Enlarged brain in angular vault

Low frontal

Bar-like supraorbital torus

No chin

FRONTAL VIEW

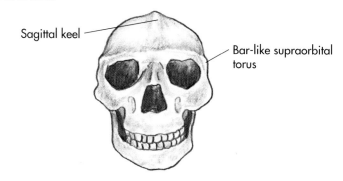

Sagittal keel

Bar-like supraorbital torus

PENTAGONAL REAR VIEW

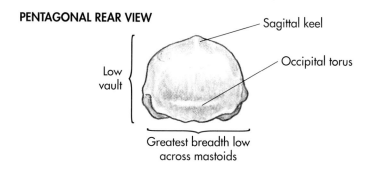

Sagittal keel

Occipital torus

Low vault

Greatest breadth low across mastoids

FIGURE 13.6   Major features of *Homo erectus* include increased brainsize, an angular vault, and cranial superstructures.

The jaw of *H. erectus* was as robust and powerfully built as the rest of the cranial complex. The proportions of the mandible contrast with the small teeth in some of the earlier *H. erectus* specimens from Africa (Wolpoff, 1999). The premolar roots are also more complex than those of modern humans (Wood and Collard, 1999). The lingual (tongue) sides of the incisors are concave, with ridges along their edges forming the shape of a tiny shovel; referred to as **shovel-shaped incisors.** Some researchers have attempted to link ancient Asian *H. erectus* populations with modern Asian people, based on this apparent continuity of incisor shape (see Chapter 15). However, because most *H. erectus* specimens from all regions possess this trait, as do Neandertals, it seems more likely that it is a primitive trait for the genus that may or may not suggest a link between modern and ancient Asian populations.

Body Size and Shape   Despite the large numbers of *H. erectus* skulls and teeth that have been found over the past century, what we know of the postcranial skeleton comes from just three partial skeletons and some isolated bones, mostly from

shovel-shaped incisors
Anterior teeth which on their lingual (tongue) surface are concave with two raised edges that make them look like tiny shovels.

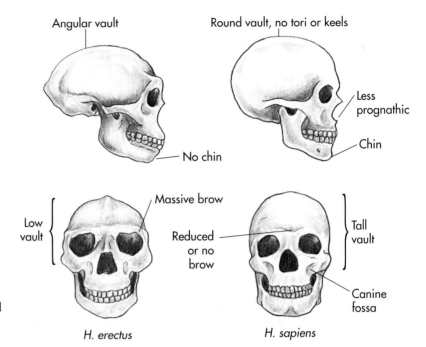

FIGURE 13.7 Compared with modern humans, *Homo erectus* has a larger face, lacks a chin, and has a more angular vault and smaller brain.

East Africa. The most important of these is the remarkably complete KNM-WT 15000 skeleton—the Nariokotome boy—found in 1984 on the western side of Lake Turkana in Kenya by Alan Walker and Richard Leakey, whose discovery is described at the beginning of this chapter (Figure 13.9). These specimens suggest not only that *H. erectus* was robustly proportioned but also that some individuals were very tall as adults, between five and a half and six feet (Walker, 1993; McHenry and Coffing, 2000) and the lower limb was long. The long bones of the arms and legs are thick; the femur is **platymeric**, which means it is flattened from front to back, and the tibia is **platycnemic**, flattened from side to side. These features are distinctive to *H. erectus* but not *H. sapiens* and do not differentiate *H. erectus* from later Neandertals or archaic *H. sapiens*.

platymeric   A bone that is flattened from front to back.

platycnemic   A bone that is flattened from side to side.

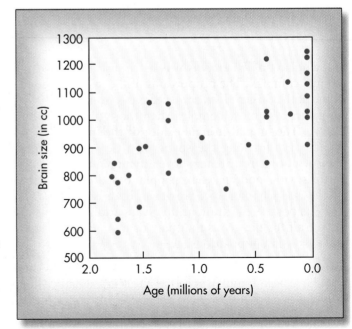

FIGURE 13.8 Although average brain size increases gradually through time in *H. erectus*, individuals with small brains are present even late in time. Dots represent individual fossils.

In addition to being tall, *H. erectus* in Africa may also have been narrow-hipped, at least based on reconstructions of pelvis shape in KNM-WT 15000 by Chris Ruff (Figure 13.10). These body proportions—long and linear—seem to follow the latitudinal gradient seen in modern humans adapted to tropical environments (see Chapter 6) and suggest that *H. erectus* was dissipating heat in much the same way that we do, that is, by sweating. This ability to dissipate heat may have allowed *H. erectus* to be more active during midday.

HOMO ERECTUS VERSUS HOMO ERGASTER

As was the case with *H. habilis,* opinions differ about whether *H. erectus* constitutes one widely dispersed, variable species or two (or more) distinct species, *H. erectus* and *H. ergaster.* The argument centers mainly around the early African (and Georgian) forms of *H. erectus* that some researchers recognize as *H. ergaster,* using the mandible KNM-ER 992 as the type specimen. The main differences between *H. ergaster* and *H. erectus* are summarized in Table 13.3 (on page 368) and include more gracile crania with less pronounced browridges in African forms and more robust and thicker-browed Asian forms, with larger teeth and more pronounced cranial superstructures (keels and tori, discussed previously). There are also archaeological differences, with some of the African forms found in association with somewhat more advanced tools, whereas even later forms of Asian *H. erectus* continue to make Oldowan-like tools, (see "The Lifeways of *H. erectus*" on page 376). In practice, *H. ergaster* is used to refer to early African *H. erectus* specimens and is considered by many to be only a slight regional variant of the pan–Old World species *H. erectus* (Rightmire, 1993; Antón, 2003). Here we will consider *H. ergaster* a regional variant or subspecies of *H. erectus.*

HOMO ERECTUS AROUND THE WORLD

If we accept *H. erectus* as a single, widely dispersed species, then it represents more than 1.5 million years of time and a broad geographic range (Figure 13.11 on page 366). Known *H. erectus* sites range in age from about 1.8 million years to 100,000

FIGURE 13.9 Dr. Emma Mbua of the National Museum of Kenya stands next to the skeleton of the Nariokotome *H. erectus* boy.

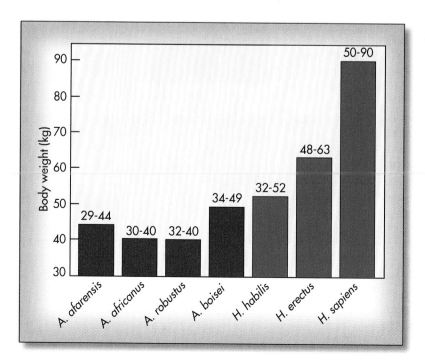

FIGURE 13.10 Body weight estimates from fossil remains show that *H. erectus* had a larger body than earlier hominids.

Figure 13.11 **THE GENUS *HOMO* THROUGH TIME**

The genus *Homo,* characterized by changes in the dentition, first appeared in the fossil record about 2.3 million years ago. The genus eventually developed larger brain and body sizes and spread out of Africa around 1.8 million years ago.

At 1.7 million years old the Dmanisi fossils are among the oldest hominids outside Africa.

The recently discovered Bouri hominid is one of a long lineage of hominids from the Middle Awash Ethiopia.

Fragmentary remains of *H. antecessor* are the earliest accepted remains in Europe.

KNM-WT 15000, the Nariokotome boy was a member of *H. erectus* who stood about 5'6" at his death and might have reached 6' tall had he lived to adulthood.

Koobi Fora, Kenya has yielded abundant fossil remains including the largest and smallest skulls of *H. habilis* (KNM-ER1470 and 1813) that some scientists prefer to assign to two separate species.

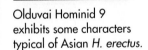

Olduvai Hominid 9 exhibits some characters typical of Asian *H. erectus.*

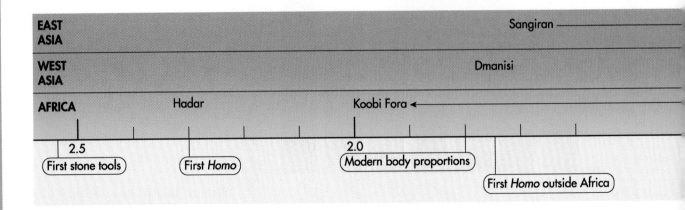

EAST ASIA				Sangiran ————
WEST ASIA				Dmanisi
AFRICA	Hadar		Koobi Fora ◄———————	

2.5   2.0

(First stone tools)   (First *Homo*)   (Modern body proportions)

(First *Homo* outside Africa)

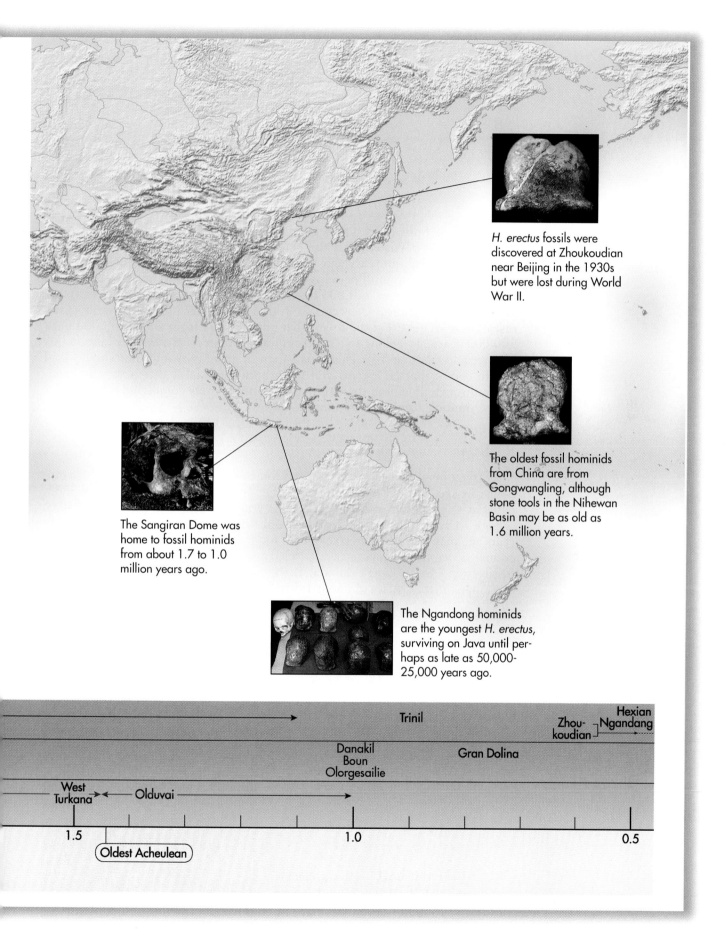

H. erectus fossils were discovered at Zhoukoudian near Beijing in the 1930s but were lost during World War II.

The oldest fossil hominids from China are from Gongwangling, although stone tools in the Nihewan Basin may be as old as 1.6 million years.

The Sangiran Dome was home to fossil hominids from about 1.7 to 1.0 million years ago.

The Ngandong hominids are the youngest *H. erectus*, surviving on Java until perhaps as late as 50,000-25,000 years ago.

Trinil

Hexian
Zhou-   Ngandang
koudian

Danakil   Gran Dolina
Boun
Olorgesailie

West
Turkana → ← Olduvai

1.5   1.0   0.5

Oldest Acheulean

TABLE 13.3	Comparison of *H. ergaster* and Classic *H. erectus*		
	REGION	SKELETON	DATE (MYA)
H. ergaster	E. Africa Rep. Georgia	Thinner cranial bones Less pronounced browridges	1.8–1.0
H. erectus	Asia	Thicker cranial bones More pronounced browridges	1.8–0.05
* MYA = millions of years ago			

years (and perhaps much younger in Indonesia). *H. erectus* is found first in Africa (where it persisted until about 1.0 million years ago), in the Republic of Georgia at 1.7 million years ago, in island Southeast Asia by about 1.8 million years ago (persisting until perhaps 100,000 years ago), and only later in continental Asia from about 800,000 to about 200,000 years ago. There is controversy as to whether *H. erectus* is found in Western Europe, with many researchers arguing that the fossils that appear there from about 800,000 until 200,000 years ago belong to a different lineage than *H. erectus* (see later in this chapter and Chapter 14). This broad span of geography and time should lead you to expect that *H. erectus* will show both geographic differences and evolution through time. And these sources of variation only compound the difficulty of determining species definitions.

AFRICAN ORIGINS

The earliest fossil evidence for *H. erectus* comes from Koobi Fora in Kenya 1.8 million years ago. The oldest remains are a largely complete cranium, KNM-ER 3733, dated at 1.78 million years old and with a cranial capacity of only about 850 cc (Figure 13.12). Slightly older remains from Koobi Fora of 1.89 and 1.95 million years ago may also be *H. erectus* but are too fragmentary or are parts of the postcranial skeleton that cannot be identified to species with certainty. Many other fossils from East Turkana exhibit anatomy similar to that of 3733 and provide an age range for the species of about 1.5 to 1.78 million years (or older). The most

FIGURE 13.12 The cranium of early African *H. erectus* KNM-ER 3733 is nearly 1.8 million years old.

exciting recent find is the partial cranium of a subadult from Ileret, Kenya (part of the Koobi Fora Formation), dated to 1.55 million years ago, that has a very small cranial capacity and some characteristics more typically found in Asian *H. erectus* (Leakey et al., 2003), arguing that African and Asian *H. erectus* should be included in a single species.

From the western side of Lake Turkana between 1.5 and 1.6 million years ago comes the nearly complete and quite tall Nariokotome *H. erectus* skeleton of a boy between 8 and 11 years old when he died. His age is based on the pattern of tooth eruption (he had just gotten his permanent premolars but still retained his baby canine), and the large range comes from our not knowing if the timing of the boy's development was more like ours (if so, he would be about 11 years of age) or more like that of an ape (if so, he would be closer to 8 years of age).

Important African *H. erectus* fossils also come from Olduvai Gorge, where the largest-brained African *H. erectus,* OH 9, with a cranial capacity of a little more than 1,000 cc, dates to about 1.47 million years ago (Figure 13.13). In addition, some of the latest *H. erectus* in Africa are also the smallest including OH 12, from Oldvuai, dated to perhaps as little as 780,000 years ago, with a capacity of only 727 cc, and the recently discovered Olorgesailie homind at about 900,000 years old (Potts et al 2004). These fossils highlight the differences in size in *H. erectus.*

H. erectus from the Bouri Formation of the Middle Awash, Ethiopia (Asfaw et al., 2002), and the Danakil Depression in Eritrea are around 1 million years old (Abbate et al. 1998) (Figure 13.14 on page 370). Another Ethiopian site, Konso-Gardula, has very ancient (1.8 million years old) fragmentary *H. erectus* fossils and the oldest known *H. erectus*–associated stone tools. The Bouri lineage in particular will prove significant for understanding the evolution of genus *Homo* because it also contains fossils of the earliest *H. sapiens.*

THE FIRST AFRICAN DIASPORA: REPUBLIC OF GEORGIA

About 50 miles southwest of Tbilisi, the capital city of the Republic of Georgia, lies the village of Dmanisi. Nearby, beneath a medieval village built at the confluence of two rivers, a stunning series of finds in the 1990s changed our understanding of when humans left the cradle of Africa (see Figure 9.11). Excavations by an international Georgian and German team headed by Leo Gabunia and David Lordkipanidze discovered evidence of early *H. erectus*–like hominids outside Africa at approximately 1.7 million years ago and associated with Oldowan-like stone

FIGURE 13.13 Olduvai Hominid 9, *H. erectus* from Olduvai Gorge, Tanzania, is nearly 1.5 million years old.

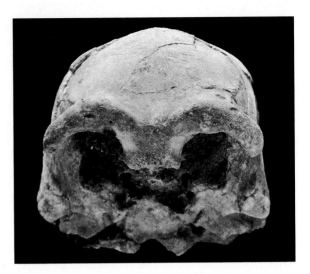

FIGURE 13.14 *Homo erectus* from Bouri Formation of the Middle Awash, Ethiopia, is about one million years old.

tools. Since 1991, at least four crania and some postcranial remains have been found in a small area (16 m²) beneath the medieval village (Figure 13.15).

The Dmanisi hominids are very similar to early African *H. erectus*, or so-called *H. ergaster* (Table 13.4). They are small-brained (less than 800 cc) but differ in anatomy from more primitive small-brained *H. habilis*. The Dmanisi hominids are linked to *H. erectus* by their premolar and molar tooth structure, the development of browridges, and their high cranial vault. They are markedly more similar to the early African *H. erectus* fossils than they are to contemporary, Asian *H. erectus* (Gabunia et al., 2000). But compared with early African *H. erectus*, the Dmanisi hominids are small (Gabunia et al., 2001).

The Dmanisi skulls show conclusively that early humans had migrated out of Africa at nearly the same time that *H. erectus* first appears in Africa. Thus, shortly after the emergence of *H. erectus* in Africa, the species moved out of the African continent and into other regions and other ecosystems.

DISPERSAL INTO EAST ASIA

The oldest Asian *H. erectus* are from island Southeast Asia, particularly the island of Java, and date to about 1.6–1.8 million years ago. However, 1.8 million years ago sea level was substantially lower than it is today, and Java and nearby islands were part of mainland Asia (Figure 13.16). So colonizing the far reaches of Asia meant only walking a long distance, not crossing water. Although travel through continental Asia is necessary to reach Southeast Asia, so far the earliest evidence of *H. erectus* on the eastern part of the continent is only about 1.5 million years old.

FIGURE 13.15 (a) Drs. David Lordkipanidze and Leo Gabunia study crania of *H. erectus* from Dmanisi, Georgia. (b) The Dmanisi cranium (right) shows similarities to early African *H. erectus* including the Nariokotome boy (left).

(a)

(b)

TABLE 13.4	Dmanisi Hominids Compared with Other Early Hominids		
TAXON	BRAIN SIZE (CC)	BODY HEIGHT (IN.)	BODY WEIGHT (LB.)
Dmanisi	650–780	58	105
H. sapiens	1,350	63–69	108–128
African H. erectus	700–1,067	63–71	123–145
Asian H. erectus	800–1,250	—	—
Earliest Homo	500–750	39–63	70–132
A. africanus	448	45–54	66–90

Source: Gabunia (2001).

Indonesia The very first *H. erectus* fossil ever found, and thus the type specimen for the species, was discovered in 1891 in Indonesia (Figure 13.17 on page 372). A few years earlier, a young doctor named Eugene Dubois left Amsterdam by steam ship in search of human fossils in the Dutch East Indies (now called Indonesia). Following Darwin's lead, Dubois considered the tropics a likely cradle of humankind. But he also thought that Asia was a more likely spot for the origin of humans than Africa because African apes, with their primitive appearance and robust facial features, seemed unlikely human antecedents, whereas the slender-bodied, monogamous Asian gibbons and modern humans seemed more similar. (Shipman, 2001). Dubois went to Indonesia to find the missing link between the two.

FIGURE 13.16 Landbridge connections between continental Asia and Indonesia during glacial periods (and low sea level) extend as far as Wallace's line.

FIGURE 13.17 The skull cap from Trinil, Java, is the type specimen for *H. erectus* and is about 900,000 years old.

In October 1891, in the banks of the Solo River near the village of Trinil, Java, Dubois's team unearthed a large, round fossil (Figure 13.17), the **calotte** or skullcap of an early human. Although only the top of the skull was found, Dubois could see that it was hominid and that in life it possessed a large brain, in a robust cranium more primitive than that of any hominid known at that time. He named the species *Pithecanthropus erectus* ("the upright ape-man"), and this specimen, Trinil 2, also nicknamed Java Man, became the type specimen for the species.

The team later found a fossilized femur that Dubois believed to be of the same individual, thereby proving to him that the creature was fully bipedal. However, Dubois's claims were met with much skepticism in part because of preconceived ideas about evolution or about which characters had appeared first in our evolutionary history. Although by the 1940s *P. erectus* was classified in our own genus as *H. erectus* and recognized as a primitive hominid intermediate between the apes and modern people, Dubois himself died well before this, embittered about his treatment by the scientific community.

The volcanic sediments of Java have yielded a wealth of other *H. erectus* fossils. These include the most ancient specimen from Java, a child's **calvaria** or braincase from the site of Mojokerto dated to about 1.8 million years ago, and a series of fossils from the Sangiran dome region, dated to between 1.7 and 1.0 million years ago. These early Indonesian *H. erectus* have cranial capacities between about 800 and 1,000 cc.

The volcanic sediments of Java provide the ideal context for estimating the radiometric age of the fossil hominids using the argon–argon technique (see Chapter 9). A series of samples from more than 80 m of section at Sangiran conducted by two different research groups have yielded a well-stratified sample ranging from about 1.7 to about 1.0 million years ago for the hominid-bearing parts (see Figure 9.14) (Swisher et al., 1994; Larick et al., 2001). There is some controversy about the precise ages of individual fossils because many have been discovered not by scientists but by farmers making rice fields; however, it is clear that the entire section is older than 1.0 million years.

The latest surviving *H. erectus* are also from Java and represent the youngest *H. erectus* anywhere in the world. A series of partial crania and other fossilized remains were excavated in the 1930s at the site of Ngandong in eastern Java. Using uranium series and electron spin resonance (ESR) methods (see Chapter 9), Carl Swisher and colleagues recently redated the fauna associated with the Ngandong hominids (but not the hominids themselves) to a remarkably recent 27,000–53,000 years ago (Swisher et al., 1996). More recently, a different radiometric technique has suggested ages for one of the Ngandong hominids of perhaps as young as 80,000 years. Previously thought to have been present at least 250,000 to 500,000

calotte The skullcap, or the bones of the skull, excluding those that form the face and the base of the cranium.

calvaria The braincase; includes the bones of the calotte and those that form the base of the cranium but excludes the bones of the face.

FIGURE 13.18 Ngandong calottes from Java are the youngest *H. erectus* fossils at perhaps 27,000–50,000 years old.

years ago, *H. erectus* may have survived in this island refuge even while going extinct in other parts of the world. However, because the excavations were performed so long ago, the data at hand cannot answer all the criticisms of the ages (Figure 13.18). Recent finds on Flores dating to 18,000 may also support a young age for *H. erectus* (Box 15.1 on page 427).

Since Indonesia achieved independence in 1945, a series of other fossils have been recovered by Indonesian scientists Teuku Jacob, Fachroel Aziz, and Sartono. These finds have helped us to understand the anatomy and evolution of *H. erectus*, but tools are almost entirely lacking in Indonesia. Tools of an Oldowan-like technology have been found, but they are few, and none were found in association with fossil hominids.

China   Although perhaps the best known of the *H. erectus* remains, the fossils from China are younger than those in Africa or earliest Indonesia, spanning only from about 800,000 to about 200,000 years ago. However, sites with stone tools in the Nihewan Basin also indicate there was likely an early Pleistocene (approximately 1.6 million years old) hominid presence, although there are no new fossils from these sites (Zhu et al., 2004). The earliest Chinese fossils, fragmentary, and crushed remains from Gongwangling, are not much help in understanding evolution in *H. erectus*. Even more ancient finds from Longuppo with an age of perhaps 1.8 million years ago are of uncertain taxonomic status and may not be hominids. The most numerous and best preserved are the so-called Peking Man fossils discovered in the 1930s in China and dated between about 600,000 and 300,000 years ago.

The story of the famed Peking Man fossils is one of discovery and loss. Chinese paleontologist Pei Wenshong discovered the original skull in December 1929 at a quarry site, Chou Kou Tien (now transliterated as Zhoukoudian), not far from modern Beijing (Figure 13.19 on page 374). Along with Davidson Black, a Canadian anatomist, he described and initially named the fossil *Sinanthropus pekinensis* ("Chinese human from Peking"). After Black's untimely death, Franz Weidenreich, a Jewish anatomist who had fled his native Germany during the Nazi era, took over anatomical work on Zhoukoudian.

In the mid-1930s, Japan invaded China before the American entry into World War II, and work at Zhoukoudian stopped. Fear spread that the Zhoukoudian *H. erectus* fossils, objects of great cultural and historical value, would be confiscated, destroyed, or taken as gifts to the Japanese emperor, a noted naturalist. So Weidenreich made extensive measurements, drawings, and plaster casts of the fossils. The fossils were then placed in the care of the United States Marines, who guarded them on a train from Beijing to the coast, where they were to be put on

FIGURE 13.19 (a) The site of Zhoukoudian outside of Beijing, China, spans several hundred thousand years and (b) yielded numerous *H. erectus* calottes.

(a)　　　　　　　　　　　　　　(b)

a ship for San Francisco. The train arrived at the Chinese coast on December 7, 1941, the day of the Japanese attack on Pearl Harbor. The Marines were taken prisoner, and the crates of fossils have never been found (Shipman, 2001).

Because of Weidenreich's careful molding and measuring of the Zhoukoudian fossils, at least we have replicas of the Peking Man fossils, comprising more than a dozen calvaria and hundreds of associated teeth and bone fragments (Weidenreich, 1943). They represent as many as forty individuals who lived nearby Zhoukoudian between 600,000 and 250,000 years ago. Although it was originally described as a habitation cave where *H. erectus* lived, used fire, and cooked meals, more recent archaeological work at the site has found that it is not a cave at all but a series of sediment-filled cracks in the rock, rather than a habitation site (Goldberg et al., 2001). In addition to the Zhoukoudian material, other Chinese *H. erectus* have been discovered including the more recently discovered Nanjing and Hexian crania, which are morphologically very similar to the Zhoukoudian finds (Wu and Poirier, 1994). In most ways, *H. erectus* from China looks like other Asian *H. erectus*.

Despite their similarities, Chinese *H. erectus* also show some regional differences from the Indonesian *H. erectus* in their frontal and occipital regions (Antón, 2003). These differences may reflect the intermittent isolation of these two groups from each other during the oscillating sea levels of the Pleistocene. Recall from Chapter 9 that sea level rose and fell periodically with the interglacial and glacial periods. Each time it rose, continental and island Southeast Asia, and the hominids and land mammals living on them, were cut off from each other. These periods of separation might last 10,000 to 50,000 years, that is many many generations of fossil hominids, and could have led to some genetic (and morphological) differences between the populations through time.

Unlike island Southeast Asia, China lacks Pleistocene volcanic sediments, posing a problem for the radiometric aging of hominid sites there. Earlier volcanics provide good age control of Jurassic and Cretaceous sites such as those in which the feathered dinosaurs of Liaoning are found. But younger volcanics are missing. Thus Chinese hominid ages are established by relative methods such as biostratigraphy or lithostratigraphy, loess stratigraphy, or, more recently, uranium series or ESR ages (see Chapter 9). At Zhoukoudian, for example, U-series and ESR age estimates on fauna suggest that the multiple layers at the site were occupied over a time span of several hundred thousand years. The earliest ages associated with hominids are nearly 600,000 years and the youngest a bit more than 200,000 years (Grün et al., 1997). U-series dates suggest that the site represents a long time period, although it may be even older than previous estimates, with the youngest hominid layers being perhaps 400,000 years old (Shen and Wang, 2000).

THE STATUS OF *HOMO ERECTUS* IN EUROPE

The status of *H. erectus* in Europe is a subject of debate among paleoanthropologists. We know that early humans that somewhat resembled *H. erectus* occupied Europe during the same time period that *H. erectus* occurred in Asia. However, most of the fossils discovered so far that are complete enough for us to assess their taxonomy differ from the typical *H. erectus* seen in Africa, Asia, or Southeast Asia. Many of the European fossils resemble *H. sapiens* as well as *H. erectus* and Neandertals, and they may well be transitional, or archaic, forms of *H. sapiens*. The later middle Pleistocene European fossils, those dated between 500,000 and 200,000 years ago, are likely to be ancestral only to Neandertals and are discussed in Chapter 14. However, the last decade has seen important but confusing finds from about 800,000 years ago from Spain that we discuss here.

Hominid fossils recovered from Gran Dolina in the Sierra de Atapuerca region of Spain by a team led by J. M. Bermudez de Castro and J. L. Arsuaga (1997) have been dated to nearly 800,000 years ago, more than 200,000 years older than any other known hominids in western Europe (Figure 13.20). The Atapuerca fossils come from a region rich in human fossils, including the more recent material from Sima de los Huesos (see Chapter 14).

The Gran Dolina fossils were found in the oldest of a series of deposits in the Sierra de Atapuerca that were exposed when a road cut was made for a now abandoned rail line. Intensive excavation began in the early 1990s, and the sample of fossils recovered so far consists of young individuals, between 3 and 18 years of age at the time they died. The fossils are interesting because they exhibit a mix of characteristics, some of which appear to foreshadow Neandertals, others of which seem to link the fossils to modern humans. In particular, the presence of a **canine fossa** (an indentation on the maxilla above the canine root) has been used to argue that the Gran Dolina fossils represent a previously unknown hominid species, *Homo antecessor,* which may have been the common ancestor of both Neandertals and modern *H. sapiens* (Arsuaga et al., 1999). However, many researchers are skeptical of this new classification, because the species *H. antecessor* was based largely on characters exhibited in a child's partial crania, characters the child might have lost as it aged. Another adult calvaria, Ceprano, from Italy is said to be 800,000 years old and a member of *H. antecessor.* However, it lacks the critical facial bones that define that species. It also differs anatomically from typical *H. erectus* and, more importantly, may not be nearly as old as is claimed. Only the discovery of more complete adult fossils will settle the question of the identity of *H. antecessor.* Regardless of whether

canine fossa An indentation on the maxilla above the root of the canine, an anatomical feature usually associated with modern humans that may be present in some archaic *Homo* species in Europe.

FIGURE 13.20 The Gran Dolina locality in Spain has yielded the oldest fossil hominids in Europe.

you accept *H. antecessor* as a valid taxon or lump the Gran Dolina remains into *H. heidelbergensis* or archaic *H. sapiens* (see Chapter 14), anatomically they cannot be classified as *H. erectus*, suggesting that this taxon may never have made it into Europe.

THE LIFEWAYS OF *HOMO ERECTUS*

From the fossils and stone tools associated with *H. erectus* and from their own anatomy we can begin to piece together how these early *Homo* lived. The species is associated with two different tool technologies that show *H. erectus* possessed advanced cognitive skills. *H. erectus* appears to have undergone a dietary shift to a more heavily meat-based diet than its predecessors and this shift seems to have fueled both its dispersal from Africa and a different pattern of growth.

HOMO ERECTUS AND THE EARLY STONE AGE

From 1.8 to about 1.5 million years ago in Africa, only Oldowan type tools are found with *H. erectus*. And the earliest tools found outside Africa at Dmanisi in the Republic of Georgia are also Oldowan-like assemblages (Gabunia et al., 2001). However, starting at approximately 1.4 million years ago in Africa some *H. erectus* are found with a different tool technology called the **Acheulean** tradition. This tradition persists until about 250,000 years ago and is made by a number of different species of the genus *Homo*. Together, the Oldowan and Acheulean are known as the **Early Stone Age** or **Lower Paleolithic**.

Acheulean assemblages are characterized by specifically shaped tools called hand axes and cleavers that are worked on two sides. Both are thus a **biface**, tool whose cutting edge is formed by the removal of flakes from opposing sides of the piece. The scars left by the removal of these flakes meet to form the sharp edge. A **hand axe** is a bifacially worked, symmetrical, teardrop-shaped tool (Figure 13.21). A **cleaver** has a broader working end where the point of the teardrop would have been in a hand axe (Figure 13.21).

For the first time in human prehistory we see hominids making standardized tools that clearly indicate they had a plan or mental template in mind. Hand axes and cleavers were highly uniform in appearance. They were made from stone cobbles or larger flakes that had been carefully selected for size and weight. The tool maker roughed out the axe first, then refined the product with more subtle flaking to achieve a particular shape.

Acheulean Stone tool industry of the early and middle Pleistocene characterized by the presence of bifacial hand axes and cleavers. This industry is made by a number of *Homo* species, including *H. erectus* and early *H. sapiens*.

Early Stone Age (or Lower Paleolithic) The earliest stone tool industries including the Oldowan and Acheulean industries, called the ESA in Africa and the Lower Paleolithic outside Africa.

biface A stone tool that has been flaked on two faces or opposing sides forming a cutting edge between the two flake scars.

hand axe Type of Acheulean bifacial tool, usually teardrop-shaped, with a long cutting edge.

cleaver Type of Acheulean bifacial tool, usually oblong with a broad cutting edge on one end.

FIGURE 13.21 The Acheulean industry is typified by hand axes and cleavers.

Indeed, one of the most extraordinary aspects of the Acheulean industry is its persistence and uniformity over great spans of time and space. We first see hand axes at about 1.5 million years ago, and they persist almost unchanged until about 250,000 years ago. In comparison, how many of our tools do you think will still be in use 1.2 million years from now and in nearly the same form they have today? This conservatism is also found across vast geographic areas. Hand axes appear in western and northern Europe, in East and North Africa, and in the Near East. (However, as we saw, they are very rare, or absent, in the east Asian *H. erectus* sites.) The uniformity of hand axe appearance suggests that they were used for specific purposes and in standard ways.

The advantages of the hand axe and cleaver over the simple flake are their ability to hold a sharp edge for a long period of time, the greater length of their working edge, and their generally convenient size, which allows them to be used for holding and cutting without fatigue. Nick Toth and Kathy Schick think that hand axes and cleavers are best seen as tools specifically developed for the butchery of large animals (Box 13.1). The circular pattern of flaking around the perimeter of the axe leads some scholars to consider them primitive versions of a circular saw in which more flaking was done as earlier edges became worn and dull.

But other hypotheses for the use of hand axes cannot be discounted. A recent study found evidence of fossilized *phytoliths*, microscopic mineral particles from plants (see Chapter 9), on the cutting edge of some hand axes. Their presence suggests that the tool was used to scrape plant material. This could have meant the users of the tools were sharpening a wooden spear, or perhaps stripping bark from wood for building or eating. Alternatively, hand axes might also have been used as digging implements, much as traditional foraging people today use sticks to dig for edible roots and potato-like tubers. Some archaeologists think they may have been used as projectiles, thrown at prey animals or even at hominid enemies. Although it seems unlikely, it is also possible that hand axes were simply raw material, the cores from which flake tools were struck. *H. erectus* might have simply carried hand axes around and struck flakes off them until the axe core was exhausted.

Whatever their use, the Acheulean industry presents an innovative technology that extended over much, but not all, of *H. erectus's* Old World range. As mentioned, Asian sites yield Oldowan-like tools but no true hand axes, at least not until late in time. The division between hand axe-bearing areas and those without hand axes is called the **Movius line**, after Hallam Movius, a renowned archaeologist who first recognized this puzzling distribution (Figure 13.22 on page 378). There are two not necessarily mutually exclusive hypotheses for the Movius line. The first suggests that the absence of hand axes reflects a loss of hand axe technology in Asia caused by differences in selective pressures and raw materials between Asia and Africa. In particular, organic materials such as bamboo are inferred to have been used by the hominids. In this view, African *H. erectus* left the continent with Acheulean technology but reverted to Oldowan technology in their new environment. Alternatively, other scientists suggest that the hominids that inhabit Asia left Africa before Acheulean tools were developed, so their absence is not so much a loss of technology as a difference in the technological paths taken in Asia and Africa. This difference may result from differences in available resources and selective pressures as well.

However, it is important to recognize that there is no one-to-one correlation between a species and a technology. Oldowan tools are used by both *H. habilis* and *H. erectus* (and perhaps any number of australopithecines), and different groups of *H. erectus* use Oldowan or Acheulean tools, or both. *H. erectus* continued to make and use Oldowan industry tools in Africa and elsewhere even after Acheulean tools came into widespread use, and later hominids used Acheulean tools in Africa and Europe.

Movius line The separation between areas of the Old World in which Acheulean technology occurs and those in which it does not; named by archaeologist Hallam Movius.

FIGURE 13.22 The Movius line separates regions of the world where Acheulean hand axes were made from regions where they were not.

A HIGHER-QUALITY DIET: *HOMO ERECTUS* SUBSISTENCE

Although we assume their diet was largely plant foods, as is true for modern foraging people, there is no mistaking the archaeological evidence that *H. erectus* ate meat. About 1.8 million years ago, an important biological shift apparently occurred in the hominid lineage, in which the human form became much more modern, taller, more linear, and with a larger brain. Shortly after this time hominids left Africa and began their worldwide geographic expansion. Both these things tell us that the shift probably was associated with a major increase in the quality of the diet, which was needed to maintain a larger body and brain (Leonard and Robertson, 1997; Antón et al., 2002).

Many scientists think the adaptive shift occurred when hominids became predators (Shipman and Walker, 1989; Antón et al., 2002). As they became carnivores, their small intestine would have lengthened while the large intestine shortened because meat takes less time in the large intestine for processing. The amount of leisure time would have increased as the time needed to forage for plants decreased. Population density would have been low because predators sit atop the food chain and must exist at low densities to avoid outstripping their prey supply. But the ability to disperse may have increased as hominids became less dependent on specific plant resources and more dependent on animal resources. Migrating herds might have led hominids to follow them, and in new areas meat is fairly safe, regardless of species, whereas new plants might be poisonous or inedible.

Most scientists argue that the adaptive shift happened with the emergence of *H. erectus* about 1.8 million years ago and that *H. erectus* was the first truly predatory human species. They base their assertion on the increasingly sophisticated tools associated with *H. erectus*, which may have been used for butchering prey, and on evidence that as *H. erectus* spread its range across the Old World, they lived at low population densities in the manner of a hunting species. Alan Walker and colleagues (1982) also cite a case of death in a *Homo erectus* individual possibly caused by overconsumption of vitamin A, which is known to occur in modern people primarily from eating internal organs, such as the liver, of prey animals. In addition, it seems that human-specific tapeworms share a history with tapeworms that live in hyenas but diverged from them about 1.8 million years ago. This suggests that ancient hyenas and humans were eating the same infected animals about 1.8 million years ago, further suggesting that humans had made the shift from a largely vegetarian to a mostly meat diet.

Once meat was obtained, there is only equivocal evidence that *H. erectus* was the first hominid to prepare it for consumption by cooking it. Archaeologists working in East Africa at Koobi Fora and Chesowanja have found associations of hominid fossils, animal fossils, and burnt earth to suggest the presence of fire as early as 1.6 million years ago (Bellomo, 1994). However, it is unclear whether this was hominid-controlled fire, perhaps collected from a natural fire, or hominid-made fire, or even just a natural fire. To date, most researchers think this may be evidence of brush fires that were not human-made. The best unequivocal evidence of hominid-controlled fire comes much later in the middle Pleistocene. Although the evidence of controlled fire is questionable, some researchers hypothesize that the advent of cooking created whole new adaptive niches for *H. erectus*. They suggest that eating potato-like tubers rather than meat could have provided the higher-quality diet necessary for expansion of the human brain (Wrangham et al., 1999). Wrangham and colleagues believe that lightning-set fires on the African savanna created an opportunity for early humans to see the effects of fire on underground tubers that survive wildfires in charred form (Wrangham et al., 1999). However, during the same time period, evidence of meat eating is overwhelming, whereas the evidence of tuber cooking is scanty at best.

HOMO ERECTUS LIFE HISTORY

As adults, modern humans and *H. erectus* look remarkably different, but are they more similar as children? The discovery of the Nariokotome boy (KNM-WT 15000), the remarkably complete *H. erectus* youth discussed earlier, highlighted how little we know about growth in fossil hominids. At first this may seem unimportant, but consider this basic fact: Evolution proceeds by modifying the developmental pattern. In small ways and in larger ways, modifications of this pattern produce the differences we see in adult forms. So understanding the developmental pattern is critical to understanding hominid evolution.

As you saw in Chapter 7 and we will explore further in Chapter 17, because of our large brain, humans grow slowly and mature late compared with nonhuman primates, even chimps. This makes us extremely k-selected, even compared with the other great apes. During this long development, human maturation is characterized by two growth spurts. The first occurs in the middle of childhood, around the age of 5, and the second is the adolescent growth spurt that occurs in humans in the teenage years. (see Chapter 17 and Figures 17.8 and 17.9). Neither exists to the same degree in chimpanzees, posing the question of when during hominid evolution they arose and what their behavioral implications are.

Teeth have been the most informative structures from which we learn about development because their internal structure forms by layers deposited in cyclical patterns in daily increments during dental development. As the crown develops, a number of bands are formed, and by looking at these bands we can glean something about the age and rate of development. Work on dental microstructure by

Chris Dean and colleagues suggests that early development in *H. erectus* was fast. Based on these data, this group concluded that the Nariokotome boy would have been no more than about 8 years old at the time of death. And *H. erectus* probably reached maturity earlier than we do, perhaps around the age of 15 years. Despite this rapid maturation, *H. erectus* were certainly as k-selected as the great apes and had a relatively large brain at birth.

HOMO ERECTUS LEAVES AFRICA

The most important adaptive shift *H. erectus* made was the first migration out of Africa (Figure 13.23). This emigration meant moving across a variety of ecosystems, climates, and ecological settings. Each of these would have presented *H. erectus* with new challenges never encountered by a hominid. Most important was the move from tropical and subtropical Africa into the more seasonally cold regions of the Northern Hemisphere in Eurasia and the Far East. This change alone demonstrates the remarkable adaptability and behavioral flexibility our lineage had evolved by just under 2 million years ago. The ability to adapt to a wide range of novel environments is a hallmark of the human species.

One question remains: Why did hominids remain in Africa for more than 3 million years, only to disperse rapidly after the origin of *H. erectus*? Some of the likely causes we have suggested in this chapter form a web of ecological and morphological advantages that facilitated *H. erectus* dispersal. First, recall from Chapter 9 that world climate was beginning to undergo some severe fluctuations at the origin and slightly before the rise of *H. erectus*. The African area was cooling and drying around 2 million years ago, leading to diminished forests with larger grasslands between them. The rise of grasslands saw the increase in the quantities of herbivorous animals and the evolution of a new niche for animals (including hominids) that could eat them.

H. erectus seems to have taken advantage of these opportunities by using Oldowan tools to access animal resources it was not physically adapted to ac-

FIGURE 13.23 *H. erectus* migrated out of Africa beginning about 1.8 million years ago and is first known from Georgia and Java.

quire. The higher-quality animal diet that resulted allowed the growth of larger bodies, and their more linear body shape probably allowed greater midday activity because they coped better with the heat. Larger bodies allowed greater ranging (home range, the area an animal traverses over a year, is positively correlated to body size in mammals). As animals such as antelope migrated, hominids may have followed.

In the late Pliocene, at about the time that we see other African fauna migrating into the Near East and western Asia, we also see *H. erectus* migrating. Were they following this food resource? Earlier hominids had not migrated during earlier faunal migrations out of Africa. They may have remained in place because of their greater reliance on plant foods. So it does seem that at this point *H. erectus* was able to do something that earlier hominids were not capable of doing. It seems reasonable to assume that tool use and the access to previously inaccessible resources it allowed were fundamental to the ability to migrate. However, a complex web of factors is implicated in dispersal.

There is unlikely to have been a single directional dispersal event from Africa to Asia. Rather, random movements of multiple hominid groups over time probably led to the eventual dispersal of the species across the Old World, and some back migrations probably also occurred. Even though the entire dispersal seems a long one, consider that an average change in home range of just 1 km a year (less than a mile), over a period of 10,000 or 15,000 years, would have led to a slow dispersal, yet it would look geologically instantaneous.

Having moved into many parts of the Old World using a combination of technology and physical adaptation, and having made a shift in foraging strategy to a higher-quality diet, early *H. erectus* was poised to begin the brain size expansion and intellectual development characteristic of the genus. Through time, *H. erectus* continued a gradual development of physical and cultural evolution. But more recent species of genus *Homo* exhibited even more dramatic changes. Intelligence is a survival strategy of enormous evolutionary importance to the human lineage. In *H. erectus*, we see the beginning of what intelligence meant for the hominid lineage. Now we turn to *H. sapiens*, in which cognition and culture take on far more importance.

SUMMARY

1. **How do we define the earliest members of the genus *Homo*?**

   Genus *Homo* is defined by brain size greater than 500 cc, a smaller, less prognathic face, and smaller teeth than australopithecines possess.

2. **Why do some researchers consider the earliest genus *Homo* to be *Australopithecus*?**

   Some researchers think that the earliest known *Homo* species, such as *Homo habilis*, are so apelike they should be lumped with *Australopithecus* and that genus *Homo* should be reserved for the larger-brained, longer limbed *H. erectus* and kin that appeared later.

3. **When and where did *H. erectus* appear?**

   The earliest *H. erectus* are often called *H. ergaster* because of their small brain and body size. They appeared in East Africa and also outside Africa in the Republic of Georgia about 1.8 million years ago.

4. **What are the differences between Asian and African *H. erectus*?**

   Asian *H. erectus* are different from African *H. erectus* in having thicker-walled crania, more robust facial features, larger teeth, and more cranial superstructures.

5. **What sort of stone tools did *H. erectus* use?**

   H. erectus used both Oldowan and Acheulean tools but may have been the hominid that invented Acheulean tools.

6. **Why do we think that *H. erectus* was the first hominid that ate substantial quantities of meat?**

   H. erectus made stone tools, and there is archaeological evidence that these tools were used to butcher large animals, suggesting substantial meat consumption. In addition, its larger body and brain size and its greater range (across the Old World) suggest that *H. erectus* must have had a higher-quality diet than earlier *Homo* in order to meet its higher energetic needs.

CRITICAL THINKING QUESTIONS

1. Why is the distinction between *Australopithecus* and *Homo* becoming fuzzier as more fossils are discovered?

2. How might we interpret the fact that the earliest *H. erectus* fossils come from East Africa, but that there are other very *H. erectus*–like fossils from outside Africa at about the same time?

3. What was the main survival value of larger brain size to *H. erectus*? What could they do that earlier hominids could not that allowed them to expand the human range beyond Africa?

KEY TERMS

Oldowan
tool industry
core
flake
hammerstone
butchering site
quarrying site
home base

supraoribital torus
angular torus
occipital torus
sagittal keel
metopic keel
shovel-shaped incisor
platymeric
platycnemic
calotte

calvaria
canine fossa
Acheulean
Early Stone Age (or
    Lower Paleolithic)
biface
hand axe
cleaver
Movius line

SUGGESTED READING

Lewin, Roger. (1997). *Bones of Contention*, 2nd edition. University of Chicago Press, Chicago.

Schick, Kathy, and Toth, Nicholas. (1993). *Making Silent Stones Speak: Human Evolution and the Dawn of Technology.* Simon & Schuster, New York.

Shipman, Pat. (2001). *The Man Who Found the Missing Link*. Harvard University Press, Cambridge, MA.

Walker, Alan, and Shipman, Pat. (1996). *The Wisdom of the Bones.* Vintage Books, New York.

Wolpoff, Milford. (1999). *Paleoanthropology,* 2nd edition. McGraw-Hill, New York.

Chapter 14

ARCHAIC *HOMO SAPIENS* AND NEANDERTALS

I N AN OPEN COAL PIT IN GERMANY, a huge mechanical shovel grinds away at the earth, stripping away not only vast amounts of coal but also Holocene and Pleistocene deposits. Scientists monitor the activity, ready to intervene should something more interesting than coal be exposed. Over the years, archaeologists have identified a number of Lower Paleolithic sites in the pit, which are located several meters below the ground. The sites date to about 400,000 years ago: the Middle Pleistocene.

The material found at these sites is what we might expect given their age and location. The inventory includes flint tools and flakes, combined with the remains of extinct elephants, bovids, deer, and horses. No hominid remains are found, which is unfortunate given the scarcity of fossils from this critical period in human evolution. But after several years of excavation, archaeologist Hartmut Thieme discovered something that was even more scarce, and perhaps more significant, than additional fossil remains: four large wooden spears.

The spears are impressive: Two of them measure more than 2.25 m (7 feet) in length. Three of them are sharpened at one end. They are carefully shaped and their weight is distributed to make them aerodynamically efficient. It remains possible that they could have been used as lances and thrust at prey rather than thrown. The fourth is smaller (less than 1 m long) and sharpened at both ends. Thieme classifies it tentatively as a throwing stick or as a small thrusting spear. Three smaller wooden implements, made from the branches of trees, were also found. Although the function of these implements is not clear, they each had a groove cut into one end that could have been used to hold flints, perhaps creating a composite cutting or chopping tool.

Thieme believes that the discovery of these wooden spears and the butchered remains of big game provides strong evidence that Middle Pleistocene hominids were capable of organized game hunting and that they could hunt from a distance, increasing their safety. By showing us how these hominids made use of organic materials in their lives, these wooden spears provide us with a window to the past that is typically shuttered. When we look at traditional peoples throughout the world, we see that only a small and biased sample of their material cultures is preserved in the archaeological record. The discovery of these ancient spears from Germany gives us a better idea of just how much we're missing from the material cultures of extinct hominids.

In the previous chapters, we reviewed the primate and hominid fossil records primarily by starting in the past and working forward. But it may be useful to consider the past from the perspective of the present and what it can tell us about what may be missing in the fossil and archaeological records. Today, one species of hominid, *Homo sapiens*, is distributed around the globe. As a species, we share a common origin that should be traceable back to a population that existed at a certain time and place. The fossil record makes it quite clear that as hominids and as members of the genus *Homo* we definitely have an African homeland: We do not find hominids outside Africa until after 2 million years ago. But because *Homo erectus*, the presumed ancestor of all later hominid species, lived throughout the Old World in regions that were later occupied by modern humans, it is not immediately clear which *H. erectus* populations, if any, are directly ancestral to us.

Population variability further complicates the matter. Although all modern humans are members of the same species, there is clearly a substantial amount of geographic variability among human populations. Did this variability arise since we last shared a common ancestor as a species? Or is it a reflection of geographic variability that was present in ancestral, pre-*sapiens* populations? Like *H. sapiens*, the widely dispersed *H. erectus* also exhibited substantial geographic variation. A fundamental issue, which we will explore in this chapter and the next, is whether *H. sapiens* evolved from a small localized population that then replaced all other hominids existing at that time or whether the evolution of *H. sapiens* occurred in such a way that variability of ancestral populations was maintained in the transition to modern humans.

Another complicating factor is that as we go back in time, the amount of variability in the hominid fossil record increases. Many paleoanthropologists would argue that at various points in the past, more than one hominid species lived. The existence of more than one species is obvious in Africa during the period 1 to 2 million years ago, when robust australopithecines and members of the genus *Homo* lived at the same time. No one believes that robust australopithecines can be lumped into a single species with members of *Homo*.

In this chapter, we look at the hominid fossil record of the Middle to Late Pleistocene. Hominid fossils from this evolutionarily dynamic period have been found from throughout much of the Old World, but taxonomic assignments for the fossil specimens during this period in human evolution remain controversial. How many hominid species were present? What constitutes enough variation to differentiate them from one another? How do these species relate to anatomically modern humans? Are the famous Neandertals simply another type of human or something more distinct? As we will see, whether a paleoanthropologist identifies more or fewer hominid fossil species during the last 500,000 years is influenced in part by the hypotheses he or she thinks best explains the emergence of our own species.

HOMINID EVOLUTION IN THE MID-TO LATE PLEISTOCENE

As we saw in Chapter 9, the *Middle Pleistocene* dates from about 900,000 years ago (corresponding to the earliest glaciation of continental Europe) to about 125,000 years ago (Conroy, 1997). The period from 125,000 to 10,000 years ago corresponds to the *Late Pleistocene*. In the latter half of the Middle Pleistocene, the hominid fossil record begins to reveal specimens that are not "classic *H. erectus*" but that exhibit features often interpreted as being more "advanced" or derived in the direction of *H. sapiens*. These specimens often are lumped together and informally labeled "archaic *Homo sapiens*" or "advanced *H. erectus*," designations that distinguish these fossils from anatomically modern *H. sapiens* and classic *H. erectus*. Such informal labels indicate the transitional nature of these specimens between *H. erectus* and *H. sapiens* and the difficulty in achieving consensus among scientists on their phylogenetic placement in hominid evolution. Several anatomically distinguishable hominid groups were present at various times in the latter half of the Middle Pleistocene. In addition to archaic *H. sapiens*, classic *H. erectus* survived in China and Indonesia until at least 250,000 years ago and maybe later (see Chapter 13). In Europe, the earliest representatives of the Neandertals make their first appearance. Finally, although modern *H. sapiens* appears only in the Late Pleistocene, it is possible that the earliest modern humans may have made their first appearance at the very end of the Middle Pleistocene in Africa (see Chapter 15).

DEFINING ANATOMICALLY MODERN *HOMO SAPIENS*

Archaic *H. sapiens* are intermediate between classic *H. erectus* and anatomically modern *H. sapiens*. To define what *intermediate* means in this context, let us describe the features that distinguish modern humans from other hominids (Clark, 1975).

Compared with those of other members of genus *Homo*, the anatomically modern *H. sapiens* skull is large (mean capacity 1,350 cc) and gracile (Figure 14.1). Muscular ridges on the cranium are not strongly marked. Supraorbital (brow) ridges are not strongly developed or are absent altogether. The occipital region of the cranium is rounded, without development of an occipital torus and usually without an **occipital bun** (a backward-projecting bulge on of the occipital part of the skull). The forehead is rounded and more vertical than in other groups of *Homo*. Seen from behind, the maximum breadth of the skull is high (in the *parietal* region), and the vault is parallel-sided in rear view. The **mastoid process**, a protrusion from the temporal bone of the skull located behind and below the ear, is large and pyramidal. The jaws and teeth are small. The third molars (wisdom teeth) sometimes are poorly developed or even absent. Following jaw size, the face is smaller and retracted under the braincase to a greater degree than in previous hominids because the cranial base is more flexed. A *canine fossa* (a depression in the maxilla above the root of the upper canines) also develops. There is marked development of a chin. The limb bones are straight and slightly built, with the lower limb much longer than the upper.

In summary, compared with *H. erectus*, the cranium of anatomically modern *H. sapiens* is distinguished by a larger braincase and finer bone structure (see Figure 13.8 on page 364). Intermediate archaic *H. sapiens* typically exhibit a mosaic of *H. erectus* (Chapter 13) and *H. sapiens* features, in many cases retaining the robustness of classic *H. erectus* but with a larger cranial capacity and a shape more similar to anatomically modern *H. sapiens*. As we will see, the intermediate or transitional nature of archaic *H. sapiens* can pose problems for determining how these specimens should be classified and their precise phylogenetic relationship to later hominid taxa.

occipital bun A backward-projecting bulge on the occipital part of the skull.

mastoid process A protrusion from the temporal bone of the skull located behind the ear.

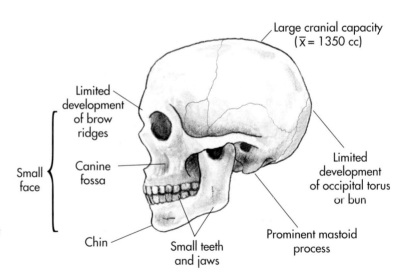

Anatomically Modern *Homo sapiens*

Large cranial capacity ($\bar{x}$ = 1350 cc)

Limited development of brow ridges

Canine fossa

Small face

Chin

Small teeth and jaws

Limited development of occipital torus or bun

Prominent mastoid process

FIGURE 14.1 Features of the skull of anatomically modern *Homo sapiens*.

ARCHAIC *HOMO SAPIENS*

Paleontologists have recovered numerous fossil specimens we informally classify as archaic *H. sapiens* from sites across the Old World, although the group is better known from remains found in Europe and Africa. Paleontological and molecular discoveries over the past two decades, along with improvements in dating techniques, have greatly increased our understanding of the place of archaic *H. sapiens* in the broader context of human evolution.

The specimens reflect an important transitional period during human evolution. Anatomically the group is diverse, but it seems to consistently differ from *H. erectus* by having larger brains (1,000–1,400 cc), more parallel-sided, taller, and less angular cranial vaults, robust but arching rather than straight supraorbital tori, and in some instances wide nasal apertures (Figure 14.2). Archaic *H. sapiens* differ from modern humans by retaining robust supraorbital tori, large faces, and thicker, lower cranial vaults. As we review the individual fossils, keep in mind that there are several phylogenetic scenarios into which they can be incorporated. Although we may call them archaic *H. sapiens*, that does not mean we consider them ancestral to later anatomically modern *H. sapiens* (although that may be a reasonable hypothesis), nor do they necessarily all represent the same species, although many scientists argue that they do.

EUROPEAN ARCHAIC *HOMO SAPIENS*

The earliest hominids in Europe (800,000 years ago) are those found at the Gran Dolina site of the Sierra de Atapuerca in Spain, described in Chapter 13. Their discoverers have provisionally assigned them to a new taxon, *Homo antecessor,* based on facial anatomy. However, the remains are generally considered too few, too fragmentary, and in some cases too developmentally young (the main remains are subadult) to make a strong case for a separate species designation. Most scientists would lump them in the general archaic *H. sapiens* category.

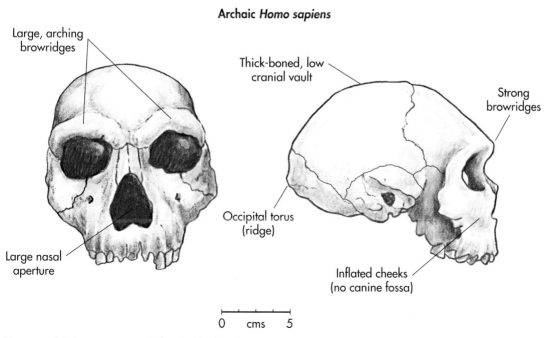

Archaic *Homo sapiens*

Large, arching browridges

Thick-boned, low cranial vault

Strong browridges

Large nasal aperture

Occipital torus (ridge)

Inflated cheeks (no canine fossa)

0   cms   5

FIGURE 14.2 Features of the skull of archaic *Homo sapiens.*

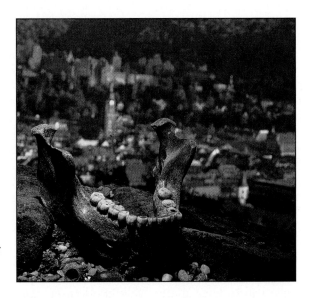

FIGURE 14.3   The Mauer mandible, discovered in Germany in 1907.

The first of the European Middle Pleistocene remains to be discovered was a mandible found in a sandpit in the village of Mauer, near Heidelberg, Germany, in 1907 (Figure 14.3; Schoetensack, 1908). Based on faunal and stratigraphic dating (no absolute dating is possible at the site), the mandible was assigned a Middle Pleistocene age of 400,000–500,000 years. Because the Mauer mandible is clearly not modern—it is quite robust and lacks a chin—it was correctly identified in 1908 as a hominid species distinct from our own. Because *Homo (Pithecanthropus) erectus* was not a generally accepted taxon at that time, the Mauer mandible was given the name *Homo heidelbergensis*.

After *H. erectus* became more definitively established, some researchers argued that the mandible should be placed in that taxon. However, others argue that the mandible differs from classic *H. erectus* in both its bony anatomy and its dentition and resembles several more complete specimens that were discovered later and are often called archaic *H. sapiens*. However, mandibles are notoriously hard to classify during this time period, and so the debate continues. For the many researchers who believe that the informal label "archaic *H. sapiens*" should be replaced with a formal species designation, because the Mauer mandible was the first of this group to be discovered and named, the species name *H. heidelbergensis* would have priority.

More complete fossils provide a more detailed picture of European hominids in the Middle Pleistocene (Figure 14.4). These include the Petralona cranium from Greece (150,000–300,000 years ago), the Steinheim cranium from Germany (200,000–250,000 years ago), the Arago 21 partial cranium from France (300,000–600,000 years ago), and the rear portion of a cranium from Swanscombe, England (200,000–250,000 years ago). Less complete remains of archaic *H. sapiens* are known from several other sites in Europe, such as Bilzingsleben and Véretesszöllös in Hungary.

The greatest trove of archaic *H. sapiens* fossils recovered from a single locality comes from a later part of the same cave system where *H. antecessor* was discovered, in Sierra de Atapuerca, Spain (Arsuaga, et al. 1997; Arsuaga, 2002) (Figure 14.5). From a cave (or pit) known as *Sima de los Huesos* (literally, the "bone pit"), Juan Luis Arsuaga and his colleagues have collected the remains of more than thirty individuals, ranging in age from 4 to 35 years. Based on faunal and absolute dating methods, the age of the site is about 300,000–400,000 years.

All these archaic *H. sapiens* specimens differ from classic *H. erectus* in vault shape and size, browridge conformation, and facial morphology, although they are similar in having thick cranial bones and less round cranial vaults. Cranial capacities of Mid-Pleistocene European fossils are between 1,100 and 1,390 cc,

(a)

(b)

FIGURE 14.4 (a) The Petralona cranium from Greece. (b) The Steinheim cranium from Germany.

making them larger brained than typical *H. erectus* specimens. The vault shape is also different in Mid-Pleistocene Europeans, exhibiting taller vaults with the greatest cranial breadth high on the parietal. The size range among these Mid-Pleistocene Europeans, especially in the sample from Sima de los Huesos, suggests that both males and females are present.

The 500,000-year-old tibia from Boxgrove in southern England, along with extensive postcranial remains from Sima de los Huesos, provide information

FIGURE 14.5 Skeletal remains from the Sima de los Huesos, Sierra de Atapuerca, Spain.

about the size and shape of the postcranial skeleton of archaic *H. sapiens* (Stringer et al., 1998; Arsuaga et al., 1997; Arsuaga, 2002). These postcrania are similar to other premodern *Homo* skeletons in being robust with strong muscle markings and thick cortical bone and in having large joint surface areas and strongly buttressed pelves.

Mid-Pleistocene European hominids are too primitive to be considered Neandertals, but those from the Sima de los Huesos exhibit several cranial features that are very Neandertal-like and seem to indicate that these fossils could be part of a population ancestral to Neandertals. Facial features that are the most Neandertal-like include a double-arched supraorbital torus and **midfacial prognathism**, the forward projection of the middle facial region, including the nose. The nasal bones actually form a shelf projecting from the face, and the cheek bones gradually recede from these rather than being perpendicular to the nose, as in our face. The nasal aperture is also quite wide. Arsuaga and his colleagues see the Sima de los Huesos hominids, along with other European archaic *H. sapiens*, as being directly ancestral to the later Neandertals and not ancestral to modern humans. We will discuss this phylogenetic model and others later.

AFRICAN ARCHAIC *HOMO SAPIENS*

The African continent has yielded at least four crania that are generally regarded as archaic *H. sapiens* because of their large cranial capacities, massive but more arching, non-barlike supraorbital tori, and less angular vaults, with their greatest width higher on the cranium. Their geological ages are not fully known. The oldest of these is likely to be the partial cranium from Bodo, Ethiopia (Figure 14.6), which preserves the face and anterior braincase and dates to as much as 600,000 years ago. The Bodo cranium is large, with a capacity of about 1,300 cc (Conroy et al., 1978). Its most extraordinary features are cut marks on the face that appear to be made by stone tools (White, 1986).

The Kabwe cranium and several postcranial elements, discovered in northern Rhodesia (present-day Zambia) at the Broken Hill limestone mine in 1921, are more complete but slightly smaller (1,280 cc) than that from Bodo (Figure 14.6). The remains are also known as Rhodesian Man or Broken Hill for their find spot. Dating of the site is uncertain, although a late Middle Pleistocene age of 125,000 years, based on faunal remains, is suggested. Both Kabwe and Bodo have large nasal apertures and somewhat prognathic midfaces with massive, arched brows. The previous classification of Broken Hill as an African Neandertal, although now discarded, may indicate its ultimate ancestry to the Neandertal lineage.

Smaller archaic *H. sapiens* crania also exist in Africa. The Ndutu partial cranium from near Olduvai Gorge in Tanzania has a cranial capacity of about 1,100 cc (Rightmire, 1990). Dates for the Ndutu cranium range from 200,000 to 400,000 years ago. The Salé partial cranium from Morocco includes most of the cranial vault but is missing the face, has a small cranial capacity (900 cc), and dates to about 200,000–250,000 years ago (Hublin, 1985). Like the Steinheim cranium from Germany, these crania may be from small females, with small cranial capacities. Although not particularly large, Ndutu and Salé share features of the cranial vault with other archaic *H. sapiens*, including a high maximum cranial breadth and rounder vaults.

Taken together, the European and African archaic *H. sapiens* specimens share many features and have a similar overall appearance. However, no African archaic *H. sapiens* have been found that possess the specific derived features reminiscent of the Neandertals, whereas in Europe, the Sima de los Huesos hominids and others are claimed by some scientists to share derived features with later Neandertals.

midfacial prognathism
The forward projection of the middle facial region, including the nose.

(a)

FIGURE 14.6 (a) The Bodo cranium (right) from Ethiopia shows signs of having been defleshed with stone tools. (b) The Kabwe cranium, from Broken Hill, Zambia.

(b)

ASIAN ARCHAIC *HOMO SAPIENS*

Fossil specimens from several sites in Asia are generally accepted as representing archaic *H. sapiens*, based on their enlarged cranial capacities. They also differ from *H. erectus* in vault and supraorbital toral shape. Reasonably complete crania have been found in China from the sites of Dali, Maba, and Jinniushan (Figure 14.7). They range in age from 130,000–200,000 years ago. The finds from Jinniushan also include some postcrania. Two other crania from Yunxian probably also represent archaic *H. sapiens* based on the shape of the browridge. However, both are heavily distorted and difficult to interpret (Li and Etler, 1992).

The oldest hominid remains on the Indian continent come from the Narmada Valley, where a partial calvaria dates to the latest part of the Middle Pleistocene (125,000–150,000 years ago). The cranium was initially classified as belonging to *H. erectus*; however, later analyses established its transitional character, indicating that it was more similar to archaic *H. sapiens* (Kennedy et al., 1991). It has an estimated cranial capacity of 1,150–1,400 cc more vertically sided vault walls, and a double-arched browridge.

Although dating is a problem for the Chinese and Indian archaic *H. sapiens*, evidence indicates that archaic *H. sapiens* probably were present in Asia by 200,000 years ago. Given some of the late dates for classic *H. erectus* in Asia (see Chapter 13), if you accept that archaic *H. sapiens* is a different species from *H. erectus*, then two distinct hominid species were present in Asia in the latter part of the Middle Pleistocene.

BEHAVIOR OF ARCHAIC *HOMO SAPIENS*

Reconstructing the behavior of archaic *Homo sapiens* poses a somewhat different problem from reconstructing the behavior of earlier hominids. Given their large brain size and probable close relationship to modern

FIGURE 14.7 Dali, a Chinese archaic *Homo sapiens*.

humans, we are compelled to consider archaic *H. sapiens* behavior from the perspective of what we know about the behavior of contemporary humans. Unfortunately, the material culture of archaic *H. sapiens* doesn't provide a comprehensive rendering of late Middle Pleistocene behavior, but archaeological excavations at many sites in the Old World dating from 150,000–500,000 years ago indicate this was a period of evolutionary, although perhaps not revolutionary, change in behavior.

STONE TOOLS

Stone tool types and distributions that characterized the Early Pleistocene were still present in the Middle Pleistocene. In Africa and Europe, where the Acheulean was well represented, Acheulean traditions—including production of bifaces (hand axes)—continued until about 150,000 years ago. In China, where hand axes were never associated with *H. erectus*, archaic *H. sapiens* are found in association with simple flake tools and cores. Together the Oldowan and Acheulean industries are known as the *Lower Paleolithic* in Europe or the *Early Stone Age* in Africa.

In the Middle Pleistocene, **Middle Paleolithic** (**Middle Stone Age**) industries that used *prepared core* technologies developed (Figure 14.8). Prepared core technologies require that the tool maker modify the original core by a number of flake removal steps in order to prepare it to produce a flake of a prescribed size and shape. Although wasteful of raw material in one sense, prepared core technology allows great control of production of a main tool type, the so-called *Mousterian* point. Such preparation in pursuit of a particular flake indicates increasing forethought and abstract thinking. Prepared core techniques include the **Levallois technique**, named for a French site near Paris where it was first discovered by scientists, even though the technique was developed in Africa between 200,000 and 300,000 years ago. In addition to prepared cores, Middle Paleolithic industries also used other flaking methods, characterized by a greater prevalence of soft hammer techniques (in which materials such as bone, antlers, or limestone were used as hammerstones), more retouched tools, and a larger variety of possibly stylized tool shapes. Tools include a number of different kinds of scrapers, made from flakes, and the previously mentioned points. The advantage of Middle Paleolithic industries, beyond the predictability of flake size and shape, is that from a given amount of raw material they produce more cutting surface

Middle Paleolithic (Middle Stone Age) Stone tool industries that used prepared core technologies.

Levallois technique A Middle Paleolithic technique that made use of prepared cores to produce uniform flakes.

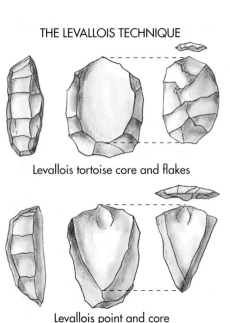

THE LEVALLOIS TECHNIQUE

Levallois tortoise core and flakes

Levallois point and core

FIGURE 14.8 The Levallois technique for making uniform flakes from a prepared core.

than Early Paleolithic techniques. Once these tool types appeared in the late Middle Pleistocene, no new tool types were introduced until the late Pleistocene.

TOOLS FROM ORGANIC MATERIALS

Based on the behavior of living nonhuman primates and humans, we assume that hominids also used tools made from organic materials that would rarely be preserved in the archaeological record. Chimpanzees fashion tools from twigs and leaves, and it is likely that early hominids did as well. Although we have seen evidence of bone tool use by the robust australopithecines in Chapter 12, modified bone or antler tools are absent from the archaic *H. sapiens* archaeological record. However, there is indirect evidence, from flake scars on stone, that these items were used as soft hammers to produce stone tools (Stringer et al., 1998).

Until recently, there was no direct evidence of wooden tool use either. However, as described at the beginning of this chapter, in 1997 archaeologist Hartmut Thieme announced the discovery of three javelin-like wooden spears and a throwing stick, along with three other worked branches, recovered from excavations in an open pit coal mine in Schöningen, Germany. They were dated to 400,000 years ago. The spears, made from the trunks of trees, were 1.82–2.30 m (5.9–7.5 feet) long and carefully sharpened at one end. They were found in close association with numerous faunal remains, and Thieme argued that the context of wooden spears with the remains of prey was evidence of large game hunting. Some researchers believe these pointed wooden sticks were not spears but only thrusting lances or that if they were spears, they would not have been very effective for large game hunting (Klein and Edgar, 2002). The three worked branches may be as significant as the spears, if Thieme's speculation that they formed the handles of stone–wood composite tools is correct. The discoveries at Schöningen establish that wooden tools probably were an important part of the toolkit of archaic *H. sapiens*. All the spears exhibit a high degree of workmanship, indicating that wood was a common medium, at least for this archaic *H. sapiens* population in Germany.

BIG GAME HUNTING

In Chapter 12, we discussed the debate about hunting or scavenging in the lives of past hominid species. In the 1960s and early 1970s, several Middle Pleistocene archaeological sites were interpreted as demonstrating that archaic *H. sapiens* or advanced *H. erectus* (as they were more likely to be considered then) were capable of big game hunting (Figure 14.9). There is little doubt that big game hunting

FIGURE 14.9 Excavations of elephant remains at Torralba, Spain.

FIGURE 14.10 Evidence for big game hunting by archaic *H. sapiens* is suggested by the association of hand axes and red deer bones at Boxgrove site, England.

would have been advantageous for some archaic *H. sapiens* (or *H. erectus*) occupying northern latitudes in Europe or Asia. In those locations, there would have been a seasonal dependence on animal food, and the ability to hunt big game would have made it easier to expand into colder areas, even if scavenging were still done. In numerous Middle Pleistocene archaeological sites, such as the Spanish sites of Ambrona and Torralba dating to 200,000–400,000 years ago (Howell, 1966), faunal remains of large game have been found in association with Acheulean artifacts. Critics point out that associations such as this do not constitute proof of hunting because they could have resulted from the activity of other animals or other nonhominid depositional forces. During the Middle Pleistocene, the sites of Ambrona and Torralba were in a swamp, and some investigators have viewed the butchered remains as being the results of scavenging elephants that were trapped in the swamp rather than hunting (Shipman and Rose, 1983). Others argue that finding large fauna in proximity with hominid artifacts at water locations may simply mean that water was important for both hominids and other animals and does not indicate a reliance on big game by either hunting or scavenging (Klein and Edgar, 2002).

However, excavations at two sites in the 1990s provide increasing evidence in support of the hypothesis that Middle Pleistocene hominids hunted big game. The Schöningen spears were found in direct association with the butchered remains of ten horses and flake tools that could be used to deflesh the carcasses. Although it is impossible to be certain that 400,000 years ago the spears were used to bring down the horses, it seems reasonable to conclude they were made to be thrown at large, living animals.

Excavations at the Boxgrove site in England (Figure 14.10) provide further evidence of big game hunting in the Middle Pleistocene (Stringer et al., 1998; Roberts and Parfitt, 1999). As you recall, this site has yielded a single, robust hominid tibia and tooth dating to about 500,000 years ago, as well as numerous remains of small and large animals in association with stone tools, mostly hand axes. Mark Roberts and his colleagues argue that big game hunting rather than scavenging explains how these animals and tools came to be deposited together: Faunal remains indicate that hominids got to the remains before carnivores or scavenging animals; stone tool cut marks always underlay carnivore teeth marks, and butchering marks indicate that eyes and tongues were removed by hominids ahead of bird scavengers. Furthermore, butchered rhinoceroses at the site were all healthy midlife adults with no apparent disease or defect, and a horse scapula (shoulder blade) recovered from the site has a clear projectile wound, a hole about

50 mm (2 inches) in diameter; it is the kind of wound that spears of the kind found at Schöningen would produce.

The hunting versus scavenging debate will go on. But the evidence seems to be mounting that archaic *H. sapiens* were capable of bringing down large game and that they did so in a cooperative manner, using Acheulean technology. At this point, however, it seems that these Middle Pleistocene hominids did not have as great an impact on the populations of large game animals as later modern *H. sapiens* had in some regions of the world in the Late Pleistocene. This may indicate that big game hunting occupied a different role in the subsistence strategies of *H. erectus* and archaic *H. sapiens* than it did for anatomically modern *H. sapiens*.

FIRE, CAMPSITES, AND HOME SITES

Evidence of the use of fire by archaic *H. sapiens* is similar to that for *H. erectus*. No proper hearths have been discovered, although ash deposits and charred bones recovered from a number of sites indicate that fire may have been used by both *H. erectus* and archaic *H. sapiens*. Archaic *H. sapiens* did not make a particularly strong impact on the landscape. Although it is reasonable to assume that they had campsites and home bases, there are few signs of them in the archaeological record; no Middle Pleistocene postholes or storage pits have been found, for example. The use of caves as shelter was also limited. Although it has been claimed that there is evidence of Acheulean "beach huts" at the site of Terra Amata in the South of France, disruption of the "living floor" of the site and the somewhat random scatter of bone and stone remains make this interpretation difficult to accept (Stringer and Gamble, 1993).

There is limited value in continuing to review all aspects of archaic *H. sapiens* cultural behavior for which we do not have evidence. Let us move on to a group of hominids who are sometimes classified as archaic *H. sapiens* but who are more commonly known as the Neandertals.

THE NEANDERTALS

The taxonomically informal term *Neandertals* refers to a group of Late Pleistocene fossil hominids whose remains have been recovered from sites dating between 27,000 and 150,000 years ago in Europe, the Near and Middle East, and western Asia. The complete or partial remains of several hundred Neandertal individuals have been discovered (Stringer and Gamble, 1993; Trinkaus, 1995). As you will recall from Chapter 9, this time period is one of extreme oscillations in temperature caused by strong glacial and interglacial cycles (see Figure 9.18) As a result of these cycles and the northern location of Neandertal sites, climate is a particularly important variable for understanding the origin and evolution of this group (Howell, 1964). At the end of their existence Neandertals and anatomically modern *H. sapiens* overlap in time and space. How they share the landscape, and indeed the relationships between them, are points of some debate.

Scientists disagree as to whether Neandertals should be considered a species within the genus *Homo* (*H. neanderthalensis*) or a subspecies within *H. sapiens* (*H. s. neanderthalensis*). As was the case for archaic *H. sapiens*, choosing a taxonomic name for the Neandertals depends on how we define a species and on the phylogenetic model for the emergence of anatomically modern *H. sapiens* to which we subscribe. At this point, there is no consensus in the field on these issues, so there is no consensus on a formal name for the Neandertals. However, there is little disagreement that "classic Neandertals" are an anatomically distinct group of hominids that lived during a short period of time and occupied a circumscribed portion of the Old World (Figures 14.11 and 14.12 on page 396).

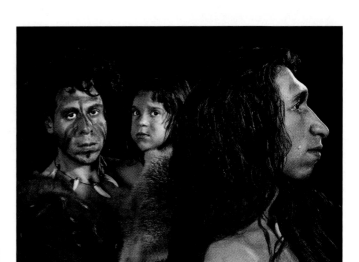

FIGURE 14.11 A scientific reconstruction of a Neandertal man.

GEOGRAPHIC AND TEMPORAL DISTRIBUTION

The largest number of Neandertal sites, including the oldest (about 150,000 years ago) and the youngest (about 27,000–30,000 years ago), are located in Western Europe (Figure 14.12). Fossil-bearing sites are plentiful in Germany (Neandertal, Ehringsdorf), Belgium (Spy, Engis), Spain (Zafarraya, Gibraltar), Italy (Guattari), and France (La Quina, La Ferrassie, St. Cesaire, La Chapelle). However, the Neandertal range extends into central Asia at the site of Teshik Tash in Uzbekistan, into the Near East (Kebara, Amud, and Tabun, Israel; Dedirayah, Syria), which

FIGURE 14.12 Distribution of Neandertal sites in Europe and western Asia.

Neandertals seemed to occupy during glacial times, and into the Middle East (Shanidar, Iraq). In addition to fossil-bearing localities, archaeological sites of the same ages span the entire region, telling us about site distribution and Neandertal movements relative to time and climate.

Most Neandertal fossils are found in caves, indicating extensive use of these areas as living sites. However, most Middle Paleolithic archaeological sites are open air localities. Cave use results in better preservation of remains and thus the better fossil record for Neandertals than for earlier hominids.

HISTORY OF NEANDERTAL DISCOVERY

From the mid-1800s until the 1930s, when *H. erectus* became a more widely accepted taxon and the South African australopithecines started to come to light, Neandertals were the core of the hominid fossil record. In the popular imagination, "Neandertal" and "caveman" became synonyms. But as the best-known representative of our evolutionary past, Neandertals also became the focus of negative portrayals and feelings (Box 14.1 on page 398). Ideas about progress along with anxiety about our animal origins cast the Neandertal in the loser's role in the evolutionary game.

The first Neandertal discovered was found at the Engis cave site in Belgium in 1830: the cranium of a small child aged 2–3 years, who even at that young age shows incipient development of a double-arched Neandertal browridge. The second Neandertal discovery, in 1848, was a nearly complete cranium from the British colony of Gibraltar on the southern coast of Spain. The significance of these finds was not fully appreciated at the time of their discovery. It took nearly 20 years for the Gibraltar cranium to be recognized as a Neandertal; although considered from the time of its discovery to be an ancient specimen, the Engis child was not "rediscovered" to be a very young Neandertal for more than a century.

The original Neandertal specimen (for which the group was named) was found in 1856 in a limestone quarry in the Neander Valley (in German, *Neanderthal*) near Düsseldorf. The quarry was dotted with caves filled with clay and debris that was removed before the limestone could be mined. The Neandertal bones were discovered in these clay deposits that had been thrown 20 m (60 feet) down a hill. The owner of the quarry saw large bones in the deposit, and thinking that they were from cave bears, contacted a local schoolteacher and natural historian, Johann Carl Fuhlrott, who identified them as human. Recognizing the potential significance of this find, Fuhlrott then contacted anatomist Professor Herman Schaafhausen, who led the scientific analysis of the discovery.

The Neandertal remains consist of a skullcap and partial skeleton, including several long bones, part of the pelvis, and the right shoulder (Figure 14.13).

FIGURE 14.13 The original Neandertal remains from the Neander Valley, Germany.

Box 14.1   Neandertal Image Makeovers

I t is definitely not a compliment to be called a Neandertal, and most of us are familiar with the stereotype of the brutish caveman. Although the origins of the stereotype have their roots in early negative portrayals of Neandertals presented by scientists, it is safe to say that the scientific appraisal of Neandertals over the past several decades has been far more positive than negative, despite debates about their status vis-à-vis anatomically modern *H. sapiens*. So why does the negative connotation of Neandertals remain in the popular culture?

Erik Trinkaus and Pat Shipman (1992) have chronicled how popular and scientific images of Neandertals have changed over the years. There seems to be ambivalence about Neandertals, especially as represented in popular media, which emerges from a pervasive unease fueled by the very existence of Neandertals in our family tree. Trinkaus and Shipman write (pp. 406-407), "They [historical Neandertal images] testify to an ongoing struggle between our willingness to accept Neandertals as close relatives and yet our abhorrence at having anything so potentially inhuman so close at hand. It is the age-old struggle between the god-like and the bestial in humans restated."

The oldest illustration of a Neandertal that Trinkaus and Shipman could track down was from a popular magazine article published in 1873. This picture of a Neandertal couple—the woman's portrayal constitutes a stereotype of Victorian notions of female passivity—and their dogs

FIGURE A   Historical reconstruction of Neandertals.

has an almost romantic quality. The Neandertal male is portrayed as a kind of "noble savage," ready to meet head-on anything that might appear at the mouth of their cave to challenge them. Clearly, this view of Neandertal men at least is not wholly negative or bestial.

The discovery of the French La Chapelle-aux-Saints Neandertal led to reconstructions of Neandertals in the popular press that were clearly not of the noble savage type. Instead, an image from a popular French publication (1909) reveals a feral and beastly Neandertal who is very unlike a modern human (Figure A). Not long after this, the analysis of the French Neandertal remains by Marcellin Boule led to recon-

structions that depicted Neandertals not necessarily as beastly but as stooped and hulking. Their physicality was emphasized over their cognition.

In scientific circles, a different view of Neandertals emerged as early as the 1930s. Anthropologist Carleton Coon produced a drawing of a Neandertal dressed in modern clothing, making the point that a Neandertal could ride on the New York subway with little notice if he were dressed correctly and given a good shave. And yet a 1950s horror movie, *The Neanderthal Man*, indicates that the more beastly view was easier to sell to the moviegoing public.

Popular views of Neandertals reflect not only deep-seated tensions about the conflict between humanity and bestiality, as Trinkaus and Shipman suggest, but also feelings about race and racial inferiority and superiority. After all, humans have a long history of considering those who do not come from their own particular group as being something less than human, even when they most obviously are. In his novel *Dance of the Tiger*, which dramatizes the demise of the Neandertals in northern Europe some 40,000 years ago, noted paleontologist Bjorn Kurten makes a point of depicting the Neandertals as light-skinned and destined to be replaced by darker-skinned modern humans from the south. Although these skin color assignments are justifiable based on scientific grounds, from a literary standpoint it is obvious that Kurten was using race as a device to make an ancient species-level conflict more poignant for twentieth-century readers.

Although the original cave where the bones were found no longer exists, the deposits from the cave were found through study of the archives of the mining company, and more than 140 years after they were initially removed (Schmitz et al., 2002), they yielded additional bones and artifacts, which indicate that there were at least three individuals in the cave. Almost unbelievably, additional remains of the original Neandertal specimen were discovered. This re-excavation allowed dating of the finds for the first time, giving them an age of 40,000 years.

Professor Schaafhausen presented his initial analyses of the Neandertal remains in 1857, a full 2 years before Darwin published *On the Origin of Species*. Schaafhausen noted the long and low shape of the skullcap, the large browridges, and the development of an occipital bun. All these distinguished this specimen from modern humans. Furthermore, the postcranial bones were very robust and marked with ridges for the attachment of large muscles; the ribs were rounded, indicating a barrel-chested individual. One of the bones of the lower left arm (the ulna) had clearly been broken and healed awkwardly; it is likely that the arm was not usable in life, and it showed some signs of atrophy due to disuse. However, Schaafhausen concluded that the left arm was the only pathological aspect of the skeleton and that otherwise it reflected the normal development of a race of men who lived in Europe long before the Romans or Celts.

The initial reception of Schaafhausen's analysis was decidedly mixed. Critics came up with a variety of arguments against the hypothesis that the Neandertal remains represented a different and extinct kind of human. One critic suggested that the robust and bowlegged individual was simply a Cossack of Mongol descent who had died during the Russian invasion of Germany in 1814. Several critics considered the Neandertal specimen to be an unfortunate individual who suffered from a variety of pathological conditions, thus explaining his unusual morphology; the obviously injured left arm lent credence to this position.

Thomas Henry Huxley, who was known as "Darwin's bulldog" for his vociferous defense of natural selection (Chapter 2), provided one of the first evolutionary analyses of the Neandertal specimen, in 1864. Although Huxley was impressed with the "pithecoid" (apelike) nature of some aspects of the skull, such as the thickness of the bones and the browridges, he concluded that the Neandertal was no ape-man or "missing link." The cranial capacity clearly exceeded that of any ape and was in the human range, and the postcranial skeleton, though robust, was essentially human. Huxley placed the Neandertal at an extreme end of variation seen in modern humans. While Huxley was presenting his analyses, British anatomist George Busk recalled the odd-looking skull from Gibraltar he had seen years before. In 1864, he presented the Gibraltar cranium as the second Neandertal specimen.

Arguments that the Neandertal specimen represented only a diseased modern human rather than a distinct fossil ancestor lost force as additional Neandertals were discovered at sites throughout Europe. By 1915, they were known from sites in Germany, Spain, Belgium, Croatia, and France. In the 1920s and 1930s, they were discovered in sites in the Middle East and as far as Uzbekistan in central Asia. We now have the remains of hundreds of Neandertal individuals recovered from dozens of sites.

Besides modern humans, Neandertals are by far the most thoroughly represented hominids in the fossil record. Given the large number of Neandertal remains available, it is possible to study aspects of their growth and development and demography, population-level variables that are impossible to realistically examine in earlier hominids. But this abundance of information does not mean there is consensus on who exactly the Neandertals were. It is likely that compared with earlier hominids, the cultural behavior of Neandertals was more complex, so it is more difficult to interpret in the context of the archaeological record.

NEANDERTAL ANATOMY: BUILT FOR THE COLD

Neandertals possess some derived features that are not present in either anatomically modern humans or archaic *H. sapiens* such as *H. heidelbergensis* (Figure 14.14 and Figure 14.15 on page 400). Therefore, many scientists think that they represent a unique evolutionary trajectory in the context of Middle and Late Pleistocene hominid evolution. Some of their derived features seem to be anticipated by the anatomy of some archaic *H. sapiens*, especially those from Sima de los Huesos, perhaps suggesting that Neandertals descended from these populations.

NEANDERTAL

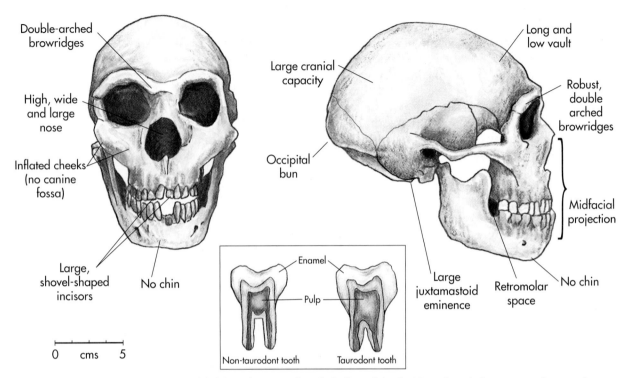

FIGURE 14.14 The Neandertal skull and teeth. Neandertals have taurodont molars.

Although the Neandertal vault is long and low, its size and shape are quite different from that of *H. erectus*. The Neandertal cranium is much larger than that of *H. erectus*; presumed females have an average cranial capacity of 1,300 cc and presumed males an average of 1,600 cc. Both figures exceed the averages seen in their modern human or *H. erectus* counterparts. Research on Neandertal brains (as studied from the impressions the brain made on the inside of the skull) suggests they were fully modern in their organization and that the large size of the brain was a function of large body size and adaptation to the cold environments in which they evolved (Holloway, 1984).

FIGURE 14.15 The faces of Neandertals (left) and anatomically modern *H. sapiens* (right) display anatomical differences including a double-arched brow and absence of a canine fossa in Neandertals.

In addition to these size differences, vault shape differs in important ways. The maximum cranial breadth in Neandertals tends to be in the middle of the cranium, giving it an oval appearance when viewed from the rear. In contrast, in humans, the maximum cranial breadth is higher on the skull, and the side walls are parallel, whereas in *H. erectus* maximum breadth is low on the vault, and the side walls slope inward, forming a pentagon in rear view. At the back of the Neandertal cranium, the occipital bone bulges posteriorly, forming the occipital bun. The mastoid process in Neandertals is smaller than in modern humans, but a ridge of bone just next to it, the **juxtamastoid eminence**, is larger than the mastoid process.

The face of the Neandertals also differs from those of *H. erectus* and modern humans. Among the most important of the derived characters of the Neandertals is their midfacial prognathism (Figure 14.15). The middle part of the face, around the nose, projects strongly anteriorly, and the cheek region is placed far posteriorly, with an even grade between the two. It is almost as if someone has grabbed the Neandertal nose and pulled it away from the cheeks, forming a smooth transition from cheek to nose. Therefore, the cheeks of Neandertals are often described as "swept back."

The face as a whole is also quite tall. Probably related to the anterior position of the midface (and upper dentition) is the presence on the rear of the mandible of a *retromolar space* between the third molar and the ascending ramus. Like earlier hominids, Neandertals show no development of a chin. Although these features are striking compared with modern humans, Erik Trinkaus (2003) points out that the large faces of Neandertals reflect continuation of a trend seen in archaic *H. sapiens*; thus, modern humans should be thought of as having small faces. Similarly, large nose size, exemplified skeletally by the large nasal aperture and projecting nasal bones, and other features in the nasal region of the Neandertals again reflect well-established evolutionary trends observed in a wide range of Middle and Late Pleistocene hominids (Franciscus, 1999, 2003).

There are also important differences between the inner ear anatomy of Neandertals and that of modern humans and *H. erectus*. The semicircular canals of the inner ear assist in maintaining balance, but there is variation in their structure even between closely related species. Although modern humans and *H. erectus* do not differ in inner ear anatomy, work by Fred Spoor and his colleagues using three-dimensional imaging shows that Neandertals have a different and probably derived inner ear anatomy (Spoor et al., 2003). The differences are so clear that they have been used to definitively identify the infant temporal bone from Arcy-sur-Cure as a Neandertal, an important identification for this site that had otherwise nondiagnostic fossil remains (Hublin et al., 1996). This is one of only two sites in which Neandertals are associated with an Upper Paleolithic (blade-based) technology known as the Châtelperronian and may also show association with symbolic remains. These clear-cut differences in ear anatomy also support the idea that the Neandertals may be a species separate from modern humans.

Three prominent features characterize Neandertal teeth (Figure 14.14):

- The anterior teeth show an unusual amount of wear that is much greater than that on the molars and is greater than among modern human populations, even those who use their anterior teeth extensively. This may indicate that Neandertals used these teeth to hold objects. Cut marks on the teeth further indicate that Neandertals held objects with their front teeth while cutting the objects, perhaps hide or pieces of meat, with stone tools.

- The upper incisors of Neandertals had built-up ridges of enamel on the side nearest the tongue (lingual surface), giving the tooth a *shovel-shaped* appearance. Shovel-shaped incisors generally are considered to provide greater resistance to wear.

juxtamastoid eminence A ridge of bone next to the mastoid process; in Neandertals, it is larger than the mastoid process itself.

● The molar teeth of Neandertals had expanded pulp cavities and fused roots, a feature known as **taurodontism**. Taurodont teeth can sustain more wear than non-taurodont teeth because they maintain a broader base for wear after the enamel of the crown has been worn away. Both taurodont molars and shovel-shaped incisors are found in modern human populations at various frequencies.

Many have speculated about why Neandertals had such prognathic faces and large noses. A popular idea is that the nose warmed cold air before it reached the respiratory system and brain. Among modern humans, however, cold-dwelling populations tend to have long and narrow noses to restrict cold airflow to the brain, whereas broad noses are found in more tropical climates and facilitate heat dissipation (Stringer and Gamble, 1993). Others argue that the prognathic midface (and the large nose associated with it) helps dissipate heavy bite loads on the anterior dentition. However, in animals and hominids that produce large bite forces, the face typically is retracted, not prognathic (remember the adaptive suite of the robust australopithecines, for example), and Neandertal muscle forces may not have been much greater than in modern human fossils with very different facial morphologies (Antón, 1996). No convincing argument for an adaptive function for the large Neandertal face and nose has yet to be generally accepted, and it may be that Neandertal facial morphology results from a variety of phylogenetic trends or evolutionary forces. In particular, genetic isolation in glacial environments may have produced the Neandertal face via genetic drift from an already prognathic ancestor, such as the Sima de los Huesos specimens.

The postcranial skeleton of the Neandertals was massive compared with that of modern humans, although Neandertals were on average shorter than Late Pleistocene humans (Figure 14.16). The chest was barrel-shaped and the limbs, espe-

taurodontism Molar teeth that have expanded pulp cavities and fused roots.

Figure 14.16 Neandertals were much more heavily built than anatomically modern humans.

cially the forearm and shin, were short. These characteristics are consistent with a body designed to conserve heat in a cold climate (see Bergman's and Allen's rules in Chapter 6), and Neandertals have been described as having "hyper-polar" bodies (Holliday, 1995). The long bones and major joints were all larger and more robust than those found in modern humans, features that Neandertals may have shared with earlier hominids and that indicate a physically demanding lifestyle. Neandertal males are estimated to have been on average 169 cm (5 ft 6.5 in) in height, with a weight of 65 kg (143 lb), whereas females were 160 cm (5 ft 3 in) and 50 kg (110 lb) (Stringer and Gamble, 1993).

The Neandertal skeleton shows evidence of very heavy muscle markings, indicating that they had very large, powerful muscles. Erik Trinkaus suggests that this powerful build indicated high levels and possibly even long hours of physically difficult activity. The energetic costs of such activity have been estimated by Mark Sorenson and Bill Leonard (2001), who suggest that physically active Neandertals would have had daily energy needs much higher than those of modern human hunter-gatherers and more similar to those of trained athletes and subsistence farmers.

Neandertal and modern human postcranial skeletons differ in several other respects. One of the most striking differences appears in the anatomy of the *pubic bone,* which forms the front part of the pelvis. The upper, anterior part of the pelvis, formed by the *superior pubic ramus,* was longer and more gracile in Neandertals than in modern humans. This is in direct opposition to the pattern established by the rest of the skeleton. Much speculation about the function of the Neandertal pubis has been offered. One thing that is clear from the complete Neandertal pelvis discovered at Kebara, Israel, is that the lengthened pubis does not result in a larger pelvic outlet, so it is not related to either increased birth efficiency or increased gestation time, as had been previously argued. The broader pelvis may simply have been the Neandertal way of establishing greater body breadth (and greater volume relative to surface area for heat retention).

GROWTH AND DEVELOPMENT

Neandertals are the only fossil group to be reasonably well represented by subadult remains of nearly all age classes from newborn (or even fetal) to adult. In Europe, the earliest Neandertal to be discovered from Engis is 2- to 3-year-old, deciduous (baby) teeth found at Spy, and a 3- to 5-year-old was found at Devil's Quarry on Gibraltar. In France, at La Ferrassie, remains of six children ranging in age from not much older than newborn to about 12 years of age were found, and at La Quina an important cranium of an 8-year-old child was discovered. Of the thousands of bone fragments at Krapina in Croatia, many of the twenty-five individuals were subadults, and in the northern Caucasus, northeast of the Black Sea, a partial skeleton of a Neandertal neonate or fetus (estimates of age range from 7 months gestational age to 2 months neonatal age) has recently been recovered from Mezmaiskaya Cave and has yielded important DNA information (Ovchinnikov et al., 2000). This infant may have been a member of one of the last surviving Neandertal populations; the date for this site is 29,000 years ago. The site representing the easternmost extent of the Neandertal range, Teshik Tash in Uzbekistan, yielded the skeleton of a 9-year-old child (Figure 14.17 on page 404). In the Near East, several infant remains have been found at Amud Cave, including a 10-month-old who clearly bears Neandertal features in its cranial anatomy (Rak et al., 1994). And the cave of Dedirayah in Syria has yielded the complete skeleton of a Neandertal child.

With a relative abundance of subadult remains, the Neandertals are the only fossil hominid group for which detailed studies on growth have been made. Recall the work by Chris Dean (Chapter 13) that indicated *H. erectus* had a faster dental

(a) (b)

FIGURE 14.17 Neandertal development and aging. (a) Remains of a child from Teshik Tash. (b) The "Old Man" from La Chapelle.

developmental rate than modern humans; this same study found Neandertals had a dental developmental rate more similar to humans. More recent studies suggest that some Neandertals may have grown even more quickly. Studies of growth of the mandible indicate that initially Neandertal children may have grown faster than modern human children but that in general growth rates are similar, even though shape changes during growth differ between the groups. Neandertals thus seem to show, for the first time in hominid evolution, growth patterns similar to our own.

HEALTH AND DISEASE

The history of Neandertal research has been strongly influenced by the recognition and interpretation of pathological conditions in bone. Recall that the type specimen from the Neander Valley was at the center of an argument over whether it was a pathological human or a distinct species or subspecies. For many years the common perception of Neandertals as primitive, shuffling creatures came from reconstructions produced by Marcellin Boule from a Neandertal skeleton from La Chapelle, France. The "Old Man" of La Chapelle-aux-Saints was found buried in a small cave in the Dordogne region of France and dates to about 40,000 years ago. The skeleton is clearly that of an older male, although in this context *old* means about 40 years of age. He suffered from numerous pathological conditions: a deformation in the pelvis, a crushed toe, severe arthritis in several of the vertebrae, and a broken rib sustained not long before death. He was missing many teeth, and the mandible and maxilla showed a significant amount of bone loss (Figure 14.17).

Boule reconstructed the Old Man as having a stooped posture and a shuffling gait, far from the upright stride of modern humans. In part Boule may have been misled by the numerous pathological conditions in the skeleton, but recent investigators who have examined the skeleton and Boule's work also believe that his interpretation of the skeleton was biased by his negative preconceptions about the "primitive" Neandertals (to be fair to Boule, the excavators of the Spy Neandertals also interpreted the skeletons as having a stooped posture). Nonetheless, Boule's appraisal and interpretation of the Old Man of La Chapelle-aux-Saints was very influential, and it formed the "scientific" basis for the negative image of Neandertals for decades.

Neandertal skeletons provide abundant evidence of traumatic injuries. The Shanidar remains from Iraq, dated to about 40,000–50,000 years ago, provide evidence of the hard lives that Neandertal individuals led (Trinkaus, 1983). Almost every one shows some type of pathological condition, most related to trauma. Shanidar 1, an older male 30–45 years old, had sustained a blow to the left side of his head, causing a break in the eye socket, and may have been blind in the left eye. The right side of his body had suffered even more extensive trauma: The lower right arm and hand were missing (the skeleton was otherwise intact and well preserved), probably because of an extensive injury that led to an atrophy of the upper right arm and shoulder; he also showed signs of injury in the right leg and foot. It is possible that this individual could have survived such injuries only with help from other Neandertals, although drawing such a conclusion based on paleopathology alone is problematic (Dettwyler, 1991).

In fact, so many Neandertals exhibit healed fractures that their cause has been sought. Some scientists believe the fractures, especially the high incidence of head and neck fractures, indicate that Neandertals were routinely getting close to dangerous prey while hunting (Berger and Trinkaus, 1995). But the spears from Schöningen suggest that Neandertals should have been able to hunt from a distance. Others see regional differences in fracture frequency and suggest that fracture rates may vary by region according to the difficulty of the substrate, with more rugged terrain and activity leading to greater fracture rates.

NEANDERTAL DNA

In the late 1990s, the original Neandertal remains again came to the attention of the scientific world when it was announced that DNA from this specimen had been successfully extracted, amplified, and sequenced (Krings et al., 1997). DNA from the recently discovered Mesmaiskaya subadult Neandertal specimens has also been extracted and analyzed (Schmitz et al., 2002). Attempts to extract DNA from fossils this old (hominids or other animals) often are unsuccessful, but the cold climate the Neandertals lived in may have helped to preserve their DNA. On visual inspection, the Neandertal specimens show an unusual preservation of collagen, an indication that conditions also favored preservation of DNA (Jordan, 1999). Neandertal DNA appears to be quite different from that of living peoples. We discuss the phylogenetic implications of this difference in Chapter 15.

NEANDERTAL BEHAVIOR

Abundant fossil and archaeological remains the Neandertals left behind should make reconstructing their past lifeways and behavior straightforward. Unfortunately, however, when we reconstruct past human behavior based on the archaeological record, we can only make inferences based on direct observation of living humans. We can be fairly certain that modern humans do not provide a particularly good model for Neandertal behavior, but we do not know how bad the fit is. Take something as fundamental to human behavior as language. It is not unreasonable to assume that the Neandertals possessed some fairly sophisticated form of spoken communication, but how did it compare to language in its ability to transmit ideas and information (see Chapter 16)? The Neandertals' large brains indicate that they were among the most cognitively sophisticated species that have ever lived, but what exactly did they do with these abilities?

MATERIAL CULTURE

Most Neandertal fossils have been found in association with the Middle Paleolithic tool industry. In general, this tool industry represents an "evolutionary" rather

FIGURE 14.18 Upper Paleolithic stone tools include blade-based tools as seen here being produced from a blade core.

than a "revolutionary" advance on past tool cultures. The prepared core techniques are more fully exploited, and there is a greater reliance on small flaked tools than in Acheulean industries. However, there is systematic variation in tool complexity. For example, the late Neandertals of Mezmaiskaya Cave possessed a clear Middle Paleolithic technology, but they made extensive use of bifaces, a feature more commonly associated with the Acheulean. Likewise, all early Neandertals and contemporaneous anatomically modern humans (such as those from Skhul and Qafzeh) are associated with Mousterian tools. This indicates that there is no reason to expect that stone tool traditions will correlate with anatomical differences between hominids.

All later anatomically modern humans and a few later Neandertals are found with the **Upper Paleolithic (Later Stone Age)**, which we discuss in more detail in Chapter 15 (Figure 14.18). The Saint-Césaire and Arcy-sur-Cure Neandertals from France are associated not with the Middle Paleolithic but rather with tools from an Upper Paleolithic industry, the **Châtelperronian** (Hublin et al., 1996). Upper Paleolithic industries are characterized by the development of blade-based technology. **Blades** are flakes that are twice as long as they are wide. In addition, Upper Paleolithic technologies use more refined flaking techniques, and an increase in the variety of flaked tools has long been considered the exclusive product of anatomically modern *Homo sapiens*.

Saint-Césaire and Arcy-sur-Cure demonstrate that Neandertals were capable of producing Upper Paleolithic technology, regardless of whether it was a completely Neandertal invention or an adoption of a modern human production technique. At some archaeological sites without hominids we find Châtelperronian and another Upper Paleolithic industry, the *Aurignacian* (which is associated with modern humans), interstratified through time in the site as if the groups were taking turns using the area. Given that most Neandertals produced Middle Paleolithic tools and only a few, late Neandertals produced Upper Paleolithic tools, it seems likely that this technology may have been borrowed from anatomically modern groups.

The development of bone tools is a prominent feature of later Upper Paleolithic industries, but they are largely absent from Middle Paleolithic assemblages. Although there have been no wood tool discoveries directly associated with Neandertal remains, the Lehringen wood spear 130,000 years old from Germany suggests that Neandertals must have made extensive use of wood. For example, many smaller Mousterian points probably were hafted to wooden shafts to form spears or lances.

The anterior dentition of the Neandertals may constitute the most unusual tool that we can recover from the archaeological record. As mentioned earlier, the anterior teeth of Neandertals are large and heavily worn compared with the back teeth, indicating that they were used in a vise-like manner. Wear patterns on the teeth indicate that both animal and vegetable matter were held in the front teeth. It is possible to imagine—but difficult to prove—any number of tasks that the Neandertals might have accomplished using their front teeth. All we can say is that it was clearly a ubiquitous practice.

COPING WITH COLD

Neandertal bodies are typical of cold-adapted populations, and their archaeological sites also give indications of behavioral adaptations to cold. One way to cope with cold is to avoid it, either by seasonally migrating over long distances or by moving as overall conditions get colder (or warmer) during all parts of the year. Middle Paleolithic archaeological deposits indicate that Neandertals were a mobile people occupying sites for short periods of time and seasonally; in general, their sites served as temporary camping, hunting, or food processing locales. But their mobility seems to have been limited: Most of the raw materials for stone tools came from within 5 km (3 miles) of where they were found, with a maximum of 80 km

Upper Paleolithic (Later Stone Age) Stone tool industries that are characterized by the development of blade-based technology.

blades Flakes that are twice as long as they are wide.

Châtelperronian An Upper Paleolithic tool industry that has been found in association with later Neandertals.

(Stringer and Gamble, 1993). Thus Neandertal mobility was not of a large enough scale to avoid seasonal cold altogether but rather probably reflected local movements necessary to exploit scarce resources within a small area.

Another way to cope with cold is through the use of fire. Charcoal deposits and ashy dump spots are commonly found in Middle Paleolithic sites, indicating that Neandertals used fire. True hearths are rare, but they have been identified in a 60,000-year-old Middle Paleolithic site in Portugal.

It is also very likely that Neandertals used animal skins and hides to protect themselves from the cold. No tools that could be used as sewing implements, such as awls or bone needles, have been found in the Middle Paleolithic; if they did use hides, it is unlikely that they were sewn. In Molodova in the Ukraine, a Middle Paleolithic site has yielded a ring of mammoth bones, approximately 5 by 8 m (15 × 24 ft.) in size, which encloses a dense concentration of artifacts, bones, and ash. Although it could be a natural deposition, many scientists believe that this site represents a living space of some kind, a wind-sheltering structure, or perhaps even a tent. It is assumed that the walls of structure probably were constructed from animal hides. As yet, there is no evidence of more substantial Neandertal structures.

As their cold-adapted bodies attest, Neandertals were able to function in more wintry climates than earlier hominids. On the other hand, the distribution of Neandertal sites through time indicates that they did migrate in and out of areas over longer periods of time depending on whether glacial or interglacial conditions persisted. For example, across the eastern Russian plain Neandertal sites are found far north only during interglacial periods and are located further south during glacial periods, as if the Neandertals were retreating in the face of the harsh glacial climate. And Neandertals never, even during interglacials, occupied as far northerly a latitude as anatomically modern humans eventually did.

Similarly, Neandertals appeared to move south into the Near East during glacial times, and modern humans occupied the region during warmer interglacials. Five prominent cave sites located on Mount Carmel in Israel have been the focus of much attention over the years (excavations in this area began in the late 1920s) because they possess either Neandertal or anatomically modern fossils. Three of these sites have produced classic Neandertals: Tabūn (dating to about 110,000 years ago), Kebara (60,000 years ago), and Amud (35,000–40,000 years ago). And two, Skhūl and Jebel Qafzeh, have yielded anatomically modern human fossils dated to about 90,000–110,000 years ago. All these hominids, Neandertal and modern human, were found in association with Mousterian (Middle Paleolithic) stone tools, which are more typically found in association with Neandertals.

Scientists long thought that the more modern-looking Skhûl and Qafzeh specimens were younger than the Neandertals, but the recent electron spin resonance and U-series dates turned that idea on its head. Neandertals clearly occupied the region for a long time, but the current evidence for occupation by modern-looking humans is more limited. If you accept Neandertals as a separate species, then it is likely that Neandertals and modern humans were alternatively using the region during varying climatic times: Neandertals during cold spells, modern humans during warmer spells. Others argue that Neandertals and modern humans could be representatives of a single, highly variable species. The Middle Eastern hominids as a group would be considered a variant on the classic Neandertal form, and the more modern features seen in some of the specimens would simply reflect local population variation. In a crossroads region (at the intersection of Africa, Europe, and Asia), it might not be surprising that this population would vary more than isolated populations.

HUNTING AND SUBSISTENCE

Stable isotope ratios of carbon and nitrogen indicate that Neandertals were heavily reliant on meat (Richards et al., 2000). They undoubtedly used all the hunting strategies known by archaic *H. sapiens* and earlier hominids. Different Neandertal sites indicate that they used a variety of subsistence strategies depending on local conditions and the game available in a given area. Although they may have scavenged meat opportunistically, there is little evidence that Neandertals engaged in scavenging on a broad scale (Marean and Assefa, 1999). In general, Neandertals appear to have been competent distance hunters and in some cases large game hunters.

An in-depth study of Neandertal subsistence has been undertaken at the site of Kebara in Israel. John Speth and Eitan Tchernov (2001) looked at faunal remains found in Middle Paleolithic deposits dating from 48,000–60,000 years ago, concentrating on a collection of 21,000 ungulate bones. Most of these bones came from two species, the mountain gazelle and the Persian fallow deer, but other kinds of deer, wild boar, and aurochs (the precursor to domestic cattle) were also hunted. Speth and Tchernov found little evidence in the processing of the bones to indicate that they were scavenged rather than hunted. In fact, a high percentage of the faunal remains were from prime adults, indicating that the Kebara Neandertals were very capable hunters. A consistent distribution of burned bones indicates that they were cooked rather than accidentally burned after consumption. Speth and Tchernov found evidence of a *midden* located along one wall of the cave, indicating that the Neandertals cleared waste and debris from the area in a consistent way.

CANNIBALISM

Many human cultures have engaged in cannibalism, although it is generally believed that it was typically undertaken in a political or ritualistic context. Because there is little evidence of ritual behavior in Neandertals, cannibalism must be classified as a kind of specialized subsistence strategy. Early claims for Neandertal cannibalism came from Italy based on a cranium (known as Guattari 1) discovered in a cave at Monte Circeo near Rome in 1939 and dated to about 60,000 years ago. The cranium is reasonably complete, but there is a large hole in its base. Early researchers claimed that it was likely that the hole in the base of the cranium had been deliberately made to facilitate access to the brain during some sort of cannibalistic rite, which was indicated by the supposed placement of the skull in a circle of stones. However, researchers today do not accept this claim: The base of the cranium is a weak part of the skull, often broken by natural forces. Thus the absence of the base of a cranium is not direct evidence of cannibalism. Furthermore, the provenance of the Guattari 1 find is open to question (Trinkaus and Shipman, 1992).

More substantial evidence of cannibalism can be found in the fragmentary remains from Krapina, Croatia, dated to about 130,000 years ago (Figure 14.19). The excavator, D. Gorjanović-Kramberger (who worked in the early twentieth century), pointed out that among the thousands of fragmentary hominid bones almost no intact long bones were present at the site, a sign that the bones may have been split open for the marrow within. He also thought that the bias toward juveniles at the site was an indication of cannibalism. Furthermore, many of the bones showed signs of burning. More recent research has definitively established that some of the bones show cut marks as well, although this is not in itself evidence of cannibalism (Russell, 1987).

The recently excavated Mousterian cave site of Moula-Guercy in France, dating to about 100,000 years ago, provides an even better case for Neandertal cannibalism (Defleur et al., 1999). Seventy-eight hominid bone fragments mixed in with several hundred animal bone fragments (mostly from red deer) constitute the fossil assemblage. Diagnostic Neandertal features are apparent in several of the fragments; furthermore, only Neandertals have ever been found at European sites

FIGURE 14.19 The Krapina remains may provide evidence of cannibalism by some Neandertals.

of this age. The hominid remains from Moula-Guercy display numerous cut marks; these are consistent with expected defleshing and butchering patterns. All crania and long bones have been broken, presumably to gain access to the brain and marrow. A key piece of evidence indicates that these remains were processed for access to meat rather than for some other purpose: The deer and other faunal remains from the site were treated in the same manner as the hominid remains. Because it is unlikely that the game species were being treated to some sort of mortuary processing that did not involve being eaten, Alban Defleur and his colleagues conclude that the Neandertals were also being eaten by other Neandertals.

BURIALS

Burial of the dead is a traditional practice in many contemporary human cultures. It can be done for different reasons and be vested with ritual significance. The notion that some Neandertals may have buried their dead goes back to the discovery of the Spy skeletons in Belgium in the 1880s (Stringer et al., 1984).

Unlike the earlier discoveries from Gibraltar and Neanderthal, the Spy Cave remains were carefully excavated. The two Spy adult skeletons were found complete and fully articulated, suggesting that they may have been intentionally buried in the cave. Since that time, numerous Neandertals have been found in caves; most excavators of these sites believed that they were deliberate burials. A large number of articulated Neandertal skeletons have been recovered in situ; many have been found in a flexed position. The sites often are littered with disarticulated animal bones; only the Neandertal bones remain in place, protected from the effects of geology or scavengers.

Further evidence of Neandertal burials came from the site of La Ferrassie in southern France (excavated in the early 1900s), where several adults and subadults, forming a burial complex, were found at a single cave site. Many researchers believe that the assemblage of individuals at the site was not an accidental grouping but indicates deliberate burial or internment. In 1938, the skeleton of a 9-year-old child found in the small cave of Teshik Tash in Uzbekistan was claimed to have been interred surrounded by six pairs of upright goat horns, reflecting some sort of ritualistic activity. Although there is no doubt that the goat horns were found near the boy, most researchers today are skeptical that they were distributed in a "meaningful" way.

In the 1950s the idea of Neandertal burial and compassionate Neandertals was further supported by the claim that the Shanidar 4 individual (an older individual) from the 40,000- to 50,000-year-old Iraqi site excavated by Ralph Solecki (1971)

FIGURE 14.20 The Kebara remains from Israel may represent a Neandertal burial.

had been buried and covered in (or on a bed of) wildflowers. A large quantity of wildflower pollen had been found in association with this burial, but there is no certainty that they were put there deliberately by Neandertal mourners. The same pollen exists in the region today and could, have been blown into the cave. Nonetheless, both the "flower burial" and the obvious survival of badly injured individuals at Shanidar led to a softer and more humanized perspective of Neandertals in the 1960s and 1970s. Even if claims of the ritual placement of a head in a center of stones or goat horns, of covering the body with flowers, or of compassionate care for the injured or disabled should all be taken with a grain of salt, it is not unreasonable to accept that some Neandertals buried their dead (Figure 14.20).

However, some investigators believe that it is possible to account for the deposition of articulated Neandertal skeletons in caves via natural forces (Gargett, 1989, 1999). One criticism, definitely valid in some cases, is that many Neandertal sites were excavated decades ago, before the development of modern excavation techniques or accurate recordkeeping. Without a clear rendering of the excavation context, it is difficult to assess the status of a claim of deliberate burial. Recent excavators of Neandertal sites, mindful of the need to provide evidence for burial rather than simply assume it, have gone to some effort to prove what was once considered the obvious. Recently excavated Neandertal infants from Amud (Hovers et al., 2000) and Mezmaiskaya Cave (Golovanova et al., 1999) are both claimed to be from deliberate burials, and the context of these discoveries strongly indicates that such small and delicate remains probably were preserved because they were shielded from damage by deliberate burial.

Neandertal burials represent a novel behavioral development of the Middle Paleolithic. Before that time we may have evidence of mortuary practices in the defleshing of the Bodo cranium and the possibly deliberate deposition of remains in the bone pit of Sima de los Huesos at Atapuereca. But there is no evidence of deliberate burial of archaic *H. sapiens* remains. On the other hand, Neandertal burials are significantly different from Upper Paleolithic burials of anatomically modern *H. sapiens* that begin to appear around 40,000 years ago. Neandertals have not been found to be interred with grave goods, objects placed with the corpse at the time of burials. On occasion a stray animal bone or horn has been found in association with a Neandertal burial, but it is very difficult to demonstrate that they were placed there deliberately.

In contrast, grave goods often are found in Upper Paleolithic burials, sometimes in great abundance. Another difference between Neandertal and Upper Paleolithic burials is that the Neandertal burials always occur in cave sites, whereas burials at open air sites are common, at least in the late Upper Paleolithic. Because it is presumed that Neandertals lived and died in open areas as well as in caves, it is apparent that either they did not bury their dead in those regions or, if they did, they did not do so in a way that prevented the disruption of the corpse by other forces.

RITUAL AND SYMBOLIC BEHAVIOR

Extrapolating from the cultural behavior of modern humans, it is easy to assume that Neandertal burial indicates some kind of ritualistic belief or significance, but the context of Neandertal burials is equally indicative of "corpse disposal" as it is of ritualized internment (Stringer and Gamble, 1993). It is clear, however, that some Neandertals dedicated a significant amount of time and energy to the burial of the dead, selecting an appropriate site, placing the body in a certain position, and covering the body with a large stone. Furthermore, chimpanzees and other mammals can show attachments to the remains of deceased infants or individuals with whom they have had a long-term relationship, even though they ultimately abandon the body. Thus even if it is impossible to know whether there was a ritual or symbolic content to the burial of the dead in Neandertals, it is reasonable to assume that when they chose to dispose of a corpse in this manner, it was both an emotional and a pragmatic decision.

If burials cannot be seen as evidence of ritualistic or symbolic behavior, then there is very little else in the Neandertal archaeological record to indicate such behaviors. A small number of incised bones have been recovered from Mousterian sites, but what these scratches might mean is beyond the scope of scientific inquiry. If Neandertals possessed something like human language, then obviously they were capable of symbolic behavior because language is reliant on symbolic representation. But there is no direct evidence of this in the archaeological record. The strongest evidence is that of personal adornment items including pierced animal teeth from Arcy-sur-Cure in France. Other engraved or incised items include a plaque or incised plate of a mammoth tooth, from the site of Tata, and an incised flint from Quinetra in the Golan Heights (Marshack, 1996; White, 2001). All these occur late in Neandertal times, with the most secure—those from Arcy-sur-Cure and Quneitra—being 55,000 years old or younger. Even if we accept these intermittent finds as symbolic behavior in Neandertals, they are qualitatively different from the systematic evidence of such behavior, including extensive personal adornment, in Upper Paleolithic sites, as we shall see in Chapter 15.

PHYLOGENETIC AND TAXONOMIC ISSUES: AN OVERVIEW

Our interpretations of taxonomic and phylogenetic relationships between late Middle and Late Pleistocene hominids depend largely on how we view the origins of anatomically modern *H. sapiens*. However, we can have a preliminary discussion based on the archaic *H. sapiens* and Neandertal fossil records.

The labels "archaic *H. sapiens*" and "Neandertal" are not taxonomically formal designations. We use informal labels because there is no consensus as to what the formal labels should be. Archaic *H. sapiens* include a widely distributed group of hominids who lived from about 150,000 to 800,000 years ago (Figure 14.21). *Neandertal* refers to a predominantly European and western Asian group of hominids who lived about 30,000–130,000 years ago. Both these groups possess features that clearly distinguish them from *H. erectus* and anatomically modern *H. sapiens*. Yet many researchers argue either that the differences are not profound enough to warrant species designations or that using such designations would

Figure 14.21 HOMINID EVOLUTION IN THE MID-TO-LATE PLEISTOCENE

Beginning about 600,000 years ago in Africa, hominids who were somewhat larger-brained than classic *H. erectus* but still cranially robust appeared in Africa, and then later in Europe and Asia. This group is usually referred to as archaic *Homo sapiens* (or by some as *H. heidelbergensis*). In Europe and western Asia, a distinct type of hominid, the Neandertals, appeared about 140,000 years ago. Their antecedents may be represented among the archaic *H. sapiens* specimens of Europe, dating up to 400,000 years ago.

BOXGROVE Evidence of big game hunting by archaic *H. sapiens* is hinted by hand axes and deer bones at the Boxgrove site, England.

NEANDERTALS Neandertal specimens are numerous enough that we can begin to understand developmental changes across their lifespan.

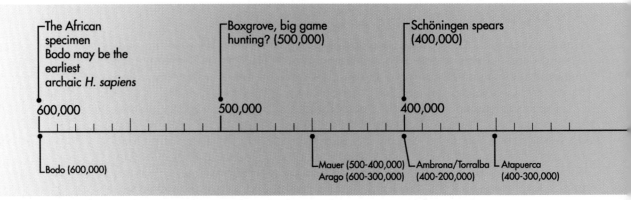

ATAPUERCA Remains of more than 30 archaic *H. sapiens* individuals have been found in the *Sima de los Huesos* at Sierra de Atapuerca, Spain.

STEINHEIM is a possible contemporary of Petralona.

The African specimen Bodo may be the earliest archaic *H. sapiens*

Boxgrove, big game hunting? (500,000)

Schöningen spears (400,000)

600,000

500,000

400,000

Bodo (600,000)

Mauer (500-400,000)
Arago (600-300,000)

Ambrona/Torralba (400-200,000)

Atapuerca (400-300,000)

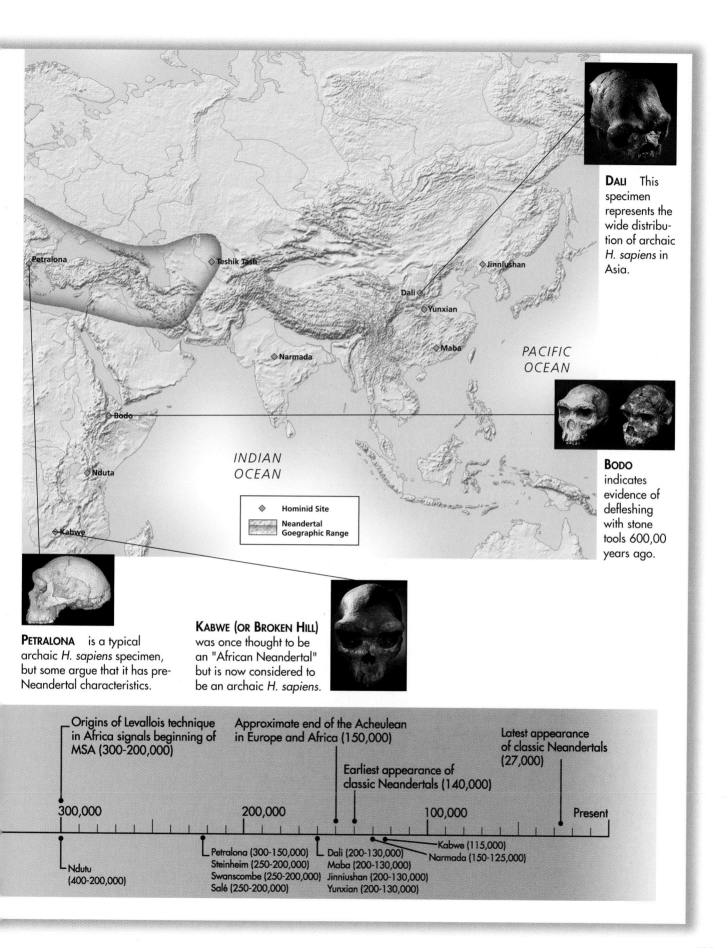

DALI This specimen represents the wide distribution of archaic *H. sapiens* in Asia.

PACIFIC OCEAN

INDIA OCEAN

Petralona

Teshik Tash

Jinniushan

Dali

Yunxian

Maba

Narmada

Bodo

Nduta

Kabwe

◇ Hominid Site

▨ Neandertal Goegraphic Range

BODO indicates evidence of defleshing with stone tools 600,00 years ago.

PETRALONA is a typical archaic *H. sapiens* specimen, but some argue that it has pre-Neandertal characteristics.

KABWE (OR BROKEN HILL) was once thought to be an "African Neandertal" but is now considered to be an archaic *H. sapiens*.

Origins of Levallois technique in Africa signals beginning of MSA (300-200,000)

Approximate end of the Acheulean in Europe and Africa (150,000)

Latest appearance of classic Neandertals (27,000)

Earliest appearance of classic Neandertals (140,000)

300,000

200,000

100,000

Present

Ndutu (400-200,000)

Petralona (300-150,000)
Steinheim (250-200,000)
Swanscombe (250-200,000)
Salé (250-200,000)

Dali (200-130,000)
Maba (200-130,000)
Jinniushan (200-130,000)
Yunxian (200-130,000)

Kabwe (115,000)
Narmada (150-125,000)

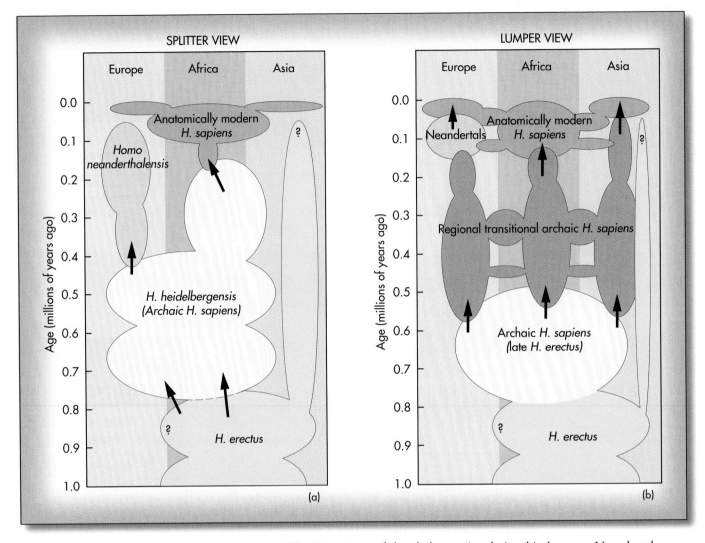

FIGURE 14.22 Two views of the phylogenetic relationship between Neandertals and modern *H. sapiens*. (a) The splitter view. (b) The lumper view.

arbitrarily impose separations on a continuous evolutionary lineage and thus be highly misleading (Figure 14.22).

From the "lumper's perspective," the informal, subspecific labels for these groups of hominids provide an acceptable solution to the problem. In the lumpers' view, archaic *H. sapiens* and Neandertals were all part of one potentially interbreeding species. Obviously, there was regional variation within the species, and variation across time as well, but lumpers see all the larger-brained hominids of the last half of the Pleistocene as part of a *single evolving species*.

The "splitter's perspective" begins with recognizing the Neandertals as a separate species: *H. neanderthalensis*. Many splitters argue that the distinctive anatomy and limited distribution of the Neandertals indicate a specialized hominid taxon fundamentally different from anatomically modern *H. sapiens*. The species designation means that Neandertals and modern humans did not or could not interbreed or did so very infrequently; it suggests that Neandertals represent an extinct type of hominid, which was ultimately replaced across its entire range by modern humans.

In the splitter's view, archaic *H. sapiens* also gets a species designation: *H. heidelbergensis*. *H. heidelbergensis* is considered a species distinct from *H. erectus*, based on the anatomical features we discussed earlier. In effect, *H. heidelbergensis* becomes the stem species for both Neandertals and anatomically modern *H. sapiens*. In Europe, *H. heidelbergensis* specimens such as Petralona and those from Sima de los Huesos are seen to be proto-Neandertals, extending the Neandertal lineage back hundreds of thousands of years. In Africa, *H. heidelbergensis* specimens such as Bodo and Kabwe are thought to be early representatives of a population from which anatomically modern *H. sapiens* evolved.

At the same time as Neandertals were living in Europe and western Asia, hominid evolutionary developments were also taking place in other parts of the world, most significantly the evolution of anatomically modern *H. sapiens*. In Chapter 15 we will more fully explore the evolutionary connections between our own species and these earlier forms. As we will see, the debate about the origins of modern humans involves not only palaeontological and archaeological data but also genetic information derived from contemporary humans and a few fossil specimens. Over the past 20 years, the quest to understand the origins of modern humans has focused on developing a synthesis of sometimes divergent and sometimes convergent molecular and palaeontological perspectives on this critical period in our history.

SUMMARY

1. **What cranial features distinguish archaic *H. sapiens* from anatomically modern *H. sapiens*?**

   Archaic *H. sapiens* are much more cranially robust than modern *H. sapiens*, with thicker cranial bones and substantial development of browridges (supraorbital tori). The face, including the jaws and the nasal aperture, tend to be larger in archaic *H. sapiens* than in modern *H. sapiens*. Cranial capacities in archaic *H. sapiens* range from 1,000 to 1,400 cc, which places them in the lower half of the modern human range, and the cranial vault is lower and longer.

2. **What cranial features distinguish Neandertals from anatomically modern *H. sapiens*?**

   Neandertal crania have double-arched browridges, an occipital bun, and substantial midfacial prognathism. Cranial capacity in Neandertals equals or exceeds that of modern humans, but the shape of the vault is longer and lower, with a maximum cranial width (when viewed from behind) at the midcranium level rather than high on the skull, as it is in modern humans. In rear view the vault is oval shaped. The mastoid eminence is smaller in Neandertals than in modern humans, but the juxtamastoid eminence is larger. The inner ear anatomy of Neandertals is also distinct from that of modern humans. Neandertals were taurodont and had retromolar spaces on their mandibles.

3. **What is the collective significance of the Near Eastern sites of Tabūn, Kebara, Amud, Skhūl, and Jebel Qafzeh?**

   These five sites, all located near one another on Mount Carmel in Israel, provide evidence that modern humans and Neandertals lived in the same area but at different times, with the earliest site, Tabūn (100,000 years ago), occupied by Neandertals; then Skhūl and Jebel Qafzeh (90,000–110,000 years ago), occupied by modern humans; followed by another, later Neandertal occupation

   indicated by fossils from Kebara (60,000 years ago) and Amud (35,000–40,000 years ago). It is possible that Neandertals lived in this area during colder periods, as they were driven southward by glaciers during ice ages, and that anatomically modern humans moved in during warmer interglacials. An alternative explanation is that they are all representatives of a single, highly variable species, located in a region that was subject to a large amount of population movement and gene flow.

4. **Why should we be wary of equating tool industries with specific hominid species or populations, especially during the Middle to Late Pleistocene?**

   Although there is some validity to generalizations associating types of hominids with specific tool industries, several counterexamples are available from specific archeological sites, especially in the later parts of the Pleistocene, to caution us against making too much of these generalizations. For example, at the Mount Carmel sites, modern humans and Neandertals are both found in association with Mousterian tools, and later classic Neandertals are found in association with Upper Paleolithic tool industries at some sites in Europe (at Saint-Césaire and Arcy-sur-Cure in France). Archaeological associations of Asian hominids cannot be easily fit into tool industry sequences developed for Europe and Africa.

5. **What is *H. heidelbergensis*?**

   H. heidelbergensis is a species name used by some researchers to refer to the majority of archaic *H. sapiens* specimens found in Europe and Africa. The type specimen for this species is the Mauer mandible found in Germany in 1907. Many researchers who accept *H. heidelbergensis* as a species also think that Neandertals are a species distinct from anatomically modern humans: *H. neanderthalensis*. *H. heidelbergensis* is seen as the ancestral species to both modern humans (in

Africa) and Neandertals (in Europe). Other researchers argue that the archaic *H. sapiens*, Neandertals, and modern humans are all part of a single polytypic species, which shows evolutionary change over the course of the later Pleistocene. Thus they do not accept *H. heidelbergensis* or *H. neanderthalensis* as valid taxa.

CRITICAL THINKING QUESTIONS

1. Besides most wood implements, what other sorts of things do you think are missing in the archaeological record of Mid- to Late Pleistocene hominids?

2. Is the label "archaic *H. sapiens*" useful or confusing?

3. What do you think of the "humanity" of Neandertals? In a broader primate context, should they be regarded as just a slightly different kind of human being?

KEY TERMS

occipital bun
mastoid process
midfacial prognathism
Middle Paleolithic
   (Middle Stone Age)

Levallois technique
juxtamastoid eminence
taurodontism
Upper Paleolithic (Later
   Stone Age)

blades
Châtelperronian

SUGGESTED READING

Stringer, Christopher, and Gamble, Clive. (1993). *In Search of the Neanderthals.* Thames and Hudson, New York.
Trinkaus, Erik, and Shipman, Pat. (1992). *The Neandertals.* Vintage Press, New York.

Wolpoff, Milford, and Caspari, Rachel. (1997). *Race and Human Evolution.* Westview Press, Boulder, Co.

Chapter 15

THE EMERGENCE AND DISPERSAL OF *HOMO SAPIENS*

THE YOUNG WOMAN SAT NEXT TO HER MOTHER and a small group of other women near the mouth of the cave. On the other side of the green valley below them rose a distant stretch of mountains. She knew that the pile of soft greenish stone by her side came from those peaks, although she had never been to the spot herself. Her brother and father had brought the stone back from a recent expedition, as they did each year about this time. From the pile she selected one of the oblong pieces of stone that her mother had cut—a blank from which she would fashion a bead—and began rounding one end of it.

As she worked she listened to the women's stories and watched her mother. Her mother was lovely, she thought, with a high forehead and strong chin, nothing like the women across the valley, with their large faces and forbidding brows. She didn't understand those women when they spoke, although they seemed kind enough.

Once the end of the blank was rounded, she took another stone and began chipping flakes out of the center of the blank, first on one side and then on the other. She furrowed her brow as she worked, wrinkling the skin on her high forehead as she noticed that her fingers were stained with the red pigment she had used the previous day, deep in the cave, to spray an outline of her hand on the rock wall. Just as she had only heard about the distant peaks, her brother had only heard about the deepest rooms of the cave where the women undertook their art and ritual.

An hour later, the two indentations merged, making a hole through the chunk of stone. Slowly and carefully she enlarged the hole, not wanting to break the piece now that she was so near to finishing. She held the small bead in her palm, rolling it about before she began polishing. Nearly another hour passed before the small bead, lustrous from polishing, was finished and dropped onto a pile of similar beads shaped by the rest of the group. Later the beads would be carefully sewn in rows onto the front of a shirt in the particular sign of their clan. Those signs would represent hundreds of hours of their labor but were critical in signaling their group's membership in a larger network of clans. One day, from one of those clans, would come a mate for her, perhaps food in scarce times, and maybe even other beads, ideas, or information. In the long run, that network would be the difference between their survival and the demise of their heavy-browed neighbors.

Modern human origins are not simply a matter of anatomy but also of behavior. No matter how cognitively sophisticated our close cousins the Neandertals or archaic *Homo sapiens* were or how close the size of their brains was to our own, they clearly did not attain a modern human level of technological or intellectual achievement. The bead described in the vignette is not much of an artifact; it is not even a tool. But it provides material evidence of personal decoration and symbolic representation. Such evidence is abundant in the archaeological record of modern humans and all but absent from the records of Neandertals and archaic *H. sapiens*.

In this chapter, we review the three distinct sources of evidence used to reconstruct the critical events surrounding the emergence of modern people. Paleontological and geological data chart the distribution in time and space of anatomically modern *H. sapiens*. Archaeological data shed light on the changes in behavior that allowed modern humans to exploit the natural world in a way that would ultimately make us the dominant species on the planet. Genetic data provide information on the web of biological relationships between us and our closest relatives. By synthesizing data from these interrelated realms, biological anthropologists attempt to address the fundamental question of our field: How did human beings evolve?

THE EMERGENCE OF MODERN HUMANS

The emergence of modern humans can be seen anatomically in a combination of cranial features that distinguish us from archaic *H. sapiens* and Neandertals (Chapter 14). To review, these include a gracile skull and postcranial anatomy, limited development of browridges or other cranial superstructures, a rounded cranium with a high maximum cranial breadth and parallel sides, a prominent mastoid process, a retracted face with a canine fossa, small teeth and jaws, and development of an obvious chin (Figure 15.1). However, large brain size does not set us apart from archaic *H. sapiens* and the Neandertals. Many Middle and Late Pleistocene hominid specimens possess cranial capacities that are easily within the modern human range (whose average is about 1,350 cc), and a number of them exceed the human mean by a substantial amount.

Despite the fact that there is no significant difference in absolute brain size, when we look at the archaeological record associated with modern humans, we find evidence of substantial behavioral differences between our close relatives and us. Between 2.5 million and 300,000 years ago, the pace of change in stone tool cultures (the Lower Paleolithic or Early Stone Age) was very slow. With the advent of the Middle Paleolithic or Middle Stone Age (MSA), many new tool types and techniques were introduced (Ambrose, 2001). However, little change took place during the MSA itself: The same tool types existed at the beginning of the MSA as at the end. In contrast, the Upper Paleolithic tool assemblages associated with modern humans in some parts of the world are radically different from those of the preceding Middle Paleolithic, and art and ornamentation, which reflect symbolic thinking, are more heavily represented. The rapid pace of change and the

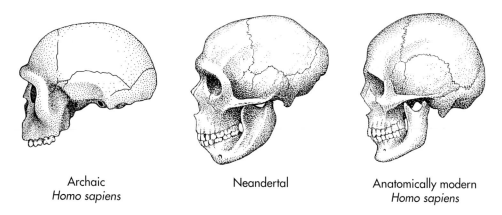

Archaic
Homo sapiens

Neandertal

Anatomically modern
Homo sapiens

FIGURE 15.1 Variations on a theme: archaic *Homo sapiens*, Neandertal, and anatomically modern *Homo sapiens* skulls.

appearance of symbolic behavior are two of the hallmarks of the Upper Paleolithic revolution, which some scientists think occurred with the sudden appearance of anatomically modern humans (Klein and Edgar, 2002). Other scientists think that different aspects of Upper Paleolithic culture appear at different times during the later MSA, thus indicating a more gradual evolution of behaviorally modern humans (McBrearty and Brooks, 2000).

MODELS OF MODERN HUMAN ORIGINS

Many scientists have attempted to assemble anatomical, behavioral, and genetic data into comprehensive models of the origins of modern humans. In the past two decades, two basic frameworks have been debated: the replacement and multiregional models. Both frameworks agree that there was an initial dispersal of *H. erectus* (or *H. ergaster*) from Africa into the rest of the Old World. However, they disagree as to what happened next.

MULTIREGIONAL AND REPLACEMENT MODELS

The **replacement models** suggest that modern humans had a localized origin— usually thought to be in Africa—and then dispersed into areas already occupied by *H. erectus* and its descendants. Replacement models thus require a second hominid dispersal from Africa. These models often are called "Out of Africa" models or "Out of Africa II," in recognition of the earlier *H. erectus* dispersal. As the word *replacement* implies, these models predict that anatomically modern humans did not interbreed substantially (or at all) with the indigenous hominids whom they ultimately replaced. One implication is that all geographic variation seen in modern humans today evolved recently, after the origin of anatomically modern humans.

    Multiregional models propose that our origins cannot be pinned down to a single population or area. Instead, gene flow, via repeated population movements and intermixing, is thought to have been extensive among Old World hominid populations. Thus the appearance of anatomically modern humans throughout the Old World resulted not from replacement of many populations by one but from the transmission of alleles underlying the modern human phenotype between populations that were in genetic contact. Therefore, multiregional models do not suggest a second dispersal from Africa. Note that the multiregional models do not call for separate and multiple origins for modern humans; rather, they suggest that modern humans originated in the context of gene flow between multiple regions.

    Although it is sometimes stated that multiregional and replacement models are irreconcilable (Wolpoff et al., 2000), this is not entirely true. Certainly, any proof of genetic contributions from regionally dispersed populations means that total replacement could not have happened. But population expansion from a single region could have been the dominant event in recent human evolution, with genetic contributions from other populations being trivial. Conversely, it is very likely that over the past 500,000 years, hominid populations in some regions have been replaced by others without interbreeding, but this does not preclude gene flow from occurring between other populations in the species.

PREDICTIONS OF THE TWO MODELS

Replacement models predict that we should first see modern human fossils in Africa and then at least two anatomically distinct lineages of hominids in each region of the Old World: Neandertals and modern humans in Europe, *Homo heidelbergensis* (archaic *H. sapiens*) and modern humans in mainland Asia, and possibly relict

replacement models
Phylogenetic models that suggest that modern humans evolved in one location and then spread geographically, replacing other earlier hominid populations without or with little admixture.

multiregional models
Phylogenetic models that suggest that modern humans evolved in the context of gene flow between Mid- to Late Pleistocene hominid populations from different regions, so there is no single location where modern humans first evolved.

populations of *H. erectus* and modern humans in Southeast Asia. Replacement further predicts that these lineages will overlap for at least a brief period of time in each region. Like the anatomy, the archaeological record would show abrupt changes in technology and behavior (as modern humans brought their technology with them to new areas), and the genetic record would indicate little overlap between the gene pools of the two lineages.

In contrast, multiregional models predict only a single evolving lineage in each region. We should see anatomical evidence of this evolution in the form of intermediate fossils with characteristics of the ancestors and the descendants. In addition, we should see regional anatomical characters continue from earlier to later populations. Likewise, the archaeological record should show evidence of behavioral continuity. And the genetic evidence should show ancient contributions to the modern gene pool, assuming there has not been a strong genetic bottleneck.

Let us now turn to the fossil, archaeological, and genetic record to see how these predictions fare against the empirical data.

ANATOMY AND DISTRIBUTION OF EARLY HUMANS

Early modern human fossil specimens are rare (Figure 15.2 on page 422). Using archaeological evidence alone to assess the early appearance of modern humans is risky because, as we have seen before, it is unwise to assert that a given tool culture is the product of a given hominid, especially in periods when significant evolutionary transformations took place. However, where we are certain that earlier hominids did not exist (such as in Australia and the Americas), we can use archaeological sites without human remains to chart the earliest appearance of modern humans.

In many cases early modern human specimens possess both derived features linking them to us and primitive features they may share with archaic *H. sapiens* or Neandertals (Pearson, 2000). For example, several early humans possess a long pubic ramus, a trait thought of as typically Neandertal. If this trait is a primitive feature inherited by both Neandertals and modern humans from their archaic *H. sapiens* or *H. erectus* ancestors (the postcranial fossil record of archaic *H. sapiens* is sparse), then it does not necessarily reflect a Neandertal ancestry for some modern human populations, supporting replacement models. Alternatively, if it is a trait unique to Neandertals it would signal Neandertal ancestry for certain modern human populations, supporting a multiregional model. Whatever its origin, a long pubic ramus seems to have been selected out of modern human populations over the last 100,000 years. In general, we should not use primitive features to exclude specimens from modern *H. sapiens* if they also possess derived features justifying their inclusion.

AFRICA

While Neandertals were evolving in Europe, a different kind of hominid was evolving in Africa: anatomically modern *H. sapiens*. As we discussed in Chapter 14, archaic *H. sapiens* fossils (Bodo and Kabwe) have been found in Africa from around 600,000 to about 200,000 years ago. Starting at about 150,000 years ago we begin to see fossils that look more, but not entirely, modern from sites such as Herto in Ethiopia, Ngaloba in Tanzania, and Florisbad in South Africa. Their anatomy typically is intermediate in form, and their ages often are imprecisely known. Slightly later, we find fully anatomically modern humans at sites such as Klasies River Mouth and Border Cave in South Africa and Aduma in Ethiopia. Although some scientists like to distinguish these two groups by calling them different subspecies, most scholars include both in *H. sapiens sapiens*.

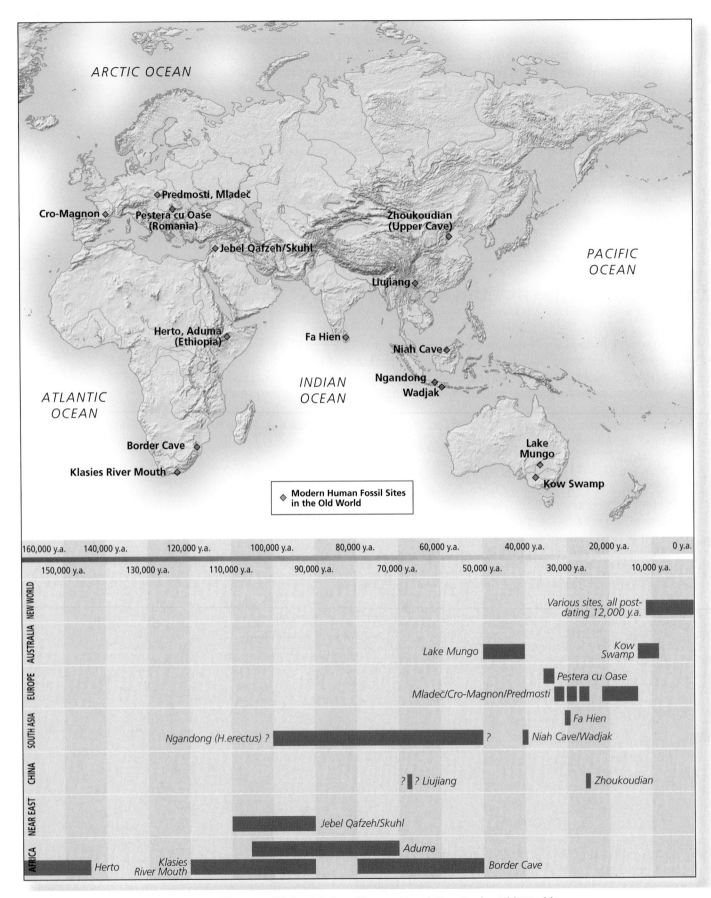

FIGURE 15.2   Modern Human Fossil Sites in the Old World.

FIGURE 15.3 Hominid remains from Herto, Ethiopia, may be the oldest anatomically modern humans yet discovered.

Perhaps the most securely dated of the earlier group of fossils are the recent discoveries from the Herto locality in the Middle Awash region of Ethiopia (Figure 15.3). Herto dates to about 160,000–154,000 years ago and yielded the crania of two adults and one juvenile (White et al., 2003). Like other African specimens from this period, the Herto crania "sample a population that is on the verge of anatomical modernity but not yet fully modern" (White et al., 2003, p. 745).

The later group, represented by Aduma in Ethiopia and Border Cave and Klasies River Mouth in South Africa, date to about 120,000–50,000 years ago. Aduma preserves cranial remains dated to 105,000–70,000 years ago (Haile-Selassie et al., 2004). A partial adult cranium from Border Cave in South Africa dates to 80,000–50,000 years ago. Fragmentary cranial and postcranial remains from Klasies River date to 120,000–90,000 years ago (Rightmire and Deacon, 1991). For the most part early *H. sapiens sapiens* are found with typical MSA tool assemblages. But at Border Cave, the Howeison's Poort industry may be considered an advanced MSA assemblage because it features microliths.

This sequence of fossils provides evidence that *H. sapiens sapiens* was well established throughout Africa by 100,000 years ago. Furthermore, a series of specimens dating from 200,000–100,000 years ago provide strong evidence of the African transformation of archaic *H. sapiens* to anatomically modern humans.

NEAR EAST

The Near East is the only region outside Africa to have yielded reliable evidence of modern humans earlier than 60,000 years ago. As discussed in Chapter 14, anatomically modern *H. sapiens* dating to 110,000–90,000 years ago have been found at the sites of Skūhl and Qafzeh, located on Mt. Carmel in Israel. The Near East sits between Africa and Asia, so if modern humans (or modern human morphology) first evolved in Africa sometime after 150,000 years ago, then the Skūhl and Qafzeh hominids (Figure 15.4) could be considered the first sign of an expansion out of Africa, which only later (60,000–40,000 years ago) spread into Asia, Australia, and Europe. Neandertals are known to have occupied the Near East for tens of thousands of years, usually associated with glacial periods. Many scientists have interpreted the correlation of anatomically modern human specimens with warm (interglacial) periods and of later Neandertals with cold (glacial) periods as a sharing of this area by these two groups through time. Both Neandertals and early *H. sapiens sapiens* in the Near East are associated with MSA tool assemblages.

EUROPE

Scores of Neandertal remains have been recovered in Europe that date to 100,000–30,000 years ago. However, modern human skeletal remains do not appear in Europe until late. An Upper Paleolithic assemblage known as the Aurignacian, so far found only in association with *H. sapiens sapiens,* appeared in Europe about 40,000 years ago, but only later skeletal remains have been found,

FIGURE 15.4 Anatomically modern humans from the Israeli cave sites of Skūhl and Qafzeh may be the earliest found outside of Africa.

FIGURE 15.5 The Oase 1 mandible, earliest modern human in Europe.

from perhaps around 36,000 years ago. A mandible recently discovered in the Carpathian region of Romania, at the site of Peştera cu Oase ("cave with bones"), is so far the oldest modern human in Europe, dating to 36,000–34,000 years ago (Trinkaus et al., 2003). Like other early modern human specimens, the Oase 1 mandible is robust and is argued to exhibit a mix of clearly derived features aligning it with anatomically modern *H. sapiens* (such as development of the chin) and primitive features (such as its robustness and anatomy of the mandibular foramen) linking it to Neandertals (Figure 15.5). The left mandibular foramen (a small hole in the mandible through which nerves and blood vessels pass) of Oase 1 has an anatomy that may be a derived feature of Neandertals and other early modern humans from Europe not seen in human populations today. Although it is an insignificant biological feature, this is the kind of diagnostic trait that can become quite important in debates about phylogenetic relationships among Late Pleistocene hominids.

The Central European sites of Mladeč and Předmostí, both located in the Czech Republic, have yielded numerous specimens of anatomically modern *H. sapiens,* which also display characters that may align them with Neandertals (Smith, 1984). These sites date to 35,000–25,000 years ago, with the Předmostí site being somewhat younger than Mladeč. Both were discovered in the late nineteenth century; unfortunately, the Předmostí remains were destroyed during World War II. Hominids from both sites show a large degree of sexual dimorphism, with the males displaying a more robust cranial anatomy (such as the presence of browridges). Several crania, probably representing males, show development of an occipital bun or hemi-bun. Though not as fully developed as the Neandertal occipital bun, this feature, in combination with the development of browridges, has been argued by some scholars to show Neandertal ancestry in these early human remains.

In contrast, early Upper Paleolithic human postcranial skeletons appear to be tropically adapted, lacking the cold-adapted proportions we saw in Neandertal skeletons. That is, they have narrower, more linear body proportions of the limbs and thorax, associated with humans living in tropical climates who easily dissipate heat. Some scholars interpret this to be evidence that modern humans migrated from tropical Africa to cold Europe more quickly than their skeleton could adapt to the climatic shift. If true, this would support a replacement model.

The best-known early anatomically modern humans from Europe come from the Cro-Magnon rock shelter located in the Dordogne region of France, which includes a number of Neandertal sites as well. The Cro-Magnon remains were discovered in 1868 and consist of at least four adults (with partial crania and mandibles) and an infant, along with an assortment of other cranial and postcranial remains (Gambier, 1989). The site dates to about 27,000 years ago, or well after the first appearance of modern humans in Europe.

Cro-Magnon 1 (or the "Old Man" of Cro-Magnon) shows a striking anatomical contrast to Neandertals from the same region (Figure 15.6). Cro-Magnon 1 has a gracile cranium that combines a very small face with a large and bulbous cranial vault (bony abnormalities on the surface of his skull may have been the result of a fungal infection). It was not very difficult for archaeologists to develop an evolutionary scenario in western Europe whereby the Middle Paleolithic Neandertals were replaced over a short period of time by Upper Paleolithic modern humans, sometime between 40,000–30,000 years ago. However, according to critics of this scenario, the Cro-Magnon 1 specimen is not particularly representative of early modern humans in Europe (including those from central Europe and even some of the other Cro-Magnon individuals), who show a more mosaic pattern of archaic and modern features.

Given their late appearance, it is not surprising that European anatomically modern humans are found only with Upper Paleolithic technologies. In fact, in western Europe there appears to be a one-to-one correlation between *H. sapiens sapiens* and the Aurignacian technology. As we saw in Chapter 14, a different Upper Paleolithic technology, the Châtelperronian, is contemporaneous with the Aurignacian but appears to be a Neandertal technology. Whether the Châtelperronian is a Neandertal innovation or the result of Neandertals mimicking *H. sapiens sapiens* remains a point of debate.

FIGURE 15.6 The "Old Man" of Cro-Magnon, from the Dordogne region of France.

ASIA AND SOUTHEAST ASIA

In Asia there is a gap in the hominid fossil record between about 100,000 and 40,000 years ago. Archaic or premodern *H. sapiens* are known from a number of sites dating from 250,000–100,000 years ago in China (Etler, 1996), but anatomically modern humans do not appear until perhaps as early as 65,000 years ago in China and possibly 40,000 years ago in Indonesia.

Dating is a problem for establishing the earliest human remains in Asia. In China, the site of Liujiang has been dated to at least 18,000 years ago, perhaps as old as 67,000 years, but there is some question as to the provenience of the human remains recovered from that site (Shen et al., 2002). Well-accepted dates of 25,000 years ago have been obtained for the site of Hebei and for the Upper Cave at Zhoukoudian (approximately 42 km southwest of Beijing). Although clearly modern humans, the three Upper Cave skulls differ anatomically from one another and are not similar to skulls of contemporary east Asian peoples. Stringer and Andrews (1988) suggest that the Upper Cave skulls most closely resemble early modern humans from the European sites of Mladeč and Předmostí (Figure 15.7). This indicates that both European and Asian early modern human populations had a common origin (presumably Africa) and that there is little evidence of regional continuity.

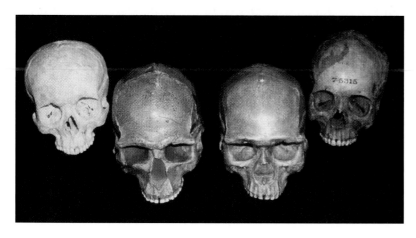

FIGURE 15.7 Fossil remains of anatomically modern humans from the Czech Republic and from China (center crania) are more robust than recent human crania but are otherwise anatomically identical. All four crania are *Homo sapiens sapiens*.

FIGURE 15.8 The Niah Cave complex in Borneo.

The earliest *H. sapiens sapiens* in Southeast Asia are equally problematic. Specimens such as the "Deep Skull" from the Niah Cave complex in Borneo (Figure 15.8) and Wadjak from Java (one of the first specimens discovered by Eugene Dubois's team) have been assigned dates of 40,000 years ago, but complex stratigraphy and provenience issues make such dates highly provisional.

The possible evolutionary relationships of these Asian modern humans exemplify contrasting views of the origin of all modern humans: Some researchers argue that they represent the culmination of an unbroken evolutionary trajectory in China and Indonesia that began with variants of *H. erectus* in each area and that extends to contemporary East Asian populations (Wolpoff et al., 1994); other researchers (e.g., Stringer and Gamble, 1993) argue that the Upper Cave individuals do not resemble modern Asians in any meaningful way, nor do the early Indonesians represent modern Indonesians, and that both may represent a migration into the region by individuals of an early, geographically undifferentiated modern human group. Filling the Asian fossil gap between 100,000 and 40,000 years ago will be essential in resolving some of these issues.

AUSTRALIA

Although Australia is separated by water from the major Eurasian land mass, evidence suggests that modern humans were in Australia before they were in Europe (Figure 15.9). To get to Australia modern humans almost certainly had to go through island Southeast Asia, so the ages of the earliest Australian occupation are also relevant to the peopling of Southeast Asia. During glacial maxima, when sea levels are lowest, Australia and New Guinea form a single land mass known as Sahul. Sahul is at all times separated by water from the land mass Sunda, which forms from some of the islands of Southeast Asia. Although all kinds of primates, including extinct hominids, occupy or occupied Sunda, only modern humans were able to disperse themselves throughout Sahul. However, a stunning recent discovery from Flores, Indonesia, shows that at least one other hominid was able to make the jump from Sunda (Box 15.1). Some scientists argue that the settlement of Australia, New Guinea, and other islands of Melanesia was a fundamental advance in

FIGURE 15.9 Aboriginal Australian art.

Box 15.1   The Little People of Flores

Homo sapiens never co-existed with *Homo erectus*. Or did they? Conventional wisdom has held that *H. erectus* went extinct in the Middle Pleistocene after giving rise to *Homo sapiens*. But as we saw in Chapter 13, geochronologists estimate that the Ngandong *H. erectus* from Java lived somewhere between 50,000 and 25,000 years ago, overlapping in time and space with modern humans who reached the region by as early as 60,000 years ago (Swisher et al., 1996). Recent discoveries on the island of Flores suggest another group lived just 18,000 years ago (sediments at the site range in age from 95,000 to 13,000 years ago). At the cave of Liang Bua where Indonesian archaeologists led by R.P. Soejono have been excavating since 1976, the remains of a diminutive hominid were recovered (Brown et al. 2004). Analyses by Peter Brown show that the skull had a cranial capacity of 380 cc (Figure A), and the postcranial skeleton suggests a female biped that stood just about a meter tall, about the size of the *A. afarensis* skeleton "Lucy." Stone tools at the site may be associated with the hominid.

Although some call it a new species, *H. floresiensis,* Brown's description makes it difficult to distinguish from *H. erectus* except on the basis of its small size. Teuku Jacob argues it is just a small, pathological human, claims that can be resolved by fur-

FIGURE A   The skull from Flores is tiny, less than one third of the capacity of a modern human skull.

ther study of the skull. A common phenomenon for large mammals that colonize small islands (Flores is about 1400 km^2) is to become, over many generations, smaller. In fact the fossil record of Flores yields the remains of a dwarfed elephant as well. This size reduction (called "insular dwarfism") is related to two selective pressures on large island mammals: fewer resources favor smaller individuals who need less food to survive and fewer predators mean that having a small body doesn't increase the chance of being eaten. The Liang Bua hominid seems to indicate such a process. Per-

haps a few members of *H. erectus* were washed onto the island on natural rafts during a storm. Stranded there they were isolated from other members of their species. Their isolation may explain not only their small size but also their survival. In their island refuge they did not come into competition for resources with and were not replaced by modern humans until much later than other archaic hominids. If it is archaic the hominid from Flores reminds us that it may have been only a few thousand years since we last shared the Earth with another hominid species.

the behavior of modern humans over earlier hominids (Noble and Davidson, 1996), in part because settlement of these islands could have been accomplished only by using a boat or raft of some kind.

The earliest human remains from Australia come from a site in the southeastern part of the continent known as Lake Mungo. Two incomplete skeletons from burials, along with other fragmentary remains and some cremations, have been found and recently dated to 40,000 years ago (Figure 15.10). Flake tools from Lake Mungo date to 50,000 years ago, which matches the earliest archaeological dates in Australia (Bowler et al., 2003). Mungo I, the buried remains of a young female, shows clear signs of having been cremated; the other burial, Mungo III, is of an old male whose body was covered with red ochre. These are the earliest known examples of such mortuary practices. Both specimens are anatomically modern *H. sapiens,* and they both exhibit a gracile build.

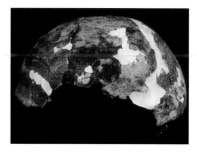

FIGURE 15.10   Partially cremated skull from Lake Mungo, Australia.

FIGURE 15.11 Evidence of regional continuity? (a) The anatomically modern Willandra Lakes Hominid 50 Calvaria from Australia and (b) a later *Homo erectus* cranium from Ngandong, Indonesia.

(a)

(b)

Other Australian sites, such as Kow Swamp and Willandra Lakes, have yielded a number of reasonably complete crania that are substantially more robust than those of the Lake Mungo people. They are also substantially younger, dating to 13,000–9,500 years ago. The Kow Swamp individuals are interesting, however, because their thick cranial bones and moderate development of browridges have been argued to demonstrate their close affinities with the latest *H. erectus* found at the site of Ngandong in Indonesia (Wolpoff et al., 1984). We saw in Chapter 14 that Ngandong may be a relict population of *H. erectus* that persisted on Java until less than 100,000 years ago and perhaps as late as 25,000 years ago, although these dates are controversial (Swisher et al., 1996). If true, this finding would support a replacement model of human origins (Figure 15.11).

However they arose, it seems clear that anatomically modern humans had the ability to cross large bodies of open water and colonize Australia by at least 50,000 if not 60,000 years ago.

ARCHAEOLOGY OF MODERN HUMAN ORIGINS

The material culture of modern humans extends from simple stone tools to complex mechanical devices. There is no doubt that the archaeological remains of later modern humans reflect cultural and individual behaviors that are substantially more complex than those indicated by the archaeological remains of earlier hominids or even of the earliest *H. sapiens sapiens*. It is important to explore the archaeology of the earliest modern humans if we are to understand the behaviors that allowed them to become the dominant hominid species throughout the world by about 40,000 years ago.

STONE AND OTHER TOOLS

We can look at the changes in tool cultures or industries associated with the emergence of anatomically modern *H. sapiens* as a tale of two continents: Europe and Africa. For many years, the European archaeological record, in conjunction with the rich trove of hominid remains recovered from European sites, stood as the basic model to explain the emergence of modern people. Over the past few decades, however, increasing research into the archaeology of Africa has provided a new context for understanding human origins.

The very earliest modern humans, those dating to 100,000 years ago or earlier in Africa and the Near East, are found with MSA assemblages that are indistinguishable in most ways from those of earlier hominids (or later Neandertals). Thus there is no one-to-one correlation between the appearance of modern anatomy and Upper Paleolithic technology.

The European Upper Paleolithic and the African Later Stone Age are distinguished from the MSA by a greater reliance on the standardized production of blades: long flakes that could be used as blanks to produce a variety of different flaked tools. A number of blades could be taken off a prepared stone core in a systematic manner (see Figure 14.18 on page 406). Refinements in tool flaking techniques also distinguish Upper Paleolithic and Later Stone Age tool industries from the MSA. For example, long, exquisitely flaked blades from the Solutrean industry of Europe demonstrate the extraordinary level of skill of Upper Paleolithic tool makers (Figure 15.12).

Microliths are another common feature of Upper Paleolithic and Later Stone Age tool industries, which appeared after 25,000 years ago in most regions. Microliths are small, flaked tools that probably were designed to be attached to wood or bone. Arrowheads are a kind of microlith and appear for the first time around 13,000–10,000 years ago. The rate and kind of change in tool types and flaking techniques also increase from the MSA to the Upper Paleolithic and Later Stone Age.

Another striking feature of the Upper Paleolithic and Later Stone Age is the vastly greater use of tools made from bone, ivory, antler, and shell. These were ground, polished, and drilled to form objects such as harpoons, spearthrowers, awls, needles, and buttons. (Such materials were used at a much cruder level and very rarely in earlier stone industries.) Upper Paleolithic Europeans also produced well-known examples of representational cave art and other artistic or ritual objects.

With one or two exceptions, the appearance of Upper Paleolithic tool industries in Europe coincided with the appearance of anatomically modern humans. In the nineteenth century, the shift from the Mousterian to the Upper Paleolithic was considered to represent a behavioral or cultural revolution that occurred when modern humans replaced Neandertals in Europe. For decades many scientists believed that the European archaeological record reflected similar replacement events in other parts of the world. However, given the relatively late appearance of modern humans in Europe, it seems unlikely that Europe should be considered a model for the original appearance of modern humans.

Because anatomically modern humans first appeared in Africa more than 100,000 years ago, we should assess whether a cultural revolution in the African archaeological record accompanied the appearance of this new biological type. It was long thought that the Middle Paleolithic of Europe and MSA of Africa were roughly contemporaneous and reflected a similar level of technological development. However, many archaeological elements thought to be uniquely associated with the Upper Paleolithic and Later Stone Age actually made their first appearance in the MSA of Africa (McBrearty and Brooks, 2000). These innovations did not appear suddenly in a single locality but in different sites at different times. For example, blades are known from several sites, dating from 75,000 years ago to perhaps as early as 280,000 years ago in East Africa. Flake technologies based on the production of points rather than scrapers (a hallmark of the Mousterian in Europe) are also abundant in African MSA sites, some dating to 235,000 years ago.

More surprisingly, microliths (Figure 15.13 on page 430), which are typically associated with the late Upper Paleolithic, were being made in the MSA 65,000 years ago. The site of Mumba in Tanzania shows a continuous sequence of the development of microlith technology, starting from larger flake tools. In South Africa, the Howieson's Poort industry (dating to 70,000–60,000 years ago) is also characterized by an abundance of microliths. At Border Cave, the Howieson's Poort industry is found in association with anatomically modern human remains. Tools made from bone have also been found at a variety of African MSA sites.

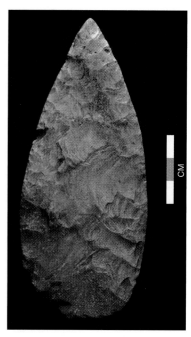

FIGURE 15.12 Upper Paleolithic refinement in stone tool production, a Solutrean blade.

microliths Small, flaked stone tools probably designed to be hafted to wood or bone; common feature of Upper Paleolithic and Later Stone Age tool industries.

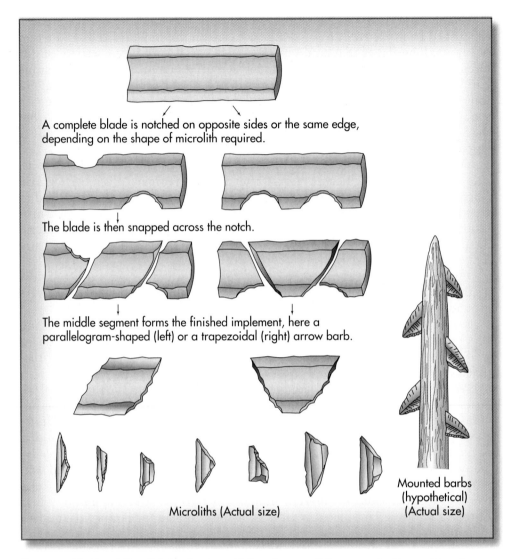

A complete blade is notched on opposite sides or the same edge, depending on the shape of microlith required.

The blade is then snapped across the notch.

The middle segment forms the finished implement, here a parallelogram-shaped (left) or a trapezoidal (right) arrow barb.

Microliths (Actual size)

Mounted barbs (hypothetical) (Actual size)

FIGURE 15.13 Microlith Production. Although mocroliths are typically considered an Upper Paleolithic technology, their origins can be traced to the Middle Stone Age of Africa.

Sally McBrearty and Alison Brooks (2000) suggest that the transition to the kind of cultural assemblage we associate with modern humans was more evolutionary than revolutionary. The European perspective, which may indeed represent the rapid replacement of the Middle Paleolithic by the Upper Paleolithic there, may not be representative of what happened in Africa, the region where modern humans first appeared. However, we should pause at this point to reflect on what modernity really means. The appearance of certain tool types often has been the basis for inferring the appearance of modern behavior. However, it is not clear that these archaeological signals are good proxies for modernity. Can modern behavior, like modern anatomy, be signaled by the appearance of a single derived character or the presence of a single tool type, however briefly it appears in the record? Or is it indicated only by the presence of a comprehensive package of behaviors that signifies a different set of interactions with the world?

SUBSISTENCE

Much evidence supports the idea that modern humans had an advantage in their ability to exploit a wider variety of foodstuffs than those used by Neandertals or archaic *H. sapiens*. Ultimately, the human ability to exploit natural resources for food led to the development of agriculture, starting about 12,000 years ago, which allowed a sustained increase in population growth. However, by expanding their subsistence base in other ways, early anatomically modern humans may have established a pattern of increased population growth relative to other hominids at the very origins of our species, long before the introduction of agriculture.

One example is the use of aquatic resources, such as fish and shellfish. Although there is earlier evidence of the limited use of marine resources, including use by some Neandertal populations, aquatic resources become a widespread and systematic part of human subsistence only in the Upper Paleolithic and Later Stone Age. However, a number of MSA coastal sites show exploitation of marine mammals, fish, shellfish, and tortoises earlier than 40,000 years ago. Perhaps they signal an earlier shift to modern behavior on that continent.

Besides archaeological remains, other sources of information point to the expansion of subsistence patterns in modern humans. *Microwear analyses* show that wear patterns on Neandertal teeth were more similar to those seen in modern human populations (Inuit and Fuegians) that have highly carnivorous diets (Lalueza et al., 1996). In contrast, Upper Paleolithic wear patterns indicate a diet incorporating a greater amount of vegetable matter. Similarly, stable isotope analyses of Neandertals (dating from 130,000 to 28,000 years ago) and Upper Paleolithic burials (aged 26,000–20,000 years) indicate that whereas the Neandertal diet relied on terrestrial herbivores, the Upper Paleolithic people were eating a more varied diet that included a substantial aquatic component, which could have come from fish, mollusks, or shorebirds (Richards et al., 2001; see Chapter 9 for a review of the stable isotope methods).

SETTLEMENT OF THE NEW WORLD AND PACIFIC ISLANDS

As evidenced by their distribution, modern humans clearly had a greater ability to exploit new environments. Although it is difficult to prove, the ability of modern humans to exploit completely new environments seems to demonstrate their ability to dominate environments that were already occupied by other hominids. Modern humans also had the ability to enter into regions that earlier hominids could not. Australia was the first of these areas, followed by the Americas and the remote islands of the Pacific.

The Americas   During ice ages, when sea levels are at their lowest, the Old and New Worlds are connected via the Bering Land Bridge, a broad swath of land (more than 2,000 km wide at its maximum) linking eastern Siberia with western Alaska (Figure 15.14 on page 432). This bridge was open and ice free only periodically, most recently between 75,000 and 45,000 years ago and again 25,000–11,000 years ago (Mandryk, 1992). Even when the land bridge was ice free, crossing it was no walk in the park but seems rather to have entailed a level of technological or subsistence development not reached by earlier hominids. Alternatively, we know that at least some modern human populations had watercraft by about 40,000 years ago, as demonstrated by the successful over-water colonization of Australia. Colonization of the New World via the coast of Siberia and Alaska or along the Pacific Rim may have been possible (Fagan, 2001).

FIGURE 15.14   Routes for the human colonization of the New World and Pacific islands.

By around 13,000 years ago, Paleo-Indian sites of the Clovis culture, which is distinguished by a characteristic finely flaked point, appeared all over North America. Additional Paleo-Indian sites appear not much later at sites in Central and South America. For many years the Clovis people were considered the first colonizers of the New World. However, scholars continue to argue over whether a pre-Clovis settlement existed.

Archeological sites aside, Paleo-Indian skeletal remains are rare. The earliest of them, such as Kennewick Man from Washington State (8,400 years old), the Browns Valley skull from Minnesota (8,700 years old), and the Warm Mineral Springs crania from Florida (perhaps 10,000 years old), exhibit features that differentiate them from recent Native American populations (Figure 15.15). This qualitative assessment has

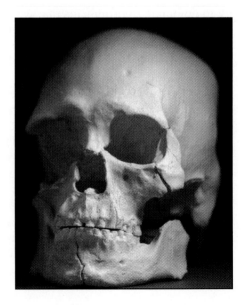

FIGURE 15.15   Paleoindian skeletal remains are rare. Kennewick man pictured here was discovered eroding from a riverbed and is about 9,000 years old.

been confirmed in a quantitative study comparing eleven early Paleo-Indian crania with crania from other populations (Jantz and Owsley, 2001). The Paleo-Indian sample showed a great degree of internal heterogeneity, and only 1 of the eleven fossils showed a strong resemblance to contemporary Native American populations. The settlement history of the Americas is clearly complex and is being addressed by genetic, linguistic, archaeological, and paleontological researchers.

The Pacific   The last regions of the world to be colonized by humans are the Pacific Islands. Although people crossed the ocean between Sunda and Sahul about 50,000 years ago and inhabited islands such as New Britain off the east coast of Papua New Guinea as early as 28,000 years ago, most of the Pacific was not colonized until 3,500 years ago or later. Only the invention of long-distance voyaging technology allowed such crossings, which settlers undertook over vast areas of ocean (Irwin, 1992). Debates continue as to how fast this expansion occurred, how much mixing there was between the expanding Southeast Asia–derived populations and the indigenous New Guinea populations, and thus how purely Asian the source population was.

Genetic, archaeological, and linguistic data seem to indicate that the source people for the peopling of the Pacific came from somewhere in East Asia or island Southeast Asia and moved into New Guinea, fusing with peoples and cultures there and then into Polynesia (Kirch, 2001). The earliest expansion of these peoples in the Pacific often is traced by their archeological sites, characterized by a pottery style called Lapita. The Lapita peoples appeared earliest in Near Oceania (the Bismarck archipelago) around 3,500 years ago and from there spread to Fiji (around 3,000 years ago) and then further out to Tonga, Samoa, and Far Oceania. Presumably in outrigger canoes, they brought with them pigs, dogs, rats, agricultural crops, and enough food and water to survive their journey. Once on these remote islands, humans did what we do best. They modified the landscape, took advantage of new natural resources, and interacted with the environment in symbolic ways. The archaeological records of most islands reveal strong impact (extinction of land birds, evidence of forest clearing for agriculture) on the available resources after the arrival of humans.

These settlements mark the end of the initial colonization of the globe by humans. Although the rest of human history on Earth will be marked by both dispersal and migration, no longer is it into ecosystems never before occupied by humans.

SYMBOLISM

Perhaps the most striking difference between later modern humans and earlier hominids is the extent to which modern human archaeological assemblages incorporate clear evidence of symbolic behavior. Remember the scant and debatable evidence of Neandertal symbolism reviewed in the last chapter. In contrast, by 50,000–40,000 years ago modern humans apparently dedicated large percentages of their time to symbolic acts such as creating and presumably wearing ornamentation, making cave and portable art, and burying their dead. All this suggests that symbolic behavior had a survival value for modern humans and that their relationship to the world and to other hominids may have been ordered by symbols.

Burials   As we saw in the last chapter, the significance and even the existence of Neandertal burials are debated, and their symbolic implications are questioned as well. By about 40,000 years ago these questions became moot for modern humans because evidence of new mortuary practices including cremation appeared at Lake Mungo in Australia at this time. In Europe, Upper Paleolithic burials (the earliest of which date to about 28,000 years ago) differ from Mousterian burials

FIGURE 15.16 Anatomically modern humans left archaeological clues, including evidence of burials that indicated ritual and symbolic behavior were important parts of their culture.

in several ways. Whether found in caves or open air sites, they are composed of burial pits. More important perhaps, a number of Upper Paleolithic burials are impressively elaborate in terms of the amount of grave goods associated with them and the number and arrangement of bodies they contain (Figure 15.16). For many interpreters of these sites, a ritualistic component in the burial is obvious. Variation in the quality of grave goods or bodily adornment between different burials may also indicate variation in social status. Obviously, not every Upper Paleolithic burial is an elaborate affair complete with an abundance of finely made grave goods. However, such burials are completely absent in the earlier archaeological records. Interestingly, evidence of deliberate burial of any kind in the later MSA is quite scanty, and Aurignacian burials are also scarce.

Art and Ornamental Objects Unlike the equivocal engravings of Neandertals, the artistic expression of Upper Paleolithic humans is astounding (Figure 15.17). Cave art and *petroglyphs* (rock carvings) occur not only in Europe but also in Africa and Australia. The earliest cave art in Europe appeared about 32,000 years ago at Chauvet, France, and is complex in its technique and representation. Rock art appeared in Africa about 26,000 years ago at Apollo 11 cave in Namibia, and somewhat earlier than that in Australia, at places such as Carpenter's Gap, which may be 40,000 years old. The rock art of Australia, which spans thousands of years, provides a particularly rich record of human artistic expression. The animals represented on cave walls such as Chauvet were once interpreted as sympathetic magic to assist in hunting success. But when compared with animals found in faunal assemblages from archaeological sites of the same period, these images suggest that people were mostly drawing animals they did not hunt. Perhaps the animals had some other symbolic or ritual importance for them.

FIGURE 15.17 Abundant cave art after about 30,000 years ago is evidence of the importance of symbolic behavior for modern human cultures.

(a)

(b)

(c)

FIGURE 15.18 Portable artwork including (a) zoomorphic figures such as this horse and (b, c) Venus figurines appear frequently in the archaeological sites of anatomically modern humans, suggesting that symbolic behavior played an important role in their lives.

Red ochre (iron oxide) and the color red were of great significance to Upper Paleolithic and other modern people. Evidence from one of the Lake Mungo burials in Australia indicates that the body may have been covered with red ochre. At the Qafzeh site, dating to about 92,000 years ago, seventy-one red ochre pieces, including some that were flaked or marked in some way, were found in association with remains of anatomically modern humans, and several stone artifacts were stained with red ochre, although there was no evidence that the bodies themselves were covered in ochre (Hovers et al., 2003). Erella Hovers and her colleagues suggest that the form and distribution of the red ochre pieces indicate they were deliberately mined from a variety of local sources.

Portable art is prevalent in modern human archaeological sites (Figure 15.18). The most famous of these pieces are the Venus figurines that represent various female figures, often interpreted as fertility totems. However, other figurines also exist, including many zoomorphic statuettes.

Personal ornamentation is perhaps the most prolific form of symbolic behavior in the Upper Paleolithic. Upper Paleolithic European burials often are covered in beads and bear other indications that the dead were buried in elaborately decorated garments (Stringer and Gamble, 1993). Thousands of beads, both isolated and associated with bodies, have been found at Upper Paleolithic sites. Experimental work by Randall White suggests that most beads were attached to garments and took a few hours each to make. Thus, the Upper Paleolithic peoples invested a huge amount of time into this form of symbolism. Particular materials seem to have been chosen for bead making, mostly representing scarce resources including ivory, talc, and nonlocal shells. In addition to beads, pendants of animal teeth are also found, but like the cave paintings they represent animals that were not food staples for Upper Paleolithic peoples. Especially abundant are perforated fox canines, red deer vestigial canines, and reindeer teeth (Figure 15.19). There are even examples of pendants made from human molars.

FIGURE 15.19 Personal ornamentation including pendants such as this ivory piece from Arcy-sur-Cure in France are often found with modern humans but rarely with Neandertals.

These elaborate displays of human symbolic behavior occur late in the archaeological record of modern humans, about 40,000 years ago or later, not with the earliest moderns. However, several examples of perforated shell, bone, and stone have been found at MSA African sites earlier in time, and perforated shell beads have recently been argued to be present at 73,000 years ago at Blombos in South Africa (Henshilwood et al., 2004) If these prove on further inspection to be worked beads, they would represent the earliest known ornamentation and important support for a gradual accumulation of modern human behaviors.

The extensive evidence of artistic abilities of Late Pleistocene modern humans, expressed in a wide range of media over a large number of populations, stands in stark contrast to the paucity of evidence for such activities in Neandertals and other hominids. Of course, this does not mean that earlier hominids were incapable of symbolic or artistic expression. Indeed, two examples of putative anthropomorphic carvings have been found in Middle Acheulean (approximately 400,000–250,000 years ago) deposits from Morocco and Israel (Bednarik, 2003), which may give us a hint of the artistic abilities of archaic *H. sapiens*. Nonetheless, even though modern humans may not have been the only type of hominid capable of inventing art, it is clear that symbolic behavior took on a whole new significance with the evolution of our species.

MOLECULAR GENETICS AND HUMAN ORIGINS

Since the mid-1980s, molecular geneticists have focused on the issue of modern human origins and the genetic histories of contemporary human populations. In general, geneticists approach these issues by making phylogenetic trees derived from different parts of the genome (see Chapters 3 and 10). These phylogenetic trees are based on the variability in these genetic systems observed in contemporary humans. In most studies, scientists use variability in DNA sequences to make the trees. However, they also use other kinds of genetic information, and trees can be based on, for example, variation in proteins, microsatellites (short, repeating DNA segments), and DNA haplotypes.

In looking at modern human origins, geneticists have used two types of data. The first considers living human genetic variation with the goal of identifying the **most recent common ancestor (MRCA)** of all people living today. The second set of data attempts to isolate DNA sequences from fossil *H. sapiens* and other hominids such as Neandertals. These ancient DNA analyses then consider the difference between the ancient groups and the extent of relatedness between them.

In a phylogenetic tree, the MRCA is indicated by the deepest node from which all contemporary variants can be shown to have evolved. Because all living people are genetically related to each other, the deepest node in a phylogenetic tree corresponds to a basic biological reality: All the variation we observe today evolved from a common ancestor. However, identifying the deepest node poses some problems. First, in large, complex datasets we can construct a huge number of possible phylogenetic trees. Thus, any particular tree represents a statistical model, which incorporates our assumptions about population size, the effects of natural selection, and other factors. Second, after identifying the deepest node in a tree, researchers want to know the date of the node. Putting a date to the node representing the MRCA entails calibration and an accurate determination of rates of genetic change (setting the molecular clock; see Chapter 10). Finally, we need to remember that the MRCA need not have been an anatomically modern human. Genetic data provide no insights into what the bodies carrying the genes looked like.

At a fundamental level, the biological issue of modern human origins can be addressed only by both genetic and anatomical (paleontological) data. The molecular

most recent common ancestor (MRCA) In a phylogenetic tree, the MRCA is indicated by the deepest node from which all contemporary variants can be shown to have evolved.

identification of the MRCA does not give us any idea about the physical or behavioral changes that led to the establishment of our species; the fossil record has no direct information about whether any past species or populations had any descendants.

MITOCHONDRIAL DNA

Research on the evolution of anatomically modern humans entered a golden age in the mid-1980s. In 1987, Rebecca Cann and her colleagues published a pioneering analysis of mitochondrial DNA (mtDNA) variation in living humans. As we discussed in Chapter 3, mitochondrial DNA is transmitted maternally (only through the mother), has a relatively rapid rate of evolution, and does not undergo recombination. Cann and her colleagues constructed a phylogenetic tree based on sequence differences distributed throughout the mtDNA genome; the mtDNA came from a large group of people representing several populations. The tree was quite complex, and there was much overlap between individuals from different populations. There was one exception: At the deepest node (representing the MRCA), on one side of the tree there was a cluster of mtDNA lineages represented exclusively in Africa. Although African mtDNA lineages were also found on the other side of the tree, the exclusive African cluster indicated that the MRCA lived in Africa. Cann and her colleagues suggested a tentative date for the MRCA between 90,000 and 180,000 years ago (Figure 15.20). Although an mtDNA phylogeny traces the lineages down to a single mtDNA source, it is important to remember that there was more than one female in the population at the time; we should not think of the mtDNA studies as identifying an African Eve.

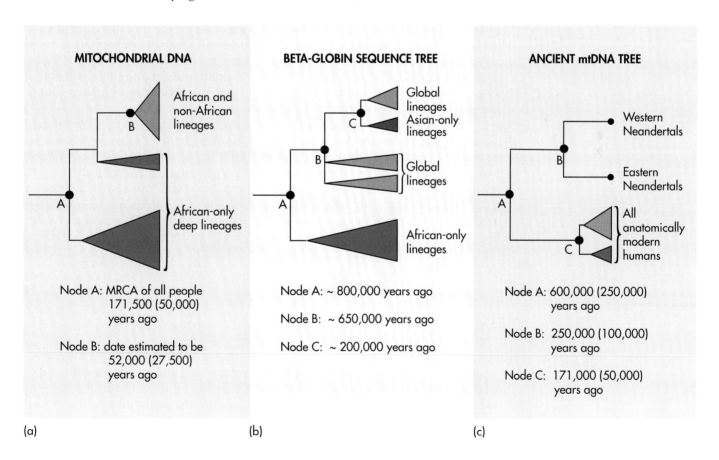

(a)   (b)   (c)

FIGURE 15.20 Three phylogenetic representations of modern human origins: (a) mtDNA, (b) beta globin gene, and (c) ancient mtDNA.

More recent analyses of the entire mtDNA genome broadly confirm the findings of the original study by Cann and her colleagues (Ingman et al., 2000). Max Ingman and his colleagues found that three of the deepest branches of the tree were exclusively African, with the next deepest being a mixture of Africans and non-Africans (Figure 15.20). All non-African mtDNA branches are of a very similar depth. Ingman and colleagues argue that such a pattern would arise if mtDNA lineages evolved initially for some time in Africa, followed by a migration out of Africa of a small number of individuals. This resulted in a population bottleneck, followed by a population expansion, with all later Eurasian mtDNA lineages derived from this initial small population that left Africa. Ingman and colleagues put the date of the MRCA for the whole tree at 171,500 (±50,000) years ago, somewhat earlier than that found in the Cann et al. study. The date of the earliest clade that included African and non-African mtDNA was 52,000 (±27,500) years ago.

THE Y CHROMOSOME

The Y chromosome is in some ways the male equivalent of mtDNA. Like mtDNA, it is transmitted across generations in only one sex, in this case males. Although parts of the Y chromosome undergo recombination, a large portion does not, and studies of this portion have been widely used in evolutionary research (Mitchell and Hammer, 1996; Stumpf and Goldstein, 2001; Jobling and Tyler-Smith, 2003). Phylogenetic analyses of the Y chromosome are based on both sequence and haplotype data. Haplotypes are combinations of mutations found together on a single chromosome; we can analyze them phylogentically or calculate population frequencies for different haplotypes (Chapter 6). There are at least eighteen major haplotype groups for the Y chromosome. Haplotypes are useful for tracing population movements and demographic events that have occurred across human history (Box 15.2 discusses a recent event illuminated by the Y chromosome).

The Y chromosome data seem to support the mtDNA story. Several estimates of a date for the Y chromosome MRCA have been suggested; most researchers accept an estimate of 100,000–180,000 years ago. Thus, the variation we observe in the Y chromosome and mtDNA of living humans appears to have evolved within similar timeframes. For both, the MRCA is dated with some confidence to less than 200,000 years ago. The Y chromosome and mtDNA data also both place the location of the MRCA in Africa. As was the case for the mtDNA, the deepest Y chromosome lineages are found exclusively in Africa, indicating evolution there first, followed by a population expansion into other parts of the world.

MRCAS FOR NUCLEAR GENES

Although the Y chromosome is part of the nuclear genome, it is a special case because such a large proportion of it is nonrecombining and it has a small number of genes that are subject to natural selection. The remainder of the nuclear genome affords countless opportunities for reconstructing the evolutionary histories of human populations.

Large-scale compilations of protein allele data (see Chapter 6) are generally consistent with the evolutionary picture provided by mtDNA and the Y chromosome (Cavalli-Sforza et al., 1994; Cavalli-Sforza and Feldman, 2003), especially in locating the MRCA in Africa. In a phylogenetic tree derived from an analysis of

Box 15.2   The Genghis Khan Effect

Y chromosome haplotypes can be an important tool in understanding the genetic histories of human populations. In a survey of more than 2,000 men from Asia using more than thirty-two genetic markers, Tatiana Zerjal and her colleagues (2003) found a Y chromosome lineage that exhibited an unusual pattern. Given the large number of markers used, most men in the survey had a unique haplotype; if two men shared a haplotype, they were always from the same population. However, one group consisted of very similar haplotypes clearly derived from a single Y chromosome ancestral haplotype; Zerjal and colleagues called this haplotype the star cluster (reflecting the emergence of these similar variants from a common source). The interesting thing about the star cluster lineage is that it is found in sixteen different populations, distributed across Asia from the Pacific Ocean to the Caspian Sea. What could explain this wide distribution?

The MRCA for this cluster was dated to about 1,000 years ago. Zerjal and her colleagues point out that the distribution of populations in which the lineage is found corresponds roughly to the maximum extent of the Mongol Empire, which reached its peak under Genghis Khan (c. 1162–1227) (Figure A). Khan and his close male relatives are known to have fathered many children (thousands, according to some historical sources). The lineage appears to have originated in Mongolia, where populations today have

FIGURE A   Genghis Khan spread more than fear across Eurasia.

some of the highest frequencies of star cluster haplotypes.

The Mongols were notoriously brutal and efficient conquerors, and as they expanded their empire across Asia, they killed many thousands of people. In many areas, relatives of Genghis Khan established dynastic lineages that ruled for centuries after the Mongol Empire proper fell apart (as a unified entity, it did not last long after the death of Genghis Khan). One additional population outside the Mongol Empire also has a high frequency of the star cluster Y chromosome: the Hazaras of Pakistan (and Afghanistan). This is puzzling at first glance, but the Hazaras

may have a Mongol origin; in fact, many Hazaras consider themselves to be direct male-line descendants of Genghis Khan. The star cluster pattern is absent from other Pakistani populations.

The star cluster lineage clearly has its roots in Mongolia, and its spread across Asia seems to be linked to the expansion of the Mongol Empire. This distribution could have resulted from the migration of a group of Mongols carrying the haplotype or may even reflect the Y chromosome carried specifically by Genghis Khan and his relatives. Zerjal and her colleagues favor the latter explanation. They point out that there is still a substantial amount of haplotype diversity in Mongolian populations; therefore, it is more likely that the star cluster represents the Y chromosome found in a group of closely related individuals, namely Genghis Khan and his male relatives. Zerjal and colleagues state that the wide distribution of the star cluster lineage is evidence of "a novel form of selection in human populations on the basis of social prestige" (p. 720). With that social prestige and political power, Genghis Khan and his male descendants obviously took advantage of the many reproductive opportunities that came their way. Centuries later, we see the effects of this extraordinary history written in the structure of the Y chromosome, even though the Mongol rulers themselves disappeared long ago, physically and culturally assimilated into the populations they ruled.

allelic variation in 120 protein genes distributed in 1,915 populations, Luca Cavalli-Sforza and his colleagues show that the deepest node in the tree represents a split between African populations and all other populations.

In contrast to mtDNA and Y chromosome analyses, phylogenetic analyses of some nuclear genes (or portions of genes) and noncoding regions of chromosomes indicate MRCAs that are substantially older than 200,000 years. In the case of genes that code for proteins, this is not necessarily surprising because variation in their structures could be strongly constrained or influenced by natural selection (of course, this is also true of the coding regions of mtDNA and the Y chromosome). However, even if natural selection is involved in shaping the patterns of variability we see, the geographic origins of different alleles can provide insights into human evolutionary history.

Rosalind Harding and her colleagues (1997) analyzed a 3,000–base pair region of the beta-globin gene (one of the chains of the hemoglobin protein). They calculated an MRCA for the gene as existing 800,000 years ago, with the oldest sequence coming from Africa (Figure 15.20b). This finding does not contradict the mtDNA and Y chromosome results because the variation in this gene could have arisen and evolved in Africa before a population expansion out of Africa less than 200,000 years ago. However, Harding and her colleagues also found Asia-specific beta-globin sequences that had MRCAs more than 200,000 years ago. This would indicate that Asian populations that existed before 200,000 years ago made unique genetic contributions to the contemporary human genome, a finding that is difficult to reconcile with the mtDNA and Y chromosome results. Harding and her colleagues also found evidence of gene flow between Asian and African populations during the last several hundred thousand years.

Results broadly similar to those for the beta-globin gene have been obtained in other studies of the nuclear genome (Zhao et al., 2000). These findings support the beta-globin results in that an ancient MRCA (>400,000 years old) is identified, with the deepest root of the tree indicating an African origin, and the MRCA for regional variation outside Africa is found to be more than 200,000 years old. Again, these kinds of results indicate a more complex picture of the genetic origins of our species than those suggested by mtDNA and Y chromosome analyses.

ANCIENT DNA

Ancient DNA (aDNA) recovered from fossils can provide a direct window into the genetics of past populations. Unfortunately, only a small percentage of fossil remains actually preserve any DNA. Several factors influence whether DNA will be intact enough for phylogenetic analysis. Age is a critical factor. Although in the early days of ancient DNA research (the late 1980s and early 1990s) many claims were made for the recovery of DNA from very ancient samples (more than 1 million years old), many subsequent research studies indicate that recovering usable DNA from fossils older than 100,000 years is extremely unlikely (Wayne et al., 1999). Temperature and humidity are also critical to whether DNA will be preserved: Cold and dry is better than warm and wet. In terms of hominid fossils, this suggests those from northern Europe and northern Asia are the most likely to provide intact DNA, whereas hominids in the tropics such as portions of Africa and Southeast Asia are least likely.

Ancient DNA from eight Neandertal individuals and seven fossil modern humans has been recovered and analyzed. Ancient samples from archaic *H. sapiens* specimens have not yet been obtained. The Neandertal samples include two from the Feldhofer Cave, Germany, the original site of the Neandertal's discovery (Krings et al., 1997; Schmitz et al., 2002), three from the Vindija Cave in Croatia (Krings et al., 2000; Serre et al., 2004), one from Mezmaiskaya Cave in the northern Caucasus (Ovchinnikov et al., 2000), and one each from Engis in Belgium and La Chapelle-aux-Saints in France (Serre et al., 2004). The modern human samples include two from Mladeč in Czechoslovakia, one each from Cro-Magnon, Abri Pataud, and La Madeleine in France (Serre et al., 2004), and two from Italy (Caramelli et al., 2003). More than twenty-five Neandertals and forty fossil humans were sampled to achieve these few results.

All of these studies agree that the Neandertal samples all fall outside the range of variation that has been observed in modern humans (Figure 15.20c). Furthermore, Neandertal samples cluster together as a clade separate from living humans on a phylogenetic tree. Sequence variation in the Neandertal sample is approximately equivalent to the level of variation observed in living modern human groups. Researchers estimate that the MRCA for modern humans and Neandertals lived between 365,000 and 853,000 years ago. An MRCA date for the western (Feldhofer and Vindija) and eastern (Mezmaiskaya) Neandertal samples has been estimated to be between 151,000 and 352,000 years ago. More importantly, ancient DNA from Neandertals also falls outside the range of variation found in ancient DNA from fossil modern humans. And all fossil humans fail to show any Neandertal DNA or any intermediate sequences and are much closer to living human DNA, despite being closer in age to the Neandertal remains.

Many researchers think that the Neandertal ancient DNA data strongly support the replacement model of modern human origins. However, some analysts (e.g., Nordborg, 1998; Relethford, 2001) argue that a small number of divergent mtDNA sequences from Neandertals does not rule out the possibility that they may have interbred with anatomically modern humans; it is not that difficult to construct mathematical population models that can account for the mtDNA data in the context of modern human–Neandertal admixture. At this time, the Neandertal genetic data do not support including Neandertals in *H. sapiens,* but they cannot be used to definitely rule out such a possibility.

INTERPRETING MODELS OF HUMAN ORIGINS

Let us now look at how our three sets of data, paleontology, archaeology, and genetics, are interpreted with respect to the origin of modern humans.

PALEONTOLOGY AND ARCHAEOLOGY

As originally developed by Milford Wolpoff, Wu Xin Zhi, and Alan Thorne (1984), the multiregional model proposed that *local regional anatomical continuity* provides strong evidence of the multiregional origins of modern humans (see also Wolpoff et al., 1994; Wolpoff and Caspari, 1997). *Local regional continuity* means we can trace a particular evolutionary trajectory through a suite of anatomical features shared by fossil specimens in a particular region; we can identify this regional anatomical pattern despite the fact that there has been a substantial amount of morphological evolution between *H. erectus* and anatomically modern *H. sapiens.* For example, widely dispersed populations of *H. erectus* exhibited regional anatomical variation (see Chapter 13), and that regional variation may have been retained in later hominid populations living in the same area.

In contrast to the multiregional model, the replacement model suggests that the earliest modern humans should look very different from the local populations they replaced and should exhibit regional continuity in only one source region, Africa (Bräuer, 1984; Stringer and Andrews, 1988). Anatomically modern humans first appeared in Africa between 200,000 and 100,000 years ago. Fossil lineages from archaic *H. sapiens* at Bodo to Herto, Aduma, and Klasies River Mouth provide evidence of an African origin of *H. sapiens sapiens* that predates such a lineage elsewhere in the world. At the same time as anatomically modern humans appear in Africa, archaic *H. sapiens* populations in Europe seem to be evolving into classic Neandertals. Because of their physical distinctiveness, Neandertals are seen to reflect a separate evolutionary trajectory from modern humans in Africa (and later in Europe), and thus are likely to have ultimately constituted a separate species. From about 40,000 to 30,000 years ago, Neandertals and anatomically modern humans appear to overlap in time and space in Europe, although they are physically and culturally distinct. By about 30,000 years ago modern humans replaced Neandertals in Europe.

In contrast, multiregional model proponents argue that the occasional appearance of occipital buns in modern human crania, the appearance of a retromolar gap in some early human fossils, and the general robustness of early European modern human fossils, especially those from central Europe, are all evidence of regional continuity (Smith, 1984). However, that some of these transitional populations, such as Vindija and Mladeč, reveal no sign of genetic admixture in their ancient DNA (Vindija is entirely Neandertal-like, Mladeč entirely modern human-like), does not support the multiregional position.

Asia and Australia may provide the best evidence of multiregional evolution, although the gap in the fossil record between about 100,000 and 40,000 years ago poses an interpretive challenge. In Asia, regional continuity between *H. erectus* and modern humans may provide evidence of multiregionalism. Multiregional proponents argue that regional characters seen in *H. erectus* in China and Indonesia are mirrored in modern humans in China and Australia. For example, the high vertical frontal lobe of Chinese *H. erectus* is considered continuous with that seen in Chinese modern humans. The sagittal keel, occipital torus, and supraorbital tori of Indonesian *H. erectus* are suggested to continue through, in lesser degrees, to modern human Australians. Likewise, multiregional proponents argue that the Ngandong hominids represent morphological and temporal intermediates between *H. erectus* and some modern Australians (Frayer et al., 1993).

Alternatively, replacement proponents counter that Ngandong is morphologically *H. erectus* and potentially overlaps in time and space with modern humans of the region (Antón, 2003; Swisher et al., 1996). In addition, replacement proponents suggest that early modern humans from Asia more closely resemble modern human specimens from other regions of the world than they do earlier Asian *H. erectus* (Stringer and Andrews, 1988).

Filling the fossil gap between 100,000 and 40,000 years ago in Asia is particularly important for paleontological advocates of the multiregional continuity model because fossils from this time period could be critical for strengthening the argument for local continuity in this region. It would also be important for offsetting the increasing evidence from Africa establishing that continent as the source of anatomically modern humans.

It is probably safe to say that within the palaeoanthropological community, there is more support for the replacement viewpoint than for the multiregional model of evolution. However, is equally safe to say that the field is far from consensus on the issue and that many palaeoanthropologists think that the fossil record provides at least some support in some regions for multiregional evolution.

MOLECULAR GENETICS

Genetic data from both living humans and fossil remains provide some clear support for a replacement model of human origins. Although the molecular data can say nothing about the anatomy of the MRCA, the picture presented by mtDNA and the Y chromosome is easy to reconcile with the paleontological replacement model, which places the origins of anatomically modern humans in Africa during roughly the same time period of the MRCA for these molecular phylogenies. The divergent mtDNA sequences of the Neandertals provide further support for a replacement event in Europe, especially in light of the fact that early modern humans in Europe have mtDNA that is well within the range of variation seen in contemporary humans. According to estimates from several genetic systems, modern humans may have evolved from a population of about 10,000 breeding individuals that existed about 100,000 years ago (Harpending et al., 1998).

For many years, there were few molecular challenges to replacement models of human origins, but data primarily from nuclear genes appear to strongly indicate MRCAs that significantly predate the MRCAs suggested by mtDNA and the Y chromosome. The most ancient lineages of these nuclear genes tend to come from Africa, but not all do, and some of the lineages outside Africa predate 200,000 years ago (Harding et al., 1997; Takahata et al., 2001).

Alan Templeton (2002) has provided a combined analysis of haplotype trees derived from mtDNA, the Y chromosome, two regions of the X chromosome, and six autosomal nuclear sequences. He argues that his analysis indicates the existence of extensive gene flow between populations throughout the Old World, dating to at least 500,000 years ago and probably longer. Several population expansions out of Africa are indicated in the analysis dating back to the original dispersal 1.7 million years ago and including the expansion indicated by mtDNA and the Y chromosome of approximately 100,000 years ago.

Templeton suggests that the expansion of cranial capacity that begins to appear about 500,000–400,000 years ago in archaic *H. sapiens* also coincides with genetic evidence for another out-of-Africa expansion (in the context of gene flow). Templeton's analysis is far-reaching and maybe overreaching (Cann, 2002), but it clearly indicates that the molecular data do not unequivocally support a replacement model. Other geneticists argue that natural selection, specifically balancing selection, could maintain alleles with deep lineages despite later population bottlenecks (Harpending and Rogers, 2000).

There is no simple answer to the question, Where did modern humans come from? (Table 15.1 on page 444). Genetic, paleontological, and archaeological data can be woven together to produce several different scenarios to explain our complex origins. Some of the controversy surrounding the issue derives from scientific success as new dating methods, new archaeological and fossil discoveries, and innovative genetic approaches have all provided an unprecedented amount of information devoted to a single evolutionary event. The controversy over which particular model of human origins is correct should not blind us to the fact that we know far more about the biological and cultural evolution of our own species than ever before.

TABLE 15.1   **Comparing Replacement and Multiregional Models of Human Origins**

	FACT	REPLACEMENT INTERPRETATION	MULTIREGIONAL INTERPRETATION
Paleontological Record, Middle Pleistocene	Between about 200,000 and 500,000 years ago, archaic *H. sapiens* lived in Africa, Europe, and Asia. Fully modern humans and classic Neandertals appeared by 125,000 years ago.	Archaic *H. sapiens* in Europe evolved into Neandertals. African archaic populations evolved into anatomically modern *Homo sapiens*.	Neandertals and modern humans are not separate evolutionary lineages. Neandertals are transitional to European modern humans.
Paleontological Record, Late Pleistocene	The anatomically modern human phenotype first appeared outside Africa 90,000–100,000 years ago in the Middle East.	Anatomically modern humans replaced preexisting hominids throughout the Old World without or with little genetic mixings. Similarities between early anatomically modern humans from widely dispersed populations are best explained by evolution from a common source population in Africa.	Anatomically modern humans arose from extensive gene flow between Middle and Late Pleistocene hominid populations throughout the Old World. Some fossils show transitional anatomy.
Recent DNA Studies	mtDNA and the Y chromosome phylogenies indicate greatest variability in Africa, suggesting that the most recent common ancestor (MRCA) of modern humans lived in Africa 150,000–200,000 years ago. Nuclear gene sequences indicate MRCAs that significantly predate 200,000 years ago. Furthermore, deep lineages of these trees have been traced to variants that appear to have originated outside Africa.	mtDNA and the Y chromosome support an African origin for modern humans and indicate a population expansion out of Africa starting about 100,000 years ago. Nuclear gene sequences reflect the age of the first dispersal (*H. erectus*) from Africa and do not preclude another dispersal by modern *H. sapiens* about 100,000 years ago. They are inconsistent with a complete replacement event.	Nuclear gene sequences indicate extensive gene flow between Old World populations over the last 500,000 years and perhaps longer. Diverse ancient Old World populations contributed to the modern human gene pool.
Ancient DNA	Ancient DNA from Neandertal and modern human fossils of the same age differ more from one another than does the DNA of living human groups. Differences between Neandertal and modern human DNA are not as great as those between chimp species. Even some fossils considered transitional in anatomy do not have transitional DNA.	Neandertals are a separate species that did not make a substantial genetic contribution to modern humans. Neandertals were replaced across their range 30,000–40,000 years ago.	Differences between Neandertals and humans are less than those between chimp species and do not support a separate species for Neandertals.

SUMMARY

1. **How do modern humans differ anatomically from earlier hominids?**

   The emergence of modern humans can be seen anatomically in a combination of cranial features that distinguish us from archaic *H. sapiens* and Neandertals. These include a gracile skull and postcranial anatomy, limited development of browridges or other cranial superstructures, a rounded cranium with a high maximum cranial breadth and parallel sides, a prominent mastoid process, a retracted face with a canine fossa, small teeth and jaws, and development of an obvious chin.

2. **How do replacement models explain the origin of modern humans?**

   Replacement models of modern human origins argue that our species evolved initially in one location (Africa) and then spread out from that location, replacing all other hominid populations without interbreeding with them. All regional variation—genetic or anatomical—that we now observe in contemporary human populations has arisen since that replacement event occurred.

3. **How do multiregional models explain the origin of modern humans?**

   Multiregional models suggest that *H. erectus* hominids distributed throughout the Old World have formed one widely distributed species with substantial gene flow between its diverse populations. Genetic innovations that arose in one population of the species were passed by gene flow to other populations in different regions. Regional variation in *H. erectus* and other Mid- to Late Pleistocene taxa is considered to have been maintained even as local *H. erectus* populations made the transition to anatomically modern human form.

4. **How do Upper Paleolithic and Middle Paleolithic tools differ?**

   Although they may occur sporadically in the Middle Paleolithic, the main distinguishing feature of Upper Paleolithic stone tools is a reliance on blades and microliths. In addition, Upper Paleolithic industries show a greater reliance on tools made from material other than stone, such as bone, antler, and shell.

5. **What is an MRCA?**

   In a phylogenetic tree, the most recent common ancestor (MRCA) is indicated by the deepest node from which all contemporary variants can be shown to have evolved. Because all living people are genetically related to each other, the deepest node in a phylogenetic tree corresponds to a basic biological reality: All the variation we observe today evolved from a common ancestor.

CRITICAL THINKING QUESTIONS

1. What do you think is the significance of early signals of modern behavior in the archaeological record of Africa? How would you define modern behavior?

2. What might be the importance of modern humans using symbolic behavior to interact with their environment? What advantages and disadvantages would this have for them?

3. Why do you think humans kept expanding into new territories? Do you think we will continue to, and where will those areas be?

KEY TERMS

replacement models
multiregional models

microliths

most recent common
   ancestor (MRCA)

SUGGESTED READINGS

Klein, Richard G., and Edgar, Blake. (2002). *The Dawn of Human Culture*. Wiley, New York.
Smith, Fred, and Spencer, Frank (eds.). (1984). *The Origins of Modern Humans*. Alan R. Liss, New York.

Wells, Spencer. (2003). *The Journey of Man: A Genetic Odyssey*. Princeton University Press, Princeton, NJ.

PART V
BIOLOGY AND BEHAVIOR OF MODERN HUMANS

Chapter 16
EVOLUTION OF THE BRAIN AND LANGUAGE

O N THE MORNING OF APRIL 12, 1861, Professor Paul Broca walked through the surgical ward of the Bicêtre hospital in Paris. An eminent scientist and surgeon and later a member of the French Senate, Broca walked like a man who was used to people getting out of his way. He was there that morning to meet a patient, named Leborgne, who was gravely ill with a gangrenous infection of his entire right leg. Broca was not particularly concerned with Leborgne's infection. Rather, he was interested in Leborgne as a neurological patient with a long history of abnormal behavior.

At the time of Broca's meeting with Leborgne, scientists interested in the human brain were embroiled in a fundamental debate about the nature of brain function. Some argued that the functions of the brain were evenly distributed throughout the brain; they believed that there were no regions of the brain that were specialized for any particular behavior or function. Others, such as Broca, believed that at least some of the functions of the brain were based in, or localized to, certain specific areas. Unfortunately for the advocates of localization, the pseudoscience of phrenology held a similar viewpoint, although the phrenologists believed they could define localized, functional areas of the brain based on the external morphology not of the brain but of the skull. That the phrenologists' claims were not based on empirical studies did not prevent phrenology from becoming a popular fad, famous throughout the world.

When Broca examined Leborgne, he found a 50-year-old man who was very weak and could no longer walk. His vision was poor, but his hearing was still good. He clearly understood what was being said to him, but he had only one response to any question asked of him: "Tan." As Broca talked to his caregivers (Leborgne had been under care for more than 20 years), his parents, and other patients on the ward, he learned that Leborgne had suffered from seizures as a child but had recovered from them. At age 30, however, Leborgne lost the ability to speak, at which time he was first admitted to the Bicêtre hospital. Starting 10 years after losing his speech, Leborgne had slowly developed a paralysis in his right arm and then his right leg, which eventually confined him to his bed.

Leborgne was not senile or insane, although the other patients generally considered him to be egotistical and rude. Because almost the only word he could say was *tan*, he became known as Tan to the rest of the hospital. The other word he could say was an expletive that he uttered when agitated or angry. Broca inadvertently elicited this expletive while repeating a test that Leborgne found tiresome.

Leborgne died only 5 days after meeting Broca, on the morning of April 17. Within 24 hours, Broca had performed an autopsy on the patient, and on that same day, obviously with some sense of urgency, he discussed Leborgne's case at a meeting of the Society of Anthropology, an organization he had founded in 1859 (which was the first anthropological organization in the world). Broca described in careful detail the damage he had found on the outer (lateral) surface of the left hemisphere of Leborgne's brain, a region that he concluded must have a specialized function involving the articulation of speech.

Broca had identified a language area of the brain. Later neuroscientists called this part of the brain Broca's area in honor of his demonstration of the localization of function in the human brain.

Although the human species possesses many features that help to make us unique, it is our complex behavior and extraordinary traditional and material cultures that set us apart from all other animals. Our behavior is ultimately the product of an anatomical feature: the human brain. Complex cultural behavior is made possible by a specific behavioral adaptation—**language**—which has evolved since the hominid lineage split from the great apes. The study of the evolution of brain and language highlights the relationship between our behavior and our biology.

In this chapter, we will review the evolution of the human brain and language. The human brain is a structure of great complexity, and it produces behaviors that are of unparalleled sophistication in the animal world. Yet we need to keep in mind that the human brain is assembled from the same basic cellular parts as found in most other animals, and its basic structural organization is reflected in the brains of both closely and distantly related species. At some point in hominid evolution, changes in the brain led to appearance of a species that behaved more like us and less like our ape cousins. Compared with the brains of our closest relatives, the human brain is larger, and it exhibits important differences in its functional organization.

Some of these organizational differences in the human brain reflect the evolution of language. When we consider the fundamental importance of language to human social existence, it is not surprising that it is a behavior that is well represented in the functional organization of the brain. Language has also help shaped the anatomy of the throat, leading to the development of an organ of speech capable of producing an extraordinary range of sounds.

We will never know exactly when our hominid ancestors started to communicate with one another using a system of communication that was more like language and less like the forms of communication used by other primates. Language, and the soft tissues that produce it, do not fossilize. But with a greater understanding of brain function and of the natural history of language, anthropologists, linguists, psychologists, and other scientists in recent years have turned to the problem of language origins with increasing enthusiasm.

OVERVIEW OF THE BRAIN

Before addressing the evolution of the hominid brain and language, it is necessary to briefly review some neuroanatomy. The central nervous system consists of two main parts: the spinal cord and the brain. The spinal cord is a thick bundle of nerve fibers that runs through the bony canal formed by the vertebrae of the spine. It is the structure through which all the nerves of the body connect to the brain. The spinal cord passes through the foramen magnum of the skull (which you read about in Chapter 11 in connection with the evolution of bipedality), where it connects to the brain.

The brain consists of three major parts: the **brain stem**, the **cerebellum**, and the **cerebrum** (Figure 16.1). As its name suggests, the brain stem sits at the base of the brain and connects directly to the spinal cord. The brain stem is important in the regulation and control of complex motor patterns, in breathing, and in the regulation of sleep and consciousness. The cerebellum, or "little brain," sits tucked in under the rest of the brain, behind the brain stem. It is densely packed with nerve cells, or **neurons**. The cerebellum is important in the control of balance, posture, and voluntary movements.

The cerebrum is the part of the brain that has undergone the most obvious changes over the course of human evolution. It is divided almost evenly along the sagittal midline into *left* and *right hemispheres*. The hemispheres can differ subtly in morphology and more substantially in function. The outer surface of the cerebrum is crisscrossed by a complex arrangement of grooves known as **sulci** (singular, **sulcus**), which gives the human cerebrum its characteristic wrinkled appearance. The sulci divide the surface of the brain into a series of thick bands or ridges, which are called **gyri** (singular, **gyrus**). Although there is individual variation, several basic sulci divide the brain into functional regions that are common to almost everyone.

language The unique system of communication used by members of the human species.

brain stem The part of the brain that controls basal metabolic rates, respiration, pulse, and other basic body functions.

cerebellum The "little brain" tucked under the cerebrum, and important in the control of balance, posture, and voluntary movement.

cerebrum The largest part of the human brain, which is split into left and right hemispheres. Seat of all "higher" brain functions.

neurons The basic cellular units of the nervous system. A neuron consists of a cell body and specialized processes called dendrites (which receive inputs from other neurons) and axons (outgrowths through which neurons send impulses to other neurons).

sulci (sing., sulcus) Grooves on the surface of the brain that divide the hemispheres into gyri.

gyri (sing., gyrus) Ridges on the surface of the brain that are formed by sulci.

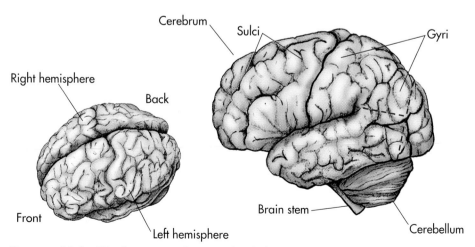

FIGURE 16.1 The human cerebrum is divided into two hemispheres, which are themselves divided by sulci into gyri.

FIGURE 16.2 A cross-section through the cerebral cortex, which is then divided into gray and white matter.

cerebral cortex The layer of gray matter that covers the surface of the cerebral hemispheres, divided into functional regions that correspond to local patterns of neuronal organization.

neurotransmitters Chemical agents that facilitate communication between neurons across the synapse.

myelin Fatty substance that sheaths neuronal axons, facilitating the transmission of electrical impulses along those axons.

If we look at a cross-section through the cerebrum (Figure 16.2), we notice that its outer surface is actually formed by a rim of tissue (4–6 mm thick) that follows the surface down into the valleys formed by the sulci; this is the **cerebral cortex**. The cerebral cortex is made of *gray matter* (which looks more brown in the living brain). Gray matter consists mostly of the cell bodies of neurons. Neurons have a characteristic structure (Figure 16.3). From the cell body, there emerge branchlike outgrowths through which neurons communicate with one another: The *dendrites* receive inputs from other neurons, and the *axon* is the outgrowth through which one neuron sends a signal to another neuron. Neurons can have many dendrites but only one axon. The junction where the axon of one cell meets the dendrite of another cell is called a *synapse*. Communication across the synapse is facilitated by chemical agents known as **neurotransmitters**. The human nervous system consists of about 100 billion neurons. Because each neuron may form synapses with thousands or even millions of other neurons, the web of communication that forms among neurons must be of mind-boggling complexity.

Gray matter makes up about 55–60% of the cerebrum. The rest of the cerebrum is composed of *white matter,* which forms the core of the hemisphere. The white matter is made up predominantly of the axons of neurons. Axons are sheathed in a white, fatty substance known as **myelin**, which facilitates the transmission of the electrical impulse along the axon. Diseases such as *multiple sclerosis*, which results from the demyelination of axons in different parts of the nervous system, demonstrate how important myelin is for normal nerve transmission. The *corpus callosum* is a large band of white matter located in the center of the brain. It is composed of axons linking the neurons of the two cerebral hemispheres. Studies of patients who have had their corpus callosum surgically severed to prevent the

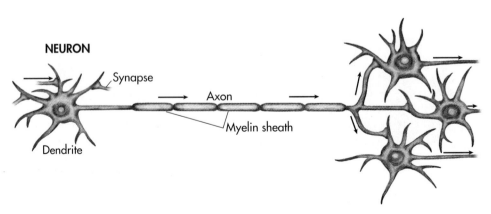

FIGURE 16.3 A neuron forming synapses with three other neurons.

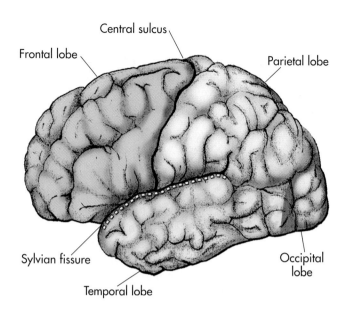

FIGURE 16.4 The major lobes of the cerebrum.

recurrence of seizures have yielded many insights into how the two hemispheres work together and separately.

MAJOR DIVISIONS OF THE CEREBRUM

Each of the hemispheres is divided into four major sectors, or *lobes* (Figure 16.4). Two of the major boundaries of the lobes are formed by the *Sylvian fissure* and the *central sulcus*. The *frontal lobe*, which makes up about 38% of the hemisphere (Allen et al., 2002), is the part of the brain located just behind your forehead. The *parietal lobe* (about 25% of the hemisphere) is just behind the frontal lobe on the other side of the central sulcus. Below the Sylvian fissure, the *temporal lobe* (22%) forms the "thumb" of the hemisphere, as it appears in a side view. The *occipital lobe* (9–10%) forms the "knob" at the back of the hemisphere. In chimpanzees and other primates, the occipital lobe is clearly separated from the other lobes by the *lunate sulcus,* a semicircular sulcus running in an arc along the posterior (back) lateral surface of the hemisphere. In humans, the lunate sulcus often is missing or present only as a minor sulcus that does not indicate a functional boundary for the occipital lobe. We will discuss the lunate sulcus later in connection with what it might tell us about the importance of reorganization of brain functions in hominid brain evolution.

Another major part of the cerebrum—not by size but by function—is the *limbic system*. The limbic system is buried within the hemispheres in the midline region of the brain and is composed of several interrelated structures. The limbic system is most notable for being the seat of emotion (Ledoux, 1996).

PRIMARY AND ASSOCIATION AREAS OF THE CEREBRAL CORTEX

Different regions of the cerebrum have different functions. As we saw earlier, the limbic regions encompass regions of the brain important for producing emotions, and some of its regions are critically important for forming new memories. The cerebral cortex is divided into two kinds of functional areas. **Primary cortex** is involved directly with either motor control or input from the senses. *Primary motor* regions are concentrated in the frontal lobe, just in front of the central sulcus. *Primary sensory* regions are distributed throughout the cerebrum.

Most of the human cerebral cortex is not primary cortex but rather **association cortex**. We can think of the association cortex as the regions where the processing

primary cortex Regions of the cerebral cortex that are involved directly with motor control or sensory input.

association cortex Parts of the cerebral cortex where inputs from primary motor and sensory cortex are processed.

FIGURE 16.5
Pierre Paul Broca, a pioneer
neuroscientist and
anthropologist.

of primary inputs or information occurs. It is generally believed that in mammals, as brain size increases, the proportion of the brain devoted to association rather than primary regions also increases. Some association areas receive inputs from only one primary area, and other regions receive inputs from multiple primary regions. Anything that we think of as a higher-level function, such as thought, decision making, art, or music, originates in association cortices.

METHODS FOR STUDYING BRAIN STRUCTURE AND FUNCTION

Several different methods for studying brain structure and function have developed over the past 150 years. Broca's study of his patient Tan included two methods. One was the *autopsy,* for many years the only way scientists had of studying brain structure, in which the brain is examined and described after a person's death. Broca (Figure 16.5) combined the autopsy with the *lesion method,* which correlates a behavioral abnormality in a living person with a brain abnormality observed at autopsy. Broca observed a lesion in the left lateral frontal lobe in a man with impoverished speech production, thus allowing him to make the inference that this region is important in speech. The lesion method relies on "natural experiments": observations of people who have sustained a brain injury (for example, via stroke or infection) and who also exhibit a behavioral deficit. It has also been used widely as an experimental tool using animals as subjects; much of what we know about mammalian brain function comes from such studies.

Over the past 20 years, the development of a field called *neuroimaging* has revolutionized the study of the brain. Noninvasive methods allow us to observe the structure and function of the brain in living, healthy people under controlled experimental conditions. **Magnetic resonance imaging** (**MRI**) is the most commonly used method to study brain structure in living individuals (Figure 16.6). A magnetic resonance image of the brain is essentially a high-resolution map of water concentration in the brain. It provides good contrast between gray and white matter and cerebrospinal fluid. For the study of brain function and activity, scientists use techniques such as *positron emission tomography* (PET) scanning and *functional MRI.* These methods show which parts of the brain are activated during a cognitive act (thinking of a word, listening to a sound, remembering an emotion) by identifying areas where metabolism or blood flow has increased.

Although recent technological advances have provided us with some extraordinary tools for examining the brain, the study of the evolution of brain structure and function, or **paleoneurology,** remains for the most part dependent on the study of endocasts. *Endocasts* are impressions of the interior part of the cranium, from which we can make inferences about the size and structure of the brain (see Tobias, 1971, for an overview) (Figure 16.7). Scientists make endocasts from fossil skulls, or in rare cases endocasts form naturally during fossilization (see Chapter 12). Unfortunately, the brain is separated from the inside of the cranium by several protective tissue layers and cerebrospinal fluid; therefore, endocasts are inevitably a

magnetic resonance imaging (MRI)   A technique for visualizing body tissues (including the nervous system) based on radiofrequency emissions from particular atomic nuclei, especially hydrogen. It works essentially as a map of water concentration in different tissues of the body.

paleoneurology   The study of the evolution of brain structure and function.

FIGURE 16.6   On the left, a portion of the surface of the brain as seen in an MRI. On the right, the same portion of the brain shown during surgery.

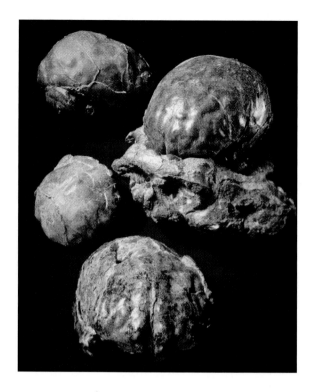

FIGURE 16.7 Endocasts from South African australopithecines.

poor reflection of the brain's anatomy. Nonetheless, they provide us with the only source of direct information we have about the brain structure of extinct species.

ISSUES IN HOMINID BRAIN EVOLUTION

Now we are ready to tackle some specific issues in hominid brain evolution. Understandably, most of the important questions examine ways in which the human brain is different from the brains of other primates and mammals. But there are many ways in which our brains are similar to those of other mammals. We use the same neurotransmitters and share a basic cellular architecture. We have gray matter and white matter and, like most mammals, have some basic sulci and gyri around which functional regions are organized.

BRAIN SIZE AND ENCEPHALIZATION

One of the defining features of the genus *Homo*, and especially our own species, is large brain size. But what do we mean by "large"? In absolute terms, the human brain weighs in at about 1,300 g, and human cranial capacities usually are reported to be in the region of 1,300–1,400 cc. These are average figures, and there is much variation in brain size. However, for purposes of cross-species comparisons, the 1,350-cc estimate for the volume of the typical human brain is good enough.

Look at the cranial capacities of various primates listed in Table 16.1 on page 454. As you can see, humans have the largest brains among primates. The second largest brains belong to the gorillas. Among the Old World monkeys, baboons appear to have relatively large brains. As discussed in Chapter 7, among the New World monkeys, spider monkeys have substantially larger brains than their close relatives, howler monkeys. To put these data in a broader zoological context, cattle have brains of about 486 cc and horses of about 609 cc—somewhat larger than that seen in a great ape (Figure 16.8 on page 454). The bottle-nosed dolphin has a brain volume of about 1,118 cc, which is nearly human-sized (Hofman, 1988).

TABLE 16.1	Cranial Capacities, Body Weights, and EQs of Several Primate Species		
SPECIES	CRANIAL CAPACITY (CC)	BODY WEIGHT (KG)	EQ
APES			
Homo sapiens, male	1,424.5	71.9	4.32
Homo sapiens, female	1,285.2	57.2	4.64
Gorilla gorilla (gorilla), male	537.4	169.5	0.85
Gorilla gorilla (gorilla), female	441.4	71.5	1.34
Pan troglodytes (chimpanzee)	388.6	83.7	1.48
Pongo pygmaeus (orangutan), male	393.1	87.7	1.08
Pongo pygmaeus (orangutan), female	341.2	37.8	1.69
Hylobates lar (gibbon)	98.3	5.5	2.10
OLD WORLD MONKEYS			
Papio anubis (baboon), male	166.4	23.5	1.18
Papio anubis (baboon), female	141.4	11.9	1.69
Cercocebus albigena (gray-cheeked mangabey)	97.3	7.69	1.63
Colobus guerza (black and white colobus)	75.4	9.05	1.11
NEW WORLD MONKEYS			
Ateles geoffroyi (spider monkey)	126.4	6.00	2.55
Alouatta palliata (howler monkey)	62.8	6.55	1.18
Saimiri sciureus (squirrel monkey)	24.4	0.68	2.58

Note: Values from Kappelman (1996), using Martin's (1983) formula for EQ. New World monkey values calculated from Harvey et al. (1987). If male and female values are not shown, midpoint values between male and female averages are shown.

Encephalization Quotients   Many scientists find absolute brain size values to be of limited usefulness in understanding brain evolution or the relationship between brain size and behavior. After all, it comes as no surprise that bigger animals have bigger brains than smaller animals, but just because a big animal has a big brain, that does not mean that the animal is more intelligent. Scientists try to deal with this issue by measuring the **encephalization** of a species, which is a measure of brain

encephalization   A measure relating brain size to body size in a species.

HORSE: weight, 400kg; cranial capacity 600cc
CHIMPANZEE: weight, 80kg; cranial capacity, 400cc

FIGURE 16.8 Chimpanzees and horses have brains that are similar in size.

size relative to body size. Researchers such as Harry Jerison (1991) and Robert Martin (1983) have shown that the relationship between brain size and body size is somewhat more complicated than a simple linear relationship. By looking at large numbers of mammal species, they derived equations that allow us to calculate the expected brain size for a mammal of any size. The **encephalization quotient (EQ)** is a ratio of the actual brain size to the expected size. Thus mammals that have EQs greater than 1.00 have brains that are larger than expected for a mammal of their size; an EQ less than 1.00 means that it is smaller than expected.

Returning to Table 16.1, we see that humans have the largest brains not only in absolute but also in relative terms, as measured by the EQ. In general, anthropoid primates have EQs greater than 1.00, indicating that their brains are larger than would be expected for mammals of their size. So even though cattle and horses have brains that are ape-sized in absolute terms, their EQs are smaller than those of apes because of their larger body sizes. It is generally assumed that the larger brain size in anthropoid primates has evolved in conjunction with the evolution of complex social behavior and adaptation to the arboreal environment.

Can we say that mammals with higher EQs are in some sense "smarter" than those with lower EQs? Yes and no. Terrence Deacon (1997) points out that the encephalization quotient is derived from both brain size *and* body size and that there is a tendency to overlook the fact that animals face strong selection pressures that shape body size as well as brain size. Among dog breeds, for example, chihuahuas are more encephalized than German shepherds; artificial selection on chihuahuas has driven body size down at a faster rate than brain size (Figure 16.9). But no one would argue that a chihuahua is smarter than a German shepherd. In anthropoids, small or even dwarfed species, such as the squirrel monkey in the New World or the talapoin monkey in the Old World, have high EQs. Again, rather than interpreting this as a sign of large brain size, we could also see it as an example of selection for small body size (which is probably more correct).

Colobine monkeys tend to have lower EQs than cercopithecine monkeys (see the mangabey versus the colobus in Table 16.1). There is no evidence that colobine behavior is in some sense less sophisticated than cercopithecine behavior. As discussed in Chapter 7, colobine monkeys are adapted to a leafy diet; this digestive requirement has driven selection for greater gut and body size, resulting in lower EQs. Colobines are still more encephalized than a typical mammal. Gorillas, who have large brains in absolute size, also have low EQs. Again, their low-quality, leafy diet (as well as other factors, such as protection from predation) may have driven selection for larger body size, leaving them with EQs lower than their closest relatives, the other apes. On the other hand, in a comparison of two closely related species sharing a particular environment, such as the spider and howler monkeys discussed in Chapter 7, it is reasonable to hypothesize that larger brain size in the spider monkey may have evolved as a result of the greater cognitive demands of frugivory. In summary, the EQ is a potentially valuable indicator of cognitive ability but we need to remember that it is a function of both brain and body size.

Sex Differences in Primate Brain Size In almost all primate species, males have larger brains than females. In the three highly sexually dimorphic species listed in Table 16.1 (orangutans, gorillas, and baboons), the absolute brain size differences are large, as are the body size differences. In each case, EQs for the females are substantially larger than for males. The EQ for

encephalization quotient (EQ) The ratio of the actual brain size of a species to its expected brain size based on a statistical regression of brain to body size based on a large number of species.

FIGURE 16.9 Encephalization is a function of both brain size and body size.

male gorillas is below 1.0, indicating that their brains are smaller than we would expect for a mammal their size. There is strong selection for male body size in highly sexually dimorphic primate species, but there is no reason to suppose that there are profound differences in the level of behavioral sophistication between the sexes.

Even in less sexually dimorphic primate species, such as rhesus macaques and humans, males have larger brains than females. This is true after we correct for body size (Holloway, 1980; Falk et al., 1999). Although we could speculate on the selection forces on behavior or other biological processes that might drive such a sex difference, one conclusion is that the sex difference in brain size observed in humans is not a function of recent evolution for higher cognitive function in hominids but seems to reflect a general primate trend (Falk et al., 1999).

BRAIN SIZE AND THE FOSSIL RECORD

In the previous chapters, you read that increasing brain size is a characteristic of genus *Homo*. A compilation of average cranial capacities of different hominid fossil taxa is presented in Table 16.2. (Please note that the *H. sapiens* values in Tables 16.1 and 16.2 differ because they are based on different samples.) As you can see, the different groups can be sorted to some extent according to their cranial capacities and EQs. Of course, this comes as no surprise because cranial capacity is one of the morphological features we use to classify specimens into different taxonomic groups.

Early Hominids and Robust *Australopithecus* Brain size increases from the early australopithecines (*A. afarensis* and *A. africanus*) to the "robust australopithecines," or *Paranthropus*. The early australopithecines have cranial capacities in the range of 400–500 cc, whereas the later *A. robustus* and *A. boisei* are in the 475–530 cc range. The early australopithecines have cranial capacities similar in size to those seen in chimpanzees, orangutans, and female gorillas, whereas the cranial capacities of the paranthropines are more similar to those seen in male gorillas. (Although the mean for male gorillas is around 530 cc, Schultz [1969] reports that at least one gorilla had a cranial capacity of 750 cc.)

Are the robust australopithecines species more encephalized than the earlier australopithecines? Are graciles and robusts more encephalized than the contemporary great apes? Answers to these questions depend on estimates of body mass and brain size. As we have already seen, gorillas have large brains, but they also have large bodies, especially male gorillas, so they are not impressively encephalized.

TABLE 16.2	Average Cranial Capacities for Fossil Hominids (adult specimens only)			
TAXON	NUMBER OF SPECIMENS	AVERAGE CRANIAL CAPACITY (CC)	RANGE (CC)	ESTIMATED EQ
A. afarensis	2	450	400–500	1.87
A. africanus	7	445	405–500	2.16
A. robustus and A. boisei	7	507	475–530	2.50
H. habilis	7	631	509–775	2.73–3.38
H. erectus	22	1,003	650–1,251	3.27
Archaic H. sapiens	18	1,330	1,100–1,586	3.52
H. neanderthalensis	19	1,445	1,200–1,750	4.04
Modern H. sapiens (older than 8,000 years)	11	1,490	1,290–1,600	5.27

Sources: Aiello and Dean (1990), Kappelman (1996), and Holloway (1999).

Note: Estimated EQs are not derived using all the specimens included in the second column.

(They are impressively big.) Estimating body mass of fossilized individuals is very difficult and depends on how well sizes of available parts of the skeleton correlate to overall body size. EQs calculated for any individual fossil specimen therefore should be taken with a grain of salt. Henry McHenry (1992; see also Kappelman, 1996) estimates that *A. afarensis*, *A. africanus*, and *A. robustus* had male body sizes of 40–45 kg and female sizes of 30–32 kg; *A. boisei* was about 10% larger. These estimates indicate that these hominids were smaller than contemporary great apes; given that their cranial capacities were at least as large, we can conclude that gracile and robust australopithecines were indeed more encephalized than the great apes. In addition, the brain size increase seen in the robust forms relative to the earlier forms is also likely to reflect an increase in encephalization.

Early *Homo* and *Homo erectus*   Hominid fossils assigned to *Homo habilis* or early *Homo* have cranial capacities substantially larger on average (by 25–30%) than those seen in *Australopithecus* or the great apes. Although the smallest early *Homo* specimens (for example, KNM-ER 1813, which has a cranial capacity of 509 cc) and the largest gorillas may overlap in cranial size, the relatively small habiline body size, estimated by McHenry (1992) to be 52kg for males and 32kg for females, combined with the larger brain size, represents an increase in encephalization over earlier hominids. As you read earlier, the appearance of *H. habilis* roughly coincides with the appearance of stone tools in the archaeological record, providing evidence of at least one kind of cognitive evolution.

The average cranial capacity of fossils assigned to *H. erectus* shows an even more profound jump than *H. habilis* in both relative and absolute size compared with earlier hominid taxa. Although both brain and body size increased in *H. erectus*, brain size may have increased relatively more quickly leading to an increase in encephalization (Kappelman 1996). As discussed in Chapter 13, *H. erectus* was widely distributed geographically and exhibited gradual change over its more than 1 million years in existence. On average, the earliest *H. erectus* specimens (such as KNM-ER 3883 and KNM-ER 3733) have smaller cranial capacities than later specimens. Thus the range of cranial capacities seen in *H. erectus* specimens is quite large (from 650–1250cc), which is one reason that some investigators have justified splitting the taxon into two or more species. The recently discovered Dmanisi crania from Georgia, dating to 1.75 million years ago, have cranial capacities of between 600 and 780cc; the smallest of these is a subadult (Vekua et al. 2002). Their cranial capacities are well within the range of *H. habilis* and *H. erectus*, but their cranial anatomy links them with *H. erectus*.

Archaic *Homo sapiens*, Neandertals, and Modern *Homo sapiens*   Cranial capacities in the modern range are found in both archaic *H. sapiens* and Neandertal specimens. Indeed, one of the apparent paradoxes of the later hominid fossil record is that Neandertal cranial capacities often exceed the average cranial capacity of modern humans (see Tables 16.1 and 16.2). Even the archaic *H. sapiens* mean is within the range of modern *H. sapiens*. The increase in average cranial capacity from *H. erectus* to the later *Homo* species is quite profound and undoubtedly exceeds any increase in body size. Thus the hominid trend for increasing brain size and encephalization continues through the appearance of archaic *H. sapiens* and Neandertals.

What about the apparent decline in brain size in modern humans compared with Neandertals and even with earlier modern humans? We should keep in mind that there may be some kind of sampling bias (for example, toward larger males); after all, we have only small numbers of fossils available to compare with large numbers of modern humans. More critically, John Kappelman (1996) points out that the larger body size of archaic *H. sapiens* and Neandertals (see Chapter 14), relative to modern humans, often is overlooked or underemphasized. Thus modern humans are more encephalized than Neandertals because their bodies are much smaller but their brains are almost as large as Neandertal brains (Figure 16.10).

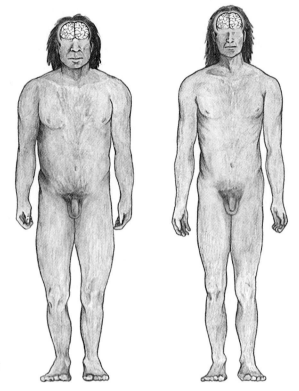

FIGURE 16.10 Although Neandertal brain sizes fall well within (or exceed) the modern human range, their EQ is lower than modern humans because they had larger bodies.

Brain size increase and increased encephalization have characterized hominid evolution over the past 3–4 million years (Figure 16.11). These trends have become more marked over the past 2 million years, as absolute brain size has nearly tripled. During the past 2 million years, increases in brain size have outpaced increases in body size, thus leading to increasingly encephalized hominids. Al-

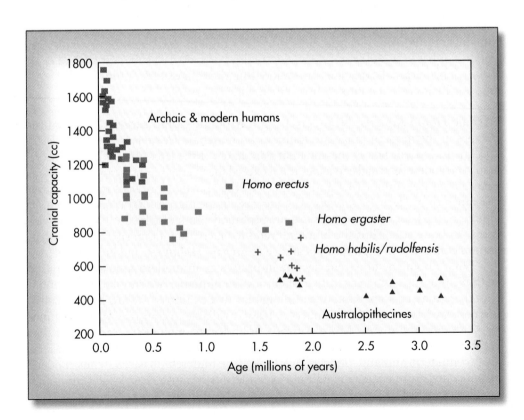

FIGURE 16.11 Cranial capacity has increased approximately fourfold over the last 3.5 million years of hominid evolution.

Box 16.1 The Ten-Percent Myth: Evolution and Energy

We have all heard the myth that we humans use only 10% of our brains. Indeed, it is apparent that not only have many people heard it but they believe it. Psychologist Barry Beyerstein (1999) has spent many years researching the origins of this mistaken idea. Although he cannot pinpoint its origins with precision, he has shown that it has been around for quite some time. One of first groups that latched onto and spread the myth was the early self-improvement ("positive thinking") industry. For example, a 1929 advertisement states that "scientists and psychologists tell us that we use only about TEN PERCENT of our brain power" and that by enrolling in the course being advertised, a person might tap some of that brain that is not being used. The advertisement uses the 10% figure as though it were common knowledge. This indicates that the origins of the myth must date to significantly earlier than 1929. Although Beyerstein has tried to identify the "scientists and psychologists" who may have said something like this, he has so far failed to find any specific reference to it in the literature.

Even if the 10% figure came from a scientist working at the turn of the twentieth century, the state of the art of neuroscience was not particularly advanced at that time.

Most people would agree that any sweeping scientific pronouncement, based on little empirical research, is eventually due for some reconsideration. Indeed, there is plenty of evidence from neurology and psychology that the 10% figure is wholly untenable; it is basically neuro-nonsense.

One of the most compelling arguments against the 10% myth comes from the perspective of energy and evolution. The brain uses a lot of energy. In humans, it accounts for about 2% of the body mass but uses about 16–20% of the total energy and oxygen consumed by the body. It is an "expensive tissue" (Aiello and Wheeler, 1995). The brain cannot store significant energy reserves, and is extremely vulnerable if the oxygen supply is cut off.

From an evolutionary standpoint, maintaining such an expensive organ only to use 10% of it does not make any sense. When you consider that there are other costs associated with large brain size (such as birth difficulties; see Chapter 17), if we used only 10% of the brain, there would have been substantial fitness benefits in reducing the brain to a more efficient and less costly size. This did not happen, of course, as brain expansion has characterized evolution in genus *Homo*.

Leslie Aiello and Peter Wheeler point out that the brain is not the only expensive tissue in the body. The heart, kidney, liver, and gastrointestinal tract consume at least as much energy as the brain. Human bodies use energy at about the rate that would be expected for a mammal our size. Given that our brains are much larger than would be expected for a mammal our size, how do we maintain the expected energy consumption rate? Aiello and Wheeler argue that a tradeoff with one of the other expensive tissues has occurred. Specifically, at the same time as the brain has increased in size in human evolution, it appears that the stomach and intestines have decreased in size. These size reductions presumably have been accompanied by a reduction in energy use. The smaller gastrointestinal tract also indicates a reliance on higher-quality, easier-to-digest foods (such as meat).

The complex relationship between behavior, brain size, diet, and gut size is one of the most fascinating problems in the study of human evolution. Although it is tempting to see brain size and gut size as engaged in a neat tradeoff, the situation probably was a bit more complex than that. Nonetheless, Aiello and Wheeler make clear that we have to pay for what we have: a large, energy-hungry brain. And a brain that wastes 90% of its volume could never have evolved.

though brain size and encephalization are not everything, expanding brain size in the hominid lineage clearly reflects an adaptation, given how "expensive" brain tissue is (Box 16.1).

BRAIN REORGANIZATION

We have direct fossil evidence of the expansion of the hominid brain over the past 4 million years. As the brain has expanded, its functional organization has also changed. We know this by comparing our brains with those of our closest relatives, such as the chimpanzee, or of the rhesus macaque, an animal often used as the primate standard in experimental neurological research. For example, there are parts of the brains that are essential for normal language production. Because other primates do not have language, obviously some reorganization of the brain has accompanied the evolution of language ability. Although scientists debate the relative importance of reorganization and expansion in hominid brain evolution, it is quite reasonable to assume that both processes have been crucial.

FIGURE 16.12 View of the bottom surface of the human brain. The olfactory bulbs are small structures located on the underside of the frontal lobes.

Investigators have tried to trace the evolution of other aspects of brain organization via both comparative anatomy and the examination of fossil endocasts. Reorganization can occur in three ways: An anatomical region of the brain (linked to some function) can become larger or smaller compared with the rest of the brain, functional regions of the brain can shift or change position (which may or may not be associated with regional expansion or contraction), or new behaviors may lead to the evolution of new functional fields, which would supplant or enhance previously existing functional associations in those areas.

We will discuss examples illustrating the first two kinds of reorganization in this section but will save the third for the section on language later in this chapter. Several studies have shown that when we look at large numbers of mammal species, the anatomical organizations of their brains are remarkably uniform in terms of the relative size of one structure compared with another or with the whole brain (Jerison, 1991; Finlay and Darlington, 1995). This is true whether the brains are big or little. Of course, as with any statistical generalization, there are exceptions. What we want to know is, What exceptions are present in the human brain and when did they evolve?

Olfactory Bulbs   In the human brain, the **olfactory bulbs**, which control our sense of smell, are small, knoblike structures found on the bottom of the frontal lobes in each hemisphere (Figure 16.12). Compared with other mammals, anthropoids have olfactory bulbs that are small for their overall brain size (Jerison, 1991), measuring only about 0.1 cc in volume (Stephan et al., 1981). In contrast, wolves have olfactory bulbs that are about 6 cc in volume, a 60-fold advantage over the human-sized olfactory bulb. Humans have olfactory bulbs that are about the same size as those found in strepsirhine species whose brains are only 1–2% the size of human brains.

Humans reflect (in more extreme form) a basic trend in olfactory bulb reduction that we can see in all living anthropoids. We presume that this reduction occurred as other sensory domains (such as vision) and higher-level cognition became more important, reducing reliance on the sense of smell. Studies of endocasts of the Oligocene primate *Aegyptopithecus* may indicate that olfactory bulb reduction was already present in this early anthropoid (Radinsky, 1979).

Frontal Lobes   Olfactory bulbs are a good example of reorganization by size reduction in the human brain. At the other end of the spectrum, many brain investigators (such as Deacon, 1997, but see also Holloway, 1968) have argued that one of the largest regions of the brain, the frontal lobe, has expanded over the course of hominid evolution, relative to the rest of the brain. Scientists believe that the **prefrontal region**—the parts of the frontal lobe that do not include the primary motor regions—has shown a marked relative expansion. In other words, we

olfactory bulbs   Knoblike structures located on the underside of the frontal lobes, that form the termination of olfactory nerves running from the nasal region to the brain.

prefrontal region   The association cortex of the frontal lobes, located forward of the primary motor region of the precentral gyrus and the supplemental motor areas.

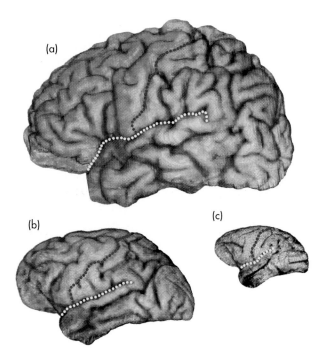

FIGURE 16.13 The frontal lobe (green) bounded by the Sylvian fissure (yellow line) and central sulcus (red line), in a (a) human, (b) chimpanzee, and (c) gibbon.

may have a larger prefrontal region (and frontal lobe) than we would expect given the size of the human brain.

Why should we expect that humans have evolved a larger frontal lobe relative to overall brain size? The functions of the frontal lobe seem to coincide with many of the higher functions that we associate with intelligence, specifically with the kind of intelligence that we seem to have more of than any other animal, such as forming goals and devising plans to attain them. It is not unreasonable to predict that given our apparent reliance on these functions, our prefrontal region should be large.

However, recent MRI studies of human, ape, and monkey brains conducted by Katerina Semendeferi and her colleagues (2000, 2002) indicate that the frontal lobe is not proportionally larger in human brains (Figure 16.13). They found that the frontal lobe makes up about 36–37% of the hemisphere in humans, orangutans, chimpanzees, and gorillas. It is proportionally larger in humans and great apes than in gibbons (29%) and in a combined sample of rhesus macaque and cebus monkeys (31%). These results indicate that we and the great apes may share a small increase in relative frontal lobe size.

The high forehead of modern humans compared with the sloping foreheads of close relatives such as Neandertals and archaic *H. sapiens* might seem to be an obvious indication of frontal lobe expansion. As you recall in Chapter 14, Neandertals and archaic *H. sapiens* differ substantially from modern humans in the anatomy of the forehead and eye orbits: In general, their foreheads slope backward from large browridges. Looking at profiles of frontal bones in cross-section, Fred Bookstein and his colleagues (1999) found that despite differences in external morphology of the frontal region, the internal morphology was remarkably similar, indicating that the shape of the frontal lobe probably was also similar in these groups.

Primary Visual Regions   The *primary visual region* is the part of the brain where visual information from the eyes is initially processed. Although it is present in the occipital lobes in both humans and other primates, in humans the primary visual region is located in a sulcus on the inner surface of the lobe, whereas in primates the primary visual cortex encompasses most of the lobe's outer surface. Furthermore, the visual cortex is smaller than we would expect for a primate brain its size: It is only about 1.5 times larger than the visual cortex of a chimpanzee or

FIGURE 16.14 Primary visual processing areas (blue) in (a) a human (lateral and mesial views) and (b) a chimpanzee. In humans, the primary visual areas surround the calcarine sulcus. In chimpanzees the lunate sulcus forms the anterior boundary.

gorilla, whereas the brain as a whole is about 3 times larger (Stephan et al., 1981). The reduction and shift of the visual region in primates presumably has allowed the expansion of the parietal association cortex, a region where sensory information from different sources is processed and synthesized. But the controversy about visual reorganization has been not about whether but about when it occurred.

The beginnings of the controversy go back to when Raymond Dart (1925) published his initial description of the Taung child (*A. africanus*) skull and endocast. In nonhuman primates, the primary visual region of the occipital lobe is reliably separated from the rest of the brain by the **lunate sulcus**, a well-defined sulcus that is almost always present. In contrast, in humans the lunate sulcus often is absent or very poorly developed. Furthermore, the lunate sulcus in humans does not mark the primary visual region; that is marked by a different sulcus (the calcarine sulcus) located on the interior surface of the occipital lobe (Figure 16.14).

When Dart analyzed the Taung endocast, he confidently marked the lunate sulcus in a posterior, "human-like" position. He interpreted this to mean that despite the apelike size of the Taung brain, it showed evidence of human-like brain reorganization. This conclusion was accepted for many years, but in the 1980s a vigorous debate about the location of the lunate sulcus in Taung and other australopithecines broke out between Ralph Holloway and Dean Falk, two of the most experienced paleoneurologists working in the field (see Falk, 1980, 1983b, 1985a, 1985b, 1989, 1991; Holloway, 1981, 1984, 1988, 1991; Holloway and Kimbel, 1986). Falk argued that Dart's positioning of the lunate was incorrect and that it was in a more apelike position. Holloway, who initially accepted Dart's placement, argued that Falk's positioning of the lunate on the endocast was also anatomically untenable. To make a long story short, it seems reasonable to conclude today that we do not know where the lunate sulcus was in australopithecines and whether the primary visual region was in a more apelike than human-like position. However the lunate sulcus debate was useful in making the methods for examining and interpreting endocasts more explicit. But even without a definitive resolution of this debate, it remains a fact that the primary visual cortex of the human brain has been reorganized over the course of hominid evolution.

LANGUAGE: BIOLOGY AND EVOLUTION

Much of what makes human behavior more complex and more sophisticated than the behavior of other animals depends on our possession of spoken language. It is one thing to possess sophisticated cognitive abilities—to make plans, to draw complex cause-and-effect relationships between the things you see in the environment, and to think in terms of the past, present, and future—but without the ability to

lunate sulcus A prominent sulcus on the lateral side of the hemisphere of most nonhuman primates, which divides the primary visual cortex of the occipital lobe from the rest of the cerebrum.

convey these thoughts to other members of the social group, their usefulness for enhancing survival and reproductive success would be limited.

Language is an adaptation. It is easy to imagine that a social group of hominids who possess language would have an advantage over a social group of hominids who did not. But language ability is as much an anatomical as a behavioral adaptation. As we will see, modern humans are designed by natural selection—in the anatomy of their throats and respiratory system and in various aspects of the structure and function of their brains—to produce language.

WHAT IS LANGUAGE?

Language is the system of communication used by members of the human species. Although linguists differ on which features are most critical in defining language, they all tend to agree on certain critical aspects that make language a unique form of animal communication.

1. *Language is spoken.* Although we can represent language using nonverbal symbols (sign language and writing), and nonverbal cues are important in human communication, language is fundamentally expressed verbally. We are anatomically specialized both to produce language and to process language-oriented sounds.

2. *Language is semantic.* The words we use in language have meanings; they are linked to real-world objects, events, or actions. Although other animals may have some semantic elements in their communication systems (for example, honeybees convey the position of food sources via their "dance"), the human semantic universe is orders of magnitude larger than that found in any other species. Each speaker of a human language knows the meaning of thousands of words. Obviously, different languages use different words, which can be learned only via *traditional transmission* in a cultural context.

3. *Language is phonemic.* Words are assembled from small sound elements known as *phonemes.* Phonemes are the building blocks of words. They have no intrinsic meaning. There is no biological limit to the combinations of phonemes that we can use to produce words. The association between a word and the object or action it represents is arbitrary. For example, *mosquito* is a large word for a small thing, and *whale* is a small word for a big thing. Onomatopoeic words (such as *buzz*) are an exception, but they form only a small percentage of the words in any language.

4. *Language is grammatical.* Although there is a limit to the number of words a person can know, there is no limit to the numbers of ways these words can be strung together to produces phrases or sentences. All languages have a *grammar,* an implicit system governing how word classes are defined and used; the rules of word order (syntax) also form an important part of a grammar. Native speakers of a language are grammatical experts, adept at identifying violations of syntax and word classes. For example, a native speaker of English would have no trouble identifying this phrase as nongrammatical: "Through I midterm slept my." As a child acquires its first language, he or she assimilates the grammatical rules of language subconsciously.

THE EVOLUTION OF GRAMMAR

The place of grammar in defining language and studying its evolution has been a point of controversy over the years. One school of linguistic thought, led by Noam Chomsky (1967), placed grammar at the center of the linguistic universe. Chomsky and his followers (such as Jackendoff, 1994) argued that by studying the

Pidgin	Hawaiian Creole English
Building – high place – wall part – time – now-time – and then – now temperature every time give you.	Get one (There is an) electric sign high up on da wall of da building show you what time an' temperature get (it is) right now.

FIGURE 16.15   A comparison of pidgin and Hawaiian Creole.

general grammatical rules of language, we can find a "deep structure," which in turn is a reflection of a "mental grammar" found in the brains of all people. Evidence of the existence of mental grammar comes from language acquisition in children. With little apparent effort, children master the rules of grammar (some of them extraordinarily complex) of any language to which they are exposed. Linguist Steven Pinker (1994) has called this ability the language instinct: Children appear to be genetically specialized to learn language.

An interesting piece of evidence of the relationship between children and a possible deep structure of language comes from the study of *pidgins* and *creoles*. Pidgins are simplified, nongrammatical communication systems that have arisen in areas where speakers of different languages need to communicate with each other but do not spend enough time around each other to learn each other's languages (new colonial situations, fishers from different countries meeting on the seas). In contrast, creoles are grammatical languages that have arisen and developed, typically in colonial situations (such as in Hawaii or New Guinea), in the context of an ongoing situation of linguistic change or instability (Figure 16.15). It has long been noticed that creole languages around the world converge on a similar grammatical structure. Linguist Derek Bickerton (1983, 1990) suggests that the source of this convergence is not a common language of origin but the fact that creoles are invented by children who share a common, biologically based, deep structure for language. The first generation of children growing up in these disrupted linguistic environments will not tolerate a nongrammatical system of communication, and they impose a linguistic structure on the language around them, thus leading to the development of creoles.

Many advocates of the deep grammar point of view believe that language represents a cognitive process that is fundamentally different from that underlying any other form of animal communication. However, several recent evolutionary theorists of language have argued against the existence of a universal mental grammar (Savage-Rumbaugh and Rumbaugh, 1993; Hurford, 1991; Schoenemann, 1999). Savage-Rumbaugh and Rumbaugh believe that syntax and grammar must develop once anyone tries to go beyond a two-word utterance; rules have to exist to let the listener know what the speaker is talking about. They write (1993, p. 106–107), "Whatever commonalities there are among grammars may well exist because only a limited number of solutions to the same problem are workable, given the constraints placed on the problem itself." Thus grammars inevitably emerge, but there is no universal grammar. Such a position is consistent with the view that human language exhibits evolutionary continuity with other forms of animal communication, because it does not posit a zoologically unique cognitive mechanism, such as a deep mental grammar, for the evolution of language (Figure 16.16).

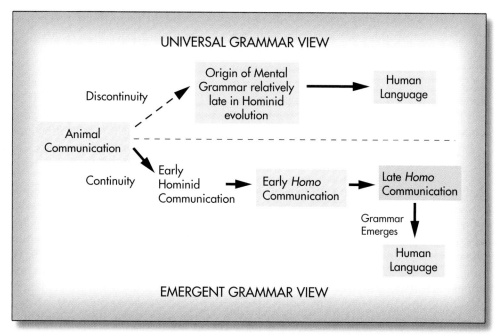

FIGURE 16.16 The Universal Grammar and Emergent Grammar viewpoints lead to very different scenarios of the evolution of language.

LANGUAGE IN THE BRAIN

We can define a *language area* of the brain as any part of the brain that is activated during the production or comprehension of speech. The classical language regions are found around the left Sylvian fissure, or *perisylvian language area* (Figure 16.17). In the frontal lobe, there is *Broca's area*. As we saw earlier, a lesion in Broca's area causes a disruption in speech production (an *aphasia*), yet comprehension remains intact. At the posterior end of the Sylvian fissure, spanning the top of the temporal lobe and the bottom of the parietal lobe, another language area was identified by German physician Carl Wernicke in 1874. *Wernicke's area* lesions cause a person to have difficulties in speech comprehension. People with Wernicke's area aphasia produce fluent but nonsensical speech, substituting one word for another or producing incomprehensible strings of words. Wernicke predicted that because it is likely that his area and Broca's area are in communication, different lesions in the white matter joining the two should produce aphasias with different symptoms. These *conduction aphasias* have been observed; for example, a lesion in the projection from Wernicke's area to Broca's area (via a bundle of axons called the *arcuate fasciculus*) causes someone to produce fluent, nonsensical speech while retaining comprehension (Damasio and Damasio, 1989).

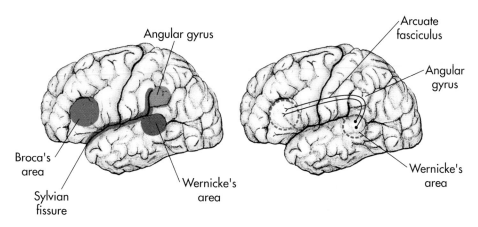

FIGURE 16.17 The major language areas of the left hemisphere of the brain. The connection between Wernicke's and Broca's areas passes through the angular gyrus.

Wernicke's insights about conduction aphasias taught us to think about language as the product of interactive networks in the brain rather than of just one or two areas. In addition to Broca's and Wernicke's areas, the perisylvian language areas include several other regions important for speech. In the frontal lobe, Broca's area sits just in front of the motor strip controlling the tongue and mouth, which are obviously involved in speech production. Along the top of the temporal lobe lies the primary auditory cortex, which is essential for speech perception. The angular gyrus in the parietal lobe is important for the comprehension of written language. This is not surprising because projections from the primary visual cortex in the occipital lobe pass through the angular gyrus on the way to Wernicke's area.

Language Lateralization When a function of the brain typically and consistently occurs in only one of the hemispheres, we say that function is *lateralized*. In 95% of people, the perisylvian language area is in the left hemisphere. Most people are also right-handed, and because motor control of one side of the body is housed in the opposite side of the brain, it is very likely that right-handedness and language ability evolved in tandem. The classical view that both language and right-handedness are associated with the left hemisphere has led to the notion of left hemisphere dominance over the right hemisphere (except in about half of the left-handers—who make up about 10% of the population—who have right hemisphere dominance).

Although it is easy to focus on the classical left perisylvian regions as the seat of language, keep in mind that lesions in other parts of the brain also disrupt normal speech. Lesions in the right hemisphere (of people with left hemisphere language dominance) disrupt the musical or *prosodic* elements of speech. Prosody is essential for speech to sound normal; otherwise, it would have the flat sound of computer-synthesized speech. Lesions in the right inferior frontal lobe (opposite Broca's area) lead to deficits in the production of normal prosody in speech, and lesions in the right hemisphere opposite Wernicke's area lead to deficits in the comprehension of prosody in speech (Nolte, 2002). Neuroimaging studies have shown that the numerous parts of the brain dedicated to in the control of the lips, tongue, larynx, and voluntary control of the diaphragm are active during speech production (Wise et al., 1999).

LANGUAGE IN THE THROAT

Although there is little evidence that evolving language capabilities has cost us anything in terms of brain function—just the opposite, in fact—it is quite clear that the rearrangement of the anatomy of our throats for language purposes has introduced new risks in everyday life that our ancestors did not have to worry about (Laitman, 1984; Lieberman, 1991). To offset these risks, there must have been a strong selective advantage for the development of language abilities over the course of hominid evolution.

The *supralaryngeal airway* is a more precise way to describe the parts of the throat and head that have undergone changes during hominid evolution (Figure 16.18). As the name suggests, it is that part of the airway that is above the *larynx*, or voice box. The larynx sits at the top of the *trachea* and has vocal folds (vocal cords), which can modulate the passage of air through the trachea to produce different sounds. The cavity above the larynx, at the back of the mouth, is known as the *pharynx*. The posterior part of the tongue, the epiglottis, and the soft palate form the boundaries of the pharynx.

When we compare the supralaryngeal airway of a human with that of a more typical mammal, such as a chimpanzee, we can see several differences that have profound functional implications (Figure 16.18). First, the larynx in humans is much

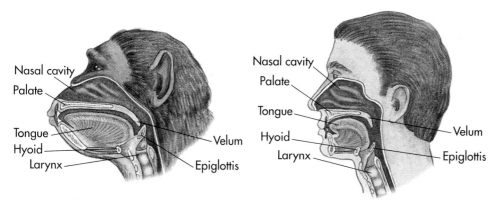

FIGURE 16.18 The supralaryngeal airway in a chimpanzee and a human. Note the relatively low position of the larynx in the human and how the back of the thickened and shortened tongue forms the front part of the pharynx.

lower than in other mammals. The new position of the larynx leads to an expansion of the pharynx. This expanded pharynx, whose anterior wall is formed uniquely in humans by a shortened and rounded tongue, is much more efficient for modifying the stream of air passing through the larynx to generate a greater variety of sounds, leading to fully articulate speech. In other mammals, the small pharynx has very little capacity for modifying the sounds produced by the larynx; supralaryngeal modification of sound can be done only by alteration of the shape of the oral cavity and lips (Laitman, 1984) (Box 16.2 on page 468).

These changes in anatomy have a profound cost, however: they greatly increase the risk of choking on food or liquid. There is too much distance between the human larynx and nasal cavity for a sealed connection to form between the two, as it does in the typical mammal. The epiglottis and soft palate are separated by the rear part of the tongue. Everything we swallow must pass over the incompletely sealed opening of the larynx, which greatly increases the risk of choking and suffocation. Interestingly, human babies less than 1 year old have a supralaryngeal anatomy that more closely resembles the mammalian norm. This allows them to drink, swallow, and breathe at the same time, which greatly enhances their suckling ability. During the second year, the larynx begins the shift to the adult position, which increases their risk of choking while increasing their ability to produce articulate speech. Darwin noted in *On the Origin of Species* that the position of the trachea in the human throat was an example of natural selection working with what history makes available to it.

LANGUAGE ABILITY AND THE FOSSIL RECORD

The brain and supralaryngeal tract—anatomical structures that demonstrate most clearly our adaptations associated with the production of spoken language—are composed primarily of soft tissues that do not fossilize. However, we do have endocasts, which might preserve information about gross changes in the brain that might be associated with the development of language. In addition the supralaryngeal tract is connected by muscles and ligaments to bony structures at the base of the cranium and in the neck. It is possible some insights into the evolution of the soft tissues of the throat may be gained by examining these bony structures.

BOX 16.2   Ape Language Studies

Few scientific developments in the twentieth century captured the public's imagination as much as the extraordinary spectacle of great apes communicating with their handlers and others via sign language (see Lieberman [1984] and Ristau [1999] for historical overviews). Although there had been several attempts to teach apes raised in close contact with humans to talk, these all failed miserably. Humans are adapted to produce the sounds of spoken language, and apes are not. In 1965, a husband-and-wife team of psychologists named Allen and Beatrix Gardner had the idea to train a 10-month-old chimpanzee named Washoe to communicate using American Sign Language, thereby bypassing the inherent vocal limitations of chimpanzees. Although Washoe was disadvantaged in starting her language training at an advanced age and her handlers were not expert ASL signers, she still managed to obtain a substantial number of signs (at least 132) in her initial 4 years of training, used them appropriately, and even coined novel two-word combinations, such as *water bird* for swan and *metal hot* for cigarette lighter. Washoe was also observed signing to herself and to other chimpanzees. In overall language skill, Washoe reached the level of a 2- or 3-year-old human child. Using ALS, she had no trouble making her wishes known to her handlers: "You go car gimme orange. Hurry" (quoted from Lieberman, 1984, p. 248).

Other investigators taught sign language to other apes, such as a gorilla and an orangutan. In some "ape language" studies, hand sign language was not used; rather, chimpanzees were taught to communicate via symbols they could point to or via a kind of keyboard. But even as some investigators were initiating and expanding research into the language skills of great apes, a backlash against such research started to grow. Many scientists were critical of the idea that the word *language* could be used in association with the communication skills displayed by Washoe and the other signing apes. Crit-

ics claimed that the signing apes were exhibiting nothing more than a "Clever Hans" phenomenon. Clever Hans was a horse who amazed people in Europe around the turn of the twentieth century with his counting and adding abilities until it was discovered that his numerical skills (which he expressed by stomping with one hoof) were actually unintentionally cued by his trainer. Although it was easy to refute the Clever Hans claims about signing apes (by using substitute handlers, setting up situations where cuing would have been impossible, or secretly videotaping), after the publication of Terrace's book funding dried up for further ape language studies. (Gibbons, 1991).

Despite the critics, in the 1980s Sue Savage-Rumbaugh and Duane Rumbaugh initiated a sign language research project with bonobos, using symbols (lexigrams) that could be pointed to in sequence to generate phrases. One of their subjects, a young male named Kanzi, picked up the language without being taught, by simply observing his mother as she was being taught (Figure A). He has since become the most proficient sign language ape yet studied, mastering hundreds of symbols and generating thousands of novel combinations of symbols, often referring to objects and situations not in his immediate vicinity (Savage-Rumbaugh and Rumbaugh, 1993). His ability to comprehend simple and complex sentences in spoken English, even though he had never been explicitly taught to do so, is also striking. At 5 years of age, his grasp of spoken English exceeded that of a 2-year-old child. For a fascinating account of Kanzi's life, training, and personality, see Savage-Rumbaugh, Shanker, and Taylor (1998).

FIGURE A   Kanzi talks using his keyboard language.

No one would argue that Kanzi and the other signing apes have *human language,* but they do provide us with several insights into the evolution of human language. First, a certain level of linguistic competence is present as part of the general cognitive abilities of great apes and presumably of the common ancestor we shared with them. Second, the research with Kanzi indicates that comprehension exceeds production in the apes. This means that the "speaker–receiver" issue probably was not a problem in the evolution of language: The evolution of speech production skills would not have been limited by the ability of listeners to understand that speech. Third, the learning situation (exposure at a young age to a rich linguistic environment) is critical for language acquisition. We did not know about the language abilities of apes until they were placed in an environment where they could be expressed. Critics of the studies have argued, why would they have such capacity and never use it? But, all reasonably complex, behaviorally sophisticated animals have new skills they can develop given the proper environmental stimuli. Language abilities in hominids did not evolve from nothing, but reflect an enhancement and elaboration of abilities found in their pongid ancestors and cousins.

Endocasts and the Evolution of Brain Asymmetries Because language in the brain is associated with a leftward lateralization of function, it is possible that asymmetries in gross brain structure may be pronounced enough that they could be seen in endocasts. In most modern humans, the left occipital lobe protrudes further back than the right occipital, and the right frontal lobe protrudes more forward than the left. Other primates also show this pattern, but Holloway and de Lacoste-Lareymondie (1982) found that the left occipital and right frontal pattern is found most often in contemporary humans and in hominids, including australopithecines and the KNM-ER 1470 *H. habilis* specimen. Although this asymmetry may not be directly related to language or handedness, it does reflect an asymmetric pattern that may be unique to hominids.

Another region of the brain that might also show evidence of asymmetry in an endocast is Broca's area. The endocast of 1470 has a well-preserved left inferior frontal region (the location of Broca's area). Anthropologists interested in hominid endocasts tend to agree that 1470 resembles humans more than pongids in the anatomical complexity in the region corresponding to Broca's area (Holloway, 1976, 1999; Falk, 1983b; Tobias, 1987). A similar claim has been made for a recently discovered Indonesian *H. erectus* specimen, Sambungmacan 3 (Broadfield et al., 2001). Although this specimen has protrusions in the inferior frontal lobe on both left and right hemispheres, the total size of the protrusion is larger in the left hemisphere, indicating the possible presence of a Broca's area in that hemisphere.

Base of the Cranium and Hyoid Bone According to some investigators, the bony remains of fossil hominids yield real clues to the form and position of the supralaryngeal tract, offering insights into the vocal abilities of these earlier hominids. However, most of these claims are somewhat controversial and reflect the inherent difficulty of reconstructing complex soft tissue structures from fossil remains.

Jeffrey Laitman (1984; Laitman and Heimbuch, 1982; Laitman and Reidenberg, 1988) has argued that the degree of *flexion* of the *basicranium* is an anatomical marker of larynx position (Figure 16.19). His studies show that among living mammals, human adults are unique in that they have a pronounced degree of basicranial flexion; the more flexed the base of the cranium, the lower the larynx and the wider range of sounds that can be produced. Laitman and Reidenberg suggest that the degree of flexion seen in the base of *H. erectus* crania is greater than that seen in pongids and australopithecines and may signal the beginning of the lowering of the larynx to a more human-like position. These claims are controversial, and other investigators (Arensburg et al., 1990) believe that the basic premise of a correlation between variation in the cranial base and vocal abilities has yet to be proven.

Reconstructions of the Neandertal vocal tract have been equally controversial. Philip Lieberman (1984, 1991) claims that because of their long palate and other factors, the shape of the Neandertal tongue would be different from a modern human's, the pharynx would not be as large, and the larynx would be higher up in the throat. In fact, Lieberman argues that it would be impossible to put a

FIGURE 16.19 The base of the human cranium is more flexed than the base of the chimpanzee cranium.

FIGURE 16.20 The hyoid bone from a Neandertal and a chimpanzee. The Neandertal hyoid is much more similar to those found in modern humans.

human supralaryngeal tract into a Neandertal because the larynx would have to be placed in the chest cavity. Lieberman suggests that Neandertals would be missing phonetic elements present in human spoken language. Like claims about the basicranium and language ability, these claims have also been the subject of much criticism (such as Falk, 1975).

A potentially more direct source of evidence about the speech abilities of Neandertals has come with the discovery of a Neandertal **hyoid bone** from Kebara Cave, Israel, dating to about 60,000 years ago (Arensburg et al., 1990). The hyoid is a small, free-floating bone (that is, it does not articulate with any other bones) that sits in the throat in front of the larynx and in close association (via muscles and ligaments) with the mandible, larynx, and other structures. Arensburg and colleagues argue that the Kebara hyoid is essentially human-like in its size and shape and very distinct from that of a chimpanzee, for example (Figure 16.20). The hyoids of chimpanzees and other apes have a boxlike body with two narrow, flaring horns, whereas the human hyoid has a much more regular horseshoe shape. Because the Kebara hyoid was found with a mandible and neck vertebrae, its location in the living individual could be suggested because these are the bony structures with which the hyoid makes soft tissue connections. According to Arensburg and colleagues, its position was human-like within a neck that was similar in length to human necks. Thus they conclude that the larynx was also in a human-like position and that Neandertals were fully capable of producing speech. Critics point out that other mammals, such as pigs, have human-like hyoids, and they do not talk.

SCENARIOS OF LANGUAGE EVOLUTION

The absence of direct evidence concerning the evolution of language ability means that there are many theories or models for how it might have occurred (Hewes, 1999). Most are untestable, although it is possible to assess the plausibility of some of the claims based on contemporary data. Since the 1980s, scenarios about the evolution of language have proliferated as new kinds of information have become available to researchers. We will discuss and assess three of these speculative models.

Throwing and Language Evolution   In the 1980s, neuroscientist William Calvin (1982, 1983) suggested that there was an intimate connection between the evolution of one-armed throwing ability, handedness, and language. Calvin pointed out that language and throwing are both lateralized activities (left hemisphere dominance). The throwing of projectiles is clearly important in hunting by humans, and it is reasonable to assume that expert throwing ability could have been an important adaptation in hominid evolution. Calvin argued that because the motor strip controlling the hand and arms is close to important centers for speech control, the evolution of language could have "piggybacked" on the evolution of throwing ability.

Calvin's hypothesis is fascinating, and it attempts to tie together several different kinds of information. Some problems with it include the fact that regions in the brain controlling throwing and speech are not really that close to each other, and there is no way to determine whether language piggybacked on throwing or vice

hyoid bone A small "floating bone" in the front part of the throat, which is held in place by muscles and ligaments.

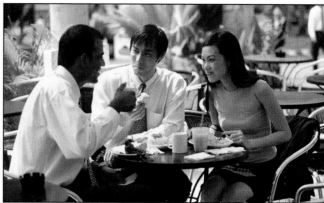

FIGURE 16.21   Language facilitates social interaction among humans. In apes, grooming one another is an essential part of social interaction, while gossiping may have a similar function in human communication.

versa. Nonetheless, the model is useful in that it highlights the potentially profound importance of the evolution of throwing ability, which is indeed a lateralized behavior just like language.

Language as a Replacement for Grooming   As you learned in Chapter 8, one of the main ways in which primate social groups maintain group cohesion is by social grooming (Figure 16.21). Primatologist Robin Dunbar (1993, 1997) points out that although humans may gain comfort from touch, they do not actually engage in very much social grooming. In looking at a wide range of primate species, Dunbar found that there was a positive statistical relationship between time spent grooming, brain size, and social group size. In other words, primates with larger brains lived in larger social groups, which required them to spend more time grooming in order to maintain social cohesiveness.

Humans are an exception to this pattern. Dunbar hypothesized that at some point in human evolution, with selection pressures to increase group size, hominids replaced social grooming with social language. Dunbar argues (based on empirical studies) that most of what people talk about is other people and their relationships (that is, gossip). Through such discussions, language maintains its primary role as a social reinforcer.

Like Calvin's throwing model, Dunbar's model weaves the evolution of language into other aspects of hominid evolution. It is also has the basic chicken-and-egg problem: Did we evolve language in order to have larger group sizes, or did larger group sizes (and brain size) evolve because we evolved language? Furthermore, the grooming hypothesis does not say much about language per se but simply about one of the many ways language can be used (although gossip obviously is one of the more important ways). Dunbar's hypothesis brings home a fundamental point, however. At some point during our evolution, hominids stopped living in primate-like social groups of small size and started living in larger, ethnicity- or culture-based societies. Without language, such a transition would have been impossible.

Symbols and Sex   In his model of language origins, anthropologist Terrence Deacon (1997) emphasizes symbols as the key feature of human language. The ordering of words in even a simple sentence constitutes a manipulation and application of symbols that goes beyond that seen in any other animal. Language puts us in a world fully shaped by symbols. Early hominids would have had a verbal and nonverbal communication system similar to those seen in other primates. They would have adopted symbolic communication slowly, in the context of the preexisting communication system. As the use of symbols increased, however, the costs of learning and mastering them would also increase. But because humans have clearly evolved a symbolic system of communication, the benefits must have outweighed the costs.

Deacon suggests that symbolic communication may have first arisen in the context of the maintenance of exclusive sexual and provisioning relationships. His scenario posits that around 2 million years ago, at the onset of genus *Homo*, male hominids began provisioning sexual partners and their offspring in the context of an exclusive relationship. Deacon argues that these hominids were living in multimale, multifemale groups, as you would find in chimpanzees today, in which paternity would be difficult to establish. Because cooperative hunting increases the chances for success, there would be a conflict between selection for paternity certainty and for a social lifestyle.

Nonhunting gibbons solve this problem by being monogamous. Deacon suggests that hominids solved it by evolving symbolic language, which reinforced the pair bond between a male and a female within a social group, ensuring sexual exclusivity for the male and provisioning for the female. Symbols would also be useful in communicating to others in the social group that such an exclusive relationship exists (Figure 16.22).

A weakness of Deacon's model is its emphasis on pair bonds, which is a controversial issue in hominid evolution (see Chapter 11). However, it does not really require that pair bonds exist, only that exclusive and identifiable sexual and provisioning relationships are present within a larger social group. For example, establishing an exclusive relationship between one male and two females would also benefit from symbolic communication. Deacon's theory asserts that the reproductive advantages conferred by a component of language—symbolic communication—at a specific moment in hominid evolution may have initiated the journey down the path to full-blown human language.

BRAIN SIZE, LANGUAGE, AND INTELLIGENCE

If there is a fundamental issue in understanding the evolution of human behavior, it is interpreting the relationships of brain size, language, and intelligence. We have not been too concerned with defining what intelligence is. People interested in material culture, such as archaeologists, have tended to look for clues of intelligence in stone

FIGURE 16.22 Symbolic language may have helped reinforce exclusive sexual relationships within social groups in later hominid evolution.

tool remains, attempting to define the level of technical intelligence our ancestors may have had (Wynn, 1999) while acknowledging that these tools may represent only a biased sample of the total material culture repertoire of past hominids. But if language ability is closely tied to level of intelligence, tools give us little to go on. As Thomas Wynn (p. 284) has said, "Tools tell us little about language . . .. [They] are not windows to symbolic behavior." It is also quite clear that the level of sophistication we observe in stone tool production does not correlate very much or at all with changes in brain size over hominid evolution. This does not mean that no insights into human cognition are to be gained from the archaeological record but that stone tools must be considered in a broader investigatory context (Mithen, 1996).

In contrast to archaeologists, scientists more interested in the behavior of living animals and humans have emphasized the importance of social behavior in the lives of past hominids as the driving force behind the increase in intelligence (Byrne and Whiten, 1988; see Dunbar's grooming model of language evolution described earlier). They argue that technical aspects of intelligence have been emphasized over the social aspects. That may be true, but a reasonable view is that both technical and social intelligences were critical in human evolution. Theorists of intelligence have emphasized the multifaceted nature of intelligence in the real world (Gardner, 1993; Sternberg, 1990), which goes beyond things such as IQ test scores. As we discussed earlier, increases in brain size tend to be distributed throughout the structure rather than localized to specific regions (with some exceptions, of course). Thus selection for one aspect of intelligence that is localized to one part of the brain will lead to size increases in other parts of the brain. This might in turn lead to the appearances of new capabilities that may themselves be selected for (see Calvin's model of throwing and language evolution described earlier).

Although we lack direct information about the evolution of brain functional organization, intelligence, and language, we are developing a clearer and more sophisticated understanding of what happened in human evolution over the past several million years. Increases in knowledge about brain structure and function, the nature of language as an evolving system, the communicatory behavior of humans and other animals, and the hominid fossil and archaeological record means that our speculations are both informed and constrained by a growing scientific database.

SUMMARY

1. What are primary and association areas of the cerebral cortex?

The cerebral cortex is the gray matter (mostly neuron cell bodies) that lines the surface of the brain. Primary cortex is involved directly with motor control or with the initial processing of sensory input. The association cortex is the region of the cortex where processing of information from one or more primary (or other association) areas occurs.

2. What does encephalization mean?

Encephalization is a measure of brain size relative to body size. Because larger brain size correlates with larger body size, it is often useful to look at brain size in relation to body size to gain an impression of overall cognitive ability. We can derive an encephalization quotient by looking at many species and determining the typical brain–body size relationship. Species with larg-

er than expected brains given their body sizes have encephalization quotients that are greater than 1.0. Although the term *encephalization* puts the emphasis on the brain size part of the equation, body size is an equal contributor.

3. How does the cranial capacity of modern humans compare with that seen in Neandertals and some archaic *Homo sapiens*?

Cranial capacities in Neandertals tend on average to be larger than those seen in modern *Homo sapiens*, and some archaic specimens have cranial capacities that are well within the human range. The (estimated) lean body mass of Neandertals and archaic *Homo sapiens* probably was substantially greater than that for modern humans; thus encephalization is greater in modern humans than in these recently extinct hominids.

4. **Are primary olfactory and visual areas in modern humans smaller or larger than expected?**

Compared with that of some other mammals and the prosimians, the olfactory region of the human brain is much smaller than we would expect relative to overall brain size. The primary visual region in the occipital lobe is also smaller than expected compared with that of other primates. Functional reorganization of the primary visual areas of the occipital lobe has occurred in the hominid lineage because its position in modern humans is substantially different from that in our closest ape relatives. When this occurred in hominid evolution is not known, although there has been much debate on the topic, centered on determining the position of the lunate sulcus in fossil endocasts.

5. **What are four hallmarks of human language?**

First, language is spoken. An evolutionary tradeoff indicates the importance of language as a biological adaptation: Anatomical changes in the throat that allow humans to produce the large variety of sounds in spoken language make us uniquely susceptible to choking. Second, language is semantic. Words have meanings that correspond to real-world objects, events, or actions. Third, language is phonemic. The words used in language are composed of small sound elements knows as phonemes. There are no semantic constraints on how these elements can be combined. Finally, language is grammatical. The ways in which words are combined in language are governed by implicit rules relating to word classes and proper word ordering in phrases or sentences. All native speakers of a language can easily detect violations of grammatical rules.

6. **What are two areas of the brain that are part of the network that underlies the production of spoken language?**

Broca's area is in the frontal lobe; Wernicke's area spans the top of the temporal lobe and bottom of the parietal lobe at the end of the Sylvian fissure. In 95% of people these language areas are located in the left hemisphere. In people who are left hemisphere dominant for language, the right hemisphere region corresponding to Broca's area controls the prosodic (musical) aspects of speech.

7. **Why is the Kebara Neandertal hyoid bone important in debates about the evolution of language?**

The hyoid is a small bone that sits at the front of the throat. Reconstructions of the soft tissue of the throat—specifically of the supralaryngeal airway—are controversial because they were based on the anatomy of the base of the cranium, mandible, and other structures, without the hyoid, until the discovery of the Kebara hyoid. This bone appears to be very human-like and indicates that Neandertals may have been capable of producing all the sounds that modern humans are capable of producing. Given the inherent uncertainties in soft tissue reconstruction, this claim has not gone unchallenged.

CRITICAL THINKING QUESTIONS

1. Which is more important: increases in brain size over hominid evolution or reorganization of brain function?

2. Chihuahuas are more encephalized than German shepherds. Does that mean that they are smarter than German shepherds? Why is this relevant to brain evolution in primates?

3. Provide your own assessments of the three theories of language evolution presented in this chapter. Do you think such speculative theories are useful for understanding how language may have evolved?

4. From an evolutionary perspective, what is intelligence? Defend or refute the statement "Human beings are smarter than chimpanzees."

KEY TERMS

language
brain stem
cerebellum
cerebrum
neuron
sulci (sing., sulcus)
gyri (sing., gyrus)
cerebral cortex

neurotransmitters
myelin
primary cortex
association cortex
magnetic resonance
   imaging (MRI)
paleoneurology
encephalization

encephalization quotient
  (EQ)
olfactory bulbs
prefrontal region
lunate sulcus
hyoid bone

SUGGESTED READING

Calvin, William H. and Ojemann, George A. (1994). *Conversations with Neil's Brain*. Perseus Books, Reading, MA.

Deacon, Terrence W. (1997). *The Symbolic Species*. Norton, New York.

Lieberman, Philip. (1991). *Uniquely Human*. Harvard University Press, Cambridge, MA.

Pinker, Steven. (1994). *The Language Instinct*. HarperPerennial, New York.

Chapter 17

BIOMEDICAL ANTHROPOLOGY

FICVS *foliis palmatis*
Ficus sativa fructu majori violaceo oblongo: cute
lacera Tourn Inst Amoen Acad Vol I p 245

L UNCHTIME ON A LATE SUMMER DAY 20,000 years ago in the southwestern part of what is now France: A small group of boys have been playing since midmorning, exploring the caves that are common in their region, looking for old stone tools that have been left behind by hunting parties. They are starting to get hungry. They know not to head back to their village for food: The morning and evening meals will be provided by their parents and other adults in the tribe, but they are on their own between those two meals.

At this time of year, the boys do not mind foraging on their own. It has been a rainy and warm summer, and a large variety of nuts, berries, and seeds are beginning to ripen. Because the summer growing season has been a good one, small game such as rabbits and squirrels are well fed and will make a good meal if the boys can manage to catch one. They spend an hour or two moving from site to site where food can be found, covering a couple of miles in the process. They see a rabbit and spend 20 minutes very quietly trying to sneak up on it before realizing that it is no longer in the area. Even without the rabbit, they are all happy with the amount of food they managed to find during their midday forage. In mid-afternoon, they stop by a stream for a rest, and then one by one they fall asleep.

LUNCHTIME ON A LATE SUMMER DAY in the early twenty-first century, at a middle school in the United States: A large group of children line up in the cafeteria to get their lunch. They have spent the morning behind desks, doing their school work. They have had one short recess, but they will not have another during the afternoon. They have a physical education class only once a week because budget cutbacks have meant that their school can afford only one gym teacher for more than 1,200 students.

As the children pass through the cafeteria line, most of them ignore the fruit, vegetables, and whole-wheat breads. Instead, they choose foods high in fat, salt, and sugar: chicken nuggets, fries, and cake. The children do not drink the low-fat milk provided but instead favor sweet sodas and fruit-flavored drinks. After they sit down, the children have 15 minutes to finish their meals. Most of them would say that they really like the food the cafeteria gives them. When they are finished, they return to their classrooms for more instruction.

At first glance, children in developed countries in the early twenty-first century are much healthier than their counterparts who lived 20,000 years ago. They are bigger and more physically mature for their age, and unlike their Paleolithic ancestors they can reasonably expect to live well into their 70s. They have been vaccinated against several potentially life-threatening viral illnesses, and they need not worry that a small cut, a minor broken bone, or a toothache will turn into a fatal infection. They are blissfully free of parasites.

On the other hand, a child from 20,000 years ago might have grown up more slowly than a contemporary child, but upon reaching adulthood he would have had a strong, lean body, with much more muscle than fat. He would not have spent a lifetime consuming more calories than he expended. If he were lucky enough to avoid infectious disease, injury, and famine, in his middle and old age he would have been less likely to suffer from heart disease, high blood pressure, diabetes, and even some kinds of cancer than an adult living today.

Health and illness are fundamental parts of the human experience. The individual experience of illness is produced by many factors. Illness is a product of our genes and culture, our environment and evolution, the economic and educational systems we live under, and the things we eat. When we compare how people live now and how they lived 20,000 years ago, it is apparent that it is difficult to define a healthful environment. Is it the quantity of life (years lived) or the quality that matters most? Are we healthier living as our ancestors did, even though we cannot recreate those past environments, or should we rejoice in the abundance and comfort that a steady food supply and modern technology provide us?

Biomedical anthropology is the subfield of biological anthropology concerned with issues of health and illness. Biomedical anthropologists bring the traditional interests of biological anthropology—evolution, human variation, genetics—to the study of medically related phenomena. Like medicine, biomedical anthropology is a biological science, which relies on empiricism and hypothesis testing and, when possible, experimental research to further the understanding of human disease and illness. Biomedical anthropology is also like cultural medical anthropology in its comparative outlook and its attempt to understand illness in the context of specific cultural environments.

In this chapter, we will look at many aspects of human health from both biocultural and evolutionary perspectives. We will see how health relates to growth, development, and aging, and we will look at an aspect of human variation—skin color—that provides an informative example of the way health factors shape human variation. We will then consider infectious disease and the problems associated with evolving biological solutions to infectious agents that can also evolve. Finally, we will examine the interaction between diet and disease and the enormous changes in diet our species has gone through since the advent of modern agriculture. But before going on to those topics, let us briefly consider some basic concepts from an allied discipline, epidemiology, which provides the quantitative foundations for population-level health research.

EPIDEMIOLOGY: BASIC TOOLS FOR BIOMEDICAL ANTHROPOLOGY

Biomedical anthropology is particularly concerned with understanding the expression of disease at the population level. Another health science with a population-level outlook is **epidemiology**. Epidemiology is the quantitative study of the occurrence and cause of disease in populations. Compared with anthropologists, epidemiologists are "number-crunchers," looking for broad-scale statistical associations between ill health and the factors that produce it in specific populations (Figure 17.1). In the same way that understanding the cell is essential for developing a proper understanding of anatomical structure, familiarity with some of the basic statistical tools of epidemiology is essential for the anthropologist's understanding of the distribution of disease in human populations.

RATES: MORTALITY, INCIDENCE, AND PREVALENCE

The most basic epidemiological statistic is the *rate* of disease per 1,000 individuals, or even 1,000,000 for rare conditions. We define rate as

Rate = Events/Population at risk

The *event* is the disease or condition you are interested in. It is important to specify the population at risk. For instance, we should calculate the ovarian cancer rate for adult women, not for the population as a whole.

biomedical anthropology The subfield of biological anthropology concerned with issues of health and illness.

epidemiology The quantitative study of the occurrence and cause of disease in populations.

FIGURE 17.1 Epidemiologists look for the causes of disease, such as toxic waste and industrial pollution, at the population level.

Mortality rates are measures of the probability of dying within a population over a given period of time. The *crude death rate* is defined as

Crude death rate = (All deaths during a calendar year/Population at midyear) × 1,000 = Deaths per 1,000

We have to be wary in interpreting crude death rates. For example, in 1997 the death rate in Pennsylvania was 10.6/1,000, whereas in Utah it was only 5.6/1,000. Does this mean that we would all be better off living in Utah rather than Pennsylvania? Not necessarily. The birth rate in Utah for that year was 21.2/1,000, whereas in Pennsylvania it was only 11.8/1,000. What is this telling us? Age is an important variable in determining a person's chance of dying in a given period of time. We can infer from these data that Utah has a much younger population than Pennsylvania. The different *age structures* of the two states undoubtedly explain much of the difference in crude death rate between them.

Two of the most important epidemiological statistics are **incidence rate** and **prevalence rate**. They are defined as follows:

Incidence rate = (Number of new cases of a disease/Total population)/ Period of time (usually a year)

Prevalence rate = Total number of cases of a disease at a given time/ Total population

Incidence rate is the occurrence of new cases of a disease. The higher the incidence rate, the more new cases are developing over a period of time. A change in incidence rate indicates a change in the balance of ecological factors that influence the expression of a disease, which could result from some naturally occurring factor or the development of an effective intervention program. Incidence rates of diagnosed cases of AIDS peaked in the United States in the early 1990s, with more than 106,000 new cases in 1993 (starting from only a handful of cases in 1981), and then leveled off to a steady 40,000 new cases per year starting in 1997 (Stine, 2003). This decline in incidence rate undoubtedly was caused by changes in behavior brought about by AIDS education programs. If a vaccine for AIDS were developed, the incidence rate would plummet.

incidence rate The number of new occurrences of a disease over a given period of time divided by the population size.

prevalence rate The number of existing cases of a disease divided by the population (or the population at risk).

The prevalence rate is a function of both incidence and *duration*. Changes in the prevalence rate of a disease do not necessarily tell us anything about the incidence rate. For example, with the introduction of new drugs to treat AIDS, people who develop the condition are now surviving longer than ever. Fifty percent of the people in the United States who were diagnosed with AIDS in 1995 were still alive in 2002 (Stine, 2003). Because the drugs only control the symptoms of AIDS and do not cure it, the prevalence rate may actually *increase* as a result of these new treatments with increased duration of illness, while the incidence rate remains the same. In contrast, a disease that kills quickly—or, looking on the bright side, is quickly cured—could have an incidence rate higher than its prevalence rate.

EPIDEMIOLOGICAL TRANSITIONS

In 1971, Abdel Omran coined the term *epidemiological transition* to describe changes in the patterns of disease and mortality in developed countries. In less-developed societies, most deaths are caused by infectious diseases. In developed countries that have passed through the epidemiological transition of the twentieth century, the most common causes of death are chronic diseases of old age. Infectious disease rates dropped dramatically in developed countries thanks to better nutrition and hygiene, a better understanding of how infectious agents cause illness, and widespread use of antibiotics and vaccinations.

Table 17.1 lists the top 10 causes of death in the United States in 1900 and 2000. The death rate from accidents holds almost the same position in both lists, although the death rate from accidents in 2000 was about half the 1900 rate. The three big causes of death in 2000—heart disease, cancer, and stroke—are all pri-

TABLE 17.1	Top 10 Causes of Death in the United States, 1900 and 2000		
RANK	CAUSE OF DEATH	DEATHS PER 100,000	PERCENTAGE OF ALL DEATHS
1900			
1	Pneumonia	202	12
2	Tuberculosis	194	11
3	Diarrhea and enteritis	140	8
4	Heart disease	137	8
5	Kidney disease	81	5
6	Accidents	76	4
7	Stroke	73	4
8	Diseases of early infancy	72	4
9	Cancer	64	4
10	Diphtheria	40	2
2000			
1	Heart disease	258	30
2	Cancer	201	23
3	Stroke	61	7
4	Chronic respiratory disease	44	5
5	Accidents	36	4
6	Diabetes mellitus	25	3
7	Influenza and pneumonia	24	3
8	Alzheimer disease	18	2
9	Kidney disease	14	2
10	Septicemia	11	1

Sources: R. D. Grove and A. M. Hetzel, *Vital Statistics Rates of the United States, 1940–1960* (Washington, DC: U.S. GPO 1988); U.S. National Center for Health Statistics, *National Vital Statistics Report,* 50 (15): 2002.

CHOLERA *TRAMPLES THE VICTOR & THE VANQUISH'D BOTH.*

FIGURE 17.2 Before the advent of vaccination and antibiotics, infectious diseases such as cholera were the scourge of human populations.

marily diseases of old age, accounting for 60% of all deaths. In 1900, they accounted for only 16% of deaths. In 1900, people were at risk from a variety of infectious diseases. In 2000, the infectious diseases that made the top ten list—pneumonia, influenza, and septicemia—were all diseases to which older, chronically ill people are particularly vulnerable.

The concept of an epidemiological transition, which is based on an evolutionary and comparative view of diseases in populations, fits in well with much biomedical anthropological research. Anthropologist George Armelagos (1997) and colleagues have argued that Omran's epidemiological transition is in fact the second epidemiological transition. The first occurred with the introduction of agriculture, which in turn led to the development of large urban populations. These larger populations became the setting for the spread of infectious diseases, many of which still plagued large cities in 1900 (Figure 17.2).

BIOCULTURAL AND EVOLUTIONARY APPROACHES TO DISEASE

Epidemiology provides the quantitative foundation for biomedical anthropology's mission to understand the evolutionary and cultural factors underlying human disease. Although these factors are interrelated, within biomedical anthropology the biocultural and evolutionary approaches provide insights into the population-level expression of disease from somewhat different perspectives.

THE BIOCULTURAL APPROACH

The *biocultural approach* recognizes that when we are looking at something as complex as human illness, both biological and cultural variables offer important insights. The biocultural view recognizes that human behavior is shaped by both our evolutionary and our cultural histories and that, just as human biology does, our behavior influences the expression of disease at both the individual and population levels (Wiley, 1992, 2004).

An example of an illness that can be understood only in light of both biology and culture is *anorexia nervosa,* a kind of self-starvation in which a person fails to maintain a minimal normal body weight, is intensely afraid of gaining weight, and exhibits disturbances in the perception of his or her body shape or size (Figure 17.3) (American Psychiatric Association, 1994). The anorexic person fights weight gain by not eating, purging (vomiting) after eating, or exercising excessively. The

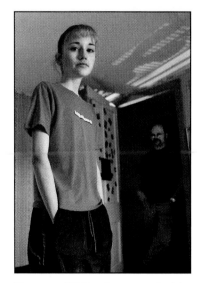

FIGURE 17.3 A teenaged girl with anorexia.

prevalence rate for anorexia is about 0.5–1.0%; about 90 percent of sufferers are female, many of them young. Anorexia is a serious illness with both long- and short-term increases in mortality. For example, at 6–12 years' follow-up, the mortality rate is 9.6 times the expected rate (Nielsen, 2001).

An ideal of female attractiveness emphasizing thinness often is thought to provide a cultural stress leading to the development of anorexia. Obviously, because not all girls living in this environment become anorexic, there are undoubtedly biological factors that also make some individuals more likely than others to have the illness. Anorexia is also found in non-Western cultures. However, anorexic patients in Hong Kong do not have the "fat phobia" we associate with Western anorexia but rather exhibit a generalized avoidance of eating (Katzman and Lee, 1997). This indicates that even though anorexia is not limited to Western cultures, the focus on fat is shaped by the Western cultural concerns with obesity, thinness, and weight loss.

Most young women maintain their body weight without starving themselves, habitually purging, or even dieting. In a 1-year longitudinal study of the eating and dieting habits of 231 American adolescent girls, medical anthropologist Mimi Nichter and colleagues (1995) showed that most of the subjects maintained their weight by watching what they eat and trying to follow a healthful lifestyle rather than taking more extreme measures. Anthropological studies such as this are important because clinicians are not as interested in what the healthy population is doing, and they help to provide a biocultural context for the expression of disease.

THE EVOLUTIONARY APPROACH

Biological anthropologists have long looked at disease from an evolutionary perspective. In the 1990s, Randolph Nesse and George C. Williams (1994) coined a new term *evolutionary medicine* to describe a "Darwinian approach" to understanding disease. Nesse and Williams argued that the evolutionary perspective provides several insights into the expression of disease.

- *Defenses versus defects.* Every disease produces certain signs and symptoms. A *defect* results from the disease process itself, whereas a *defense* is a part of the body's attempt to fight the disease. For example, a fair-skinned person with pneumonia may present with a cough and darkening skin color. The darkening skin color is a defect, caused by the fact that the person's hemoglobin is not carrying sufficient oxygen. The cough is a defense—an adaptation—that evolved as a mechanism to eject infectious material from the throat and lungs.

- *Infection and "arms races."* The environment is filled with infectious agents or **pathogens**, such as bacteria and viruses. As our bodies evolve defenses to fight them, they too are evolving to combat our defenses. A familiar example is the evolution of *antibiotic resistance* in bacteria. Antibiotics were first introduced in the 1930s. By 1944, some strains of staphylococcal bacteria were showing signs of resistance to penicillin, and today 95% are penicillin resistant. As a result we have to use other antibiotics to fight them.

- *Environmental mismatch.* Human bodies did not evolve to deal with most aspects of modern life, including fatty diets, low reproductive rates, and noise. Thus certain diseases may be considered to be the result, in whole or part, of the mismatch between our bodies, adapted for life in a hunter-gatherer environment, and contemporary environments. We will discuss examples of these diseases later in the chapter.

- *Pleiotropic gene effects.* We have many genes or alleles that probably did not lead to adaptations in past environments but were simply harmless. However, in

pathogens Organisms and entities that can cause disease.

modern environments these genes may be expressed in new ways. For example, because we now live longer, we have to deal with genes that cause diseases such as Alzheimer disease and cancer, which are typically expressed only in old age.

- *Design compromises.* A classic example of an evolutionary design compromise leading to human suffering is back pain. The S-shaped spine we evolved in order to walk upright clearly predisposes us to developing back pain (Figure 17.4). This shape, combined with a sedentary lifestyle, causes 50–80% of all people in industrialized society to suffer from lower back pain at some point in their lives (Anderson, 1999).

Biomedical anthropology sits at the intersection of evolutionary and biocultural approaches to health and illness. A central concept of biomedical anthropology is adaptation. As we have discussed in previous chapters, an adaptation is a feature or behavior that serves over the long term to enhance fitness in an evolutionary sense. But we can also look at adaptation in the short term; this is known as *adaptability* (Chapter 6). A basic question biomedical anthropologists try to answer is, To what extent is adaptability itself an adaptation? For example, the life history stages that all people go through have been shaped by natural selection, but our biology must be flexible enough to cope with the different environmental challenges we will face over a lifetime.

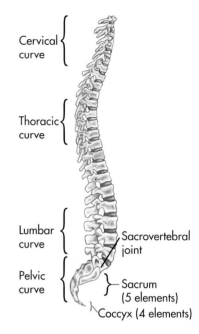

FIGURE 17.4 The S-curve in the human vertebral column—a result of the evolution of bipedality—makes humans highly susceptible to back injury and pain.

BIRTH, GROWTH, AND AGING

All animals go through the processes of birth, growth, and aging. Normal growth and development are not medical problems per se, but the process of growth is a sensitive overall indicator of health status (Tanner, 1978). Therefore, studies of growth and development in children provide useful insights into the nutritional or environmental health of populations.

HUMAN CHILDBIRTH

Nothing should be more natural than giving birth. After all, the survival of the species depends on it. However, in industrialized societies birth usually occurs in hospitals. Of the more than 4 million births in the United States in 2000, more than 90% occurred in hospitals; in 2001, 24.4% of all births were Cesarean deliveries (MacDorman et al., 2002). In 1900, only 5% of U.S. births occurred in a hospital (Wertz and Wertz, 1989). At that time, given the high risk of contracting an untreatable infection, hospitals were seen as potentially dangerous places to give birth.

Human females are not that much larger than chimpanzee females, yet they give birth to infants whose brains are nearly as large as the brain of an adult chimpanzee and whose heads are very large compared with the size of the mother's pelvis (Trevathan, 1999). The easiest evolutionary solution to this problem would be for women to have evolved larger pelves, but too large a pelvis would reduce bipedal efficiency. Wenda Trevathan points out that the shape as well as the size of the pelvis is a critical factor in the delivery of a child. Not only is there a tight fit between the size of the newborn's head and the mother's pelves, but the baby's head and body most rotate or twist as they pass through the birth canal, which is a process that introduces other dangers (such as the umbilical cord wrapping around the baby's neck). In contrast to humans, birth is easy in the great apes. Their pelves are substantially larger relative to neonatal brain size, and the shape of their quadrupedal pelvis allows a more direct passage of the newborn through the birth canal (Figure 17.5 on page 484).

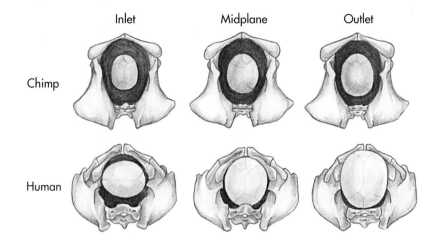

FIGURE 17.5 Compared to a chimpanzee, the human newborn has relatively little room to spare as it passes through the birth canal.

In traditional cultures, women usually give birth with the assistance from a midwife (almost always a woman). Trevathan (1999) points out that although women vary across cultures in their reactions to the onset of labor, in almost all cases, the reaction is emotion-charged and results in the mother seeking assistance from others. She suggests that this behavior is a biocultural adaptation. A human birth is much more likely to be successful if someone is present to assist the mother in delivery. Part of the assistance is in actually supporting the newborn through multiple contractions as it passes through the birth canal, but much recent research has shown that the emotional support of mothers provided by birth assistants is also of critical importance (Klaus and Kennell, 1997). Such emotional support often is lacking in contemporary hospital deliveries, although there has been some effort in recent years to remedy this situation (Figure 17.6).

PATTERNS OF HUMAN GROWTH

The study of human growth and development is known as **auxology**. All animals go through stages of growth that are under some degree of genetic control. However, the processes of growth and development can be acutely sensitive to environmental conditions. Thus patterns of growth that emerge under different

auxology The science of human growth and development.

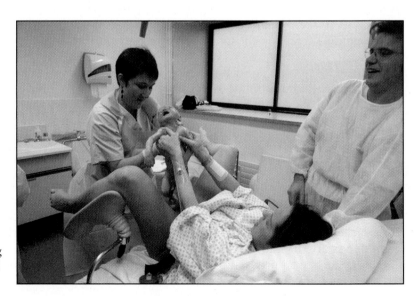

FIGURE 17.6 Women giving birth in traditional cultures usually receive help from other women, or midwives. Midwife-assisted births are also becoming increasingly common in hospital settings.

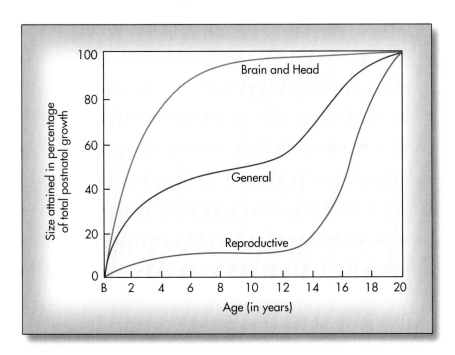

FIGURE 17.7 Different parts of the body mature at different rates. "General" refers to the body as whole, the major organ systems (non-reproductive), musculature, and blood volume.

environmental conditions can provide us with clear examples of *biological plasticity* (Mascie-Taylor and Bogin, 1995) (Chapter 6).

Looking at human growth, we can imagine an optimal environment in which an individual will reach his or her genetic potential. However, most environments are not optimal. We can view growth responses to nonoptimal environments in two different ways (Schell, 1995). The anthropological model views the way humans grow in high-stress environments (with a lack of food, heavy infectious disease load, and pollution) in the context of nongenetic adaptation, or adaptability. Growth patterns are responses to environmental conditions, which may actually enhance survival. On the other hand, the medical approach assumes that any deviation from optimal growth patterns is evidence of ill health. The biomedical anthropological approach incorporates both these perspectives.

We chart growth and development using several different measures including height, weight, and head circumference. Cognitive skills, such as those governing the development of language, also appear in a typical sequence as the child matures. We can also assess age by looking at dentition or sexual reproductive capacity. Different parts of the body mature at different rates (Figure 17.7). For example, a nearly adult brain size is achieved very early, whereas physical, and reproductive maturation all come later in childhood and adolescence.

STAGES OF HUMAN GROWTH

In the 1960s, Adolph Schultz (1969) proposed a model of growth in primates that incorporated four stages shared by all primates. This model is presented in Figure 17.8 on page 486. In general, as life span increases across primate species, each stage of growth increases in length as well.

The Prenatal or Gestational Stage   The first stage of growth is the prenatal or gestational stage. This begins with conception and ends with the birth of the newborn. As indicated in Figure 17.8, gestational length increases across primates with increasing life span but is not simply a function of larger body size. Gibbons have a 30-week gestation, compared with the approximately 25-week gestation of baboons, even though they are much smaller. Growth during the prenatal period is extraordinarily rapid. In humans, during the *embryonic stage* (first 8 weeks after

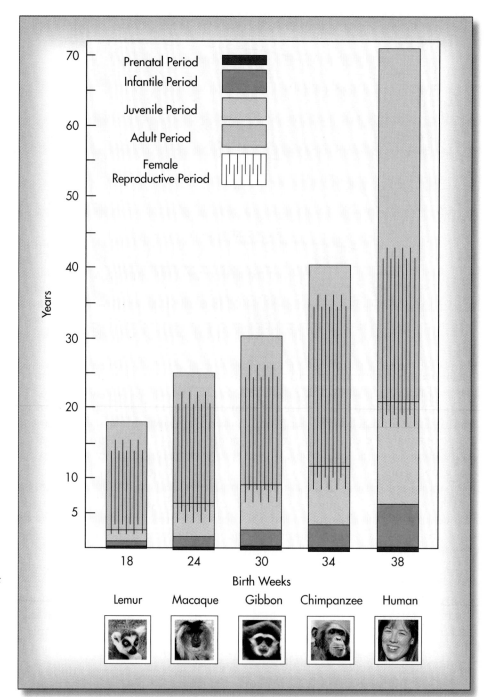

FIGURE 17.8 The four stages of life expressed in five different primates. Note that gestation length increases with increased lifespan, and the long post-reproductive (female) lifespan seen in humans but not in other primates.

teratogens Substances that cause birth defects or other abnormalities in the developing embryo or fetus during pregnancy.

conception), the fertilized ovum (0.005 milligrams) increases in size 275,000 times. During the remainder of the pregnancy (the *fetal period*), growth continues at a rate of about 90 times the initial weight (the weight at the end of the embryonic stage) per week, to reach a normal birth weight of about 3,200 g.

Although protected by the mother both physically and by her immune system, the developing embryo and fetus are highly susceptible to the effects of some substances in their environment. Substances that cause birth defects or abnormal development of the fetus are known as **teratogens**. The most common human teratogen is alcohol. *Fetal alcohol syndrome* (FAS) is a condition seen in children that results from "excessive" drinking of alcohol by the mother during pregnancy. At this point, it is not exactly clear what the threshold for excessive drinking is or whether binge drinking or a prolonged low level of drinking is worse for the fetus (Thackray and Tifft, 2001). Nonetheless, it is clear that heavy maternal drinking can lead to the development of characteristic facial abnormalities and behavioral problems in children. It is estimated that between 0.5 and 5 in 1,000 children have some form of alcohol-related birth defect.

Although they are not teratogens, other substances in the environment may affect the developing fetus. Pollutants such as lead and polychlorinated biphenyls may cause low birth weight and other abnormalities. Excessive noise in the environment has been conclusively linked to reduced prenatal growth (Schell, 1991).

Infancy, Juvenile Stage, Adolescence, and Adulthood Schultz defined the three stages of growth following birth—infancy, juvenile stage, and adulthood—with reference to the appearance of permanent teeth. Infancy lasts from birth until the appearance of the first permanent tooth. In humans, this tooth usually is the lower first molar, and it appears at 5–6 years of age. The juvenile stage begins at this point and lasts until the eruption of the last permanent tooth, the third premolar, which can occur anywhere between 15 and 25 years of age. Adulthood follows the appearance of the last permanent tooth.

Tooth eruption patterns provide useful landmarks for looking at stages of growth across different species of primates, but they do not tell the whole story. Besides length of stages, there is much variation in the patterns of growth and development in primate species. Barry Bogin (1999) suggests that the four-stage model of primate growth is too simple and does not reflect patterns of growth that may be unique to humans. In particular, he argues that during *adolescence,* humans have a growth spurt that reflects a species-specific adaptation.

Bogin places the end of the juvenile period, and the beginning of adolescence, at the onset of *puberty.* The word *puberty* literally refers to the appearance of pubic hair, but as a marker of growth it refers more comprehensively to the period during which there is rapid growth and maturation of the body (Tanner, 1978). The age at which puberty occurs is tremendously variable both within and between populations, and even within an individual, different parts of the body may mature at different rates and times. Puberty tends to occur earlier in girls than boys. In industrialized societies, almost all children go through puberty between the ages of 10 and 14 years (Figure 17.9).

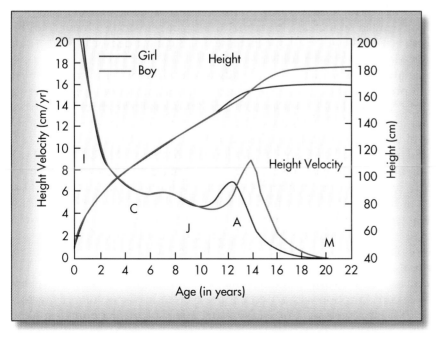

FIGURE 17.9 The adolescent growth spurt in humans is seen as a "bump" in the height curve and a "spike" in the height velocity curve.

Adolescence begins with puberty. During adolescence, maturation of the primary and secondary sexual characteristics continues. In addition, there is an *adolescent growth spurt*. According to Bogin (1993, 1999), the expanding database on primate maturation patterns indicates that the adolescent growth spurt—and therefore adolescence—is most pronounced in humans. Why do we need adolescence? From an evolutionary standpoint, the early stages of mammalian growth are fairly self-explanatory. There must be a gestational stage and period of dependence on the mother for nutrition (infancy). The length of the juvenile stage, most of which occurs after brain size has reached adult proportions, varies widely among mammal species. There is a cost to a prolonged juvenile stage because it delays the onset of full sexual maturity and the ability to reproduce. But the juvenile stage is also necessary as a training period during which younger animals can learn their adult roles and the social behaviors necessary to survive and reproduce within their own species. The evolutionary costs of delaying maturation are offset by the benefits of social life. Among mammals, the juvenile stage is longest in highly social animals, such as wolves and primates.

Humans are the ultimate social animal. Bogin argues that the complex social and cultural life of humans, mediated by language, requires an extended period of social learning and development: adolescence. In support of the view that adolescence is a period necessary for social learning, recent research on human brain growth has demonstrated that although approximate adult brain size is reached around 6–7 years of age, there is also an adolescent period of growth in the gray matter (neurons) of some parts of the brain, including the frontal and parietal lobes (Giedd et al., 1999; Sowell et al., 1999). These are both areas substantially devoted to higher brain functions (such as decision making). Thus, the uniquely human adolescent growth spurt includes the brain.

THE SECULAR TREND IN GROWTH

One of the most striking changes in patterns of growth identified by auxologists is the *secular trend in growth*. By using data collected as long ago as the eighteenth century, they demonstrated that in industrialized countries, children have been growing larger and maturing more rapidly with each passing decade, starting in the late nineteenth century in Europe and North America (Figure 17.10). The secular trend started in Japan after World War II, and it is just being initiated now in parts of the developing world. In Europe and North America, since 1900, children at 5–7 years of age averaged an increase in stature of 1–2 cm per decade (Tanner, 1978). In Japan between 1950 and 1970, the increase was 3 cm per decade in 7-year-olds and 5 cm per decade in 12-year-olds.

The secular trend in growth undoubtedly is a result of better nutrition (more calories and protein in the diet) and a reduction in the impact of diseases during infancy and childhood. We find evidence for this over the short term from *migration studies,* which have shown that changes in the environment (from a less healthful to a more healthful environment) can lead to the development of a secular trend in growth. Migration studies look at a cohort of the children of migrants born and raised in their new country and compare their growth with either their parents' growth (if the children have reached adulthood) or that of a cohort of children in the country from which they immigrated. Recent migration studies of Mayan refugees from Guatemala to the United States show evidence of a secular trend in growth (Bogin, 1995). Mayan children raised in California and Florida were on average 5.5 cm taller and 4.7 kg heavier than their counterparts in Guatemala.

The secular trend in growth in industrialized societies has been so pervasive that it tends to obscure variation within populations caused by socioeconomic factors (Tanner, 1978). However, we can measure the effect of the economy on child

FIGURE 17.10   The secular trend in growth as measured in Swedish (a) girls and (b) boys between 1883 and 1968.

growth in some locales. Deborah Crooks (1999) looked at the growth of children in a rural, eastern Kentucky county at the edge of the Appalachian Mountains where 35% of the children live below the poverty level. Crooks found mild but persistent patterns of short stature among the children, with 21.7% of them having a stature below the fifteenth percentile of a broader U.S. sample. Among girls, "stunted growth" was about twice as common in this county as elsewhere in the United States (9.1% versus 5%).

Although the secular trend in growth appears to be a simple relationship between increased stature and industrialization, at the individual level the interplay of causative factors (genetics, economic stature, and nutritional availability) is highly complex.

MENARCHE AND MENOPAUSE

Another hallmark of the secular trend in growth is a decrease in the age of **menarche**—a girl's first menstrual period—seen throughout the industrialized world. From the 1850s until the 1970s, the average age of menarche in European and North American populations dropped from around 16–17 years to 12–13 years (Figure 17.11 on page 490) (Tanner, 1978; Coleman and Coleman, 2002). A recent comprehensive study of U.S. girls (sample size of 17,077) found that the age of menarche was 12.9 years for white girls and 12.2 years for black girls (Herman-Giddens et al., 1997). This does not reflect a substantial drop in age of menarche since the 1960s.

In cultures undergoing rapid development, changes in the age of menarche have been measured over short periods of time. Among the Bundi of highland Papua New Guinea, age of menarche dropped from 18.0 years in the mid-1960s to 15.8 years for urban Bundi girls in the mid-1980s (Worthman, 1999). Over the long term, the rate of decrease in age of menarche in most of the population was in the range 0.3–0.6 years per decade. For urban Bundi girls, the rate is 1.29 years per decade, which may be a measure of the rapid pace of modernization in their society.

menarche   The onset of a girl's first menstrual period.

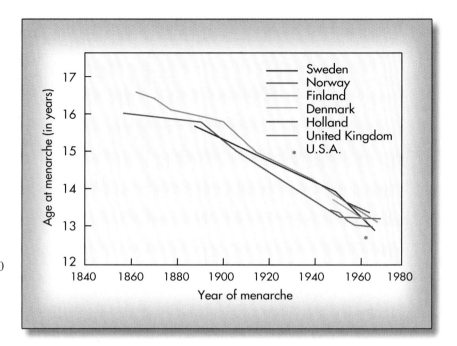

FIGURE 17.11 The declining age of menarche over the past 150 years has been measured in many European countries, and has also been observed more recently in developing countries.

Menarche marks the beginning of the reproductive life of women, whereas **menopause** marks its end. Menopause is the irreversible cessation of fertility that occurs in all women before other parts of the body show other signs of advanced aging (Peccei, 2001a). Returning to Figure 17.8, note that of all the primate species illustrated, only in humans does a significant part of the life span extend beyond the female reproductive years. In fact, as far as we know, humans are unique in having menopause (with the exception of a species of pilot whale). Menopause has occurred in the human species for as long as recorded history (it is mentioned in the Bible), and there is no reason to doubt that it has characterized older human females since the dawn of *Homo sapiens*. Although highly variable, menopause usually occurs around the age of 50 years.

Menopause occurs when women run out of eggs for ovulation. All the eggs a human female will ever have are produced during the fifth month of gestation. These eggs are in an arrested stage of meiosis and are known as *oocytes*. At birth a girl has 2 million oocytes in her ovaries, but that number drops to 400,000 at puberty. Over the course of her lifetime, a woman ovulates only about 400 mature eggs. The rest of the eggs are lost through programmed cell death or *atresia*. If human females maintained the rate of atresia they have for most of their adult life, they would have enough oocytes to last until they were 70 years old. However, the rate of atresia increases starting at age 40, with menopause resulting by about the age of 50. There is no strong evidence that the secular trend in growth has influenced the age of menopause in any way (Peccei, 2001b).

At first glance, menopause looks to be a well-defined, programmed life history stage. Why does it occur? Jocelyn Peccei (1995) suggests a combination of factors, including adaptation, physiological tradeoff, and an artifact of the extended human life span. Some adaptive models focus on the potential fitness benefits of having older woman around to help their daughters raise their children, or the grandmothering hypothesis (Hill and Hurtado, 1991). Kristen Hawkes (2003) proposes that menopause is the most prominent aspect of a unique human pattern of longevity and that this pattern has been shaped largely by the inclusive fitness benefits derived by postmenopausal grandmothers who contribute to the care of their grandchildren. In support of this idea, a recent study of Finnish and Canadian historical records indicates that women who had long postreproductive lives had

menopause   The postreproductive period in the lives of women, after the cessation of ovulation and menses.

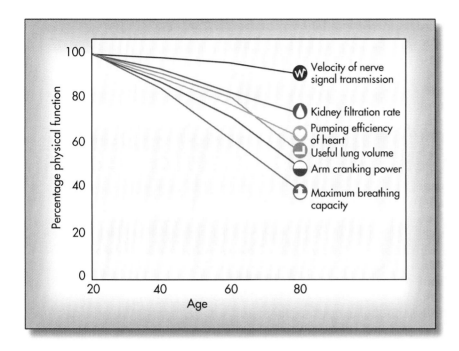

FIGURE 17.12 The effects of aging can be seen in the decline in function of many physiological systems.

greater lifetime reproductive success (Lahdenpera et al., 2004). Peccei suggest that an alternative to the grandmothering hypothesis may be more plausible: the mothering hypothesis. She argues that the postreproductive life span of women allows them to devote greater resources to the (slowly maturing) children they already have and that this factor alone could account for the evolution of menopause.

AGING

Compared with almost all other animal species, humans live a long time, at least as measured by maximum life span potential (approximately 120 years). But the body begins to age, or undergo **senescence**, starting at a much younger age. Many bodily processes actually start to decline in function starting at age 20, although the decline becomes much steeper starting between the ages of 40 and 50 (Figure 17.12). The physical and mental changes associated with aging are numerous and well known, either directly or indirectly, to most of us (Schulz and Salthouse, 1999).

Why do we age? We can answer from both the physiological and the evolutionary standpoints (Figure 17.13 on page 492). From a physiological perspective, several theories or models of aging have been offered (Nesse and Williams, 1994; Schulz and Salthouse, 1999). Some have focused on DNA, with the idea that over the lifetime, the accumulated damage to DNA, in the form of mutations caused by radiation and other forces, leads to poor cell function and ultimately cell death. Higher levels of DNA repair enzymes are found in longer-lived species, so there may be some validity to this hypothesis, although in general the DNA molecule is quite stable. Support for the DNA damage theory of aging comes from a rare (1 in 10 million people) autosomal recessive disorder known as *Werner syndrome* (Kirkwood, 2002). When they are young, people with this condition suffer from a variety of ailments that are common in the elderly (such as cataracts and osteoporosis). Werner syndrome is caused by an abnormal form of the enzyme *helicase*, which unwinds DNA during replication, repair, and gene expression. This disease provides evidence that accumulating DNA errors can cause aging.

Another model of aging focuses on the damage that *free radicals* can do to the tissues of the body (Finkel and Holbrook, 2000). Free radicals are molecules that contain at least one unpaired electron. They can link to other molecules in

senescence Age-related decline in physiological or behavioral function in adult organisms.

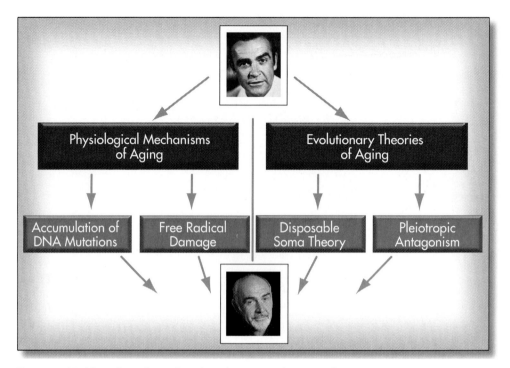

FIGURE 17.13   Physiological and evolutionary theories of aging.

tissues and thereby cause damage to those tissues. Oxygen free radicals, which result from the process of oxidation (as the body converts oxygen into energy), are thought to be the main culprit for causing the bodily changes in aging. Antioxidants, such as vitamins C and E, may reduce the effects of free radicals, although it is not clear yet whether they slow the aging process. Further evidence for the free radical theory of aging comes from diseases in which the production of the body's own antioxidants is severely limited. These diseases seem to mimic or accelerate the aging process. For example, an enzyme called *superoxide dismutase* (SOD) is an antioxidant usually produced by our bodies. People who do not make this enzyme (they are homozygous for an abnormal SOD gene) develop a familial form of the degenerative nerve disease *amyotrophic lateral sclerosis* (Lou Gehrig's disease). Both the DNA and free radical models of aging emphasize that the damage caused by these processes accumulates over the lifetime.

In wild populations, aging is not a major contributor to mortality: Most animals die of something besides old age, as humans did before the modern age. Thus aging per se could not have been an adaptation in the past because it occurred so rarely in the natural world (Kirkwood, 2002). Two nonadaptive evolutionary theories of aging are the *disposable soma theory* (Kirkwood and Austad, 2000) and the *pleiotropic gene theory* (Williams, 1957; Nesse and Williams, 1994). Both take the position that old organisms are not as evolutionarily important as young organisms. The disposable soma theory posits that it is more efficient for an organism to devote resources to reproduction rather than maintenance of a body. After all, even a body in perfect shape can still be killed by an accident, predator, or disease. Therefore, organisms are better off devoting resources to getting their genes into the next generation rather than fighting the physiological tide of aging.

The pleiotropic gene theory has a similar logic, although it comes at the problem from a different angle. As you recall, *pleiotropy* refers to the fact that most genes have multiple phenotypic effects. For all organisms, the effects of natural selection are more pronounced based on the phenotypic effects of the genes during the earliest rather than later phases of reproductive life. The simple reason for this is that a much higher proportion of organisms live long enough to reach the early reproductive phase than the proportion who make it until the late reproductive phase. For example, imagine that a gene for calcium metabolism helps a younger animal heal more quickly from wounds and thus increase its fertility (Nesse and Williams, 1994). A pleiotropic effect of that same gene in an older animal might be the development of calcium deposits and heart disease; this "aged" effect has little influence on the lifetime fitness of the animal. Aging itself may be caused by the cumulative actions of pleiotropic genes that were selected for their phenotypic effects in younger bodies but have negative effects as the body ages. A key point of the pleiotropic model of aging is that you cannot select against senescence because the effects of natural selection are always more pronounced earlier rather than later in the life span.

HUMAN VARIATION AND HEALTH: SKIN COLOR

Like human growth and development, skin color provides us with a means to explore issues of adaptation and adaptability in a biomedical anthropological context. Skin color offers us one the most visible examples of the interaction between the phenotype and the environment and the importance of evolutionary forces such as natural selection and migration in the expression of disease.

The skin is one of the largest and most complex organs of the body (Robins, 1991; Molnar, 2002). It has two main components: the thick *dermis* and the much thinner *epidermis*, which covers it (Figure 17.14). The dermis is a connective tissue layer consisting of collagen and other fibers, sweat and sebaceous glands, hair follicles, and hair. The epidermis is a thin layer of tissue consisting mostly (95%) of epithelial cells called *keratinocytes*, with 5% pigment cells, or **melanocytes**. Keratinocytes are synthesized at the base of the epidermis and migrate over the course of 4–6 weeks to the surface, where they are shed. Thus the epidermis is a continually renewing tissue layer.

Skin has several important functions. It a fluid barrier, keeping the body protected from most chemicals in the environment. It is extremely important in *thermoregulation* (maintaining body temperature in the normal range) thanks to blood vessels located in the dermis and the cooling effects of the evaporation of sweat on the surface of the body. Skin also plays a critical function in the metabolism of

melanocytes Cells in the epidermis that produce melanin.

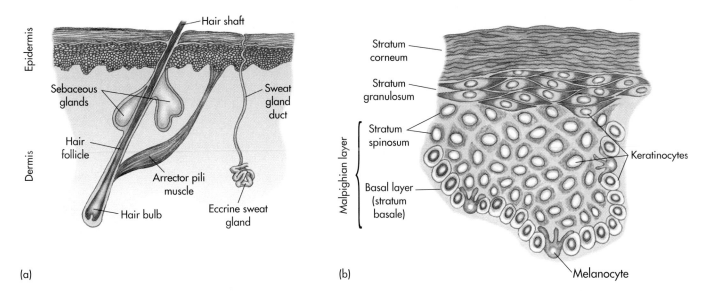

(a)   (b)

FIGURE 17.14 The structure of skin (a) and epidermis (b) at the microscopic level.

various vitamins. As we will see, this function may be critical to our understanding of the evolution of skin color in human populations.

The color of skin is produced by a combination of three substances. *Oxidized hemoglobin* in red blood cells contributes red, and *carotene* (which is derived from the diet) makes a small contribution in the yellow range to overall skin color. By far the most important component of skin color is **melanin**, a dark pigment produced by the melanocytes of the epidermis. Like neurons, with which they share a common embryonic origin, melanocytes are cells that consist of a cell body and long processes known as dendrites. The melanin in melanocytes is packaged into an organelle in the cytoplasm known as the *melanosome*. Through its dendrites, the melanocyte deposits mature melanosome in the keratinocytes surrounding it. Skin color is produced by a combination of melanosome size, the density of melanosomes within each keratinocyte, and the distribution of melanosome-bearing keratinocytes (Robins, 1991). People with darker skin have more melanin in their epidermis than people with lighter skin.

The distribution of skin color in the populations of the world follows a fairly orderly pattern, especially in the Old World. People with the darkest skin live at the equator or in the tropics (Figure 17.15). As you go north or south to higher latitudes, skin color becomes progressively lighter. In the New World, skin color does not follow such an orderly distribution, probably because of the recent migration (less than 15,000 years ago) of peoples to the New World from temperate Asia. Migration patterns over the past few hundred years have further disrupted this or-

melanin   A dark pigment produced by the melanocytes of the epidermis, which is the most important component of skin color.

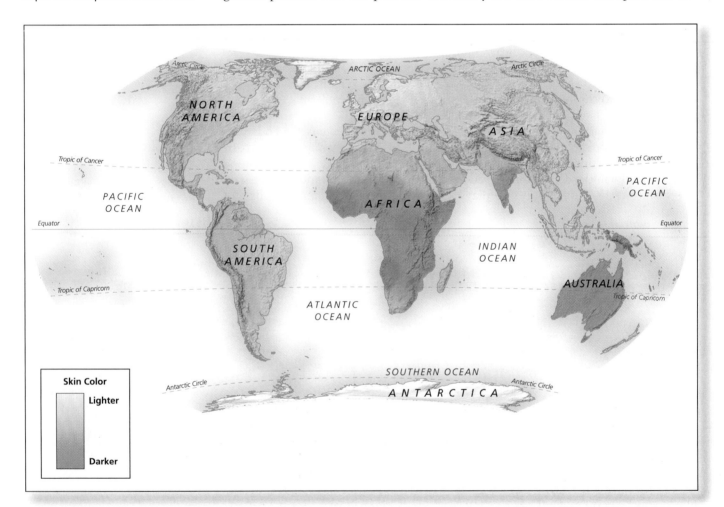

FIGURE 17.15   World map of the distribution of skin color. Note that darker skin colors are found near the equator, especially in the Old World.

derly picture, with people from higher latitudes moving to places with an abundance of sun (for example, people of northern European ancestry living in Australia) and people from equatorial regions moving to places where there is not so much sun (for example, people of west African ancestry living in the northeast United States). Such migrations and mixings are nothing new. For example, Khoisan (formerly Hottentot) peoples have lived in the temperate climate of South Africa for thousands of years and have substantially lighter skin color than Bantu-speaking Zulu people, who came to the area from equatorial Africa only 1,000 years ago (Jablonski and Chaplin, 2002). Of course, the lightest South Africans are the descendants of northern Europeans who immigrated to the region over the past few hundred years.

Reconstructing the evolution of skin color depends on explaining the advantages of dark skin in more abundant sunlight and of light skin in less abundant sunlight. Many attempts to explain this pattern have been based on diseases or conditions associated with having the "wrong" skin color for the environment.

ADVANTAGES AND DISADVANTAGES OF LIGHT AND DARK SKIN COLOR

Electromagnetic energy from the sun comes to the earth not only in the form of visible light but also in the form of *ultraviolet radiation* (UVR), which is below the wavelength for visible light. Although much of the UVR is absorbed by the ozone layer, enough reaches the earth to profoundly affect the biology of many organisms, including human beings.

Sunburn and Skin Cancer   In humans, the two most visible effects of UVR are sunburn and skin cancer. Sunburn causes congestion of subcutaneous capillaries, destruction of skin cells, and edema (collection of fluids under the skin), and it can permanently damage skin. Besides being uncomfortable, sunburn can be very serious because it may interfere with the body's ability to cool itself and lead to the development of wounds that are highly vulnerable to infection. Ultraviolet radiation also damages DNA, which in turn leads to the development of skin cancer. Most skin cancers, though unsightly, are benign. However, cancer of the melanocytes, *malignant melanoma,* spreads easily throughout the body and must be treated early.

Melanin blocks or filters out incoming UV waves. Thus people with more melanin or the ability to temporarily produce more melanin in response to light (that is, *tanning*) are less susceptible to the effects of UVR than people who have less melanin. As most of us know, very light-skinned people who cannot tan are very susceptible to sunburn. They are also more susceptible to skin cancer. People from the British Isles who have migrated to sunnier climates provide an example of the effects of increased UVR on light skin. In Britain, the skin cancer rate is 28 per 100,000 in males and 15 per 100,000 in females. In Queensland, Australia, much of which is tropical, the rates are 265 and 156 per 100,000. Despite the health risks of skin cancer in light-skinned peoples today, for most of human history it was probably protection against sunburn that provided the greater fitness benefit because cancer typically takes its toll later in life.

Vitamin D Synthesis   Vitamin D is an essential compound in calcium metabolism and is necessary for the normal development of bones and teeth. Dietary sources of vitamin D are not common, although it is present in large quantities in some fish oils and to a much lesser degree in eggs and butter. Most people get their vitamin D from the sun, or, more accurately, UVR in the sun causes a photochemical reaction in the epidermis, converting *7-dehydrocholesterol* (7-DHC) into a precursor of vitamin D, which is transformed in the kidney into vitamin D over a period of 2–3 days. Vitamin D deficiency leads to the development of a serious medical condition known as *rickets*. Because calcium metabolism is disrupted, children with rickets have bones that are severely weakened. The bones can become deformed or are prone to breakage. Rickets can range from very mild to quite severe and can even result in death. On the other side of the coin, vitamin D toxicity can also have important health consequences, but it is almost impossible to get enough vitamin D via exposure to sunlight to cause toxicity (Robins, 1991).

Because melanin blocks the effects of UVR, people with darker skin cannot synthesize vitamin D as efficiently as people with lighter skin. Dark skin takes six times longer to make vitamin D as light skin (Holick et al., 1981). In the tropics, this is not an issue because intense sunlight is readily available and seasonality is minimal. At the higher latitudes, the sunlight is less intense, and seasonality means that during certain times of the year, access to sunlight is nearly cut off. Cold weather necessitates covering the skin, further limiting the skin's exposure to direct sunlight. Vitamin D synthesis in the skin is very efficient, however, so even the exposure of a limited amount of skin (as little as 20 cm^2) to sunlight can provide sufficient vitamin D.

Rickets was first recognized to be a major health problem in the industrialized cities of northern Europe and North America at the beginning of the twentieth century. The cities' northern location and smoky pollution limited exposure to sunlight, and it was very dark in the dingy, overcrowded tenements where factory workers and their children lived. Up to 90% of children in these cities suffered from some degree of rickets (Robins, 1991). In the 1920s, rates for rickets in African American children in the United States were two to three times higher than for European American children. The epidemiology of rickets led to the development of the *vitamin D hypothesis* for the evolution of skin color (Murray, 1934; Loomis, 1967). In a nutshell, this hypothesis proposes that the evolution of lighter skin color—starting from darker-skinned ancestry—occurred in areas with less sunlight as a direct result of selection for more efficient vitamin D synthesis. Impaired movement or childbearing ability (if the pelvis is affected) in rickets would provide the negative consequences of vitamin D deficiency that would drive the selection for light skin color.

Folate (Folic Acid)　Folate is a B vitamin essential for DNA synthesis and cell replication, and exposure to UVR in the dermis causes the breakdown of folate in the bloodstream. This effect is particularly pronounced in people with light skin, who do not filter out UVR as efficiently as people with dark skin (Branda and Eaton, 1978). Deficiencies in folate during pregnancy can cause neural tube birth defects in the developing embryo. Jablonski and Chaplin (2000, 2002) propose that retention of folate may be a critical factor in the evolution of dark skin color in places with strong sunlight.

SKIN COLOR AND HEALTH: EVOLUTIONARY SYNTHESIS

Diseases associated with skin and skin color provide several potential insights into the evolution of skin color. Jablonski and Chaplin (2000, 2002) have mapped out the distribution of UVR on the earth and used it to create a map of the predicted distribution of skin color. They found that the skin color prediction was very accurate for the Old World. Indigenous peoples of the New World tropics do not have skin as dark as predicted. However, as we discussed previously, they are recent arrivals to that region, and thus we can explain the mismatch between skin color and UVR exposure by historical factors. Jablonski and Chaplin suggest that the distribution of skin color in human populations is maintained by a balance between the contrasting effects of UVR on vitamin D synthesis and on folate degradation. Although Jablonski and Chaplin focus on the role of vitamin metabolism, factors such as resistance to sunburn and skin cancer, and even protection from cold injury (light-skinned Europeans are less likely to suffer from frostbite than people of African descent) may have also contributed to the evolution of the distribution of skin color. Although there may have been some primary driving force in the evolution of skin color, the different evolutionary models are not mutually exclusive.

INFECTIOUS DISEASE AND BIOCULTURAL EVOLUTION

Our bodies provide the living and reproductive environment for a wide variety of viruses, bacteria, single-celled eukaryotic parasites, and more biologically complex parasites, such as worms. As we develop defenses to combat these disease-causing organisms, they in turn are evolving ways to get around our defenses. Understanding the nature of this arms race and the environments in which it is played out may be critical to developing more effective treatments in the future.

Infectious diseases are those in which a biological agent, or pathogen, parasitizes or infects a *host*. Human health is affected by a vast array of pathogens. These pathogens usually are classified taxonomically (such as bacteria or viruses), by their *mode of transmission* (such as sexually transmitted, airborne, or waterborne), or by the organ systems they affect (such as respiratory infections, encephalitis, or "food poisoning" for the digestive tract). Pathogens vary tremendously in their survival strategies. Some pathogens can survive only when they are in a host, whereas others can persist for long periods of time outside a host. Some pathogens live exclusively within a single host species, whereas others can infect multiple species or may even depend on different species at different points in their life cycle.

FIGURE 17.16 A child suffering from malaria, one of the most common and deadly infectious diseases.

HUMAN BEHAVIOR AND THE SPREAD OF INFECTIOUS DISEASE

Human behavior is one of the critical factors in the spread of infectious disease. Actions we take every day influence our exposure to infectious agents and determine which of them may or may not be able to enter our bodies and cause an illness. Food preparation practices, toiletry habits, sex practices, whether one spends time in proximity to large numbers of adults or children—all these can influence a person's chances of contracting an infectious disease. Another critical factor that influences susceptibility to infectious disease is overall nutritional health and wellbeing. People weakened by food shortage, starvation, or another disease (such as cancer) are especially vulnerable to infectious illness (Figure 17.16). Of course, it works both ways. Some studies indicate that children in areas where the parasitic worm *Ascaris* is common show improved nutritional status after receiving medication to treat the infection, even without changes in diet (Mascie-Taylor, 1993; Brown and Gilman, 1986).

Just as individual habits play an important role in the spread of infectious disease, so can widespread cultural practices. Sharing a communion cup has been linked to the spread of bacterial infection, as has the sharing of a water source for ritual washing before prayer in poor Muslim countries (Mascie-Taylor, 1993). Cultural biases against homosexuality and the open discussion of sexuality gave shape to the entire AIDS epidemic, from its initial appearance in gay communities to delays by leaders in acknowledging the disease as a serious public health problem. A fascinating example of the influence of cultural practices on the spread of an infectious disease involves a condition known as *kuru* (Box 17.1 on page 498).

Agriculture Agricultural populations are not necessarily more vulnerable to infectious disease than hunter-gatherer populations. However, by virtue of their larger population size, agricultural populations are likely to play host to all the diseases that affect hunter-gatherer populations and others that can be maintained only in larger populations. This is the basis of the first epidemiological transition discussed earlier. For example, when a child is exposed to measles, his or her immune system takes about 2 weeks to develop effective antibodies to fight the disease. This means that in order to be maintained in a population, the measles virus needs to find a new host every 2 weeks; in other words, there must be a pool of twenty-six new children available over the course of a year to host the measles virus. This is

BOX 17.1 Kuru, Cannibalism, and Prion Diseases

One of the most striking examples of a specific cultural practice contributing to the spread of an infectious disease is the case of *kuru*, a disease that once afflicted members of the Fore tribe in highland New Guinea (Gajdusek and Zigas, 1957; Goldfarb, 2002). Kuru is a progressive neuromuscular disorder that advances from tremors in the arms and legs to total paralysis over the course of a year. Behavioral changes, such as dementia, accompany the physical changes.

The kuru epidemic among the Fore started in the early twentieth century, and by the mid-1940s there were more than 200 new cases a year appearing in a population of only about 12,000 individuals. Over the course of the epidemic, approximately 3,000 people were killed by kuru, all of them members of the Fore ethnic group or related in some way. About three-quarters of the victims were women, with children forming the next largest group afflicted.

Because kuru tended to appear in families, it was initially thought to be a genetic disease. Scientific investigations of kuru started in the late 1950s, which was about the same time as the sickle cell trait and anemia balanced polymorphism was being worked out. Therefore, it is not surprising that some investigators suggested kuru was also being maintained as a balanced polymorphism of some kind. They were shown to be wrong, however, when Carleton Gajdusek and colleagues (1966) demonstrated that they could transmit kuru to chimpanzees by injecting them with tissue extracts from kuru victims.

We now know that kuru is a *prion disease*, one of a family of diseases that affect the tissues of the brain (they are also

called transmissible spongiform encephalopathy [TSE] diseases), leading to both muscular degeneration and behavioral abnormalities (Sy et al., 2002). They are almost always fatal. All humans (and many other mammals) make the prion protein, especially in brain tissue. The exact function of the protein is still unknown.

Prion diseases can be genetic: A mutation in the prion gene can lead to familial versions of TSE diseases (such as fatal familial insomnia), and spontaneous mutations in the prion gene are also a major cause. However, the striking thing about prion diseases is that they are also communicable. If a person with a normal prion protein is exposed to the abnormal, disease-causing prion protein, the abnormal prion protein can "seed" a transformation of the normal protein to the disease-causing form, leading to the development of a TSE disease. Unlike bacteria or viruses, the prion is a transmissible infectious agent that spreads without the use of a nucleic acid.

Kuru in the Fore people probably can be traced back to a mutation that arose in

FIGURE A   A victim of kuru.

the prion gene of a person living sometime at the end of the nineteenth century. But it did not spread through the population as a genetic disease would have. Instead, the transmission of kuru in the Fore was caused almost entirely by ritual cannibalism undertaken during funeral rites, usually by relatives of the deceased. Such rites were almost always directed by women, and cannibalism was considered to be in the women's domain. Young children accompanying their mothers and other relatives also consumed human flesh (the youngest kuru victim recorded was 4 years old). Although other groups living near the Fore also practiced ritual cannibalism, the disease was found only among the Fore or those who were related to the Fore in some way.

The Fore stopped practicing cannibalism in the 1950s, and kuru has largely disappeared. No person born after 1960 has had the disease. However, sporadic cases occur from time to time in older individuals. This is an indication of the long latency period that can occur in these prion diseases. TSE diseases are quite rare, and although protein-based infectivity is biologically fascinating, there was no reason to view prion diseases as a public health threat. This all changed in the 1990s, when it was shown that bovine spongiform encephalopathy (BSE), or "mad cow disease," can lead to the development of prion disease in humans who have consumed beef or other products derived from a cow with BSE. Kuru went from being an example of biomedical exotica of historical interest to a model for a disease with potentially major economic and public health ramifications (Lindenbaum, 2001).

possible in a large agricultural population but almost impossible in a much smaller hunter-gatherer population (Figure 17.17).

Another difference between agricultural and nonagricultural populations is that the former tend to be sedentary, whereas the latter tend to be nomadic. Large, sedentary agricultural populations therefore are more susceptible to diseases that are transmitted by contact with human waste products, which include a variety of bac-

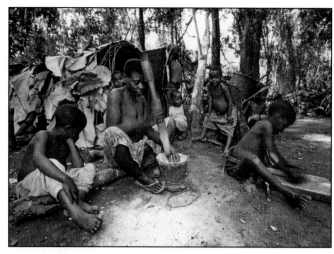

FIGURE 17.17 Risks of infectious disease increase in (left) high-density agricultural populations compared to (right) low-density, dispersed hunter-gatherer populations.

terial diseases and parasitic worms. In addition, many diseases are carried by water, and agricultural populations are far more dependent on a limited number of water sources than nonagricultural populations. Finally, agricultural populations often have domestic animals and also play host to a variety of commensal animals, such as rats, each of which is a potential carrier of diseases that may affect humans.

As mentioned in Chapter 6, specific agricultural practices may change the environment and encourage the spread of such infectious diseases as sickle cell and malaria. Slash-and-burn agriculture leads to more open forests and standing pools of stagnant water. Such pools are an ideal breeding ground for the mosquitoes that carry the protozoa that cause malaria. Agriculture that makes extensive use of irrigation and water damming brings people into contact with large flatworms of the genus *Schistoma*. These flatworms cause a disease known as *schistosomiasis*, which is often characterized by blood in the urine. *Schistoma* species have an extraordinary life cycle that involves several distinct stages lived both inside and outside its two hosts: humans and a particular snail species. Schistosomiasis can damage the bladder, kidney, liver, spleen, and intestines. The World Health Organization estimates that 200 million people may be infected with the parasite and that 200,000 die annually from its effects (Figure 17.18).

Mobility and Migration The human species is characterized by its mobility. One price of this mobility has been the transmission of infectious agents from one population to another, leading to uncontrolled outbreaks of disease in the populations that have never been exposed to the newly introduced diseases.

The Black Death in Europe (1348–1350) is one example of just such an outbreak (Figure 17.19 on page 500). The Black Death was bubonic plague, a disease caused by the bacterium *Yersinia pestis*. The bacterium is transmitted by the rat flea, which lives on rats. When the fleas run out of rodent hosts, they move to other mammals, such as humans. The bacteria can quickly overwhelm the body, causing swollen lymph nodes (or buboes, hence the name) and in more severe cases leading to infection of the respiratory system and blood. It can kill very quickly. An outbreak of bubonic plague was recorded in China in the 1330s, and by the late 1340s it had reached Europe. In a single Italian city, Florence, a contemporary report placed the number dying between March and October 1348 at 96,000. By the end of the epidemic, a third of Europeans (25–40 million) had been killed, and the economic and cultural life of Europe was forever changed.

Similar devastation awaited the native peoples of the New World upon the arrival of European explorers and colonists after 1492. Measles, smallpox, influenza,

FIGURE 17.18 Two children with schistosomiasis.

FIGURE 17.19   The Black Death spread over much of Europe in a three-year period in the middle of the fourteenth century.

whooping cough, and sexually transmitted diseases exacted a huge toll on native populations throughout North and South America, the Island Pacific, and Australia. Some populations were completely wiped out, and others had such severe and rapid population depletion that their cultures were destroyed. In North America, for example, many communities of native peoples lost up to 90% of their population through the introduction of European diseases (Pritzker, 2000). Infectious diseases often reached native communities before the explorers or colonizers did, giving the impression that North America was an open and pristine land waiting to be filled.

INFECTIOUS DISEASE AND THE EVOLUTIONARY ARMS RACE

As a species, we fight infectious diseases in many ways. However, no matter what we do, parasites and pathogens continuously evolve to overcome our defenses. Over the last 50 years, it appeared that medical science was gaining the upper hand on infectious disease, at least in developed countries. However, despite real advances, infectious diseases such as the virus that causes AIDS and antibiotic-resistant bacteria remind us that this primeval struggle will continue.

The Immune System   One of the most extraordinary biological systems that has ever evolved is the vertebrate immune system, the main line of defense in the fight against infectious disease. At its heart is the ability to distinguish self from nonself. The immune system identifies foreign substances, or **antigens**, in the body and synthesizes **antibodies,** which comprise a class of proteins known as **immunoglobulins,** which are specifically designed to bind to and destroy specific antigens (Figure 17.20).

antigens   Whole or part of an invading organism that prompts a response (such as production of antibodies) from the body's immune system.

antibodies   Proteins (immunoglobulins) formed by the immune system that are specifically structured to bind to and neutralize invading antigens.

immunoglobulins   Proteins produced by B lymphocytes that function as antibodies.

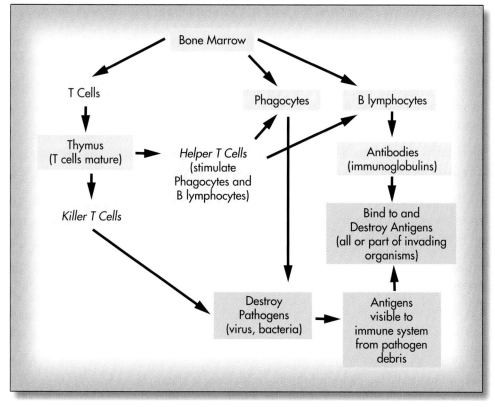

FIGURE 17.20 The immune system has several different components that work in concert.

Antibodies are produced by white blood cells known as *B lymphocytes.* These originate in the bone marrow and circulate between lymph tissue and the bloodstream. Another class of lymphocytes, *T cells,* is also critical in the immune response. *Helper T cells* lead to the activation of B lymphocytes to produce antibodies and stimulate the production of specialized cells called *phagocytes,* which destroy infectious agents, such as viruses, by engulfing and destroying them. One of the most extraordinary qualities of the immune system is its ability to remember previous exposures to an antigen, thus priming the system in case later exposures to the antigen occur. This is the immunological basis of *vaccination* (discussed in more detail in the next section), whereby exposure to a killed or inactivated form of an antigen such as a virus protects an individual from developing an illness upon later exposure to the active form of the antigen. The memory function of the immune system is carried out by specialized T and B lymphocytes.

The immune system is a complex mechanism that has evolved to deal with the countless number of potential antigens in the environment. An example of what happens when just one of the components of the immune system is not functioning occurs in AIDS. The *human immunodeficiency virus* (HIV) that causes AIDS attacks the helper T cells. As mentioned earlier, the helper T cells respond to antigens by inducing the B lymphocytes to produce antibodies, leading to the production of phagocytes; when their function is compromised, the function of the entire immune system is also compromised. This leaves a person with HIV infection vulnerable to a host of opportunistic infections, a condition that characterizes the development of AIDS.

Cultural and Behavioral Interventions Although the immune system does a remarkable job fighting infectious disease, it is obviously not always enough. Even before the basis of infectious diseases was understood, humans took steps to limit their transmission. Throughout the Old World, people with leprosy were shunned and forced to live apart from the bulk of the population. This isolation amounted to *quarantine*, in recognition of the contagious nature of their condition.

One of the most effective biocultural measures developed to fight infectious diseases is vaccination. The elimination of *smallpox* as a scourge of humanity is one of the great triumphs of widespread vaccination. Smallpox is a viral illness that originated in Africa some 12,000 years ago and subsequently spread throughout the Old World (Barquet and Domingo, 1997). It was a disfiguring illness, causing pustulent lesions on the skin, and it was often fatal. Smallpox killed millions of people upon its introduction to the New World; in the Old World, smallpox epidemics periodically decimated entire populations. In 180 A.D., a smallpox epidemic killed 3.5–7 million people in the Roman Empire, precipitating the first period of its decline.

Numerous remedies were used to combat the spread of smallpox. In some cultures, children were exposed to people with mild cases of smallpox in the hopes that it would strengthen their resistance to the disease. In China, powdered scabs of smallpox sores were blown into the nostrils of healthy people. Women in the harems of the Turkish Ottoman Empire were inoculated on parts of their body where the smallpox scars (which result in the area of the vaccination) could not be seen. The Turkish method was to make four or five small scratches on the skin and introduce some pus from an infected person into them. This method was introduced to England (and Western medicine) in the early eighteenth century, and early medical statisticians verified its success at preventing the development of serious forms of the illness (although 2–3% of the people vaccinated by this method died). We now have much safer forms of vaccination against smallpox, which have led to the total eradication of this horrible disease (Figure 17.21).

The most recently developed forms of intervention against infectious disease are drug based. The long-term success of these drugs will depend on the inability of the infectious agents to evolve resistance to their effects. Overuse of anti-infectious drugs may actually hasten the evolution of resistant forms by intensifying the selection pressures on pathogens.

Evolutionary Adaptations   The immune system is the supreme evolutionary adaptation in the fight against infectious disease. However, specific adaptations to disease that do not involve the immune system are also quite common (Jackson,

KINE POCK INOCULATION.

Rules to be attended to during the Vaccination.

1. THE diet to be the same as before vaccination.
2. Scratching or rubbing the arm, or shoving up the sleeve should be avoided as much as possible.
3. In case an itching sensation of the vaccinated part should give the patient uneasiness, a little vinegar applied to the part will give immediate relief.
4. No matter to be transferred from the person inoculated to another person.   Taking it from another often becomes a snare to individuals, and the source of spurious matter.   But even those, who by chance have had the genuine disease in that way, have no certainty of it—and who would wish to have it upon uncertainties ?
5. Women, who do house work, should avoid washing and baking on the 7th and 8th days, the usual time for the symptoms.
6. No danger of washing the hands and face in cold water during the disease.
7. Women may without hesitation receive the Kine Pock in all circumstances without exception, at home or travelling by land or water.
8. No danger of vaccinating children at the period of teething.
9. Labouring men and mechanics need not abstain from their customary employment, provided their indisposition does not require it.
10. Children should never be lifted by the arms,* especially when under the inoculation.   The arm should not be bound up, nor confined in tight sleeves.

OBSERVATIONS.

1. It occasions no other disease.   On the contrary, it has often been known to improve health ; and to remedy those diseases, under which the patient before laboured.
2. It leaves behind no blemish, but a *blessing* ;—one of the greatest ever bestowed on man ;—*a perfect security against the future infection of the small-pox.*
N. B. Save the scab for examination.   B. WATERHOUSE.

* No prudent person, who is aware of the tenderness of the bone of a young child, would ever lift one by its arms, or lead a child a mile by one arm.

Cambridge, July 3, 1809.

FIGURE 17.21 Early instructions for administration of the smallpox vaccine. Note in the last lines that it was considered to be a "blessing."

2000). For example, a class of enzymes known as *lysozymes* attack the cell wall structure of some bacteria. Lysozymes are found in high concentrations in the tear ducts, salivary glands, and other sites of bacterial invasion.

The sickle cell allele has spread in some populations because it functions as an adaptation against malaria. Another adaptation to malaria is the Duffy blood group (see Chapter 6) In Duffy-positive individuals, the proteins Fya and Fyb are found on the surface of red blood cells. These proteins facilitate entry of the malaria-causing protozoan *Plasmodium vivax*. Duffy-negative individuals do not have Fya and Fyb on the surface of their red blood cells, so people with this phenotype are resistant to vivax malaria. Many Duffy-negative people are found in parts of Africa where malaria is common; others who live elsewhere have African ancestry.

DIET AND DISEASE

It seems that there are always conflicting reports on what particular parts of our diet are good or bad for us. Carbohydrates are good one year and bad the next. Fats go in and out of fashion. From a biocultural anthropological perspective, American attitudes toward diet and health at the turn of the twenty-first century provide a rich source of material for analysis. For example, what do you think when you hear the word *cholesterol?* On one hand, this steroid alcohol is essential for the synthesis of many steroid hormones in the body, and its consumption is normal and necessary. On the other, high blood serum levels of cholesterol increase the risk of heart disease. Some people feel as if having high cholesterol is a sign of moral failure or weakness. Thus cholesterol has gone from being just a molecule to being a nutritional boogeyman, to be avoided via the consumption of low-cholesterol and cholesterol-free foods.

Despite all the confusion about diet, we all have the same basic nutritional needs. We need energy (measured in calories or kilojoules) for body maintenance, growth, and metabolism. Carbohydrates, fat, and proteins are all sources of energy. We especially need protein for tissue growth and repair. In addition to energy, fat provides us with essential fatty acids important for building and supporting nerve tissue. We need vitamins, which are basically organic molecules that our bodies cannot synthesize but that we need in small quantities for a variety of metabolic processes. We also need a certain quantity of inorganic elements, such as iron and zinc. For example, with insufficient iron, the ability of red blood cells to transport oxygen is compromised, leading to anemia. Finally, we all need water to survive.

In this section, we will look at reconstructions of the typical *Paleolithic diet*, which theoretically reflects the kinds of foods people ate during the pre-agricultural part of human history. Many researchers believe that our bodies are evolved for functioning in this kind of nutritional environment. We will then consider how agriculture changed everything, at least in terms of the human diet. New foods were introduced, but variety was lost, and problems associated with specific dietary deficiencies (other than total calories) became common in some agricultural populations. Ultimately, however, the legacy of modern agriculture is not scarcity but abundance, and we will see how we as a species are not particularly well adapted to living in an environment of continuous nutritional abundance.

THE PALEOLITHIC DIET

For most of human history, people lived in small groups and subsisted on wild foods that they could collect by hunting or gathering. Obviously, diets varied in different areas: Sub-Saharan Africans were not eating the same thing as Native Americans on the northwest Pacific Coast. Nonetheless, S. Boyd Eaton and Melvin Konner (Eaton and Konner, 1985; Eaton et al., 1999) argue that we can reconstruct an *average*

TABLE 17.2 Comparison of Paleolithic and Contemporary Diets

DIETARY COMPONENT	PALEOLITHIC DIET	CONTEMPORARY DIET
Energy (calories)	High caloric intake and expenditure to support active lifestyle and large body size.	More sedentary lifestyle uses fewer calories, yet caloric consumption often exceeds expenditure
Micronutrients (vitamins, antioxidants, folic acid, iron, zinc)	High consumption (65–70% of diet) of foods rich in micronutrients, such as fruits, roots, nuts, and other noncereals.	Low consumption of foods rich in micronutrients.
Electrolytes (sodium, calcium, and potassium, needed for a variety of physiological processes)	High consumption of potassium relative to sodium (10,500 mg/day vs. 770 mg/day). High blood pressure is rare in contemporary hunter-gatherers with high potassium/sodium ratios.	Low consumption of potassium relative to sodium (3,000 mg/day vs. 4,000 mg/day). High sodium intake from processed foods is associated with high blood pressure.
Carbohydrates	Provide about 45–50% of daily calories, mostly from vegetables and fruits, which are rich in amino acids, fatty acids, and micronutrients.	Provide about 45–50% of daily calories, mostly from processed cereal grains, sugars, and sweetners, which are low in amino acids, fatty acids, and micronutrients.
Fat	Provides about 20–25% of daily calories, mostly from lean game animals, which have less fat and saturated fat than domestic animals, leading to lower serum cholesterol levels.	Provides about 40% of calories, mostly from meat and dairy products. Some contemporary diets, such as from Japan and the Mediterranean region, are low in total or saturated fat and are associated with lower heart disease rates.
Protein	High consumption, providing about 30% of daily calorie intake, mostly from wild game that is low in fat.	Recommended daily allowance about 12% of total calories. High protein intake has been associated with higher heart disease rates, probably because contemporary high-protein diets also tend to be high in fat.
Fiber	50–100 g/day. High-fiber diets sometimes are considered risky because of loss of micronutirents, but this would be less of a worry in a Paleolithic diet rich in micronutrients.	20 g/day.

Paleolithic diet from a wide range of information derived from paleoanthropology, epidemiology, and nutritional studies. A comparison of the average Paleolithic and contemporary diets is presented in Table 17.2 (Eaton et al., 1999).

As we can see, the contemporary diet is not simply a more abundant version of the hunter-gatherer diet. It differs fundamentally in both composition and quality. Compared with contemporary diets, the hunter-gatherer diet can be characterized as being high in micronutrients, protein, fiber, and potassium and low in fat and sodium. Total caloric and carbohydrate intake is about the same in both diets, but hunter-gatherers typically were more active than contemporary peoples and thus needed more calories, and their carbohydrates came from fruits and vegetables rather than processed cerals and refined sugars.

The comparison between hunter-gatherer and contemporary diets indicates that increasing numbers of people are living in nutritional environments for which their bodies are not necessarily well adapted. With few exceptions (such as the evolution of lactose tolerance) there has not been enough time, or strong enough selection pressures, for us to develop adaptations to this new nutritional environment. Indeed, because most of the negative health aspects of contemporary diets (obesity, diabetes, cancer) become critical only later in life, it is likely that health problems associated with the mismatch between our bodies and our nutritional environment will be with us for some time.

AGRICULTURE AND NUTRITIONAL DEFICIENCY

The essential paradox of the development of agriculture is that although it allowed the establishment of large population centers—which in turn led to the development of large-scale, stratified civilizations with role specialization—from a nutritional standpoint, most people led lives that were inferior to the lives of hunter-gatherers. Agricultural peoples often suffered from *nutritional stress* as dependence on a few crops made their large populations vulnerable to both chronic nutritional shortages and occasional famines. The "success" of agricultural peoples relative to hunter-gatherers came about not because agriculturalists lived longer but because there were more of them.

FIGURE 17.22   Enamel defects due to malnutrition in a child from the Illinois Valley (600–1200 A.D.).

An example of the decline in health associated with the intensification of agriculture comes from paleopathological research in the Illinois Valley (Cook, 1979; Cook and Buikstra, 1979). Over the period 600–1200 A.D., the people there went from lives that were characterized predominantly by subsistence based on hunting and gathering (with some trade for agricultural products) to an agricultural economy with significant maize production. Population centers increased in size. However, at the same time, signs of malnutrition also increased. Enamel defects in tooth development became more common, and we can associate them with higher death rates during the weaning years (Figure 17.22). Skeletal growth rates slowed. Specific skeletal lesions associated with malnutrition also increased in frequency.

With their dependence on a single staple cereal food, agricultural populations throughout the world have been plagued by diseases associated with specific nutritional deficiencies. As in the Illinois Valley, many populations of the New World were dependent on maize as a staple food crop. Dependence on maize is associated with the development of *pellagra*, a disease caused by a deficiency of the B vitamin *niacin* in the diet. Pellagra causes a distinctive rash, diarrhea, and mental disturbances, including dementia. Ground corn is low in niacin and in the amino acid tryptophan, which the body can use to synthesize niacin. Even into the twentieth century, poor sharecroppers in the southern United States and poor farmers in southern Europe, both groups that consumed large quantities of cornmeal in their diets, were commonly afflicted with pellagra. Some maize-dependent groups in Central and South America were not so strongly affected by pellagra because they processed the corn with an alkali (lye, lime, ash) that released niacin from the hull of the corn.

In Asia, rice has been the staple food crop for at least the last 6,000 years. In China, a disease we now call *beriberi* was first described in 2,697 B.C. Although it was not recognized at that time, beriberi is caused by a deficiency in vitamin B1 or *thiamine*. Beriberi is characterized by fatigue, drowsiness, and nausea, leading to a variety of more serious complications related to problems with the nervous system (especially tingling, burning, and numbness in the extremities) and ultimately heart failure. Rice is not lacking in vitamins; however, white rice, which has been polished and milled to remove the hull, has been stripped of most of its vitamin content, including thiamine. Recognition of an association between rice overdependence and beriberi began to develop in the late nineteenth century, when the Japanese navy reported that beriberi could be eliminated among its sailors (half of whom contracted the disease) by increasing the meat, vegetables, and fish in their diets.

AGRICULTURE AND ABUNDANCE: THRIFTY, NONTHRIFTY, AND THRIFTY-PLEIOTROPIC GENOTYPES

The advent of agriculture ushered in a long era of nutritional deficiency for most people. However, the recent agricultural period, as exemplified in the developed nations of the early twenty-first century, is one of nutritional excess, especially in terms of the consumption of fat and carbohydrates of little nutritional value other than calories. The amount and variety of foods available to people in contemporary societies are unparalleled in human history.

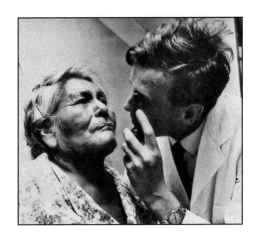

FIGURE 17.23 Pima Indian woman receiving an eye exam. Eye problems are a common result of diabetes.

In 1962, geneticist James Neel introduced the idea of a *thrifty genotype,* a genotype that is very efficient at storing food in the body in the form of fat, after observing that many non-Western populations that had recently adopted a Western or modern diet were much more likely than Western populations to have high rates of obesity, diabetes (especially Type 2 or non–insulin-dependent diabetes), and all the health problems associated with those conditions (see also Neel, 1982). Populations such as the Pima-Papago Indians in the southwest United States have diabetes rates of about 50%, and elevated rates of diabetes have been observed in Pacific Island–, Asian-, and African-derived populations with largely Western diets (Figure 17.23).

According to Neel, hunter-gatherers needed a thrifty genotype to adapt to their nonabundant nutritional environments; in contrast, the thrifty genotype had been selected against in the supposedly abundant European environment through the negative consequences of diabetes and obesity. The history of agriculture and nutritional availability in Europe makes the evolution of a *non-thrity genotype* unlikely (Allen and Cheer, 1996); Europe was no more nutritionally favored than other agricultural or hunter-gatherer populations. However, the notion of a thrifty genotype retains validity. At its heart is the idea that we are adapted to a lifestyle and nutritional environment far different from those we find in contemporary populations.

Douglas Crews and Linda Gerber (1994; Gerber and Crews, 1999) have proposed a refinement and expansion of the thrifty genotype model that they call the *thrifty-pleiotropic genotype* model. Whereas Neel concentrated primarily on energy intake, they point out that the thrifty genotype should apply to any nutrient in the environment that is (or was) potentially scarce. Thus we should expect negative health consequences for the overconsumption of a variety of nutrients: Excess cholesterol consumption leads to heart disease, excess salt consumption leads to high blood pressure, and so on. The deficiency syndromes of agriculture are part of this adaptive balance: Too little of a nutrient can also lead to disease. The pleiotropic aspect of Crews and Gerber's model is based on the observation that most of the diseases associated with overconsumption are chronic illnesses that have their effects late in life; they are to some extent a consequence of aging. If the efficiency of the thrifty genotype increases reproductive fitness early in life, the negative pleiotropic consequences in middle and old age will not be selected against, even in an environment of nutritional abundance.

We have seen how growth patterns, infectious disease exposure, nutritional status, and a host of other health-related issues are fundamentally changed by the adoption of new cultural practices and technologies. Conditions such as rickets and diabetes have been called diseases of civilization because they seem to be a direct result of the development of the industrialized urban landscape and food production. But this label is misleading. Rickets could also be called a disease of migration and maladaptation to a specific environment. Diabetes could be characterized as a disease of nutritional abundance, which was certainly *not* a characteristic of civilization for most of human history.

Biomedical anthropology is interested in understanding the patterns of human variation, adaptation, and evolution as they relate to health issues. This entails an investigation of the relationship between our biologies and the environments we live in. Understanding environmental transitions helps us understand not only the development of disease but also the mechanisms of adaptation that have evolved over thousands of years of evolution. Change is the norm in the modern world. In the future, we should expect human health to be affected by these changes. By their training and interests, biological anthropologists will be in an ideal position to make an important contribution to understanding the dynamic biocultural factors that influence human health and illness.

SUMMARY

1. **What is the difference between incidence rate and prevalence rate? How do they relate to each other?**

   The incidence rate is the rate at which new cases of a disease appear in a population over a certain period of time (usually a year). The prevalence rate is the total number of cases of disease divided by the population size at any given time. Prevalence is a function of both incidence and the duration of the disease. For example, a disease with a low incidence rate but a long duration could have a higher prevalence rate than a disease with a high incidence rate that is quickly cured or quickly fatal.

2. **Why are both biocultural and evolutionary approaches important in biomedical anthropology?**

   Biomedical anthropology is concerned with the processes of adaptation and adaptability with reference to health and human variation. In evolutionary terms, this encompasses how human biology adapts to stressful environments by evolving adaptations to overcome them; in addition, understanding the mismatch between biological adaptations and current environments can also provide insights into human health. Humans must also respond to environment stress in the short term. Human adaptability studies show that biological plasticity and biocultural traditions can have a profound effect on health status.

3. **What are the four stages of growth seen across primates? Why is adolescence possibly a fifth stage of growth unique to humans?**

   The four stages of growth are prenatal or gestational, infancy, juvenile stage, and adulthood. Barry Bogin argues that humans have a unique stage of growth, adolescence, that begins with puberty and is marked by a growth spurt not seen in other mammals. Adolescence may also provide an extended time period for human children to better learn their adult behavioral roles.

4. **What is the secular trend in growth?**

   It has been demonstrated in several populations at different times that stature and weight increase with the advent of development, industrialization, and improved nutrition. This trend plateaus when the population reaches its genetic potential. Migration studies provide further evidence of the secular trend in growth by comparing growth between migrant populations living in nutrition-rich environments and nonmigrant populations in nutrition-poor environments.

5. **What are some of the selection pressures influencing the distribution of skin color around the world?**

   The main selection pressure is exposure to UVR. However, there are several ways in which exposure to UVR can influence the evolution of skin color. In areas of high UVR (high sunlight), selection for dark skin as a protection from sunburn and skin cancer may have occurred; dark skin color may also prevent the breakdown of folic acid. In northern latitudes with less direct sunlight exposure, light skin color may have been selected in order to facilitate vitamin D synthesis. Low vitamin D levels can cause the disease known as rickets.

6. **Why are agricultural populations more susceptible to infectious disease than hunter-gatherer populations?**

   Agricultural populations are larger than hunter-gatherer populations, providing a larger pool of potential hosts who have not developed antibodies to the pathogen. They are more sedentary, which makes them more susceptible to diseases transmitted in human waste. Agricultural populations are also more dependent on only a few water sources, making them more susceptible to waterborne diseases. Finally, they live in close proximity to both domestic animals and commensals (such as rats) and therefore are susceptible to diseases they carry or transmit.

7. **What are pellagra and beriberi?**

Both are vitamin deficiency diseases. Pellagra is caused by niacin deficiency and is seen in populations that have corn or maize as a staple cereal. Ground corn is low in niacin and the amino acid tryptophan, which the body uses to synthesize niacin. Beriberi is a disease common in populations where polished white rice is a staple cereal. It is caused by a deficiency in thiamine, which is present in the rice hull but is removed during processing to make white rice.

CRITICAL THINKING QUESTIONS

1. Is aging an adaptation or an indirect byproduct of natural selection acting on other biological, physiological, genetic factors?

2. What do we mean when we say there is an evolutionary arms race between pathogens and hosts?

3. Should everyone adopt the Paleolithic diet? Why or why not?

KEY TERMS

biomedical anthropology
epidemiology
incidence rate
prevalence rate
pathogens

auxology
teratogens
menarche
menopause
senescence
melanocytes

melanin
antigens
antibodies
immunoglobulins

SUGGESTED READINGS

Bogin, Barry. (2001). *The Growth of Humanity.* Wiley-Liss, New York.

Nesse, Randolph M. and Williams, George C. (1994). *Why We Get Sick: The New Science of Darwinian Medicine.* Times Books, New York.

Tanner, J. M. (1978). *Fetus into Man.* Harvard University Press, Cambridge.

Trevathan, Wenda, Smith, E. O., and McKenna, J. J. (eds.) (1999). *Evolutionary Medicine.* Oxford University Press, New York.

Chapter 18

The Evolution of Human Behavior

DEBATES ABOUT THE RELEVANCE OF BIOLOGICAL AND evolutionary approaches to understanding human behavior have a long history. One of the liveliest periods in this ongoing intellectual dialogue (to use a polite term) was the mid-1970s. During this period, new evolutionary and ecological approaches to understanding animal behavior were starting to be applied to human behavior. Increasing knowledge about the sophisticated social behavior of other primates further fueled the effort to place human behavior in a broader evolutionary and zoological context.

In early 1978, the American Association for the Advancement of Science held a meeting in Washington, D.C., which attempted to bring together representatives from all sides in the sociobiology "debate". Two of the most prominent scientists to attend the meeting were Edward Wilson, a proponent of the evolutionary study of human behavior (which was then called sociobiology), and Stephen Jay Gould, who cautioned that arguments about the biological basis of human behavior historically had been used to justify racist and sexist ideologies. Many of Wilson's critics accused him of arrogance for suggesting that evolutionary explanations of human behavior would come to dominate thinking in the traditional social sciences. In contrast, proponents of sociobiology felt that Wilson and other workers in the field were being unfairly accused of holding political and ideological views that they themselves found to be repugnant. Advocates on both sides of the debate were fueled by arrogance and righteousness, a volatile combination.

Sociologist of science Ullica Segerstråle attended this landmark meeting. She describes the extraordinary scene when Wilson faced some of his more enthusiastic critics:

"The two-day symposium featured about twenty speakers in all. As a member of the audience, I can say that for those who anticipated a public showdown, it was somewhat disappointing to sit through rather technical talks dealing with animal sociobiology. . . . But there was anticipation in the air, particularly in the session where both Wilson and Gould were to speak. The ballroom was filled to capacity. Would Gould demolish sociobiology? Would Wilson stand up to Gould? By now, the audience wanted some action. The result exceeded anybody's expectation.

"What happens is a total surprise. The session has already featured Gould, among others, and Wilson is one of the later speakers. Just as Wilson is about to begin, about ten people rush up on the speaker podium shouting 'Racist Wilson you can't hide, we charge you with genocide!' While some take over the microphone and denounce sociobiology, a couple of them rush up behind Wilson (who is sitting in his place) and pour a pitcher of ice-water over his head, shouting 'Wilson, you are all wet!' Then they quickly disappear again. Great commotion ensues but things calm down when the session organizer steps up to the microphone and apologizes to Wilson for the incident. The audience gives Wilson a standing ovation. Now Gould steps up to the microphone saying that this kind of activism is not the right way to fight sociobiology—here he has a Lenin quote handy, on 'radicalism, an infantile disorder of socialism.' For his valiant handling of the situation, Gould, too, gets a standing ovation. (The audience does not quite know how to react to any of this but applauding seems somehow right.) Wilson—still wet—gives his talk, in spite of the shock of the physical attack. . . . his calmly delivered talk is something of an anticlimax" (Segerstråle, 2000).

We are fortunate that most debates about the evolution of human behavior do not end (or begin) with someone being doused with water. But the incident provides an indication of just how heated these debates can become. They reflect a basic conflict over whether human behavior is "in the genes" or is a product of our culture and upbringing: the old nature versus nurture debate. The nurture, or cultural, side accuses the nature, or evolutionary, side of being *genetic determinists,* people who believe that all observed behavioral differences between individuals, the sexes, or populations can be ascribed only to differences in genetics. The genetic side accuses the cultural side of embracing the logic of creationism: That once culture evolved, the rules of the game changed, and we were no longer subject (at the behavioral level) to the forces of evolution, which are so readily apparent in the animal world.

As you might expect, neither of these two extreme views reflects the views of most biological anthropologists. Biological anthropologists, with their appreciation for the biology and behavior of our closest primate relatives, understand that human bodies and human behavior evolved. Although behaviors do not fossilize, we can draw inferences about how they may have evolved by examining contemporary human and nonhuman primate behavior and biology.

Biological anthropologists also understand the importance of culture and experience in shaping human behavior. Behavioral plasticity is one of the critical adaptations that accompanied the evolution of a large brain. But many behavioral scientists today believe that although a large brain does confer on humans the ability to adopt a wide range of behaviors, some patterns of behavior we observe across cultures and populations are most directly explained by evolution and natural selection. The behaviors are not genetically determined but reflect the interactions of genes and environments that yield patterns of behavior we can analyze statistically.

To understand the evolutionary foundations of contemporary human behavior we need to apply the same logic and inferences that we use when studying other evolutionary phenomena. We can use the vast amount of information we have about human behavior and look for patterns that are consistent with evolutionary models. We can also take advantage of "natural experiments" that provide unusual combinations of variables and allow us to gain new perspectives on human behavior. The same principles that we use to make inferences about the phylogenetic relationships of the Old World monkeys, the adaptive value of the trunk of an elephant, the plumage of the male peacock, or the social behavior of prairie dogs can also guide our inferences about the evolution of human behavior. However, human behavior occurs in a cultural context. Like the medical anthropology approach to health and illness (discussed in Chapter 17), a comprehensive understanding of the evolution of human behavior entails a biocultural perspective.

In this chapter, we will address several aspects of human behavior from an evolutionary perspective. These include the ecology and demography of traditional human societies, patterns of human behavior that have been shaped by sexual selection, the interaction between culture and biology in the expression of language, and the emergence of behavioral disease in an evolutionary context. We recognize, of course, that each of these topics can be productively analyzed from a cultural or nonevolutionary perspective; these other perspectives may provide alternative or complementary analyses to those provided here. However, as we have emphasized throughout this text, the biological anthropological approach is defined both by evolutionary theory and by the quest to understand the human species—including human behavior—in a biocultural context. Therefore, this chapter focuses on these evolutionary and biocultural explanations of human behavior.

STUDYING THE EVOLUTION OF HUMAN BEHAVIOR

Evolutionary approaches to understanding behavior did not make much of an impact through the first half of the twentieth century. A major development in the study of the evolution of behavior was the publication of G. C. Williams's book *Adaptation and Natural Selection* (1966). Williams saw the evolution of social behavior in terms of benefits not to the group as a whole but to the individuals who made up the group (and their genes). Following on this work and others, in 1975 zoologist Edward O. Wilson published a book called *Sociobiology: The New Synthesis.* For a variety of social and political reasons, which are beyond the scope of this text (see Segerstråle, 2000; Alcock, 2001), Wilson's book became a lightning rod for critics of evolutionary interpretations of human behavior. Wilson defined **sociobiology** simply as the science of the biological basis of social behavior. Only a small part of his book was dedicated to humans, with most of it focusing on examples and discussions drawn from the animal world, especially the insects that were the main focus of his research. Although a classic work, *Sociobiology* was not *The Origin of Species:* It emerged from an intellectual climate that was, at least in part, already in tune with the message.

Critics of sociobiology, such as the paleontologist and writer Stephen Jay Gould, claimed that sociobiology in general was not good science and was susceptible to political misapplication. Mindful of these criticisms, the field of the evolution of human behavior has moved away from Wilson's grand vision of human sociobiology (that it would subsume all the social sciences) and embraced several different, sometimes competing approaches to human behavior, which are seen to be complementary to or a part of traditional human behavioral sciences.

THE EVOLUTION OF HUMAN BEHAVIOR: FOUR APPROACHES

Anthropologists and other scientists interested in the evolution of human behavior use quite different approaches to the subject depending on their particular research interests and training (Figure 18.1). Four of the most common approaches are paleontological reconstructions of behavior, biocultural approaches, evolutionary psychology, and human evolutionary (or behavioral) ecology. The examples covered in this chapter make use of the latter three approaches.

Paleontological Reconstructions of Behavior In Chapters 10–15, we discussed several reconstructions of the behavior of earlier hominids. These reconstructions were based on the anatomy of extinct hominids and, when present, the archaeological remains with which they were associated. They were also based on correlations among behavior, anatomy, and ecology we have observed in nonhuman primate species and in contemporary humans, especially those living under traditional hunter-gatherer conditions. Any reconstruction of the behavior of our hominid ancestors is a synthesis of both paleontological and contemporary data. Although there are limits to how much we can learn from such reconstructions, they are the only source of information we have to understand the *sequence* of events in human behavioral evolution.

Biocultural Approaches It is clear that human cultural behavior has influenced human evolution. For example, the adoption of slash-and-burn agriculture had an indirect effect on the evolution of the sickle cell polymorphism, and the development of dairying in some populations was a direct selective factor in the evolution of lactose tolerance. As we will see in this chapter, our biological and evolutionary heritage may have shaped several patterns of behavior that are expressed in a cultural context. One aspect of human behavior that we have already discussed in detail—language—is a prime example.

sociobiology Name popularized by E.O. Wilson for the evolutionary study of animal social behavior.

FIGURE 18.1 Four approaches to studying the evolution of human behavior.

Evolutionary Psychology   **Evolutionary psychology** is characterized by an adherence to three main principles. First, human and animal behavior is not produced by minds that are general purpose devices. Rather, the mind is composed of cognitive modules—which are assumed to have an underlying neuroanatomical basis—that express specific behaviors in specific situations. Second, cognitive modules are complex design features of organisms. Because natural selection is the only way to evolve complex design features, evolutionary psychology focuses on understanding behaviors or cognitive modules as adaptations. Third, for most of our history, humans and hominids have lived in small groups as hunter-gatherers. Evolutionary psychologists believe that our evolved behavior may reflect or should be interpreted in terms of this hypothetical **environment of evolutionary adaptedness (EEA)**.

Evolutionary psychologists acknowledge that some behaviors, like some physical features, are the byproducts of other evolutionary forces and therefore should not be considered adaptations (musical ability is such a behavior, for example). Furthermore, although the EEA figures prominently in their interpretation of behavioral data, most evolutionary psychologists study the behavior of contemporary humans living in developed countries, via surveys, psychological experiments, and observations of people in day-to-day settings. They use such data to uncover the adaptations that characterized life in the EEA, whatever that may have been. Over the past decade the principles of evolutionary psychology have been elucidated by two of its main proponents, anthropologist John Tooby and psychologist Leda Cosmides (Barkow et al., 1992; Tooby and Cosmides, 2000).

Human Evolutionary (or Behavioral) Ecology   In contrast to evolutionary psychology, which focuses more on psychological experiments and surveys of people living in developed countries, **human evolutionary ecology** focuses on the ecological factors that influence reproductive success in the few remaining

evolutionary psychology
Approach to understanding the evolution of human behavior that emphasizes the selection of specific behavioral patterns in the context of the environment of evolutionary adaptedness.

environment of evolutionary adaptedness (EEA)   According to evolutionary psychologists, the critical period for understanding the selective forces that shape human behavior; exemplified by hunter-gatherer lifestyles of hominids before the advent of agriculture.

human evolutionary ecology
Approach to understanding the evolution of human behavior that attempts to explore ecological and demographic factors important in determining individual reproductive success and fitness in a cultural context.

hunter-gatherer populations. Among the groups studied most intensely have been the Yanomamö of Amazonia (Chagnon, 1988, 1997), the Aché of Paraguay (Hill and Hurtado, 1996), and the Hadza of Tanzania (Hawkes et al., 2001). Topics of interest to human evolutionary ecologists include the relationship between status and reproductive success, demographic effects of tribal warfare and aggression, and the underlying social impact of hunting and food sharing. Researchers use data on contemporary hunter-gatherer groups to refine models that purport to reconstruct the behavior of extinct hominids.

BEHAVIORAL PATTERNS AND EVOLUTION

Although we talk about investigating human *behavior*, in reality scientists study different human *behaviors*. Human behavioral phenomena can be observed at the individual, cultural, or even species-wide levels. Biological and evolutionary explanations of different behavioral patterns vary depending on the contexts in which those behaviors are expressed. But to understand the natural history of human behavior, it is important to remember the mosaic nature of its evolution. Just as different parts of the human body evolved at different points in our past, different aspects of human behavior may reflect different evolutionary periods.

Cognitive Universals   As a species we share many behaviors by virtue of our shared biology. These **cognitive universals** include behaviors studied by cognitive scientists, such as sensory processing, the basic emotions, consciousness, motor control, memory, and attention (Gazzaniga, et al 1998). Language also is typically included among the cognitive behaviors shared by all people. At a biological level, we share the neurological mechanisms underlying some of these cognitive universals with many other mammalian species. For example, much of what we know about the specifics of visual processing comes from experimental work on cats and monkeys. Other universals, such as language, clearly have emerged fully only in the hominid lineage (although we may study its biological antecedents by looking at other species).

Given the universal, and in many cases cross-species, expression of these cognitive processes, it is reasonable to assume they are biological adaptations that have been shaped by natural selection. Although cognitive universals have a basic common expression in all people, we often see variation in the way they are expressed. It is likely that this variation results from both environmental and genetic factors, in the same way, for example, that variation in stature arises within and between populations.

Cross-Cultural Universals   When we look across the diverse cultures of the world, it is easy to notice that many commonalities emerge, which can be called **cross-cultural universals** (Brown, 1991). For example, all cultures have a language. We also find that each culture develops rituals and traditions to mark and recognize status. They develop systems for identifying and naming kin. They organize social and occupational roles along sex and gender lines. Standards of sexual attractiveness and beauty may show common patterns across cultures. Many biological anthropologists argue that common cultural practices did not develop independently over and over again but rather reflect underlying genetic factors that are widely distributed in our species. If we cannot find a common cultural origin for a widespread behavioral pattern observed across cultures, then it is reasonable to hypothesize that the pattern may reflect a common biological origin. This is especially true if we find the behavior in a majority of human cultures or if we can show it to be associated with a common ecological variable. One way to look at this is that we are not "hardwired" to develop these behaviors but rather are "prewired" to express them given a proper ecological or cultural environment (Marcus, 2004).

cognitive universals Cognitive phenomena such as sensory processing, the basic emotions, consciousness, motor control, memory, and attention that are expressed by all normal individuals.

cross-cultural universals Behavioral phenomena, such as singing, dancing, and mental illness, that are found in almost all human cultures, but are not necessarily exhibited by each member of a cultural group.

Remember that cross-cultural universals are not individual universals. For example, we could say that singing and dancing are cross-cultural universals, but that does not mean that all members of every culture sing and dance. Similar forms of behavioral disease are found in different cultures, so in one sense we can say that mental illnesses are a cross-cultural universal, even if only a small proportion of the population develops these conditions.

Within-Culture Variation   Male and female mammals may adopt different sexual and reproductive strategies because of their differential investment in time and energy in each offspring. How has this mammalian pattern been rendered in a human cultural context? Do we see evidence that humans have evolved away from typical primate patterns? If so, how and why has this *within-culture variation* happened? Variation in behavior correlated with age may also have been shaped by evolutionary pressures. Is the young, risk-taking male a Western cultural construct or a cross-cultural phenomenon amenable to evolutionary theorizing? Although age and sex are the primary biological variables that figure into studies of the evolution of within-culture variation, we can study other aspects of within-culture variation from an evolutionary perspective.

Biological Constraints on Human Behavior   People are capable of doing just about anything, and any number of behaviors shaped by culture are not easily explained in a bioevolutionary context. On the other hand, when we look across cultures, there seem to be some *constraints* on what people do, which in turn lead to behavioral convergences across cultures. Unlike cross-cultural universals, behavioral convergences that arise from biological constraints are not the primary result of biological processes. A nonbehavioral example of a behavioral convergence is footwear. Footwear tends to converge on a similar basic shape, which is functionally constrained by the shape and action of the human foot. In a similar fashion, human behavior may be channeled into similar patterns by constraints imposed by our neurobiology. A basic issue in the evolution of behavior is determining whether any given behavior is an adaptation or simply the result of a biological constraint on behavior. Of course, similar debates arise about anatomical features as well.

TRADITIONAL LIVES IN EVOLUTIONARY ECOLOGICAL PERSPECTIVE

Over the past three decades human evolutionary ecologists have undertaken intensive study of several traditional cultures to better understand the interplay between biological and cultural factors in human behavior and human behavioral evolution. Studies of traditional hunter-gatherers and traditional agricultural cultures are important because their lifestyles reflect more closely the selective environments (the EEA) that shaped hominid evolution, until the advent of agriculture and large-scale societies starting about 10,000 years ago.

Evolutionary ecology represents a profound theoretical departure from traditional cultural anthropology. Investigating the complex interplay between behavior, culture, and ecology, evolutionary ecologists typically live for extended periods of time with the groups they are studying (as cultural anthropologists do) (Figure 18.2 on page 516). However, they differ from other cultural anthropologists, in their reliance on quantitative research methods, which are necessary to test evolutionary hypotheses.

QUANTIFICATION IN EVOLUTIONARY ECOLOGY RESEARCH

To rigorously test evolutionary hypotheses and to discover how ecological factors affect human behavior, evolutionary ecologists must collect quantifiable data. These data include birth, death, and marriage statistics (that is, demographic variables), nutritional data, and calculations of daily energy expenditure. Some evolutionary

FIGURE 18.2 Evolutionary ecologists live and do research in contemporary cultures that maintain all or some aspects of their traditional lifeways, such as these tribespeople from New Guinea.

ecologists use sophisticated mathematical models to try to understand human cultural behavior in an evolutionary context (Boyd and Richerson, 1988). Let's look at a couple of examples of quantitative research in human evolutionary ecology.

Wealth, Reproductive Success, and Survival   One of the basic tenets of human evolutionary ecology is that cultural success should be related to increased fitness (Irons, 1979). William Irons tested this hypothesis in a study of fertility and mortality among the tribal Turkmen of Iran. In this culture, wealth (in terms of money, jewelry, and consumable goods) is a primary measure of cultural success. Irons found that for men, fertility and survivorship were higher for the wealthier half of the population than for the poorer half (Figure 18.3); survivorship was significantly higher for the wealthier women, but there was no difference in fertility. He also found that male reproductive success was more variable among men than among women (that is, the difference between the richer and poorer halves was more pronounced for men than for women), as predicted by sexual selection theory.

Monique Borgerhoff Mulder (1987, 1990) looked at the relationship between wealth and reproductive success in a different population, the Kipsigis of Kenya

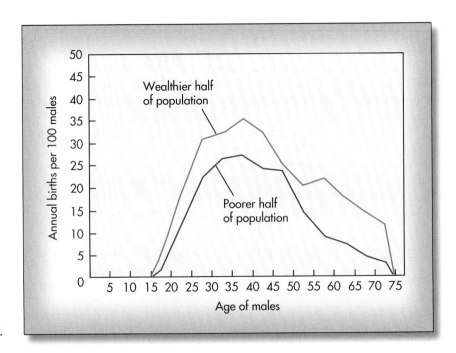

FIGURE 18.3 Male Turkmen in the wealthier half of the population had higher fertility rates than those in the poorer half.

FIGURE 18.4
The Kipsigis of Kenya.

(Figure 18.4). The Kipsigis are a pastoral people who moved into Kenya from northeastern Africa in the late eighteenth century. The wealth of a Kipsigis man is defined in terms of his land holdings, the number of animals he has, and his household possessions. Borgerhoff Mulder found that all these measures correlate strongly to amount of land owned, so she used that as her primary statistic of wealth.

The Kipsigis practice polygyny, which means that a man can have more than one wife at a time. When a man wants to marry a young woman, he approaches her parents with an offer of **bridewealth,** a payment that can equal up to a third of an average man's wealth. Borgerhoff Mulder looked at wealth and reproductive success among Kipsigis men in a series of different age groups and found a strong correlation between wealth and number of offspring. For example, in a group of forty-four men who were circumcised between 1922 and 1930 (circumcision marks coming of age), there was a very high correlation between number of offspring and acres of land owned (Figure 18.5). Ownership of 30 acres correlated to having fifteen to twenty surviving offspring, whereas men with 90 acres had twenty-five to thirty offspring. In

bridewealth   Payment offered by a man to the parents of a woman he wants to marry.

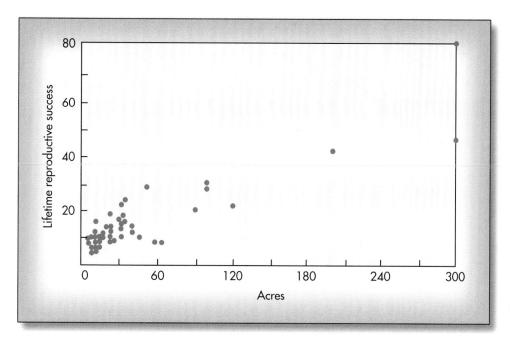

FIGURE 18.5   The relationship between number of acres a Kipsigis man owns and the number of offspring he has during his lifetime.

general, the fertility of the wives of richer and poorer men was approximately the same. Wealthier men have more children because they can have more wives, being able to afford more bridewealth payments. And although larger families may lead to increased wealth, Borgerhoff Mulder found no evidence that this was the causal direction: Wealthier men were able to afford large families, not the other way around.

The Turkmen and Kipsigis studies, and others done elsewhere, support the hypothesis that one measure of cultural success—wealth—correlates with reproductive success. However, this correlation does not generally hold for developed, urbanized, capitalist cultures, where higher socioeconomic status typically is not associated with a higher birth rate. This is an important example of the kind of fundamental biocultural change that can occur in a society when it transforms from an undeveloped to a developed economy.

Physiology and Ecology   Another method for quantifying the relationship between cultural and ecological factors in human behavior is to look at the way physiological measures vary across ecological contexts. For example, Peter Ellison (1990, 1994) developed a method of measuring levels of reproductive hormones in saliva as a noninvasive means to assess reproductive function in women living in diverse environments.

Progesterone is a steroid hormone produced by the corpus luteum and the placenta that prepares the uterus for pregnancy and helps maintain pregnancy once fertilization has occurred. Progesterone levels measured in saliva correlate with ovarian function. Ellison and his colleagues found that salivary progesterone levels are strongly correlated with age over the course of a woman's reproductive life (between about ages 15 and 50 years). Progesterone levels increase from a baseline level at the end of puberty, peaking between 25 and 30 years of age and dropping off thereafter. Ellison suggests that ovarian function matures at approximately the same age as the pelvis becomes structurally mature (early to mid-20s).

Studies among two traditional agricultural groups, the Lese of Zaire and the Tamang of Nepal, and women from the Boston area showed that the basic age-dependent curve of salivary progesterone production was the same in all three populations (Figure 18.6). Ellison believes that this pattern probably represents a fundamental feature of human reproductive physiology. This discovery refines our view of the female reproductive years as an evolved life history stage (beginning at menarche and ending at menopause).

progesterone   A steroid hormone produced by the corpus luteum and the placenta, which prepares the uterus for pregnancy and helps maintain pregnancy once fertilization has occurred.

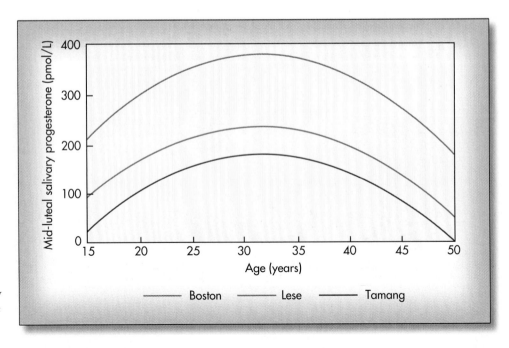

FIGURE 18.6   The age-dependent curve of salivary progesterone levels in three populations.

Although the shapes of the progesterone-versus-age curves were the same in Boston, Lese, and Tamang women, the amount of progesterone produced varied among the groups. Boston women, who presumably had the most nutritionally rich environment with few infectious diseases, had higher progesterone levels at every age than the other two populations. Ellison suggests that chronic stress that delays growth and maturation, such as nutritional deficiencies, could lead to lower levels of ovarian function throughout the lifetime. Such a stress-response relationship could be adaptive because in a stressful environment it may be better to devote more effort and energy to body maintenance and survival rather than reproduction.

HUNTING, GATHERING, AND THE SEXUAL DIVISION OF LABOR

Recent research on contemporary hunter-gatherer groups has revolutionized our knowledge of how people without agriculture acquire the food they eat and how hunting and gathering patterns in hominids may have evolved. It has become increasingly clear that earlier speculations (Lee and DeVore, 1968) were based on inadequate understanding of hunter-gatherer lifeways. The concept of "man the hunter, women the gatherer" (Box 18.1 on page 520) reflects a division of labor between the sexes in all human cultures, but it is all too easy to turn it into a simplistic, stereotypical picture of evolved, hardwired gender roles (Bird, 1999; Panter-Brick, 2002). Furthermore, observing sex differences in food acquisition practices is not the same as explaining why they exist.

In almost every traditional foraging culture, both men and women devote a substantial portion of their time and energy to the search for and acquisition of food. And in almost every culture, despite the fact that they live in the same environment, men and women exploit different aspects of that environment when acquiring food, leading to a pronounced sexual division of labor. For example, among the aboriginal peoples of Mer Island in the Coral Sea, both men and women forage for food on the coral reef. Men concentrate on using large spears to kill large fish swimming around the edges of the reef while women walk the dry part of the reef, collecting shellfish or catching small fish or octopus with small spears (Figure 18.7). Women almost always succeed in bringing home a reasonable amount of food, whereas the men have much more variable success (Bird, 1999). In the Hadza of Tanzania, men concentrate on large game hunting while women focus almost exclusively on foraging for berries, nuts, fruits, and roots (O'Connell et al., 1992; Hawkes et al., 1997).

There are several models for the origins of the sexual division of labor. The *cooperative provisioning model,* based on the study of monogamous birds, predicts that the sexual division of labor occurred as a result of the evolution of monogamous

FIGURE 18.7 The evolutionary significance of "Man the Hunter" (or in this instance "Man the Fisher") has been debated for decades.

Box 18.1   "Man the Hunter"

In 1966 about fifty anthropologists who studied the lifeways of traditional foraging people gathered in Chicago for a conference to examine the status of the world's hunter-gatherers. Perhaps the foremost scientific conclusion that came out of the meeting was that the importance of meat in the diets of foraging people had been exaggerated. This was deeply ironic because the most influential and ultimately notorious perspective to emerge from the meeting came to be known as "Man the Hunter."

Sherwood Washburn and Chet Lancaster contributed to the conference a paper called "The Evolution of Hunting." It set out to explain how and why the human brain had experienced a 3.5-fold increase in size and complexity since the dawn of humanity. Washburn and Lancaster claimed that "our intellect, interests, emotions, and basic social life—all are evolutionary products of the success of the hunting adaptation." They were referring mainly to our more recent human ancestors in the Pleistocene. In their view, hunting for game animals was the soul of the human experience. However, they noted that the sexes had different roles in many traditional societies when it comes to acquiring meat. According to Washburn and Lancaster, men hunt while women gather. This view put men in the important role of obtaining the highest-quality nutrients and the calories that their households would use.

Hunting requires communication and coordination of action between the hunters.

According to Washburn and Lancaster this placed an evolutionary premium on intelligence and communicative ability in order to successfully track and hunt down potentially dangerous prey. Moreover, Washburn and Lancaster linked the deep human love of hunting to the equally deep human love of going to war and to acts of aggression in general. That it is almost always males who commit these acts reinforced the idea that men—rather than women—occupied the role of clever-minded forager, meat provider, and conqueror in human societies. Ever since, many theories of human evolution have focused on male activities rather than female as the core human adaptations.

The eventual response to Washburn and Lancaster's "Man the Hunter" model was angry and its impact long-lasting. Many anthropologists were angered by the suggestion that a hallmark in our ancestry was affected by natural selection for male cognitive abilities, implying that women were merely carried along in some genetic linkage. Anthropologists Adrienne Zihlmann and Nancy Tanner pointed out that in some of the traditional societies most vaunted for the man's role in hunting, up to 85% of the protein obtained by a household came not from men at all but from women performing the less glamorous role of gathering foods such as nuts, tubers, and small animals. The role of human females had been neglected in "Man the Hunter," according to its critics, because

of the gender politics of scientific advances and the failure to appreciate the role of women in foraging.

The influence of the backlash to "Man the Hunter" permeates all fields of anthropology. In the study of nonhuman primates, it contributed to a reappraisal of the way in which the field was practiced. Observers had always tended to focus more on the behavior of males than females because they are often bolder and therefore more visible. The practice of observational primatology was made more systematic when it was recognized that females also played a central role in the primate group. More recent theoretical advances made it clear that females rather than males often are the central players around whom the mating system is structured. This backlash led eventually to an engendering of the field of archaeology; it was recognized that the role of women in early human societies had long been ignored in favor of the often more visible role of men. Stone tools made for butchering carcasses persist in the fossil record, whereas the implements of gathering made and used by women might not. Women nevertheless perform critical tasks and occupy spheres of influence in antiquity that go far beyond where the largely male archaeological community had considered them for decades. Archaeologists today refer to the failure of an earlier generation of scholars to consider the role of women as a Paleolithic glass ceiling.

relationships, because it would allow the pair to more fully exploit the environment if they did not compete with each other for resources (see discussion of Lovejoy's model in Chapter 11). An alternative model, the *conflict model*, suggests that hominid males and females were already exploiting the environment in fundamentally different ways before males began contributing energy and resources to females and their young (Bird, 1999). The "sexual division of labor" is not really a division but reflects the fact that males and females have different problems to overcome (conflicts) in the course of mating, reproduction, and parenting.

It is nonsensical to ask whether hunting or gathering is more important. Neither provides more energy than the other on a regular basis. The productivity of hunting and gathering varies by season, environment, and a host of other factors (Kaplan et al., 2000). Women and men do vary in the *package size* of the food they focus on acquiring. Women concentrate on small foodstuffs that tend to be predictable, immobile, and obtainable while caring for infants and young children. Even though she almost always receives assistance from others, including female relatives and the father of her children, an individual woman is responsible primarily for feeding herself and her children.

Men concentrate on obtaining foods in large sizes that they cannot consume at once by themselves and that they redistribute to families or the larger social group. These foods almost always come in the form of dead animals, which may be obtained by hunting, trapping, fishing, or even scavenging. In some Melanesian societies, however, men compete to grow the largest yams, which, although they are too fibrous to eat, can be distributed and used for propagation of new plants (Weiner, 1988). Big yams aside, animals provide protein and fat in quantities not available from any other source, and animal food is almost always highly prized in human cultures. As Hilliard Kaplan and colleagues (2000, p. 174) state, "The primary activity for adult males is hunting to provide nutrients for others. . . . [Hunting] is a fundamental feature of the human life-history adaptation." But why do males provide nutrients for others?

Why Do Men Hunt and Share Meat?   As we discussed in Chapter 11, male co-operative hunting and meat sharing, which we see in chimpanzees, may have a long history in hominid evolution. As hominids became more adept at hunting larger game that could not be butchered, transported, or consumed by a single individual, meat sharing could become a central component of human culture. A fascinating aspect of big game hunting in many cultures is that the hunter or hunters most responsible for the catch may have little to say about how the meat is distributed. Research among the Hadza in Tanzania shows that a successful hunter may not even be able to recoup his losses via reciprocal altruism later (Hawkes et al., 2001).

The *tolerated theft model* of hunting and meat sharing explains meat sharing in part by suggesting that defending a large kill takes more energy than it is worth; in other words, it may pay off in the long run to tolerate the "theft" of meat (that is, sharing) rather than to work hard to defend a kill (which may be too large for a single individual to consume). The reward for hunting would come not from the meat itself but from the increase in social status and prestige, which reflects on family members as well (Figure 18.8). In effect then, large animal hunting becomes

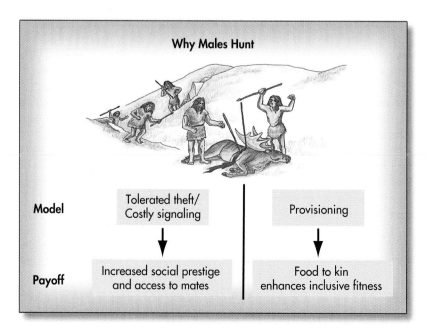

FIGURE 18.8   Models for the evolution of hunting by males.

a form of *costly signaling* (Bird, 1999), which ultimately increases the opportunities for males to acquire new mates. In the tolerated theft model, large game hunting did not evolve primarily as a means of paternal provisioning, although females and their young definitely benefit from males' hunting activity.

Critics of the tolerated theft or costly signaling model argue that because most of the food that is shared after a hunt goes to close kin or reproductive partners, sharing enhances the fitness of the male hunter and therefore should be considered an adaptation (Hill and Kaplan, 1993); they suggest that the provisioning itself, not the costly signaling, is the fitness-enhancing aspect of the behavior. Kaplan and colleagues (2000) propose that hunting and meat sharing intensified in hominid evolution in the context of a pair bond and paternal investment in the young. Part of their evidence for this hypothesis is that reproductive-age women in hunter-gatherer populations almost always receive nutritional support from men. Because most of that support comes in the form of animals that have been hunted, and such altruistic behavior is much more likely to have evolved in the context of provisioning kin, paternal investment via hunting may be an adaptation, not simply a secondary result of hunting for social prestige.

In the costly signaling model, hunting by men and meat sharing evolved in the context of sexual selection. Hunting itself is not seen as a critical behavior in hominid evolution, and nutritional benefits to children may be an incidental outcome of the process (Bird, 1999). In contrast, advocates of the provisioning model give hunting and meat sharing a central role in hominid evolution: They argue that it was a prime impetus in the evolution of a larger brain and increased longevity (Kaplan et al., 2000). Studies of the Aché in Paraguay show that hunters do not achieve peak hunting proficiency until they are in their 40s (Walker et al., 2002).

Resolution of the debate about why men hunt—for mates and prestige, as Kristen Hawkes, Rebecca Bird, and others argue, or to provision, as Hilliard Kaplan, Kim Hill, and their colleagues suggest—will require further study. Unfortunately, the limited number of cultures that still practice a hunter-gather lifestyle (mostly in marginal environments) may make obtaining new data on the issue difficult. Obviously there is merit to both views, but they cannot both be correct because they posit divergent views on the importance of hunting in hominid evolution.

SEXUAL SELECTION AND HUMAN BEHAVIOR

The study of human sexual behavior has been revolutionized over the past 25 years by the development of an evolutionary perspective on human reproductive strategies, sex and gender differences in behavior, and cross-cultural patterns of attractiveness and mate selection (Symons, 1979; Fisher, 1992; Buss, 2003). This evolutionary perspective is based in large part on the fact that humans are mammals. Male and female mammals vary profoundly in their energetic investment in producing offspring. Female mammals provide not only eggs but also a body in which fetal growth takes place. After birth, they are obligated to provide milk and care for offspring until the age of weaning. Males are obligated to provide sperm at the time of conception, and that is all. Subsequent investment, which can take the form of provisioning a pregnant or lactating female or providing food for the young, is not required, and in many species, including most primate species, males do not directly participate or invest in rearing of young.

Mammalian males and females also vary in their reproductive potential. The energetic costs of gestation and lactation limit a female mammal's reproductive potential; she can only have a limited number of offspring in her lifetime. On the other hand, sperm production does not impose much of a limit on a male mammal's reproductive potential. Given their potential energetic investment in reproduction, we would expect mammalian females to be choosier when selecting mates than males. Males should also be choosy, but if they are successful in impregnat-

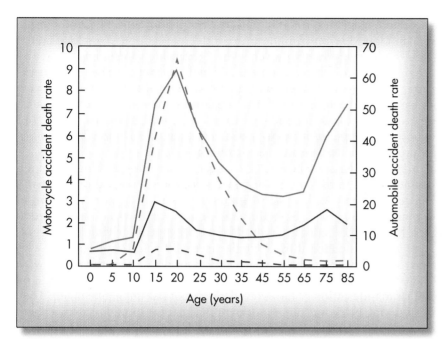

FIGURE 18.9 Risk of death from motorcycle accidents (dashed lines) and passenger car accidents (solid lines) per 100,000 US population during 1980-1986 for males (green lines) and females (maroon lines).

ing a large number of females, choosing a specific, high-quality mate is less of an issue. In general, mammalian males compete for access to females, and mammalian females should choose high-quality males, however that is defined. We can also expect males to vary more in their reproductive success than females. For example, there may be a large number of males that never reproduce, whereas almost every female will find a reproductive partner.

Research on human mate selection and standards of attractiveness in different cultures indicate that women tend to value resource-providing ability in their partners, whereas men tend to value youth and appearance (indicators of reproductive potential) in their potential partners (Buss, 2003). These observations are consistent with predictions derived from mammalian evolutionary biology. Of course, these are statistical patterns generated from surveys of large numbers of individuals. Obviously, different cultures define sexual attractiveness differently, and there is much individual variation in sexual preferences. Nonetheless, according to many evolutionary researchers, the statistical patterns of sexual behavior that are observed across cultures are not easily explained by cultural convergence. Instead, they may reflect underlying behavioral trends that have been shaped by natural selection.

RISK-TAKING BEHAVIOR

When we look across human cultures, we find that as a group young adult males (ages 15–29) have the highest death rates from accidents or violence (Figure 18.9). For example, death rates in motor vehicle accidents for 20-year-old Americans are three to four times higher in men than women (Hill and Chow, 2002). Young males do not die from accidents more often because they are unlucky but because they are more likely to put themselves in risky situations (Figure 18.10). Proclivity toward risk-taking behavior in males may reflect a significant sex difference in human behavior, which may have a long evolutionary history (Low, 2000).

Why should males engage in risk-taking behavior more than females? Bobbi Low (2000) argues that the reason goes back to general sex differences in mammalian biology. For a female mammal, the costs associated with risk-taking behavior are unlikely to outweigh the benefits. She is likely to be able to find mates and fulfill her reproductive potential throughout her lifetime, so she has no

FIGURE 18.10 Risk-taking behavior by young males.

particular need to engage in risk-taking behavior to acquire mates. On the other hand, male mammals vary much more in reproductive success. A male mammal may engage in high-risk, potentially very costly (even life-threatening) activities because such behaviors could have a potentially high reproductive benefit. For example, aggressive behavior between male mammals over access to females is very common; it has clearly been selected for in the context of sexual access to mates. Females may also find risk-taking in males to be attractive because they may consider it a manifestation of ambition or "good genes" or a proxy for the ability to provide resources for the female and her offspring.

Elizabeth Hill and Krista Chow (2002) suggest that risky or binge drinking may also be understood in the context of sexual selection for risk-taking behavior. First, among college-age people, risky drinking is about 50% more common in men than women (48% versus 33%, although figures vary depending on criteria for defining a binge), and males are more likely to engage in driving after drinking. The peak age for alcohol abuse in males is 15–29 years. College men who were not married were twice as likely to engage in binge drinking as those who were married. These aspects of risky drinking in young men suggest to Hill and Chow that it is another manifestation of the evolved pattern of risk-taking behavior. They argue that risk-taking behaviors are not deviant but that we should recognize them as an evolved response to environmental instability. With specific reference to risky drinking at the individual level, Hill and Chow suggest that dealing with instability in the person's family or work life may be one avenue of therapy or treatment for alcohol abuse.

INBREEDING AVOIDANCE AND INCEST TABOOS

Evolutionary factors may have played an important role in shaping not only mate choice preferences but also mate choice aversions. Inbreeding is defined as reproduction between close relatives. Close inbreeding has two major biological costs. First, a highly inbred population or species loses genetic variability over time. This means that when environments or other selective forces change, the population does not have the variability to respond to these changes via natural selection. Second, when close relatives interbreed, it increases the likelihood that lethal or debilitating recessive alleles will be expressed. Because relatives share a high percentage of their alleles, there is a good chance they will both possess a lethal recessive that may be passed on to their offspring. Studies of a wide range of mammal species have demonstrated that inbred individuals suffer from greater mortality or loss of fitness, a phenomenon known as **inbreeding depression**, relative to less inbred individuals in the same species (Mettler et al., 1988). Studies of inbreeding in humans clearly demonstrate the potentially harmful effects of reproduction between first-degree relatives (such as father and daughter or sister and brother) and between relatives who share 25% of their alleles (such as uncle and niece or grandparent and grandchild). Offspring of first-degree relatives (who share 50% of alleles) are far more likely than other children to be stillborn or to die within the first year of life, and physical and mental abnormalities are much more common among them.

Only a very small proportion of all human births are the result of matings between first-degree relatives. Sexual contact between close relatives is rare, and the proportion of those contacts in which pregnancy could occur (in which both parties are sexually mature and sexual intercourse takes place) is also very small (Van den Berghe, 1983). Across the world's cultures, 2–3% allow matings between close relatives, but this is usually only among elites, and it has the primary goal of consolidating resources or political power.

Inbreeding Avoidance and Incest Rules   All human cultures have rules and traditions that regulate sexual contact and reproductive relationships. **Incest** is any violation of such rules by members of a kin group. *Incest rules* are sometimes explicit

inbreeding depression   Lesser fitness of offspring of closely related individuals compared with the fitness of the offspring of less closely related individuals, caused largely by the expression of lethal or debilitating recessive alleles.

incest   A violation of cultural rules regulating mating behavior.

(stated in legal or customary form) and sometimes implicit (followed but not overtly stated or codified). Definitions of kin vary from culture to culture and do not always closely follow biological patterns of relatedness. For example, in American culture, sexual contact between stepparents and stepchildren is generally regarded as being incestuous, although from a biological standpoint a pregnancy that resulted from such a mating would not constitute inbreeding.

Both cultural and biological scientists agree on the universality of cultural rules governing sexual relations between close kin—the *incest taboo*—but they differ on why it exists. For many years, Freudian ideas dominated cultural explanations of the incest taboo: Incest rules were necessary to prevent people from acting on their "natural" desire to commit incest. The evidence that people innately desire to commit incest is very slight, and the Freudian viewpoint, despite its historical popularity, has little cross-cultural, empirical support (Thornhill, 1991). Biological theories of inbreeding avoidance have focused on the fact that mechanisms that encourage outbreeding should be selected for; the cross-cultural universality of the incest taboo (which is essentially a mechanism for outbreeding) is taken to be evidence that such an adaptive mechanism may be present in the human species as a whole.

A basic social science criticism of the biological evolutionary view of inbreeding avoidance asks, Why do cultures make laws against it? If it is biological, the argument goes, then there should be no need to have cultural laws or institutions to prevent it. Nancy Thornhill's (1991) analysis of incest rules suggests that most of them are more concerned with regulating sexual (and economic and power) relationships between more distantly related kin; incest taboos among close relatives are more likely to be implicit than explicit. Thus the assumption that most cultures regulate inbreeding between close relatives using explicit cultural rules is unfounded.

Brother-Sister Inbreeding and the Westermarck Hypothesis Finnish anthropologist Edvard Westermarck (1891) long ago suggested, in what became known as the *Westermarck hypothesis,* that siblings raised together develop an aversion to seeing each other as reproductive partners when they are adults. In order for the aversion to develop, siblings must be in proximity to one another during a *critical period,* usually thought to encompass the first 5 years of life. The psychological mechanism governing this aversion may be an adaptation because it was probably selected for as a mechanism to promote outbreeding.

Evidence for the Westermarck hypothesis comes from a variety of sources, including some natural experiments. In the the mid-twentieth century, the *kibbutz* movement in Israel led to the establishment of numerous small, independent communities dedicated to socialist and egalitarian principles. Similarly aged boys and girls were raised communally in "children's houses" in some of these kibbutzim (Shepher, 1983) (Figure 18.11). In his groundbreaking study, anthropologist Joseph Shepher found that of 2,769 marriages between children raised in kibbutzim, only 14 united couples who had been reared in the same children's house. Shepher interpreted these results as strong evidence for the Westermarck hypothesis. The child-rearing arrangement in the kibbutz "fooled" biology (and the psychological mechanism leading to sexual aversion) by bringing unrelated children into close proximity with one another during the critical period. In usual circumstances, children raised in close proximity to one another are close relatives, and there should be strong selection pressures against them mating with one another. Thus kibbutz children raised in the same children's house saw each other as siblings and did not see their housemates as potential spouses.

Similar evidence supporting the Westermarck hypothesis has been obtained from the study of *sim-pua* marriages in Taiwan (Wolf, 1966, 1970). Sim-pua is a form of arranged marriage whereby a girl is adopted into a household at a young age and then later expected to marry a biological son of the same family when

FIGURE 18.11 Children in a kibbutz.

motherese (infant-directed speech) Emotive spoken language used by mothers and other adults when addressing prelinguistic babies and children.

they are older. These marriages were found to have much higher rates of divorce and lower numbers of offspring than non–sim-pua marriages. Anthropologist Arthur Wolf, who conducted the research, suggests that these marriages often failed because of a sexual aversion that developed between the adopted sister and her brother/groom who were raised in close proximity during the critical period.

The Westermarck hypothesis is supported by evidence from these diverse natural experiments and is based on a strong theoretical foundation in the context of the biological costs of close inbreeding. It applies only to sibling inbreeding avoidance, of course. Clearly, different biological or cultural mechanisms would have to regulate intergenerational inbreeding avoidance.

LANGUAGE-RELATED CROSS-CULTURAL BEHAVIORS

In Chapter 16 we discussed the evolution of language, a behavior (in a very large sense) that almost all scientists agree is a biological universal in our species. It is not surprising that something as pervasive and essential as language has multiple effects on several aspects of human behavior (Box 18.2). Many anthropologists believe that language is what makes human culture possible. Indeed, when we look at the central place of language in defining a specific culture, we could argue that cultural diversity is inevitable given that languages themselves evolve and diverge. And yet, even beyond the basic biology and structure of language, cross-cultural patterns emerge that we can best explain from a broader evolutionary perspective.

MOTHERESE OR INFANT-DIRECTED SPEECH

Human infants are remarkably proficient at acquiring language. If they are placed in an environment where language is used, they will pass through a series of stages that, typically by the age of 3 years, result in a fully linguistically competent human being (Pinker, 1994). *Language development* entails training of both the mind and the body: the body to produce sounds and the mind to put them in the correct order to produce language. A critical stage in language development in babies is *babbling*. Starting at about 7–8 months of age, babies start to say syllables such as *ba-ba* or *da-da*. This is the beginning of the production of spoken language. Even babies who are born deaf babble as they learn sign language (Petitto and Marentette, 1991) (Figure 18.12). The difference is that they babble with their hands.

The stages of language development that babies go through form a kind of cross-cultural behavioral universal. But language development is so clearly biologically hardwired, and babies have so little cultural exposure, that it does not make much sense to think of it in terms of cross-cultural universals. In contrast, the way adults talk to babies seems to be much more of a culturally influenced behavior.

As we look at how adults talk to babies in different cultures with very different languages, we find striking similarities in their use of **motherese** or **infant-directed speech** (Ferguson, 1964; Fernald et al., 1989). Compared with adult-directed speech, speech directed at infants tends to be slower, higher-pitched, and more repetitive, with shorter utterances and longer pauses. Most of us are familiar with what "baby-talk" sounds like; it tends to sound the same in a wide variety of languages (Figure 18.13 on page 528). In fact, one study has shown that native English-speaking mothers could differentiate between adult- and infant-directed Hindi language song excerpts with much greater success than chance suggests (Trehub et al., 1993).

Although motherese is not universal, it is widespread and found in diverse cultures that do not share a recent common origin. One idea about motherese is that

FIGURE 18.12 A deaf baby attempting to sign.

Box 18.2 Reading, Writing, and Evolution

Reading and writing are *not* human cross-cultural universals. After all, most traditional cultures do not or did not have writing systems. The invention of writing, which has occurred several times in diverse locations, is recent; even the oldest writing systems are only a few thousand years old. We did not evolve to read and write, although it is quite clear that almost all people, no matter what their particular cultural or biological heritage, are capable of learning these skills.

The ability to learn to read is clearly part of our shared biological heritage, even if it is not a biologically evolved behavior. Neuroscientist Stanislas Dehaene (2003) believes that although our brains have not been shaped by evolution specifically to read, our brains have shaped the writing systems that cultures develop: "I suggest that writing systems themselves were subjected to selective pressure and had to evolve within constraints fixed by our primate visual system" (p. 33).

Dehaene points out that our brains are truly adept at reading. For example, we recognize that EVOLUTION, *evolution*, evolution, eVoLuTiOn, and e v o l u t i o n are all the same word, despite their varied appearances. On the other hand, we also easily recognize that subtle differences, such as that between "but" and "butt," can signal profound differences in meaning. Of course, reading piggybacks on spoken language, whose neural basis has been shaped by natural selection. Neuroimaging research by Dehaene and his col-

FIGURE A Chinese characters.

leagues (Dehaene et al., 1997; Dehaene, 2003) indicates that many parts of our brain are activated by reading. However, a part of the cortex of the left temporal lobe, located near the boundary of the occipital lobe, is invariably activated during reading in all individuals. Furthermore, no matter what the language, whether it uses an alphabet-based writing system, as in English, or a character-based system, such as Japanese Kanji, activation in this region occurs not only during the reading of actual words but also during the recognition of wordlike sequences of letters. As children learn to read, activation in this region increases, whereas adults with *dyslexia* show reduced levels of activation.

In primates, this "reading region" is devoted almost exclusively to visual recognition, especially of complex visual forms. Although part of the temporal lobe, the region is located close to the occipital lobe, which is concerned primarily with visual processing. In humans, the reading region seems to be adapted primarily to identifying objects based on their shape, no matter what their size or orientation (Dehaene, 2003). For example, even without specific training, it is not hard to recognize letters that are upside down (a skill many of us discover while sitting across the desk of a supervisor). Children often have difficulty distinguishing the letters *p, q, d,* and *b.* Given that the reading region may be concerned primarily with shape, this is not too surprising. All these letters have the same shape, varying only in their orientation in space. The development of reading behavior specifically entails training and refining the shape recognition ability associated with this small part of the temporal lobe. It is interesting that this region is not a classic spoken language area, although the left lateralization of activation follows the spoken language pattern.

Dehaene proposes that our brain biology constrains the cultural expression of human writing systems and that it should be possible to identify features common to all writing systems (Figure A). Although written Chinese and English are profoundly different in some ways, from a neurobiological perspective they obviously share some basic similarities as well.

it is not directly related to teaching language but instead strengthens the emotional bond between mother and infant (Fernald, 1992). Compared with adult-directed speech, infant-directed speech is less emotionally inhibited; more emotional forms of adult-directed speech more closely resemble infant-directed speech (Trainor et al., 2000). There can be no doubt that babies do not understand the words in baby-talk, but it clearly provokes some response or adults would not persist with it. Anne Fernald argues that motherese helps establish emotional communication between the mother and infant before the development of verbal language. As we learned in Chapter 8, the mother-infant relationship is the fundamental relationship in primate societies, and it is based in part on the development of a strong emotional bond between mother and child. Motherese may serve as an

FIGURE 18.13 Motherese may be just one of many ways the emotional bond between mother and child is reinforced.

adaptation to facilitate the emotional development of the mother-infant bond, which is expressed through the mother's spoken language.

BASIC COLOR TERMS

A trip to the paint store or a glance at a large box of crayons could lead you to believe that there is an almost unlimited number of color names. But if we look beyond the "peach parfaits" and "iceberg whites" of the world, we see that we can limit the number of *basic color terms* to a much smaller number. Anthropological linguists Brent Berlin and Paul Kay published a groundbreaking study in 1969 in which they analyzed color terms used by native informants speaking a wide range of languages and found significant constraints on the ways in which languages identify color (color term data on more than 100 languages are now available [Kay and Berlin, 1997]).

Berlin and Kay defined basic color terms as single words used to describe colors that can be applied to a wide range of objects, that are widely known within a culture, and that are not subsumed into a more inclusive color category (for example, *green* is a basic color term but *lime* is not). Berlin and Kay did not find that the actual words used to describe colors are similar cross-culturally; rather, the naming of colors appears to follow a systematic and perhaps evolved pattern. In cultures that identify only two *focal colors*, or colors that exemplify the basic color categories, these always correspond to black and white (light and dark). In cultures that have three color terms, the named colors are always black, white, and red. In cultures with four terms, the colors are black, white, red, and blue/green/yellow. Above four color terms, patterns are still evident, although they are more variable and complex. The cross-cultural distribution of color terms suggests a cultural evolutionary scenario for developing color terms: The black versus white distinction came first, followed by the addition of red and then other colors.

English has eleven focal colors: black, white, red, yellow, green, blue, brown, purple, pink, orange, and gray. In contrast, the Dani of New Guinea recognize only two colors: *mola* for bright, warm colors and *mili* for dark colors (Figure 18.14). Although these are the only two color terms that the Dani use, the color terms themselves do not constrain the Dani perception of the variety of colors in the world. In a series of studies, psychologist Eleanor Rosch (Heider) found that Dani people have no trouble remembering or differentiating between colors or hues for which they have no name (Heider 1972).

English Color Terms	Dani Color Terms
black	
white	
red	
yellow	*mili*
green	
blue	
brown	*mola*
purple	
pink	
orange	
gray	

FIGURE 18.14 English and Dani basic color terms.

Color naming patterns probably are constrained by factors related to the physiology of color vision and perception, although there is much debate about how the physiology of color vision is converted into the psychology of color naming (Dedrick, 1996). Color vision is extremely important to anthropoid primates, including human beings, and our color vision system reflects a long evolutionary history; it comes as no surprise that cultural color naming behaviors might be strongly influenced by this adaptation to the environment. Since 1969, a vast amount of research has been done on color naming, and the cross-cultural sequence of acquiring color terms probably is more complicated than outlined above especially as we get beyond four color terms. Nonetheless, given the infinite number of colors and names that human perception and language could generate, there can be little doubt that this cultural behavior is constrained by some aspect of our perceptual biology.

BEHAVIORAL DISEASE

We once thought mental illnesses and behavioral diseases were limited to "civilized" cultures (Allen, 1997). However, studies of the cross-cultural distribution of mental illness show that many behavioral diseases are expressed in much the same way in different cultures (Murphy, 1976) (Figure 18.15). In modern biological psychiatry, we consider mental illnesses to result primarily from the interaction of genetic predispositions and environmental factors. Because many genetically influenced behavioral disorders are common, and we cannot explain their prevalence by mutation rate or environmental factors alone, it is reasonable to explore the evolutionary factors that may underlie their distribution. Note that this does *not* mean we should necessarily consider the behavioral diseases themselves to be adaptive, but rather that we may better understand them in the context of behavioral phenotypes shaped by natural selection.

DEPRESSION AND NATURAL SELECTION

Psychiatrists define *mood* as a persistent emotional state. Over the course of a lifetime, all people go through periods of high or low mood. Changes in mood in response to the environment or particular events are only natural. For example, low mood, or *minor depression*, is a perfectly reasonable response to an unhappy event, such as the death of a loved one. On the other hand, when depression gets out of hand and strongly affects a person's ability to function or care for himself or herself, then it is clearly not an adaptive behavioral phenotype. Psychiatrists say that

FIGURE 18.15 A Yoruban with a psychotic disorder.

FIGURE 18.16   Grieving behavior can have common expressions in different cultures.

a person has *major depression* if he or she suffers from 2 or more weeks of depressed mood or impaired enjoyment, disturbed sleep and appetite, psychomotor changes (such as restlessness or feeling slowed down), reduced concentration, excessive guilt, or suicidal thoughts or actions (American Psychiatric Association, 1994). Major depression is surprisingly common, with about 16.2% of Americans suffering from it at some point in their lives (Kessler et al., 2003).

Why is major depression so common? In its severe form, depression is clearly not adaptive because it not only leads to increased mortality via suicide but also diminishes a person's ability to respond to all kinds of environmental and social stimuli. The genetics underlying mood are undoubtedly complex, but many studies have shown that there is a genetic component to developing major depression, and two specific alleles have been identified (Caspi et al., 2003; Zubenko et al., 2002). The alleles that cause some people to become clinically depressed have an additive effect, exacerbating a normal tendency toward developing (minor) depression that all people share. It is likely that, as with other phenotypes influenced by multiple genes (such as stature), there is a normal distribution in the expression of mood, with people at one extreme suffering from major depression.

Minor Depression as an Adaptation   Evolutionary psychiatrist Randolph Nesse (2000) suggests that, in general, minor depression, or low mood, is a psychological and physiological mechanism that regulates our behavior when we are placed in any situation that might constitute an adaptive challenge. Minor depression is common because decreased motivation or activity is beneficial in many situations. For example, over the course of hominid evolution, the loss of a loved one probably signaled a number of things: a dangerous situation, loss of information, loss of a contributing member to the community or family, and loss of future contributors to the community (in the case of children). Whatever the particular situation, temporary low mood would encourage the surviving individuals to disengage from activity in the short term, allowing them to establish new goals and directions (Figure 18.16).

Major depression is increasing in developed countries and becoming a larger health problem. Why? Nesse suggests that another possible adaptive function of low mood is to dissuade people from wasting energy in the pursuit of unreachable goals. Most people living in hierarchical societies (in which resources and power are not distributed equally) face an ongoing conflict between their knowledge of a more prosperous life and their inability to achieve it. According to Nesse, the contemporary media culture exacerbates this conflict by presenting a range of unachievable goals while promoting the pursuit of such goals as a cultural ideal.

In the environments in which it evolved, low mood is a short-term adaptation to a transient challenge; once the challenge or event is over, mood improves. However, in contemporary urbanized societies, people live in an environment in which challenges to status or goal achievement are ongoing, encouraging the development of persistent low mood. This persistent low mood can slip into major depression in genetically susceptible individuals.

Of course, Nesse's hypothesis on the adaptive nature of depression is speculative. However, we know that mood is important in all social primates: Whether or not we want to say they are "happy" or "sad," it is clear that we can see social primates exhibiting high or low mood (Chapter 8). Mood has been shaped by millions of years of evolution in a social context. Thus socio-cultural factors, such as the development of a media culture, may indeed be playing a role in the expression of mood and the increased development of major depression.

SCHIZOPHRENIA

Schizophrenia is the chronic brain disease most typically associated with cultural notions of "crazy" behavior or "insanity." It is found in almost all human cultures, with a lifetime prevalence typically estimated to be somewhere between 0.5% and 1.0% (Jablonsky et al., 1992). Although that percentage seems low, it translates into nearly 3 million people with schizophrenia in the United States alone. Schizophrenia is characterized by several symptoms, including delusions (often of a paranoid nature), auditory hallucinations, disorganized speech, grossly disorganized or catatonic behavior, and negative symptoms, which are characterized by emotional flattening, not talking, or not moving (American Psychiatric Association, 1994). Age of onset typically is the late teens into the twenties (usually a bit later in females than males), and the course of illness is highly variable.

Schizophrenia is clearly a genetic disease. Evidence of its origin comes from a variety of sources; among them is the fact that a family history of schizophrenia is associated with a much higher risk of developing the disease. However, concordance rates for identical twins tend to be no higher than 50% (Gottesman and Shields, 1982), indicating that some people carry the alleles that predispose development of schizophrenia but do not develop the illness.

Why Is Schizophrenia So Common? The basic evolutionary question about schizophrenia is, Why is it so common? The estimated prevalence rate of 1% is much higher than can be maintained via mutation rate alone, whether schizophrenia is caused by the effect of a single major allele or of multiple alleles. In addition, numerous studies conducted over the past century have shown that people with schizophrenia, particularly males, have reduced fertility and fitness (Nimgaonkar et al., 1997). This is not surprising because the disease strikes at an age when people are entering their reproductive years.

Because schizophrenia is associated with reduced fertility and is a genetic condition, the alleles underlying the condition eventually should be eliminated from the population by negative selection. This does not seem to be happening. If anything, over the past 200 years schizophrenia seems to be getting more rather than less common, and it may be more common in large, developed societies than in traditional ones (Allen, 1997). The clinical schizophrenia phenotype itself obviously is not adaptive because it leads to demonstrably reduced fitness. Individuals who carry schizophrenia-causing alleles but who do not develop the disease may have some characteristics that help them to reproductively compensate for the loss of alleles in individuals who have full-blown schizophrenia.

The Schizophrenia Genotype as a Balanced Polymorphism Since the 1960s, numerous theories have been offered to explain the evolution of schizophrenia (see Polimeni and Reiss, 2003, for a review). Given the reduced fitness of individuals who have schizophrenia and the current understanding of the genetics underlying the condition, it is reasonable to suggest that schizophrenia alleles are being maintained in human populations as a balanced polymorphism. Although some argue that schizophrenia is simply a byproduct of human brain evolution, several researchers have looked at the alternative phenotypes associated with the schizophrenia genotype to explain how a small reproductive advantage (on the order of 5% [Kidd, 1975]) in the relatives of schizophrenic patients could maintain the alleles in the population.

The earliest exploration of the evolution of schizophrenia modeled it along the lines of sickle cell anemia (Chapter 6), describing it as a balanced polymorphism maintained by heterozygous advantage (Huxley et al., 1964). The problem with this view is that genetic studies show that schizophrenia is not an autosomal recessive illness. Allen and Sarich (1988) suggested that if schizophrenia is a balanced polymorphism, it is maintained in a *frequency-dependent* manner (Chapter 6). Following from the profound social dysfunction associated with clinical schizophrenia, they suggest that the primary advantage of relatives of schizophrenic patients is asociality. Interactive social groups provide benefits to the individuals that live within them, and the individuals within them must devote time and energy to the maintenance of the social group. Asocial individuals (such as those who carry alleles underlying the development of schizophrenia) may receive the benefits of social group living without investing as much in the maintenance of the group as a whole. Because a social group has only so many asocial roles (and there are more of them in more complex societies), there is a frequency-dependent limit to the spread of schizophrenia genotypes; a social group cannot be maintained if there are too many asocial individuals living in it. Other suggested possible reproductive advantages in relatives of people with schizophrenia include creativity, disease resistance, and pain resistance.

PSYCHOACTIVE SUBSTANCE USE AND ABUSE

The consumption of *psychoactive substances* (drugs) seems to be a cross-cultural human universal, and its history dates back tens of thousands of years. The most commonly consumed psychoactive substances are alcohol, tobacco, betel nut (used throughout South and Southeast Asia and Oceania), opium and its derivatives, coca and cocaine (coca leaves are a mild stimulant when chewed; cocaine is a concentrated form of the active ingredient), cannabis (marijuana), caffeine, and khat (chewed in East Africa) (Smith, 1999; Sullivan and Hagen, 2002) (Figure 18.17). Contemporary psychoactive drugs for the most part appeared with the development of agriculture, starting 10,000–15,000 years ago. Preagricultural peoples undoubtedly used available psychoactive substances in plants, although large and steady quantities of such substances did not become available until the development of agriculture (Smith, 1999).

Psychoactive drugs generally work by mimicking the effects of neurotransmitters found in the nervous system or by stimulating the production of neurotransmitters that influence behavior or mood. Biological research on *drug addiction,* or *substance dependence,* indicates that both genetic and environmental factors play key roles in the development of drug dependence. A person with a substance dependence problem exhibits the following: tolerance to the effects of a drug, leading to the use of increasing amounts; psychological or physiological withdrawal if the drug is removed, making giving up the drug difficult; and use of the drug despite knowledge of the negative consequences of continued usage.

Genetic Polymorphisms Associated with Psychoactive Substance Dependence
Much biological research on drug dependence has focused on the neurotransmitter *dopamine*. Dopamine is an important component of the pleasure and reward system in the brain. Stimulants, opiates, nicotine, and THC (the active ingredient in marijuana) all affect this neurotransmitter system (Enoch and Goldman, 1999). Kenneth Blum and colleagues (1996) suggest that a whole range of addictive behaviors (including drug addiction, gambling addiction, and so on) may be related to polymorphisms in dopamine receptor genes. Specifically, individuals with

FIGURE 18.17   Worldwide map of traditional psychoactive substance use.

severe addiction problems may be much more likely to carry an allele associated with a reduction in the total number of dopamine receptors. These individuals appear to need more of a stimulus (drug or activity) to derive a sense of reward or pleasure. Therefore, they are at higher risk for increased drug usage and ultimately substance dependence. Blum and colleagues call this constellation of behaviors *reward deficiency syndrome.*

In contrast to reward deficiency syndrome, a different polymorphism may make addiction to a specific drug—alcohol—less likely than usual (Enoch and Goldman, 1999). *Ethanol* (the "alcohol" we consume) is metabolized first to acetaldehyde by the enzyme *alcohol dehydrogenase* (ADH) and then to acetate by *aldehyde dehydrogenase* (ALDH). Acetaldehyde is the chemical that produces facial flushing, tachychardia (increased heart rate), and nausea in some people after the consumption of alcohol. In most people acetaldehyde does not accumulate in the body because it is quickly converted to acetate (Figure 18.18 on page 534). However, alleles found in some East Asian populations lead to a buildup of acetaldehyde in the body, either increasing its rate of synthesis or decreasing its rate of conversion to acetate. For example, an allele *ALDH2*2* (due to a single amino acid substitution in ALDH) is found with a frequency of 35% in the Japanese population. This allele leads to a buildup of acetaldehyde in the body, leading to facial flushing and other unpleasant side effects after even modest alcohol consumption. *ALDH2*2* heterozygotes and homozygotes both experience facial flushing; their risk of developing alcoholism is one-tenth to one-fourth that of those who do not possess the allele. No *ALDH2*2* homozygote individual has ever been observed to be an alcoholic, presumably because their physiology prevents them from ever consuming enough alcohol to become dependent on it.

Evolutionary Psychology Theories about Psychoactive Substance Use and Abuse
Randolph Nesse and Kent Berridge (1997) have taken the view that psychoactive substances are an evolutionarily novel feature of the contemporary environment. They argue that psychoactive drug use cannot be adaptive because it so

FIGURE 18.18　Genetic variation in the metabolism of alcohol.

fundamentally disrupts longstanding emotional mechanisms that have been shaped by natural selection. Drugs that simulate positive emotions (heroin, cocaine, alcohol, marijuana, and amphetamine) send false signals of fitness benefit, which in turn has the potential to disrupt a person's entire biological system of "wants" and "likes." Drugs that block negative emotions or reduce anxiety are potentially even more disruptive because they remove the body's signals to take action or to avoid potential threats.

Roger Sullivan and Ed Hagen (2002) provide a different evolutionary analysis of human psychoactive substance use. They argue that hominids have probably had a long-term evolutionary relationship with psychoactive substances. With the exception of alcohol, most of the active ingredients of commonly used psychoactive drugs are formed naturally in plants and are similar to neurotransmitters found in the brain. Sullivan and Hagen argue that we benefit from consuming small quantities of these neurotransmitter-like chemicals in the same way that we need to consume small quantities of essential vitamins and minerals. An interesting point raised by Sullivan and Hagen is that in many traditional cultures, no distinction is made between drugs and food. People consume "food" for sustenance and to have more energy; for example, some traditional cultures classify tobacco as a "food." Much psychoactive substance use in traditional cultures is associated not with developing a hedonic rush ("getting high") but with gaining increased stamina in a marginal environment (such as the Australian desert or Andean mountains). Even today, nonhedonic substances constitute most drug consumption (caffeine, nicotine, arecoline in betel nuts). Sullivan and Hagen hypothesize that psychoactive drug use in past environments could have been adaptive (providing increased stamina and neurotransmitters), although it may not be so in contemporary environments, which are characterized by easy access to both food and psychoactive substances.

EPILOGUE

The place of humans in the natural world has been the major theme of this book. We have explored this topic from a wide variety of perspectives, including the fossil record, the behavior of living nonhuman primates, the lives of people in traditional societies, the workings of the brain, and the biology of modern people. However, our explorations of these diverse topics have been linked by a single common thread: evolutionary theory.

You've now completed a comprehensive look at your own evolutionary past, and at the place of humankind in the history of the world. As you have seen, the evidence of our past is present in us today. It's visible in our DNA, our hominid anatomy, our physiological adaptations, and even in aspects of our behavior. Many people live in denial or in ignorance of this evolutionary past. In contrast, we feel that embracing and understanding it is critical to being an enlightened citizen of the twenty-first century.

It is important to keep in mind, however, that to embrace an evolutionary perspective of humankind is not to deny the importance of culture in our lives. We have seen that culture may be the most fundamental of human traits. Many aspects of the biology of modern people are influenced in some way by culture, while at the same time our cultural nature is a direct outgrowth of our biology.

This book has been concerned with our evolutionary past, but the most pressing question for humankind in the early twenty-first century is whether our species will survive long enough to experience significant evolutionary change. Environmental degradation, overpopulation, warfare and a host of other problems plague our species. It is safe to say that no species in Earth's history has contended with so many self-induced problems and survived. But of course no other species has had the capability to solve problems and change its world for the better the way that we humans have.

SUMMARY

1. **What are four approaches to understanding the evolution of human behavior?**

   The four approaches are palaeontological reconstructions of behavior, evolutionary psychology, biocultural anthropology, and human evolutionary (or behavior) ecology. All approaches are interested in understanding human behavior in an evolutionary context, although they differ in the kinds of data they use and the methods they use to collect those data.

2. **How are human evolutionary ecologists similar and dissimilar to traditional cultural anthropologists?**

   Traditional cultural anthropologists and human evolutionary ecologists both typically engage in intensive fieldwork conducted in traditional and nontraditional communities. Human evolutionary ecologists tend to be more quantitative than cultural anthropologists and focus on collecting data on population structure, reproductive factors, energetic expenditure, and nutrition, which can be used to test evolutionary and ecological hypotheses.

3. **What is the sexual division of labor? In what ways is it manifest in traditional cultures around the world?**

   In the older anthropological literature, the sexual division of labor is characterized by men being hunters and women being gatherers. More recent formulations suggest that men focus on collecting "large package" foodstuffs (such as big game) and women on "small package" items (which include plant material or small game). These differences are manifest in different cultural and ecological environments.

4. **Why are young males deemed risk-takers by researchers interested in the evolution of behavior?**

   Young males (15–30 years of age) have higher accident rates and engage in more apparently antisocial and aggressive behavior than any other sex-age group. This can be understood in terms of sexual selection theory, in which young males who take large risks may ultimately derive from them large reproductive advantages. Although this is not true in contemporary societies, the risk-taking behaviors are still manifest in young males trying to establish themselves in society as a whole.

5. **How does the Westermarck hypothesis explain the rarity of sibling inbreeding in cultures around the world?**

   The Westermarck hypothesis explains the rarity of offspring produced through sibling matings by suggesting that a developmental psychological mechanism exists whereby young children raised in proximity to one another (who would typically be closely related) grow up to not consider each other as potential reproductive partners. The aversion to mating develops only if the children are raised together during a critical period in the first several years of life.

6. **What is the empirical evidence underlying the claim that there are biological constraints on naming color terms?**

Across a wide range of cultures, if a culture has only two basic color terms, they correspond to black and white. If there are three color terms, then they are black, white, and red. The fourth color term added is blue/green/yellow. The cultural convergence in basic color terms may result from the physiology of color perception in humans.

7. **In what ways might minor depression be considered an adaptation? How are major and minor depression different?**

Minor depression, or low mood, is a normal response to a variety of events that occur in the lives of individuals. It may be adaptive in that it causes an individual to inhibit his or her actions at a time when low activity may be temporarily beneficial. Low mood prevents individuals from pursuing unrealistic goals and wasting energy. Persistent low mood, or major depression, is not adaptive because it leads not only to increased rates of suicide but also to other behavioral patterns that increase mortality.

8. **Why is it argued that schizophrenia is a phenotype maintained by a balanced polymorphism?**

Schizophrenia is a genetically influenced brain disease, and as a group, people with schizophrenia have lower fitness than other members of the population. The prevalence of schizophrenia (approximately 1%) remains high compared with the mutation rate. Thus schizophrenia is not being selected out of human populations, despite being a genetic condition with low fitness. This indicates that it is being maintained as a balanced polymorphism through the enhanced fitness of nonschizophrenic carriers of schizophrenia alleles.

9. **Give two examples that illustrate how people vary biologically in their responses to psychoactive substances. How do these relate to the tendency to develop substance dependence?**

Some individuals have alleles that cause them to have fewer receptors for the neurotransmitter dopamine, which is important in the brain's reward system. These individuals appear to need a greater amount of a stimulant (such as drugs or gambling) before they derive a sense of reward from the substance or activity. This predisposes them to developing addictive behaviors and substance dependence. In contrast, individuals who possess the *ALDH2*2* allele for alcohol metabolism rarely develop alcoholism. The reason is that this allele leads to the buildup of acetaldehyde in the body after the consumption of even limited amounts of alcohol. Acetaldehyde is a toxic substance that can cause facial flushing, rapid heart rate, and nausea. Individuals with the *ALDH2*2* allele do not become alcoholics because they cannot consume enough alcohol to become dependent on it.

CRITICAL THINKING QUESTIONS

1. Why is it necessary to approach the evolution of human behavior from diverse viewpoints?

2. Defend or critique the following statement: Human psychoactive substance use is an adaptive behavior in many environments.

3. Human evolutionary ecologists uncover many cultural patterns of behavior that make sense in light of evolutionary theory. What does this say about the motivations of individuals living in human societies? Should we regard people in general as operating as "fitness maximizers" no matter what they are doing?

4. How should society deal with young male risk-takers? Does the evolutionary perspective help us understand and deal with the antisocial or unduly aggressive behavior of some young adult males? Can increases in the aggressive or antisocial behavior of young females be explained in an evolutionary context?

5. Drawing on what you have learned while reading this textbook, can you think of any areas in which understanding the evolutionary history of our species could directly lead to a betterment of the contemporary human condition?

KEY TERMS

sociobiology
evolutionary psychology
environment of
   evolutionary
   adaptedness (EEA)
human evolutionary
   ecology

cognitive universals
cross-cultural universals
polygyny
bridewealth
progesterone
inbreeding
inbreeding depression

incest
motherese (infant-
   directed speech)

SUGGESTED READING

Alcock, J. (2001). *The Triumph of Sociobiology.* Oxford University Press, New York.

Allman, W. F. (1995). *The Stone Age Present.* Touchstone, New York.

Barkow, J.H., Tooby J., and Cosmides, L. (1992). *The Adapted Mind.* Oxford University Press, New York.

Barrett, L., Dunbar, R., and Lycett, J. (2002). *Human Evolutionary Psychology.* Princeton University Press, Princeton.

Betzig, L. (editor). (1997). *Human Nature: A Critical Reader.* Oxford University Press, New York.

Fox, R. (1983). *The Red Lamp of Incest.* University of Notre Dame Press, Notre Dame, Indiana.

Low, Bobbi S. (1999). *Why Sex Matters.* Princeton University Press, Princeton, NJ.

APPENDIX A

FORENSIC ANTHROPOLOGY

NEW YORK CITY, SEPTEMBER 11, 2001: The city is beginning the most massive job of unearthing and identifying bodies ever faced by any government.

"There's never been an effort like this in terms of identification and recovery of the dead in history. It's going to be a terrible job," said forensic anthropologist Clyde Snow, who is considered the world's leading expert on body identification.

"This is so unprecedented," forensics expert Lawrence Kobilinsky of John Jay College in Manhattan, said. "There has never been anything that comes close to what we're facing."

The New York City Medical Examiner's office has been marshaling forces from several states and dozens of agencies, preparing to receive, process and identify up to 20,000 bodies, all victims of Tuesday's attack on the World Trade Center, although nobody is sure how many people are buried in the debris.

—Laurie Garrett, for the Associated Press

In the days after the attack on the World Trade Center in New York on September 11, 2001, forensic anthropologists from around the country were called in to help identify the victims (although the death toll thankfully was lowered from original estimates of 20,000 to fewer than 3,000). This may have been our first real-life introduction to their work, but most of us have seen forensic scientists in popularized form on such television shows as *C.S.I.* and *Crossing Jordan*.

The field of forensic anthropology traces its professional origins to the 1970s, when the physical anthropology section of the American Academy of Forensic Sciences (AAFS) was formed, although anatomists and biological anthropologists have been assisting in human skeletal identification since the late 1800s. Nearly all forensic anthropologists are also biological anthropologists who have advanced training in the field of human osteology, with specialized training in identifying human remains, differentiating the results of trauma, determining time since death, and applying the rules of evidence collection and documentation.

Forensic anthropology is an applied branch of biological anthropology in which principles of osteology and skeletal biology are used in legal or criminal investigations (see Chapter 1). This process means reconstructing the circumstances not only of homicides but also of accidental deaths, suicides, war crimes, and combat deaths. Forensic anthropologists differ from pathologists and medical ex-

aminers in having an anthropological perspective and a hard tissue focus. That is, they bring a broad perspective of natural human variation, human osteology, and natural selection to their work. Because the morphological form of the skeleton of a human or any other animal is dictated by its function in life and its evolutionary history, the forensic anthropologist can reconstruct what happened to a victim just before, around the time of, and after his or her death and determine the probable age, sex, and ancestry of the victim from skeletal remains. Usually the forensic anthropologist is involved when soft tissue remains are absent or too badly decomposed to help with identification and assessment of the cause and manner of death. In addition, forensic anthropologists must work in accordance with the rules not only of science but also of the courts. They must be able to convince their colleagues of their findings, and their findings must withstand the scrutiny of lawyers, juries, and judges.

In the medico-legal community each state has medical examiners or coroners who are legally responsible for signing death certificates and determining the cause and manner of death of people not in the care of a doctor. They also have the authority to consult other experts in their investigations, including forensic anthropologists. Forensic anthropologists work on staff as permanent members of a state medical examiner's office or a police agency or for the federal government, including the Federal Bureau of Investigation, the Armed

Forces Institute of Pathology, and the Joint Prisoner of War/Missing in Action Accounting Command (JPAC). They also work as outside consultants, in which case their primary work usually is at a museum or university. Whatever their position, forensic anthropologists are one kind of specialist in a web of forensic science experts that also includes forensic pathologists, forensic geneticists, forensic odontologists, and forensic entomologists (bug experts). Collectively, the aim of these scientists is to assist in identification and to elucidate the events surrounding a person's death.

THE INVESTIGATIVE PROCESS

The forensic investigative process generally begins at the scene of recovery, with the most immediate work being done on site where the body is found or is thought to be buried (Figure A.1). First, the area is cordoned off to limit disturbance of the scene. The forensic anthropologist surveys the area for additional remains and may undertake an excavation, using archaeological techniques to retrieve additional remains and plot their position and that of associated items such as bullets, clothing, and jewelry. The forensic anthropologist determines in the field whether the remains are human or nonhuman (they could be those of a dog or deer, for instance) and, based on the bones, whether more than one individual is present. Once recovered, the remains are removed to the lab for more detailed examination. There they are logged into evidence files, and a strict *chain of custody* is established to ensure that they cannot be tampered with in case they become evidence in a court case.

Back in the lab the remains may be cleaned of adhering soft tissue and dirt, then laid out in anatomical position, the way they would have looked in the skeleton in life (Figure A.2). An osteological inventory is made of each bone present. Most adult humans have 206 bones, many of which are extremely small (see Appendix B).

FIGURE A.2 Forensic anthropologists working at a temporary morgue following the recovery of remains from a flooded cemetery in Georgia.

The bodies of fetuses and children contain many more bones because many bones develop separately and fuse together only later in life. Often, a long-deceased and hidden body consists of no more than a few fragments. The forensic anthropologist therefore must be a skilled osteologist very familiar with patterns of interpopulational and intrapopulational human variation.

Once the inventory has been completed, the scientist determines age, sex, and ancestry. He or she examines the skeleton for signs of *premortem* disease or trauma, which occurred while the person was alive; *perimortem* changes, which occurred around the time of death; and *postmortem* changes, which occurred after death. The forensic anthropologist also notes any other potential identifying features, such as clothing or soft tissue that remained on the corpse. From these combined data the forensic anthropologist puts together a written report that documents his or her methods and conclusions. This report goes to the person or agency that hired the forensic anthropologist.

When skeletal material has been fragmented during a disaster (as in the World Trade Center crime scene), forensic scientists may rely heavily on comparisons with DNA reference samples, typically obtained from relatives of the victims.

THE KEY FORENSIC DIAGNOSES

Forensic anthropologists seek to identify the victim and the elements that reveal the cause and manner of his or her death. The identification process can be extraordinarily difficult if key parts of the skeleton that provide easy identification, such as the teeth, are missing. (To use DNA for identification, the scientist must have some knowledge of who the victim might have been to find living relatives to whom DNA can be matched.) The forensic anthropologist seeks information about several features that may be clues to identity: the age, sex, and ancestry of the remains (Snow, 1982).

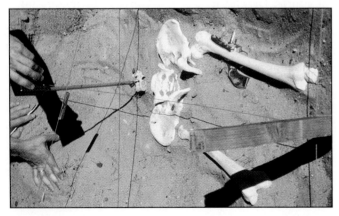

FIGURE A.1 Forensic anthropologists use archaeolgical excavation techniques to recover remains.

FIGURE A.3   Since bone changes in size and shape as an individual grows, bone anatomy helps to provide an age estimate, particularly in children. Foot bones (a) and vertebrae (b) from an archaeological site are shown from younger (left) to older (right).

AGE

As the human body develops, from fetus to old age, dramatic changes occur in the skeleton and teeth. Humans have two sets of teeth of different shapes and sizes that erupt at fairly predictable ages. Which teeth are present can help distinguish between children of different ages and between older subadults and adults of the same size. The long bones of the arms and legs acquire characteristic bony growths at their ends (the epiphyses), which are present as separate bones while the person is still growing rapidly. The lengths and proportions of bones change in predictable ways as children grow, and in small children the degree of closure of the cranial bones (covering the fontanelles, or "soft spots" of the skull) also changes with age. Thus a number of skeletal systems can be used to assess subadult age (Figure A.3).

In adults, age is harder to determine because growth is essentially complete. Some of the last epiphyses to fuse, such as the clavicle and top of the ilium, can be used to estimate age in young adults. Wear or attrition to parts of the skeleton helps in assessing age in older adults. For example, the pubic symphysis of the innominate, the auricular surface of the sacrum, and the end of the fourth rib near the sternum all show predictable degenerative changes. Research on skeletons of known age collected in the 1900s, such as those housed in the Hamman-Todd collection in Cleveland and the Terry Collection in Washington, D.C., has helped to define these standards.

Whenever scientists determine age, they always report it as a range (such as 35–45 years) rather than as a single number. This range reflects the individual variation in growth and aging in the human population and denotes the person's biological rather than chronological age (age in years). The hope is that it also encompasses the person's age at the time of death.

SEX

The sex of a discovered set of remains may provide an immediate clue to identity. The two parts of the skeleton that most readily reveal sex are the pelvis and the skull, and sex characteristics are more prominent in an adult skeleton than in a child. Because of selective pressures for bipedality and childbirth, human females have evolved pelves that provide a large birth canal (see Chapter 11). This affects the shape of the innominate and sacrum; the pubis is longer in females than in males, the sacrum is broader and shorter, and the sciatic notch of the ilium is broader (Figure A.4 on page 542). Scientists can determine sex with 95–98% accuracy using the human pelvis.

The skull is also a useful indicator of sex, at least in adults. Male skulls are more robust on average than female skulls of the same population. However, these differences are relative and population dependent; some human populations are more gracile than others. Typical features scored in sex estimation are the mastoid process of the temporal bone and the muscle markings of the occipital bone, which are larger in males; the shape and size of the browridge and orbital rim, which are less developed and sharper in females; the chin, which is squarer in males; and the frontal bone, which is more vertical in females (Figure A.4). These differences form a continuum and provide successful sex estimates in perhaps 80–85% of cases when the population is known.

ANCESTRY

In days long past, biological anthropologists tried to assign people to racial categories, which amounted to little more than pigeonholes that reinforced racist stereotypes. Race as a biological construct may have dubious validity (see Chapter 6), but we have learned that the geographic

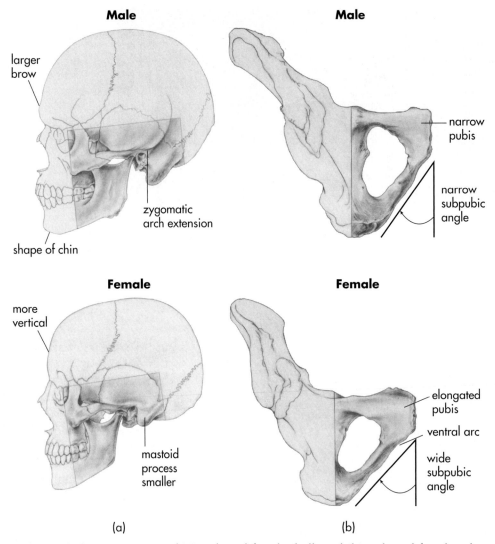

FIGURE A.4   Comparison of (a) male and female skulls and (b) male and female pelves.

conditions in which an organism's ancestors evolved influence the anatomy of that being. The term *ancestry* takes into account the place of geographic origin, which corresponds to biological realities in ways that the term *race* does not.

Forensic assessments of ancestry usually are made from the skull but can also include the postcrania. Both measurements and study of the nonmetric features of the skull, such as certain anatomical characters of the teeth and the presence or absence of minor bony structures, are helpful. Scientists base ancestry assessments on research in skeletal populations of known ancestry. An isolated skull can be measured and compared using multivariate statistics with the University of Tennessee Forensic Data Bank of measurements from crania of known ancestry. This process provides a likely assignment of ancestry and a range of possible error. However, human variation is such that many people exist in

every population whose skulls do not match well with most other skulls of similar geographic origin.

The ability to even partially assign ancestry can be useful in several forensic contexts. Missing person reports often provide an identification of ancestry, and although this is not based directly on the skeleton, a skeletal determination of ancestry may suggest a match that could be confirmed by other more time-consuming means (such as dental record comparisons or DNA analysis). In another context, forensic anthropologists are still working to identify the remains of soldiers killed in the Vietnam War, thirty years after that conflict ended. If a local contact leads a forensic team to a field where an American soldier was reportedly buried, the team will begin to search and excavate. Upon finding human remains, the forensic anthropologist confirms that the skeleton is likely to be that of an American, not that of a Vietnamese person.

HEIGHT

Physical stature is reflected in the length of the bones that contribute to a person's height. Physical anthropologists have developed formulas for estimating stature based on long bone length, such as that of the femur or tibia, using skeletal remains of individuals of known stature. These formulas allow an estimate of the height of a victim based on incomplete remains, although the formulas vary by population, partly because different body shapes result from ecological rules such as Bergmann's and Allen's rules (Chapter 6). Like age, stature is estimated as a range (for example, 5′10″ to 6′ 0″) that captures the person's true height at the time of death.

TIME SINCE DEATH

One of the more difficult tasks for a forensic anthropologist is determining how long the victim has been dead. This assessment is so complicated that at least one research program in forensic anthropology, at the University of Tennessee, maintains an outdoor morgue in which bodies are left to decompose under a variety of conditions so researchers can learn how natural processes affect the rate of decay. In general, bodies left on the surface of the ground decompose most quickly and those buried in the ground most slowly. Each medium has its own diagnostic markers of time since death. However, temperature and humidity are the primary factors affecting decay rate because they in turn influence the insect activity, which has become the most useful indicator of time since death, and because they affect other physiological rates of decay. The timing of insect life cycles is well known, and their preferences for tissue types and extent of decay are also well studied. Forensic entomologists therefore are important members of any forensic team.

PREMORTEM INJURY OR DISEASE

Injuries and sickness suffered by a victim in life can leave lasting marks on the skeleton. Arthritis and infections of bone show up clearly in skeletal remains. Old healed injuries, such as broken leg or arm bones or gunshot wounds, also leave their mark (Figure A.5). Such premortem injury can be key evidence for police investigating a death and for forensic scientists trying to reconstruct the circumstances of the death. Old injuries can also be matched to premortem x-rays taken when a victim sought medical attention. Orthopedic implants and pins often resolve issues of identity. In addition, lifestyle may leave an indelible mark on the skeleton; an athlete who uses one side of the body for intense activity (such as a baseball pitcher or tennis player) will have a more robustly developed arm on that side. Surfers tend to develop one big toe that is larger than the other.

FIGURE A.5 Bone fractures that occur before death show signs of healing. Note the foreshortened tibia (upper) due to a massive healed fracture and the less severe fracture on the proximal (right) end of the lower tibia.

PERIMORTEM TRAUMA

One of the most critical tasks a forensic anthropologist undertakes is amassing evidence that may help investigators understand the cause and manner of death (whether homicide, suicide, or accident). Perimortem trauma is the physical evidence of activity that happened around the time of death, either slightly before or slightly after. We can differentiate it from premortem injury because in perimortem trauma no healing is evident at the trauma site.

A medical examiner can use evidence of perimortem trauma to infer cause of death. The presence of telltale fractures of the hyoid, a small bone in the neck, suggests strangulation, for example. Perimortem trauma may also indicate a perpetrator's intent to hide or dispose of a body. For example, circular saws and reciprocating saws leave different marks on bone and sometimes leave portions of themselves embedded in bone. Experts can identify types of blades and sometimes make direct matches to tools owned by a suspect.

POSTMORTEM TRAUMA

Taphonomists study the ways in which natural processes affect the body from death to decomposition and discovery (Chapter 9). They attempt to distinguish naturally caused bone changes from those that appear to be human-created. For forensic investigations, taphonomic analysis may help to determine the length of time the victim was dead and the nature of perimortem trauma. But forensic anthropologists must be careful to distinguish postmortem events from perimortem events because postmortem events do not suggest cause or manner of death. Although neither perimortem nor postmortem trauma shows healing, they can be differentiated from one another because bones broken in the perimortem interval retain an organic component and therefore break differently from those that dry out after death; think of the difference between how a small living tree branch bends when you try to break it, whereas a dried stick on the ground snaps.

Postmortem events may also rule out a crime if they suggest that marks on bone are made by natural causes, rather than knives, guns, or chainsaws, or if they show that the skeleton is of ancient rather than forensic interest. For instance, Willey and Leach (2003) cite a case in which forensic anthropologists sought to identify a human skull found in a suburban yard. The skull was discolored in a variety of ways that, turned out to most closely resemble the way in which skulls are sometimes treated when collected as trophies of war. As it turned out, the skull in question was a souvenir brought home from the Vietnam War by a man who had since moved away from the area, leaving the skull in his garage.

CHEMICAL AND MOLECULAR ANALYSIS

Sometimes the evidence for cause of death is clear: a skull fracture or gunshot wound. But often the evidence is much less obvious, and then chemical and molecular analyses of bone may answer questions surrounding a death. In these cases forensic anthropologists usually collaborate with another forensic specialist to build a better case.

Chemical tests on bone can identify some poisons even long after soft tissues have decomposed. Some years ago, the body of former U.S. president Zachary Taylor was exhumed and an age-old hypothesis was tested (Maples and Browning, 1994). Taylor had been president in the years leading up to the Civil War. He was adamantly antislavery and had many enemies in Washington. He died several days after suffering a bout of severe indigestion, leading many of his supporters to think he was poisoned by political enemies. Forensic anthropologist William Maples was part of the forensic team that exhumed the body. The team tested levels of arsenic, the most widely used poison at the time and the only one that would have lingered in the body long enough to have killed Taylor days after he ingested it. They found that arsenic levels in Taylor's body tissues (toenails and bones) matched those found on his clothes and were within the normal limits for a person living in the mid-nineteenth century. Taylor died from something he ate, they concluded, but not at the hands of conspirators.

The rise of technologies able to establish kinship using DNA analysis has given forensic scientists a powerful new tool for identifying victims and establishing the presence of an alleged perpetrator at a crime scene. DNA testing can use tiny samples of hair, skin, blood, and other body fluids and even bone. Where admissible in a court of law, such testing can lead the prosecution to ask for a conviction or the defense to claim mistaken identity of the defendant. Forensic scientists use a variety of tests, including DNA profiling (examining gene sequences that only kin would be likely to share), DNA typing (isolating particular segments of the genetic sequence for analy-

sis), and DNA fingerprinting (the original DNA test, in which the same segments of DNA are lined up to examine the degree of similarity between samples from two people) (Nafte, 2000).

APPLICATIONS OF FORENSIC ANTHROPOLOGY

Although forensic anthropologists most often work on cases of lone victims of homicide, suicide, or accidental death, they are also called to the scene of mass fatalities, the search for soldiers killed in combat, and human rights abuses that result in hidden or mass graves.

MASS FATALITIES

The attacks on the World Trade Center brought many forensic anthropologists to the scene, as did the Oklahoma City bombing case 7 years earlier. And forensic anthropologists play key roles in the attempt to identify victims of earthquakes, plane crashes, floods, and other natural and human-wrought disasters. The United States has regional emergency response teams called Disaster Mortuary Teams (DMORT) that include pathologists, forensic anthropologists, and forensic odontologists who are mobilized in response to national mass disasters such as the World Trade Center fire and collapse. Military forensic experts respond when U.S. citizens or military are involved in mass fatalities abroad.

In 1994 a DMORT team responded to an unusual mass disaster. Flooding of historic proportions caused the remains from a cemetery in Albany, Georgia, to surface. The lids of the concrete vaults in which coffins were placed during burial were removed by the floodwaters, causing coffins to float to the surface and into the town of Albany. Some remains were separated entirely from their coffins. The DMORT team recovered the remains and established a morgue to process them, to attempt to forensically identify them, and to reconnect them to their place of interment (Figure A.2). Of the 415 disinterred remains, the DMORT team was able to positively identify 320 people.

WAR DEAD

U.S. forensic anthropologists first became involved in the identification of those who died in war when the Central Identification Laboratory (CIL) in Hawaii (CILHI) was formed to aid in the identification of those missing in action during World War II. Since then the skeletal remains of U.S. soldiers and civilians from World War II, the Korean War, the Vietnam War, and other military actions have been recovered and identified by this group of anthropologists, now part of JPAC. JPAC teams travel around the world to identify and recover U.S. soldiers lost in the wars of the twentieth century. The remains are brought back to the CIL, thoroughly examined, and identified. In addition to standard forensic anthropological techniques, JPAC teams also extensively use forensic DNA techniques to reach a positive identification so that remains may be returned to the next of kin.

Not only does this group of forensic anthropologists help in identifying missing personnel, but they have also undertaken some of the most important systematic research used in all forensic work. For example, Dr. Mildred Trotter, an early director of CILHI, developed regression analyses for determining stature from long bone lengths based on the skeletal remains of soldiers who died in the Korean War. This large body of work remains a standard in forensic analyses today and would not have been possible without the detailed medical histories of these military personnel.

WAR CRIMES AND GENOCIDE

Finally, forensic anthropologists may play a key role in uncovering mass graves and identifying bodies in them, and they may be important witnesses in the investigation of war crimes. Whether in Cambodia, Rwanda, Bosnia, or Iraq, when repressive regimes crack down on their citizens, they often attempt to intimidate the population through mass murder. The mass graves that are left contain the bodies of hundreds or even thousands of victims, whose loved ones spend lifetimes attempting to locate them and determine their fate. Forensic anthropologists help to identify the victims for the sake of surviving family members and may provide key evidence in reconstructing a mass crime scene in an effort to bring those responsible to justice. Forensic anthropologists in these areas work for both government and private groups such as Physicians for Human Rights, the International Commission for Missing Persons, and the United Nations.

For example, the effort to exhume mass graves in the former Yugoslavia began in 1996 under the auspices of the United Nations (UN) and in particular the International Criminal Tribunal for the former Yugoslavia (ICTY), in partnership with Physicians for Human Rights. Some of these exhumations concentrated in eastern Croatia on a grave site known as Ovcara, which contained victims from a massacre in Vukovar. The Vukovar massacre occurred in November 1991, and the mass grave site was located in 1992 based on information from a person who had escaped the massacre. Excavation waited until 1996 because of continuing hostilities in the region (although the site was guarded by the UN for the entire time).

The forensic teams consisted of scientists from around the world and included forensic anthropologists and archaeologists, pathologists, evidence technicians, radiologists, odontologists, autopsy technicians, and computer scientists. The teams exhumed about 200 bodies from Ovcara, nearly all of them males. Mapping the grave site took more than a month. The remains were autopsied in Zagreb with the goals of constructing a biological profile (age, sex, and stature) that would help in identification and interpreting perimortem trauma to understand the cause of death. Many of the victims had multiple gunshot wounds and other forms of trauma. Biological profiles were compared with the medical and dental records of missing people, a task hampered by the destruction of hospitals and other medical facilities during the war, and lists of identifying characteristics (including tattoos) provided by family members of missing people. Through these comparisons about half of the 200 were positively identified. This evidence has been used in the prosecution of war crimes by the UN-ICTY, including the case against the region's former leader, Slobodan Milosevic.

Forensic anthropologists apply the method and theory of biological anthropology to the investigation of recent deaths. Their work, whether on cases of lone victims of homicide, suicide, or accidental death or at the scene of mass fatalities, helps bring closure to grieving relatives and bring criminals to justice.

PRIMATE AND HUMAN COMPARATIVE ANATOMY

FIGURE B.1 The Axial and Appendicular Skeletons.

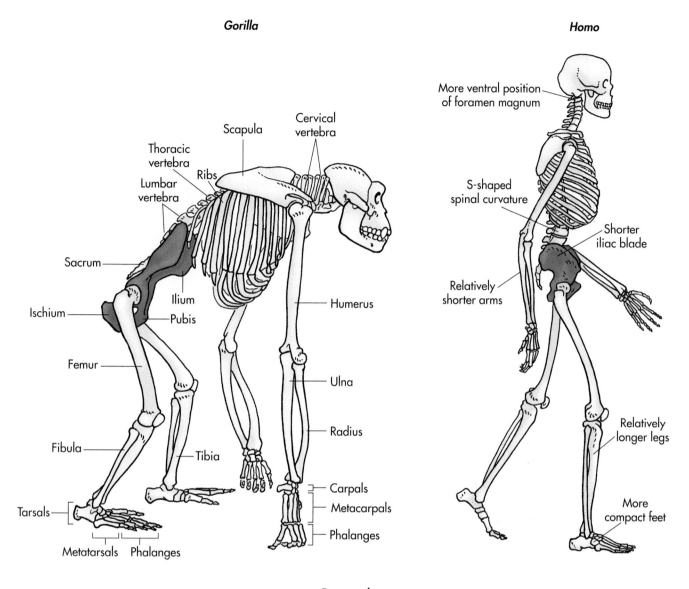

FIGURE B.2 Comparisons of *Gorilla*, *Homo* and *Proconsul* skeletons.

Human Skull

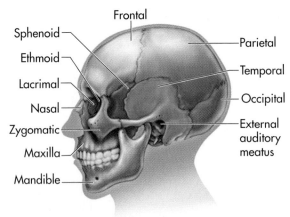

(a) The major bones of the skull and face

Sphenoid · Ethmoid · Lacrimal · Nasal · Zygomatic · Maxilla · Mandible · Frontal · Parietal · Temporal · Occipital · External auditory meatus

(b) Lower surface of skull

Zygomatic · Palatine · Vomer · Sphenoid · Foramen magnum · Occipital · Maxilla

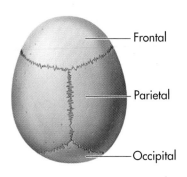

(c) Top view of skull

Frontal · Parietal · Occipital

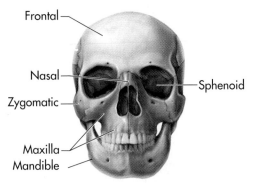

(d) Front view of skull showing facial bones

Frontal · Nasal · Zygomatic · Maxilla · Mandible · Sphenoid

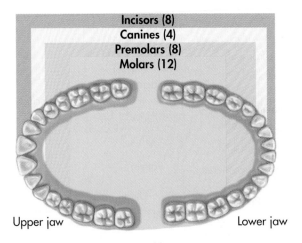

Incisors (8)
Canines (4)
Premolars (8)
Molars (12)

Upper jaw · Lower jaw

(e) Upper and lower jaws

FIGURE B.3   (a, b, c) The major bones of the skull and face, (d) facial bones and, (e) dentition.

The Vertebral Column

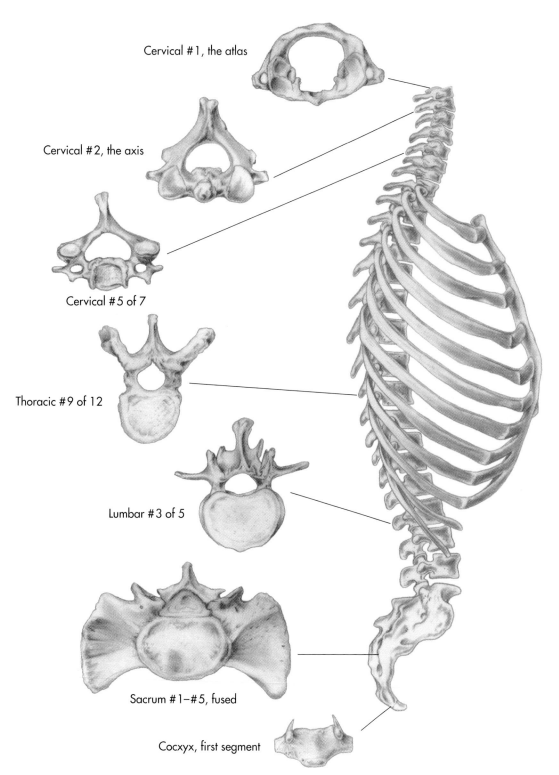

Cervical #1, the atlas

Cervical #2, the axis

Cervical #5 of 7

Thoracic #9 of 12

Lumbar #3 of 5

Sacrum #1–#5, fused

Cocxyx, first segment

FIGURE B.4 The Vertebral Column. The human vertebral column consists of 7 cervical, 12 thoracic, 5 lumbar, 5 fused sacral, and 4 or 5 diminutive coccygeal vertebrae.

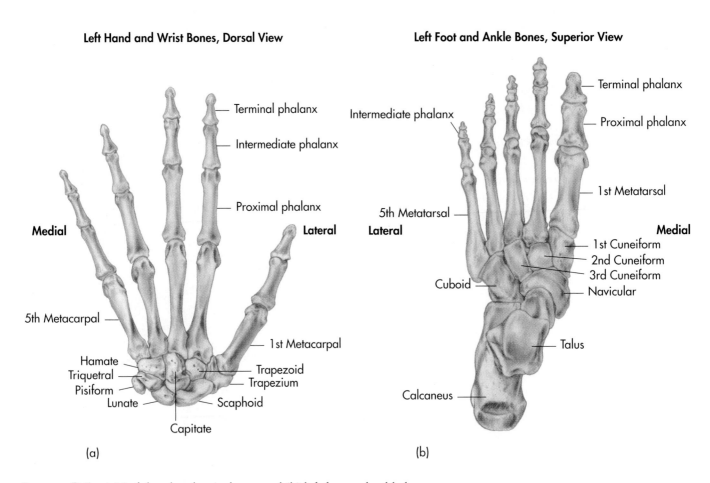

Left Hand and Wrist Bones, Dorsal View

Terminal phalanx

Intermediate phalanx

Proximal phalanx

Medial

Lateral

5th Metacarpal

1st Metacarpal

Hamate

Triquetral

Pisiform

Lunate

Trapezoid

Trapezium

Scaphoid

Capitate

(a)

Left Foot and Ankle Bones, Superior View

Terminal phalanx

Proximal phalanx

Intermediate phalanx

1st Metatarsal

5th Metatarsal

Lateral

Medial

1st Cuneiform

2nd Cuneiform

3rd Cuneiform

Navicular

Cuboid

Talus

Calcaneus

(b)

FIGURE B.5   (a) Left hand and wrist bones and (b) left foot and ankle bones.

APPENDIX C

THE HARDY–WEINBERG EQUILIBRIUM

In Chapter 5, we introduced the Hardy–Weinberg equilibrium in the context of our discussion of the forces of evolutionary change. Population genetics provides the mathematical underpinnings of evolutionary theory, and the Hardy–Weinberg equilibrium is at the heart of mathematical and quantitative approaches to understanding evolutionary change in diploid organisms. In this appendix, we will briefly go over a derivation of the Hardy–Weinberg equilibrium and show some applications of the equilibrium in evolutionary research.

Throughout the discussion, we will use the simplest case to illustrate our examples: a single gene (or locus) with two alleles, A and a. The frequency of A in the population is represented by p; the frequency of a is represented by q. By definition, $p + q = 1$.

DERIVATION OF THE HARDY–WEINBERG EQUILIBRIUM

The Hardy–Weinberg equilibrium states that, given known allele frequencies p and q, we can represent the genotype frequencies by $AA = p^2$, $Aa = 2pq$, and $aa = q^2$. Furthermore, these allele frequencies remain constant from generation to generation if the following conditions are met:

- Large population size (or theoretically infinite population size), which minimizes the influence of genetic drift on allele frequencies

- Random mating (no inbreeding or assortative or disassortative mating)

- No mutation

- No gene flow

- No natural selection

Let us begin by considering a specific example, where the allele frequency of A is 0.6 ($p = 0.6$) and that of a is 0.4 ($q = 0.4$). To look at this another way, the probability that any given sperm or egg will carry A is 0.6, and the probability that it will carry a is 0.4. Thus under conditions of totally random mating with no other evolutionary forces in effect (under equilibrium conditions), the probability of producing a zygote with a homozygous AA genotype is $(0.6)(0.6) = 0.36$. We can represent the probabilities of all the genotypes occurring in a modified Punnett square:

		SPERM	
		FREQ(A) = p = 0.6	FREQ(a) = q = 0.4
EGGS	freq(A) = p = 0.6	freq(AA) = p^2 = (0.6)(0.6) = 0.36	freq(Aa) = pq = (0.6)(0.4) = 0.24
	freq(a) = q = 0.4	freq(Aa) = pq = (0.6)(0.4) = 0.24	freq(aa) = q^2 = (0.4)(0.4) = 0.16

This gives us a population with genotype frequencies of 0.36 (for AA), 0.48 (for Aa), and 0.16 (for aa). What are the allele frequencies for this population? For A, it is $0.36 + (0.5)(0.48) = 0.36 + 0.24 = 0.6$, which is what the frequency of A was originally. The allele frequency of a is $0.16 + (0.5)(0.48) = 0.16 + 0.24 = 0.40$, which is the original frequency of a. This demonstrates that allele frequencies are maintained in equilibrium under conditions of random mating and in the absence of other evolutionary forces.

The general equation for the distribution of genotypes for a population in Hardy–Weinberg equilibrium is given by the equation

$$p^2 + 2pq + q^2 = 1$$

We can derive this equation directly from the modified Punnett square.

The constancy of allele frequencies over generations is shown by the following equations. Let p' equal the allele frequency of A in the first generation. From the preceding example we see that

$$p' = (\text{frequency of } AA) + (0.5)(\text{frequency of } Aa)$$

We want to count only half the alleles for A in the heterozygotes. Substituting the allele frequency values from the Hardy–Weinberg equation, we get

$$p' = p^2 + (0.5)(2pq)$$

Because $(0.5)(2pq) = pq$, we now have

$$p' = p^2 + pq$$

Which, factoring out p, is the same thing as

$$p' = p(p + q)$$

As you recall, $p + q = 1$; therefore,

$$p' = p$$

This demonstrates that allele frequencies remain constant in a population in Hardy–Weinberg equilibrium.

One of the main uses of the Hardy–Weinberg equation is to determine if a population is *not* in equilibrium. We do this by comparing observed allele frequencies with observed genotype frequencies. If the observed genotype frequencies are significantly different from those expected based on the allele frequencies (which we usually check by using a chi-square statistical test), then we can say the population is not in equilibrium. This result indicates that one of the assumptions of the Hardy–Weinberg equilibrium is being violated and that an evolutionary force may be acting on the population or acted on the population in the past to produce the non-equilibrium distribution of alleles.

Another application of the Hardy–Weinberg equation is to estimate the frequency of heterozygotes in a population. As we discussed in Chapter 6, it is particularly useful for estimating the frequency in a population of carriers of a recessive autosomal illnesses, such as Tay–Sachs disease or cystic fibrosis. The recessive allele frequency is simply

$$q = \sqrt{\text{frequency of autosomal recessive condition}}$$

And the dominant allele frequency is

$$p = 1 - q$$

Thus the frequency of heterozygous carriers = $2pq$.

HARDY–WEINBERG AND NATURAL SELECTION

The Hardy–Weinberg equilibrium can help us mathematically model the effects of any of the forces of evolution (mutation, genetic drift, gene flow, and natural selection). Let us consider how to use the Hardy–Weinberg equation to understand how natural selection may affect the distribution of allele frequencies in a population. In these equations, we assume that nat-

ural selection is the only force of evolution acting on the population.

In the simple case of one gene with two alleles, we have three possible genotypes that are subject to natural selection. To model the change in allele frequencies, we need to know not the absolute fitness of each genotype (which we could measure as its likelihood of survival) but rather the genotypes' fitness relative to each other. Relative fitness usually is represented by the letter w; thus we have

$$w_{AA} = \text{relative fitness of } AA$$
$$w_{Aa} = \text{relative fitness of } Aa$$
$$w_{aa} = \text{relative fitness of } aa$$

Let's say that the homozygous genotype AA has the highest fitness; its relative fitness w_{AA} therefore would be equal to 1. The relative fitnesses of Aa and aa are lower, such that

$$w_{AA} = 1.0$$
$$w_{Aa} = 0.8$$
$$w_{aa} = 0.4$$

Let's also assume starting allele frequencies of $p = 0.7$ and $q = 0.3$.

If the population were in Hardy–Weinberg equilibrium, the expected genotype frequencies after one generation would be

$$p^2 = (0.7)(0.7) = 0.49 \text{ for } AA$$
$$2pq = 2(0.7)(0.3) = 0.42 \text{ for } Aa$$
$$q^2 = (0.3)(0.3) = 0.09 \text{ for } aa$$

However, natural selection is working on this population and affecting the survival of the different genotypes. So the genotype frequencies after selection are

$$w_{AA}\, p^2 = 1.0(0.7)(0.7) = 0.49 \text{ for } AA$$
$$w_{Aa}\, 2pq = 0.8(2)(0.7)(0.3) = 0.336 \text{ for } Aa$$
$$w_{aa}\, q^2 = 0.4(0.3)(0.3) = 0.036 \text{ for } aa$$

The frequency of p after natural selection has acted on the population is

$$p' = [(0.49) + (0.5)(0.336)] / (0.49 + 0.336 + 0.036)$$
$$= 0.658/0.862$$
$$= 0.763$$

The frequency of q is

$$q' = 1 - p' = 1 - 0.763 = 0.237$$

So after only one generation of natural selection operating at these levels, there is a substantial change in allele frequencies, with A going from 0.7 to 0.763 and a decreasing from 0.3 to 0.237. Following this through five generations, the allele frequencies would be

GENERATION	1	2	3	4	5
p	0.763	0.813	0.852	0.883	0.907
q	0.237	0.187	0.148	0.117	0.093

In the case of a lethal autosomal recessive condition (such as Tay–Sachs disease), in which the relative fitness of the recessive homozygote is 0 and for the other two genotypes it is 1, we can represent the change in allele frequency of the recessive allele by a simple equation (which is derived from the Hardy–Weinberg equation):

$$q_g = q_0/(1 + gq_0)$$

where g is the number of generations passed, q_G is the frequency of a in generation g, and q_0 is the starting frequency of a. Consider a founding population in which the allele frequency of a lethal recessive is 0.20. Over ten generations, the frequency of this allele will decrease to

$$q_{10} = 0.2/[1 + (10)(0.2)]$$
$$= 0.2/3$$
$$= 0.067$$

Of course, a small founding population violates one of the conditions of the Hardy–Weinberg equilibrium (infinite population size), but we can ignore that for the sake of this example.

APPENDIX D

METRIC–IMPERIAL CONVERSIONS

METRIC UNIT	IMPERIAL EQUIVALENT
1 centimeter	0.39 inches
1 meter	3.28 feet
1 kilometer	0.62 miles
1 kilogram	2.20 pounds
454 grams	1 pound
1 gram	0.035 ounces
1 liter	1.06 quarts
400 cubic centimeters	24.4 cubic inches
1 square kilometer	0.39 square miles
1 square kilometer	247 acres
0 degrees Celsius	32 degrees Fahrenheit

Glossary

ABO blood type system   Refers to the genetic system for one of the proteins found on the surface of red blood cells. Consists of one gene with three alleles: A, B, and O.

acclimatization   Short-term changes in physiology that occur in an organism in response to changes in environmental conditions.

acetabulum   The cup-shaped joint formed by the ilium, ischium, and pubis at which the head of the femur attaches to the pelvis.

Acheulean   Stone tool industry of the early and middle Pleistocene characterized by the presence of bifacial hand axes and cleavers. This industry is made by a number of *Homo* species, including *H. erectus* and early *H. sapiens*.

activity budget   The pattern of waking, eating, moving, socializing, and sleeping that all nonhuman primates engage in each day.

adapoids   Family of mostly Eocene primates, probably ancestral to all strepsirhines.

adaptability   The ability of an individual organism to make positive anatomical or physiological changes after short- or long-term exposure to stressful environmental conditions.

adaptation   A trait that increases the reproductive success of an organism, produced by natural selection in the context of a particular environment.

adaptationism   A premise that all aspects of an organism have been molded by natural selection to a form optimal for enhancing reproductive success.

adaptive radiation   The diversification of one founding species into multiple species and niches.

alleles   Alternative versions of a gene. Different alleles are distinguished from one another by their different effects on the phenotypic expression of the same gene.

Allen's rule   Stipulates that in warmer climates, the limbs of the body are longer relative to body size to dissipate body heat.

allopatric speciation   Speciation occurring via geographic isolation.

amino acids   Molecules that form the basic building blocks of protein.

anagenesis   Evolution of a trait or a species into another gradually over a period of time.

analogous   Having similar traits due to similar use, not due to shared ancestry.

angular torus   A thickened ridge of bone at the posterior angle of the parietal bone.

anthropoid   Member of the primate suborder Anthropoidea that includes the monkeys, apes, and hominids.

anthropology   The study of humankind in a cross-cultural context. Anthropology includes the subfields cultural anthropology, linguistic anthropology, archaeology, and biological anthropology.

anthropometry   The measurement of different aspects of the body, such as stature or skin color.

antibodies   Proteins (immunoglobulins) formed by the immune system that are specifically structured to bind to and neutralize invading antigens.

antigens   Whole or part of an invading organism that prompts a response (such as production of antibodies) from the body's immune system.

arboreal hypothesis   Hypothesis for the origin of primate adaptation that focuses on the value of grasping hands and stereoscopic vision for life in the trees.

archaeology   The study of the material culture of past peoples.

argon–argon (^{40}Ar/^{39}Ar)   Radiometric technique modified from K–Ar that measures ^{40}K by proxy using ^{39}Ar. Allows measurement of smaller samples with less error.

artifacts   The objects, from tools to art, left by earlier generations of people.

association cortex   Parts of the cerebral cortex where inputs from primary motor and sensory cortex are processed.

Australopithecines   The common name for members of the genus *Australopithecus*.

autoimmune diseases   Occur when a body's immune system attacks its own tissues.

autosomal dominant disease   A disease that is caused by a dominant allele; only one copy needs to be inherited from either parent for the disease to develop.

autosomal recessive disease   A disease caused by a recessive allele; one copy of the allele must be inherited from each parent for the disease to develop.

autosomes   Any of the chromosomes other than the sex chromosomes.

auxology   The science of human growth and development.

balanced polymorphism   A stable polymorphism in a population in which natural selection prevents any of the alternative phenotypes (or underlying alleles) from becoming fixed or being lost.

base   Variable component of the nucleotides that form the nucleic acids DNA and RNA. In DNA, the bases are adenine, guanine, thymine, and cytosine. In RNA, uracil replaces thymine.

Bergmann's rule   Stipulates that body size is larger in colder climates to conserve body temperature.

biface   A stone tool that has been flaked on two faces or opposing sides forming a cutting edge between the two flake scars.

binomial nomenclature   Linnaean naming system for all organisms, consisting of a genus and species label.

biocultural anthropology   The study of the interaction between biology and culture, which plays a role in most human traits.

biological anthropology   The study of humans as biological organisms, considered in an evolutionary framework; sometimes called physical anthropology.

biological species concept   Defines species as interbreeding populations reproductively isolated from other such populations.

biomedical anthropology   The subfield of biological anthropology concerned with issues of health and illness.

biostratigraphy   Relative dating technique using comparison of fossils from different stratigraphic sequences to estimate which layers are older and which are younger.

blades   Flakes that are twice as long as they are wide.

blending inheritance   Discredited nineteenth-century idea that genetic factors from the parents averaged-out or blended together when they were passed on to offspring.

brachiation   Mode of arm-hanging and arm-swinging that uses a rotating shoulder to suspend the body of an ape or hominid beneath a branch or to travel between branches.

brain stem   The part of the brain that controls basal metabolic rates, respiration, pulse, and other basic body functions.

breccia   Cement-like matrix of fossilized rock and bone. Many important South African early humans have been found in breccias.

bridewealth   Payment offered by a man to the parents of a woman he wants to marry.

butchering site   A place where there is archaeological evidence of the butchering of carcasses by hominids. The evidence usually consists of tool cut marks on fossilized animal bones or the presence of the stone tools themselves.

calibrated relative dating techniques   Techniques that can be correlated to an absolute chronology.

calotte   The skullcap, or the bones of the skull, excluding those that form the face and the base of the cranium.

calvaria   The braincase; includes the bones of the calotte and those that form the base of the cranium but excludes the bones of the face.

canine fossa   An indentation on the maxilla above the root of the canine, an anatomical feature usually associated with modern humans that may be present in some archaic *Homo* species in Europe.

captive study   Primate behavior study conducted in a zoo, laboratory, or other enclosed setting.

Catarrhini   Infraorder of the order Primates that includes the Old World monkeys, apes, and hominids.

catastrophism   Theory that there have been multiple creations interspersed by great natural disasters such as Noah's flood.

centromere   Condensed and constricted region of a chromosome. During mitosis and meiosis, location where sister chromatids attach to one another.

cerebellum   The "little brain," tucked under the cerebrum, and important in the control of balance, posture, and voluntary movements.

cerebral cortex   The layer of gray matter that covers the surface of the cerebral hemispheres, divided into functional regions that correspond to local patterns of neuronal organization.

cerebrum   The largest part of the human brain, which is split into left and right hemispheres. Seat of all "higher" brain functions.

cervical vertebrae   The seven neck vertebrae.

Châtelperronian   An Upper Paleolithic tool industry that has been found in association with later Neandertals.

chromatin   The diffuse form of DNA as it exists during the interphase of the cell cycle.

chromosome   Discrete structures composed of condensed DNA and supporting proteins.

chronometric dating techniques   Techniques that estimate the age of an object in absolute terms through the use of a natural clock such as radioactive decay or tree ring growth.

cladistics   Method of classification using ancestral and derived traits to distinguish patterns of evolution within lineages.

cladogenesis   Evolution through the branching of a species or a lineage.

cladogram   Branching diagram showing evolved relationships among members of a lineage.

cleaver   Type of Acheulean bifacial tool, usually oblong with a broad cutting edge on one end.

cline   The distribution of a trait or allele across geographic space.

coccyx   The fused tail vertebrae that are very small in humans and apes.

co-dominant   In a diploid organism, two different alleles of a gene that are both expressed in a heterozygous individual.

codon   A triplet of nucleotide bases in mRNA that specifies an amino acid or the initiation or termination of a polypeptide sequence.

cognitive universals   Cognitive phenomena such as sensory processing, the basic emotions, consciousness, motor control, memory, and attention that are expressed by all normal individuals.

compound temporonuchal crest   Bony crest at the back of the skull formed when an enlarged temporalis muscle approaches enlarged neck (nuchal) muscles, present in apes and *A. afarensis*.

convergent evolution   Similar form or function brought about by natural selection under similar environments rather than shared ancestry.

core   The raw material source (a river cobble or a large flake) from which flakes are removed.

core area   The part of a home range that is most intensively used.

CP₃ complex   Combination of canine and first premolar teeth that form a self-sharpening apparatus.

cranial crests   Bony ridges on the skull to which muscles attach.

creation science   A creationist attempt to refute the evidence of evolution.

cross-cultural universals   Behavioral phenomena, such as singing, dancing, and mental illness, that are found in almost all human cultures, but are not necessarily exhibited by each member of a cultural group.

crossing over Exchange of genetic material between homologous chromosomes during the first prophase of meiosis; mechanism for genetic recombination.

cultural anthropology The study of human societies, especially in a cross-cultural context; the subdivision of anthropology that includes ethnology, archaeology, and linguistics.

culture The sum total of learned traditions, values, and beliefs that groups of people, and a few species of highly intelligent animals, possess.

cytoplasm In a eukaryotic cell, the region within the cell membrane that surrounds the nucleus; it contains organelles, which carry out the essential functions of the cell, such as energy production, metabolism, and protein synthesis.

data The scientific evidence produced by an experiment or by observation, from which scientific conclusions are made.

daughter isotope (product) The isotope that is produced as the result of radioactive decay of the parent isotope.

deduction A conclusion that follows logically from a set of observations.

deletion mutation A change in the base sequence of a gene that results from the loss of one or more base pairs in the DNA.

deme A local, interbreeding population that is defined in terms of its genetic composition (for example, allele frequencies).

dental apes Early apes exhibiting Y-5 molar patterns but monkey-like postcranial skeletons.

dental arcade The parabolic arc that forms the upper or lower row of teeth.

deoxyribonucleic acid (DNA) A double-stranded molecule that is the carrier of genetic information. Each strand is composed of a linear sequence of nucleotides; the two strands are held together by hydrogen bonds that form between complementary bases.

diastema Gap between anterior teeth.

diploid number Full complement of paired chromosomes in a somatic cell. In humans, the diploid number is 46 (23 pairs of different chromosomes).

directional selection Natural selection that drives evolutionary change by selecting for greater or lesser frequency of a given trait in a population.

diurnal Active during daylight hours.

dominance hierarchy Ranking of individual primates in a group that reflects their ability to displace, intimidate, or defeat group mates in contests.

dominant In a diploid organism, an allele that is expressed when present on only one of a pair of homologous chromosomes.

Duffy blood group Red blood cell system useful for studying admixture between African- and European-derived populations.

Early Stone Age (or Lower Paleolithic) The earliest stone tool industries including the Oldowan and Acheulean industries, called the ESA in Africa and the Lower Paleolithic outside Africa.

ecological intelligence Hominid intelligence and brain size increase theorized as a result of benefits of navigating and foraging in a complex tropical forest ecosystem.

ecological species concept Defines species based on the uniqueness of their ecological niche.

ecology The study of the interrelationships of plants, animals, and the physical environment in which they live.

electron spin resonance (ESR) Electron trap technique that measures the total amount of radioactivity accumulated by a specimen such as tooth or bone since burial.

electron trap techniques Radiometric techniques that measure the accumulation of electrons in traps in the crystal lattice of a specimen.

encephalization A measure relating brain size to body size in a species.

encephalization quotient (EQ) The ratio of the actual brain size of a species to its expected brain size based on a statistical regression of brain to body size based on a large number of species.

endocast A replica (or cast) of the internal surface of the braincase that reflects the impressions made by the brain on the skull walls. Natural endocasts are formed by the filling of the braincase by sediments.

endoplasmic reticulum (ER) An organelle in the cytoplasm consisting of a folded membrane.

environment of evolutionary adaptedness (EEA) According to evolutionary psychologists, the critical period for understanding the selective forces that shape human behavior; exemplified by hunter-gatherer lifestyles of hominids before the advent of agriculture.

environmentalism The view that the environment has great powers to directly shape the anatomy of individual organisms.

enzyme A complex protein that is a catalyst for chemical processes in the body.

epidemiology The quantitative study of the occurrence and cause of disease in populations.

estrus Hormonally influenced period of sexual receptivity in some female mammals, which corresponds to the timing of ovulation.

ethnic group A human group defined in terms of sociological, cultural, and linguistic traits.

ethnobiology The study of how traditional cultures classify objects and organisms in the natural world.

ethnography The practice of cultural anthropology. Ethnographers study the minute-to-minute workings of human societies, especially non-Western societies.

ethnology The study of human societies, their traditions, rituals, beliefs, and the differences between societies in these traits.

eukaryote A cell that possesses a well-organized nucleus.

eutheria Mammals that reproduce with a placenta and uterus.

evolution A change in the frequency of a gene or a trait in a population over multiple generations.

evolutionary psychology   Approach to understanding the evolution of human behavior that emphasizes the selection of specific behavioral patterns in the context of the environment of evolutionary adaptedness.

evolutionary species concept   Defines species as evolutionary lineages with their own unique identity.

experimentation   The testing of a hypothesis.

falsifiable   Able to be shown to be false.

female philopatry   Primate social system in which females remain and breed in the group of their birth, whereas males emigrate.

femoral condyles   The enlarged inferior end of the femur that forms the top of the knee joint.

field study   Primate behavior study conducted in the habitat in which the primate naturally occurs.

fission–fusion   Form of mating system seen in chimpanzees, bonobos, and a few other primates in which there are temporary subgroups but no stable, cohesive groups.

fission–fusion polygyny   Type of primate polygyny in which animals travel in foraging parties of varying sizes instead of a cohesive group.

fission track dating   Radiometric technique for dating non-crystalline materials using the decay of ^{238}Ur and counting the tracks that are produced by this fission. Estimates the age of sediments in which fossils are found.

fitness   Reproductive success.

flake   The stone fragment struck from a core, thought to have been the primary tools of the Oldowan.

folivores   Animals who eat a diet composed mainly of leaves or foliage.

foramen magnum   Hole in the occipital bone through which the spinal cord connects to the brain.

forensic anthropology   The study of human remains applied to a legal context.

fossils   The preserved remnants of once-living things, often buried in the ground.

founder effect   A component of genetic drift theory, stating that new populations that become isolated from the parent population carry only the genetic variation of the founders.

frequency-dependent balanced polymorphism   Balanced polymorphism that is maintained because one (or more) of the alternative phenotypes has a selective advantage over the other phenotypes only when it is present in the population below a certain frequency.

frugivorous   An animal that eats a diet composed mainly of fruit.

gametes   The sex cells: sperm in males and eggs (or ova) in females.

gene   The fundamental unit of heredity. Consists of a sequence of DNA bases that carries the information for synthesizing a protein (or polypeptide) and occupies a specific chromosomal locus.

gene flow   Movement of genes between populations.

genetic bottleneck   Temporary dramatic reduction in size of a population or species.

genetic code   The system whereby the nucleotide triplets in DNA and RNA contain the information for synthesizing proteins from the 20 amino acids.

genetic drift   Random changes in gene frequency in a population.

genotype   The genetic makeup of an individual. *Genotype* can refer to the entire genetic complement or more narrowly to the alleles present at a specific locus on two homologous chromosomes.

geological time scale (GTS)   The categories of time into which Earth's history is usually divided by geologists and paleontologists: eras, periods, and epochs.

geology   The study of the earth.

geomagnetic polarity time scale (GPTS)   Time scale composed of the sequence of paleomagnetic orientations of sediments through time.

gluteal muscles   Gluteus maximus, medius, and minimus, the muscles of walking, which have undergone radical realignment in habitual bipeds.

gradualism   Darwinian view of slow, incremental evolutionary change.

group selection   Notion largely discredited by the rise of Darwinian theory proposing that animals act for the good of their social group or of their species.

gyri (sing., gyrus)   Ridges on the surface of the brain that are formed by sulci.

half-life   The time it takes for half of the original amount of an unstable isotope of an element to decay into more stable forms.

hammerstone   A stone used for striking cores to produce flakes or bones to expose marrow.

hand axe   Type of Acheulean bifacial tool, usually teardrop-shaped, with a long cutting edge.

haploid number   The number of chromosomes found in a gamete, representing one from each pair found in a diploid somatic cell. In humans, the haploid number is 23.

haplorhine (Haplorhini)   Infraorder of the order Primates that includes the anthropoids and the tarsier.

haplotypes   Combinations of alleles (or at the sequence level, mutations) that are found together in an individual.

hard object feeding   Chewing tough, hard-to-break food items such as nuts or fibrous vegetation.

Hardy–Weinberg equilibrium   The theoretical distribution of alleles in a given population in the absence of evolution, expressed as a mathematical equation.

hemoglobin   Protein found in red blood cells that transports oxygen.

heritability   The proportion of total phenotypic variability observed for a given trait that can be ascribed to genetic factors.

heterodont   Tooth array in which different teeth have different forms and functions.

heterozygous   Having two different alleles at the loci for a gene on a pair of homologous chromosomes (or autosomes).

heterozygous advantage   With reference to a particular genetic system, the situation in which heterozygotes have a selective advantage over homozygotes (for example, sickle cell disease); a mechanism for maintaining a balanced polymorphism.

home base Archaeological term for an area to which early hominids may have brought tools and carcasses and around which their activities were centered.

home range The spatial area used by a primate group.

hominid A member of the primate family Hominidae, distinguished by bipedal posture and, in more recently evolved species, large brain.

homodont Having teeth that are uniform in form, shape, and function.

homologous chromosomes Members of the same pair of chromosomes (or autosomes). Homologous chromosomes undergo crossing over during meiosis.

homology Similarity of traits resulting from shared ancestry.

homozygous Having the same allele at the loci for a gene on both members of a pair of homologous chromosomes (or autosomes).

hormone A natural substance (often a protein) produced by specialized cells in one location of the body that influences the activity or physiology of cells in a different location.

human biology Subfield of biological anthropology dealing with human growth and development, adaptation to environmental extremes, and human genetics.

human evolutionary ecology Approach to understanding the evolution of human behavior that attempts to explore ecological and demographic factors important in determining individual reproductive success and fitness in a cultural context.

human leukocyte antigen (HLA) system Class of blood group markers formed by proteins expressed on the surface of white blood cells (leukocytes).

hylobatid (Hylobatidae) Member of the gibbon, or lesser ape, family.

hyoid bone A small "floating bone" in the front part of the throat, which is held in place by muscles and ligaments.

hypothesis A preliminary explanation of a phenomenon. Hypothesis formation is the first step of the scientific method.

ilium The blade of the innominate to which gluteal muscles attach.

immunoglobulins Proteins produced by B lymphocytes that function as antibodies.

immutability (or fixity) Stasis, lack of change.

inbreeding Mating between close relatives.

inbreeding depression Lesser fitness of offspring of closely related individuals compared with the fitness of the offspring of less closely related individuals, caused largely by the expression of lethal or debilitating recessive alleles.

incest A violation of cultural rules regulating mating behavior.

incidence rate The number of new occurrences of a disease over a given period of time divided by the population size.

inclusive fitness Reproductive success of an organism plus the fitness of its close kin.

infanticide The killing of infants, either by members of the infant's group or by a member of a rival group.

innominate bones (os coxae) The pair of bones that compose the lateral parts of the pelvis; each innominate is made up of 3 bones that fuse during adolescence.

insertion mutation A change in the base sequence of a gene that results from the addition of one or more base pairs in the DNA.

intelligent design A creationist school of thought that proposes that natural selection cannot account for the diversity and complexity of form and function seen in nature.

ischium Portion of the innominate bone that forms the bony underpinning of the rump.

isotopes Variant forms of an element that differ based on their atomic weights and numbers of neutrons in the nucleus. Both stable and unstable (radioactive) isotopes exist in nature.

juxtamastoid eminence A ridge of bone next to the mastoid process; in Neandertals, it is larger than the mastoid process itself.

karyotype The complete chromosomal complement of an individual; usually based on a photograph of the chromosomes visualized under the microscope.

kin selection Principle that animals behave preferentially toward their genetic kin; formulated by William Hamilton.

k-selected Reproductive strategy in which fewer offspring are produced per female, interbirth intervals are long, and maternal investment is high.

lactose intolerant The inability to digest lactose, the sugar found in milk; most adult mammals (including humans) are lactose intolerant as adults.

language The unique system of communication used by members of the human species.

Levallois technique A Middle Paleolithic technique that made use of prepared cores to produce uniform flakes.

linguistic anthropology The study of language, its origins, and use; also called anthropological linguistics.

linkage Genes that are found on the same chromosome are said to be linked. The closer together two genes are on a chromosome, the greater the linkage and the less likely they are to be separated during crossing over.

lithostratigraphy The study of geologic deposits and their formation, stratigraphic relationships, and relative time relationships based on their lithologic (rock) properties.

locus The location of a gene on a chromosome. The locus for a gene is identified by the number of the chromosome on which it is found and its position on the chromosome.

lumbar vertebrae The five vertebrae of the lower back.

lunate sulcus A prominent sulcus on the lateral side of the hemisphere of most nonhuman primates, which divides the primary visual cortex of the occipital lobe from the rest of the cerebrum.

Lysenkoism Soviet-era research program that tried to apply Lamarckian thinking to agricultural production.

macroevolution Evolution of major phenotypic changes over relatively short time periods.

magnetic resonance imaging (MRI)   A technique for visualizing body tissues (including the nervous system) based on radiofrequency emissions from particular atomic nuclei, especially hydrogen. It works essentially as a map of water concentration in different tissues of the body.

male philopatry   Primate social system in which males remain and breed in the group of their birth, whereas females emigrate.

mastoid process   A protrusion from the temporal bone of the skull located behind the ear.

material culture   The objects or artifacts of past human societies.

maternal–fetal incompatibility   Occurs when the mother produces antibodies against an antigen (for example, a red blood cell surface protein) expressed in the fetus that she does not possess.

matrilineal   Pattern of female kinship in a primate social group.

megadontia   Enlarged teeth.

meiosis   Cell division that occurs in the testes and ovaries and leads to the formation of sperm and ova (gametes).

melanin   A dark pigment produced by the melanocytes of the epidermis, which is the most important component of skin color.

melanocytes   Cells in the epidermis that produce melanin.

menarche   The onset of a girl's first menstrual period.

Mendel's law of independent assortment   Genes found on different chromosomes are sorted into sex cells independently of one another.

Mendel's law of segregation   The two alleles of a gene found on each of a pair of chromosomes segregate independently of one another into sex cells.

menopause   The postreproductive period in the lives of women, after the cessation of ovulation and menses.

messenger RNA (mRNA)   Strand of RNA synthesized in the nucleus as a complement to a specific gene (transcription). It carries the information for the sequence of amino acids to make a specific protein into the cytoplasm, where at a ribosome it is read and a protein molecule is synthesized (translation).

metatarsals   Five foot bones that join the tarsals to the toes and form a portion of the longitudinal arch of the foot.

metatheria   Mammals that reproduce without a placenta, including the marsupials.

metopic keel   Longitudinal ridge or thickening of bone along the midline of the frontal bone.

microevolution   The study of evolutionary phenomena that occur within a species.

microliths   Small, flaked stone tools probably designed to be hafted to wood or bone; common feature of Upper Paleolithic and Later Stone Age tool industries.

Middle Paleolithic (Middle Stone Age)   Stone tool industries that used prepared core technologies.

midfacial prognathism   The forward projection of the middle facial region, including the nose.

mitochondria   Organelles in the cytoplasm of the cell where energy production for the cell takes place. Contains its own DNA.

mitochondrial DNA (mtDNA)   Small loop of DNA. Found in the mitochondria. It is clonally and maternally inherited.

mitosis   Somatic cell division in which a single cell divides to produce two identical daughter cells.

molecular clock   A systematic accumulation of genetic change that can be used to estimate the time of divergence between two groups if relative rates are constant and a calibration point from the fossil record is available.

monogamy   A mating pair bond; primates can be socially monogamous but still mate occasionally outside the pair bond.

monogenism   Ancient belief that all people are derived from a single creation.

most recent common ancestor (MRCA)   In a phylogenetic tree, the MRCA is indicated by the deepest node from which all contemporary variants can be shown to have evolved.

motherese (infant-directed speech)   Emotive spoken language used by mothers and other adults when addressing prelinguistic babies and children.

Movius line   The separation between areas of the Old World in which Acheulean technology occurs and those in which it does not; named by archaeologist Hallam Movius.

multiregional models   Phylogenetic models that suggest that modern humans evolved in the context of gene flow between Mid- to Late Pleistocene hominid populations from different regions, so there is no single location where modern humans first evolved.

muscles of mastication   The chewing muscles: masseter, temporalis, medial and lateral pterygoids.

mutation   An alteration in the DNA, which may or may not alter the function of a cell. If it occurs in a gamete, it may be passed from one generation to the next.

myelin   Fatty substance that sheaths neuronal axons, facilitating the transmission of electrical impulses along those axons.

natural selection   Differential reproductive success over multiple generations.

neocortex   The part of the brain that controls higher cognitive function; part of the cerebrum.

neurons   The basic cellular units of the nervous system. A neuron consists of a cell body and specialized processes called dendrites (which receive inputs from other neurons) and axons (outgrowths through which neurons send impulses to other neurons).

neurotransmitters   Chemical agents that facilitate communication between neurons across the synapse.

nocturnal   Active at night.

nondisjunction error   The failure of homologous chromosomes (chromatids) to separate properly during cell division. When it occurs during meiosis, it may lead to the formation of gametes that are missing a chromosome or have an extra copy of a chromosome.

nuchal plane   Flattened bony area of the occipital posterior to the foramen magnum, to which neck muscles attach.

nucleotide   Molecular building block of nucleic acids DNA and RNA; consists of a phosphate, sugar, and base.

nucleus   In eukaryotic cells, the part of the cell in which the genetic material is separated from the rest of the cell (cytoplasm) by a plasma membrane.

null hypothesis   The starting assumption for scientific inquiry, that one's research results occur by random chance. One's hypothesis must challenge this initial assumption.

observation   The gathering of scientific information by watching a phenomenon.

occipital bun   A backward-projecting bulge on the occipital part of the skull.

occipital torus   A thickened horizontal ridge of bone on the occipital bone at the rear of the cranium.

Oldowan   The tool industry characterized by simple, usually unifacial core and flake tools.

olfactory bulbs   Knoblike structures located on the underside of the frontal lobes that form the termination of olfactory nerves running from the nasal region to the brain.

omomyoids   Family of mostly Eocene primates, probably ancestral to all haplorhines.

ontogeny   The life cycle of an organism from conception to death.

optically stimulated luminescence (OSL)   Electron trap technique that uses light to measure the amount of radioactivity accumulated by crystals in sediments (such as sand grains) since burial.

osteodontokeratic culture   A bone, tooth, and horn toolkit envisioned by Raymond Dart to be made by *Australopithecus*.

osteology   The study of the skeleton.

paleoanthropology   The study of the fossil record of ancestral humans and their primate kin.

paleomagnetism   The magnetic polarity recorded in ancient sediments. Reversed or normal direction is used to correlate with the geomagnetic polarity time scale to infer an age for a site.

paleoneurology   The study of the evolution of brain structure and function.

paleontology   The study of extinct organisms, based on their fossilized remains.

paleopathology   The study of ancient diseases in the skeletons of ancestral human populations or other animals.

paleosol   Ancient soil.

paradigm   A conceptual framework useful for understanding a body of evidence.

parapatric speciation   Speciation occurring when two populations have continuous distributions and some phenotypes in that distribution are more favorable than others.

parent isotope   The original radioactive isotope in a sample.

particulate inheritance   The concept of heredity based on the transmission of genes (alleles) according to Mendelian principles.

pathogens   Organisms and entities that can cause disease.

pedigree   A diagram used in the study of human genetics that shows the transmission of a genetic trait over several generations of a family.

phalanges   Bones that form the fingers and toes.

phenology   The leafing and fruiting cycles of a forest.

phenotype   An observable or measurable feature of an organism. Phenotypes can be anatomical, biochemical, or behavioral.

phenylketonuria (PKU)   Autosomal recessive condition that leads to the accumulation of large quantities of the amino acid phenylalanine, which causes mental retardation and other phenotypic abnormalities.

phylogeny   An evolutionary tree indicating relatedness and divergence of taxonomic groups.

physical anthropology   The study of humans as biological organisms, considered in an evolutionary framework.

phytoliths   Silica bodies produced by some plants, especially grasses, that can be used to indicate the presence of certain types of vegetation at a fossil site.

platycnemic   A bone that is flattened from side to side.

platymeric   A bone that is flattened from front to back.

Platyrrhini   Infraorder of the order Primates that is synonymous with the New World monkeys, or ceboids.

pleiotropy   The phenomenon of a single gene having multiple phenotypic effects.

plesiadapiforms   Mammalian order or suborder of mammals that may be ancestral to later Primates, characterized by some but not all of the primate trends.

point mutation   A change in the base sequence of a gene that results from the change of a single base to a different base.

polyandry   Mating system in which one female mates with multiple males.

polygenic traits   Phenotypic traits that result from the combined action of more than one gene; most complex traits are polygenic.

polygenism   Ancient belief that people are derived from multiple creations.

polygynandrous   Primate social system consisting of multiple males and multiple females.

polygynous   Mating system consisting of at least one male and more than one female.

polygyny   Mating system in which one man is allowed to take more than one wife.

polymerase chain reaction (PCR)   Method for amplifying DNA sequences using the Taq polymerase enzyme. Can potentially produce millions or billions of copies of a DNA segment starting from a very small number of target DNA.

polymorphic   Two or more distinct phenotypes (at the genetic or anatomical levels) that exist within a population.

polypeptide   A molecule made up of a chain of amino acids.

polytypic species   Species that consist of a number of separate breeding populations, each varying in some genetic trait.

pongid (Pongidae)   One of the four great ape species: gorilla, chimpanzee, bonobo, or orangutan.

population   An interbreeding group of organisms.

population genetics   The study of genetic variation within and between groups of organisms.

postorbital bar   A bony ring encircling the lateral side of the eye but not forming a complete cup around the eye globe.

postorbital constriction   The pinching-in of the cranium just behind the orbits where the temporalis muscle sits. Little constriction indicates a large brain and small muscle; great constriction indicates a large muscle, as in the robust australopithecines.

potassium–argon (K–Ar) dating   Radiometric technique using the decay of ^{40}K to ^{40}Ar in potassium-bearing rocks; estimates the age of sediments in which fossils are found.

prefrontal region   The association cortex of the frontal lobes, located forward of the primary motor region of the precentral gyrus and the supplemental motor areas.

prehensile tail   Grasping tail possessed by some species of the primate families Cebidae and Atelidae.

prevalence rate   The number of existing cases of a disease divided by the population (or the population at risk).

primary cortex   Regions of the cerebral cortex that are involved directly with motor control or sensory input.

primate   Member of the mammalian order Primates, including prosimians, monkeys, apes, and humans, defined by a suite of anatomical and behavioral traits.

primatology   The study of the nonhuman primates and their anatomy, genetics, behavior, and ecology.

progesterone   A steroid hormone produced by the corpus luteum and the placenta, which prepares the uterus for pregnancy and helps maintain pregnancy once fertilization has occurred.

prognathic face   Projection of the face well in front of the braincase.

prokaryotes   Single-celled organisms, such as bacteria, in which the genetic material is not separated from the rest of the cell by a nucleus.

prosimian   Member of the primate suborder Prosimii that includes the lemurs, lorises, galagos, and tarsiers.

proteins   Complex molecules formed from chains of amino acids (polypeptide) or from a complex of polypeptides. They function as structural molecules, transport molecules, antibodies, enzymes, and hormones.

protein synthesis   The assembly of proteins from amino acids which occurs at ribosomes in the cytoplasm and is based on information carried by mRNA.

prototheria   Mammals that reproduce by egg-laying, then nurse young from nipples. The Australian platypus and echidna are the only living monotremes.

provenience   The origin or original source (as of a fossil).

pubis   Portion of the innominate that forms the anterior part of the birth canal.

punctuated equilibrium   Model of evolution characterized by rapid bursts of change, followed by long periods of stasis.

qualitative variation   Phenotypic variation that can be characterized as belonging to discrete, observable categories.

quantitative variation   Phenotypic variation that is characterized by the distribution of continuous variation (expressed using a numerical measure) within a population (for example, in a bell curve).

quarrying site   An archaeological site at which there is evidence that early hominids were obtaining the raw material to make stone tools.

race   In biological taxonomy, same thing as a subspecies; when applied to humans, sometimes incorporates both cultural and biological factors. The term is not used by biological anthropologists today.

racism   A prejudicial belief that members of one ethnic group are superior in some way to those of another.

radiocarbon dating   Radiometric technique that uses the decay of ^{14}C in organic remains such as wood and bone to estimate the time since death of the organism.

radiometric dating   Chronometric techniques that use radioactive decay of isotopes to estimate age.

recessive   In a diploid organism, refers to an allele that must be present in two copies (homozygous) in order to be expressed.

recognition species concept   Defines species based on unique traits or behaviors that allow members of one species to identify each other for mating.

recombination   The rearrangement of genes on homologous chromosomes that occurs during crossing over in meiosis. Source of variation that arises out of sexual reproduction and is important for increasing rates of natural selection.

reductionism   Paradigm that an organism is the sum of many evolved parts and that organisms can best be understood through an adaptationist approach.

regulatory genes   Guide the expression of structural genes without coding for a protein themselves.

relative dating techniques   Dating techniques that establish the age of a fossil only in comparison to other materials found above and below it.

relative rate test   A means of determining whether molecular evolution has been occurring at a constant rate in two lineages by comparing whether these lineages are equidistant from an outgroup.

replacement models   Phylogenetic models that suggest that modern humans evolved in one location and then spread geographically, replacing other earlier hominid populations without or with little admixture.

reproductive isolating mechanisms (RIMS)   Any factor—behavioral, ecological, or anatomical—that prevents a male and female of two different species from hybridizing.

reproductive potential   The possible offspring output by one sex.

reproductive strategy   The evolved pattern of behaviors by which a primate ensures its reproductive success.

reproductive tactics   The social behaviors a primate uses to achieve mating success.

reproductive variance   A measure of variation from the mean of a population in the reproductive potential of one sex compared with the other.

rhesus (Rh) system   Blood type system that can cause hemolytic anemia of the newborn through maternal–fetal incompatibility if the mother is Rh-negative and the child is Rh-positive.

ribonucleic acid (RNA)   Single-stranded nucleic acid that performs critical functions during protein synthesis and comes in three forms: messenger RNA, transfer RNA, and ribosomal RNA.

ribosomes   Structures composed primarily of RNA, which are found on the endoplasmic reticulum. They are the site of protein synthesis.

r-selected Reproductive strategy in which females have many offspring, interbirth intervals are short, and maternal investment per offspring is low.

sacrum The fused vertebrae that form the back of the pelvis.

sagittal crest Bony crest running lengthwise down the center of the cranium on the parietal bones; for the attachment of the temporalis muscles.

sagittal keel Longitudinal ridge or thickening of bone on the sagittal suture not associated with any muscle attachment.

scientific method Standard scientific research procedure in which a hypothesis is stated, data are collected to test it, and the hypothesis is either supported or refuted.

secondary compounds Toxic chemical compounds found in the leaves of many plants which the plants use as a defense against leaf-eating animals.

semi-free ranging Primate behavior study conducted in a large area that is enclosed or isolated in some way so the population is captive.

senescence Age-related decline in physiological or behavioral function in adult organisms.

sex chromosomes In mammals, chromosomes X and Y, with XX producing females and XY producing males.

sexual dimorphism Difference in size, shape, or color, between the sexes.

sexual receptivity Willingness and ability of a female to mate, also defined as fertility.

sexual selection Differential reproductive success within one sex of any species.

shovel-shaped incisor Anterior teeth which on their lingual (tongue) surface are concave with two raised edges that make them look like tiny shovels.

sickle cell disease An autosomal recessive disease caused by a point mutation in an allele that codes for one of the polypeptide chains of the hemoglobin protein.

social intelligence Hominid intelligence and brain size increase theorized as a result of benefits of being politically or socially clever when living with others; sometimes called Machiavellian intelligence.

sociality Group living, a fundamental trait of haplorhine primates.

social system The grouping pattern in which a primate species lives, including its size and composition, evolved in response to natural and sexual selection pressures.

sociobiology Name popularized by E. O. Wilson for the evolutionary study of animal social behavior.

somatic cells The cells of the body that are not sex cells.

speciation Formation of one or more new species via reproductive isolation.

species An interbreeding group of animals or plants that are reproductively isolated through anatomy, ecology, behavior, or geographic distribution from all other such groups.

stabilizing selection Selection that maintains a certain phenotype by selecting against deviations from it.

stem cells Undifferentiated cells found in the developing embryo that can be induced to differentiate into a wide variety of cell types or tissues. Also found in adults, although adult stem cells are not as totipotent as embryonic stem cells.

strata Layers of rock.

stratigraphy The study of the order of rock layers and the sequence of events they reflect.

strepsirhine (Strepsirhini) Infraorder of the order Primates that includes the prosimians, excluding the tarsier.

structural genes Genes that contain the information to make a protein.

subspecies A group of local populations that share part of the geographic range of a species and can be differentiated from other subspecies based on one or more phenotypic traits.

sulci (sing., sulcus) Grooves on the surface of the brain that divide the hemispheres into gyri.

supraorbital torus Thickened ridge of bone above the eye orbits of the skull; a browridge.

sympatric speciation Speciation occurring in the same geographic location.

systematics Branch of biology that describes patterns of organismal variation.

taphonomy The study of what happens to the remains of an animal from the time of death to the time of discovery.

tarsals Foot bones that form the ankle and arches of the foot.

taurodontism Molar teeth that have expanded pulp cavities and fused roots.

taxon A group of organisms assigned to a particular category.

taxonomy The science of biological classification.

technical intelligence Hominid intelligence and brain size increase modeled as a result of tool use and extractive foraging.

tephrostratigraphy A form of lithostratigraphy in which the chemical fingerprint of a volcanic ash is used to correlate across regions.

teratogens Substances that cause birth defects or other abnormalities in the developing embryo or fetus during pregnancy.

territory The part of a home range that is defended against other members of the same species.

theory of inheritance of acquired characteristics Discredited theory of evolutionary change proposing that changes that occur during the lifetime of an individual, through use or disuse, can be passed on to the next generation.

theory of mind Ability to place oneself into the mind of others; necessary for possessing an awareness of the knowledge or cognitive ability of others and for imitating or teaching others.

thermoluminescence (TL) Electron trap technique that uses heat to measure the amount of radioactivity accumulated by a specimen such as a stone tool since its last heating.

thoracic vertebrae The twelve vertebrae of the thorax that hold the ribs.

tool industry A particular style or tradition of making stone tools.

transfer RNA (tRNA) RNA molecules that bind to specific amino acids and transport them to ribosomes to be used during protein synthesis.

trinucleotide repeat diseases A family of autosomal dominant diseases that are caused by the insertion of multiple copies of a three–base pair sequence (CAG) that codes for the amino acid glutamine. Typically, the more copies inserted into the gene, the more serious the disease.

twin method A method for estimating the heritability of a phenotypic trait by comparing the concordance rates of identical and fraternal twins.

type specimen According to the laws of zoological nomenclature, the anatomical reference specimen for the species definition.

uniformitarianism Theory that the same gradual geological process we observe today was operating in the past.

Upper Paleolithic (Later Stone Age) Stone tool industries that are characterized by the development of blade-based technology.

uranium series (U-series) techniques Radiometric techniques using the decay of uranium to estimate an age for calcium carbonates including flowstones, shells, and teeth.

vertebral column The column of bones, and cartilaginous disks, that houses the spinal cord and provides structural support and flexibility to the body.

visual predation hypothesis Hypothesis of the origin of primate adaptation that focuses on the value of grasping hands and stereoscopic vision for catching small prey.

X-linked disorders Genetic conditions that result from mutations to genes on the X chromosome. They are almost always expressed in males, who have only one copy of the X chromosome; in females, the second X chromosome containing the normally functioning allele protects them from developing X-linked disorders.

zygomatic arch The bony arch formed by the zygomatic (cheek) bone and the temporal bone of the skull.

zygote A fertilized egg.

BIBLIOGRAPHY

Abbate E, Albianelli A, Azzaroli A, et al. 1998. A one million year old *Homo* cranium from the Danakil (Afar) depression of Eritrea. *Nature* 393:458–460.

Adcock GJ, Dennis ES, Easteal S, et al. 2001. Mitochondrial DNA sequences in ancient Australians: Implications for modern human origins. *Proceedings of the National Academy of Sciences* 98:537–542.

Aiello L, Dean C. 1990. *An Introduction to Human Evolutionary Anatomy*. Academic Press, London.

Aiello LC, Wheeler P. 1995. The expensive-tissue hypothesis. *Current Anthropology* 36:199–221.

Alcock J. 2001. *The Triumph of Sociobiology*. Oxford University Press, New York.

Allen JS. 1989. Franz Boas's physical anthropology: The critique of racial formalism revisited. *Current Anthropology* 30:79–84.

Allen JS. 1997. Are traditional societies schizophrenogenic? *Schizophrenia Bulletin* 23:357–364.

Allen JS, Cheer SM. 1996. The non-thrifty genotype. *Current Anthropology* 37:831–842.

Allen JS, Damasio H, Grabowski TJ. 2002. Normal neuroanatomical variation in the human brain: An MRI-volumetric study. *American Journal of Physical Anthropology* 118:341–358.

Allen JS, Damasio H, Grabowski et al. 2003. Sexual dimorphism and asymmetries in the gray-white composition of the human cerebrum. *NeuroImage* 18:880–899.

Allen JS, Sarich VM. 1988. Schizophrenia in an evolutionary perspective. *Perspectives in Biology and Medicine* 32:132–153.

Allison AC. 1954. Protection afforded by sickle-cell trait against malarial infection. *British Medical Journal* 1:290–294.

Altmann J. 1980. *Baboon Mothers and Infants*. Harvard University Press, Cambridge, MA.

Alvarez LW, Alvarez W, Asaro F, Michel HV. 1980. Extraterrestrial cause for the Cretaceous–Tertiary extinction. *Science* 208:1095–1108.

Alvarez W. 1997. *T. rex and the Crater of Doom*. Princeton University Press, Princeton, NJ.

Ambrose SH. 2001. Paleolithic technology and human evolution. *Science* 291:1748–1753.

American Psychiatric Association. 1994. *Diagnostic and Statistical Manual of Mental Disorders*, 4th ed. American Psychiatric Association, Washington, DC.

Anderson R. 1999. Human evolution, low back pain, and dual-level control. In *Evolutionary Medicine* (WR Trevathan, EO Smith, JJ McKenna, eds.), pp. 333–349. Oxford University Press, Oxford.

Andersson S. 1992. Female preference for long tails in lekking Jackson's widow-birds: Experimental evidence. *Animal Behavior* 43:379–388.

Andrews PJ. 1989. Palaeoecology of Laetoli. *Journal of Human Evolution* 18:173–181.

Antón SC. 1996. Tendon-associated bone features of the masticatory system in Neandertals. *Journal of Human Evolution* 31:391–408.

Antón SC. 2002. Evolutionary significance of cranial variation in Asian *Homo erectus*. *American Journal of Physical Anthropology* 118:301–323.

Antón SC. 2003. A natural history of *Homo erectus*. *Yearbook of Physical Anthropology* 46:126–170.

Antón SC, Leonard WR, Robertson M. 2002. An ecomorphological model of the initial hominid dispersal from Africa. *Journal of Human Evolution* 43:773–785.

Antón SC, Swisher CC III. 2001. Evolution and variation of cranial capacity in Asian *Homo erectus*. In *A Scientific Life: Papers in Honor of Professor Dr. Teuku Jacob* (E Indriati, SC Antón, J Kurtz, eds.), pp. 25–39. Bigraf Publishing, Yogyakarta, Indonesia.

Aoki K. 1986. A stochastic model of gene-culture coevolution suggested by the "cultural-historical hypothesis" for the evolution of adult lactose absorption in humans. *Proceedings of the National Academy of Sciences* 83:2929–2933.

Ardrey R. 1966. *The Territorial Imperative*. Atheneum, New York.

Arensburg B, Schepartz LA, Tillier AM, et al. 1990. A reappraisal of the anatomical basis for speech in Middle Paleolithic hominids. *American Journal of Physical Anthropology* 83:137–146.

Armelagos G. 1997. Disease, Darwin, and medicine in the third epidemiological transition. *Evolutionary Anthropology* 5:212–220.

Arsuaga JL. 2002. *The Neanderthal's Necklace*. Four Wall Eight Windows, New York.

Arsuaga JL, Martines A, Garcia A, Lorenzo C. 1997. The Sima de los Huesos crania (Sierra de Atapuerca, Spain). A comparative study. *Journal of Human Evolution* 33:219–281.

Arsuaga JL, Martínez I, Lorenzo C, et al. 1999. The human cranial remains from Gran Dolina Lower Pleistocene site (Sierra de Atapuerca, Spain). *Journal of Human Evolution* 37:431–457.

Asfaw B, Gilbert WH, Beyene Y, et al. 2002. Remains of *Homo erectus* from Bouri, Middle Ethiopia. *Nature* 416:317–320.

Asfaw B, White TD, Lovejoy CO, et al. 1999. *Australopithecus garhi*: A new species of early hominid from Ethiopia. *Science* 284:629–635.

Atran S. 1998. Folk biology and the anthropology of science: Cognitive universals and cultural particulars. *Behavioral and Brain Sciences* 21:547–609.

Barkow JH, Cosmides L, Tooby J, eds. 1992. *The Adapted Mind: Evolutionary Psychology and the Generation of Culture*. Oxford University Press, New York.

Barquet N, Domingo P. 1997. Smallpox: The triumph over the most terrible ministers of death. *Annals of Internal Medicine* 127:635–642.

Bateson W. 1900–1901. Problems of heredity as a subject for horticultural investigation. *Journal of the Royal Horticultural Society* 25:54–61.

Bateson W. 1902. *Mendel's Principles of Heredity: A Defence*. Cambridge University Press, Cambridge.

Beall CM. 2001. Adaptations to altitude: A current assessment. *Annual Review of Anthropology* 30:423–456.

Beall CM, Decker MJ, Brittenham GM, et al. 2002. An Ethiopian pattern of human adaptation to high-altitude hypoxia. *Proceedings of the National Academy of Sciences* 99:17215–17218.

Beall CM, Steegman AT. 2000. Human adaptation to climate: Temperature, ultraviolet radiation, and altitude. In *Human Biology: An Evolutionary and Biocultural Perspective* (S Stinson, B Bogin, R Huss-Ashmore, D O'Rourke, eds.), pp. 163–224. Wiley-Liss, New York.

Beals KL, Smith CL, Dodd SM. 1984. Brain size, cranial morphology, climate, and time machines. *Current Anthropology* 25:301–330.

Beard CK, Qi T, Dawson MR, Wang B, Li C. 1994. A diverse new primate fauna from middle Eocene fissure fillings in southeastern China. *Nature* 368:604–609.

Bearder SK, Honess PE, Ambrose L. 1995. Species diversity among galagos with special reference to mate recognition. In *Creatures of the Dark: The Nocturnal Prosimians* (L Alterman, GA Doyle, MK Izard, eds.), pp. 1–22. Plenum, New York.

Bednarik RG. 2003. A figurine from the African Acheulian. *Current Anthropology* 44:405–413.

Behe M. 1996. *Darwin's Black Box.* The Free Press, New York.

Behrensmeyer AK, Hill A, eds. 1980. *Fossils in the Making.* University of Chicago Press, Chicago.

Bellomo RV. 1994. Methods of determining early hominid behavioral activities associated with the controlled use of fire at FxJj 20 Main, Koobi Fora, Kenya. *Journal of Human Evolution* 27:173–195.

Benefit BR. 1999. *Victoriapithecus*, the key to Old World monkey and catarrhine origins. *Evolutionary Anthropology* 7:155–174.

Benefit BR, McCrossin ML. 1995. Miocene hominoids and hominid origins. *Annual Review of Anthropology* 24:237–256.

Benefit BR, McCrossin ML. 2002. The Victoriapithecidae, Cercopithecoidea. In *The Primate Fossil Record* (WC Hartwig, ed.), pp. 241–253. Cambridge University Press, Cambridge.

Benit P, Rey F, Blandin-Savoja F, et al. 1999. The mutant genotype is the main determinant of the metabolic phenotype in phenylalanine hydroxylase deficiency. *Molecular Genetics and Metabolism* 68:43–47.

Berger T, Trinkaus E. 1995. Patterns of trauma among the Neandertals. *Journal of Archaeological Science* 22:841–852.

Berlin B. 1992. Ethnobiological Classification: Principles of Categorization of Plants and Animals in Traditional Societies. Princeton University Press, Princeton, NJ.

Berlin B, Kay P. 1969. *Basic Color Terms: Their Universality and Evolution.* University of California Press, Berkeley.

Bermudez de Castro JM, Arsuaga JL, Carbonell E, et al. 1997. A hominid from the lower Pleistocene of Atapuerca, Spain: Possible ancestor to Neandertals and modern humans. *Science* 276:1392–1395.

Berry WBN. 1968. *Growth of a Prehistoric Time Scale Based on Organic Evolution.* WH Freeman, San Francisco.

Betzig L, ed. 1997. *Human Nature: A Critical Reader.* Oxford University Press, New York.

Beyerstein BL. 1999. Whence cometh the myth that we only use 10% of our brains? In *Mind Myths* (S Della Sala, ed.), pp. 3–24. Wiley, New York.

Bickerton D. 1983. Pidgin and creole languages. *Scientific American* 249:116–122.

Bickerton D. 1990. *Language and Species.* University of Chicago Press, Chicago.

Bird R. 1999. Cooperation and conflict: The behavioral ecology of the sexual division of labor. *Evolutionary Anthropology* 8:65–75.

Bix HP. 2000. *Hirohito and the Making of Modern Japan.* HarperCollins, New York.

Blixt S. 1975. Why didn't Gregor Mendel find linkage? *Nature* 256:206.

Bloch JI, Silcox MT. 2001. New basicrania of Paleocene–Eocene *Ignacius:* Re-evaluation of the Plesiadapiform–Dermopteran link. *American Journal of Physical Anthropology* 116:184–198.

Blum K, Cull JG, Braverman ER, Comings DE. 1996. Reward deficiency syndrome. *American Scientist* 84:132–145.

Blumenschine RJ. 1986. Carcass consumption sequences and the archaeological distinction of scavenging and hunting. *Journal of Human Evolution* 15:639–659.

Blumenschine RJ. 1987. Characteristics of an early hominid scavenging niche. *Current Anthropology* 28:383–407.

Boas F. 1912. Changes in the bodily form of descendants of immigrants. *American Anthropologist* 14:530–533.

Boas F. 1938(1911). *The Mind of Primitive Man,* rev. ed. Macmillan, New York.

Boas F. 1940. *Race, Language, and Culture.* University of Chicago Press, Chicago.

Boesch C, Boesch H. 1989. Hunting behavior of wild chimpanzees in the Taï National Park. *American Journal of Physical Anthropology* 78:547–573.

Bogin B. 1993. Why must I be a teenager at all? *New Scientist* 137:34–38.

Bogin B. 1995. Plasticity in the growth of Mayan refugee children living in the United States. In *Human Variability and Plasticity* (CGN Mascie-Taylor, B Bogin, eds.), pp. 46–74. Cambridge University Press, Cambridge.

Bogin B. 1999. Evolutionary perspective on human growth. *Annual Review of Anthropology* 28:109–153.

Boinski S. 1987. Mating patterns in squirrel monkeys (*Saimiri oerstedi*). *Behavioral Ecology & Sociobiology* 21:13–21.

Boinski S. 1994. Affiliation patterns among male Costa Rican squirrel monkeys. *Behaviour* 130:191–209.

Bookstein F, Schäfer K, Prossinger H, et al. 1999. Comparing frontal cranial profiles in archaic and modern *Homo* by morphometric analysis. *Anatomical Record (New Anat.)* 257:217–224.

Borgerhoff Mulder M. 1987. On cultural and reproductive success: Kipsigis evidence. *American Anthropologist* 89:617–634.

Borgerhoff Mulder M. 1990. Kipsigis women's preferences for wealthy men: Evidence for female choice in mammals. *Behavioral Ecology and Sociobiology* 27:255–264.

Borries C, Launhardt K, Epplen C, et al. 1999. DNA analyses support the hypothesis that infanticide is adaptive in langur monkeys. *Proceedings of the Royal Society of London* B 266:901–904.

Bottini N, Meloni GF, Finocchi A, et al. 2001. Maternal-fetal interaction in the ABO system: A comparative analysis of healthy mothers and couples with recurrent spontaneous abortion suggests a protective effect of B incompatibility. *Human Biology* 73:167–174.

Bowler JM, Johnston H, Olley JM, et al. 2003. New ages for human occupation and climatic change at Lake Mungo, Australia. *Nature* 421:837–840.

Boyd R, Richerson P. 1988. *Culture and the Evolutionary Process.* University of Chicago Press, Chicago.

Boyd WC. 1950. *Genetics and the Races of Man.* Little, Brown, Boston.

Brace CL, Xinag-qing S, Zhen-biao Z. 1984. Prehistoric and modern tooth size in China. In *The Origins of Modern Humans: A World Survey of the Fossil Evidence* (F Smith, F Spencer, eds.), pp. 485–516. Alan R. Liss, New York.

Brain CK. 1981. *The Hunters or the Hunted? Introduction to African Cave Taphonomy.* University of Chicago Press, Chicago.

Branda RF, Eaton JW. 1978. Skin color and nutrient photolysis: An evolutionary hypothesis. *Science* 201:625–626.

Bräuer G. 1984. The "Afro-European *sapiens* hypothesis" and hominid evolution in East Asia during the Late Middle and Upper Pleistocene. *Courier Forschunginstitut Senckenberg* 69:145–165.

Britten RJ. 2002. Divergence between samples of chimpanzee and human DNA sequences is 5%, counting indels. *Proceedings of the National Academy of Sciences* 99:13633–13635.

Broadfield DC, Holloway RL, Mowbray K, et al. 2001. Endocast of Sambungmacan 3: A new *Homo erectus* from Indonesia. *The Anatomical Record* 262:369–379.

Broca P. 1861. Remarks on the seat of the faculty of articulated language, following an observation of aphemia (loss of speech) [in French]. *Bulletin de la Société Anatomique* 6:330–357. English translation by CD Green available at psychclassics.yorku.ca/Broca/aphemie-e.htm.

Brockelman WY, Reichard U, Treesucon U, Raemakers JJ. 1998. Dispersal, pair formation, and social structure in gibbons (*Hylobates lar*). *Behavioral Ecology and Sociobiology* 42:329–339.

Brooks J Langdon. 1984. *Just Before the Origin*. ToExcel Publishing, New York.

Broom R. 1947. Discovery of a new skull of the South African ape-man, *Plesianthropus*. *Nature* 159:672.

Brown DE. 1991. *Human Universals*. McGraw-Hill, New York.

Brown FH. 1983. Correlation of Tulu Bor Tuff at Koobi Fora with the Sidi Hakoma Tuff at Hadar. *Nature* 306:210.

Brown FH. 1992. Methods of dating. In *The Cambridge Encyclopedia of Human Evolution* (S Jones, R Martin, D Pilbeam, eds.), pp. 179–186. Cambridge University Press, Cambridge.

Brown KH, Gilman R. 1986. Nutritional effects of intestinal helminths with special reference to ascariasis and strongyloidiasis. In *The Interaction of Parasitic Diseases and Nutrition* (C Chagas, GT Keusch, eds.), pp. 213–232. Pontifica Academia Scientarium, Vatican City.

Brown P, Sutikana T, MJ Morwood, et al. Due (2004) A new small-bodied hominid from the Late Pleistocene of Flores, Indonesia. *Nature* 431:1055–1061.

Browner CH, Ortiz de Montellano BR, Rubel AJ. 1988. A methodology for cross-cultural ethnomedical research. *Current Anthropology* 29:681–702.

Brues AM. 1977. *People and Races*. Macmillan, New York.

Brunet M, Beauvilain A, Coppens Y, et al. 1995. The first australopithecine 2,500 kilometres west of the Rift Valley (Chad). *Nature* 378:273–275.

Brunet M, Beauvilain A, Coppens Y, et al. 1996. *Australopithecus bahrelghazali*, une nouvelle espece d'hominide ancien de la region de Koro Toro (Tchad). *Comptes Rendus des Seances de l'Academie des Sciences* 322:907–913.

Brunet M, Guy F, Pilbeam D, et al. 2002. A new hominid from the Upper Miocene of Chad, Central Africa. *Nature* 418:145–151.

Bshary R, Noë R. 1997. The formation of red colobus–diana monkey associations under predation pressure from chimpanzees. *Proceedings of the Royal Society of London* B 264:253–259.

Buckley GA. 1997. A new species of *Purgatorius* (Mammalia; Primatomorpha) from the Lower Paleocene Bear Formation, Crazy Mountains Basin, South-Central Montana. *Journal of Palaeontology* 71:149–155.

Bumpus HC. 1899. The elimination of the unfit as illustrated by the introduced sparrow, *Passer domesticus*. *Biol. Lectures, Marine Biological Laboratory, Woods Hole* 209–226.

Bunn HT, Ezzo JA. 1993. Hunting and scavenging by Plio-Pleistocene hominids: Nutritional constraints, archaeological patterns, and behavioural implications. *Journal of Archaeological Science* 20:365–398.

Buss DM. 2003. *The Evolution of Desire*. Basic Books, New York.

Byrne RW. 1995. *The Thinking Ape*. Oxford University Press, Oxford.

Byrne RW, Whiten A, eds. 1988a. Machiavellian Intelligence: Social Expertise and the Evolution of Intellect in Monkeys, Apes, and Humans. Clarendon, Oxford.

Byrne RW, Whiten A. 1988b. Towards the next generation in data quality: A new survey of primate tactical deception. *Behavioral and Brain Sciences* 11:267–273.

Calvin WH. 1982. Did throwing stones shape hominid brain evolution? *Ethology and Sociobiology* 3:115–124.

Calvin WH. 1983. *The Throwing Madonna*. McGraw-Hill, New York.

Calvin WH, Ojemann GA. 1994. Conversations with Neil's Brain: The Neural Nature of Thought and Language. Perseus Books, Reading, MA.

Cande SC, Kent DV. 1995. Revised calibration of the geomagnetic polarity timescale for the Late Cretaceous and Cenozoic. *Journal of Geophysical Research* 100:6093–6095.

Cann RL. 2001. Genetic clues to dispersal in human populations: Retracing the past from the present. *Science* 291:1742–1748.

Cann RL. 2002. Tangled genetic routes. *Nature* 416:32–33.

Cann RL, Stoneking M, Wilson AC. 1987. Mitochondrial DNA and human evolution. *Nature* 325:31–36.

Caramelli D, Lalueza-Fox C, Vernesi C, et al. 2003. Evidence for a genetic discontinuity between Neandertals and 24,000-year-old anatomically modern Europeans. *Proceedings of the National Academy of Sciences* 100:6593–6597.

Cartmill M. 1974. Rethinking primate origins. *Science* 184:436–443.

Caspi A, Sugden K, Moffitt TE, et al. 2003. Influence of life stress on depression: Moderation by a polymorphism in the 5-HTT gene. *Science* 301:386–389.

Cavalli-Sforza LL, Bodmer WF. 1999(1971). *The Genetics of Human Populations*. Dover, Mineola, NY.

Cavalli-Sforza LL, Feldman MS. 2003. The application of molecular genetic approaches to the study of human evolution. *Nature Genetics* (suppl.) 33:266–275.

Cavalli-Sforza LL, Menozzi P, Piazza A. 1994. *The History and Geography of Human Genes*. Princeton University Press, Princeton, NJ.

Chagnon NA. 1988. Life histories, blood revenge, and warfare in a tribal population. *Science* 239:985–992.

Chagnon NA. 1997. *Yanomamö: The Fierce People*. Holt, Rinehart, and Winston, New York.

Chakravarti A, Chakraborty R. 1978. Elevated frequency of Tay–Sachs disease among Ashkenazic Jews unlikely by drift alone. *American Journal of Human Genetics* 30:256–261.

Chargaff E. 1950. Chemical specificity of nucleic acids and mechanism for their enzymatic degradation. *Experientia* 6:201–209.

Charles-Dominique P. 1977. *Ecology and Behaviour of Nocturnal Prosimians*. Columbia University Press, New York.

Cheney DL, Seyfarth RM. 1991. *How Monkeys See the World*. University of Chicago Press, Chicago.

Cheney D, Seyfarth RM, Andelman SJ, Lee PC. 1988. Reproductive success in vervet monkeys. In *Reproductive Success* (TH Clutton-Brock, ed.), pp. 384–402. University of Chicago Press, Chicago.

Chomsky N. 1967. The formal nature of language (Appendix A). In *Biological Foundations of Language* (EH Lenneberg, ed.), pp. 397–442. Wiley, New York.

Clark WEL. 1975. *The Fossil Evidence for Human Evolution*. University of Chicago Press, Chicago.

Clarke RJ. 1998. First ever discovery of a well-preserved skull and associated skeleton of *Australopithecus*. *South African Journal of Science* 94:460–464.

Clarke RJ, Tobias PV. 1995. Sterkfontein Member 2 foot bones of the oldest South African hominid. *Science* 269:521–524.

Coghlan A. 2003. A sad farewell for Dolly the sheep, the world's first cloned mammal. *New Scientist* 177:5.

Coleman L, Coleman J. 2002. The measurement of puberty: A review. *Journal of Adolescence* 25:535–550.

Collard M, Wood B. 2000. How Reliable Are Human Phylogene Hypothesis? *Proceedings of the National Academy of Sciences*. Vol.: 97:5003–5006

Conroy GC. 1997. *Reconstructing Human Origins*. Norton, New York.

Conroy GC, Jolly CJ, Cramer D, Kalb JE. 1978. Newly discovered fossil hominid skull from the Afar depression, Ethiopia. *Nature* 275:67–70.

Cook D. 1979. Subsistence base and health in the lower Illinois Valley: Evidence from the human skeleton. *Medical Anthropology* 4:109–124.

Cook D, Buikstra JE. 1979. Health and differential survival in prehistoric populations: Prenatal dental defects. *American Journal of Physical Anthropology* 51:649–664.

Cooke GS, Hill AVS. 2001. Genetics of susceptibility to human infectious disease. *Nature Reviews: Genetics* 2:967–977.

Cords M. 1990. Vigilance and mixed-species association of some East African forest monkeys. *Behavioral Ecology and Sociobiology* 26:297–300.

Covert HH. 2002. The earliest fossil primates and the evolution of the prosimians: Introduction. In *The Primate Fossil Record* (WC Hartwig, ed.), pp. 13–20. Cambridge University Press, Cambridge.

Crews DE, Gerber L. 1994. Chronic degenerative diseases and aging. In *Biological Anthropology and Aging* (DE Crews, R Garruto, eds.), pp. 154–181. Oxford University Press, New York.

Crooks D. 1999. Child growth and nutritional status in a high-poverty community in eastern Kentucky. *American Journal of Physical Anthropology* 109:129–142.

Cuatrecasas PD, Lockwood H, Caldwell J. 1965. Lactase deficiency in the adult: A common occurrence. *Lancet* 1:14–18.

Curtin RA, Dolhinow P. 1978. Primate behavior in a changing world. *American Scientist* 66:468–475.

Dagosto M. 1993. Postcranial anatomy and locomotor behavior in Eocene primates. In *Postcranial Adaptation in Nonhuman Primates* (DL Gebo, ed.), pp. 567–593. Northern Illinois University Press, DeKalb.

Damasio A. 1994. *Descartes' Error*. Avon Books, New York.

Damasio H, Damasio AR. 1989. *Lesion Analysis in Neuropsychology*. Oxford University Press, New York.

Dart RA. 1925. *Australopithecus africanus:* The man-ape of South Africa. *Nature* 115:195–199.

Darwin C. 1839. Journal of Researches into the Geology and Natural History of the Various Countries Visited by H.M.S. *Beagle*. Colburn, London.

Darwin C. 1859. On the Origin of Species by Means of Natural Selection; or, The Preservation of Favoured Races in the Struggle for Life. John Murray, London.

Darwin C. 1871. The Descent of Man and Selection in Relation to Sex. J. Murray, London.

Dawkins R. 1976. *The Selfish Gene*. Oxford University Press, New York.

Deacon TW. 1990. Fallacies of progression in theories of brain-size evolution. *International Journal of Primatology* 11:193–236.

Deacon TW. 1997. The Symbolic Species: The Co-Evolution of Language and the Brain. Norton, New York.

De Bonis L, Koufos G. 1993. The face and mandible of *Ouranopithecus macedoniensis:* Description of new specimens and comparisons. *Journal of Human Evolution* 24:469–491.

Dedrick D. 1996. Color language universality and evolution: On the explanation for basic color terms. *Philosophical Psychology* 9:497–524.

Defleur A, White T, Valensi P, Slimak L, Crégut-Bonnoure E. 1999. Neanderthal cannibalism at Moula-Guercy, Ardèche, France. *Science* 286:128–131.

Dehaene S. 2003. Natural born readers. *New Scientist* 179:30–33.

Dehaene S, Dupoux E, Mehler J, et al. 1997. Anatomical variability in the cortical representation of first and second language. *NeuroReport* 8:3809–3815.

De Heinzelen J, Clark JD, White T, et al. 1999. Environment and behavior of 2.5 million-year-old Bouri hominids. *Science* 284:625–628.

Deino AL, Renne PR, Swisher CC. 1998. ^{40}Ar/^{39}Ar dating in paleoanthropology and archaeology. *Evolutionary Anthropology* 6:63–75.

Delgado RA, van Schaik CP. 2000. The behavioral ecology and conservation of the orangutan (*Pongo pygmaeus*): A tale of two islands. *Evolutionary Anthropology* 9:201–218.

Delson E. 1980. Fossil macaques, phyletic relationships and a scenario of deployment. In *The Macaques: Studies in Ecology, Behavior, and Evolution* (DG Lindburg, ed.), pp. 10–30. Van Nostrand Reinhold, New York.

d'Errico F, Blackwell LR, Berger LR. 2001. Bone tool use in termite foraging by early hominids and its impact on understanding early hominid behaviour. *South African Journal of Science* 97:71–75.

Dettwyler KA. 1991. Can paleopathology provide evidence for "compassion"? *American Journal of Physical Anthropology* 84:375–384.

de Waal FBM. 1982. *Chimpanzee Politics*. Johns Hopkins University Press, Baltimore.

de Waal FBM, Lanting F. 1997. *Bonobo: The Forgotten Ape*. University of California Press, Berkeley.

de Waal Malefijt A. 1968. *Homo monstrosus*. *Scientific American* 219:112–118.

Di Fiore A, Rendall D. 1994. Evolution of social organization: A reappraisal for primates by using phylogenetic methods. *Proceedings of the National Academy of Sciences* 91:9941–9945.

Digby L. 1995. Infant care, infanticide, and female reproductive strategies in polygynous groups of common marmosets (*Callithrix jacchus*). *Behavioral Ecology and Sociobiology* 37:51–61.

Disotell TR. 1999. Human evolution: Origins of modern humans still look recent. *Current Biology* 9:R647–R650.

Dobzhansky T. 1973. Nothing in biology makes sense except in the light of evolution. *American Biology Teacher* 35:125–129.

Dunbar RIM. 1983. Reproductive Decisions: An Economic Analysis of Gelada Baboon Social Strategies. Princeton. Princeton University Press.

Dunbar, RIM. 1992. Neocortex size as a constraint on group size in primates. *Journal of Human Evolution* 20:469–493.

Dunbar RIM. 1993. Coevolution of neocortical size, group size, and language in humans. *Behavioral and Brain Sciences* 16:681–735.

Dunbar R. 1997. *Grooming, Gossip, and the Evolution of Language*. Harvard University Press, Cambridge, MA.

Durham WH. 1991. *Coevolution: Genes, Culture, and Human Diversity*. Stanford University Press, Stanford, CA.

Eaton SB, Eaton SB III, Konner MJ. 1999. Paleolithic nutrition revisited. In *Evolutionary Medicine* (WR Trevathan, EO Smith, JJ McKenna, eds.), pp. 313–332. Oxford University Press, Oxford.

Eaton SB, Konner MJ. 1985. Paleolithic nutrition. A consideration of its nature and current implications. *New England Journal of Medicine* 312:283–289.

Eldredge N, Gould SJ. 1972. Punctuated equilibrium: An alternative to phyletic gradualism. In *Models in Paleobiology* (TJM Shopf, ed.), pp. 82–115. Freeman, Cooper, and Co., San Francisco.

Ellison PT. 1990. Human ovarian function and reproductive ecology: New hypotheses. *American Anthropologist* 92:933–952.

Ellison PT. 1994. Advances in human reproductive ecology. *Annual Review in Anthropology* 23:255–275.

Endler J. 1983. Natural and sexual selection on color patterns in poeciliiad fishes. *Environmental Biology of Fishes* 9:173–190.

Endler J. 1986. *Natural Selection in the Wild*. Princeton University Press, Princeton, NJ.

Engels F. 1896. The part played by labor in the transition from ape to man.

Ennattah NS, Sahi T, Savilahti E, et al. 2002. Identification of a variant associated with adult-type hypolactasia. *Nature Genetics* 30:233–237.

Enoch MA, Goldman D. 1999. Genetics of alcoholism and substance abuse. *Psychiatric Clinics of North America* 22:289–299.

Etler DA. 1996. The fossil evidence for human evolution in Asia. *Annual Review of Anthropology* 25:275–301.

Evernden JF, Curtis GH. 1965. Potassium–argon dating of Late Cenozoic rocks in East Africa and Italy. *Current Anthropology* 6:643–651.

Eyre-Walker A, Keightley PD. 1999. High genomic deleterious mutation rates in hominids. *Nature* 397:344–347.

Fagan BM. 2001. *People of the Earth*, 10th ed. Prentice Hall, Upper Saddle River, NJ.

Fairbanks DJ, Rytting B. 2001. Mendelian controversies: A botanical and historical review. *American Journal of Botany* 88:737–752.

Fairburn HR, Young LE, Hendrich BD. 2002. Epigenetic reprogramming: How now, cloned cow? *Current Biology* 12:R68–R70.

Falk D. 1975. Comparative anatomy of the larynx in man and chimpanzee. *American Journal of Physical Anthropology* 43:123–132.

Falk D. 1980. A reanalysis of South African australopithecine natural endocasts. *American Journal of Physical Anthropology* 53:525–539.

Falk D. 1983a. Cerebral cortices of East African early hominids. *Science* 221:1072–1074.

Falk D. 1983b. The Taung endocast: A reply to Holloway. *American Journal of Physical Anthropology* 60:479–489.

Falk D. 1985a. Apples, oranges, and the lunate sulcus. *American Journal of Physical Anthropology* 67:313–315.

Falk D. 1985b. Hadar AL 162-28 endocast as evidence that brain enlargement preceded cortical reorganization in hominid evolution. *Nature* 313:45–47.

Falk D. 1989. Ape-like endocast of "ape-man" Taung. *American Journal of Physical Anthropology* 80:335–339.

Falk D. 1990. Brain evolution in *Homo*: The "radiator" theory. *Behavioral and Brain Sciences* 13:333–381.

Falk D. 1991. Reply to Dr. Holloway: Shifting positions on the lunate sulcus. *American Journal of Physical Anthropology* 84:89–91.

Falk D, Conroy G. 1983. The cranial venous sinus system in early hominids: Phylogenetic and functional implications for *Australopithecus afarensis*. *Nature* 306:779–781.

Falk D, Froese N, Sade DS, Dudek BC. 1999. Sex differences in brain/body relationships of rhesus monkeys and humans. *Journal of Human Evolution* 36:233–238.

Feathers JK. 1996. Luminescence dating and modern human origins. *Evolutionary Anthropology* 5:25–36.

Feibel CS. 1999. Tephrostratigraphy and geological context in paleoanthropology. *Evolutionary Anthropology* 8:87–100.

Feibel CS, Brown FH, McDougall I. 1989. Stratigraphic context of fossil hominids from the Omo Group deposits, northern Turkana Basin, Kenya and Ethiopia. *American Journal of Physical Anthropology* 78:595–622.

Feldman MW, Cavalli-Sforza LL. 1989. On the theory of evolution under genetic and cultural transmission with application to the lactose absorption problem. In *Mathematical Evolutionary Theory* (MW Feldman, ed.), pp. 145–173. Princeton University Press, Princeton, NJ.

Ferguson CA. 1964. Baby talk in six languages. *American Anthropologist* 66:103–114.

Fernald A. 1992. Human maternal vocalizations to infants as biologically relevant signals: An evolutionary perspective. In *The Adapted Mind* (JH Barkow, L Cosmides, J Tooby, eds.), pp. 391–428. Oxford University Press, New York.

Fernald A, Taeschner T, Dunn J, et al. 1989. A cross-language study of prosodic modifications in mothers' and fathers' speech to preverbal infants. *Journal of Child Language* 16:477–501.

Finkel T, Holbrook NJ. 2000. Oxidants, oxidative stress and the biology of ageing. *Nature* 408:239–247.

Finlay BL, Darlington RB. 1995. Linked regularities in the development and evolution of mammalian brains. *Science* 268:1578–1584.

Fischbeck KH. 2001. Polyglutamine expansion neurodegenerative disease. *Brain Research Bulletin* 56:161–163.

Fisher H. 1992. *Anatomy of Love*. Fawcett Columbine, New York.

Fisher RA. 1958. *The Genetical Theory of Natural Selection*, 2nd ed. Dover Publications, New York.

Fleagle JG. 1998. *Primate Adaptation and Evolution*, 2nd ed. Academic Press, San Diego, CA.

Fleagle JG, Kay RF. 1987. The phyletic position of the Parapithecidae. *Journal of Human Evolution* 16:483–532.

Fleagle JG, Rosenberger AL, eds. 1990. The platyrrhine fossil record. *Journal of Human Evolution* 19:1–254.

Fleagle JG, Stern JT, Jungers WL, et al. 1981. Climbing: A biomechanical link with brachiation and with bipedalism. *Symposia of the Zoological Society of London* 48:359–375.

Fleagle JG, Tejedor MF. 2002. Early platyrrhines of southern South America. In *The Primate Fossil Record* (WC Hartwig, ed.), pp. 161–173. Cambridge University Press, Cambridge.

Foley RA, Lee PC. 1991. Ecology and energetics of encephalization in hominid evolution. *Philosophical Transactions of the Royal Society of London* B 334:223–232.

Fossey D. 1983. *Gorillas in the Mist*. Houghton Mifflin, Boston.

Franciscus RG. 1999. Neandertal nasal structures and upper respiratory tract "specialization." *Proceedings of the National Academy of Sciences* 96:1805–1809.

Franciscus RG. 2003. Internal nasal floor configuration in *Homo* with special reference to the evolution of Neandertal facial form. *Journal of Human Evolution* 44:701–729.

Frayer D, Wolpoff MH, Smith FM, et al. 1993. Theories of modern human origins: The paleontological test. *American Anthropologist* 95:14–50.

Frisancho AR, Baker PT. 1970. Altitude and growth: A study of the patterns of physical growth of a high altitude Peruvian Quechua population. *American Journal of Physical Anthropology* 32:279–292.

Furuichi T. 1987. Sexual swelling, receptivity, and grouping of wild pygmy chimpanzee females at Wamba, Zaïre. *Primates* 28:309–318.

Gabunia L, Antón SC, Lordkipanidze D, et al. 2001. Dmanisi and dispersal. *Evolutionary Anthropology* 10:158–170.

Gabunia L, Vekua A, Lordkipanidze D, et al. 2000. Earliest Pleistocene cranial remains from Dmanisi, Republic of Georgia: Taxonomy, geological setting, and age. *Science* 288:1019–1025.

Gagneux P, Wills C, Gerloff U, et al. 1996. Mitochondrial sequences show diverse evolutionary histories of African hominoids. *Proceedings National Academy Sciences* 96:5077–5082.

Gajdusek DC, Gibbs CJ Jr, Alpers M. 1966. Experimental transmission of a kuru-like syndrome to chimpanzees. *Nature* 209:794–796.

Gajdusek DC, Zigas V. 1957. Degenerative disease of the central nervous system in New Guinea: The endemic occurrence of "kuru" in the native population. *New England Journal of Medicine* 257:974–978.

Galdikas BMF. 1985. Subadult male sociality and reproductive tactics among orangutans at Tanjung Putting. *American Journal of Primatology* 8:87–99.

Galdikas BMF, Wood JW. 1990. Birth spacing patterns in humans and apes. *American Journal of Physical Anthropology* 83:185–191.

Galik K, Senut B, Pickford M, et al. 2004. External and internal morphology of the BAR 1002'00 *Orrorin tugenensis* femur. *Nature* 305:1450–1453.

Gambier D. 1989. Fossil hominids from the early Upper Paleolithic (Aurignacian) of France. In *The Human Revolution: Behavioral and Biological Perspectives on the Origins of Modern Humans* (P Mellars, C Stringer, eds.), pp. 194–211. Princeton University Press, Princeton, NJ.

Ganzhorn HU, Kappeler PM. 1993. *Lemur Social Systems and Their Ecological Basis*. Plenum, New York.

Garber PA. 1989. Role of spatial memory in primate foraging patterns: *Saguinus mystax* and *Saguinus fuscicollis*. *American Journal of Primatology* 19:203–216.

Garber P. 1997. One for all and breeding for one: Cooperation and competition as a tamarin reproductive strategy. *Evolutionary Anthropology* 5:187–199.

Gardner H. 1993. *Frames of Mind: The Theory of Multiple Intelligences*, 2nd ed. Basic Books, New York.

Gargett RH. 1989. Grave shortcomings: The evidence for Neandertal burial. *Current Anthropology* 30:157–190.

Gargett RH. 1999. Middle Paleolithic burial is not a dead issue: The view from Qafzeh, Saint-Césaire, Amud, and Dederiyeh. *Journal of Human Evolution* 37:27–90.

Garner KJ, Ryder OA. 1996. Mitochondrial DNA diversity in gorillas. *Molecular Phylogenetics and Evolution* 6:39–48.

Gautier-Hion A, Quris R, Gautier JP. 1983. Monospecific vs. polyspecific life: A comparative study of foraging and antipredatory tactics in a community of *Cercopithecus* monkeys. *Behavioral Ecology and Sociobiology* 12:325–335.

Gazzaniga MS, Ivry RB, Mangun GR. 1998. *Cognitive Neuroscience: The Biology of the Mind*. Norton, New York.

Gebo DL. 1996. Climbing, brachiation, and terrestrial quadrupedalism: Historical precursors of hominid bipedalism. *American Journal of Physical Anthropology* 101:55–92.

Gebo DL, MacLatchy L, Kityo R, et al. 1997. A hominoid genus from the early Miocene of Uganda. *Science* 276:401–404.

Gerber LM, Crews DE. 1999. Evolutionary perspectives on chronic degenerative diseases. In *Evolutionary Medicine* (WR Trevathan, EO Smith, JJ McKenna, eds.), pp. 443–469. Oxford University Press, Oxford.

Gibbons A. 1991. Déjà vu all over again: Chimp-language wars. *Science* 251:1561–1562.

Giedd JN, Blumenthal J, Jeffries NO, et al. 1999. Brain development during adolescence: A longitudinal MRI study. *Nature Neuroscience* 2:861–863.

Gingerich PD. 1976. Cranial anatomy and evolution of early Tertiary Plesiadapidae (Mammalia, Primates). *Museum of Paleontology, University of Michigan, Papers on Paleontology* 15:1–140.

Gislén A, Dacke M, Kröger RHH, et al. 2003. Superior underwater vision in a human population of sea gypsies. *Current Biology* 13:833–836.

Glander KE, Wright PC, Seigler DS, Randrianasolo VB. 1989. Consumption of cyanogenic bamboo by a newly discovered species of bamboo lemur. *American Journal of Primatology* 19:119–124.

Gleason TM, Norconk MA. 2002. Predation risk and antipredator adaptation in white-faced sakis, *Pithecia pithecia*. In *Eat or Be Eaten: Predation Sensitive Foraging among Primates* (LE Miller, ed.), pp. 169186. Cambridge University Press, Cambridge.

Godfrey LR, Jungers WL. 2002. Quaternary fossil lemurs. In *The Primate Fossil Record* (WC Hartwig, ed.), pp. 97–121. Cambridge University Press, Cambridge.

Godinot M, Dagosto M. 1983. The astragalus of *Necrolemur* (Primates, Microchoerinae). *Journal of Paleontology* 57:1321–1324.

Goldberg A, Wrangham RW. 1997. Genetic correlates of social behaviour in chimpanzees: Evidence from mitochondrial DNA. *Animal Behaviour* 54:559–570.

Goldberg E. 2001. *The Executive Brain: Frontal Lobes and the Civilized Mind*. Oxford University Press, New York.

Goldberg P, Weiner S, Bar-Yosef O, Xu Q, Liu J. 2001. Site formation processes of Zhoukoudian, China. *Journal of Human Evolution* 41:483–530.

Goldfarb LG. 2002. Kuru: The old epidemic in a new mirror. *Microbes and Infection* 4:875–882.

Goldsmith ML. 1999. Ranging behavior of a lowland gorilla (*Gorilla g. gorilla*) group at Bai Hokou, Central African Republic. *International Journal of Primatology* 20:1–23.

Golovanova LV, Hoffecker JF, Kharitonov VM, Romanova GP. 1999. Mezmaiskaya Cave: A Neanderthal occupation in the northern Caucasus. *Current Anthropology* 40:77–86.

Goodall J. 1963. Feeding behaviour of wild chimpanzees: A preliminary report. *Symposium of the Zoological Society of London* 10:39–48.

Goodall J. 1968. Behaviour of free-living chimpanzees of the Gombe Stream area. *Animal Behaviour Monographs* 1:163–311.

Goodall J. 1968. *In the Shadow of Man*. National Geographic Society, Washington, DC.

Goodall J. 1986. *The Chimpanzees of Gombe: Patterns of Behavior*. Harvard University Press, Cambridge, MA.

Goodman M. 1962. Immunochemistry of the primates and primate evolution. *Annals of the New York Academy of Sciences* 102:219–234.

Goodman M. 1963. Serological analysis of the systematics of recent hominoids. *Human Biology* 35:377–436.

Goodman M. 1999. The genomic record of humankind's evolutionary roots. *American Journal of Human Genetics* 64:31–39.

Goodman M, Porter CA, Czelusniak J, et al. 1998. Toward a phylogenetic classification of primates based on DNA evidence complemented by fossil evidence. *Molecular Phylogenetics and Evolution* 9:585–598.

Goodman SM, O'Connor S, Langrand O. 1993. A review of predation on lemurs: Implications for the evolution of social behavior in small, nocturnal primates. In *Lemur Social Systems and Their Ecological Basis* (PM Kappeler, JU Ganzhorn, eds.), pp. 51–66. Plenum, New York.

Gossett TF. 1965. *Race: The History of an Idea in America.* Schocken Books, New York.

Gottesman II, Shields J. 1982. *Schizophrenia: The Epigenetic Puzzle.* Cambridge University Press, Cambridge.

Gould SJ, Lewontin RC. 1979. The spandrels of San Marco and the Panglossian paradigm. *Proceedings of the Royal Society of London* B 205:581–598.

Grant PR. 1986. *Ecology and Evolution of Darwin's Finches.* Princeton University Press, Princeton, NJ.

Gravlee CC, Bernard HR, Leonard WR. 2003. Heredity, environment, and cranial form: A reanalysis of Boas's immigrant data. *American Anthropologist* 105:125–138.

Groves C. 2001. *Primate Taxonomy.* Smithsonian Institution Press, Washington, DC.

Grün R, Huang PH, Huang W, et al. 1998. ESR and U-series analyses of teeth from the paleoanthropological site of Hexian, Anhui Province, China. *Journal of Human Evolution* 34:555–564.

Grün R, Huang PH, Wu X, et al. 1997. ESR analysis of teeth from the paleoanthropological site of Zhoukoudian, China. *Journal of Human Evolution* 32:83–91.

Grün R, Stringer CB. 1991. Electron spin resonance dating and the evolution of modern humans. *Archaeometry* 33:153–199.

Grün R, Stringer CB, Schwarcz HP. 1991. ESR dating of teeth from Garrod's Tabun Cave collection. *Journal of Human Evolution* 20:231–248.

Guglielmino CR, Desilvesteri A, Berres J. 2000. Probable ancestors of Hungarian ethnic groups: An admixture analysis. *Annals of Human Genetics* 64:145–159.

Gursky S. 1994. Infant care in the spectral tarsier (*Tarsius spectrum*) Sulawesi, Indonesia. *International Journal of Primatology* 15:843–853.

Gursky S. 1995. Group size and composition in the spectral tarsier, *Tarsius spectrum:* Implications for social organization. *Tropical Biodiversity* 3:57–62.

Haile-Selassie Y, Asfaw B, White TD. 2004. Hominid cranial remains from Upper Pleistocene deposits at Aduma, Middle Awash, Ethiopia. *American Journal of Physical Anthropology* 123:1–10.

Haile-Selassie Y, White T, Suwa G. 2004. Late Miocene teeth from Middle Awash Ethiopia and early hominid dental evolution. *Science* 303:1503–1505.

Haller JS. 1970. The species problem: Nineteenth-century concepts of racial inferiority in the origin of man controversy. *American Anthropologist* 72:1321–1329.

Hamilton WD. 1964. The genetical evolution of social behaviour, I and II. *Journal of Theoretical Biology* 7:1–52.

Hammer MF, Redd AJ, Wood ET, et al. 2000. Jewish and Middle Eastern non-Jewish populations share a common pool of Y-chromosome biallelic haplotypes. *Proceedings of the National Academy of Sciences* 97:6769–6774.

Hansson GC. 1988. Cystic fibrosis and chloride-secreting diarrhoea. *Nature* 333:711.

Harcourt AH. 1978. Strategies of emigration and transfer by primates, with particular reference to gorillas. *Zeitschrift für Tierpsychologie* 48:401–420.

Harding RM, Fullerton SM, Griffiths RC, et al. 1997. Archaic African and Asian lineages in the genetic ancestry of modern humans. *American Journal of Human Genetics* 60:772–789.

Hardy GH. 1908. Mendelian proportions in a mixed population. *Science* 28:49–50.

Harpending HC, Batzer MA, Gurven M, et al. 1998. Genetic traces of ancient demography. *Proceedings of the National Academy of Sciences* 95:1961–1967.

Harpending H, Rogers A. 2000. Genetic perspectives on human origins and differentiation. *Annual Review in Genomics and Human Genetics* 1:361–385.

Harrison GA, Tanner JM, Pilbeam DR, Baker PT. 1988. *Human Biology,* 3rd ed. Oxford University Press, Oxford.

Harrison T, Gu Y. 1999. Taxonomy and phylogenetic relationships of early Miocene catarrhines from Sihong, China. *Journal of Human Evolution* 37:225–277.

Hartwig WC. 1994. Patterns, puzzles and perspectives on platyrrhine origins. In *Integrative Paths to the Past: Paleoanthropological Essays in Honor of F. Clark Howell* (RS Corruccini, RL Ciochon, eds.), pp. 69–94. Prentice Hall, Englewood Cliffs, NJ.

Harvey P, Martin RD, Clutton-Brock TH. 1987. Life histories in comparative perspective. In *Primate Societies* (BB Smuts, DL Cheney, RM Seyfarth, RW Wrangham, TT Struhsaker, eds.), pp. 181–196. University of Chicago Press, Chicago.

Hassold T, Hunt P. 2001. To err (meiotically) is human: The genesis of human aneuploidy. *Nature Reviews: Genetics* 3:280–291.

Hauser MD, Sulkowski GM. 2001. Can rhesus monkeys spontaneously subtract? *Cognition* 79:239–262.

Hausfater G. 1975. Dominance and reproduction in baboons (*Papio cynocephalus*). In *Contributions to Primatology,* vol. 7. Karger, Basel.

Hawkes K. 2003. Grandmothers and the evolution of human longevity. *American Journal of Human Biology* 15:380–400.

Hawkes K, O'Connell JF, Blurton Jones NG. 1997. Hadza women's time allocation, offspring production, and the evolution of long postmenopausal life spans. *Current Anthropology* 38:551–577.

Hawkes K, O'Connell JF, Blurton Jones NG. 2001. Hadza meat sharing. *Evolution and Human Behavior* 22:113–142.

Heider ER. 1972. Universals in color naming and memory. *Journal of Experimental Psychology* 93:10–20.

Henshilwood C, d'Errico F, Vanhaeren M, et al. 2004. Middle Stone Age shell beads from South Africa. *Science* 304:404.

Herman-Giddens ME, Slora E, Wasserman RC, et al. 1997. Secondary sexual characteristics and menses in young girls seen in office practice: A study from the Pediatric Research in Office Settings Network. *Pediatrics* 99:505–512.

Hewes GW. 1999. A history of the study of language origins and the gestural primacy hypothesis. In *Handbook of Human Symbolic Evolution* (A Lock, CR Peters, eds.), pp. 571–595. Blackwell, Oxford.

Hey J. 2001. The mind of the species problem. *Trends in Ecology and Evolution* 16:326–329.

Hill EM, Chow K. 2002. Life-history theory and risky drinking. *Addiction* 97:401–413.

Hill EM, Ross L, Low B. 1997. The role of future unpredictability in human risk-taking. *Human Nature* 8:287–325.

Hill K, Hurtado AM. 1991. The evolution of premature reproductive senescence and menopause in human females: An evaluation of the "grandmother hypothesis." *Human Nature* 2:313–350.

Hill K, Hurtado AM. 1996. *Aché Life History: The Ecology and Demography of a Foraging People.* Aldine de Gruyter, New York.

Hill K, Kaplan H. 1993. On why male foragers hunt and share food. *Current Anthropology* 34:701–706.

Hirszfeld L, Hirszfeld H. 1919. Essai d'application des methods au problème des races. *Anthropologie* 29:505–537.

Hladik CM. 1975. Ecology, diet and social patterns in Old and New World Primates. In *Socioecology and Psychology of Primates* (RH Tuttle, ed.), pp. 3–35. Mouton, The Hague.

Hocket CF. 1960. The origin of speech. *Scientific American* 203:88–111.

Hodgen MT. 1964. *Early Anthropology in the Sixteenth and Seventeenth Centuries.* University of Pennsylvania Press, Philadelphia.

Hofman M. 1988. Size and shape of the cerebral cortex. II. The cortical volume. *Brain, Behavior and Evolution* 32:17–26.

Hohmann G, Fruth B. 1993. Field observations on meat sharing among bonobos (*Pan paniscus*). *Folia Primatologica* 60:225–229.

Holick MF, MacLaughlin JA, Doppelt SH. 1981. Regulation of cutaneous previtamin D3 photosynthesis in man: Skin pigment is not an essential regulator. *Science* 211:590–593.

Holliday TW. 1995. Body size and proportions in the late Pleistocene western Old World and the origins of modern humans. PhD dissertation, University of New Mexico, Albuquerque.

Holloway RL. 1968. The evolution of the primate brain: Some aspects of quantitative relations. *Brain Research* 7:121–172.

Holloway RL. 1976. Paleoneurological evidence for language origins. *Annals of the New York Academy of Sciences* 280:330–348.

Holloway RL. 1980. Within-species brain–body weight variability: A reexamination of the Danish data and other primate species. *American Journal of Physical Anthropology* 53:109–121.

Holloway RL. 1981. Revisiting the South African Taung australopithecine endocast: The position of the lunate sulcus as determined by stereoplotting technique. *American Journal of Physical Anthropology* 56:43–58.

Holloway RL. 1984. The poor brain of *Homo sapiens neanderthalensis*: See what you please. In *Ancestors: The Hard Evidence* (E Delson, ed.), pp. 319–324. Alan R. Liss, New York.

Holloway RL. 1984. The Taung endocast and the lunate sulcus: A rejection of the hypothesis of its anterior position. *American Journal of Physical Anthropology* 64:285–287.

Holloway RL. 1991. On Falk's 1989 accusations regarding Holloway's study of the Taung endocast: A reply. *American Journal of Physical Anthropology* 84:87–88.

Holloway RL. 1999. Evolution of the human brain. In *Handbook of Human Symbolic Evolution* (A Lock, CR Peters, eds.), pp. 74–125. Blackwell, Oxford.

Holloway RL, de LaCoste-Lareymondie MC. 1982. Brain endocast asymmetry in pongids and hominids: Some preliminary findings on the paleontology of cerebral dominance. *American Journal of Physical Anthropology* 58:101–110.

Holloway RL, Kimbel WH. 1986. Endocast morphology of Hadar hominid AL 162-28. *Nature* 321:536–537.

Hollox EJ, Poulter M, Zvarik M, et al. 2001. Lactase haplotype diversity in the Old World. *American Journal of Human Genetics* 68:160–172.

Hooton EA. 1916. The relation of physical anthropology to medical science. *Medical Review of Reviews* April:260–264.

Hooton EA. 1946. *Up from the Ape*, rev. ed. Macmillan, New York.

Hovers E, Ilani S, Bar-Yosef O, Vandermeersch B. 2003. An early case of color symbolism: Ochre use by modern humans in Qafzeh Cave. *Current Anthropology* 44:491–522.

Hovers E, Kimbel WH, Rak Y. 2000. The Amud 7 skeleton: Still a burial. Response to Gargett. *Journal of Human Evolution* 39:253–260.

Howell FC. 1964. Pleistocene glacial ecology and the evolution of "classic Neandertal" man. *Southwestern Journal of Anthropology* 8:377–410.

Howell FC. 1966. Observations on the earlier phases of the European Lower Paleolithic. *American Anthropologist* 68:111–140.

Howell FC. 1994. A chronostratigraphic and taxonomic framework of the origins of modern humans. In *Origins of Anatomically Modern Humans* (MH Nitecki, DV Nitecki, eds.), pp. 253–319. Plenum, New York.

Howell WM, Calder PC, Grimble RF. 2002. Gene polymorphisms, inflammatory diseases and cancer. *Proceedings of the Nutritional Society* 61:447–456.

Howells WW. 1973. *Cranial Variation in Man.* Papers of the Peabody Museum, Cambridge, MA.

Hrdy SB. 1977. *The Langurs of Abu.* Harvard University Press, Cambridge, MA.

Hrdy SB, Whitten PL. 1987. Patterning of sexual activity. In *Primate Societies* (BB Smuts, DL Cheney, RM Seyfarth, RW Wrangham, TT Struhsaker, eds.), pp. 370–384. University of Chicago Press, Chicago.

Hublin JJ. 1985. Human fossils from the North African Middle Pleistocene and the origin of *Homo sapiens*. In *Ancestors: The Hard Evidence* (E Delson, ed.), pp. 283–288. Alan R. Liss, New York.

Hublin JJ, Spoor F, Braun M, et al. 1996. A late Neanderthal associated with Upper Paleolithic artefacts. *Nature* 381:224–226.

Hunt KD. 1996. The postural feeding hypothesis: An ecological model for the evolution of bipedalism. *South African Journal of Science* 92:77–90.

Hurford JR. 1991. The evolution of the critical period for language acquisition. *Cognition* 40:159–201.

Huxley J, Kettlewell HBD. 1965. *Charles Darwin and His World*

Huxley J, Mayr E, Osmond H, Hoffer A. 1964. Schizophrenia as a genetic morphism. *Nature* 204:220–221.

Ingman M, Kaessmann H, Pääbo S, Gyllensten U. 2000. Mitochondrial genome variation and the origin of modern humans. *Nature* 408:708–713.

Irons W. 1979. Cultural and biological success. In *Evolutionary Biology and Human Social Behavior* (NA Chagnon, W Irons, eds.), pp. 257–272. Duxbury Press, North Scituate, MA.

Irwin G. 1992. *The Prehistoric Exploration and Colonisation of the Pacific.* Cambridge University Press, New York.

Isaac GL. 1978. The food-sharing behavior of proto-human hominids. *Scientific American* 238:90–108.

Isbell L, Young T. 1996. The evolution of bipedalism in hominids and reduced group size in chimpanzees: Alternative responses to decreasing resource availability. *Journal of Human Evolution* 30:389–397.

Ishida H, Pickford M. 1997. A new late Miocene hominoid from Kenya: *Samburupithecus kiptalami* gen et sp. nov. *Comptes Rendus de l'Academie des Sciences de Paris* 325:823–829.

Jablensky A, Sartorius N, Ernberg G, et al. 1992. Schizophrenia: Manifestations, incidence and course in different cultures: A World Health Organization Ten-Country Study. *Psychological Medicine* 20(suppl.):1–97.

Jablonski NG, Chaplin G. 1993. Origin of habitual terrestrial bipedalism in the ancestor of the Hominidae. *Journal of Human Evolution* 24:259–280.

Jablonski NG, Chaplin G. 2000. The evolution of human skin coloration. *Journal of Human Evolution* 39:57–106.

Jablonski NG, Chaplin G. 2002. Skin deep. *Scientific American* 287:74–81.

Jackendoff R. 1994. *Patterns in the Mind: Language and Human Nature.* Basic Books, New York.

Jackson FLC. 2000. Human adaptations to infectious disease. In *Human Biology: An Evolutionary and Biocultural Perspective*

(S Stinson, B Bogin, R Huss-Ashmore, D O'Rourke, eds.), pp. 273–293. Wiley-Liss, New York.

Janson CH. 1985. Aggressive competition and individual food consumption in wild brown capuchin monkeys (*Cebus apella*). *Behavioral Ecology and Sociobiology* 18:125–138.

Janson CH, Goldsmith ML. 1995. Predicting group size in primates: Foraging costs and predation risks. *Behavioral Ecology* 6:326–336.

Jantz RL, Owsley DW. 2001. Variation among early North American crania. *American Journal of Physical Anthropology* 114:146–155.

Jarman PJ. 1974. The social organization of antelope in relation to their ecology. *Behaviour* 48:215–267.

Jeffreys AJ, Wilson V, Thein SL. 1985. Hypervariable "minisatellite" regions in human DNA. *Nature* 314:67–73.

Jensen-Seaman M, Kidd KK. 2001. Mitochondrial variation and biogeography of eastern gorillas. *Molecular Ecology* 10:2240–2247.

Jerison HJ. 1991. Brain size and the evolution of mind. In *59th James Arthur Lecture on the Evolution of the Human Brain, 1989*. Columbia University Press, New York.

Jobling MA, Tyler-Smith C. 2003. The human Y chromosome: An evolutionary marker comes of age. *Nature Reviews Genetics* 4:598–612.

Johannsen W. 1911. The genotype conception of heredity. *American Naturalist* 45:129–159.

Johanson D, Edey M. 1981. *Lucy: The Beginnings of Humankind*. Simon & Schuster, New York.

Johanson DC, Lovejoy CO, Kimbel WH, et al. 1982. Morphology of the Pliocene partial hominid skeleton (AL 288-1) from the Hadar Formation, Ethiopia. *American Journal of Physical Anthropology* 57:403–452.

Johanson DC, Taieb M. 1976. Plio-Pleistocene hominid discoveries in Hadar, Ethiopia. *Nature* 260:293–297.

Johanson DC, White TD. 1979. A systematic assessment of early African hominids. *Science* 202:321–330.

Jolly CJ. 1970. The seed-eaters: A new model of hominid differentiation based on a baboon analogy. *Man* 5:1–26.

Jones FW. 1916. *Arboreal Man*. Edward Arnold, London.

Jordan P. 1999. *Neanderthal*. Sutton Publishing, Phoenix Mill, Gloucestershire.

Kaessmann H, Heissig F, von Haeseler A, Pääbo S. 1999. DNA sequence variation in a non-coding region of low recombination on the human X chromosome. *Nature Genetics* 22:78–81.

Kandel ER, Schwartz JH, Jessell TM. 2000. *Principles of Neural Science*, 4th ed. McGraw-Hill, New York.

Kano T. 1992. *The Last Ape*. Stanford University Press, Stanford, CA.

Kaplan H, Hill K, Lancaster J, Hurtado AM. 2000. A theory of human life history evolution: Diet, intelligence, and longevity. *Evolutionary Anthropology* 9:156–185.

Kappelman J. 1996. The evolution of body mass and relative brain size in hominids. *Journal of Human Evolution* 30:243–276.

Karn MN, Penrose LS. 1951. Birth weight and gestation time in relation to maternal age, parity, and infant survival. *Annals of Eugenics* 16:147–161.

Katzman MA, Lee S. 1997. Beyond body image: The integration of feminist and transcultural theories in the understanding of self starvation. *International Journal of Eating Disorders* 22:385–394.

Kay P, Berlin B. 1997. Science imperialism: There are nontrivial constraints on color naming. *Behavioral and Brain Science* 20:196–201.

Keith A. 1923. Man's posture: Its evolution and disorders. *British Medical Journal* 1:451–454, 499–502, 545–548, 587–590, 624–626, 669–672.

Keith A. 1940. Blumenbach's centenary. *Man* 40:82–85.

Kennedy KA, Sonakia A, Chiment J, Verma KK. 1991. Is the Narmada hominid an Indian *Homo erectus*? *American Journal of Physical Anthropology* 86:475–496.

Kessler RC, Berglund P, Demler O, et al. 2003. The epidemiology of major depressive disorder. *Journal of the American Medical Association* 289:3095–3105.

Kevles DJ. 1985. *In the Name of Eugenics*. Alfred A. Knopf, New York.

Kidd K. 1975. On the magnitude of selective forces maintaining schizophrenia in the population. In *Genetic Research in Psychiatry* (R Fieve, D Rosenthal, H Brill, eds.), pp. 135–145. Johns Hopkins University Press, Baltimore.

Kimbel WH, Rak Y, Johanson DC. 2004. *The Skull of Australopithecus afarensis*. Oxford University Press, New York.

Kirch PV. 2001. *On the Road of the Winds: An Archaeological History of the Pacific Islands before European Contact*. University of California Press, Berkeley.

Kirkpatrick M. 1982. Sexual selection and the evolution of female choice. *Evolution* 36:1–12.

Kirkpatrick RC. 1998. Ecology and behavior of the snub-nosed and douc langurs. In *The Natural History of the Doucs and Snub-Nosed Langurs* (NG Jablonski, ed.), pp. 155–190. World Scientific, Singapore.

Kirkwood TBL. 2002. Evolution theory and the mechanisms of aging. In *Brocklehursts' Textbook of Geriatric Medicine and Gerontology*, 6th ed. (R Tallis, HM Fillit, eds.), pp. 31–35. Churchhill Livingstone, Edinburgh and New York.

Kirkwood TBL, Austad SN. 2000. Why do we age? *Nature* 408:233–238.

Klaus MH, Kennell JH. 1997. The doula: An essential ingredient of childbirth revisited. *Acta Paediatrica* 86:1034–1036.

Klein RG, Edgar B. 2002. *The Dawn of Human Culture*. Wiley, New York.

Klug WS, Cummings MR. 2003. *Concepts of Genetics*. Prentice Hall, Upper Saddle River, NJ.

Knott CD. 1998. Social system dynamics, ranging patterns, and male and female strategies in wild Bornean orangutans (*Pongo pygmaeus*). *American Journal of Physical Anthropology* 26(suppl.):140.

Koda Y, Tachida H, Liu Y, et al. 2001. Contrasting patterns of polymorphisms at the ABO-secretor gene (FUT2) and plasma (1,3)fucosyltransferase gene (FUT6) in human populations. 747–756.

Kornberg A. 1960. Biological synthesis of DNA. *Science* 131:1503–1508.

Kostianovsky M. 2000. Evolutionary origin of eukaryotic cells. *Ultrastructural Pathology* 24:59–66.

Krings M, Capelli C, Tschentscher F, et al. 2000. A view of Neandertal genetic diversity. *Nature Genetics* 26:144–146.

Krings M, Geisert H, Schmitz RW, et al. 1999. DNA sequence of the mitochondrial hypervariable region II from the Neandertal type specimen. *Proceedings of the National Academy of Sciences* 96:5581–5585.

Krings M, Stone A, Schmitz RW, et al. 1997. Neandertal DNA sequences and the origin of modern humans. *Cell* 90:19–30.

Kummer H. 1968. *Social Organization of Hamadryas Baboons*. University of Chicago Press, Chicago.

Lahdenpera M, Lummaa V, Helle S, et al. 2004. Fitness benefits of prolonged post-reproductive lifespan in women. *Nature* 428:178–181.

Laidlaw SA, Kopple JD. 1987. Newer concepts of the indispensable amino acids. *American Journal of Clinical Nutrition* 46:593–605.

Laitman J. 1984. The anatomy of human speech. *Natural History* 92:20–27.

Laitman JT, Heimbuch RC. 1982. The basicranium of Plio-Pleistocene hominids as an indicator of their upper respiratory systems. *American Journal of Physical Anthropology* 59:323–343.

Laitman JT, Reidenberg JS. 1988. Advances in understanding the relationship between skull base and larynx, with comments on the origins of speech. *Human Evolution* 3:101–111.

Lalueza C, Perez-Perez A, Turbon D. 1996. Dietary inferences through buccal microwear analysis of middle and upper Pleistocene human fossils. *American Journal of Physical Anthropology* 100:367–387.

Larick R, Ciochon RL, Zaim Y, et al. 2001. Early Pleistocene $^{40}Ar/^{39}Ar$ ages for Bapang Formation hominids, Central Java, Indonesia. *Proceedings of the National Academy of Science* 98:4866–4871.

Larsen CS, Matter RM, Gebo DL. 1998. *Human Origins: The Fossil Record*, 3rd ed. Waveland Press, Prospect Heights, IL.

Larson E. 1997. Summer of the Gods: The Scopes Trial and America's Continuing Debate over Science and Religion. Harvard University Press, Cambridge, MA.

Larson E. 2001. Evolution's Workshop: God and Science on the Galapagos Islands. Basic Books, New York.

Latimer B, Ward C. 1993. The thoracic and lumbar vertebrae. In *The Nariokotome* Homo erectus *Skeleton* (A Walker, R Leakey, eds.), pp. 266–293. Harvard University Press, Cambridge, MA.

Leakey LSB. 1959. A new fossil skull from Olduvai. *Nature* 184:491–493.

Leakey LSB. 1962. A new lower Pliocene fossil primate from Kenya. *Annals of the Magazine of Natural History* 4:689–696.

Leakey MG, Feibel CS, McDougall I, Walker A. 1995. New four-million-year-old hominid species from Kanapoi and Allia Bay, Kenya. *Nature* 376:565–571.

Leakey MG, Spoor F, Brown FH, et al. 2001. New hominid genus from eastern Africa shows diverse middle Pliocene lineages. *Nature* 410:433–440.

Leakey MG, Spoor F, Brown FH, et al. 2003. A new hominid calvaria from Ileret (Kenya). *American Journal of Physical Anthropology* 36(suppl.):136.

Leakey R, Lewin R. 1978. *People of the Lake: Mankind and Its Beginnings*. Doubleday, New York.

LeBlanc S, Register K. 2003. *Constant Battles: The Myth of the Peaceful, Noble Savage*. St. Martin's Press, New York.

Ledoux J. 1996. *The Emotional Brain*. Touchstone, New York.

Lee RB, DeVore I, eds. 1968. *Man the Hunter*. Aldine, Chicago.

Lee-Thorp JA, van der Merwe NJ, Brain CK. 1994. Diet of *Australopithecus robustus* at Swartkrans from stable carbon isotope analysis. *Journal of Human Evolution* 27:361–372.

Le Gros Clark WE, Thomas DP. 1952. The Miocene lemuroids of East Africa. *Fossil Mammals of Africa* 5:1–20.

Leigh SR. 1992. Cranial capacity evolution in *Homo erectus* and early *Homo sapiens*. *American Journal of Physical Anthropology* 87:1–13.

Leighton M. 1993. Molding diet selectivity by Bornean orangutans: Evidence for integration of multiple criteria for fruit selection. *International Journal of Primatology* 14:257–313.

LeMay M. 1985. Asymmetries of the brains and skulls of nonhuman primates. In *Cerebral Lateralization in Nonhuman Species* (SD Glick, ed.), pp. 233–245. Academic Press, Orlando, FL.

Leonard WR, Robertson ML. 1997. Rethinking the energetics of bipedality. *Current Anthropology* 38:304–309.

Li T, Etler DA. 1992. New Middle Pleistocene hominid crania from Yunxian in China. *Nature* 357:484–487.

Lieberman P. 1984. *The Biology and Evolution of Language*. Harvard University Press, Cambridge, MA.

Lieberman P. 1991. Uniquely Human: The Evolution of Speech, Thought, and Selfless Behavior. Harvard University Press, Cambridge, MA.

Lifton RJ. 1986. *The Nazi Doctors*. Basic Books, New York.

Lindee MS. 2000. Genetic disease since 1945. *Nature Reviews Genetics* 1:236–241.

Lindenbaum S. 2001. Kuru, prions, and human affairs: Thinking about epidemics. *Annual Review in Anthropology* 30:363–385.

Littlefield A, Lieberman L, Reynolds LT. 1982. Redefining race: The potential demise of a concept in physical anthropology. *Current Anthropology* 23:641–655.

Livingstone FB. 1958. Anthropological implications of sickle cell gene distribution in West Africa. *American Anthropologist* 60:533–562.

Ljung BO, Bergsten-Brucefors A, Lindgren G. 1974. The secular trend in physical growth in Sweden. *Annals of Human Biology* 1:245–256.

Loomis WF. 1967. Skin-pigment regulation of vitamin D biosynthesis in man. *Science* 157:501–506.

Lovejoy CO. 1978. A biomechanical review of the locomotor diversity of early hominids. In *Early Hominids of Africa* (CJ Jolly, ed.), pp. 403–429. St. Martin's, New York.

Lovejoy CO. 1988. The evolution of human walking. *Scientific American* 259:118–125.

Lovejoy OW. 1981. The origin of man. *Science* 211:341–350.

Low BS. 2000. *Why Sex Matters*. Princeton University Press, Princeton, NJ.

Lowe JJ, Walker MJC. 1997. *Reconstructing Quaternary Environments*, 2nd ed. Prentice Hall, Essex, England.

Ludwig KR, Renne PR. 2000. Geochronology on the paleoanthropological time scale. *Evolutionary Anthropology* 9:101–110.

MacDorman MF, Minino AM, Strobino DM, Guyer B. 2002. Annual summary of vital statistics: 2001. *Pediatrics* 110:1037–1052.

Mackintosh NJ. 1998. *IQ and Human Intelligence*. Oxford University Press, Oxford.

MacLatchy L, Gebo D, Kityo R, Pilbeam D. 2000. Postcranial functional morphology of *Morotopithecus bishopi*, with implications for the evolution of modern ape locomotion. *Journal of Human Evolution* 39:159–183.

Maggioncalda AN, Sapolsky RM, Czekala NM. 1999. Reproductive hormone profiles in captive male orangutans: Implications for understanding development arrest. *American Journal of Physical Anthropology* 109:19–32.

Malenky RK, Kuroda S, Vineberg EO, Wrangham RW. 1994. The significance of terrestrial herbaceous foods for bonobos, chimpanzees and gorillas. In *Chimpanzee Cultures* (RW Wrangham, WC McGrew, FB de Waal, PG Heltne, eds.), pp. 59–75. Harvard University Press, Cambridge, MA.

Mandryk C. 1992. Paleoecologist finds corridor ice-free but forbidding. *Mammoth Trumpet March* 1992.

Maples WR, Browning M. 1994. *Dead Men Do Tell Tales*. Broadway Books, New York.

Marcus G. 2004. *The Birth of the Mind*. Basic Books, New York.

Marean C. 1989. Sabertooth cats and their relevance for early hominid diet. *Journal of Human Evolution* 18:559–582.

Marean CW, Assefa Z. 1999. Zooarcheological evidence for the faunal exploitation behavior of Neandertals and early modern humans. *Evolutionary Anthropology* 8:22–37.

Marks J. 1992. Chromosomal evolution in primates. In *The Cambridge Encyclopedia of Human Evolution* (S Jones, R Martin, D Pilbeam, eds.), pp. 298–302. Cambridge University Press, Cambridge.

Marks J, Schmid CW, Sarich VM. 1988. DNA hybridization as a guide to phylogeny: Relations of the Hominoidea. *Journal of Human Evolution* 17:769–786.

Marshack A. 1996. A Middle Paleolithic symbolic composition from the Golan Heights: The earliest known depictive image. *Current Anthropology* 37:357–365.

Martin RD. 1983. Human brain evolution in an ecological context. In *52nd James Arthur Lecture on the Evolution of the Human Brain, 1982*. Columbia University Press, New York.

Mascie-Taylor CGN. 1993. The biological anthropology of disease. In *The Anthropology of Disease* (CGN Mascie-Taylor, ed.), pp. 1–72. Oxford University Press, Oxford.

Mascie-Taylor CGN, Bogin B, eds. 1995. *Human Variability and Plasticity*. Cambridge University Press, Cambridge.

Matisoo-Smith E, Roberts RM, Allen JS, et al. 1998. Patterns of prehistoric mobility in Polynesia revealed by mitochondrial DNA from the Pacific rat. *Proceedings of the National Academy of Sciences* 95:15145–15150.

Mayr E. 1942. *Systematics and the Origin of Species*. Columbia University Press, New York.

Mayr E. 1963. *Animal Species and Evolution*. Harvard University Press, Cambridge, MA.

Mayr E. 1983. How to carry out the adaptationist program. *American Naturalist* 121:324–334.

Mazurek R. 1999. Back from the dead. *New Scientist* 164:40.

McBrearty S, Brooks AS. 2000. The revolution that wasn't: A new interpretation of the origin of modern human behavior. *Journal of Human Evolution* 39:453–563.

McCown TD, Kennedy KAR, eds. 1971. *Climbing Man's Family Tree*. Prentice Hall, Englewood Cliffs, NJ.

McCracken RD. 1971. Lactase deficiency: An example of dietary evolution. *Current Anthropology* 12:479–517.

McCrossin ML, Benefit BR. 1993. Recently recovered *Kenyapithecus* mandible and its implications for great ape and human origins. *Proceedings of the National Academy of Sciences USA* 90:1962–1966.

McCrossin ML, Benefit BR, Gitau S, Blue KT. 1998. Fossil evidence for the origins of terrestriality among Old World higher primates. In *Primate Locomotion: Recent Advances* (EL Strasser, JG Fleagle, AL Rosenberger, HM McHenry, eds.), pp. 353–396. Plenum, New York.

McDermott F, Grün R, Stringer CB, Hawkesworth CJ. 1993. Mass-spectrometric U-series dates for Israeli Neanderthal/early modern hominid sites. *Nature* 363:252–255.

McDougall I. 1985. K–Ar and $^{40}Ar/^{39}Ar$ dating of the hominid-bearing Pliocene–Pleistocene sequence at Koobi Fora, Lake Turkana, northern Kenya. *Geological Society America Bulletin* 96:159–175.

McElroy A, Townsend PK. 1996. *Medical Anthropology in Ecological Perspective*, 3rd ed. Westview Press, Boulder, CO.

McFadden et al. 1999. Global ecology and biogeography Journal of 8:137–149.

McGrew WC. 1992. *Chimpanzee Material Culture*. Cambridge University Press, Cambridge.

McHenry HM. 1991. Sexual dimorphism in *Australopithecus afarensis*. *Journal of Human Evolution* 20:21–32.

McHenry HM. 1992. Body size and proportions in early hominids. *American Journal of Physical Anthropology* 87:407–431.

McHenry HM. 1994. Behavioral ecological implications of early hominid body size. *Journal of Human Evolution* 27:77–87.

McHenry HM, Coffing K. 2000. *Australopithecus* to *Homo*: Transformations in body and mind. *Annual Review of Anthropology* 29:125–146.

McKusick VA, Eldridge R, Hostetler JA, Egeland JA. 1964. Dwarfism in the Amish. *Transactions of the Association of American Physicians, Philadelphia* 77:151–168.

McNeil WH. 1976. *Plagues and People*. Doubleday, New York.

Meehan JP. 1955. Individual and racial variations in vascular response to cold stimulus. *Military Medicine* 116:330–334.

Meier B, Albibnac R, Peyrieras A, et al. 1987. A new species of Hapalemur (Primates) from South East Madagascar. *Folia Primatologica* 48:211–215.

Meindl RS. 1987. Hypothesis: A selective advantage for cystic fibrosis heterozygotes. *American Journal of Physical Anthropology* 74:39–45.

Melnick D, Hoelzer GA. 1996. Genetic consequences of macaque social organization and behavior. In *Evolution and Ecology of Macaque Societies* (JE Fa, DG Lindburg, eds.), pp. 412–442. Cambridge University Press, Cambridge.

Mendel G. 1866. Versuche über Pflanzenhybriden [Experiments in plant hybridization]. *Verhandlungen des Naturforschenden Vereines in Brünn, Bd. IV für das Jahr 1865*, 3–47.

Menzel CR. 1991. Cognitive aspects of foraging in Japanese monkeys. *Animal Behaviour* 41:397–402.

Mettler LE, Gregg TG, Schaffer HE. 1988. *Population Genetics and Evolution*. Prentice Hall, Upper Saddle River, NJ.

Meyer D, Thomson G. 2001. How selection shapes variation of the human major histocompatibility complex: A review. *Annals of Human Genetics* 65:1–26.

Milton K. 1980. The Foraging Strategy of Howler Monkeys: A Study in Primate Economics. Columbia University Press, New York.

Milton K. 1981. Distribution patterns of tropical food plants as a stimulus to primate mental development. *American Anthropologist* 83:534–548.

Milton K. 1982. Dietary quality and demographic regulation in a howler monkey population. In *The Ecology of a Tropical Forest* (EG Leigh, AS Rand, DM Windsor, eds.), pp. 273–289. Smithsonian Institution Press, Washington, DC.

Milton K. 1999. A hypothesis to explain the role of meat-eating in human evolution. *Evolutionary Anthropology* 8:11–21.

Mintz L. 1977. *Historical Geology: The Science of a Dynamic Earth*. Charles E. Merrill, Columbus, OH.

Mitani JC. 1985. Responses of gibbons (*Hylobates muelleri*) to self, neighbor and stranger song duets. *International Journal of Primatology* 6:193–200.

Mitani JC, Gros-Louis J, Manson JH. 1996. Number of males in primate groups: Comparative tests of competing hypotheses. *American Journal of Primatology* 38:315–332.

Mitchell RJ, Hammer MF. 1996. Human evolution and the Y chromosome. *Current Opinion in Genetics and Development* 6:737–742.

Mithen S. 1996. *The Prehistory of the Mind*. Thames and Hudson, London.

Mittermeier RA, Konstant WR, Rylands AB. 2002. Priorities for primate conservation in the first decade of the 21st century. XIXth Congress of International Primatological Society, Beijing, China (abstract).

Molnar S. 2002. *Human Variation,* 5th ed. Prentice Hall, Upper Saddle River, NJ.

Montagu A. 1974. *Man's Most Dangerous Myth: The Fallacy of Race,* 5th ed. Oxford University Press, London.

Moran EF. 2000. *Human Adaptability,* 2nd ed. Westview Press, Boulder, CO.

Morell V. 1995. Ancestral Passions: The Leakey Family and the Quest for Humankind's Beginnings. Simon & Schuster, New York.

Moya-Sola S, Kohler M. 1996. The first *Dryopithecus* skeleton: Origins of great ape locomotion. *Nature* 379:156–159.

Mullis K. 1990. The unusual origins of the polymerase chain reaction. *Scientific American* April:56–65.

Murphy J. 1976. Psychiatric labeling in cross-cultural perspective. *Science* 191:1019–1028.

Murray FG. 1934. Pigmentation, sunlight, and nutritional disease. *American Anthropologist* 36:438–445.

Myrianthopoulos NC, Aronson SM. 1966. Population dynamics of Tay–Sachs disease. I. Reproductive fitness and selection. *American Journal of Human Genetics* 18:313–327.

Nafte M. 2000) *Flesh and Bone: An Introduction to Forensic Anthropology.* Carolina Academic Press, Durham, NC.

Neel JV. 1962. Diabetes mellitus: A thrifty genotype rendered detrimental by "progress"? *American Journal of Human Genetics* 14:353–362.

Neel JV. 1982. The thrifty genotype revisited. In *The Genetics of Diabetes Mellitus* (J Kobberling, R Tattersall, eds.), pp. 283–293. Academic Press, London.

Nesse RM. 1994. An evolutionary perspective on substance abuse. *Ethology and Sociobiology* 15:339–348.

Nesse RM. 2000. Is depression an adaptation? *Archives of General Psychiatry* 57:14–20.

Nesse RM, Berridge KC. 1997. Psychoactive drug use in evolutionary perspective. *Science* 278:63–66.

Nesse RM, Williams GC. 1994. *Why We Get Sick: The New Science of Darwinian Medicine.* Times Books, New York.

Newman RW, Munroe EH. 1955. The relation of climate and body size in U.S. males. *American Journal of Physical Anthropology* 13:1–17.

Newton PN. 1987. The variable social organization of Hanuman langurs (*Presbytis entellus*), infanticide, and the monopolization of females. *International Journal of Primatology* 9:59–77.

Nichter M, Ritenbaugh C, Nichter M, Vuckovic N, Aickin M. 1995. Dieting and "watching" behaviors among adolescent females: Report of a multimethod study. *Journal of Adolescent Health* 17:153–162.

Nielsen S. 2001. Epidemiology and mortality of eating disorders. *Psychiatric Clinics of North America* 24:201–214.

Nimgaonkar VL, Ward SE, Agarde H, et al. 1997. Fertility in schizophrenia: Results from a contemporary US cohort. *Acta Psychiatrica Scandinavica* 95:364–369.

Nishida T. 1990. *The Chimpanzees of the Mahale Mountains.* University of Tokyo Press, Tokyo.

Noble W, Davidson I. 1996. *Human Evolution, Language and Mind.* Cambridge University Press, Cambridge.

Nolte J. 2002. The Human Brain: An Introduction to Its Functional Anatomy, 5th ed. Mosby, St. Louis.

Nordborg M. 1998. On the probability of Neanderthal ancestry. *American Journal of Human Genetics* 63:1237–1240.

Nowak RM, Paradiso JL. 1983. *Walker's Mammals of the World,* 4th ed. John Hopkins University Press, Baltimore.

Oakley K. 1963. Analytical methods of dating bones. In *Science in Archaeology* (D Brothwell, E Higgs, eds.). Basic Books, New York.

O'Connell JF, Hawkes K, Blurton Jones NG. 1992. Patterns in the distribution, site structure, and assemblage composition of Hadza kill-butchering sites. *Journal of Archaeological Science* 19:319–345.

Ogonuki N, Inoue K, Yamamoto Y, et al. 2002. Early death of mice cloned from somatic cells. *Nature Genetics* 30:253–254.

Omran AR. 1971. The epidemiologic transition: A theory of the epidemiology of population change. *Milbank Memorial Fund Quarterly* 49:509–538.

Online Mendelian Inheritance in Man. 2000. McKusick-Nathans Institute for Genetic Medicine, Johns Hopkins University, Baltimore, and National Center for Biotechnology Information, National Library of Medicine, Bethesda. URL: http://www.ncbi.nlm.nih.gov/omim/.

Ovchinnikov IV, Götherström A, Romanova GP, et al. 2000. Molecular analysis of Neanderthal DNA from the northern Caucasus. *Nature* 404:490–493.

Palombit RA. 1994. Extra-pair copulations in a monogamous ape. *Animal Behaviour* 47:721–723.

Panter-Brick C. 2002. Sexual division of labor: Energetic and evolutionary scenarios. *American Journal of Human Biology* 14:627–640.

Parish AR. 1996. Female relationships in bonobos (*Pan paniscus*). *Human Nature* 7:61–96.

Parra EJ, Marcini A, Akey J, et al. 1998. Estimating African American admixture proportions by use of population-specific alleles. *American Journal of Human Genetics* 63:1839–1851.

Partridge TC, Granger DE, Caffee MW, Clarke RJ. 2003. Lower Pliocene hominid remains from Sterkfontein. *Science* 300:607–612.

Paterson HEH. 1986. Environment and species. *South African Journal of Science* 82:62–65.

Paterson JD. 1996. Coming to America: Acclimation in macaque body structures and Bergmann's rule. *International Journal of Primatology* 17:585–611.

Pearson OM. 2000. Postcranial remains and the origin of modern humans. *Evolutionary Anthropology* 9:229–247.

Peccei JS. 1995. The origin and evolution of menopause: The altriciality–lifespan hypothesis. *Ethology and Sociobiology* 16:425–449.

Peccei JS. 2001a. A critique of the grandmother hypothesis: Old and new. *American Journal of Human Biology* 13:434–452.

Peccei JS. 2001b. Menopause: Adaptation or epiphenomenon? *Evolutionary Anthropology* 10:43–57.

Peschken CA, Esdaile JM. 1999. Rheumatic diseases in North America's indigenous peoples. *Seminars in Arthritis and Rheumatism* 28:368–391.

Petitto LA, Marentette PF. 1991. Babbling in the manual mode: Evidence for the ontogeny of language. *Science* 251:1493–1496.

Pickford M, Senut B. 2001. "Millennium Ancestor," a 6-million-year-old bipedal hominid from Kenya: Recent discoveries push back human origins by 1.5 million years. *South African Journal of Science* 97:2–22.

Pickford M, Senut B, Gommery D, Treil J. 2002. Bipedalism in *Orrorin tugenensis* revealed by its femora. *Concise Review Papers Paleoevolution* 1:191–203.

Pilbeam D. 1982. New hominoid skull material from the Miocene of Pakistan. *Nature* 295:232–234.

Pinker S. 1994. *The Language Instinct.* HarperPerennial, New York.

Pinker S, Bloom P. 1990. Natural language and natural selection. *Behavioral and Brain Sciences* 13:707–784.

Polimeni J, Reiss JP. 2003. Evolutionary perspectives on schizophrenia. *Canadian Journal of Psychiatry* 48:34–39.

Potts R. 1984. Home bases and early hominids. *American Scientist* 72:338–347.

Potts R. 1988. Early Hominid Activities at Olduvai. Aldine, Chicago.

Pritzker BM. 2000. *A Native American Encyclopedia.* Oxford University Press, New York.

Pusey A, Williams J, Goodall J. 1997. The influence of dominance rank on the reproductive success of female chimpanzees. *Science* 277:828–831.

Radinsky L. 1979. The fossil record of primate brain evolution. In *49th James Arthur Lecture on the Evolution of the Human Brain, 1979.* American Museum of Natural History, New York.

Rak Y, Kimbel WH, Hovers E. 1994. A Neandertal infant from Amucd Cave, Israel. *Journal of Human Evolution* 26:313–324.

Rasmussen DT. 2002. The origin of primates. In *The Primate Fossil Record* (WC Hartwig, ed.), pp. 5–9. Cambridge University Press, Cambridge.

Ratjen F, Döring G. 2003. Cystic fibrosis. *Lancet* 361:681–689.

Reed KE. 1997. Early hominid evolution and ecological change through the African Plio-Pleistocene. *Journal of Human Evolution* 32:289–322.

Reed TE. 1969. Caucasian genes in American Negroes. *Science* 165:762–768.

Relethford JH. 2001. Absence of regional affinities of Neandertal DNA with living humans does not reject multiregional evolution. *American Journal of Physical Anthropology* 115:95–98.

Remis MJ. 1997a. Ranging and grouping patterns of a western lowland gorilla group at Bai Hokou, Central African Republic. *American Journal of Primatology* 43:111–133.

Remis MJ. 1997b. Western lowland gorillas (*Gorilla gorilla gorilla*) as seasonal frugivores: Use of variable resources. *American Journal of Primatology* 43:87–109.

Richard A. 1992. Aggressive competition between males, female-controlled polygyny and sexual monomorphism in a Malagasy primate, *Propithecus verreauxi. Journal of Human Evolution* 22:395–406.

Richards MP, Pettitt PB, Stiner MC, Trinkaus E. 2001. Stable isotope evidence for increasing dietary breadth in the European mid–Upper Paleolithic. *Proceedings of the National Academy of Sciences* 98:6528–6532.

Richards MP, Pettitt PB, Trinkaus E, et al. 2000. Neanderthal diet at Vindija and Neanderthal predation: The evidence from stable isotopes. *Proceedings of the National Academy of Sciences* 97:7663–7666.

Richmond BG, Strait DS. 2000. Evidence that humans evolved from a knuckle-walking ancestor. *Nature* 404:382–385.

Rightmire GP. 1993. *The Evolution of* Homo erectus, *Comparative Anatomical Studies of an Extinct Human Species.* Cambridge University Press, New York.

Rightmire GP, Deacon HJ. 1991. Comparative studies of Late Pleistocene human remains from Klasies River Mouth, South Africa. *Journal of Human Evolution* 20:131–156.

Ristau CA. 1999. Animal language and cognition projects. In *Handbook of Human Symbolic Evolution* (A Lock, CR Peters, eds.), pp. 644–685. Blackwell, Oxford.

Roberts DF. 1978. *Climate and Human Variability.* Cummings, Menlo Park, CA.

Roberts MB, Parfitt SA. 1999. *A Middle Pleistocene Hominid Site at Eartham Quarry, Boxgrove, West Sussex.* English Heritage Archaeological Report 17. English Heritage, London.

Roberts MB, Stringer CB, Parfitt SA. 1994. A hominid tibia from Middle Pleistocene sediments at Boxgrove, U.K. *Nature* 369:311–313.

Robins AH. 1991. *Biological Perspectives on Human Pigmentation.* Cambridge University Press, Cambridge.

Rodman PS, McHenry HM. 1980. Bioenergetics and the origin of hominid bipedalism. *American Journal of Physical Anthropology* 52:103–106.

Rose MD. 1984. Food acquisition and the evolution of positional behavior: The case of bipedalism. In *Food Acquisition and Processing in Primates* (DJ Chivers, BA Wood, A Bilsborough, eds.), pp. 509–524. Plenum, New York.

Rosenberg KR, Trevathan WR. 1996. Bipedalism and human birth: The obstetrical dilemma revisited. *Evolutionary Anthropology* 4:161–168.

Rosenberger AL. 2002. Platyrrhine paleontology and systematics: The paradigm shifts. In *The Primate Fossil Record* (WC Hartwig, ed.), pp. 151–159. Cambridge University Press, Cambridge.

Ross C, Williams B, Kay RF. 1998. Phylogenetic analysis of anthropoid relationships. *Journal of Human Evolution* 35:221–306.

Rowe JH. 1965. The Renaissance foundations of anthropology. *American Anthropologist* 67:1–20.

Rowell TE. 1988. Beyond the one-male group. *Behaviour* 104:189–201.

Russell MD. 1987. Bone breakage in the Krapina hominid collection. *American Journal of Physical Anthropology* 72:373–379.

Ruvolo M. 1997. Molecular phylogeny of the hominoids: Inferences from multiple independent DNA sequence data sets. *Molecular Biology and Evolution* 14:248–265.

Ryan MJ. 1990. Sexual selection, sensory systems, and sensory exploitation. *Oxford Surveys in Evolutionary Biology* 7:156–195.

Sabater-Pi J, Bermejo M, Ilera G, Vea JJ. 1993. Behavior of bonobos (*Pan paniscus*) following their capture of monkeys in Zaïre. *International Journal of Primatology* 14:797–804.

Sanders WJ, Bodenbender BE. 1994. Morphometric analysis of lumbar vertebra UMP 67-28: Implications for spinal function and phylogeny of the Miocene Moroto hominoid. *Journal of Human Evolution* 26:203–237.

Sarich VM, Wilson AC. 1967. Immunological time scale for hominid evolution. *Science* 158:1200–1203.

Sauther ML. 2002. Group size effects on predation sensitive foraging in wild ring-tailed lemurs (*Lemur catta*). In *Eat or Be Eaten: Predation Sensitive Foraging among Primates* (LE Miller, ed.), pp. 107–125. Cambridge University Press, Cambridge.

Sauther ML, Sussman RW, Gould L. 1999. The socioecology of the ringtailed lemur: Thirty-five years of research. *Evolutionary Anthropology* 8:120–132.

Savage-Rumbaugh S, Lewin R. 1994. *Kanzi: The Ape at the Brink of the Human Mind.* New York: Wiley.

Savage-Rumbaugh S, Rumbaugh D. 1993. The emergence of language. In *Tools, Language, and Cognition in Human Evolution* (KR Gibson, T Ingold, eds.), pp. 86–108. Cambridge University Press, Cambridge.

Savage-Rumbaugh S, Shanker SG, Taylor TJ. 1998. *Apes, Language, and the Human Mind.* Oxford University Press, New York.

Schaaffhausen H. 1858. Zur Kentiss der ältesten Rassenschädel. *Archiv für Anatomie* 5:453–488.

Schell L. 1991. Pollution and human growth: Lead, noise, polychlorobiphenyl compounds and toxic wastes. In *Applications of Biological Anthropology to Human Affairs* (CGN Mascie-Taylor, GW Lasker, eds.), pp. 83–116. Cambridge University Press, Cambridge.

Schell L. 1995. Human biological adaptability with special emphasis on plasticity: History, development and problems for future research. In *Human Variability and Plasticity* (CGN Mascie-Taylor, B Bogin, eds.), pp. 213–237. Cambridge University Press, Cambridge.

Schell LM, Hills EA. 2002. Polluted environments as extreme environments. In *Human Growth from Conception to Maturity* (G Gilli, LM Schell, L Benso, eds.), pp. 249–261. Smith-Gordon, London.

Schick K, Toth N. 1993. Making Silent Stones Speak: Human Evolution and the Dawn of Technology. Simon & Schuster, New York.

Schick KD, Toth N, Garufi G, et al. 1999. Continuing investigations into the stone tool-making and tool-using capabilities of a Bonobo (*Pan paniscus*). *Journal of Archaeological Science* 26:821–832.

Schiller F. 1979. *Paul Broca: Founder of French Anthropology, Explorer of the Brain*. University of California Press, Berkeley.

Schmitz RW., Serre D, Bonani G, et al. 2002. The Neandertal type site revisited: Interdisciplinary investigations of skeletal remains from the Neander Valley, Germany. *Proceedings of the National Academy of Sciences* 99:13342–13347.

Schoenemann PT. 1999. Syntax as an emergent characteristic of the evolution of semantic complexity. *Mind and Machines* 9:309–346.

Schoenemann PT, Budinger TF, Sarich VM, Wang WSY. 2000. Brain size does not predict general cognitive ability within families. *Proceedings of the National Academy of Sciences* 97:4932–4937.

Schoetensack O. 1908. Der unterkiefer des *Homo heidelbergensis* aus den Sanden von Mauer bei Heidelberg. W. Engelmann, Leipzig.

Schultz AH. 1969. *The Life of Primates*. Universe Books, New York.

Schulz R, Salthouse T. 1999. *Adult Development and Aging: Myths and Emerging Realities*. Prentice Hall, Upper Saddle River, NJ.

Schuman LM. 1953. Epidemiology of frostbite: Korea. In *Cold Injury: Korea 1951–52*, pp. 205–568. Army Medical Research Laboratory Report 113, Ft. Knox.

Scriver CR, Gregory DM, Sovetts D, et al. 1985. Normal plasma free amino acid values in adults: The influence of some common physiological variables. *Metabolism* 34:868–873.

Segerstråle U. 2000. *Defenders of the Truth: The Battle for Science in the Sociobiology Debate*. Oxford University Press, New York.

Seiffert ER, Simons EL, Attia Y. 2003. Fossil evidence for an ancient divergence of lorises and galagos. *Nature* 422:421–424.

Semendeferi K, Damasio H. 2000. The brain and its main anatomical subdivisions in living hominoids using magnetic resonance imaging. *Journal of Human Evolution* 38:317–332.

Semendeferi K, Damasio H, Franks R, Van Hoesen GW. 1997. The evolution of the frontal lobes: A volumetric analysis based on three-dimensional reconstructions of magnetic resonance scans of human and ape brains. *Journal of Human Evolution* 32:375–388.

Semendeferi K, Lu A, Schenker N, Damasio H. 2002. Humans and large apes share a large frontal cortex. *Nature Neuroscience* 5:272–276.

Serre D, Langaney A, Chech M, et al. 2004. No evidence of Neandertal mtDNA contribution to early modern humans. *PLoS Biology* 2:E57.

Seymour RM, Allan MJ, Pomiankowski A, Gustafsson K. 2004. Evolution of the human ABO polymorphism by two complementary selective pressures. *Proceedings of the Royal Society of London* B. 22:1065–1072 Vol. 22: 1065–1072

Shapiro HL. 1939. *Migration and Environment*. Oxford University Press, Oxford.

Shell ER. 2002. *The Hungry Gene: The Science of Fat and the Future of Thin*. Atlantic Monthly Press, New York.

Shen G, Wang J. 2000. Chronological studies on Chinese middle–late Pleistocene hominid sites, actualities and prospects. *Acta Anthropologica Sinica* 19(suppl.):279–284.

Shen G, Wang W, Wang Q, et al. 2002. U-series dating of Liujiang hominid site in Guangxi, southern China. *Journal of Human Evolution* 43:817–829.

Shepher J. 1983. *Incest: A Biosocial View*. Academic Press, New York.

Sherman PW. 1977. Nepotism and the evolution of alarm calls. *Science* 197:1246–1253.

Shipman P. 1981. *Life History of a Fossil*. Harvard University Press, Cambridge, MA.

Shipman P. 1986. Scavenging or hunting in early hominids. *American Anthropologist* 88:27–43.

Shipman P. 2001. *The Man Who Found the Missing Link*. Harvard University Press, Cambridge, MA.

Shipman P, Rose J. 1983. Evidence of butchery and hominid activities at Torralba and Ambrona. *Journal of Archaeological Science* 10:475–482.

Shipman P, Walker A. 1989. The costs of becoming a predator. *Journal of Human Evolution* 18:373–392.

Shipman P, Walker AC, Van Couvering JA, et al. 1981 The Fort Ternan hominoid site, Kenya: Geology, age, taphonomy and paleoecology. *Journal of Human Evolution* 10:49–72.

Sibley CG, Ahlquist JE. 1984. The phylogeny of the hominoid primates, as indicated by DNA–DNA hybridization. *Journal of Molecular Evolution* 20:2–15.

Sikes N. 1994. *Journal of Human Evolution* 27:25–45.

Sillen A. 1988. Elemental and isotopic analyses of mammalian fauna from southern Africa and their implications for paleodietary research. *American Journal of Physical Anthropology* 76:49–60.

Simons EL. 1987. New faces of *Aegyptopithecus* from the Oligocene of Egypt. *Journal of Human Evolution* 16:273–290.

Simons EL. 1995. Egyptian Oligocene primates: A review. *Yearbook of Physical Anthropology* 38:199–238.

Simoons FJ. 1970. Primary adult lactose intolerance and the milking habit: A problem in biological and cultural interrelations. 2. A cultural historical hypothesis. *American Journal of Digestive Diseases* 15:695–710.

Simpson GG. 1961. *Principles of Animal Taxonomy*. Columbia University Press, New York.

Small MF. 1989. Female choice in nonhuman primates. *Yearbook of Physical Anthropology* 32:103–127.

Smith CI, Chamberlain AT, Riley MS, et al. 2003. The thermal history of human fossils and the likelihood of successful DNA amplification. *Journal of Human Evolution* 45:203–217.

Smith EO. 1999. Evolution, substance abuse, and addiction. In *Evolutionary Medicine* (WR Trevathan, EO Smith, JJ McKenna, eds.), pp. 375–406. Oxford University Press, New York.

Smith FH. 1984. Fossil hominids from the Upper Pleistocene of central Europe and the origin of modern Europeans. In *The Origins of Modern Humans* (FH Smith, F Spencer, eds.), pp. 137–210. Alan R. Liss, New York.

Smith GE. 1913. The evolution of man. Annual Report of the Board of Regents of the Smithsonian Institution 1912:553–572.

Smith MT. 1998. Genetic adaptation. In *Human Adaptation* (GA Harrison, H Morphy, eds.), pp. 1–54. Berg, Oxford.

Smith SS. 1965(1810). An Essay on the Causes of the Variety of Complexion and Figure in the Human Species. Belknap Press-Harvard University Press, Cambridge, MA.

Smuts BB. 1985. *Sex and Friendship in Baboons*. Aldine, New York.

Snow CC. 1982. Forensic anthropology. *Annual Review of Anthropology* 11:97–131.

Solecki R. 1971. *Shanidar: The First Flower People*. Knopf, New York.

Solter D. 2000. Mammalian cloning: Advances and limitations. *Nature Reviews: Genetics* 1:199–207.

Sommer V. 1994. Infanticide among the langurs of Jodhpur: Testing the sexual selection hypothesis with a long-term record. In *Infanticide and Parental Care* (S Parmigiani, F vom Saal, eds.), pp. 155–198. Harwood Academic Publishers, London.

Sommer V, Reichard U. 2000. Rethinking monogamy: the gibbon case. In *Primate Males: Causes and Consequences of Variation in Group Composition* (PM Kappeler, ed.), pp. 159–168. Cambridge University Press, Cambridge.

Sorensen M, Leonard WR. 2001. Neandertal energetics and foraging efficiency. *Journal of Human Evolution* 40:483–495.

Sowell ER, Thompson PM, Holmes CJ, et al. 1999. *In vivo* evidence for post-adolescent brain maturation in frontal and striatal regions. *Nature Neuroscience* 2:859–861.

Sparks CS, Jantz RL. 2002. A reassessment of human cranial plasticity: Boas revisited. *Proceedings of the National Academy of Sciences* 99:14636–14639.

Spencer F, ed. 1997. *History of Physical Anthropology*. Garland, New York.

Speth JD, Tchernov E. 2001. Neandertal hunting and meat-processing in the Near East. In *Meat-Eating and Human Evolution* (CB Stanford, HT Bunn, eds.), pp. 52–72. Oxford University Press, New York.

Spoor F, Hublin JJ, Braun M, Zonneveld F. 2003. The bony labyrinth of Neanderthals. *Journal of Human Evolution* 44:141–165.

Spurdle AB, Jenkins T. 1996. The origins of the Lemba "Black Jews" of southern Africa: Evidence from p12F2 and other Y-chromosome markers. *American Journal of Human Genetics* 59:1126–1133.

Stanford CB. 1998a. *Chimpanzee and Red Colobus: The Ecology of Predator and Prey*. Harvard University Press, Cambridge, MA.

Stanford CB. 1998b. The social behavior of chimpanzees and bonobos: Empirical evidence and shifting assumptions. *Current Anthropology* 39:399–420.

Stanford CB. 1999. *The Hunting Apes*. Princeton University Press, Princeton, NJ.

Stanford CB. 2001. The subspecies concept in primatology: The case of mountain gorillas. *Primates* 42:309–318.

Stanford CB. 2002. Arboreal bipedalism in Bwindi chimpanzees. *American Journal of Physical Anthropology* 119:87–91.

Stanford CB, Nkurunungi JB. 2003. Sympatric ecology of chimpanzees and gorillas in Bwindi Impenetrable National Park, Uganda. Diet. *International Journal of Primatology* 24:901–918.

Stanford CB. 2003. *Upright*. Houghton Mifflin, Boston.

Stanton W. 1960. *The Leopard's Spots: Scientific Attitudes toward Race in America 1815–59*. University of Chicago Press, Chicago.

Steadman DW. 2003. *Hard Evidence: Case Studies in Forensic Anthropology*. Prentice Hall, Upper Saddle River, NJ.

Stedman HH, Kozyak BW, Nelson A, et al. 2004. Myosin gene mutation correlates with anatomical changes in the human lineage. *Nature* 428:415–418.

Steegman AT. 2003. Climate, racial category, and body proportions in the U.S. *American Journal of Physical Anthropology* 36(suppl.):199–200.

Steno N. 1669. *De Solido intra Solidum Naturaliter Contento*. Dissertatio Prodromus, Florence.

Stephan H, Frahm H, Baron G. 1981. New and revised data on volumes of brain structures in insectivores and primates. *Folia Primatologica* 35:1–29.

Stern JT, Susman RL. 1983. The locomotor anatomy of *Australopithecus afarensis*. *American Journal of Physical Anthropology* 60:279–317.

Sternberg R. 1990. *Metaphors of Mind: Conceptions of the Nature of Intelligence*. Cambridge University Press, Cambridge.

Steudel KL. 1996. Limb morphology, bipedal gait, and the energetics of hominid locomotion. *American Journal of Physical Anthropology* 99:345–355.

Stewart C, Disotell TR. 1998. Primate evolution: in and out of Africa. *Current Biology* 8:R582–R588.

Stewart R, Pryzborski S. 2002. Non-neural adult stem cells: Tools for brain repair? *BioEssays* 24:708–713.

Stine GJ. 2003. *AIDS Update 2003*. Prentice Hall, Upper Saddle River, NJ.

Stocking GW. 1987. *Victorian Anthropology*. The Free Press, New York.

Stringer CB. 1994. Out of Africa: A personal history. In *Origins of Anatomically Modern Humans* (MH Nitecki, DV Nitecki, eds.), pp. 149–172. Plenum, New York.

Stringer CB, Andrews P. 1988. Genetic and fossil evidence for the origin of modern humans. *Science* 239:1263–1268.

Stringer CB, Gamble C. 1993. *In Search of the Neanderthals*. Thames and Hudson, New York.

Stringer CB, Grün R, Schwarcz HP, Goldberg P. 1989. ESR dates for the hominid burial site of Es Skhul in Israel. *Nature* 338:756–758.

Stringer CB, Hublin JJ, Vandermeersch B. 1984. The origin of anatomically modern humans in Western Europe. In *The Origins of Modern Humans* (FH Smith, F Spencer, eds.), pp. 51–136. Alan R. Liss, New York.

Stringer CB, Trinkaus E, Roberts MB, et al. 1998. The Middle Pleistocene human tibia from Boxgrove. *Journal of Human Evolution* 34:509–547.

Strum SC. 1981. Processes and products of change: Baboon predatory behavior at Gilgil, Kenya. In *Omnivorous Primates*. (RSO Harding, G Teleki, eds.), pp. 255–302. Columbia University Press, New York.

Stumpf MPH, Goldstein DB. 2001. Genealogical and evolutionary inference with the human Y chromosome. *Science* 291:1738–1742.

Sullivan RJ, Hagen EH. 2002. Psychotropic substance-seeking: Evolutionary pathology or adaptation? *Addiction* 97:389–400.

Susman R, ed. 1984. *The Pygmy Chimpanzee*. Plenum, New York.

Susman RL, Stern JT, Jungers WL. 1984. Arboreality and bipedality in the Hadar hominids. *Folia Primatologica* 43:113–156.

Sussman RL. 1991. Primate origins and the evolution of angiosperms. *American Journal of Primatology* 23:209–223.

Sussman RL. 1992. Male life history and intergroup mobility among ringtailed lemurs (*Lemur catta*). *International Journal of Primatology* 13:395–413.

Suwa G, Asfaw B, Beyene Y, et al. 1997. The first skull of *Australopithecus boisei*. *Nature* 389:489–92.

Swisher CC, Curtis GH, Jacob T, et al. 1994. Age of the earliest known hominids in Java, Indonesia. *Science* 263:1118–1121.

Swisher CC III, Rink WJ, Antón SC, et al. 1996. Latest *Homo erectus*, in Java: Potential contemporaneity with *Homo sapiens* in Southeast Asia. *Science* 274:1870–1874.

Sy MS, Gambetti P, Wong BS. 2002. Human prion diseases. *Medical Clinics of North America* 86:551–571.

Symons D. 1979. *The Evolution of Human Sexuality*. Oxford University Press, New York.

Szalay FS. 1975. Where to draw the nonprimate–primate taxonomic boundary. *Folia Primatologia* 23:158–163.

Szalay FS. 1981. Phylogeny and the problems of adaptive significance: The case of the earliest primates. *Folia Primatologica* 34:1–45.

Szalay FS, Delson E. 1979. *Evolutionary History of the Primates*. Academic Press, New York.

Takahata N, Lee SH, Satta Y. 2001. Testing multiregionality of modern human origins. *Molecular Biology and Evolution* 18:172–183.

Tan CL. 1999. Group composition, home range size, and diet of three sympatric bamboo lemur species (genus *Hapalemur*) in Ranomafana National Park, Madagascar. *International Journal of Primatology* 20:547–566.

Tanner JM. 1978. *Fetus into Man*. Harvard University Press, Cambridge, MA.

Tanner NM, Zihlman AL. 1976. Women in evolution part 1: Innovation and selection in human origins. *Signs: Journal of Women, Culture, and Society* 1:585–608.

Tappen M. 2001. Deconstructing the Serengeti. In *Meat-Eating and Human Evolution* (CB Stanford, HT Bunn, ed.), pp. 13–32. Oxford University Press, New York.

Tattersall I. 1986. Species recognition in human paleontology. *Journal of Human Evolution* 15:165–175.

Taylor RE. 2000. Fifty years of radiocarbon dating. *American Scientist* 88:60–67.

Templeton AR. 2002. Out of Africa again and again. *Nature* 416:45–51.

Terborgh J. 1983. *Five New World Primates*. Princeton University Press, Princeton, NJ.

Terrace H. 1979. *Nim*. Knopf, New York.

Thackray HM, Tifft C. 2001. Fetal alcohol syndrome. *Pediatrics in Review* 22:47–55.

Thieme H. 1997. Lower palaeolithic hunting spears from Germany. *Nature* 385:807–810.

Thornhill NW. 1991. An evolutionary analysis of rules regulating human inbreeding and marriage. *Behavioral and Brain Sciences* 14:247–293.

Tobias PV. 1971. *The Brain in Hominid Evolution*. Columbia University Press, New York.

Tobias PV. 1987. The brain of *Homo habilis*: A new level of organization in cerebral evolution. *Journal of Human Evolution* 16:741–761.

Tomasello M, Savage-Rumbaugh S, Kruger A. 1993. Imitative learning of actions on objects by children, chimpanzees and enculturated chimpanzees. *Child Development* 64:1688–1705.

Tooby J, Cosmides L. 2000. Toward mapping the evolved functional organization of mind and brain. In *The New Cognitive Neurosciences*, 2nd ed. (MS Gazzaniga, editor-in-chief), pp. 1167–1178. MIT Press, Cambridge, MA.

Toth N. 1985. Archaeological evidence for preferential right-handedness in the Lower and Middle Pleistocene, and its possible implications. *Journal of Human Evolution* 14:607–614.

Toth N, Schick K, Savage-Rumbaugh S. 1993. *Pan* the tool-maker: Investigations into the stone tool-making and tool using capabilities of a bonobo (*Pan paniscus*). *Journal of Archaeological Science* 20:81–91.

Trainor LJ, Austin CM, Desjardins RN. 2000. Is infant-directed speech prosody a result of the vocal expression of emotion? *Psychological Science* 11:188–195.

Trehub SE, Unyk AM, Trainor LJ. 1993. Maternal singing in cross-cultural perspective. *Infant Behavior and Development* 16:285–295.

Trevathan WR. 1987. *Human Birth: An Evolutionary Perspective*. Aldine de Gruyter, Hawthorne, NY.

Trevathan WR. 1999. Evolutionary obstetrics. In *Evolutionary Medicine* (WR Trevathan, EO Smith, JJ McKenna, eds.), pp. 183–207. Oxford University Press, Oxford.

Trevathan W, Smith EO, McKenna JJ, eds. 1999. *Evolutionary Medicine*. Oxford University Press, Oxford.

Trinkaus E. 1983. *The Shanidar Neandertals*. Academic Press, New York.

Trinkaus E. 1995. Neanderthal mortality patterns. *Journal of Archaeological Science* 22:121–142.

Trinkaus E. 2003. Neandertal faces were not long; modern human faces were short. *Proceedings of the National Academy of Sciences* 100:8142–8145.

Trinkaus E, Moldovan O, Milota S, et al. 2003. An early modern human from the Petera cu Oase, Romania. *Proceedings of the National Academy of Sciences* 100:11231–11236.

Trinkaus E, Shipman P. 1992. *The Neandertals*. Vintage Press, New York.

Turner CG. 1989. Teeth and prehistory in Asia. *Scientific American* 260:88–91, 94–96.

Turner CG. 1990. Major features of Sundadonty and Sinodonty, including suggestions about East Asian microevolution, population history, and late Pleistocene relationships with Australian aboriginals. *American Journal of Physical Anthropology* 82:295–317.

Tutin CEG. 1996. Ranging and social structure of lowland gorillas in the Lopé Reserve, Gabon. In *Great Ape Societies* (WC McGrew, LF Marchant, T Nishida, eds.), pp. 58–70. Cambridge University Press, Cambridge.

Tuttle RH. 1981. Evolution of hominid bipedalism and prehensile capabilities. *Philosophical Transactions of the Royal Society of London* B 292:89–94.

Tyson E. 1972 (1699). *Orang-outang sive Homo sylvestris*: or the anatomy of a pygmie. In *Climbing Man's Family Tree* (TD McCown, KAR Kennedy, eds.), pp. 41–48. Prentice Hall, Englewood Cliffs, NJ.

Van den Berghe PL. 1983. Human inbreeding avoidance: Culture in nature. *Behavioral and Brain Sciences* 6:91–123.

Vandermeersch B. 1985. The origin of the Neandertals. In *Ancestors: The Hard Evidence* (E Delson, ed.), pp. 306–309. Alan R. Liss, New York.

van Schaik CP, Hörstermann M. 1994. Predation risk and the number of adult males in a primate group: A comparative test. *Behavioral Ecology and Sociobiology* 35:261–272.

van Schaik CP, Monk KR, Yarrow Robertson JM. 2001. Dramatic decline in orang-utan numbers in the Leuser ecosystem, northern Sumatra. *Oryx* 35:14–25.

van Schaik CP, van Hoof JARAM. 1983. On the ultimate causes of primate social systems. *Behaviour* 85:91–117.

Van Valen L. 1976. Ecological species, multispecies, and oaks. *Taxon* 25:233–239.

Van Valen L, Mellin GW. 1967. Selection in natural populations. VII. New York babies (fetal life study). *Annals of Human Genetics* 31:109–127.

Vasey N. 1996. Feeding and ranging behavior of red ruffed lemurs (*Varecia variegata rubra*) and white-fronted lemurs (*Lemur fulvus albifrons*). *American Journal of Physical Anthropology* (suppl. 22):234–235.

Vekua A, Lordkipanidze D, Rightmire GP, et al. 2002. A new skull of early *Homo* from Dmanisi, Georgia. *Science* 297:85–89.

Venter JC, Adams MD, Myers EW, et al. 2001. The sequence of the human genome. *Science* 291:1304–1351.

Vervaecke H, van Elsacker L, Möhle U, et al. 1999. Inter-menstrual intervals in captive bonobos (*Pan paniscus*). *Primates* 40:283–289.

Videan E, McGrew WC. 2001. Are bonobos (*Pan paniscus*) really more bipedal than chimpanzees (*Pan troglodytes*)? *American Journal of Primatology* 54:233–239.

Vollrath D, Nathans J, Davis RW. 1988. Tandem array of human visual pigment genes at Xq28. *Science* 240:1669–1672.

Volta U, Bellentani S, Bianchi G, et al. 2001. High prevalence of celiac disease in Italian general population. *Digestive Diseases and Sciences* 46:1500–1505.

Von Koenigswald GHR. 1952. *Gigantopithecus blacki* von Koenigswald, a giant fossil hominoid from the Pleistocene of southern China. *Anthropological Papers of the American Museum of Natural History* 43:291–326.

Walker A, Leakey R, eds. 1993a. *The Nariokotome* Homo erectus *Skeleton*. Harvard University Press, Cambridge, MA.

Walker AC, Leakey RE, Harris JM, Brown FH. 1986. 2.5-myr *Australopithecus boisei* from west of Lake Turkana, Kenya. *Nature* 322:517–522.

Walker A, Shipman P. 1996. *The Wisdom of the Bones*. Vintage Books, New York.

Walker AC, Teaford M. 1989. The hunt for *Proconsul*. *Scientific American* 260:76–82.

Walker A, Zimmerman MR, Leakey REF. 1982. A possible case of hypervitaminosis A in *Homo erectus*. *Nature* 296:248–250.

Walker R, Hill K, Kaplan H, McMillan G. 2002. Age-dependency in hunting ability among the Ache of eastern Paraguay. *Journal of Human Evolution* 42:639–657.

Walsh PD, Abernethy KA, Bermejo M, et al. 2003. Catastrophic ape decline in western equatorial Africa. *Nature* 422:611–614.

Walter RC, Aronson JL. 1982. Revisions of K/Ar ages for the Hadar hominid site, Ethiopia. *Nature* 296:122–127.

Ward CV. 1997. Functional anatomy and phylogenetic implications of the hominoid trunk and hindlimb. In *Function, Phylogeny and Fossils: Miocene Hominoid Evolution and Adaptation* (DR Begun, CV Ward, MD Rose, eds.), pp. 101–130. Plenum, New York.

Washburn SL. 1968. Speculation on the problem of man's coming to the ground. In *Changing Perspectives on Man* (B Rothblatt, ed.), pp. 191–206. University of Chicago Press, Chicago.

Watanabe H, Fujiyama A, Hattori M, et al. 2004. DNA sequence and comparative analysis of chimpanzee chromosome 22. *Nature* 429:382–388.

Watson JD, Crick FHC. 1953a. Genetical implications of the structure of deoxyribonucleic acid. *Nature* 171:964–967.

Watson JD, Crick FHC. 1953b. A structure for deoxyribonucleic acid. *Nature* 171:737–738.

Watts DP. 1989. Infanticide in mountain gorillas: New cases and a reconsideration of the evidence. *Ethology* 81:1–18.

Wayne RK, Leonard JA, Cooper A. 1999. Full of sound and fury: The recent history of ancient DNA. *Annual Review in Ecology and Systematics* 30:457–477.

Weidenreich F. 1943. The skull of *Sinanthropus pekinensis*: A comparative study of a primitive hominid skull. *Palaeontologica Sinica* D10:1–485.

Weiner A. 1988. *The Trobrianders of Papua New Guinea*. Holt, Rinehart, and Winston, New York.

Weiner J. 1994. *The Beak of the Finch*. Vintage Books, New York.

Weiss KM. 2002. Goings on in Mendel's garden. *Evolutionary Anthropology* 11:40–44.

Wertz RC, Wertz DC. 1989. *Lying-In: A History of Childbirth in America*. Yale University Press, New Haven, CT.

Westermarck EA. 1891. *The History of Human Marriage*. Macmillan, New York.

Wheeler PE. 1991. The thermoregulatory advantages of hominid bipedalism in open equatorial environments: The contribution of increased convective heat loss and cutaneous evaporative cooling. *Journal of Human Evolution* 21:107–115.

White TD, Moore RV and Suwa G. 1984. Hadar biostratigraphy. *Journal of Vertebrate Paleontology* 4:575–581.

White M. 2001. *Leonardo: The First Scientist*. Griffin, New York.

White R. 2001. Personal ornaments from Grotte du Renne at Arcy-sur-Cure. *Athena Review* 2:41–46.

White TD. 1986. Cut marks on the Bodo cranium: A case of prehistoric defleshing. *American Journal of Physical Anthropology* 69:503–509.

White TD, Asfaw B, DeGusta D, et al. 2003. Pleistocene *Homo sapiens* from Middle Awash, Ethiopia. *Nature* 423:742–747.

White TD, Harris JM. 1977. Suid evolution and correlation of African hominid localities. *Science* 198:13–21.

White TD, Suwa G, Asfaw B. 1994. *Australopithecus ramidus*, a new species of early hominid from Aramis, Ethiopia. *Nature* 371:306–312.

Whiten A, Goodall J, McGrew WC, et al. 1999. Cultures in chimpanzees. *Nature* 399:682–685.

Wiens JJ. 2001. Widespread loss of sexually selected traits: How the peacock lost its spots. *Trends in Ecology and Evolution* 16:517–523.

Wiley A. 1992. Adaptation and the biocultural paradigm in medical anthropology: A critical review. *Medical Anthropology Quarterly* 6:216–236.

Wiley AS. 2004. *An Ecology of High-Altitude Infancy: A Biocultural Perspective*. Cambridge University Press, Cambridge.

Willey P, Leach P. 2003. The skull on the lawn: trophies, taphonomy and forensic anthropology. In *Hard Evidence: Case Studies in Forensic Anthropology* (DW Steadman, ed.), pp. 176–188. Prentice Hall, Upper Saddle River, NJ.

Williams DR. 2003. The biomedical challenges of space flight. *Annual Review in Medicine* 54:245–256.

Williams GC. 1957. Pleiotropy, natural selection, and the evolution of senescence. *Evolution* 11:398–411.

Williams GC. 1966. *Adaptation and Natural Selection*. Princeton University Press, Princeton, NJ.

Williams RJ. 1956. *Biochemical Individuality*. University of Texas Press, Austin.

Wilson EO. 1975. *Sociobiology: The New Synthesis*. Harvard University Press, Cambridge, MA.

Wise RJ, Greene J, Buchel C, Scott SK. 1999. Brain regions involved in articulation. *Lancet* 353:1057–1061.

WoldeGabriel G, White TD, Suwa G, et al. 1994. Ecological and temporal placement of early Pliocene hominids at Aramis, Ethiopia. *Nature* 371:330–333.

Wolf AP. 1966. Childhood association, sexual attraction, and the incest taboo: A Chinese case. *American Anthropologist* 68:883–898.

Wolf AP. 1970. Childhood association and sexual attraction: A further test of the Westermarck hypothesis. *American Anthropologist* 72:503–515.

Wolff G, Wienker T, Sander H. 1993. On the genetics of mandibular prognathism: Analysis of large European noble families. *Journal of Medical Genetics* 30:12–16.

Wolpoff MH. 1999. *Paleoanthropology*, 2nd ed. McGraw-Hill, New York.

Wolpoff M, Caspari R. 1997. *Race and Human Evolution*. Westview Press, Boulder, CO.

Wolpoff M, Hawks J, Caspari R. 2000. Multiregional, not multiple origins. *American Journal of Physical Anthropology* 112:129–136.

Wolpoff MH, Senut B, Pickford M, Hawks J. 2002. Paleoanthropology: *Sahelanthropus* or *"Sahelpithecus"*? *Nature* 419:581–582.

Wolpoff MH, Thorne AG, Smith FH, et al. 1994. Multiregional evolution: A world-wide source for modern human populations. In *Origins of Anatomically Modern Humans* (MH Nitecki, DV Nitecki, eds.), pp. 175–199. Plenum, New York.

Wolpoff MH, Zhi WX, Thorne AG. 1984. Modern *Homo sapiens* origins: A general theory of hominid evolution involving the fossil evidence from east Asia. In *The Origins of Modern Humans* (FH Smith, F Spencer, eds.), pp. 411–484. Alan R. Liss, New York.

Wood B, Collard M. 1999. The changing face of genus *Homo*. *Evolutionary Anthropology* 8:195–207.

Worthman CM. 1999. Evolutionary perspectives on the onset of puberty. In *Evolutionary Medicine* (WR Trevathan, EO Smith, JJ McKenna, eds.), pp. 135–163. Oxford University Press, Oxford.

Wrangham RW. 1980. An ecological model of female-bonded primate groups. *Behaviour* 75:262–292.

Wrangham RW, Jones JH, Laden G, et al. 1999. Cooking and human origins. *Current Anthropology* 40:567–594.

Wu R, Dong X. 1985. *Homo erectus* in China. In *Palaeoanthropology and Palaeolithic Archaeology in the People's Republic of China* (R Wu, JW Olsen, eds.), pp. 79–89. Academic Press, New York.

Wu X, Poirer FE. 1995. *Human Evolution in China: A Metric Description of the Fossils and a Review of the Sites*. Oxford University Press, New York.

Wynn TG. 1999. The evolution of tools and symbolic behaviour. In *Handbook of Human Symbolic Evolution* (A Lock, CR Peters, eds.), pp. 263–287. Blackwell, Oxford.

Wynne-Edwards VC. 1962. *Animal Dispersion in Relation to Social Behaviour*. Oliver & Boyd, Edinburgh.

Yamashita N. 2002. Diets of two lemur species in different microhabitats in Beza Mahafaly Special Reserve, Madagascar. *International Journal of Primatology* 23:1025–1051.

Yarrow Robertson JM, van Schaik CP. 2001. Causal factors underlying the dramatic decline of the Sumatran orang-utan. *Oryx* 35:26–38.

Yellen JE. 1991. Small mammals: !Kung San utilization and the production of faunal assemblages. *Journal of Anthropological Research* 10:1–26.

Yule GU. 1902. Mendel's laws and their probable relations to intra-racial heredity. *New Phytologist* 1:193–207, 222–238.

Zahavi A. 1975. Mate selection: A selection for a handicap. *Journal of Theoretical Biology* 53:205–214.

Zerjal T, Xue Y, Bertorelle G, et al. 2003. The genetic legacy of the Mongols. *American Journal of Human Genetics* 72:717–721.

Zhao Z, Jin L, Fu YX, et al. 2000. Worldwide DNA sequence variation in a 10-kilobase noncoding region on human chromosome 22. *Proceedings of the National Academy of Sciences* 97:11354–11358.

Zhu RX, Potts R, Xie F, et al. 2004. New evidence on the earliest human presence at high northern latitudes in northeast Asia. *Nature* 431:559–562.

Zubenko GS, Hughes HB, Maher BS, et al. 2002. Genetic linkage of region containing the *CREB1* gene to depressive disorders in women from families with recurrent, early-onset, major depression. *American Journal of Medical Genetics* 114:980–987.

CREDITS

Cave Art: Parts I, II, III, IV and V: Berna Villiers/Douglas Mazonowicz

Part I: xx, © The Natural History Museum of London; AP Wide World Photos; Rikard Larma/ Getty Images, Inc – Liaison; Craig Stanford; William F. McComas, Ph.D.

Chapter 1: 1, Craig Stanford; © William F. McComas **4,** Fig. 1.2, Fred Spoor; Fig. 1.3, © The Natural History Museum of London; **5,** Fig. 1.4, AP Wide World Photos; Fig. 1.5, Rickard Larma/Getty Images Inc., Liaison; **6,** Fig. 1.6, AP Wide World Photos; **6,** Fig. 1.7, Craig Stanford; **7,** Fig. 1.8, AP Wide World Photos; **8,** Fig. 1.9, Roger Ressmeyer/Corbis/Bettmann; **10,** Fig. 1.11, Craig Stanford; **13,** Fig. 1.12, AP Wide World Photos; **14,** Fig. 1.13, Michael T. Sedam/ Corbis/Bettmann.

Chapter 2: 17, The Granger Collection, New York/ Archive/Photo Researchers, Inc.**; 19,** Fig. 2.1, Corbis/Bettmann; **20,** Fig. 2.3, Corbis/Bettmann; **21,** Fig. 2.4, Courtesy of the Library of Congress; **22,** Fig. 2.5, Corbis/Bettmann; **23,** Fig. 2.6, Leonard de Selva/ Corbis/Bettmann; **24,** Fig. 2.7, © Science Photo Library/Photo Researchers, Inc.; Fig. 2.8, Stock Montage, Inc./Historical Pictures Collection; **25,** Fig. 2.10, Corbis/Bettmann; **26,** Fig. 2.11, Archive/Photo Researchers, Inc.; **26** Fig. 2.12, Dorling Kindersley; **27,** Fig. 2.13, © William F. McComas; **28,** Fig. 2.14, © William F. McComas; Fig. 2.15, © William F. McComas; **30,** Fig. 2.17, Craig Stanford; **31,** Fig. 2.18a, Craig Stanford; Fig. 2.18b, Craig Stanford/Jane Goodall Research Center; Fig. 2.18c, Craig Stanford; Fig. 2.18d, AP Wide World Photos; Fig. 2.19, Library of Congress; **32,** Fig. A, Getty Images, Inc./Hulton Archive; **34,** Fig. 2.21b, Yann Arthus-Bertrand/Corbiss/Bettmann; Fig. 2.21c, Michael P. Gadomski/Photo Researchers, Inc.; **36,** Fig. 2.22, Kurt Wilson.

Part II: 40, CNRI/ Photo Researchers, Inc.; Oliver Meckes and Nicole Ottawa/ Photo Researchers, Inc.; The Ohio Historical Society; Renne Purse/ Photo Researchers, Inc.

Chapter 3: 41, Dan McCoy/ Rainbow; **44,** Fig. 3.1, Hartsoeker, N. Essay de dioptrique, Paris, 1694, p. 230. National Library of Medicine; **47,** Fig. A, © Reuters NewMedia Inc./CORBIS, **51,** Fig. 3.5a, AP Wide World Photos; Fig. 3.5b, The Novartis Foundation; **56,** Fig. 3.10, I. Kiselva and Don. W. Fawcett/ Visuals Unlimited; **60,** Fig. A, Dr. William S. Klug; **62,** Fig. 3.15, CNRI/Photo Researchers, Inc.; **64,** Fig. 3.16, Reproduced with permission from *Nature Reviews Genetics*, Vol. 2, No. 4, pp. 280–91. © 2001 Macmillan Magazines Ltd.; **69,** Fig. 3.20c, Dr. Elisabeth Matisoo-Smith, University of Auckland.

Chapter 4: 72, Cynthia Hart/Corbis/Bettmann; **75,** Fig. 4.1, Paramount Pictures/Picture Desk, Inc./Kobal Collection; **76,** Fig. 4.2, John Sholtis/Amgen Inc.; **77,** Fig. 4.3, Mark Richards/ Corbis/Bettmann; **78,** Fig. 4.5, Getty Images Inc.-Hulton Archive; **82,** Fig. 4.9, Klug, William S., and Cummings, Michael R., *Concepts of Genetics*, Seventh Edition, © 2003 Reprinted by permission of Pearson Education, Upper Saddle River, N.J.; **84,** Fig. 4.11, Oliver Meckes and Nichole Ottawa/Photo Researchers, Inc.; **86,** Fig. 4.14, Barent (Bernard) van Orley (c. 1492–1541), *Portrait of Charles V as a boy*. Oil on Wood. Herve Lewandowski/Musee Louvre, Paris. RMN Reunion des Nationaux/Art Resource, NY; **89,** Fig. 4.16, Mary Evans Picture Library/ Photo Researchers, Inc.; **91,** Fig. A, American Philosophical Society; **92,** Fig. 4.18, The Ohio Historical Society; **93,** Fig. 4.20, Robin Nelson/Black Star; **96,** Fig. 4.21, McGill University/ Montreal Children's Hospital.

Chapter 5: 99, American Museum of Natural History; **103,** Fig. 5.2, Craig Stanford; **103,** Fig. 5.3, University of Chicago Divisions of Biological Sciences, Ecology, and Evolution. Reprinted by permission; **105,** Fig. 5.4, Centers for Disease Control (CDC); **107,** Fig. 5.6, Renne Purse/Photo Researchers, Inc.; **108,** Fig. 5.7, © The New Yorker Collection 2004 Carolita Johnson from cartoonbank.com. All Rights Reserved; **116,** Fig. A, Fig B, Craig Stanford; **118,** Fig. 5.12a, Fig. 5.12b, Craig Stanford; **120,** Fig. 5.14, Reuters/Mike Segar/ Corbis/Bettmann; **121,** Fig. 5.15, The Royal Society of London; **123,** Fig. 5.16, Craig Stanford.

Chapter 6: 126, Jose Luis Pelaez/ Corbis/Bettmann; **129,** Fig. 6.1, Jeff Greenberg/ PhotoEdit; **132,** Fig. 6.3, Art Resource, N.Y.; **134,** Fig. 6.4, The Granger Collection, New York; **137,** Fig. A, George Catlin (1796–1872), Eeh-nis-kim, Crystal Stone, Wife of the Chief. 1832. Oil on Canvas. 29" x 24". Smithsonian American Art Museum, Washington, D.C./Art Resource, N.Y.; Fig. B, Courtesy of

the Library of Congress; **139,** Fig. 6.5, Dorling Kindersley; **143,** Fig. 6.7, The Jews of Africa; **146,** Fig. 6.10, Cavalli-Sforza, Luca, *The History and Geography of Human Genes*, © 1994 Princeton University Press. Reprinted by permission of Princeton University Press; **150,** Fig. 6.12, Mathieu Laboureur/ Peter Arnold, Inc.; **151,** Fig. 6.13, Dorling Kindersley; **155,** Fig. A, NASA/John F. Kennedy Space Center; **156,** Fig. 6.15a, Michael S. Quinton/ National Geographic Image Collection; Fig. 6.15b, Terry W. Eggers/ Corbis/Bettmann; **157,** Fig. 6.16a, Adrian Arbib/ Corbis/Bettmann; Fig. 6.16b, Yvette Cardozo/ Index Stock Imagery, Inc.; **158,** Fig. 6.17, Dr. Andrea Wiley/James Madison University; **159,** Anna Gislen, PhD/Lund University.

Part III: 162, Craig Stanford.

Chapter 7: 163, Craig Stanford; **165,** Fig. 7.1, Craig Stanford; Fig. 7.2, Craig Stanford; **168,** Fig. 7.6a,b (photos), Craig Stanford; **169,** Fig. 7.6c,d (photos), Craig Stanford; **173,** Fig. 7.8, Schultz; **176,** Fig. 7.10, Craig Stanford; Juergen and Christine Sohns/ Animals Animals/Earth Scenes; Michael Dick/ Animals Animals/Earth Scenes; Michael and Patricia Fogdon/ Corbis/Bettmann; George D. Lepp/ Corbis/Bettmann; **178,** Fig. 7.11, Dorling Kindersley; **178,** Fig. 7.12, Joseph Van Os / Image Bank/Getty Images; **179,** Figs. 7.13, 7.14, 7.15, 7.16, Craig Stanford; **180,** Fig. 7.17, Dorling Kindersley; **180,** Fig. 7.18, Michael Dick/ Animals Animals/Earth Scenes; Fig. 7.19, Juergen and Christine Sohns/ Animals Animals/Earth Scenes; **181,** Fig. 7.20, Dorling Kindersley; **181,** Fig. 7.21, Michael and Patricia Fogdon/ Corbis/Bettmann; **182,** Figs. A, B, Craig Stanford; **183,** Figs. C, D, E, F, Craig Stanford; **184,** Fig. 7.22, Dorling Kindersley; **184,** Fig. 7.23, Craig Stanford; **185,** Fig. 7.24, Mickey Gibson/ Animals Animals/Earth Scenes; Figs. 7.25, 7.26, Craig Stanford; **186,** Figure 7.27, Dorling Kindersley; **187,** Figs. 7.28, 7.29, 7.30, 7.31, Craig Stanford; **188,** Figs. 7.32, 7.33, Craig Stanford; **189,** Fig. 7.34, Dorling Kindersley; **189,** Fig. 7.35, Craig Stanford; **190,** Fig. 7.36, Dorling Kindersley; **190,** Fig. 7.37, George D. Lepp/ Corbis/Bettmann; **191,** Fig. 7.39, 7.40, Craig Stanford; **192,** Fig. A, Craig Stanford; **194,** Figs. 7.41, 7.42, Craig Stanford; **195,** Fig. 7.43; **196,** Fig. 7.44, Craig Stanford; **197,** Fig. 7.45, Craig Stanford; **203,** Fig. 7.48, Craig Stanford; **205,** Fig. 7.49, Craig Stanford.

Chapter 8: 208, Martin Harvey/Gallo Images; **210,** Fig. 8.1, Fig. 8.2, Craig Stanford; **211,** Fig. 8.3, Fig. 8.4, Craig Stanford; **213,** Fig. 8.5a, Fig. 8.5b, Craig Stanford; **216,** Fig. 8.8, Craig Stanford; **217,** Fig. 8.9, Craig Stanford; **218,** Fig. A, Craig Stanford; **219,** Fig. B, Fig. C, Craig Stanford; **220,** Fig. 8.10, Craig Stanford; **222,** Fig. A, Craig Stanford; **223,** Fig. B, Frans Lanting Photography; **224,** Fig. 8.11a, Fig. 8.11b, Craig Stanford; **225,** Fig. 8.12, Strier, K. B., 1994, "Myth of the Typical Primate," *Yearbook of Physical Anthropology* 37:233–71. Copyright © 1994, Wiley-Liss, Inc. Reprinted by permission of Wiley-Liss, Inc., a subsidiary of John Wiley & Sons, Inc.; **226,** Fig. 8.13, Craig Stanford; **227,** Fig. 8.14, Craig Stanford; **228,** Fig. 8.15, Reprinted with permission from American Association for the Advancement of Science. Copyright 1991 AAAS. Fig. 2 from Pussey et al., *Science* 277:828–31; Fig. 8.16, Craig Stanford; **230,** Fig. 8.17, R. W. Wrangham, 1980, "An Ecological Model of Female-Bonded Primate Groups," *Behavior* 75:262–300. Reprinted by permission Koninklyke Brill Netherlands.

Part IV: 232, © Carr Clifton; Copyright Susan C. Antón; Meave Leakey, Fred Spoor / National Museums of Kenya; John Krigbaum; Randall White.

Chapter 9: 233, David Muench/ Muench Photography, Inc.; **236,** Fig. 9.2a, Breck P. Kent; Fig. 9.2b, E. J. Tarbuck; **237,** Fig. 9.3a, Carr Clifton Photography; Fig. 9.3b, Michael Collier; **244,** Fig. 9.8 (photos), E. J. Tarbuck; **245,** Fig. 9.10a, Fig. 9.10b, Copyright Susan C. Antón; **246,** Fig. A, Corbis/Bettmann; Fig. B, Courtesy The Natural History Museum Picture Library, **249,** Fig. 9.11a, Copyright Susan C. Antón/ Carl Swisher; Fig. 9.11b, Copyright Susan C. Antón; **252,** Figs. 9.14a, b,d,e,f, Copyright Susan C. Antón; Fig. 9.14c, Kenneth Garrett Photography/Copyright Susan C. Antón; **256,** Fig. 9.16, Photo Courtesy of Craig Feibel; **262,** Fig. 9.20, Copyright Susan C. Antón.

Chapter 10: 267, Illustration Courtesy of P. Wynne, Ian Tattersall and American Museum of Natural History; **272,** Fig. 10.2a, K. D. Rose, 1995, "The Earliest Primates," from *Evolutionary Anthropology* 3:159–73. Reprinted with permission of Wiley-Liss, Inc., a subsidiary of John Wiley & Sons, Inc.; Fig. 10.2b, Illustration Courtesy of P. Wynne, Ian Tattersall & American Museum of Natural

History; Fig. 10.2c, William K. Sacco, Peabody Museum of Natural History, Yale University; **275,** Fig. A, Photo by P. Wynne. Courtesy Dept. of Library Services, American Museum of Natural History; **276,** Fig. 10.4, Reprinted with permission of Cambridge University Press; **279,** Fig. 10.6b, Elwyn L. Simons, M.D. / Duke University Primate Center; 280, Fig. 10.7a, William K. Sacco, Peabody Museum of Natural History, Yale University; 10.7b, From *A Photographic Atlas for Physical Anthropology* by Whitehead, P.F., Sacco, W.K., and Hochgraf, S.B.; **281,** Fig. 10.9, Corbis/Bettmann; **282,** Fig. 10.10, Monte L. McCrossin, PhD and Brenda Benefit, Ph.D.; **286,** Fig. 10.11, Dorling Kindersley; **286,** Fig. 10.14a, b, Peabody Museum of Archaeology and Ethnology; **287,** Fig. 10.15a, b, Russell L. Ciochon, University of Iowa; **290,** Fig. 10.17, Reprinted from "Evolutionary Relationship of New World Monkeys" in *Primate Adaptation and Evolution* by John G. Fleagle, 1988, by Academic Press; Peabody Museum of Archaeology and Ethnology; William K. Sacco, Peabody Museum of Natural History, Yale University; Monte L. McCrossin, PhD.

Chapter 11: 298, Kenneth Garrett Photography; **300,** Fig. 11.1 (left), Stephen Wilkes/Image Bank/Getty Images; Fig. 11.1 (middle), Jonathan Chester/ Lonely Planet Images/Photo 20-20; Fig. 11.1 (right), Getty Images/Digital Vision; **301,** Fig. 11.2, The Far Side(R) by Gary Larson © 1982 FarWorks, Inc. All Rights Reserved. Used with Permission; Fig. 11.3, AP Wide World Photos; **302,** Fig. 11.4, Milford Wolpoff, *Paleoanthropology,* Second Edition, Figure 38. Reprinted by permission of McGraw Hill Companies; Fig. 11.5, Kenneth Garrett Photography; **309,** Fig. A, Frank Lane Picture Agency/Michael Gore/ Corbis/Bettmann; **313,** Fig. 11.13, Michael Nichols/NGS Image Collection; **315,** Fig. 11.14, Craig Stanford; **317,** Jules Perrier/ Corbis/Bettmann.

Chapter 12: 320, Kenneth Garrett Photography; **324,** Fig. 12.2b, Craig Stanford; **325,** Fig. 12.3, Dorling Kindersley; **326,** Fig. 12.4, Michel Brunet; **327,** Fig. 12.6, © 2003 Tim D. White/ Brill Atlanta; **328,** Fig. A, Eugene Cernan/ NASA/Science Photo Library/ Photo Researchers, Inc.; **332,** Fig. 12.8, Michel Brunet; Kenneth Garrett Photography; Jeffrey K. McKee; Institute of Human Origins, Arizona State University; Pat Shipman/Alan Walker/ National Museums of Kenya; © 2003 Tim D. White/Brill Atlanta; **334,** Fig. 12.9, Alan Walker/ National Museums of Kenya; **335,** Fig. 12.11, Institute of Human Origins, Arizona State University; **336,** Fig. 12.13, Meave Leakey, Fred Spoor / National Museums of Kenya; Fig. 12.14, © 1999 David L. Brill/Brill Atlanta; **339,** Fig. 12.16, Carl Swisher; Fig. 12.17, Kenneth Garrett Photography; **340,** Figs. 12.18, 12.19, Kenneth Garrett Photography; **341,** Fig. 12.21, Jeffrey K. McKee; **343,** Fig. 12.24, Alan Walker/ National Museums of Kenya; **345,** Fig. 12.26, Jeffrey K. McKee.

Chapter 13: 352, Javier Trueba/ Madrid Scientific Films; **355,** Fig. 13.2, Kenneth Garrett Photography; **358,** Fig. 13.4, Chris Johns/ National Geographic Image Collection; **365,** Fig. 13.9, Alan Walker/ National Museums of Kenya; **366,** Fig. 13.11, Javier Trueba/ Madrid Scientific Films; Copyright Susan C. Antón; © 2001 David L. Brill/Atlanta; Pat Shipman/Alan Walker/ National Museums of Kenya; Kenneth Garrett Photography; Copyright Susan C. Antón; **368,** Fig. 13.12, Kenneth Garrett Photography; **369,** Fig. 13.13, Copyright Susan C. Antón; **370,** Fig. 13.14, © 2001 David L. Brill/Atlanta; Fig. 13.15a,b, Copyright Susan C. Antón; Fig. 13.16, Dorling Kindersley; **372,** Fig. 13.17, Kenneth Garrett Photography; **373,** Fig. 13.18, Kenneth Garrett Photography; **374,** Fig. 13.19a, Carl Swisher; Fig. 13.19b, Copyright Susan C. Antón; **375,** Fig. 13.20, Javier Trueba/ Madrid Scientific Films; **378,** Fig. 13.22, Dorling Kindersley; **380,** Fig. 13.23, Dorling Kindersley.

Chapter 14: 383, Kenneth Garrett Photography; **388,** Fig. 14.3 Kenneth Garrett Photography; **389,** Fig. 14.4a, Courtesy of and copyright by Eric Delson; Fig. 14.4b, Kenneth Garrett Photography; Fig. 14.5, Javier Trueba/ Madrid Scientific Films; **391,** Fig. 14.6a, Photo by Willard Whitson/ Courtesy the Library, American Museum of Natural History; Fig. 14.6b, Kenneth Garrett Photography; Fig. 14.7, Kenneth Garrett Photography; **393,** Fig. 14.9, F. Clark Howell; **394,** Fig. 14.10, Copyright Susan C. Antón; **396,** Fig. 14.11, Kenneth Garrett Photography/ National Geographic Image Collection; Figure 14.12, Dorling Kindersley; **397,** Fig. 14.13, Kenneth Garrett Photography; **398,** Fig. A, © Chris Hellier/CORBIS; **400,** Fig. 14.15, Prof. Milford Wolpoff/Univ. of Michigan; **404,** Fig. 14.17a, Prof. Milford Wolpoff/Univ. of Michigan; Fig. 14.17b, John Reader/Science Photo Library; **409,** Fig. 14.19, Kenneth Garrett Photography; **410,** Fig. 14.20, Tel Aviv University, Sackler School of Medicine, Department of Anatomy and Anthropology/Brill Atlanta; **412,** Fig. 14.23, Copyright Susan C. Antón; Kenneth Garrett Photography; John Reader/Science Photo Library; Javier Trueba/ Madrid Scientific Films; Courtesy of and copyright by Eric Delson;

Prof. Milford Wolpoff/Univ. of Michigan; Photo by Willard Whitson, Courtesy the Library, American Museum of Natural History.

Chapter 15: 417, Ulmer Museum; **422,** Fig. 15.2, Dorling Kindersley; **423,** Fig. 15.3, © 2001 David L. Brill/Atlanta; Fig. 15.4, Kenneth Garrett Photography; **424,** Fig. 15.5, Erik Trinkaus/Romanian Academy; Fig. 15.6, John Reader/ Photo Researchers, Inc.; Fig. 15.7, The Natural History Museum, London; **426,** Fig. 15.8, John Krigbaum; Fig. 15.9, Penny Tweedie/ Corbis/Bettmann; **427,** Fig. A, Dr. Peter Brown University of New England; Fig. 15.10, The Granger Collection, New York; **428,** Fig. 15.11a,b, Prof. Milford Wolpoff/Univ. of Michigan; **429,** Fig. 15.12, Randall White; **432,** Fig. 15.15, AP Wide World Photos; **434,** Fig. 15.16, Randall White; Fig. 15.17, Kenneth Garrett Photography; **435,** Fig. 15.18a, Randall White; Fig. 15.18b, Kenneth Garrett Photography; Fig. 15.18c, Randall White; Fig. 15.19, Randall White; **439,** Fig. A, The Granger Collection, New York.

Part V: 446 Hanna Damasio, M.D.; Cary Wolinsky/ Aurora & Quanta Productions Inc.; William Sallaz/Duomo/ Corbis/Bettmann.

Chapter 16: CHAPTER OPENING PHOTOS credits, 450, Fig. 16.2, Hanna Damasio, M.D.; **452,** Fig. 16.5, National Library of Medicine; Fig. 16.6, Hanna Damasio, M.D.; **453,** Fig. 16.7, John Reader/SPL/ Photo Researchers, Inc.; **459,** Fig. 16.9, Jorg and Petra Wegner/ Animals Animals/Earth Scenes; **460,** Fig. 16.12, Visuals Unlimited; **461,** Fig. 16.13a,b,c, Hanna Damasio, M.D., Dr. Katerina Semendeferi/UCSD; **462,** Fig. 16.14a,b,c, Hanna Damasio, M.D.; **467,** Fig. 16.18, Reprinted by permission of the publisher from *Uniquely Human: The Evolution of Speech, Thought, and Selfless Behavior* by Philip Lieberman, p. 55, Cambridge, Mass.: Harvard University Press, © 1991 by the President and Fellows of Harvard College; **468,** Fig. A, © Yerkes Regional Primate Research Center, Emory University; **471,** Fig. 16.21 (left), EyeWire Collection/ Getty Images–Photodisc; Fig. 16.21 (right), Yang Liu/ Corbis/Bettmann.

Chapter 17: 476, Philip de Bay/ Corbis/Bettmann; **479,** Fig 17.1, Gabe Palmer/ Corbis/Bettmann; **481,** Fig. 17.2, National Library of Medicine; Fig. 17.3, AP/Wide World Photos; **484,** Fig. 17.5, "Fig. 8.2: Pelvic inlet, midplane, and outlet of chimpanzees and humans" from *Evolutionary Medicine,* edited by Wenda Trevathan and E. O. Smith, copyright 1999 by Oxford University Press, Inc. Used by permission of Oxford University Press, Inc.; Fig. 17.7, Vo Trung Dung/ Corbis/ Bettmann; **485,** Fig. 17.8, Reprinted by permission of the publisher from *Fetus Into Man: Physical Growth From Conception to Maturity* by J. M. Tanner, p. 16, Cambridge, Mass.: Harvard University Press, Copyright 1978, 1989 by J. M. Tanner; **487,** Fig. 17.9, B. Bogin (2001) *The Growth of Humanity,* p. 4. This material is used by permission of Wiley-Liss, a subsidiary of John Wiley & Sons, Inc.; **490,** Fig. 17.11, Reprinted by permission of Harvard University Press, *Fetus Into Man: Physical Growth From Conception to Maturity* by J. M. Tanner. Also see Rona, 1978, p. 264 : Rona, R.J., Swan A.V. and Altman D.G., 1978, "Social factors and height of primary schoolchildren in England and Wales," Journal of Epidemiology and Community Health, 32, 147–54; **492,** Fig. 17.13 (top), Corbis/ Bettmann; Fig. 17.13 (bottom), Fafael Roa/ Corbis/Bettmann; **494,** Fig. 17.15, Dorling Kindersley; **497,** Fig. 17.16, WHO/ National Library of Medicine; **498,** Fig. A, National Institute of Health; **499,** Fig. 17.17 (left), Sheldon Collins/ Corbis/Bettmann; Fig. 17.17 (right), Sheldon Collins / Corbis/Bettmann; Fig. 17.18, WHO/ National Library of Medicine; **500,** Fig. 17.19, Dorling Kindersley; **502,** Fig. 17.21, National Library of Medicine; **505,** Fig. 17.22, Courtesy of Della Collins Cook; **506,** Fig. 17.23, National Library of Medicine.

Chapter 18: 509, National Gallery, London/SuperStock; **516,** Fig. 18.2, Jack Fields/ Corbis/Bettmann; **517,** Fig. 18.4, Corbis/Bettmann; **519,** Fig. 18.7, Cary Wolinsky/ Aurora & Quanta Productions Inc.; **523,** Fig. 18.9, Life History Theory and Risky-Drinking, E.M. Hill and K. Chow, Addiction 97:401–13, Reprinted by permission; Fig. 18.10, William Sallaz/Duomo/ Corbis/Bettmann; **525,** Fig. 18.11, Tom Spiegel/ Corbis/Bettmann; **526,** Fig. 18.12, Courtesy of Laura-Ann Petitto/ Photo by Jeff DeBelle; **527,** Fig. A, Digital Vision Ltd.; **528,** Fig. 18.13, Owen Franken/ Corbis/Bettmann; **529,** Fig. 18.15, Reproduced with permission from Dr. Jane M. Murphy, *Science* 1976. Copyright 2006 American Association for the Advancement of Science; **530,** Fig. 18.16 (left), Peter Turnley/ Corbis/Bettmann; Fig. 18.16 (middle), David Turnley/ Corbis/Bettmann; Fig. 18.16 (right), Shaul Schwarz/ Corbis/Bettmann; **533,** Figure 18.17, Dorling Kindersley.

Appendices A, B: 540, Figs. A.1, A.2, Paul Sledzik; **541,** Fig. A.3, Copyright Susan C. Antón; **543,** Fig. A.5, Paul Sledzik; **542,** Fig. A.4, and **549,** B.4, **550,** B.5 *Forensic Anthropology Training Manual* by Karen Ramey Burns, illustrations by Joanna Wallington.

INDEX

Note: Entries in **bold** indicate glossary terms. Page numbers followed by *f* indicate figures and by *t*, tables.

RITE AID PHARMACY

With us, it's personal.

Store #05976
2620 EL CAMINO REAL
SANTA CLARA, CA 95051
(408) 241-0919

Register #5 Transaction #413724
Cashier #59765169 4/17/07 10:34AM

1 BF SPORT SPRV SPF 36 4.7Z	10.48 T
1 ARRID XX AER FRSH 6Z	4.99 T
1 RA OILFRE FACEBLCK 30SPF3	5.99 T
1 FINGER LIGHT	1.99 T

4 Items   Subtotal   23.46
                    Tax   1.94
                  Total   25.40
   *PAID BY DEBIT   25.40
 DEBIT card * #XXXXXXXXXX2017
App # AUTO
Ref # 432385
Card Present

                Tendered   25.40
               Cash Change   .00

****

Tell us about our service
and you will be entered
to win

$10,000

Call TOLL FREE
Disponible en Español, llame

1-800-734-5383

Enter Code:
0417 1005 9760 5083

Entry code expires 14 days from the
date of this receipt
For Official Rules Call 1-800-RITE-AID
****

****
We're Medicare experts
Ask your pharmacist for a FREE
Medicare Prescription Plan Guide today
****

Internet Refills at RiteAid.com
powered by drugstore.com
1-800-RITEAID for customer service